S0-BYF-815

Management Information Systems

THIRD EDITION

Management Information Systems

THIRD EDITION

DAVID KROENKE

RICHARD HATCH

McGraw-Hill, Inc.
New York St. Louis San Francisco Auckland Bogotá
Caracas Lisbon London Madrid Mexico City Milan
Montreal New Delhi San Juan Singapore
Sydney Tokyo Toronto

Mitchell **McGRAW-HILL**

Watsonville, CA 95076

Management Information Systems, *Third Edition*

Copyright © 1994, 1992, 1989 by **McGraw-Hill, Inc.** All rights reserved. Printed in the United States of America. Except as permitted under the United States Copyright Act of 1976, no part of this publication may be reproduced or distributed in any form or by any means, or stored in a database or retrieval system, without the prior written permission of the publisher.

5 6 7 8 9 0   DOH DOH   9 0 9 8 7 6 5

ISBN 0-07-035938-5

Sponsoring editor: Erika Berg

Director of production: Jane Somers

Project management: Greg Hubit, Bookworks

Text design and illustration: Gary Palmatier, Ideas to Images

Photo research: Sarah Bendersky

Composition: Ideas to Images

Cover design: John Edeen

Cover photograph: Bill Schwob Photography

Printer and binder: R. R. Donnelley & Sons Company

Library of Congress Card Catalog No. 93-79560

Information has been obtained by Mitchell McGraw-Hill from sources believed to be reliable. However, because of the possibility of human or mechanical error by our sources, Mitchell McGraw-Hill, or others, Mitchell McGraw-Hill does not guarantee the accuracy, adequacy, or completeness of any information and is not responsible for any errors or omissions or the results obtained from use of such information.

INTERNATIONAL EDITION

Copyright © 1994

Exclusive rights by McGraw-Hill, Inc. for manufacture and export. This book cannot be re-exported from the country to which it is consigned by McGraw-Hill. The International Edition is not available in North America.

When ordering this title, use ISBN 0-07-113422-0

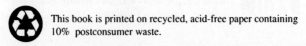

This book is printed on recycled, acid-free paper containing 10% postconsumer waste.

Brief Contents

Detailed Contents

Chapter 2

Fundamental Types of Management Information Systems 40

Chapter 3

Introduction to Information Systems Technology 86

Chapter 4

The Value Added by Information Systems

PART **II**   # Personal Management Information Systems   **169**

Chapter 5

Personal Information Systems: Applications and Goals   170

Chapter 6

Components of Personal Information Systems   220

Chapter 7

Developing Personal Information Systems   262

Module A

Developing Personal Database Applications 313

PART III Workgroup Management Information Systems 333

Chapter 8

Workgroup Information Systems: Applications and Goals 334

Chapter 9

Components of Workgroup Information Systems   382

Chapter 10

Developing Workgroup Information Systems   436

Module B

Developing an MIS for Legacy Systems' Customer Support   493

PART **IV** # Enterprise Management Information Systems **515**

Chapter 11

Enterprise Information Systems: Applications and Goals **516**

Chapter 12

Components of Enterprise Information Systems 566

Chapter 13

Developing Enterprise Information Systems 624

Module C

Development of an Enterprise Information System

Preface to the Student

THE INFORMATION AGE. You undoubtedly have heard references to it on TV and read them in the press. You know that computer systems are important in business. After all, you see computers everywhere: in department stores, airports, book shops, restaurants, and businesses in which you have worked. Computers are so common, they must be important.

But why? Why are they so prevalent? What benefits do they bring? Beyond the notion that computers perform computations very fast, what, really, do they do to help a business? Further, not all businesses benefit equally from the use of computers. Some businesses have found ways to gain substantial competitive advantage with computers, but others have wasted millions of dollars on them. What accounts for this difference?

An even more important question is this: *What do you as a future business professional need to know about computers?* Is it enough to know how to operate one? Do you need to know how to program one? Should you know how to develop an application for yourself? Or should you know how to hire someone else to develop an application for you? If so, how do you go about that? How much should you pay?

Consider your competition. Right now, other students, in other universities, are taking this same course. What are they learning? What will you need to know to compete effectively? What information systems knowledge will your future employer expect you to have? What will you be asked to do?

GOALS OF THIS TEXT

The goal of this text is to help you answer these questions. To do so, you may need to discard some common misconceptions. For example, all the sentences above that contain the word *computer* should say *information system* instead. As you will see in Chapter 1, *information systems add value* to businesses; computers are only a part of such systems.

Technical knowledge, while important, is not enough. The most successful business professionals know how to *blend technology with business.* For example, what do you need to know about local area networks? It's important to know what the IEEE 802.3 standard for local area networks is (discussed in Chapter 9). But it's far more important to know how you can use a local area network to make the group you manage more efficient and effective. In fact, the main reason you need technical knowledge is to help you find ways to make yourself and your company more competitive.

Another trait of successful business professionals is the ability to *identify potential applications of technology and then instigate their development.* Such people do not necessarily develop the systems themselves; rather, they define and manage a project in which specialists work together to develop the application.

A final desirable trait is the knowledge to *put the business before the technology.* It is tempting to take an exciting technology and run around a company looking for an application to fling it upon. Better, in fact *far* better, is to start with the business goals and objectives and then ask, What do we want to do? How do we want to do that? How, then, can technology help us?

This text is organized with these goals in mind. First, we break the application of information technology into three major levels: technology for *individuals,* technology for *workgroups,* and technology for *enterprises.* Then, for each level, we answer three key questions: First, *why do we use* information technology to support that level? Second, *what technology* is appropriate to that level? Finally, *how do we develop applications* of that technology?

Blending technology with business is seldom an easy task. (If it were, there would be less demand for the knowledge and skills you are about to gain.) Technology is precise, rigid, and concrete; business organization and management are fluid, and ambiguous. Bringing the two together will be your primary challenge. Sometimes you will not know what to do; sometimes you will want a single, definite, concrete answer, one that does not exist. This is normal and typical, and you need to experience such frustration now. Developing skills for dealing with unavoidable ambiguity is as important as any learning you can take from this course.

Preface to the Professor

MIS IS FACING A PERIOD OF UNPRECEDENTED OPPORTUNITY. In corporations throughout the world, end users are suddenly being empowered to use MIS techniques to solve important business problems. Managers often hire departmental and workgroup systems development professionals from outside the corporation. Sophisticated end users build personal systems on their own. To profit from this empowerment, *workers need practical, down-to-earth information* about how to increase their MIS productivity. That is our opportunity.

In higher education, however, a few colleagues are beginning to draw the wrong conclusions from these trends. Noting that many corporate MIS departments are being reorganized, they say, "Corporations are cutting their MIS departments, and we should too. Besides, today's students already know how to use spreadsheets, so they don't need an MIS course."

We who teach MIS must respond to these mistaken assumptions vigorously and forcefully. As MIS responsibility shifts from corporate MIS departments to users, *the need for MIS education goes up,* not down. Here's why:

■ *MIS adds value at all levels*—personal, workgroup, and enterprise—not just through the activities of the MIS department.

■ Since more MISs are being developed outside the MIS department than inside, *people at all levels need MIS knowledge.* More MIS knowledge, not less, is needed to supervise outside developers of a workgroup MIS than to assist internal MIS developers of an enterprise system.

■ The key MIS knowledge is not the technology itself; instead, the key is knowing how to use technology in creating *information systems that satisfy business needs and goals.*

As MIS professors, we know that these arguments provide a valid foundation for MIS. But for our colleagues to take us seriously, we must organize our courses to fulfill these promises.

A LOGICAL ORGANIZATION
FOR THE MIS COURSE

What is the best organization? The traditional approach is to divide the material along technology lines: a chapter on hardware, a chapter on programs, a chapter on telecommunications, a chapter on database, a chapter on systems development, and so on. We believe that such an organization makes us vulnerable to those who would cut back on MIS courses. It focuses first on technology, and business needs are an afterthought. Further, the traditional approach risks inundating students with a thousand definitions that they cannot use because they learned them in a vacuum, outside any business context.

We believe a more successful course *is driven by the needs and goals of business.* That perspective inspires a more natural and effective three-tiered approach: individual, workgroup, and enterprise. When we organize our study of information systems into these three levels, as shown in Figure 1, we gain the following benefits.

Figure 1

	WHY Use the System	WHAT Technology Is Required	HOW to Develop the System
Personal IS	Chapter 5: Using spreadsheets, DBMS, desktop publishing, etc. for personal productivity	Chapter 6: The ins and outs of PCs, graphical user interface, DOS, Unix, OS/2, and more	Chapter 7: Developing through prototyping, spreadsheet design, page layouts, choosing graphics
Workgroup IS	Chapter 8: Workgroups, collaborative work, electronic mail, group conferencing, group decision support	Chapter 9: Local area networks, ISO OSI reference model, Ethernet, IEEE 802.3, 802.5, client-server architecture	Chapter 10: The systems development life cycle, identifying and choosing vendors, the user's role in design and implementation
Enterprise IS	Chapter 11: Integrated applications, business process redesign, business network redesign, electronic data interchange, interorganizational systems	Chapter 12: Teleprocessing, distributed processing, TCP/IP, SNA, internets, EDP controls, organization of MIS departments	Chapter 13: Challenges of enterprise system development, information systems planning, CASE, outsourcing, future of MIS departments

Teaches from a Business Perspective

If your course has been organized in the traditional technology-based pattern, the course organization in Figure 1 may seem peculiar. Why, for example, have three chapters on systems development? Isn't the course rather repetitive?

No, it isn't. *The process for most effectively developing a system varies* depending on the type and size of the system. Your students' roles will vary, too.

The last time you built a spreadsheet, did you really follow the systems development life cycle? In truth, few of us do. We classify the problem as a spreadsheet problem, create a platform, and start building prototypes. When we have a prototype that seems to do the job, we implement. Certainly, a process is involved, but it is not the classical systems development life cycle. Instead, as Chapter 7 describes, personal information systems are developed through *iterative prototyping.*

The process that works best for personal systems promises disaster for workgroup systems. With more than one individual concerned, consensus on the problem definition becomes crucial. Solving only the boss's problem guarantees nothing about the effectiveness of the new system for other group members. For workgroups, the *classical systems development life cycle* process presented in Chapter 10 is crucial.

Enterprise systems are also developed using the systems development life cycle, but they involve *strategic business issues* such as information systems planning, enterprise analysis, critical success factors, CASE, outsourcing, and line MIS, all described in Chapter 13. In the traditional course organization, the significant differences between personal, workgroup, and enterprise systems development processes are obscured.

Builds on Student Expectations

When we organize the MIS course content around these three levels, we start by satisfying students' expectations to learn about personal systems. Introducing personal systems in the beginning of the course also provides an early conceptual springboard into a hands-on component of the course, if any. After establishing rapport, we shift toward the workgroup and finally the enterprise systems that are equally important but more difficult for students to appreciate early on. This progression from *personal to workgroup to enterprise systems* has proven effective starting with the first edition of this text.

Progresses in Complexity

Another advantage of the organization shown in Figure 1 is that the topics progress from *simple to complex*. Consider the technology chapters shown in the second column. Chapter 3 (not shown in the figure) provides students with a fundamental understanding of information technology, common to all types and sizes of systems. Chapter 6 builds on this foundation and discusses PCs, workstations, GUI environments, DOS and OS/2, and so on. Chapter 9 builds further to introduce local area networks, the ISO OSI reference model, IEEE 802.x, client-server processing, and so on. Finally, the technology discussion continues in Chapter 12, where enterprise systems, including teleprocessing, internets, WANs, and communications backbones are described. Each level adds sophistication to the student's understanding.

Creates Change of Pace

The spiral organization shown in Figure 1 has yet another important advantage: The natural changes of pace *renew student interest.* When we teach the use of information systems in workgroups, we begin with types of workgroups, workgroup processes, and workgroup applications in Chapter 8. This material is management-oriented. It defines *why* this type is system is used.

We then shift to the technology of workgroup systems in Chapter 9: the ISO seven-layer reference model, IEEE 802.x, client-server systems, and so on. These topics answer *what* technology is needed to build this type of system. In doing so, Chapter 9 provides a degree of concreteness students can appreciate after the managerial emphasis of Chapter 8.

Then, in Chapter 10, we define *how* workgroup systems are developed. This pattern in change of pace occurs three times: once for personal systems (Part II), once for workgroup systems (Part III), and once for enterprise systems (Part IV).

By following the organization of this text, there is a gap of several weeks between, for example, the technology discussions in Chapters 3, 6, 9, and 12. By *returning to technological topics repeatedly* over a two-to-three-month period, we believe students can digest more of the information than if it were presented all at once.

CHANGES IN THE THIRD EDITION

The fundamental organization just described has been well received by adopters of both previous editions. Therefore, we have retained it in this edition. At the same time, we have incorporated a number of important suggestions for improvements as summarized in Figure 2.

Figure 2

Change Requested	Example of Response	Benefit
Modernize data communications material	Add backbone networks in Chapter 9, routers in Chapter 12.	Students get the current state of the art.
Add ethics	New discussion of MIS ethics in Chapter 1, new ethics supplement.[1]	Students recognize the ethical implications of MIS activities.
Add new developments in workgroup computing	Chapter 2 introduces collaborative writing; new section in Chapter 8 provides group systems classification.	Students understand the relationships of MIS categories of group systems.
Further differentiate the different processes for system development	Describe the purposes of prototyping under each systems development process as in Chapters 7 and 10.	Students are prepared to choose the development methodology best suited to the job.
Add more international MIS	New section on international data communications issues in Chapter 12.	Students appreciate the multinational context of MIS and understand key international issues.
Reduce overlap with management courses	Chapter 4 revised to focus sharply on MIS concepts.	Students understand how MIS adds value.
Update the technology	New data communications technology in Chapters 9 and 12; current micro-processor technology in Chapter 6; pen-based computing in Chapter 3.	Provides a basis for understanding current technology news.
Update minicase material	New minicases throughout.	Demonstrates practical applications of concepts in business.
Improve text appearance	New photos throughout; redesigned artwork.	More graphic and interesting for students.

1. Kallman, Earnest A., and John P. Grillo, *Ethical Decision Making and Information Technology: An Introduction with Cases,* Mitchell McGraw-Hill, 1993, ISBN 0-07-033884-1.

SUMMARY OF FEATURES

This text is divided into five parts. Part I provides a foundation and introduces fundamental concepts. Parts II, III, and IV implement the three-tiered spiral organization just described. Part V highlights two special information systems topics: decision support systems and knowledge systems.

Current Topics

Every effort has been made to include discussions of the *latest technology* that is pertinent to today's information systems. The following table summarizes some of the important enhancements of this edition.

Topic	Example
Connectivity	Pages 70–71
Downsizing, outsourcing	Pages 650–658
Group systems	Pages 68–69, 159–161, 341–372
International MIS	Pages 598–599
Internetworking, backbone networks, routers	Pages 582–585
Manufacturing systems, MRPII, JIT	Pages 543–545
MIS ethics	Pages 14–15
New chip technology	Pages 225–228
Pen-based systems	Pages 222–224
Quality, continuous change	Pages 138–150

Our goal has been to retain and add the technology that promises to be most relevant to students' future careers.

Real-World Flavor

As with earlier editions, we have used many vignettes throughout this text. Their purpose is to illustrate the need for technology and motivate student understanding. Vignettes also add interest.

Legacy Systems, a software publisher that appears in many vignettes, is a fictitious company that has many of the characteristics and problems observed in consulting with actual software companies. Using Legacy has an added benefit. When we teach an aspect of Legacy's business (such as the functions of the customer support department), we are teaching about the microcomputer industry.

Students learn that software publishers have customer support departments, and they learn the services they should expect from such departments.

At the end of each core part, a module adds further real-world flavor. Modules following Chapters 7, 10, and 13 illustrate how to apply MIS principles in developing a real-life application.

In addition, each chapter includes a new application minicase with discussion questions. These minicases show how the concepts of each chapter relate to an actual business. The questions can be used to stimulate in-class discussions of concepts or for short, out-of-class essays.

Finally, the casebook described below provides practical applications of major concepts, emphasizing student understanding of the business problems and issues that are raised by MIS activities.

THE SUPPORT PACKAGE

The following supplements were designed to enhance the use of this text:

Casebook

The *Casebook for MIS: Solving Business Problems with PC Software* by David Kroenke and Sandra Dewitz (Mitchell McGraw-Hill, 1994, ISBN 0-07-035948-2) contains six brand-new cases that can be used either in classroom discussion or as the basis for hands-on software projects, or both. Cases vary from 5 to 20 pages long and emphasize issues such as MIS effectiveness and efficiency, aligning information technology to organizational objectives, analyzing costs and benefits, and business reengineering. Case material is provided for all three tiers of the course: personal, workgroup, and enterprise systems.

Of the six cases, three can be used as the basis for hands-on spreadsheet projects, two for database projects, and one for a combination spreadsheet and database project. Projects emphasize solving business problems rather than just the mechanics of particular software packages. Students are taught a four-step approach: problem analysis, design, implementation, and post-implementation review. An Instructor's Solutions Disk (ISBN 0-07-840257-3) is also available.

Supplementary Text and Casebook on Ethics

Ethical Decision Making and Information Technology: An Introduction with Cases, by Earnest A. Kallman and John P. Grillo, is designed as a case study supplement to any MIS course. Chapter 1 defines ethics. Chapter 2 relates ethics to the use of information technology. And by applying a four-step analysis process to an ethical dilemma, Chapter 3 illustrates how to reach a defensible decision. The 18 cases that follow challenge students to apply the knowledge they've gained in Chapters 1-3 to recognize, evaluate, and react responsibly to ethical dilemmas. (Mitchell McGraw-Hill, 1994, ISBN 0-07-033884-1.)

Test Bank

Dr. Norman Sondak of San Diego State University has developed the computerized test bank that accompanies this text, including over 2,500 questions. The test bank is available printed and on disk.

Instructor's Manual

The Instructor's Manual includes materials for developing a course syllabus as well as objectives, chapter outlines, and answers to questions for each chapter in the text.

Overhead Transparency Masters

Overhead transparency masters of more than 300 key figures in the text are available. Transparency masters are referenced throughout the Instructor's Manual.

ACKNOWLEDGMENTS

We thank Greg Hubit of Bookworks and Gary Palmatier of Ideas to Images for the superb production of this edition. The art and design of this text have been thoroughly (and beautifully) redone from the second edition, and we are very grateful for the time and talent of these people. Gary composed the pages of this text on a Macintosh computer in a process similar to that described by Robert Black in Chapter 7. The result was a closer collaboration between author and compositor than we have had in any previous text. The consequence is an art program and text layout that will, we hope, be both informative and easy to use.

We would like to thank the following people who have provided advice and assistance in the development of this text:

Linda Anderson, Clackamas College; Melissa Bowers, University of Tennessee at Knoxville; Bill Burrows, University of Washington; Tom Case, Georgia Southern College; Sue Conger, Georgia State University; Mary Culnan, Georgetown University; Charles Davis, University of Houston–Downtown Campus; Mark Dishaw, Boston University; Omar El Sawy, University of Southern California; Karen Forcht, James Madison University; Stephen Floyd, University of Alabama; Mike Ginzberg, Case Western Reserve University; Mike Goldberg, Pace University; John Gorgone, Bentley College; Paul Gray, Claremont College; Constanza Hagmann, Kansas State University; Thomas Hilton, Utah State University; Cheng Hsu, Rensselaer Polytechnic University; Neal Jacobs, Northern Arizona University; Eleanor Jordan, University of Texas, Austin; KarenAnn Kievet, Loyola Marymount University; Bob Keim, Arizona State University; Louise Knouse, LeTourneau College; Jay Larson, Lewis and Clark State College; Jane MacKay, Texas Christian University; Earl McKenney, U.S. Air Force Academy; Lawrence McNitt, College at Charleston; Efrem Mallach, University of Massachusetts, Lowell; M. Lynne Markus, University of California, Los Angeles; Richard Mason, Southern Methodist University; Herb Mayer, Eastern Washington University; John Melrose, University of Wisconsin at Eau Claire; Norman Pendegraf, University of Idaho; Jan Pipkin, University of South Florida; Robert Putname, West Coast University; Steve Ruth, George Mason University; John Schillak, University of Wisconsin at Eau Claire; Tom Schriber, University of Michigan; James Shannon, New Mexico State University; Laurette Simmons, Loyola College; Charles Small, Abilene Christian University; Jill Smith, University of Denver; Marion Sobol, Southern Methodist University; Ananth Srinivasen, Case Western Reserve University; David Stamper, Northern Colorado University; Ted Surynt, Stetson University; James Teng, University of Pittsburgh; Tony Verstraete, Pennsylvania State University; Christian Wagner, University of Southern California; Merrill Warkentin, Bryant College; George Widmeyer, University of Southern California; Ron Williams, Piedmont Central College.

David M. Kroenke
Seattle, Washington

Richard Hatch
San Diego State University

Foundations

PART I LAYS THE FOUNDATION FOR THIS TEXT. Chapter 1 describes the nature of MIS, identifies the three major themes of the book, and defines important terms. Chapter 2 paints the broad picture by surveying five basic types of information systems: transaction processing systems, management information systems, decision support systems, office automation systems, and executive support systems.

Chapter 3 introduces the fundamentals of information technology and discusses hardware, programs, and data. The concepts presented in Chapter 3 are the basis for subsequent discussions of technology throughout the text. Finally, Chapter 4 surveys the ways in which information systems add value to individuals and organizations. It builds a model that will be used to illustrate the benefits of information systems to organizations throughout the text.

1

Introduction to Management Information Systems

AS YOU STUDY THIS TEXT, the field of management information systems (MIS) is undergoing a profound and exciting revolution. Explosive changes in information technology are upsetting the basic assumptions that have served MIS well over the past 40 years.

In the recent past, a large company would have set up its MIS by hiring skilled MIS professionals, buying and installing a large mainframe computer, and developing applications to meet the company's particular needs. The entire process was centrally managed by MIS professionals.

Today, however, microcomputer technology has developed so rapidly that the newest $10,000 microcomputers have fully as much computing power as do $3 million mainframe computers. As a result, companies are quickly shifting tasks away from mainframe computers and onto PCs, and in the process, decentralizing MIS control and management. Subsequently, MIS professionals are assuming a very different role, managing only the few tasks that absolutely must be centralized and serving as consultants and advisors to those who manage the smaller systems.

This book focuses on three major themes, which Chapter 1 introduces. The first theme is that an information system can and must add value or some important capability to an organization and its people.

The second theme concerns the composition of information systems. This chapter introduces the five components that comprise every type of information system: hardware, programs, data, procedures, and people. Later chapters will cover the particular characteristics of these five components, for each type of information system presented.

The third and final theme of this book concerns information systems development. You will learn how to instigate information systems to facilitate personal and organizational goals. In some cases, you might instigate a system by developing it yourself. In other cases, you might hire outside consulting firms or other experts to develop a system for you and your organization. In still other cases, you might work as part of an in-house team of users and information systems professionals to develop an information system. Some of the major lessons stressed in this book concern the roles you must play in differing circumstances.

HOW MANAGEMENT INFORMATION SYSTEMS SERVE BUSINESSES

This book is first about business and second about technology. It concerns the role of technology in serving the needs of business. The following scenario may clarify the need for this orientation:

> "Ms. Silver, we've got an order for $275,000 from Ajax Distributing, and I want to get your approval before I send it through Operations. They're still late on payment."

> "OK, Harold. Have they made any payments in the last month or two?"

> [He looks at the accounts receivable report.] "They've owed us $800,000 since August. They paid $119,000 in September and $257,000 in October—nothing in November or December. Without interest, they still owe us $524,000."

> "What does Sales say about this?"

> "Frank says they're doing better since their reorganization—also since they fired Tanweather as their CEO. He wants the sale because he needs it to make his numbers this quarter, but I think he's shaky on it."

> "Me, too. Ship it COD, and tell Frank to let them know that we'll have to cut them off completely if we don't get some large payments this month!"

In this example, the activities of the sales department are being coordinated with those of the operations and accounting departments. The goal of this coordinated activity is to generate revenue without accepting excessive risk of bad debt.

Figure 1-1 shows the flow of information to these activities. Sales submits customer orders to Operations. The company has a rule that if the order is large (where *large* is defined as any dollar amount over $100,000), Operations must

Figure 1-1 Portion of a Revenue Generation System

This dataflow diagram shows part of the procedure used for processing sales orders in one large company.

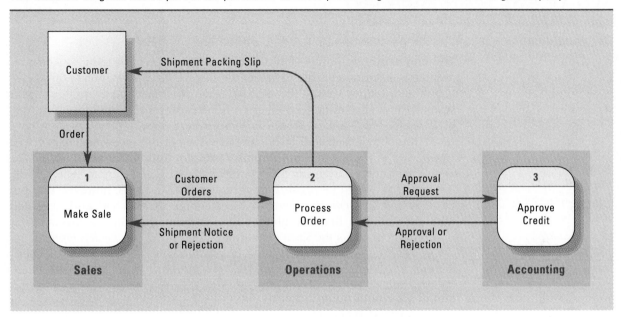

obtain the permission of Accounting before filling and shipping the order. Once permission is granted, the order can be shipped.

Figure 1-1 is the skeleton of an information system; it is a dataflow diagram. Chapter 10 discusses the use and construction of such diagrams.

The system in Figure 1-1 facilitates the goals of the organization and the individual departments. It provides for checks and balances. In the case of this example, Accounting keeps Sales from risking too much bad debt, and at the same time, Sales keeps Accounting from being too cautious. The information system coordinates the departments' activities so that the company responds as a unit.

This information system probably involves a computer-based order-entry system. Further, Accounting probably uses a computer-based system to keep track of customer debt and payments.

To the organization, however, using a certain type of computer (i.e., brand, model, size, amount of memory, efficiency, etc.) is far less important than having the appropriate information flows on a timely basis. If Ms. Silver learns about the large Ajax order after it has been shipped, then all the computer technology in the world will not cure the $275,000 bad debt.

The above example illustrates why the primary orientation of this book is not the computer, its software, or some other technology. Rather the primary emphasis is on the development and use of information systems that facilitate the goals of organizations and the people who work in them.

WHAT ARE MANAGEMENT INFORMATION SYSTEMS?

The term *management information system (MIS)* can be misleading, as it does not accurately communicate the nature of the subject. Peter Keen, one of the leaders in this field, defines MIS as "the effective design, delivery, and use of information systems in organizations."[1] Observe that this definition includes the word *organization* but does not include the word *management.*

Thus, the subject of MIS is broader than the words *management information systems* imply. This subject includes managers, but it also includes all of the other people in an organization and the structure and design of the organization as well. A better term would be *organizational information systems;* however, the term *management information systems* has become established and accepted. Remember, though, that this subject is much broader than those words indicate.

This book alters the Keen definition as follows: *MIS is the development and use of effective information systems in organizations.* The essence of Keen's definition is unchanged: the word *development* replaces the words *design* and *delivery* and places emphasis on the term *effective information systems.* An information system is effective if it helps to accomplish the goals of the people and the organization that use it.

HOW INFORMATION SYSTEMS SUPPORT ORGANIZATIONS

Take a moment and imagine a large company, say Procter & Gamble, IBM, or Bank of America. Think about the information systems in one of those companies and the myriad ways in which people, groups, departments, and divisions share information. This is a truly mind-boggling picture; clearly, to make any progress at all in studying MIS, the subject must be broken down.

Daft and Steers provide a clue for organizing the study of information systems in their book *Organizations, A Micro/Macro Approach:* "As social systems, organizations are composed of systems at different levels. Organizational scientists generally think of three levels of analysis—the individual, the group or department, and the organization itself."[2] This text models its presentation of the subject on

---

1. Keen, Peter G. W., "MIS Research: Reference Disciplines and a Cumulative Tradition," *Proceedings of the First International Conference on Information Systems,* Ephraim R. McLean, ed. Philadelphia, PA, 1980.

2. Daft, Richard L. and Richard M. Steers, *Organizations, A Micro/Macro Approach.* Glenview, IL: Scott, Foresman, 1986, pp. 7–8.

Daft and Steers's statement. Following the trend in the information systems industry, we will call systems that address the organizational level enterprise information systems.

Enterprise Information Systems

Figure 1-2 shows a portion of an organization chart for an order-processing company (e.g., a mail-order catalog company) with four major departments: Marketing, Sales, Operations, and Finance.

Figure 1-2 Three Levels of Information Systems

This portion of a large company's organization chart illustrates the three levels of information systems: enterprise, workgroup, and personal. Example MISs at each level are shown.

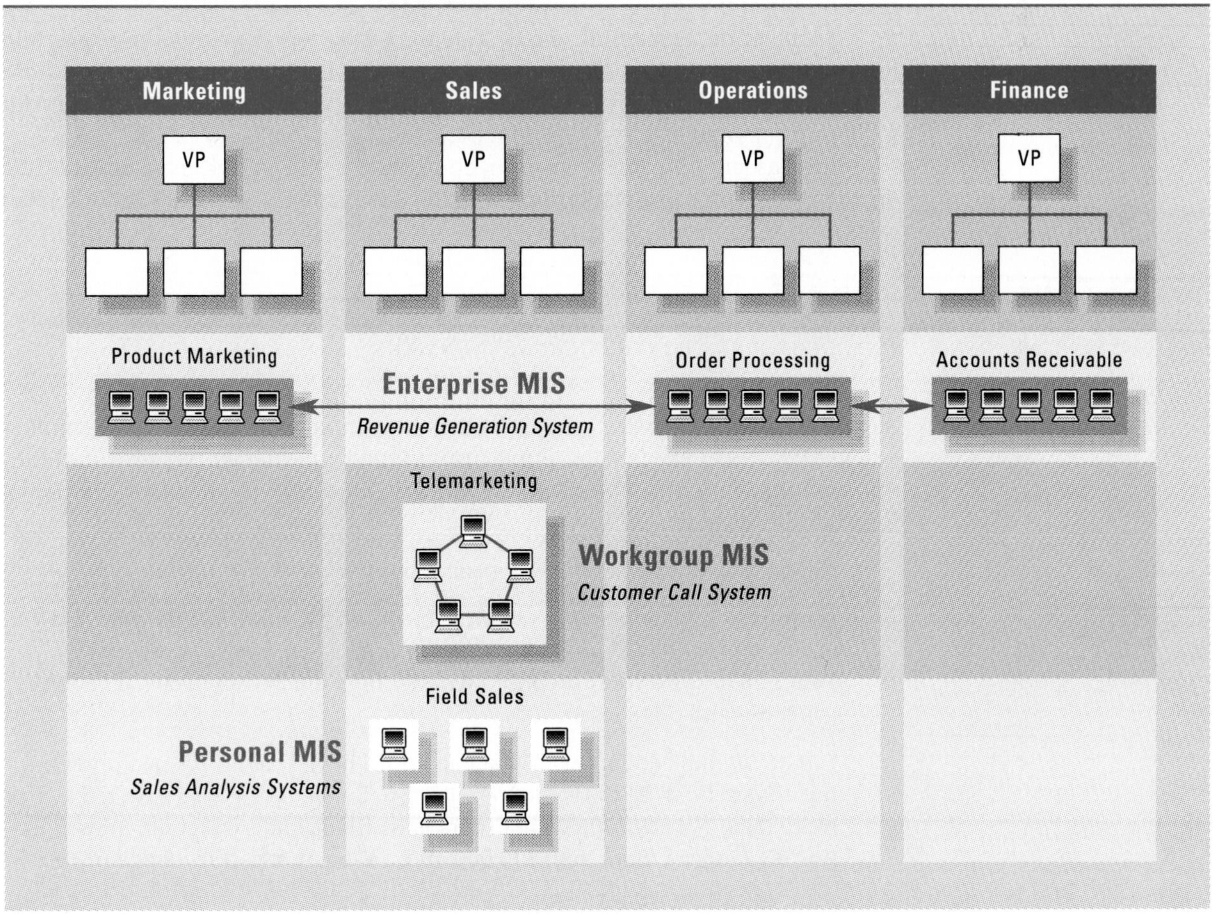

The figure shows information systems at all three levels: enterprise, workgroup, and personal. The revenue generation system is an **organizational,** or **enterprise, information system;** it integrates the revenue generation activities of all four departments across the enterprise.

Workgroup Information Systems

Figure 1-2 also provides examples of **workgroup information systems.** For example, Telemarketing calls prospective customers on a rotating basis in an attempt to make contact at least once per quarter with every active customer.

The actions of Telemarketing's representatives, however, need to be coordinated. The group does not want to miss customers or duplicate calls; furthermore, some calls require follow-up. The group as a whole cannot afford to drop the ball even when a particular representative who promised a follow-up is not working at the time it must be performed.

To meet departmental needs, Telemarketing has developed a workgroup information system. This system maintains a file of customers and assigns those customers to representatives on a rotating basis. It also keeps track of the need for follow-up calls and assigns these to representatives as well.

Just as an enterprise system coordinates the activities of individual departments, so does a workgroup system coordinate the activities of individual sales representatives.

Personal Information Systems

Suppose that, in addition to Telemarketing, the company in Figure 1-3 also employs a field sales force. These salespeople are assigned a particular territory, and they operate independently. The following scenario illustrates the need for a **personal information system:**

[Diane is talking to herself in the car. . .]

Let me think. How many hours did I spend on the freeway this week? At least 4 on Monday, 5 on Tuesday, another 3½—oh, say, 4 hours a day. That's 20 hours a week driving! I wonder how much I could sell, if I could sell more and drive less....

I've got to think about this. What can I do? I have around 100 customers, but a lot of them are low volume. Hmmm. So, anybody who's placed more than, oh, say $10,000 in orders is worth calling. And companies that could place more than $10,000 and... Wait, that's it! I'll divide my

Figure 1-3 Workgroup

The people in this workgroup coordinate their activities toward common group goals. They share access to certain data and information in working toward those goals.

customers into three groups—those who are already ordering more than $10,000, those who could, if I work it right, and those who will never order that much, either because they're too small or because of competition, or whatever. Now, who are they? I need to look at my computer files.

[Later that night, at home...]

OK, this disk has all of last year's orders for every customer. [She types on her keyboard...] "Show total sales for each customer sorted by total sales." There we go, that's it!

But, good heavens! I've only got five customers who ordered more than $10,000? OK then, who are the desirables? Well, let's see...they have the potential of ordering $10,000, they are close to my office, they have centralized purchasing, no—not really, that's not what I mean. Hmm, they're in high-growth industries.... What I need to do is build a customer file that I can relate to sales. I've got that Chamber of Commerce report on number of employees and size of revenues, and I've also got my redbook fact sheets.

Figure 1-4 Personal Information System

This personal information system provides valuable information to assist a field sales representative in working more effectively.

Next week, I'm not driving anywhere. I'm declaring a moratorium on driving. Diane, your car just broke down! Now, I'll build this customer file and work up a call list. I'll never get to sleep tonight....

This scenario illustrates a personal information system. Unlike the workgroup and enterprise systems, it does not integrate the activities of different individuals or departments. Instead, it facilitates and increases the productivity of a single individual.

HOW INFORMATION SYSTEMS SUPPORT INDIVIDUALS

As stated, this book is concerned with the use of information systems in organizations, and the levels of organizations provide a context for the use of information. We will make extensive use of these three contexts throughout this book.

At the same time, however, organizations do not directly employ information systems, type on keyboards, read reports, or interpret graphs—people do. Thus, it is important to consider how individuals use information systems *within an organizational context.*

This text is concerned about people in all sorts of jobs: managers and nonmanagers, professionals and nonprofessionals, accountants, engineers, consultants, advertising executives, and delivery drivers, among others. This diversity of people creates a need to define a common model for their activity.

Management is often defined as the process of **planning, organizing,** and **controlling** a business activity. This definition fits the activities of all types of business personnel and not just those of managers. At one end of the organizational chart, a delivery driver plans, organizes, and controls the tasks of scheduling and making deliveries. At the other end, a chief executive officer (CEO) plans, organizes, and controls the strategic direction of the company.

Planning

Individuals plan by setting objectives and determining the resources and courses of action needed to meet those objectives. Planning assumes that there will be a tomorrow and another tomorrow beyond that. Further, planning recognizes that some things cannot be produced instantaneously. Finally, planning recognizes that we have some degree of control over where we go. Unless we are very lucky, to achieve a desired state, we need to know what that state is and to aim for it.

Planning involves objectives and means. For example, Diane has set the objective of spending less of her sales workday driving. Why? There are probably several related objectives. She wants to sell more. She may also want less stress, more time for herself, more time with her family, and so forth. She wants greater personal productivity. She is aware that, if she just responds to whatever telephone calls reach her office, she is like a billiard ball bouncing from customer to customer. She may have quite satisfied customers, but that does not necessarily mean she will generate large sales or enjoy her career.

This example brings up a key concept that will appear often in this text: **productivity.** A measure of productivity is the ratio of output to input. To improve productivity, the ratio must be increased. This increase can be achieved by (1) obtaining more output for the same input, (2) obtaining the same output for less input, or (3) doing both.

Suppose Diane defines her productivity as the ratio of sales to hours worked. (Of course, she could increase sales with no change in productivity simply by working more hours—for example, by driving more.) To increase productivity, she must change something. She must cause sales to go up for the same number of hours worked, cause sales to stay the same for fewer hours worked, or do both. Diane's prime objective, then, is to increase her personal productivity.

Planning involves objectives and means. Diane must identify some means— courses of action, resources—to accomplish her goal. Diane decided to focus her time and attention on customers that will bring her the most return. She defined such customers as those likely to generate more than $10,000 in sales, and then she proceeded to identify them.

Diane's planning process is simple. It involves setting clear goals for herself; she can do this job alone. In contrast, much business planning involves workgroups or whole companies. Such cooperative planning is considerably more difficult than individual planning. Large groups, multiple goals, complicated business environments, changing technology, and uncertain industrial or economic conditions complicate the planning process.

Organizing

Organizing, the second dimension in the model of individual activity, is the process of dividing work into tasks and coordinating those tasks to achieve one or more objectives.[3] Often, organizing refers to the assignment of work to groups of people and the creation of lines of authority among those groups. The organizational chart in Figure 1-2 shows the hierarchical arrangement of work-groups and employees, each of which is responsible for a particular component of work to be done.

Organizing can also be more personal. It is the answer to the question, How am I going to get *X* done?

"Do I have to talk to them?"

"The PR agency says it's important. Sue says with all the rumors about the new legislation and its impact on international trade, she's getting 25 calls a day from the press. The agency says if you talk with *Industry Week*, you can head off a lot of the damage."

"You'd think the sky was falling in, but I suppose I'd better talk with them. Who are they sending?"

"Fitzroy and Alsop."

"Alsop's OK. But Fitzroy will want to know how this relates to sales in Swahili in 1952. Alright, then, here's the plan. Have Sue give me the press clippings, and get J. S. to give me the latest financials. I'll need to review the sales forecasts in the United States, Europe, and Japan. Get them from Frank. What's the name of his new secretary?"

"Sharon Gallagher took the job."

---

3. Schermerhorn, John R., Jr., *Management for Productivity.* New York: John Wiley & Sons, 1984, p. 177.

"Alright, have her send them over. Then dig up that report that Johnson did on sales versus international dollar values. Also, get me the weekly stock prices on our competition for the last year. I guess that's it. Oh, where's Frank this week?"

"In Tokyo."

"Good. Have Sharon get in touch with him and tell him to call me at the lodge over the weekend. I've got to talk with him before Monday."

"Anything else?"

"No, leave all this stuff on my desk. I'll take it this weekend. Who's next on the calendar?"

"Krista."

"OK. Oh, tell Sue to stop by my office before she goes home. I want to hear how nasty they're going to be. Have her bring a summary of what we're paying the PR agency. I'll call Hank over the weekend and tell him to earn those astronomical sums they charge. Leave me his home phone number."

"I'll walk down to Krista's. Call me if the sky *does* fall in."

Whatever has happened to this company has been judged detrimental to its prospects. Mr. Franklin, the CEO, needs to turn public opinion, so arrangements have been made for him to speak with the industry press. He must convey the impression that his company will be able to effectively deal with the new situation, that it is still in control of its destiny, and that business will continue as usual. He knows all of this intuitively.

Franklin has been a professional manager for 38 years. He rose to the position of CEO for many reasons—ambition, intelligence, communication skills, negotiating ability, integrity and values, and, perhaps most importantly, the ability to organize. As he speaks with his assistant, he initially challenges the need for the press meeting, but once he agrees on the necessity for the meeting, his organizational skills snap into place.

Franklin needs information. Based on prior experience, he knows the kinds of questions he will be asked, how much time he will have, and what kind and how many resources he can bring to bear during that time period. Given this knowledge, he organizes. He issues instructions that will prepare his way to the interview on Monday.

Much of the coordination will be done by Franklin's assistant, Robin. In fact, observe how Franklin organized the work so that his only tasks are assimilating information and communicating it to the press. He would say that those are the tasks he is supposed to do. Other employees whose time is less expensive to the corporation, can do footwork and coordination. His capable and effective staff indicates the success of his prior organizational activities.

Controlling

Even the best of plans can fail: The plan itself might be faulty, the organization might be wrong, people might make mistakes, circumstances might prohibit people or groups from delivering on commitments, and so forth. People control by observing business activity, comparing the actual results to the intended results, and taking corrective action when necessary.

When Ms. Silver in Accounting considers a customer's credit, she is engaged in a control activity. Her company ships goods under the terms that payment will be received within 60 days. Part of the responsibility of the finance department is to ensure that this policy is followed. Finance tracks receivables and payments, compares payments to the schedule, and makes corrections when necessary. As you saw in the previous scenario, one way to reduce risk during these occurrences is to condition or refuse future orders. Other means involve collection agencies or litigation.

Most likely, Finance recognizes that a certain amount of bad debt will occur and that some payments will be stretched out. The department undoubtedly has guidelines as to how much bad debt can be allowed and how fast collections, on the average, must be received. Part of Ms. Silver's job is to ensure that Finance achieves these goals.

Control involves three components. First, a goal, or standard, must exist, to indicate whether the process is in control. Second, observations or measurements must be made of the business activity. Finally, means of making corrections must exist.

It was stated earlier in the text that information systems are effective if they facilitate the goals and objectives of the people who use them. One way of assessing such effectiveness is to determine whether the information system facilitates the planning, organizing, and controlling of an individual's work. These criteria will be considered from time to time throughout this text.

Ethics and Information Systems

The development and use of information systems raises a number of issues involving value judgments by individuals—issues of **ethics**. For example, the following situations raise ethical problems:

- Using commercial programs without paying for them.
- Using company computer resources for personal purposes.
- Unauthorized snooping in company data or data on other employees' PCs.

- Collecting data about individuals without their knowledge or permission.

- Collecting data about individuals without safeguards against incorrect or misleading data.

- Providing access to job-required data to all employees, including those who are disabled.

- Using computers to monitor employee performance.

On some of these issues, the law may provide useful guidelines for action; on others, corporate policies or professional codes of conduct may be helpful. Lacking such sources of guidance, it is important to consider reasonable standards that can be applied in determining what to do.

Three standards are often applied.[4] First is the Golden Rule: Treat others as you would like them to treat you. Second, ask yourself whether an action serves the interests of the majority or the interests of a minority, perhaps only yourself. Third, consider how an action would appear to others if they knew about it. What would your employer think? Your customers? Although thoughtful people may honestly disagree on outcomes, most can agree on the usefulness of standards such as these.

We now turn our attention to the terms *information* and *systems.*

WHAT IS INFORMATION?

Information is an odd concept. Most people seem to understand what the word *information* means and to know when they do or do not have it. When pressed, however, these same people might find it very difficult to define the word. To clarify what this text means by its use of the word *information*, consider the following example:

Cara Rojas heads the quality assurance group at Standard-Wayne, a manufacturer of industrial electronic test instruments. Her day got off to a rough start this morning at the company weekly manager's conference. Ed Kingsley in Sales led the attack.

"Quality control is nearly out of control," he said. "Last year at this time, our customer support desk was receiving about 130 complaint calls a month, on average. Last month, we got 296 calls." Standard-Wayne customers phone the

---

4. Kallman, Ernest A. and John P. Grillo, *Ethical Decision Making and Information Technology: An Introduction with Cases.* Watsonville, CA: Mitchell McGraw-Hill, 1993.

Figure 1-5 Customer Service Desk Calls by Month

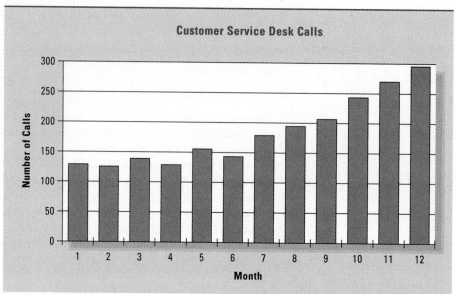

support desk when a product fails to operate correctly. Ed's chart (see Figure 1-5) showed the dramatic increase in calls. "Something simply has to be done to get our product quality back in line, or we're going to go broke staffing the support desk. Besides, if quality doesn't improve, we're going to start losing sales in a big way!"

Back in her office, Cara considered the situation. Her figures showed a steady, modest improvement in quality over the past year (see Figure 1-6), and she took pride in that record. Yet there was no doubt that Ed's numbers looked bad. She needed information to explain what was happening, but she did not know how to proceed.

"The frustrating thing," Cara told her assistant, "is that despite the problems of nearly tripling production over the past year, we've managed to keep quality up... Wait a minute! Let's look at this year's sales figures." She entered a command at her PC keyboard and created the sales graph shown in Figure 1-7.

"Look at that!" she said. "Of course there are more service desk calls. Sales increased to three times the beginning level, so there were bound to be more calls. But calls increased only by a little more than double. That means that the number of complaints per unit sold actually decreased." After a few more minutes' work at the keyboard, Cara completed the table in Figure 1-8 showing nearly a 25 percent reduction in service desk calls per 100 units sold. She enthusiastically began her memo to Ed Kingsley, with copies to the others who were in that meeting.

Figure 1-6   Manufacturing Defects per 100 Units Produced by Month

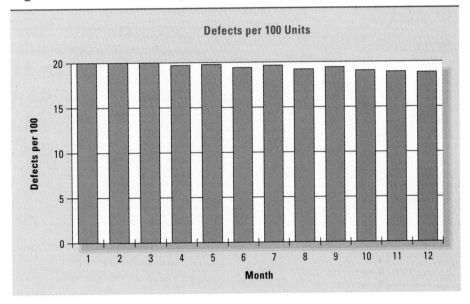

Figure 1-7   Unit Sales by Month

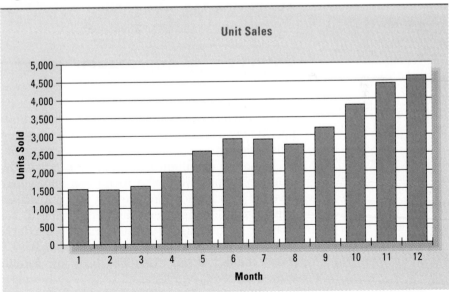

Figure 1-8   Customer Service Desk Calls
per Hundred Units Sold by Month

	Customer Service Desk Calls per Hundred Units Sold **Standard-Wayne Corporation**		
	Unit Sales	**Service Desk Calls**	**Calls per 100 Sales**
Jan	1,562	133	8.5
Feb	1,542	127	8.2
Mar	1,614	141	8.7
Apr	2,003	132	6.6
May	2,581	155	6.0
Jun	2,899	143	4.9
Jul	2,904	178	6.1
Aug	2,736	193	7.1
Sep	3,179	206	6.5
Oct	3,812	245	6.4
Nov	4,389	271	6.2
Dec	4,620	296	6.4

Definitions of Information

The term *information* is defined in a variety of ways. If you have taken a prerequisite course, you may have learned the classic information systems definition, which is, *information is knowledge derived from data.* Data, in turn, is defined as recorded facts or figures.

Another definition is, *information is data placed within a context.* For example, suppose you tell a friend that your younger sister, Toni, is about to have her 16th birthday. Your friend may grimace or chuckle at that statement. Why? Because people typically obtain their driver's license at that age. We imagine a beginning driver just learning how to let out the clutch, change gears, and so on. If your friend grimaces as you make this statement, he or she has placed the fact of your sister's birthday into a context and has thereby gained knowledge about your sister.

Other definitions of information are more mathematical. Two electrical engineers, Shannon and Weaver, define information as *the amount of uncertainty that is reduced when a message is received.*[5] To understand this definition, suppose that you are waiting for an answer to a question that can only be answered by yes or no; further suppose that the answers are equally likely. When the answer arrives, you will have reduced your uncertainty by 50 percent.

Now consider a second situation. Suppose you are waiting for the transmission of a single letter from the English alphabet and that all letters are equally likely. In this case, the odds of a particular letter arriving are 1 out of 26. When a particular letter does arrive, you have ruled out the other 25 possibilities and thus reduced your uncertainty by 25/26ths. The letter in the second example has much more information than the answer in the first.

Although the full-blown Shannon-Weaver definition is too precise to be directly applicable to most business decision making, its underlying concept is useful. That is, when we face a decision—which vendor to select, which applicant to hire, which procedure to follow—we may initially consider, say, ten plausible-looking courses of action. As we assimilate information, some of those alternatives may be revealed as unworkable. For example, if we learn that one applicant for a computer programming position has no experience with the type of programming to be done, we feel more confidence in our ability to judge that person's qualifications. Thus, the information has *reduced our uncertainty* about what to do.

A final definition was set out by the social scientist Gregory Bateson. He defined information as "a difference that makes a difference."[6] This definition turns out to be surprisingly robust. It reflects much of what people mean when they say they would like to have information.

Consider a budgeting situation. Why do organizations have budgets, and why do they keep track of expenses and compare them to budgets? The answer is that they are looking for differences in expenditures that make a difference to the department or to the enterprise.

Or, why might a company maintain an inventory control information system? Such systems exist to determine when an item needs to be ordered or whether items are being stocked and used at an acceptable rate. These reasons are differences that make a difference.

Quality assurance director Cara Rojas needed to know what was causing the unexpected number of customer service desk calls. As it turned out, the drastic increase in sales was the difference that made a difference.

This definition of information will appear in the text from time to time, particularly when it helps clarify how to proceed in the development of an information system.

---

5. Shannon, Claude E. and Warren Weaver, *The Mathematical Theory of Communication.* Urbana: University of Illinois Press, 1949.

6. Bateson, Gregory, *Steps to an Ecology of Mind.* New York: Ballantine, 1978, p. 271.

Characteristics of Good Information

Not all information statements are equal. Some are better than others. In your career, you will be presented with thousands of information statements. Since you will rely on those statements, you need to be able to assess their quality. What criteria should be applied?

First, information must be **pertinent.** It must relate to business at hand and to matters important to the person who has requested the information. Information should help the person deal, in some way, with the issues in his or her world.

Second, information must be **timely.** If your company's advertising manager makes a commitment on advertising by 1 October, market research results available on 15 September are far more valuable than those arriving on 15 October. Similarly, the finance department needs to know about an order from a questionable customer *before* the order is shipped.

Third, information must be **accurate.** If the numbers in Figure 1-8 have substantial errors, then any conclusions drawn from these values may be misleading and harmful.

In some cases, however, information accuracy depends on context. For example, people expect information statements about current and past periods to be more accurate than predictions of the future. If the year-end shareholders' report states that a total earnings of $315,687.00 was disbursed to 267,878 shares of record, for a per-share earning of $1.18, people expect those numbers to be precise.

On the other hand, if the same report predicts that next year's earnings will be $415,000, and those earnings turn out ot be $411,000, everyone will probably be delighted. People apply different criteria for accuracy, depending on the information statement and its intended use.

In addition to pertinence, timeliness, and accuracy, good information also **reduces uncertainty.** Good information involves differences that *make a difference.* Another way of saying this is that good information contains an **element of surprise.** It tells me something I did not already know. When Mr. Franklin, who is preparing to meet the press, asks for Hank's telephone number, he will be disappointed if Robin tells him that he can get it from the information operator in San Francisco. He knows where he can get it; what he doesn't know is the number itself. Characteristics of good information are listed in Figure 1-9.

Figure 1-9 Characteristics of Good Information

- Pertinence
- Timeliness
- Accuracy
- Reduced uncertainty
- Element of surprise

FIVE COMPONENTS OF AN INFORMATION SYSTEM

So far in this chapter we have addressed one important dimension of information systems: *why* they are used. Two other dimensions are also important in the study of MIS: what and how. First, *what* components comprise an information system? Second, *how* are information systems created? We will first consider the *what* question and the nature of systems in general.

Systems

A specialized body of knowledge called general systems theory offers several fundamental definitions. According to general systems theory, a **system** is a set of interrelated elements. A **purposive system** is a system that seeks a set of related goals.[7] All information systems are purposive; in this text, when we use the term *system*, we mean purposive system.

Furthermore, the systems to be presented in this text are **open systems**— that is, they interact with their environments. For example, an interaction occurs when a user enters a command and the computer system responds with a display of data.

Finally, the systems presented share a common model of action: receiving *input* from their environment, *processing* the input, and producing *output* back to their environment. This process occurs so commonly in information systems that it has a name: the **I/P/O**, or **input/process/output**, **cycle**.

Information Systems An **information system** is an open, purposive system that produces information using the I/P/O cycle. The minimal information system consists of three elements: **people, procedures,** and **data**. People follow procedures to manipulate data to produce information. In preparing to meet the press, Mr. Franklin asks that Sue create a summary of fees paid to the PR agency. To do this, Sue will go to her files, obtain data from the agency's billing statements, and process the amounts on the statements using a summarization procedure. She will then follow another procedure to present the results.

Part of Sue's job will be to determine what summarization procedure to follow. She knows Mr. Franklin wants a statement about the structure of payments made to the agency. He does not want a detail of every payment, nor does he want

---

7. Acoff, Russell L., "Towards a System of Systems Concepts," *Management Science,* Vol. 17, No. 11, July 1971, pp. 661–671.

to know just the total. From the context of the request, she can guess that he might want the information as ammunition to motivate Hank to do something regarding the press interview, or he might want it to assess the effectiveness of the agency. In either case, she will follow a procedure to provide a statement less detailed than a report listing every payment, but more detailed than a sheet giving just the total.

Data is a pool of observations. It is a collection of measurements about some aspect of the business. Data is processed to produce information—or differences that make a difference.

Computer-Based Information Systems   Information systems that include a computer are known as **computer-based information systems**. They consist of the following elements: people, procedures, data, programs, and **hardware. Programs** are instructions for computers just as procedures are instructions for people.

The computer can fulfill several roles in the production of information. First, when used as a data storage and retrieval device, the computer acts as a data librarian. Second, the computer provides processing capabilities for the production of information. Examples include calculation of totals, averages, maximums, and the like. Third, the computer serves as a communication device to obtain data or information from other computers. Finally, the computer presents information by producing tables, reports, charts, graphs, and formatted documents.

Computers and humans act as partners in an information system. Work that the humans would have to do in a manual system is delegated to the computer. To make this possible, human procedures are translated into computer programs.

Information systems are not necessarily computer-based. Since the systems considered in this text are all computer-based information systems, the term *information system* will represent the term *computer-based information system*.

Information System Components

To understand the components of an information system, consider a typical system—for instance, that used by a ticket agent at an airline counter. The agent keys something into the system, and the system responds with a screen display. Two entities are interacting here: the human and the computer. Figure 1-10a shows an information system as having two components: a person and a machine. We think of these components first because they behave in a specific way; they produce actions.

Consider the interaction of these two components. What is their interface? When the person looks at the computer screen, what medium establishes their relationship? It is data. When the person's finger touches a key on the keyboard, that action symbolizes data—the connection between the human and the computer. In this context, data can be either the user's data or the commands used to direct the computer.

Figure 1-10 Components of an Information System
(a) At its simplest, a computer-based information system involves a person and a computer. (b) A more complete analysis shows the relationships among all five components.

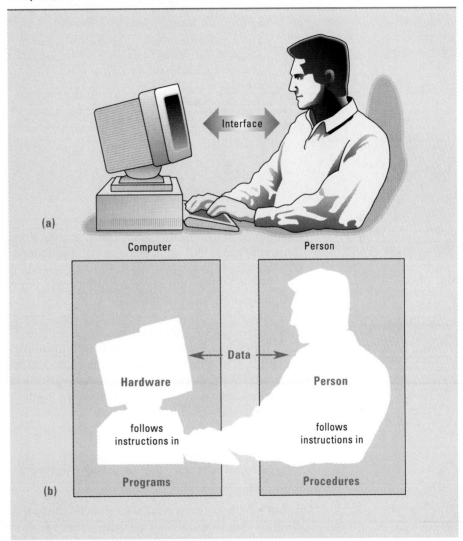

(a)

Computer   Interface   Person

Data

Hardware   **Person**

follows instructions in   follows instructions in

(b)   **Programs**   **Procedures**

Figure 1-10b shows this relationship. The information system consists of a computer that interfaces with a human via the data. The human inputs data and interprets the displayed results. The computer receives the data, processes it, stores it, and sends it back. Data creates a bridge between the computer and the human.

Figure 1-11 Relationships Among the Five Components of an Information System

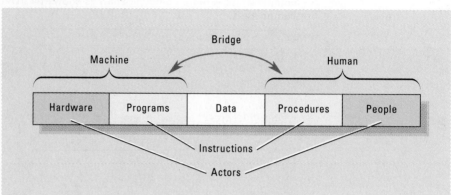

Both computers and humans are general-purpose entities. That is, both are capable of doing many things. To do one specific thing, both entities follow specific steps, which may be embodied in a set of instructions. The computer's instructions take the form of programs, and the human's instructions, the form of procedures.

Figure 1-11 summarizes this discussion. An information system has five components. On the machine side, computer hardware executes instructions in programs; on the human side, people follow instructions in procedures. Data is the interface between the machine and the human.

These five components are common to all information systems, at all levels of organization. The complexity of the components increases between personal and workgroup applications and between workgroup and enterprise applications, but the basic components remain the same. To understand this, briefly consider the system components at each level.

Components of a Personal Information System

Figure 1-12 depicts a typical personal information system. Here, an individual is using a personal computer to perform some business function. That person follows procedures to collect and key data. The personal computer is running programs that process the data and generate results.

Characteristics of personal information systems are shown in the first category listed in Figure 1-13. The single user has his or her own perspective. In a personal system, the individual usually plays three roles: **user** (using information produced to perform some business function); **operator** (starting the computer, loading the correct disks, and putting paper in the printer); and **developer** (creating the system).

Figure 1-12 Personal Information System Components

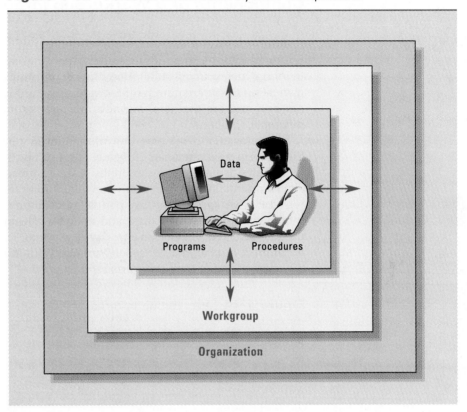

Figure 1-13 Characteristics of Systems at Each Level

Level	Number of Users	Perspective	Roles
Personal	One	Individual	User User operator User developer
Workgroup	Many, but normally fewer than 25	Group— users share similar perspective	Users User operators Professional developers
Enterprise	Many, often hundreds	Organization— Users have multiple perspectives	Users Professional operators Professional developers

Components of a Workgroup Information System

Figure 1-14 shows a workgroup information system. The figure illustrates one of several possible hardware arrangements—personal computers connected together in a *local area network* (LAN). Users follow procedures to collect, key, and share data using the interconnected hardware. The hardware operates programs that not only process the data, but also manage the communications among the different computers.

Characteristics of workgroup information systems are shown in Figure 1-13. The many users, as members of a group, share similar perspectives. All the members of the sales department, for example, share a similar view of the business and a similar orientation and perspective on their information system.

In a workgroup setting, people typically serve only two of the three information system roles: user and operator. Departmental personnel do not usually serve as developers in a workgroup system. Too much technical expertise is required. Instead, outside experts are hired either from another department in the organization or from an external source.

Figure 1-14   Workgroup Information System Components

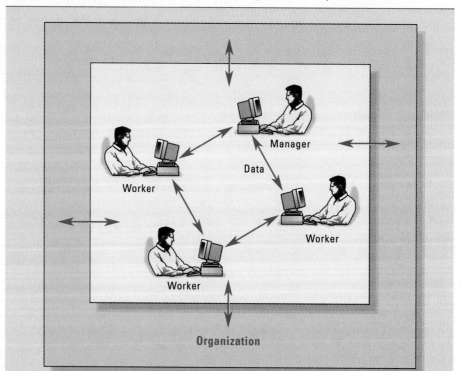

Components of an Enterprise Information System

Figure 1-15 shows one hardware possibility for an enterprise information system with its five components. The system is based around a centralized computer with terminals for users in each of the departments. People follow procedures to collect and key data and enter commands for processing. Programs process the data and coordinate the concurrent operations of the many users.

Figure 1-13 shows characteristics of enterprise information systems. The many users typically hold different perspectives on business and on the use of the information system. For example, in an order-processing system, people in the operations department need information about the components of the order, and

Figure 1-15   Enterprise Information System Components

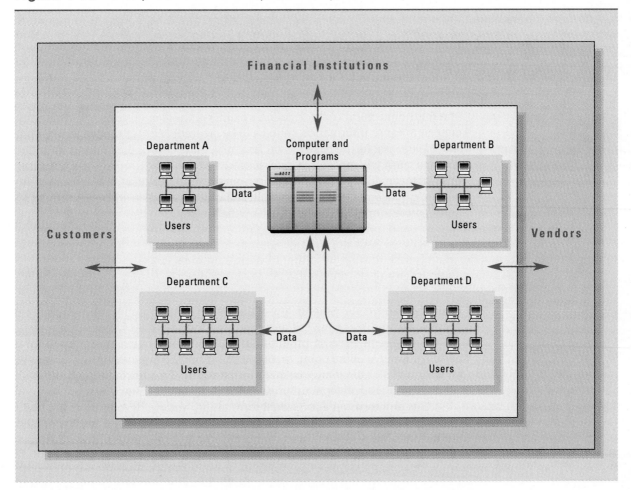

they need to know where and by what means to ship the order. People in the accounts receivable department, on the other hand, need to know how much is owed and where to send the bill. These different perspectives greatly complicate the development of enterprise information systems.

In an enterprise system, the users typically play only the role of user. Information systems professionals develop the system, and a professional staff of operators runs the equipment.

We will study the five components of an information system—hardware, programs, data, procedures, and people—in greater detail in Chapter 6 (personal systems), Chapter 9 (workgroup systems), and Chapter 12 (enterprise systems).

As we move from personal to workgroup systems, we cross an important boundary: from single to multiple users. As we move from workgroup to enterprise systems, we cross a second boundary: from single to multiple perspectives. These boundaries change the nature of the systems, as you will learn.

THE SYSTEMS DEVELOPMENT PROCESS

The third dimension of information systems is the *how* dimension. What must happen to cause information systems to be created? More to the point, what role should you, as a future business professional, play? One of the major goals of this text is to teach you the appropriate roles for systems development. In some cases, this will mean doing most of the work yourself. In other cases, it will mean hiring outside consultants to do the work. In still other cases, you will work with an in-house, professional MIS staff to develop the system.

The Systems Development Life Cycle

Figure 1-16 shows the general flow of the systems development process. Business needs arise, and someone initiates the development of an information system. The development process produces an information system that is used for a period of time. At some point, there is a change in the organization or in its need for information. This change causes a reevaluation of the business need and leads to a new systems development process, which results in a new system.

This process is an abbreviated form of the **systems development life cycle**. In this cycle, systems are developed, used, modified, redeveloped, used, modified, and so forth. Many systems in use today have been through this process dozens of times and are, tracing back through all their versions, 25 or 30 years old!

Figure 1-16 The Systems Development Life Cycle

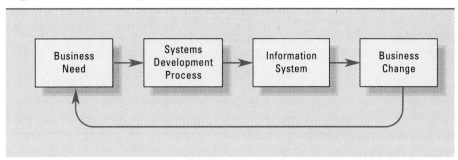

No single systems development process is universally optimum. Many processes are used, each with variations. Development processes vary, especially depending on the level of the system to be developed. Personal systems are far easier to develop than workgroup systems, which are, in turn, much easier to develop than enterprise systems.

Chapter 7 introduces systems development through prototyping, a process used to create personal systems. Chapter 10 discusses a more structured process used for the development of workgroup systems; it also discusses the use of modeling tools and outside contractors for systems development. Chapter 13 describes the individual's role in the development of enterprise information systems.

The User's Role in Systems Development

The role of the end user changes as the complexity of the information system increases. Users have the principal developmental role in personal information systems. After completing this text, you should be able to follow the development process described in Chapter 7 to create personal information systems such as those required to perform financial analyses with spreadsheets. And you should recognize that, in creating such a system, you will deal with all five of the system's components, not just with hardware and programs.

In developing workgroup systems as described in Chapter 10, users typically take a managerial role. As manager (or key member of the workgroup), you take steps to bring about the development of the system by others, and contractors, vendors, or in-house MIS professionals normally take the action roles. You need to learn to define your needs and express them to these people. Further, you need to know enough about workgroup information system development to be an informed consumer of the developers' services.

Finally, in the development of enterprise MIS, as described in Chapter 13, you will take the role of one member of a team that will create the system. Here, you need to know how to express your needs and how to ensure that those needs receive appropriate attention. You also need to understand the problems that developers face in large-scale enterprise systems development, making their needs and actions far more understandable.

HOW THIS TEXT IS ORGANIZED

Figure 1-17 summarizes the course of investigation that this book follows. As shown, the text spirals through the three dimensions of MIS. First, the *why, what,* and *how* dimensions of personal information systems are considered in Chapters 5, 6, and 7. Then, this knowledge is used as a foundation, and these same dimensions are reconsidered for workgroup information systems in Chapters 8, 9, and 10. Finally, the *why, what,* and *how* dimension for enterprise information systems are discussed in Chapters 11, 12, and 13.

In this process, topics such as computer technology and systems development methods will be discussed several times. Understanding of these topics facilitates understanding of information systems at every level: personal, workgroup, and enterprise. Since the context changes at each level, however, you should expect to learn new things about technology and development each time they are considered.

The next three chapters establish a foundation for the remainder of the book. Chapter 2 surveys common types of MISs. Chapter 3 discusses the fundamentals of information systems technology: hardware, programs, and data. Chapter 4 describes the generic ways in which information systems add value to organizations and to the people who work in them.

SUMMARY

This book describes the things you need to know to function effectively in the midst of sweeping changes that are taking place in MIS. It presents three major themes: the ways in which information systems add value to organizations and people; the composition of information systems; and the development of information systems.

MIS is the development and use of effective information systems in organizations. MIS is broader than its name implies. MIS involves management,

Figure 1-17 How the Text Is Organized

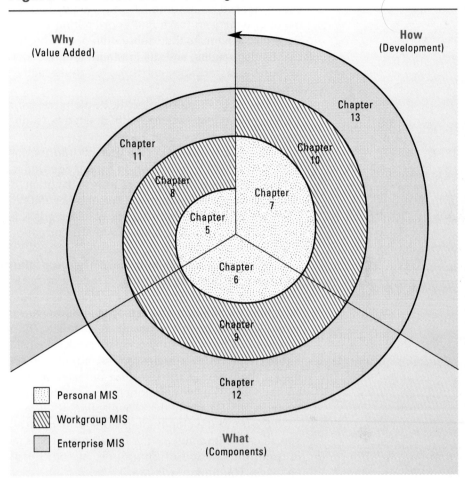

but it also concerns the needs of nonmanagement people as well as the structure and design of organizations that use information systems.

The application of MIS is broad and ubiquitous. To facilitate the study of MIS, the text investigates MIS at three organizational levels: enterprise, workgroup, and personal. Enterprise systems integrate the activity of separate departments and enable the organization to function consistently and appropriately as a single unit. Workgroup systems integrate the activity of employees in a working group so the group responds as a single unit. Personal systems facilitate the work of a single individual.

At each of these levels, the text investigates the ways that people use information systems to plan, organize, and control their work life. Planning involves setting objectives and determining the resources and courses of action needed to accomplish those objectives. Organizing is the process of dividing work into tasks and coordinating those tasks to achieve objectives. Controlling involves the observation of activity, the comparison of that activity to intended results, and the implementation of corrective activity. Information systems can facilitate all three of these activities, at all three levels of organization.

The use of information technology raises a variety of ethical issues. To respond effectively to such questions, individuals need standards for selecting actions.

There are many definitions of information. The classic MIS course definition is that information is knowledge derived from data, where data is defined as recorded facts or figures. Another definition is, information is data placed within a context. Yet another definition concerns the reduction of uncertainty when information is received. A final definition, and the one this text uses most frequently, is that information is a difference that makes a difference.

Information varies in quality. The best information is pertinent, timely, and accurate. Information should reduce uncertainty, and it usually contains an element of surprise.

Information systems are open, purposive systems consisting of at least three elements: people, procedures, and data. The computer-based information systems that form the subject of this book also include hardware and programs. People and hardware are active agents. Procedures and programs are instructions; data is the interface between human components and machine components. The five components are common to computer-based information systems at all levels of the organization, though they vary in type and quality.

Systems development occurs in a cyclical fashion. A business need serves as the impetus for the development of a system. The resulting system is used for a period of time, until, at some point, the need for the system changes. The new needs are fed back to the systems development process, and a new system or new version is created. Systems development activity varies considerably, depending on the scope and complexity of the system. As a general rule, personal systems are far easier to develop than workgroup systems, which are far easier to develop than enterprise systems. The user's role in systems development varies, depending on the level and complexity of the system.

This text approaches the study of MIS in three dimensions: *why* (benefits of information systems); *what* (components of information systems); and *how* (systems development process). It considers each of these dimensions at each level of system—personal, workgroup, and enterprise—in a spiral fashion.

KEY TERMS

MIS	Information (several definitions)	People
Organizational, or enterprise, information system	Pertinent information	Procedures
	Timely information	Data
Workgroup information system	Accurate information	Computer-based information system
	Reducing uncertainty	Hardware
Personal information system	Element of surprise	Programs
	System	User
Planning	Purposive system	Operator
Organizing	Open system	Developer
Controlling	I/P/O cycle	Systems development life cycle
Productivity	Information system	
Ethics		

REVIEW QUESTIONS

1. Describe the major changes taking place in MIS today.

2. What are the three major themes of this text?

3. What departments are involved in approving the large order in the first scenario? Why are these departments involved?

4. Explain the activity documented in Figure 1-1.

5. Define MIS. (Use the Keen definition, as altered for this text.)

6. Explain why the term *MIS* is broader than just the definition of the term *management*. What other topics does MIS involve?

7. State the three organizational levels that we will consider in this text.

8. Give an example, other than the one in this text, of an enterprise information system.

9. Give an example, other than the one in this text, of a workgroup information system.

10. Give an example, other than the one in this text, of a personal information system.

11. State the three tasks involved in most business activities.

12. Describe planning activities.

13. Describe organizing activities.

14. Describe controlling activities.

15. List six types of standards that may be applied in making ethical decisions.

16. State the classical definition of information.

17. Explain how information is related to the concept of uncertainty reduction.

18. State the definition of information that has to do with differences. Explain the meaning of this definition, and give an example.

19. List three characteristics of good information.

20. Explain why information accuracy is relative.

21. Define the term *purposive, open system*.

22. List the minimum components of an information system.

23. List the five components of a computer-based information system.

24. Explain how the five-component framework applies to information systems supporting all three levels of organization.

25. Sketch the major phases of the systems development life cycle. Why must it be a cycle?

26. Summarize how the systems development effort changes when developing information systems at the personal, workgroup, and enterprise levels.

27. What are three dimensions of MIS that this text considers? What are the major categories and topics in each dimension?

DISCUSSION QUESTIONS

1. Reread the first paragraph of this chapter. Are you surprised to find that today's changes are so far-reaching? (If so, explain why that paragraph has information for you.) Explain the three major themes of this book.

Are you disappointed at these themes? What sort of knowledge do you think you need for your future business career?

2. Consider the portion of an information system depicted in Figure 1-1. What would happen if Accounting were not involved in this system? Alternatively, suppose the key decision makers in this department become very cautious. What will happen in the organization? Is the information system to be blamed? In what way does this information system reflect corporate policy? Generalize on this idea: How do information systems reflect corporate policy in other circumstances?

3. According to the first scenario, the Ajax order is to be shipped COD. How can Harold ensure that this happens? Should he? Suppose the order had been refused. How would Harold know that it was not shipped? Should he worry about following up to ensure that it was not shipped? What information would he need to follow up in this way?

4. Why is it important to make it clear that MIS involves organizations and nonmanagement people? Describe information systems that do not involve managers. Consider professional jobs such as consulting that do not involve management. What kinds of information systems are appropriate for these people?

5. Why is it important to consider organizational structure in the design of information systems? In what ways do you think organizational structure influences MIS? In what ways does MIS influence organizational structure?

6. Describe a personal information system that facilitates a salesperson's planning activity, his or her organizing activity, and his or her controlling activity.

PROJECTS

A. Gather five examples of information. Try to be as creative as possible in selecting them. Do not restrict yourself to information produced by computer systems. Reflect on these five pieces of information, and answer the following questions:

1. What is information made of?

2. Where is the information?

3. How do you know if one of your examples contains more information than the other?

4. Consider these questions in light of the three different definitions of information presented in this chapter. Which do you think is the most appropriate definition? Modify the definition of information in any way you think appropriate, given your answers to the preceding three questions.

B. Consider the following situations. In each situation, what standards could be applied in deciding what should be done? What do you think should be done ideally? What pressures might lead a person to do something other than the ideal thing?

1. A financial planner is scheduled to present a major report on Monday. Although she had scheduled the departmental portable computer for the weekend, which includes the necessary programs to create the report, another employee with an even greater need has received that computer. She copies the needed programs and uses the copies on her personal computer at home to prepare the report.

2. Among the candidates for the position of manager of production planning is a well-qualified, visually impaired person. The job, as currently organized, requires some hours of reading each day from a video display screen. This person's interview is scheduled an hour from now.

3. Exploring data in the company database on assignment, a training department employee accidentally discovers a way to access data about the salaries of the company's executives. He prints a copy of the data and shows it to co-workers.

4. The director of marketing has discovered that department employees are sending personal messages (not involving company business) through the company electronic mail system. Some personal messages have been written during work hours; others are written during breaks, but even these use company computing resources for personal purposes. The director has proposed to access and read employees' electronic mail messages, on a spot-check basis, to ensure that all messages involve company business.

C. Tour your campus and observe some of the administrative jobs and workgroups that are in use. Find an example of an enterprise information system, a workgroup information system, and a personal information system. Describe, in general, the goals of these systems. If possible, ask the people in these jobs what the goals of the information system are. How do these goals relate to the overall goals of the organization?

D. Identify what you think are the three most important business functions that your campus library must fulfill. Describe an example enterprise information system (meaning librarywide), workgroup information system (one within the library) and personal information system to support each of these functions.

MINICASE

Parts Smarts

Three times a week, 60 managers gather in front of a wall-sized screen in the bowels of a mammoth facility at Tinker Air Force Base near Oklahoma City, Okla. But instead of plotting military strategy, these managers are planning the work for the world's largest jet engine rebuilding plant. The screen displays real-time information on the whereabouts of the hundreds of thousands of parts that they will reassemble into jet engines for B-52s, F-16s, and other military aircraft.

The information projected on the giant screen is part of the rework plant's Inventory Tracking System (ITS). Before moving to this paperless system offering detailed manufacturing information, the plant was struggling toward an uncertain future. Now, as budget cuts threaten many military bases, the Propulsion Directorate at Tinker's Air Logistics Center has emerged as the leader in the minutely complex and expensive business of rebuilding jet engines.

Because the equipment is so expensive in the first place, rebuilding jet engines and their components is a necessity. New engines cost millions of dollars to manufacture, and they wear out in just five years of routine use—sooner if they're pushed to their limits. The importance of the rebuilding process should increase even more as military budgets head further south and equipment is kept in service longer.

Michael McWaters, the civilian Operations Branch Chief who over sees ITS for Tinker, comes from an engine overhaul and maintenance background. He attributes the system's high function-to-cost ratio in part to the major role prospective users played in the design.

"It's a little difficult to get people who don't know what you're doing to build a system like this," says McWaters. "I don't want to sell the systems people short, because it was a joint effort, but the actual design came from the users."

McWaters isn't exaggerating the complexity of his work. "Planning and scheduling at the Tinker plant make a typical, new-goods manufacturing plant look like child's play in comparison," says Martin Piszczalski, director of manufacturing automation planning in the Ann Arbor, Mich., office of Yankee Group Inc. He has studied the Tinker system.

Tearing down and rebuilding the engines for lethal weapons like F-16 fighters and B-2 Stealth bombers puts some 600,000 parts in Tinker's shop at a given moment, each of which may be at any stage of the rework process—in disassembly, testing, repair, or reassembly. The typical jet engine, which may contain 3,000 to 4,000 parts, takes 65 days to tear down and reassemble. ∎

Edward Cone, excerpted from *Information Week*, August 2, 1993, pp. 36–40.

Discussion Questions

1. Describe the ITS discussed in this minicase.

2. What is the business problem that the ITS is designed to solve?

3. Why did the design for the system need to come from its users rather than from information systems professionals?

4. If a computerized inventory system were not available at Tinker's Air Logistics Center, what kind of manual system do you think would be used? Describe such a manual system.

Copyright© 1993 by **CMP Publications, Inc.,** 600 Community Drive, Manhasset, NY 11030. Reprinted from INFORMATIONWEEK with permission.

2

Fundamental Types of Management Information Systems

FIVE FUNDAMENTAL TYPES OF INFORMATION SYSTEMS are introduced in this chapter. Transaction processing systems support the operational, day-to-day activities of the organization. Management information systems facilitate the management of those day-to-day activities. Decision support systems are special-purpose applications that support the resolution of less structured problems and help make decisions in ambiguous and complicated situations. Office automation systems support interpersonal communication activities such as the preparation and communication of correspondence. Finally, executive support systems are used by senior managers to keep abreast of the organization in broad, overview terms.

The goal of this chapter is to illustrate and discuss fundamental, generic types of information systems. The terminology presented in this chapter will be used throughout the text. Chapter 3 describes the technology that underlies these systems, and Chapter 4 shows how these systems benefit organizations.

ANSWERING KEY BUSINESS QUESTIONS AT SARAH MORRIS ENTERPRISES

Sarah Morris offers public seminars and provides consulting services for improving human communication. Before starting her business, Sarah worked as a clinical psychologist for a number of years. From time to time, she was asked to give motivational and other types of presentations. She is a gifted speaker, and Sarah soon found that she was having more success making speeches than practicing psychology. As a result, she decided to become a professional public speaker. Since she frequently received requests for follow-up consulting, she decided to offer consulting services as well.

Sarah markets her seminars via direct mail, advertising, and professional associations. For direct mail, she maintains a list of customers from prior seminars, and she also sometimes buys mailing lists. She promotes herself through professional associations by speaking at workshops that the associations arrange for her. Seminar attendees often request consulting services after hearing her message. In fact, Sarah has never needed to market her consulting in any other way.

Sarah employs an administrative assistant, who answers the telephone, responds to routine questions, maintains business records, arranges for the printing of seminar materials, reserves seminar space in hotels, and makes travel arrangements. Her assistant also helps prepare and mail marketing materials.

Figure 2-1 lists the types of questions that Sarah Morris and her assistant must answer to run the business. Questions about day-to-day operations are most often answered by a transaction processing system. Questions about management of the company's affairs are usually answered by a type of management information system. Strategic questions are answered by a decision support system.

These questions are sorted in order of *structure*. The first group can be answered by looking up data in a file. These are highly structured questions. The second group involves processing of data. These are less structured questions. A question in the third group, such as "Should we increase prices?" is less quantitative than those in the second group. Analysis of data can help, but subjective judgment is also required. This group is composed of semistructured questions. The very last question is highly unstructured, and though its answer depends to some extent on information produced from data, it depends primarily on Sarah's subjective feelings, beliefs, and attitudes.

It is easier to build information systems to answer questions for more structured questions like those in the first group. The third group of questions requires a balance of information from systems and from subjective, human analysis. This situation is typical of all businesses.

We will now consider three types of information systems that support the three categories of questions.

Figure 2-1   Questions That Sarah Morris Enterprises Asks

Questions about Day-to-Day Operations

■   Is Elizabeth March enrolled in the Milwaukee seminar next week?

■   How much money has Allied Industries paid for the seven attendees at the Atlanta seminar next month?

■   What are the names of the attendees at tomorrow's seminar?

Management Questions

■   Are there sufficient attendees to justify holding the seminar in Milwaukee next week?

■   What was the profit from the seminar in Boston?

■   What's our most profitable seminar topic?

Strategic Questions

■   Should we increase prices?

■   Are follow-on seminars worth developing?

■   Is there enough consulting work?

■   Do we want to be in this business?

TRACKING OPERATIONS WITH TRANSACTION PROCESSING SYSTEMS

Transaction processing systems (TPSs) support day-to-day operations by maintaining detailed records. These systems help a company conduct its operations and keep track of its activities.

Because they are at the heart of a company's business, TPSs must do their work quickly and reliably. Key business functions, such as ticket reservations; order entry; and check, accounts payable, accounts receivable, and payroll processing depend on TPSs.

TPSs are the oldest type of information system. They were first developed in the 1950s in accounting departments of major corporations. They have been the workhorse of the information systems industry for the last 30 years. Their technology is stable.

Architecture of a TPS

Figure 2-2 shows the architecture of a typical TPS application. The graphical symbols in this figure represent various components of a TPS. These symbols are not arbitrary; they have standardized meanings that are summarized in Figure 2-3. Figure 2-2 is an example of a **systems architecture diagram**. Such diagrams are useful for documenting and understanding the major files, programs, and hardware in an information system.

According to Figure 2-2, an event occurs, such as a request for a ticket to a concert, an order for products, or the presentation of a check for payment. The event is recorded by keying it into the computer system as a **transaction**, which is a representation of the event. One or more TPS programs process the transaction against TPS data. In a ticket reservation system, this data includes the location of available seats; in an order-entry system, the data includes a list of available products, their prices, and related data; in a check-processing system, the data includes account balances and customer lists.

The TPS program generates two types of output. It sends messages back to the user terminal, and it generates printed documents. For example, a ticket reservation program displays which seats have been sold to a particular person; it also prints the tickets and, perhaps, a mailing label for sending them.

There are two fundamental types of TPSs: on-line and batch.

Figure 2-2 Architecture of a TPS Application

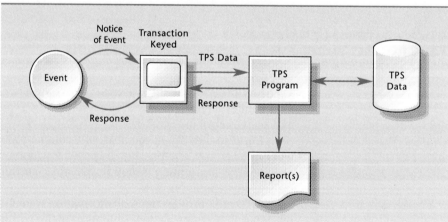

Figure 2-3 Symbols Used in Systems Architecture Diagrams

Symbol	Name	Comments
	Computer Program	Program runs on a computer, which is usually not shown.
	User Workstation	Keyboard and screen; can be terminal or microcomputer.
	Direct-Access Storage Device (DASD)	Data repository; data can be read or written in any order.
	Tape: Sequential Access Device	Data repository; data must be read and written sequentially.
	Document	Report, graphic, or manual form.
	Telecommunications Link	Telephone line or other, similar connection.

On-Line TPS

On-line interactive systems, or **on-line systems**, involve a direct connection between the user and the TPS program. The user inputs a single transaction, and the program interacts with the user to process that transaction.

For example, when a customer calls to place an order, the clerk accesses the order-entry TPS program to determine the quantities of goods in inventory. The clerk and the customer use the information that the program provides to determine the best way to meet the customer's needs. They interact directly with the program. The system in Figure 2-2 is an example. This system implements the I/P/O cycle defined in Chapter 1.

Batch TPS

Batch systems are the second type of TPS. In a batch system, transactions are grouped together and processed as a batch. For example, in a check-processing system, all checks received on a particular day may be grouped together and processed as a batch.

Figure 2-4   Entering an Order
Order entry is an essential ingredient in most TPSs.

The architecture of a typical batch-processing application is shown in Figure 2-5. Transactions are batched into a **transaction file** and sorted by an identifying value. For example, checks may be **sorted** by account number. The batch processing program uses the transaction data to update the **master file**. The checking system master file contains customer checking account data, including account balances. This data is updated to create a new customer master file with updated account balances. Reports produced include overdrawn accounts, monthly summaries, and suspicious activity.

Although batch processing is older and, for many purposes, more cumbersome than on-line processing, it does have advantages. Under some circumstances, it is more efficient than on-line transaction processing, especially when its purpose is naturally a periodic activity, such as payroll.

Figure 2-5   Architecture of a Batch-Processing Application

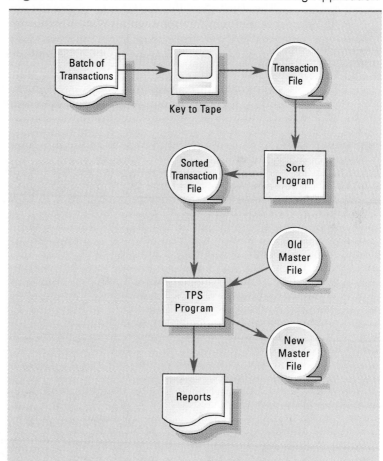

Also, because transactions are processed in batches, it is easier to control processing. For example, in an accounts payable application, it is easier to ensure that no extra checks are generated if all checks are produced in one run and the number of transactions is balanced against the number of checks generated. Such a balancing procedure is called a *control*; Chapter 12, which discusses the elements of enterprise systems, will consider such controls.

An Example TPS for Sarah Morris Enterprises

Sarah Morris Enterprises uses a TPS to keep track of customers, seminars, and course registrations. This TPS uses a set of programs called the customer/enrollment system, which Sarah purchased from an independent computer consulting company.

The structure of this system is similar to the one shown in Figure 2-2. Sarah and her assistant key transactions on a microcomputer keyboard. The data is processed by the customer/enrollment programs (the TPS programs). The customer data and the enrollment data are modified, and class enrollment and other reports are printed.

The system provides menus, forms, and reports. Figure 2-6 shows the menus. A **menu** is a list of action choices that direct the system's activity. The user selects

Figure 2-6 Customer/Enrollment System Menus

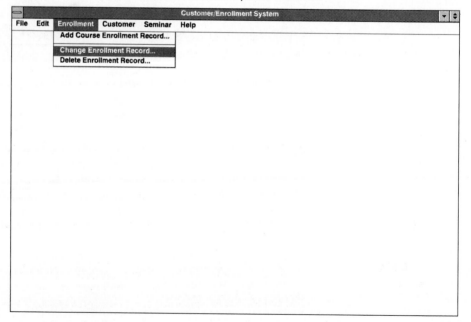

Figure 2-7 Processing a Form

(a) To enroll a customer in a seminar, the user follows the procedure in part b to fill in the screen form. (b) The user fills in either the customer number or the customer's first name and last name, and the system supplies the remaining customer information. If that information is correct, then data about this customer already exists, and the enrollment can proceed. If it is not, then the user must press <F3> to enter complete customer data before proceeding.

(a)

Customer Enrollment Form

Cust #:

Cust Last Name:

Cust First Name:

Company Name:

Course #:

Course Name:

Course Location:

Course Date:

Press <F1 > to enter data.

(b)

1. Enter Cust # or Cust Last Name, Cust First Name
2. If customer exists, the application will move the cursor to Course # and fill in Customer data. If correct, proceed with step 4.
3. Press <F3> to enter customer data. Follow instructions on that form.
4. Enter Course #. Application will fill in Course Name and other data. If incorrect, enter correct Course #.
5. Press <F1> to enter data.

from the choices presented in the menu. Some selections may cause the display of submenus, with additional choices.

A **form** on the screen is the electronic equivalent of a paper form with blanks to be filled in. The form for enrolling a customer in a seminar is shown in Figure 2-7a. It is displayed when the user selects the appropriate choice from a menu. To complete the form, the user follows the procedure in Figure 2-7b. Often, after the user has entered partial information, such as the customer name, the system uses its stored data to fill in additional information, such as the customer number.

The customer/enrollment system fits the TPS architecture shown in Figure 2-2. The TPS data comprises three tables: CUSTOMER, COURSE, and ENROLL (see Figure 2-8). The customer/enrollment programs add, delete, change, or display values in these tables of data, depending on the choices selected from menus.

The customer/enrollment system produces a variety of **reports**, including the two shown in Figure 2-9. Reports are most often displayed on the computer's screen, but either Sarah or her assistant can print them if needed. Sarah takes a copy of the seminar attendance report to a seminar to verify attendance. She (or a

Figure 2-8 Tables in Customer/Enrollment System

Format of CUSTOMER Table

Cust#	CustLname	CustFname	CoName	AreaCode	Phone	Addr1	Addr2	City	State	Zip

Format of COURSE Table

Course#	CourseName	Location	CourseDate

Format of ENROLL Table

Cust#	Course#	AmountDue	AmountPaid

Figure 2-9 Example Customer/Enrollment System Reports

SEMINAR ATTENDANCE REPORT

Date of Report: 2/2/94

Date of Seminar: 4/15/94   Location: Atlanta

Customer Name	Company Name	Amount Due	Amount Paid
Abernathy, Kathy	Forrest, Inc.	$ 795.00	$ 0.00
Ouspensky, P. D.	Self-employed	$ 795.00	$ 795.00
Smathers, Jane	Amicon	$ 795.00	$ 295.00

Total Due: $ 1,195.00

SEMINAR DATE REPORT

Date of Report: 2/2/95

Topic	Date	City	Number of Attendees	Revenue
Seminar 1	10/07/94	Atlanta	14	$ 3,347.55
Seminar 2	10/15/94	Boston	17	$ 6,798.83
Seminar 2	11/30/94	Salt Lake City	12	$ 4,388.55

local temporary assistant) also uses it to collect amounts due. Both Sarah and her assistant use the seminar date report to overview the year's activities.

In addition, Sarah or her assistant can query the data tables in an ad hoc way using a *query language processor.* This program lets users pose questions about the data using a flexible, easy-to-learn language.

The customer/enrollment TPS helps Sarah and her assistant manage the operations of the business. The system can be used to answer questions about day-to-day operations. It does not, however, address management questions or strategic questions. Other types of information systems are required for those purposes.

INFORMING MANAGERS WITH MANAGEMENT INFORMATION SYSTEMS

The second major type of information system is the **management information system (MIS)**. The term *MIS* has two very different definitions. The first was given in Chapter 1: the development and use of effective information systems in organizations. This is the **broad** and encompassing definition. The second, which concerns us now, is much narrower. It identifies a specific type of MIS. In this **narrow** definition, an MIS is an information system that facilitates management by producing structured, summarized reports on a regular and recurring basis. Such MIS outputs are produced routinely and used primarily for controlling activities, though they can also be used for planning and organizing.

Conceptually, such MISs are a level above TPS applications. They are not concerned with day-to-day operations, but rather with the longer-term management of operations. For example, in a ticket reservations system, a TPS is used to take orders and print tickets, and an MIS is used to measure and report the performance of each ticket agent. Such an MIS keeps track of the numbers and amounts of each agent's sales, and it regularly produces reports, such as the one in Figure 2-10, about agent effectiveness. The sales office manager uses this report to track agent performance, identify problems, and reward exceptional sales activity.

Architecture of an MIS

Usually, MIS applications process data that is generated by TPSs and other internal information sources. Figure 2-11 shows a typical MIS system architecture. The user submits requests for reports to the MIS programs. The programs process the

Figure 2-10   Example MIS Report for Ticket Sales Activity

SALES FOR THE WEEK OF 8 AUGUST				
Salesperson	**Hours Worked**	**Number of Sales**	**Dollar Sales**	**Dollar Sales/Hour**
Jane Adams	40	486	$ 10,692	$ 267
Mark Baker	40	654	$ 16,350	$ 409
Michelle Johnson	20	392	$ 10,192	$ 510
Bill McIntyre	40	441	$ 10,143	$ 254

Figure 2-11   Architecture of an MIS Application

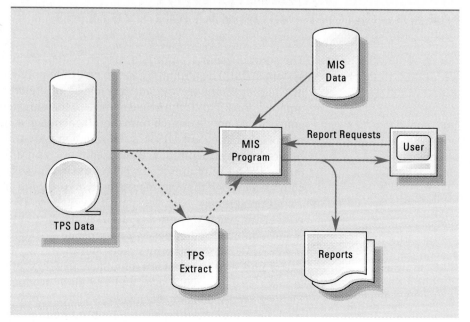

TPS data by aggregating and reformatting it to produce reports, which are either printed or displayed at the manager's workstation.

In some cases, the reports are automatically generated. For example, the MIS programs may be written to produce a certain series of reports every Monday morning or at the close of every business day.

Some MIS application programs look for certain exceptional conditions in the data and produce reports when those conditions occur. For example, Sarah Morris has an MIS application that prints the name and location of any seminar that does not have at least 10 participants 2 weeks prior to its start. Such reports are called **exception reports.**

In some cases, the MIS application does not read the operational TPS data directly. Instead, an extract of the TPS data is made, and the MIS application processes the extract. This is done for a variety of reasons—to provide security for the TPS data, to transfer data between computers when the TPS and the MIS operate on different machines, or to consolidate data to make MIS processing more efficient.

The MIS may also store and maintain data of its own. Some MIS applications have simple models of business activity that they use in processing data to generate information for the manager. If such models exist, they are static, so that the manager gets the same report with comparable data for every period. You will see an example of such a static model in the next section.

Improving Management Information at Sarah Morris Enterprises

To answer the management questions in Figure 2-1, Sarah Morris must take data from TPS applications and use it to compute revenue, costs, and profit.

She knows that her profitability depends on the seminar price, the costs of food, rooms, and services in the seminar hotel, and the number of attendees. She has developed a set of equations to determine profitability:

Profit = Revenue – Total-Expense

Revenue = *Number-of-Attendees* × *Seminar-Price*

Total-Expense = Fixed-Cost + Variable-Cost

Fixed-Cost = Hotel-Cost + Travel-Expense

Hotel-Cost = *Daily-Meeting-Room-Cost* × *Number-of-Days*

Travel-Expense = *Airfare* + (*Daily-Lodging-Cost* + \$65) × *Number-of-Days*

Variable-Cost = Material-Cost + Food-Cost

Material-Cost = \$40 × *Number-of-Attendees* + \$135

Food-Cost = (2 × *Break-Cost* + *Lunch-Cost*) × *Number-of-Attendees* × *Number-of-Days*

In these equations, the **independent variables** are italicized. The values of these variables do not depend on other variables, but rather on actual number of attendees, travel expenses, and hotel prices. Given values for each of these variables, the profitability of a seminar can be approximated from the equations.

These equations are a simple *model* of seminar profitability. In Figure 2-11, these equations would be stored on the disk labeled MIS Data. The model is used to transform the raw data into information that will be helpful to Sarah and her assistant. Such models must be static so the reports will be comparable.

These equations can be used before or after a seminar. Before a seminar, Sarah inputs estimated values for independent variables and receives a report of the seminar's expected profitability. She uses this projection to answer questions such as "Are there sufficient attendees to justify holding the seminar in Milwaukee next week?" Operational data from past seminars may be used to calculate estimates of independent variables.

After a seminar, Sarah inputs actual values of independent variables from the operational TPS data and receives a report of actual profit or loss. The report answers questions such as"What was the profit from the Boston seminar?"

MIS with a Spreadsheet Program

Sarah could compute the equations by hand or write a computer program to do it, but she did neither. Instead, she used a **spreadsheet program**. Figure 2-12 shows the screen display of a spreadsheet to compute the equations. This screen shows pre-seminar projections that assume the Milwaukee seminar may be attended by 10, 20, 25, 30, or 35 people.

After a seminar, Sarah inputs actual values of the independent variables, and the spreadsheet computes actual profitability. These actual values can be saved for future reference.

Figure 2-13 shows the profit and loss statement for all of the seminars Sarah taught in the second (calendar) quarter of 1993, showing both actual and estimated material and travel costs. This report helps Sarah determine the profitability of her seminars, and it helps her assess the accuracy of her projections and her model.

Consider the report in Figure 2-13 in light of the third definition of information in Chapter 1. The presentation of actual and estimated data helps Sarah determine *which differences make a difference.* If the actual data is not too far from estimated, Sarah will take no special action. If the actual data is quite different from estimated, Sarah must do something to improve the estimate.

Historical data such as that in Figure 2-13 helps Sarah answer questions concerning her most (or least) profitable seminar topic. She can save actual values of costs and revenue in each seminar's spreadsheet and then use the various spreadsheets to determine the answers.

Figure 2-12 Spreadsheet: Projected Profit and Loss

Sarah Morris Seminars
Projected Profit and Loss Statement, Milwaukee, September 1994

INDEPENDENT VARIABLES					
	Case 1	Case 2	Case 3	Case 4	Case 5
Num.Att.	10	20	25	30	35
Price	$ 295.00	$ 295.00	$ 295.00	$ 295.00	$ 295.00
D.Mtg.Cst.	$ 75.00	$ 75.00	$ 75.00	$ 75.00	$ 75.00
Num.Days	2	2	2	2	2
Airfare	$ 378.00	$ 378.00	$ 378.00	$ 378.00	$ 378.00
D.Ldg Cst.	$ 89.00	$ 89.00	$ 89.00	$ 89.00	$ 89.00
Brk.Cst.	$ 5.25	$ 5.25	$ 5.25	$ 5.25	$ 5.25
Lnch.Cst.	$ 17.50	$ 17.50	$ 17.50	$ 17.50	$ 17.50
REVENUE					
Total	$ 2,950.00	$ 5,900.00	$ 7,375.00	$ 8,850.00	$ 10,325.00
COSTS					
Variable					
Food	$ 560.00	$ 1,120.00	$ 1,400.00	$ 1,680.00	$ 1,960.00
Material	$ 535.00	$ 935.00	$ 1,135.00	$ 1,335.00	$ 1,535.00
Tot.Var.	$ 1,095.00	$ 2,055.00	$ 2,535.00	$ 3,015.00	$ 3,495.00
Fixed					
Travel	$ 940.00	$ 940.00	$ 940.00	$ 940.00	$ 940.00
Hotel	$ 150.00	$ 150.00	$ 150.00	$ 150.00	$ 150.00
Tot.Fixed	$ 1,090.00	$ 1,090.00	$ 1,090.00	$ 1,090.00	$ 1,090.00
Total					
Tot.Exp.	$ 2,185.00	$ 3,145.00	$ 3,625.00	$ 4,105.00	$ 4,585.00
PROFIT					
Profit	$ 765.00	$ 2,755.00	$ 3,750.00	$ 4,745.00	$ 5,740.00

Figure 2-13   Actual Second Quarter Profit and Loss Statement

Sarah Morris Seminars
Profit and Loss Statement, Second Quarter 1994

INDEPENDENT VARIABLES					
	Atlanta 15 Apr 94	Los Angeles 12 May 94	Chicago 19 May 94	Wash. D.C. 07 Jun 94	Los Angeles 22 Jun 94
Num.Att.	27	34	14	7	22
Price	$ 295.00	$ 295.00	$ 295.00	$ 295.00	$ 295.00
D.Mtg.Cst.	$ 75.00	$ 115.00	$ 95.00	$ 145.00	$ 115.00
Num.Days	2	2	2	2	2
Airfare	$ 378.00	$ 485.00	$ 279.00	$ 415.00	$ 615.00
D.Ldg.Cst.	$ 89.00	$ 135.00	$ 105.00	$ 138.00	$ 135.00
Brk.Cst.	$ 5.25	$ 6.50	$ 5.00	$ 6.75	$ 6.50
Lnch.Cst.	$ 17.50	$ 22.50	$ 19.95	$ 24.95	$ 22.50

REVENUE					
Total	$ 7,965.00	$ 10,030.00	$ 4,130.00	$ 2,065.00	$ 6,490.00

COSTS					
Variable					
Food Est.	$ 1,512.00	$ 2,414.00	$ 838.60	$ 538.30	$ 1,562.00
Food Act.	$ 1,677.78	$ 2,377.89	$ 790.55	$ 515.47	$ 1,544.28
Mat. Est.	$ 1,215.00	$ 1,495.00	$ 695.00	$ 415.00	$ 1,015.00
Mat. Act.	$ 1,177.94	$ 1,295.85	$ 675.00	$ 387.25	$ 1,123.87
T.Var.Est.	$ 2,727.00	$ 3,909.00	$ 1,533.60	$ 953.30	$ 2,577.00
T.Var.Act.	$ 2,855.72	$ 3,673.74	$ 1,465.55	$ 902.72	$ 2,668.15
Fixed					
Travel Est.	$ 940.00	$ 1,185.00	$ 889.00	$ 1,124.00	$ 1,315.00
Travel Act.	$ 1,134.67	$ 1,407.85	$ 987.46	$ 940.00	$ 1,589.25
Hotel Est.	$ 150.00	$ 230.00	$ 190.00	$ 290.00	$ 230.00
Hotel Act.	$ 167.00	$ 245.00	$ 177.00	$ 124.00	$ 385.67
T.Fixed.Est.	$ 1,090.00	$ 1415.00	$ 1,079.00	$ 1,414.00	$ 1,545.00
T.Fixed.Act.	$ 1,301.67	$ 1652.85	$ 1,164.46	$ 1,064.00	$ 1,974.92
Total					
T.Exp.Est.	$ 3,817.00	$ 5,324.00	$ 2,612.60	$ 2,367.30	$ 4,122.00
T.Exp.Act.	$ 4,157.39	$ 5,326.59	$ 2,630.01	$ 1,966.72	$ 4,643.07

PROFIT					
Profit Est.	$ 4,148.00	$ 4,706.00	$ 1,517.40	($ 302.30)	$ 2,368.00
Cum.Est.Prof.	$ 4,148.00	$ 8,854.00	$ 10,371.40	$ 10,069.10	$ 12,437.10
Profit Act.	$ 3,807.61	$ 4,703.41	$ 1,499.99	$ 98.28	$ 1,846.93
Cum.Act.Prof.	$ 3,807.61	$ 8,513.61	$ 10,031.01	$ 9,728.71	$ 12,096.71

IMPROVING DECISION MAKING WITH DECISION SUPPORT SYSTEMS

The third major type of information system is the **decision support system (DSS)**. DSSs are interactive computer-based facilities that assist decision making in less structured situations. DSSs differ from TPSs and MISs in that they do not always support an ongoing process. DSSs are often created to solve particular problems on an **ad hoc processing** basis and to study one-of-a-kind problems or opportunities. Unlike MISs, which are used for regular and recurring needs, the need for a DSS can be irregular. DSSs are designed to facilitate the solution of less-structured problems whereas MISs and TPSs are better suited for the solution of very structured problems. Therefore, in a DSS, flexibility and adaptability are critical.

For example, suppose a strike by the musicians' union forces the cancellation of opera performances. The management of the opera association wants to know the impact on revenue of each performance's cancellation. A DSS could process ticket agency data to produce this information.

Actually, the term *decision support facility* would be more accurate than the term *decision support system*. DSSs are not structured, finished systems, as are TPSs and MISs, but rather they are collections of data and data processing tools used in creative ways to manipulate data. Often, users of DSSs use the tools on their own, without help from professional information systems personnel.

Like MISs, DSSs involve **models** of business activity. Unlike MISs, however, DSS models are often quite complex. They are also dynamic; the DSS user frequently changes the models to adapt them to the changing understanding and needs of a problem. Ticket agencies, for example, may have a series of equations that predicts sales of tickets on the basis of type of performance, day of week, time of year, and so forth. As the strike progresses, the DSS users may add to or otherwise modify these equations to produce information that is important in negotiating a resolution to the strike. These models are stored as part of the DSS data.

The technology of DSSs is evolving. Both hardware and programs are becoming more powerful and better suited to DSS tasks. Expect significant improvements over the next decade or more.

Architecture of a DSS

Figure 2-14 shows the architecture of a typical DSS application. Data from the organization's TPS and MIS applications is input to the DSS programs, along with data from external sources and DSS model data. The user interacts with the DSS on-line; requests are made, models are created or adjusted, data is manipulated

Figure 2-14   Architecture of a DSS Application

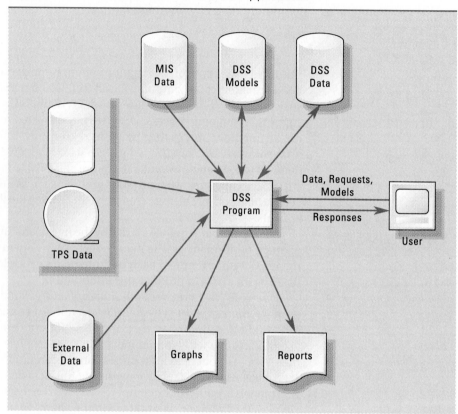

and stored, and so forth. The output of the DSS programs can be text, structured reports, or graphics.

A variety of programs support the DSS, including spreadsheet programs, personal database management systems (DBMSs), word processing packages, graphics programs, statistical packages, and other special-purpose programs. (You will learn more about such programs in subsequent chapters.)

Answering Strategic Questions at Sarah Morris Enterprises

To illustrate the type of processing typical in DSS applications, we will consider two of the strategic questions in Figure 2-1. First, "Should Sarah Morris raise her prices?" This is a typical DSS question because it is less structured, it does not occur regularly, and answering it involves a dynamic interaction between the user and the information system.

Briefly, Sarah wants to know what will happen to her revenue and profitability if she raises prices. She believes an inverse relationship exists between price and attendance: If she increases prices, attendance will decrease. Her problem is that she does not know the amount of the decrease. It may decrease only slightly, so the increase in prices will more than make up for the lost revenue, or it may decrease so much that the increase in prices will not make up for the lost revenue. She would like to know where the **break-even point** is.

In the spreadsheet in Figure 2-15, Sarah simulates what would have happened in the second quarter if she had changed her prices. She uses the equations from the spreadsheet in Figure 2-13, but inserts the actual hotel and travel cost data from her second quarter seminars. She computes a baseline case using actual attendance and her current price (Figure 2-15a). Then, she adds $100 to the price and assumes 10 and 50 percent attendance reductions. These spreadsheets are shown in Figures 2-15b and 2-15c. With a 10 percent reduction, she earns about $7,500 more with the price increase. With a 50 percent reduction, she earns about $5,000 less.

Examining these results, she guesses that she would break even assuming a 35 percent attendance reduction. She enters that level of attendance and obtains the results shown in Figure 2-15d. Her break-even point is just about 35 percent.

With this information, Sarah now needs to make subjective business decisions. Will a $100 price increase reduce attendance more than 35 percent? Is it worth the risk? If she obtains, say, a 10 percent reduction in attendance, she will earn about $7,500 more, but she will meet 10 percent fewer people, and her consulting business may suffer. Sarah will need to weigh these factors and others before making the price change.

So far, Sarah's use of the DSS has involved only a small amount of operational data and a simple spreadsheet model. To answer the question about the amount of attendance reduction due to a $100 increase, Sarah might add other models of demand. She might also access, via programs on her computer, external sources of industry data that will tell her what other companies charge for seminars.

Using TPS Data in a DSS

To determine whether developing follow-on seminars is worthwhile, Sarah can **extract** and process data from the operational TPS system.

Suppose Sarah currently offers three communications seminars. (We'll call them seminars 1, 2, and 3, though they have suitable marketing-oriented names.) Customers must attend seminar 1 before enrolling in seminar 2 or 3, which can be taken in either order. Thus, some customers take seminar 1 only, some take 1 and 2, some take 1 and 3, and some take 1, 2, and 3.

Figure 2-15 Simulating a Change in Pricing
(a) Baseline profit and loss statement.

Sarah Morris Seminars
Profit and Loss Statement, Second Quarter 1994

	Atlanta 15 Apr 94	Los Angeles 12 May 94	Chicago 19 May 94	Wash. D.C. 07 Jun 94	Los Angeles 22 Jun 94
INDEPENDENT VARIABLES					
Num.Att.	27	34	14	7	22
Price	$ 295.00	$ 295.00	$ 295.00	$ 295.00	$ 295.00
D.Mtg.Cst.	$ 75.00	$ 115.00	$ 95.00	$ 145.00	$ 115.00
Num.Days	2	2	2	2	2
Airfare	$ 378.00	$ 485.00	$ 279.00	$ 415.00	$ 615.00
D.Ldg.Cst.	$ 89.00	$ 135.00	$ 105.00	$ 138.00	$ 135.00
Brk.Cst.	$ 5.25	$ 6.50	$ 5.00	$ 6.75	$ 6.50
Lnch.Cst.	$ 17.50	$ 22.50	$ 19.95	$ 24.95	$ 22.50
REVENUE					
Total	$ 7,965.00	$ 10,030.00	$ 4,130.00	$ 2,065.00	$ 6,490.00
COSTS					
Variable					
Food	$ 1,512.00	$ 2,414.00	$ 838.60	$ 538.30	$ 1,562.00
Material	$ 1,215.00	$ 1,495.00	$ 695.00	$ 415.00	$ 1,015.00
Tot.Var.	$ 2,727.00	$ 3,909.00	$ 1,533.60	$ 953.30	$ 2,577.00
Fixed					
Travel	$ 940.00	$ 1,185.00	$ 889.00	$ 1,124.00	$ 1,315.00
Hotel	$ 150.00	$ 230.00	$ 190.00	$ 290.00	$ 230.00
Tot.Fixed	$ 1,090.00	$ 1,415.00	$ 1,079.00	$ 1,414.00	$ 1,545.00
Total					
Tot.Exp.	$ 3,817.00	$ 5,324.00	$ 2,612.60	$ 2,367.30	$ 4,122.00
PROFIT					
Profit	$ 4,148.00	$ 4,706.00	$ 1,517.40	($ 302.30)	$ 2,368.00
Cum.Prof.	$ 4,148.00	$ 8,854.00	$ 10,371.40	$ 10,069.10	$ 12,437.10

Figure 2-15 *(continued)*
(b) Projected profit and loss statements for $100 price increase, 10 percent attendance drop.

Sarah Morris Seminars
Projected Profit and Loss Statement, Second Quarter 1994
$100 Price Increase, 10 Percent Attendance Drop

INDEPENDENT VARIABLES					
	Atlanta 15 Apr 94	Los Angeles 12 May 94	Chicago 19 May 94	Wash. D.C. 07 Jun 94	Los Angeles 22 Jun 94
Num.Att.	24	31	13	6	20
Price	$ 395.00	$ 395.00	$ 395.00	$ 395.00	$ 395.00
D.Mtg.Cst.	$ 75.00	$ 115.00	$ 95.00	$ 145.00	$ 115.00
Num.Days	2	2	2	2	2
Airfare	$ 378.00	$ 485.00	$ 279.00	$ 415.00	$ 615.00
D.Ldg.Cst.	$ 89.00	$ 135.00	$ 105.00	$ 138.00	$ 135.00
Brk.Cst.	$ 5.25	$ 6.50	$ 5.00	$ 6.75	$ 6.50
Lnch.Cst.	$ 17.50	$ 22.50	$ 19.95	$ 24.95	$ 22.50
REVENUE					
Total	$ 9,480.00	$ 12,245.00	$ 5,135.00	$ 2,370.00	$ 7,900.00
COSTS					
Variable					
Food	$ 1,344.00	$ 2,201.00	$ 778.70	$ 461.40	$ 1,420.00
Material	$ 1,095.00	$ 1,375.00	$ 655.00	$ 375.00	$ 935.00
Tot.Var.	$ 2,439.00	$ 3,576.00	$ 1,433.70	$ 836.40	$ 2,355.00
Fixed					
Travel	$ 940.00	$ 1,185.00	$ 889.00	$ 1,124.00	$ 1,315.00
Hotel	$ 150.00	$ 230.00	$ 190.00	$ 290.00	$ 230.00
Tot.Fixed	$ 1,090.00	$ 1,415.00	$ 1,079.00	$ 1,414.00	$ 1,545.00
Total					
Tot.Exp.	$ 3,529.00	$ 4,991.00	$ 2,512.70	$ 2,250.40	$ 3,900.00
PROFIT					
Profit	$ 5,951.00	$ 7,254.00	$ 2,622.30	$ 119.60	$ 4,000.00
Cum.Prof.	$ 5,951.00	$ 13,205.00	$ 15,827.30	$ 15,946.90	$ 19,946.90

Figure 2-15   *(continued)*

(c) Projected profit and loss statements for $100 price increase, 50 percent attendance drop.

	Atlanta 15 Apr 94	Los Angeles 12 May 94	Chicago I9 May 94	Wash. D.C. 07 Jun 94	Los Angeles 22 Jun 94
Sarah Morris Seminars **Projected Profit and Loss Statement, Second Quarter 1994** **$100 Price Increase, 50 Percent Attendance Drop**					
INDEPENDENT VARIABLES					
Num.Att.	14	17	7	3	10
Price	$ 395.00	$ 395.00	$ 395.00	$ 395.00	$ 395.00
D.Mtg.Cst.	$ 75.00	$ 115.00	$ 95.00	$ 145.00	$ 115.00
Num.Days	2	2	2	2	2
Airfare	$ 378.00	$ 485.00	$ 279.00	$ 415.00	$ 615.00
D.Ldg.Cst.	$ 89.00	$ 135.00	$ 105.00	$ 138.00	$ 135.00
Brk.Cst.	$ 5.25	$ 6.50	$ 5.00	$ 6.75	$ 6.50
Lnch.Cst.	$ 17.50	$ 22.50	$ 19.95	$ 24.95	$ 22.50
REVENUE					
Total	$ 5,530.00	$ 6,715.00	$ 2,765.00	$ 1,185.00	$ 3,950.00
COSTS					
Variable					
Food	$ 784.00	$ 1,207.00	$ 419.30	$ 230.70	$ 710.00
Material	$ 695.00	$ 815.00	$ 415.00	$ 255.00	$ 535.00
Tot.Var.	$ 1,479.00	$ 2,022.00	$ 834.30	$ 485.70	$ 1,245.00
Fixed					
Travel	$ 940.00	$ 1,185.00	$ 889.00	$ 1,124.00	$ 1,315.00
Hotel	$ 150.00	$ 230.00	$ 190.00	$ 290.00	$ 230.00
Tot.Fixed	$ 1,090.00	$ 1,415.00	$ 1,079.00	$ 1,414.00	$ 1,545.00
Total					
Tot.Exp.	$ 2,569.00	$ 3,437.00	$ 1,913.30	$ 1,899.70	$ 2,790.00
PROFIT					
Profit	$ 2,961.00	$ 3,278.00	$ 851.70	($ 714.70)	$ 1,160.00
Cum.Prof.	$ 2,961.00	$ 6,239.00	$ 7,090.70	$ 6,376.00	$ 7,536.00

Figure 2-15 *(continued)*

(d) Projected profit and loss statements for $100 price increase, 35 percent attendance drop.

Sarah Morris Seminars
Projected Profit and Loss Statement, Second Quarter 1994
$100 Price Increase, 35 Percent Attendance Drop

INDEPENDENT VARIABLES				
Atlanta **15 Apr 94**	**Los Angeles** **12 May 94**	**Chicago** **19 May 94**	**Wash. D.C.** **07 Jun 94**	**Los Angeles** **22 Jun 94**

	Atlanta	Los Angeles	Chicago	Wash. D.C.	Los Angeles
Num.Att.	18	22	9	5	14
Price	$ 395.00	$ 395.00	$ 395.00	$ 395.00	$ 395.00
D.Mtg.Cst.	$ 75.00	$ 115.00	$ 95.00	$ 145.00	$ 115.00
Num.Days	2	2	2	2	2
Airfare	$ 378.00	$ 485.00	$ 279.00	$ 415.00	$ 615.00
D.Ldg.Cst.	$ 89.00	$ 135.00	$ 105.00	$ 138.00	$ 135.00
Brk.Cst.	$ 5.25	$ 6.50	$ 5.00	$ 6.75	$ 6.50
Lnch.Cst.	$ 17.50	$ 22.50	$ 19.95	$ 24.95	$ 22.50

REVENUE				
Total $ 7,110.00	$ 8,690.00	$ 3,555.00	$ 1,975.00	$ 5,530.00

COSTS				

Variable					
Food	$ 1,008.00	$ 1,562.00	$ 539.10	$ 384.50	$ 994.00
Material	$ 855.00	$ 1,015.00	$ 495.00	$ 335.00	$ 695.00
Tot.Var.	$ 1,863.00	$ 2,577.00	$ 1,034.10	$ 719.50	$ 1,689.00
Fixed					
Travel	$ 940.00	$ 1,185.00	$ 889.00	$ 1,124.00	$ 1,315.00
Hotel	$ 150.00	$ 230.00	$ 190.00	$ 290.00	$ 230.00
Tot.Fixed	$ 1,090.00	$ 1,415.00	$ 1,079.00	$ 1,414.00	$ 1,545.00
Total					
Tot.Exp.	$ 2,953.00	$ 3,992.00	$ 2113.10	$ 2,133.50	$ 3,234.00

PROFIT				

	Atlanta	Los Angeles	Chicago	Wash. D.C.	Los Angeles
Profit	$ 4,157.00	$ 4,698.00	$ 1,441.90	($ 158.50)	$ 2,296.00
Cum.Prof.	$ 4,157.00	$ 8,855.00	$ 10,296.90	$ 10,138.40	$ 12,434.40

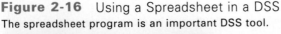

Figure 2-16   Using a Spreadsheet in a DSS
The spreadsheet program is an important DSS tool.

Sarah could develop a new follow-on seminar, say 4, that (*a*) has no prerequisites, (*b*) requires seminar 1 as a prerequisite, or (*c*) requires combinations of 1 and 2, 1 and 3, or 1, 2, and 3. Obviously, the more prerequisites required, the smaller the market. On the other hand, since Sarah is such a good speaker, someone who has been to previous seminars is more likely to attend another. Thus, a higher percentage of the smaller market may attend.

As Sarah considers these questions, she decides that she first needs to answer two preliminary questions. First, how big is the market for follow-on seminars? She would like to offer a seminar 4 that requires seminars 1, 2, and 3, but she is afraid there are too few qualified people to make it worthwhile. Second, what is the geographic pattern of the data? Are the people who have taken seminar sequences dispersed so thinly, geographically, that she cannot attract enough attendees for seminar 4 in any one city? Sarah knows that the data needed to answer these preliminary questions exists in files maintained by her operational TPS.

In fact, all the data Sarah needs to answer these questions is in her customer/enrollment TPS database. (We have not yet defined the term *database*. We will do so in the next chapter. For now, think of a database as a collection of tables of data.)

Figure 2-17 shows sample data for the CUSTOMER, COURSE, and ENROLL tables in Sarah's TPS database. The CUSTOMER table contains data about each customer; the COURSE table has data about course offerings; and the ENROLL table stores data concerning which seminars customers have taken.

Consider this data in the context of Sarah's questions. The number of people who have taken various seminars can be determined from data in the ENROLL table. The following statements, which are coded in a database query and update language called **Structured Query Language (SQL),** would produce the wanted information.

```
SELECT      COURSE#, COUNT (*)
FROM        ENROLL
GROUP BY    COURSE#
```

(Do not worry about understanding the syntax. Just realize that this language and other similar facilities can be used to obtain such an answer.)

The result of this expression is a table that contains the number of each seminar and the number of attendees. For example:

Course#	Count
100	38
110	47
120	33
200	17
210	19

The question about the geographic spread of seminar attendance can be answered by producing a report that shows the attendance for each seminar in each city. Since the name of each city in which a seminar is held is stored in the COURSE table, this report will require combining the data from the COURSE table and the ENROLL table. Figure 2-18 shows a sample of the combined table. This table can be further processed to count the number of seminar enrollments in various cities.

SQL, which was included as a general-purpose query language with Sarah's customer/enrollment system, is an industry-wide standard. This language and other query facilities can be used by noncomputer professionals like Sarah to query and create reports on operational data. Although such languages are not easy to learn thoroughly, the basics can be mastered in a half-day or so.

The processing described for Sarah Morris Enterprises is typical of a DSS. For larger organizations, there is considerably more data, and the models involved are much more complex. This discussion, however, has introduced very typical DSS applications.

Figure 2-17 Sample Data from Customer/Enrollment Database

CUSTOMER										
Cust#	CustLname	CustFname	CoName	AreaCode	Phone	Addr1	Addr2	City	State	Zip
1234	Abernathy	Kathy	Forrest, Inc.	503	555-1234	155 Elm Avenue	Dept Z	Portland	OR	89334
4459	Ouspensky	P D.	Self-employed	213	333-4459	20 North 15th	– 0 –	Los Angeles	CA	90007
3978	Williams	Jean	EDVP	703	551-0087	133 NE 133rd	Bldg. One, #332	Alexandria	VA	22345
1076	Yeats	William	Self-employed	303	722-1924	P.O. Box 143	– 0 –	Denver	CO	80219
3356	Jackson	Michelle	Classic Enterprises	312	787-5587	3398 SE 75th	Dept 245	Chicago	IL	60677
1112	Calbom	Spike	Calbom Partners	202	555-1234	P.O. Box 44456	– 0 –	Seattle	WA	98104
•	•	•	•	•	•	•	•	•	•	•
•	•	•	•	•	•	•	•	•	•	•
•	•	•	•	•	•	•	•	•	•	•

COURSE			
Course#	CourseName	Location	CourseDate
100	Seminar 1	Atlanta	10/07/94
310	Seminar 3	Tampa	01/15/95
300	Seminar 3	Philadelphia	11/05/94
210	Seminar 2	Salt Lake City	11/30/94
200	Seminar 2	Boston	10/15/94
120	Seminar 1	San Francisco	11/01/94
110	Seminar 1	Los Angeles	10/17/94
•	•	•	•
•	•	•	•
•	•	•	•

ENROLL			
Cust#	Course#	AmountDue	AmountPaid
1234	100	$ 295	$ 295
4459	100	$ 295	$ 295
1234	200	$ 495	$ 495
3978	110	$ 295	$ 295
1076	120	$ 295	$ 295
3356	120	$ 295	$ 295
1112	120	$ 295	$ 295
4459	200	$ 495	$ 495
1076	210	$ 495	$ 495
1234	300	$ 795	$ 0
4459	310	$ 795	$ 795
3356	210	$ 495	$ 495
1112	210	$ 495	$ 495
1076	300	$ 795	$ 795
1112	310	$ 795	$ 0
•	•	•	•
•	•	•	•
•	•	•	•

Figure 2-18 Combination of Data from ENROLL and
COURSE Tables, Sorted by Location and CourseDate

Cust#	Course#	AmountDue	AmountPaid	CourseName	Location	CourseDate
1234	100	$ 295	$ 295	Seminar 1	Atlanta	10/07/94
4459	100	$ 295	$ 295	Seminar 1	Atlanta	10/07/94
1234	200	$ 495	$ 495	Seminar 2	Boston	10/15/94
4459	200	$ 495	$ 495	Seminar 2	Boston	10/15/94
3978	110	$ 295	$ 295	Seminar 1	Los Angeles	10/17/94
1076	300	$ 795	$ 795	Seminar 3	Philadelphia	11/05/94
1234	300	$ 795	$ 0	Seminar 3	Philadelphia	11/05/94
1112	210	$ 495	$ 495	Seminar 2	Salt Lake City	11/30/94
1076	210	$ 495	$ 495	Seminar 2	Salt Lake City	11/30/94
3356	210	$ 495	$ 495	Seminar 2	Salt Lake City	11/30/94
1112	120	$ 295	$ 295	Seminar 1	San Francisco	11/01/94
1076	120	$ 295	$ 295	Seminar 1	San Francisco	11/01/94
3356	120	$ 295	$ 295	Seminar 1	San Francisco	11/01/94
4459	310	$ 795	$ 795	Seminar 3	Tampa	01/15/94
1112	310	$ 795	$ 0	Seminar 3	Tampa	01/15/94

Processing Knowledge with Expert Systems

Expert systems, which are a specialized type of information system, provide advice and assistance on semistructured problems. An expert system uses reasoning to render advice, make recommendations, or diagnose problems. To do this, the expert system processes input data against a knowledge base. In most expert systems today, the knowledge base consists of a set of rules.

For example, one organization uses an expert system to make recommendations to employees about the most cost-effective means of shipping parcels. The user inputs size, weight, destination, and time constraints into the expert system. The system processes this data against a knowledge base of rules that tells which companies handle specific sizes of shipments, under what time constraints, and at what costs. Thus, the system can make a recommendation about the most cost-effective transportation means.

An expert system encodes knowledge that can take a human several months, years, or even decades to learn. The shipping advisor system, for instance, contains knowledge that shipping clerks normally require several months to learn. Using this expert system, new employees can be productive far more quickly. Also, when experienced and seasoned employees are promoted or otherwise leave the department, the benefit of their knowledge is retained, since it has been incorporated into the rule base.

The term *expert system* may be misleading. Most systems today do not possess the capability of a true human expert. It might be better to think of these systems as knowledge helpers and encoders than as true experts. Chapter 15 considers expert systems.

ENHANCING COMMUNICATION EFFECTIVENESS WITH OFFICE AUTOMATION SYSTEMS

The fourth major type of information system is the **office automation system (OAS)**. These systems create, store, modify, and process interpersonal communications, whether in written, verbal, or video form.

The prevalence of microcomputers in offices, along with a veritable explosion in new communications, computer, and storage products, has caused fundamental changes in the ways that businesspeople communicate. At first, computer systems were used as **word processors**. Over time, interconnected computers let users share word processing files and send messages electronically. Today a wide variety of OASs exist.

With **electronic mail** systems, businesspeople create and send messages to one another. On **electronic bulletin boards**, files are essentially electronic posts on which people can leave public messages. Today, these systems have become more useful because high-quality graphics can be included in the messages. **Facsimile (fax)** machines have been improved and reduced in cost, so documents containing text, illustrations, and graphics can be communicated over telephone lines. Personal computers can both send and receive faxes, if they are properly equipped.

In parallel with these developments, computer technology has improved voice message systems. Business telephones are often connected to sophisticated private branch exchange (PBX) systems—computer-based switchboards that support not only **voice mail** but also flexible call-forwarding, telephone-conferencing, and the like.

In addition, companies in document-intensive industries such as insurance have developed **image-processing** systems in which documents are scanned to produce electronic images. One insurance company creates an electronic image of every document it receives. Each image is coded with date, time, critical numbers (such as customer numbers, invoice numbers, and the like), and comments. When

Figure 2-19 Types of OAS Resources

Resource	Use
Word Processor	Creates documents electronically
Electronic Mail	Sends and receives messages
Electronic Bulletin Board	Posts electronic notices
Facsimile (Fax)	Sends documents over telephone lines
Voice Mail	Supports voice mailboxes, provides sophisticated telephone facilities
Image Processing	Enables on-line access to pictures and documents
Collaborative Document Processing	Enables groups to share the drafting of documents
Video-Conferencing	Communicates face-to-face without travel
Multimedia Systems	Creates composite documents and messages

a customer calls regarding an insurance claim, the claims agent is able to electronically access all data and correspondence about that claim.

Collaborative writing systems enable groups of people to work together, in parallel, in the development of documents such as proposals. Participants use the system both to contribute their work and to review the work of others as it is developed.

Finally, large organizations use **video-conferencing** to let people communicate face-to-face without traveling. At first, such capabilities were used to connect key executives in two or three locations. Recently, such systems have been used to connect thousands of people to see and hear the same presentation.

Most of these systems have been developed in isolation from each other. **Multimedia systems**, appearing today, create messages that are composites of the separate capabilities: text, drawings, images, data, voice, and motion video. In some systems, messages are not limited to elements physically stored at any one site. Instead, they are created on demand from data assembled from many sites. Figure 2-19 summarizes types of resources provided in OASs.

OASs and New Human Capacities

Doug Englebart, one of the pioneers in OASs, predicts that the real power of such systems will not be realized by improving our productivity in working as we do today. Rather, the greatest benefit will be to let people think, communicate, and work together in new ways.[1] OASs can change the way people view, conceptualize, and solve problems.

For example, in **hypertext** systems, text, illustrations, graphics, data, programs, audio, and video can be integrated into electronic documents. Users can read such a document sequentially or at random just as books can be read. Unlike books, however, hypertext documents let users follow many different preestablished paths through the document, or users can establish their own paths. For example, in a hypertext automotive repair manual, one path might be used to repair a clutch, and another, to replace the brakes.

Hypertext versions of encyclopedias and dictionaries have been created, in which the "see also" cross-references are replaced by links to the actual text source. A reader who wants to follow the "see also" link just touches a key; the material is immediately presented. With these hypertext versions, paging through multiple volumes is no longer necessary.

The Nonarchitecture of an OAS

OAS applications vary so much in their capabilities that it is not possible to show a generic OAS architecture as it is for TPS, MIS, and DSS applications. The media involved are so disparate (computers, telephones, television screens, copy machines, graphics plotters, audio equipment, etc.) that no single chart can show any one overall architecture.

In addition, specific applications are selected to meet the needs of particular companies and workgroups, and they may change over time. The needs of an architecture firm, the technical writing group of a software house, and the operations management group for a shipyard are significantly different, and OAS applications must be selected to meet each set of needs.

The technology of OAS is exploding, leading to extremely rapid changes in the types of OAS applications that are available. Changes in hardware, programs, and data in OASs have repeatedly revolutionized applications over the past few years; capabilities that could only be dreamed about just 2 or 3 years ago will be reality in the near future.

For example, the rapidly developing technology of **virtual reality** is used by architectural firms to let clients visualize buildings that do not yet exist. Using special 3-D display technology, clients can seemingly move around in a building that only exists in a computer design, seeing what the internal spaces will look like when they are constructed.

There are at this point two important limitations on our ability to take advantage of this exploding technology. First, much of the required equipment

---

1. Engelbart, Douglas C., "A Conceptual Framework for the Augmentation of Man's Intellect," in *Computer-Supported Cooperative Work: A Book of Readings,* Irene Grief, ed. San Mateo, CA: Morgan Kaufmann, 1988, pp. 35–66.

has been developed by different vendors working independently and using different standards. Therefore, the machines often cannot communicate with one another, and it is often difficult to integrate the various capabilities into a single system. For example, it is difficult to connect computers to copying machines.

One part of the problem is technology, and another part is the nature of competition. Vendors sometimes have a negative incentive to connect to each other's equipment. Competitors often do not want to share a standard lest their equipment be readily replaceable by another company's equipment.

The lack of standardization is a short-run phenomenon. Customers show a marked preference for **connectivity**, standardized equipment that can be integrated. Digital Equipment Corporation, for example, developed a strong market share in minicomputers by providing a high degree of connectivity. Even though standards do allow for ready substitution, vendors will probably bow to customer demand for increasing standardization in the 1990s.

Today, OASs are divided into **islands of capability**. For example, there are islands of computers, islands of copying equipment, islands of telephones, and islands of video conferences. Over time, the trend toward connectivity will undoubtedly integrate the islands.

The second limitation on OAS integration concerns storage. Nontext data such as graphs or illustrations require substantially more storage than does text data; voice and video data require even more. For example, a minute of broadcast-quality motion video requires about 1 gigabyte of storage, the equivalent of 10 sets of the *Encyclopaedia Britannica*. Consequently, it is difficult with today's technology to store large volumes of nontext material in electronic form.

One approach to this problem is the use of data compression techniques to reduce storage requirements. Another is to develop extremely high-capacity storage systems such as **optical disk storage**. (See Chapter 3; if you had a hypertext version of this textbook, however, you could touch a special key and the material on optical disk storage would appear, here and now.) Certainly it appears that some solutions will be forthcoming.

Improving Communication Productivity at Legacy Systems Legacy Systems develops and sells computer software products. Each of its products is accompanied by at least one user document, and most products have three or four different documents. A typical document set consists of an installation booklet, a tutorial manual, a product capabilities manual, and a reference command summary book.

To develop documentation, Legacy has a staff of more than 30 full-time writers, augmented by free-lance writers when necessary. Typically, a group of 3 to 10 writers is assigned to create the documents for each product. More writers are needed to produce documentation for new and complicated products than for revisions or products with fewer features.

Although Legacy management devotes considerable time to product planning, rapid changes in technology and the software market sometimes necessitate dramatic changes in plans. On these occasions, Legacy's documentation group is often forced to create documents within an extremely short period of time.

Since the documents often refer to each other and to the same examples, they are best written sequentially. When product development time is short, however, writers are added to the project, and the documents are developed in parallel. Because of the cross-references, parallel development can result in chaos if it is not carefully managed.

Using a Hypertext System to Improve Legacy's Documentation To facilitate parallel documentation development, the documentation group uses a hypertext system for work in process.

When sections of documents are first assigned to particular writers, these writers develop conceptual outlines and store them in the hypertext system. All team members then review and comment on each section. Sample planning screens are shown in Figure 2-20. Cross-references (denoted by arrows) are specified.

A writer who wants one section to refer to another section indicates this to the hypertext system. The system will establish a connection so a reviewer can readily access the cross-referenced material.

Suppose an example will be used in five different sections. To refer to the example, the writer of each section instructs the hypertext system to establish a pointer. The example is stored in only one place. As the example is changed and developed, the sections that point to it automatically have access to the latest copy.

As portions of the document are finished, they are added to the hypertext system, and gradually the document comes together. All the while, every writer has access to the latest version of the work. Inconsistencies become apparent sooner, and less work is wasted or duplicated, and the quality of the finished product is higher. The hypertext system is also very useful when the documentation needs to be changed for newly developed versions of the product. It will be discussed further in a later chapter.

PROVIDING THE BIG PICTURE WITH EXECUTIVE SUPPORT SYSTEMS

The fifth major type of information system is the **executive support system (ESS)**, which supports the information needs of very senior executives by summarizing and presenting data at the highest levels of aggregation. Usually, ESSs involve presenting reports in standard formats, and they often involve graphics.

Figure 2-20 Example Pages in a Hypertext Document Used to Plan Documentation

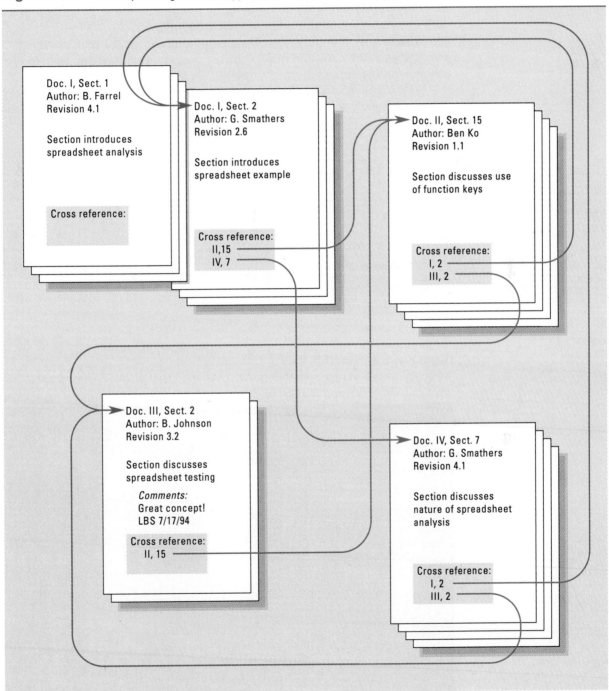

Characteristics of an ESS

The primary goal of an ESS is to obtain data from a variety of sources, integrate and aggregate that data, and display the resulting information in an easy-to-use, comprehensible format.

The characteristics of ESSs are summarized in Figure 2-21. They are easy to use and nearly always graphical, as shown in Figure 2-22. Pointing devices

Figure 2-21   Characteristics of ESSs

- Graphical
- Easy-to-use interface
- Broad, aggregated perspective
- Able to expand detail
- Provides context
- Integrates many sources of data
- Timeliness crucial

Figure 2-22   An ESS User Interface

This touch-screen system responds to the press of a finger on the display screen. Each icon represents available information.

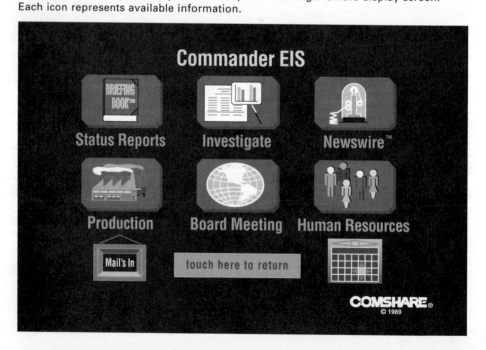

(light pens and mice, as described in the next chapter) and touch screens are often used. The goal is to require as little knowledge and skill on the part of the executive as possible.

ESSs provide broad, highly aggregated information. At the same time, they can show further detail when, for example, an executive sees something that seems curious and wants to see the underlying data.

Executives are looking for differences that make a difference. Therefore, they want to see information within a context. As with the MIS reports described for Sarah Morris, this often means that facts are shown in relation to budget or to some prior period. Because executives have a broad span interest, an effective ESS must integrate many sources of data. And since executives typically need to respond rapidly to changing circumstances, timeliness is crucial. Information that is even a week old is often not useful.

As shown in Figure 2-23, an ESS accepts data from all of the other types of information systems. It also accepts input from personnel who support the executive, such as administrative assistants.

Figure 2-23   Architecture of an ESS Application

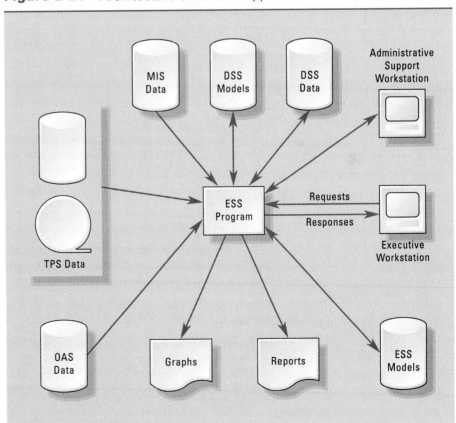

ESSs are the newest of the five categories of information systems. Many large organizations are today experimenting with ESS applications. As a result, you should expect to see further development of the ESS concept over the next few years.

Informing the CEO at Legacy Systems

The following conversation between Mr. Franklin, the CEO of Legacy Systems, and Amir Plotniki, a senior systems developer, illustrates the attitude of many executives today:

"Look, Amir, my needs are very simple. There are at least a half a dozen things I want to keep track of every day. And I don't care whether you give them to me on a computer terminal or blue paper. Just be sure I have accurate data, on time, every day!"

"I'm certain we can do it, Mr. Franklin. If you'll give me a few more minutes of your time, I'll summarize my understanding of what you need.

"First, cash. You want to know the daily balances of all liquid accounts. That includes bank accounts, managed money accounts, and investment accounts. It also includes, on the negative side, balances of the lines of credit."

"You've got it, Amir. Every day, by 8:00 A.M., either on this desk, or, if you want, on this computer."

"Good. Now, in the sales area, you want two things. You want summarized sales data that show total sales by major product line for the year, the quarter, the month, and the week so far. And you want each of those reports compared to a year ago."

"Yes. Plus the breakouts."

"Now, for the breakouts, you want the same data, but you want it broken out by the key individual products by sales regions. Would you like a table or a graph of this data?"

"Well, I don't know. I've always had a table. A graph might be nice. You tell me."

"I'll work up some examples and let you take a look at them."

"Good. The rest is basically calendar data. I want to know the key marketing events for the month and their status. The same for key development events. Finally, I want to know where the officers are. Tell me if they're in or out of the office, and if they're out, tell me where they are."

"I'm sure we can do it. I'll get back to you next week with examples. We should have the system up and running in less than a month."

"You know, Amir, I have to say it will be nice to have this system. But I'm not sure I really need it on the computer. I mean, if all of you think so, I'll give it a try. The old paper system worked well as long as everyone got their data in to Robin on time. But, I'll try it."

Figure 2-24 shows an example of several of Mr. Franklin's information needs. The cash report, shown in Figure 2-24a, lists the balances of the accounts of concern to him. The higher-level sales data is shown in the sales report in Figure 2-24b, and the executive calendar is shown in Figure 2-24c. All of this data is highly aggregated and presented in a standardized format. Mr. Franklin, like most executives, must process enormous amounts of information, and he wants this data in the same format every time so he knows exactly where to look and what to look for.

Mr. Franklin does not think that putting this data on a computer screen is of any particular benefit. In fact, it may be a detriment, because he is comfortable with paper documents and does not want to carry a laptop computer. A computer-based ESS may give him more accurate and timely information, but if it does not, then it is not worthwhile, and he will consider the manual system better.

SUMMARY

Figure 2-25 lists the purpose and characteristics of the five types of information systems we have discussed in this chapter. TPSs support operations by maintaining detailed records. Since TPS applications support operations, they must provide a quick response. Customers cannot be kept waiting in line for the computer system to accomplish its tasks. Similarly, the TPS must be reliable; failures must be rare and quickly fixed. TPSs are the oldest type of information system, and the underlying technology is relatively stable.

In a TPS, transactions are processed to update master data. In an on-line TPS, each transaction is processed immediately when it is entered. The user is typically provided menus for selecting actions and forms for entering data. In a batch TPS, transactions are batched, sorted, and processed together. Both types of TPS generate detailed reports of operational information.

MIS applications support the management of operations by producing regular reports oriented to longer-term management rather than day-to-day operations. MIS reports are standardized and recurring so their contents are comparable over time. For the same reason, models in MIS applications are

Figure 2-24   Sample Reports in the Legacy Systems ESS
(a) Cash report; (b) sales report; (c) executive calendar

(a)	CASH REPORT, 17 AUGUST 1994
Balance of Bank Accounts:	$ 4,384,119.24
Balance of Managed Accounts:	$ 14,773,248.72
Balance of Investment Accounts:	$ 23,255,004.60

(b)   SALES REPORT, 17 AUGUST 1994

	Year-to-Date Current/Last Yr.	Qtr-to-Date Current/Last Yr.	Month-to-Date Current/Last Yr.	Week-to-Date Current/Last Yr.
Spreadsheet Products	$ 31,415	$ 10,192	$ 2,716	$ 917
	$ 22,177	$ 8,001	$ 2,001	$ 491
Database Products	$ 47,614	$ 15,661	$ 3,719	$ 910
	$ 43,619	$ 13,226	$ 2,282	$ 517
Utility Products	$ 14,385	$ 4,002	$ 842	$ 183
	$ 7,405	$ 1,714	$ 149	$ 41
Totals	$ 93,414	$ 29,855	$ 7,277	$ 2,010
	$ 73,201	$ 22,941	$ 4,432	$ 1,049

(All numbers in 000s)

(c)   EXECUTIVE CALENDAR, WEEK OF 16 AUGUST 1994

	Mon	Tues	Wed	Thr	Fri
Franklin	Office	Office	St. Louis	Office	Office
Silver	Office	Office	Office	Office	Office
Jackson	Atlanta	Atlanta	Vacation	Vacation	Vacation
Chang	San Jose	San Jose	Office	Office	Office
Johnson	Office	Office	Office	Office	Office

static. Since management relies on the output of an MIS, the reports must be timely and reliable. The underlying technology is stable.

DSSs support decision making in less structured environments and situations. They are better viewed as facilities than as formalized systems.

Figure 2-25 Summary: The Five Types of MIS

Name	Purpose	Characteristics
Transaction Processing System	Support operations	Detailed, record-oriented Performance, reliability critical Supporting technology stable
Management Information System	Support management of operations	Summarized and standardized reports Regular, recurring reports Timeliness, reliability important Simple models with static structure Technology stable
Decision Support System	Support decision making in less structured situations	More a facility than a system Ad hoc response to varying needs Flexibility, adaptability critical Involves models and model building Technology evolving
Office Automation System	Support interpersonal communication	Multimedia applications Interconnectedness and reliability important Specific applications selected to meet local needs Technology exploding
Executive Support System	Support senior executive information needs	High-level, aggregated, and often standardized information Integrates many sources of data Timeliness, accuracy crucial Technology evolving

Often, DSSs are used to respond on an ad hoc basis to problems and opportunities as they develop. As such, flexibility and adaptability are crucial. DSSs often involve models of business activity; sometimes the DSS users build models as they use the system. Technology to support DSSs is evolving.

OASs exist to support interpersonal communications. Such systems are often multimedia, processing data, text, graphics, illustrations, voice, and video together. OAS applications are selected to meet corporate and workgroup needs and may vary from group to group—or even within the same group from time to time. Since the primary goal is communication, interconnectedness is critical. Reliability is also important. The technology of OASs is exploding, and you are likely to witness dramatic changes during your career.

ESS is the newest type of system, and is still evolving. Its goal is to support the information needs of senior executives with highly aggregated information in frequently standardized, often graphical, formats. An ESS integrates many sources of data. Timeliness and accuracy are vital.

KEY TERMS

TPS	MIS (narrow definition)	Electronic bulletin board
Systems architecture diagram	Exception reports	Fax
Symbols of systems components (Figure 2-3)	Independent variable	Voice mail
	Spreadsheet program	Image processing
	DSS	Collaborative writing systems
Transaction	Ad hoc processing	Video-conferencing
On-line systems	Decision support facility	Multimedia systems
Batch systems	Model (of business activity)	Hypertext
Transaction file	Break-even point	Virtual reality
Sorting (of transactions)	Extract (TPS data)	Connectivity
Master file	SQL	Island of capability
Menu	Expert system	Optical disk storage
Form	OAS	ESS
Report	Word processor	
MIS (broad definition)	Electronic mail	

REVIEW QUESTIONS

1. What does it mean to say that the questions in Figure 2-1 are sorted in order of structure?

2. Why is it easier to build an information system to answer the questions about day-to-day operations in Figure 2-1 than it is to build one to answer the strategic questions?

3. Explain the meanings of the symbols in Figure 2-3.

4. What is the function of a TPS?

5. Define the term *transaction*.

6. Describe the major elements of a TPS that could be used to keep track of software checked out from a microcomputer laboratory.

7. What is an on-line TPS?

8. Describe a situation for which an on-line TPS would be appropriate.

9. What is a batch TPS? Define the terms *transaction file* and *master file*.

10. Describe a situation for which a batch TPS would be appropriate.

11. Explain the purpose of a menu.

12. Explain the purpose of a form.

13. Explain the purpose of a query processor.

14. Explain the two ways in which the term *management information system* is used. Give the broad definition of MIS. Give the narrow definition of MIS.

15. Explain how an MIS differs from a TPS.

16. Explain the purpose of an exception report.

17. List three reasons an extract of TPS data might be created to be inputted to an MIS.

18. What is an independent variable?

19. What function did the spreadsheet program serve in the MIS used by Sarah Morris Enterprises?

20. What is a DSS?

21. Why is a DSS more of a facility than a system?

22. Explain the term *business model*. How do the models used for an MIS differ from the models used for a DSS?

23. Explain how a DSS differs from an MIS.

24. In your own words, describe how you would process the ENROLL data in Figure 2-17 to obtain the number of people who have taken particular courses.

25. Describe how you would process the data in Figure 2-18 to obtain the average revenue for each course in each city.

26. What is the function of an OAS?

27. Explain the function each of the following:

    a. Word processor

    b. Electronic mail

    c. Electronic bulletin board

    d. Facsimile (fax) machine

    e. Voice mail

    f. Image processing

    g. Collaborative document processing

    h. Video-conferencing system

    i. Hypertext

28. Describe two important limitations in the use of OASs today.

29. Describe how Legacy Systems uses the hypertext system to facilitate the parallel production of product documentation.

30. What is the purpose of an ESS?

31. Explain the difference between an ESS and a DSS.

DISCUSSION QUESTIONS

1. Suppose that Sarah Morris merges her company with another similar company that is located in a distant city.

    a. If the other company agrees to use a copy of the customer/enrollment system, how should the procedures for enrolling customers be changed? How will the two businesses coordinate their activities?

    b. In the time period immediately following the merger, what problems do you anticipate might occur in answering the questions in Figure 2-1?

    c. Consider three cases. First, suppose that Sarah Morris Enterprises and the other company decide to merge, but that each maintains its own information system. Second, suppose that they both run the customer/ enrollment application, but do so independently. Third, suppose that they develop a system in which their computers communicate and they share data. Describe how you think the business operating procedures, policies, communications, and culture will vary across these three alternatives.

2. Consider the equations that Sarah Morris uses to compute seminar profit and loss. These equations are not as specific as they could be. For example, they assume that the cost of seminar materials is the same for all seminar topics. They also make possibly unwarranted assumptions about travel costs. Change these equations so that they will more accurately represent the costs of a seminar. Under what conditions will the changes you have made be important? Under what conditions will they be unimportant?

3. Suppose that Sarah Morris decides to merge her company with another company as in question 1. Prior to the merger, she needs to establish the value of her company. Explain ways in which a DSS could be used to compute and document a valuation for her company. In what ways would such a DSS strengthen her negotiating position?

4. With regard to OASs, this chapter states that companies have a negative incentive to conform to standards. Expand on that statement. In what ways do IBM, Apple Computer, AT&T, and Xerox have such a negative incentive? Is there any way in which they would be benefited by such a standard? In general, under what conditions does a standard benefit a company, and under what conditions does a standard damage a company? Assuming there is such a negative incentive, what can customers do to cause standards to be created?

5. How might Sarah Morris use a TPS to facilitate her marketing? What functions would a sales and marketing TPS serve? What output would such a system produce? What data would it need to maintain? Would a sales and marketing TPS store any data that would improve Sarah Morris's MIS? Improve her DSS capabilities? How?

6. Consider the claim that hypertext systems will change the ways that people think. Do you think this is likely? How might it change the way individuals think? How might it change the way groups think? Is the development of hypertext systems as important a development as that of moveable type?

PROJECTS

A. On a computer with a spreadsheet program, build a model with the equations that Sarah Morris uses to compute her profit and loss statements.

1. Using the data in this chapter, verify that her break-even point on a $100 price increase is a 35 percent reduction in attendance.

2. After answering question 2 above, build a new profit and loss model using your revised equations. Compute the break-even point of a $100 price increase. Are the differences between your model and Sarah Morris's significant?

3. Assume that Sarah Morris offers three different types of seminars. The first seminar costs $295; the second, $395; and the third, $495. Assume that each seminar is offered once, and the first seminar is attended by 30 people; the second, by 20; and the third, by 15. Using the equations in this chapter, compute her total profit (or loss). Compute her total profit if there is a $100, across-the-board price increase and a 35 percent reduction in attendance. Compute the total number of people who attended both before and after the price increase. Do you recommend such an increase?

B. On a computer with a DBMS, build a database to store the data in Figure 2-17. Using the DBMS query language, determine the number of people who have attended each seminar topic. Determine the total number of people who have attended in each city. You will need to add data to demonstrate that your solution works, since there is insufficient existing data to do this in Figure 2-17.

C. Obtain information about at least two hypertext products. Is either product powerful enough to be used by Legacy Systems's documentation group? If so, explain how you would use it. If not, determine what functions and features are missing.

M I N I C A S E

Waldenbooks System Helps Book Special Orders

When superstore bookstores started popping up over the last few years, Waldenbooks Co. was faced with a problem: how to compete with stores that had three times the space—and three times the inventory—of Waldenbooks, whose 1,250 retail stores were locked into smaller mall locations.

The solution: an enterprisewide OS/2-based application that allowed the store's clerks to inform customers within 36 hours whether Waldenbooks could order a certain book for them and when it would be delivered.

"A superstore may have 18,000 to 30,000 square feet, and our stores are a lot smaller," said Jeff Kish, project manager of store systems for the Stamford, Conn., company. "With our special-order system, within 36 hours I can be confident I can ship the same book that a superstore has the room to carry."

The homegrown application, which has helped the retailer more than double its special-order business, draws on existing Waldenbooks' databases and a communications infrastructure that provides each store with nightly access to an IBM ES/9000 mainframe at the firm's home office in Stamford.

"The whole thing revolves around our titles database, which tells us what's in print and what is available from us," he said. The database, which is updated monthly, lists about 500,000 titles.

Customers can place special orders for books found in the database, which is integrated with Waldenbooks' store and warehouse inventory information as well as one of its publishers, Kish said.

Each day, individual stores enter their requests for special orders; that evening, each store's PC dials up one of two PS/2-based RemoteWare Servers at the home office using XcelleNet Inc.'s RemoteWare Communications Management System. The RemoteWare software also supports data-collection functions and provides users with tight control of the transfer process.

Once the individual stores have transmitted their special orders, a second OS/2 server on the LAN collects the orders into a single, large file for bulk transmission to the ES/9000 mainframe for batch processing.

After batch processing, the mainframe sends one large file containing all the special-order confirmations back to the OS/2 server; the server in turn runs a program that splits up that file into store-specific confirmation files, which are then distributed into the subdirectory set up for each store on the XcelleNet RemoteWare server.

The confirmation files include information on whether the order went through, when it will come back and whether the book will come from one of the retailer's two distribution centers or directly from a publisher.

Although Waldenbooks hasn't measured how effective the special-order system has been in combating the rise of superstores, Berndt and others are pleased with the increased level of service they can offer customers.

"We can now be more proactive with our customers," Berndt said. ∎

Paula Musich, excerpted from *PC Week*, March 15, 1993, pp. 41, 44.

Discussion Questions

1. Describe the business problem that the Waldenbooks special-order system is designed to solve. What benefits does the company receive from the system?

2. In the terms of this chapter, what type of information system is described in this case? Be specific.

3. An alternative possibility that Waldenbooks may have considered is to provide on-line access to its 500,000-title database so that store clerks could respond to customer questions immediately. Why do you think the company did not select this solution to its problem?

4. The data about special book orders created by this system may provide valuable information to company decision makers. Describe how it could be used (a) by an MIS and (b) by a DSS. Give an example of an MIS report created from this data. Give an example of a question that might be answered by a DSS that accesses this data.

3

Introduction to Information Systems Technology

THIS CHAPTER INTRODUCES INFORMATION SYSTEMS TECHNOLOGY. Its goal is to develop a foundation of technology that you can use throughout the book, and it considers in detail three of the five components of an information system—hardware, programs, and data.

Computer hardware can be categorized in a number of ways—most commonly by its function in relation to data. Thus, we will survey each type in turn: input hardware, processing hardware, storage hardware, and output hardware.

The chapter then considers the fundamentals of computer programs, both systems programs and applications programs. In addition, it briefly surveys computer languages. Finally, it presents the fundamentals of data representation and describes how data is stored and processed.

The purpose of this chapter is to provide a foundation for the remainder of the text. For MIS, information systems technology is important only to the degree that it accomplishes the goals and objectives of organizations and people. Therefore, we will focus on the knowledge that you, as a future user or manager, will need.

THE EVOLUTION OF INFORMATION SYSTEMS TECHNOLOGY

To study the details of information technology, a preliminary overview on its origins and evolution is essential. The main developmental trends can be understood in terms of the five components of an information system shown in Figure 3-1. The history of information technology has involved a shift in focus from left to right across these components. The industry began with an intense focus on hardware, then moved to programs, then to data, and so forth, as you will see.

Origins

The earliest ideas of computer processing extend back to **Charles Babbage,** an English inventor who designed two different types of steam-powered mechanical computers in the mid-1800s. Babbage's machines were never implemented, in spite of considerable funding by the British government. Many of the concepts that Babbage described were later used in electronic computers, but there is no evidence that the early designers of electronic computers knew about Babbage's concepts.

Although there were many early attempts at developing computers in the late 1930s and early 1940s, most people agree that the first complete electronic computer was the **ENIAC,** which became operational in 1946. That year is generally considered the computer's year of birth.

Figure 3-1   Five Components of an Information System
Programs are instructions to machines. Procedures are instructions to people. Data is the bridge between machines and people.

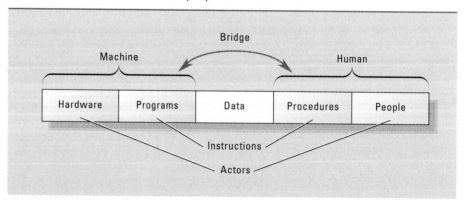

The First Generation

The ENIAC and other early computers were based on vacuum tubes, and they were exceedingly unreliable. Tube replacement was a continuous job; in computer rooms, permanent teams of technicians wound their way through banks of vacuum tubes, constantly replacing burned out tubes. Computers based on vacuum tubes are called **first-generation computers**.

The major focus of this era was to keep the machinery operating. Little attention was paid to any of the other four components in Figure 3-1. Programming was considered secretarial work, and data was an afterthought. People and procedures, such as they were, were focused on the constant need to keep the computer running. The evolution of information systems technology is summarized in Figure 3-2.

The Second Generation

By the mid- to late 1950s, vacuum tubes were replaced by transistors, and machine reliability increased dramatically. Computers of this era were called **second-generation computers**.

With the improvement in reliability, the primary focus of information technology switched from hardware to programming. People began to think about

Figure 3-2 Evolution of Information Systems Technology

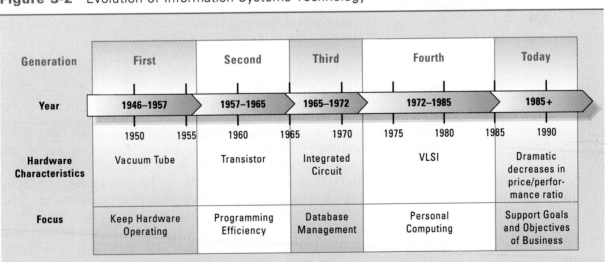

ways of making programming more efficient and programs more reliable. A new type of program, called a **compiler**, was developed. The function of a compiler is to translate program instructions from a symbolic code that people can understand to machine code, which consists of 1s and 0s. With compilers, people can write programs using instructions in a familiar form.

The Third Generation

In **third-generation computers**, transistors and other electronic components were combined on a single silicon chip called an **integrated circuit**. With such circuits, computers became smaller, faster, and even more reliable. At the same time, powerful computer languages and, subsequently, thousands of computer programs, were developed. These programs, in turn, generated more data than had ever been imagined, and the structure of that data became increasingly sophisticated. In business, the implementation of computer-based accounting systems generated countless files of accounting data.

During this stage, which occurred from the mid-1960s to the early 1970s, the focus of information technology turned to the data component. New methods and technology, called **database management**, were developed to help organizations structure and manage their data. Organizations began to view data not as something needed to drive programs, but rather as a asset to be managed in its own right.

There was no grand plan under which information systems technology was developed. In terms of the components shown in Figure 3-1, the information technology industry blindly backed its way from left to right. From a focus on hardware, the industry backed into programs; and from a focus on programs, the industry backed into data. People and procedures, though they provided the impetus for the use of information technology, were largely ignored. People were expected to adapt themselves to the needs of the technology.

The Fourth Generation

For the most part, these conditions prevailed through most of the 1970s as the early **fourth-generation computers** were developed. In this generation, electronic components were further miniaturized and condensed into **very large-scale integrated circuits (VLSI)**. One result of VLSI was that it became possible to put an entire computer on a chip. This led to the creation of microcomputers and, eventually, to the personal computer in the late 1970s.

With the advent of the personal computer, easy-to-use computing power became available to all businesspeople. Computer technology was no longer the sole province of technicians working within glass-enclosed, air-conditioned vaults. All types of businesspeople became computer literate and began to place more demands on information systems technology. People began to see information systems as an assembly of all five components and to demand that computers and programs serve them and their needs, rather than the other way around.

Information Systems Today

Today, we are witnessing a veritable explosion in information systems technology. Major changes in technology take place so rapidly that concomitant changes in software and procedures never quite catch up before the next major change is upon us. What's more, the rate of change is accelerating. And though the changes create valuable opportunities, their pace can be disconcerting to those who must try to maintain business competitiveness in a changing environment.

Major hardware developments today involve increasing miniaturization, which has meant more computer power for less money and continuing dramatic decreases in the price/performance ratio. As a result, new information systems need not be concerned only with using hardware in an extremely efficient manner; instead people and procedures can share the focus with technology. Systems developers now consider topics such as *organizational learning*—that is, ways in which organizations can adapt to improve performance toward goals and objectives. These adaptations may not even require the use of computer technology.

At the same time, systems developers are broadening their focus to include *business process redesign*. Rather than take the organization and its structure and procedures as fixed, systems developers increasingly include these components as part of the domain of their work. In this role, systems developers are as likely to recommend a change in organizational structure as they are to recommend a particular type of computer hardware.

With these historical trends in mind, we can now consider the basics of hardware, programs, and data.

COMPUTER HARDWARE

A wide variety of computer hardware exists today, and it serves many different purposes. As mentioned earlier, hardware can be categorized by the functions it serves with regard to data: inputting, processing, storing, and outputting. A typical computer hardware system is shown in Figure 3-3.

Figure 3-3 Typical Computer Hardware System

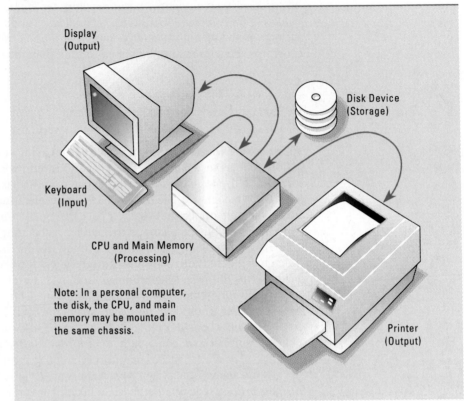

Input Hardware

Input hardware transmits data to the processing and storage hardware. The data to be input can be in **source form** that humans perceive or in **machine form** that can be electronically sensed by another computer.

The most popular device for inputting source data is the **keyboard**. This device is nearly always accompanied by a display screen, an output device used to verify that the data has been correctly keyed. For personal information systems, the keyboard and the display screen are adjacent to, or even part of, the processing and other hardware. In workgroup and organizational systems, input devices called **terminals** (nonintelligent keyboards and screens) are remote from the processing hardware. Terminals are connected via communication lines to a centralized computer.

For some applications, keyboard data entry uses a **mouse** to create a **point and click interface** (see Figure 3-4). As the mouse is moved around on a flat

Figure 3-4 Mouse Input Device
Moving the mouse on the desktop positions a pointer on the display screen.

surface, the motion of its roller-ball is translated into the movement of a pointer on the display screen. The user points at an item on the screen and clicks a mouse button to instruct the program to do something. Mice are most commonly used in graphically oriented applications like desktop publishing.

A third source-input device is a **scanner**, which transforms text or graphical images into computer-sensible data. One common application of a scanner is used in law firms, where depositions are converted from typed pages to word processing files. This saves considerable retyping. Another application is used to read graphical logos or other symbols for desktop publishing applications.

Some applications use **voice input**, in which the sound of the human voice is input to a signal interpreter. Most voice systems in use today have a small vocabulary, and many have to be trained to recognize particular voices. This training is done by having a person repetitively read a list of common words so that the signal interpreter can establish a pattern. A typical application of voice input is in a loading dock where workers call out the numbers of boxes they are carrying. In this situation, voice input is valuable because the workers' hands are busy, and they cannot use another input device.

An important emerging technology is the **pen-based system** for **handwriting input**. People use this system by writing on an electronically sensitive pad. Characters are recognized and inputted to the computer system. Such hardware is used with some personal computer systems.

Machine data input requires other types of hardware, most commonly, a **modem** for connecting a computer though a telephone line to another computer. Chapter 12 on computer communications considers modems in more detail. Other types of machine data input hardware are **light pens**, used to point at and select items on the screen, and **bar code** and other readers.

Processing Hardware

Processing hardware includes devices that compute, compare, and perform special instructions. The **central processing unit (CPU)** contains the **control unit** and the **arithmetic-logic unit (ALU)**. The control unit retrieves instructions from system memory and interprets them. The ALU executes the interpreted instructions. **System memory**, or *main memory*, holds program instructions and data for immediate processing.

The ALU includes components called **registers**, special circuitry in the ALU that performs arithmetic and other operations on data. Typically, an ALU has from 8 to 16 different registers. Data is read into a register from system memory and processed in the register, and the results are replaced in system memory. From there, results can be output to a printer or other device.

Before any data can be processed, it must reside in system memory. The transfer of data between system memory and sources outside the CPU—such as keyboard, display screen, or printer—is called **input/output (I/O)**. Most input and output devices operate very slowly compared to the speed of processing, so I/O operations are much slower than processing operations.

CPU Characteristics   Several terms are used to specify the speed of a CPU. For example, when you buy a personal computer, the salesperson may say, "That's a 32-bit processor," or ask, "Do you want the 33- or 50-megahertz version?" (see Figure 3-5). This section explains these terms.

Activities in a computer are organized in terms of *cycles*. A cycle is a unit of time required for the various components of the computer to complete a certain amount of work. Consider a human analogy. Suppose staff work is organized around a weekly meeting. At the end of each meeting, work is assigned to staff members, and they are told to report on progress at the next meeting. At that meeting, the staff regroups and new assignments are made.

Figure 3-5 Microprocessor
The 80486 microprocessor used in many of today's
microcomputers is a 32-bit processor.

Inside a microcomputer, components are assigned work. At the end of the cycle, the components regroup. Results are collected, and new work assignments are made. For some operations, multiple cycles are needed to finish a job. For example, the addition of two numbers may require 4 cycles; the division of two numbers involving fractions may require 8 or 10 cycles.

The capacities of computers are measured in terms of their speed and the amount of data that can be manipulated in a single cycle. Speed can be expressed either in cycles per second or in instructions per second. **Cycle speed** is expressed in **megahertz**, or millions of cycles per second. Instruction speed is expressed in **millions of instructions per second (MIPS)**. Since some instructions take several cycles, the speed of a computer in cycles per second is faster than the speed in instructions per second.

The amount of data that can be manipulated in a cycle (the processor's **word size**) is measured in bits, as explained in the data section later in this chapter. Relatively primitive computers (such as the early Zilog Z-80 microprocessor) were 8-bit processors; they processed 8 bits of data in a cycle. More modern microprocessors are 16-bit or 32-bit processors. Still larger computers process 64 bits in a cycle or even more.

Suppose you are shoveling dirt from a pile into a wheelbarrow. Suppose a cycle is the time required for you to move one shovelful of dirt. Speed refers to the number of cycles you make in, say, an hour. Word size is akin to the width of the shovel. You can have an 8-inch, 16-inch, or 32-inch shovel. The wider the shovel, the more dirt you move. You can increase your throughput by shortening your cycle time (shoveling faster), increase the amount of dirt you move (getting a wider shovel), or both.

System Memory The two fundamental types of system memory are **read-only memory (ROM)** and **random-access memory (RAM)**. ROM is used to hold initialization instructions for computer start-up and certain other repetitive, specialized functions. As the name implies, this memory may only be read and cannot be changed. ROM is **nonvolatile**, meaning that its contents are not lost when the computer is unpowered. Usually a computer has only a small amount of ROM memory, and it is built in by the manufacturer.

A variation of ROM is **programmable read-only memory (PROM)**. To the buyer or user of the computer, PROM acts the same as ROM. The difference lies in the way that the contents of PROM memory are filled. Whereas the contents of ROM are permanently wired into the circuitry of the chips when they are fabricated, the circuits in PROM are general purpose; their contents are programmed by the manufacturer of the device that uses them. Thus, a computer manufacturer can buy one type of PROM and program it in different ways for use in different computers.

RAM can be both read and written. RAM is where program instructions and data are held while they are being processed. In general, a program is read from a storage unit outside of the CPU and placed into RAM. When the program starts executing, the first few instructions are moved from RAM into the control unit, where they are processed. More instructions are moved into the control unit as the program proceeds. This movement is necessary because only a few instructions will fit in the control unit at one time. Hundreds of thousands of instructions will fit into RAM.

Unlike ROM, today's RAM is **volatile**. The contents of RAM are lost when the power is off. Consequently, RAM contents must be written to disk before the computer is turned off, and data may be lost if the computer suddenly loses power.

The amount of RAM varies from computer to computer, and it is specified in terms of the number of characters of data that can be stored at a time. As you will learn later in this chapter, a character of data is sometimes called a byte. A **kilobyte (K)** is 1024 bytes. A typical size for smaller system memory is 640K. Memory size may also be expressed in **megabytes (MB)**, millions of bytes. In large computers, system memory ranges as high as 500 MB or more.

Data Bus, or Processor Channel The CPU is connected to other computer devices via a **data bus**, or **processor channel**. The channel is designed and constructed by the manufacturer. The channel usually has built-in connection **ports** for keyboards, displays, printers, mice, and other I/O devices. In addition, the channel has connections for storage devices, such as disks and tapes, and possibly for other CPUs.

A processor channel for a personal computer is shown in Figure 3-6. The channel connects directly to the CPU and to a disk storage device. The channel has **expansion slots**, often used to plug in adapter boards for additional equipment such as floppy disks, plotters, printers, and light pens.

There is a difference between a CPU and a computer. The CPU is generally considered to consist of control unit and ALU. A computer, on the other hand, includes the CPU plus system memory, processor channel, power supply, and circuitry necessary to integrate the components. In a personal computer, the CPU is a **microprocessor**; the microprocessor plus data bus, power supply, and other circuitry comprises the microcomputer.

Three Categories of Processing Hardware The three categories of processor hardware are mainframe computers, minicomputers, and microcomputers. Today, the three categories overlap so much that they have lost much of their meaning.[1] This section first describes their traditional usage; then it considers current and projected changes.

Mainframe computers, as in Figure 3-7, are the largest and fastest computers. They are typically used to support large enterprise information systems with

Figure 3-6 Data Bus in a Personal Computer

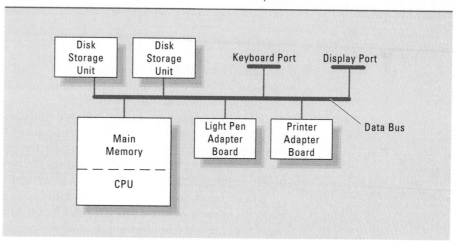

---

1. A fourth type of computer is the *supercomputer*. Such computers are much larger, faster, and more expensive than mainframes. They are not used in business applications, and so we do not consider them here.

Figure 3-7 Mainframe Computer
Mainframe computers are isolated in controlled environments, attended by information systems professionals.

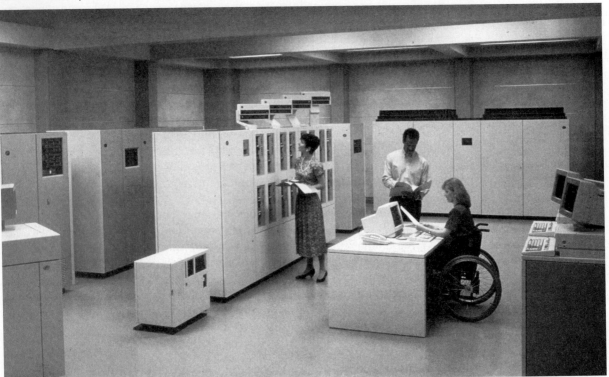

hundreds of terminals and concurrent users. Processing speeds range from 10 to more than 100 MIPS; system memories range from 32 to over 500 MB. Base prices range from $1 million to over $10 million.

Minicomputers (see Figure 3-8) are midsized computers, often used to support workgroups or corporate computing for smaller organizations. Minicomputers typically have dozens of terminals and concurrent users. Processing speeds range from 4 to over 20 MIPS, and system memories range from 24 to over 250 MB. Base prices are from $200,000 to $1 million.

Microcomputers (or micros), as shown in Figure 3-9, are the smallest computers, generally used to support a single user. Micros are also used as terminals to systems on minicomputers and mainframe computers. Sometimes micros are connected via **local area networks (LANs)** to support workgroups and small organizations. Processing speeds vary from 2 to more than 100 MIPS; memory sizes vary from 512K to over 100MB. Base prices range from less than $1,000 to over $15,000.

Figure 3-8 Minicomputer
A minicomputer typically serves a group of workers who share use of common data.

Figure 3-9 Microcomputer
A microcomputer typically supports a single user in a personal information system.

As the semiconductor industry has produced components with greater power for less money, the categories of mainframe computer, minicomputer, and microcomputer have blurred. Although it is true that mainframes are still physically largest, the processing capabilities of the three categories now heavily overlap. The minicomputer category has been overrun by micros, and large minis are now used where mainframes were previously required.

Today these "categories" are actually only sociological definitions. Each type of computer was developed to be used in a particular environment, and those environments continue even though the categories of supporting hardware have blurred.

The *enterprise computing environment* (which used to be mainframe) is a controlled environment. Computers are kept in isolated rooms, closely supervised and guarded, with elaborate temperature and humidity controls. Systems are standardized, and change is carefully implemented. A system that supports bank teller processing is a typical enterprise computing system.

The *workgroup computing environment* (which used to be minicomputer) is less rigid and controlled than the enterprise environment. Workgroup computers usually reside in the workgroup rather than in an isolated, locked area. Procedures for change are less formal. A centralized time accounting and billing system used in a large law firm is a typical workgroup computer.

The *personal computing environment* (which used to be microcomputer) is informal and flexible. A single person defines whatever controls exist; change can be made at the need of the sole user. A financial analyst using a spreadsheet program is a typical personal computer user.

Processor Architectures   Two movements currently under way may change the nature of computer processors over the next few years. The first movement is the development of **reduced instruction set computers (RISCs)**. The second is the development of parallel computing.

Conventional CPUs, or **complex instruction set computers (CISCs)** contain circuitry not only for commonly needed instructions, like adding two whole numbers, but also for less frequently needed instructions, like dividing two very large fractional numbers to produce high-precision results. Such specialized instructions may seldom be needed, but their presence adds complexity to the CPU and hence reduces its performance.

The rationale behind RISC computers is that only the most commonly used instructions need to be built in to the electronics of the CPU. Less frequently used instructions can be implemented in programs of many simple steps. With this design strategy, the CPU can be made to perform the most frequently used instructions much faster—perhaps 10 or more times faster than with CISC processors. The less frequently used instructions will be slower with RISC than with CISC, but this will have little impact on overall performance because these instructions are infrequently needed. Today, the RISC strategy is being incorporated into the design of most widely used CPU chips, either partially or completely.

A second change in processors is longer term, and it concerns the nature of CPU architecture. Every commercially successful computer today is based on an architecture first set out by the mathematician John von Neumann in the early 1940s. The **von Neumann architecture** assumes a single CPU.

In recent years, there has been promising research on a new type of computer architecture involving **parallel computing** by dozens or even hundreds of processors. These computers will have capabilities far different from those of the von Neumann class. For example, they may rival the human brain in pattern recognition. Such machines require still more advances in the state of the art, however, and it may be some years before they see commercial application. Be aware, however, that there may be major breakthroughs in computer architecture in the early part of your business career.

Storage Hardware

RAM is used to hold data and programs that are actively being processed. It cannot be used to hold all of an information system's data and programs, however, for two reasons. First, since RAM is volatile, all data is lost when the system is shut down or when there is a power failure.

Second, RAM is limited in size, and it is expensive. An organization might store many billions of bytes of data. No CPU today has that much RAM, and even if it did, the cost of storing that much data in RAM would be prohibitive. Instead, external media are used to store data and programs when they are not actively processed. Two types of magnetic *storage hardware* are the most common: disk drives and tape drives.

Disk Storage **Disks** are the most common storage medium in information systems. A disk is a circular surface coated with a substance that can readily be magnetized. Data is magnetically recorded in concentric circles called **tracks,** as shown in Figure 3-10. The starting point of each track is permanently recorded on the disk. Data is recorded and read by **read/write heads**. A few high-performance disk drives have one head for each track; most disks have a few heads that can be positioned over whichever track is to be read or written.

The CPU expects the rate of data transfer to and from a disk to be constant. Since it takes the same amount of time for each track to make one revolution, the amount of data on each track must be the same. Hence, tracks near the center of the disk have data recorded more densely than those on the outside. A **sector** is a pie-shaped section of the surface of the disk. Each track in a sector contains the same amount of data.

Some disks are hard, or inflexible. **Hard disks** are often stacked, as shown in Figure 3-11. To read such a stack of disks, a tower of read/write heads moves in and out of the disk. All of the tracks that can be read with the tower in one position

Figure 3-10 Layout of Data on a Magnetic Disk
On disk storage, data is organized into sectors and tracks.

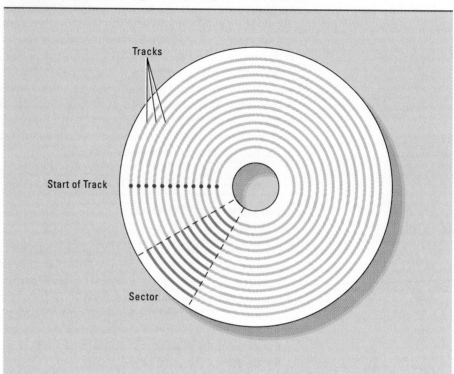

are called a **cylinder**. The read/write heads do not touch the surface of the disk. Rather, they fly over the top of it.

The advantages of hard disks include both high capacity and high speed. Capacity ranges from 40 MB to several gigabytes. A **gigabyte (GB)** is 1,000 MB, or 1 billion bytes. Speed is rated in **average access time**, the average time required to move the read/write head from one position to another and then for the disk's rotation to bring the needed data into position. Modern hard disks have average access times of 20 milliseconds or less.

On microcomputers, hard disks are permanently mounted inside the computer chassis. Several disk drives can be connected to a single computer so several gigabytes of storage is feasible. In truth, such capacities are seldom provided. Most personal computer applications require 200 MB of storage or less.

Hard disks can be permanent or removable. Removable disks are used to expand the capacity of a single disk-processing unit.

Another type of disk is a **diskette**, or **floppy disk**. Floppy disks are single-disk units that can be recorded on both sides. The two tracks that can be accessed

Figure 3-11 Stacked Hard Disks

A hard drive often includes several disks. Read/write heads for each surface of each disk are mounted on a common actuator, which moves all the heads to the corresponding tracks of the various recording surfaces, making a cylinder.

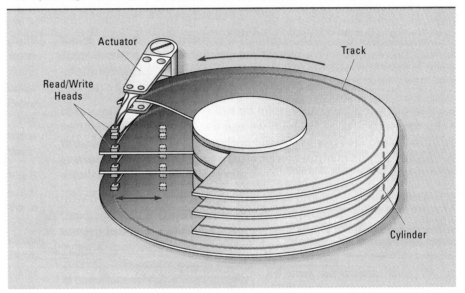

when the read/write head is in a given position are called the *cylinder*, similar to a cylinder on a stack of hard disks.

There are two standard types of diskettes. The older type is 5 1/4 inches across, and it is mounted in a flexible cover. (You should not remove the cover when processing data on the disk!) The capacity of 5 1/4-inch diskettes ranges from 360K to over 1MB. The second type of floppy disk is 3 1/2 inches across, and it is mounted in a stiff plastic cover. The capacity of this second type is greater.

Since the capacity of diskettes is low, they are used primarily to move data and programs from one computer to another and to back up critical data from the hard disk. Capacities of various types of disks are summarized in Figure 3-12.

Tape Storage The second major type of storage is **magnetic tape**, similar to the tape used in a stereo system. Data is recorded on the tape in blocks. Typically, a block consists of a number of records concatenated together. A typical tape format is shown in Figure 3-13.

The advantage of tape is that, once the tape drive has been bought, each additional tape is exceedingly cheap. The disadvantage of tape is that data can only be accessed in sequence; to read the 1000th record, the first 999 must be read first. Thus, tapes provide only **sequential access** to data. Disks provide both sequential access and **direct access**.

Figure 3-12   Disk Capacities as of 1993

Type	Size	Capacity
Diskette	5¼ inches	1.2 MB
Diskette	3½ inches	1.4 MB
Hard Disk — Microcomputer	5¼ inches	100–1000 MB
Hard Disk — Minicomputer and Mainframe Computer	10–15 inches	0.1 to 100+ GB

Figure 3-13   Typical Magnetic Tape Format

For efficient reading and writing, several data records are clustered into a single recorded block of data on a magnetic tape.

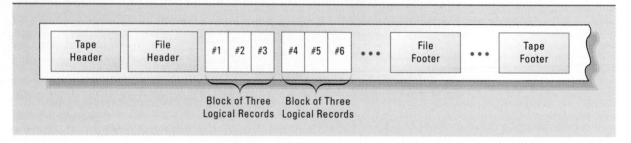

Additionally, data cannot be updated in the middle of the tape. Even if the update is the same length as the original data, positioning the tape in exactly the right spot is too difficult. If you have ever tried to replace one song with another song in the middle of one of your stereo tapes, you know the difficulty involved. To update data in the middle of a tape, a new tape must be produced. The data up to the update is copied to the new tape, then the updated data is written, and the rest of the data on the original tape is copied over.

Another disadvantage of tape is that the units used to read and write tape are expensive. Although the cost per byte of tape storage is low, the initial cost of tape drives is high. In light of these disadvantages, tape is seldom used with personal computers. Tape storage is very common in minicomputer and mainframe computer applications, however, where the initial high cost of the tape drive can be justified by the lower cost of storing large amounts of data.

Increasingly, the primary application of tape is to back up data on disk. Such backups are made to protect the data against hardware malfunction, program error, or human mistake. Tape is also used for long-term, or *archival*, storage of data that is no longer actively needed.

Optical Storage Hardware Although magnetic disk and magnetic tape are currently the primary forms of computer data storage, **optical disk storage** devices are becoming increasingly popular. Three types of optical devices exist. **CD-ROM** (compact disk–read-only memory) devices are similar to compact disks used in home stereo systems. They can hold from 500 to 700 MB of data. Their disadvantage is that, like audio compact disks, they can only be read; new data cannot be recorded.

CD-ROM devices are becoming popular for the storage and retrieval of reference materials, large amounts of data such as stock market prices, and large volumes of information as in encyclopedias. Large computer programs and multimedia applications are increasingly distributed on CD-ROMs.

CD-ROM data is recorded by using a laser to burn tiny pits in the metallic surface of a master disk along a spiral track on the underside of the disk beginning at the center and spiraling outward. The extremely close spacing of the spiral (about 16,000 turns per inch) permits a track 3 miles long. To keep the density of pits along the spiral constant, the rotational speed of the disk must change as the laser moves—faster at the center and slower at the edge.

The pattern of pits on the master disk is reproduced on the CD-ROM disks that are distributed and sold. To use the disk, you insert it into a CD-ROM drive; a laser in the drive follows the spiral track on the disk and senses the presence of the pits.

Access is somewhat slower than for data on a hard drive. First, the laser mechanism that must be moved into position for each read is much bulkier than the tiny hard drive read/write head. Second, repositioning the head requires adjusting the disk's rotational speed, and it takes some time for the new speed to become stable. Compared to the 20 milliseconds or less average access times of modern hard disk drives, the 400 milliseconds or longer access times typical of CD-ROM drives is a definite step down in performance.

A second type of optical disk is the **write-once/read-many (WORM)** optical disk. As the name implies, such disks can be written once, but every write is permanent. In the WORM drive, a laser is used on higher power to burn the pits into the surface of the disk, and on lower power to read the data. WORM devices are useful where it is important to maintain a permanent record of all data, such as transaction processing on a financial network. In such an application, the inability to erase the data is an advantage because it ensures a permanent and unchangeable audit trail of transactions. WORM disks are also used to record photographs taken with a digital camera.

Erasable optical disks are the third type of optical storage. Their drives can both read data and write data. On erasable disks, data is recorded by altering the magnetic properties of the surface of the disk so light is reflected in different ways. (One type of reflection is considered to be a 1 and another, a 0.) Data is written by heating the spot to be recorded with a laser beam, altering the magnetic properties of the metallic surface, and allowing a magnetic field to take effect. The technology of erasable optical disks is still emerging.

The primary advantage of all types of optical disks is their high-capacity, compact, durable storage. A principal disadvantage is speed; optical disks are slower than magnetic storage.

Output Hardware

Printers and video displays are by far the most common output devices. This section will discuss them and then mention several of the less common devices.

Printers Printers vary in capability from inexpensive dot matrix printers to high-priced typesetting-quality laser printers. Printers can be classified in several ways. For one, there are **character printers**, **line printers**, and **page printers**. Character printers are usually inexpensive; they print a single character at a time, and they are slow. Line printers print a line at a time. They are used mainly in enterprise computing environments for printing large volumes of standardized forms such as monthly invoices. Page printers print a page at a time, and they operate like a copier. Most page printers use lasers to create the printed image.

Impact printers strike the paper while **nonimpact printers** do not. A dot matrix printer (so called because the characters are composed of dots) strikes a ribbon, which in turn strikes the paper. In contrast, a laser printer uses photoelectric technology to print an image without any impact. Typically, impact printers are noisy; they have the advantage, however, of being able to print multiple copies at the same time.

In a **bit-mapped printer**, each dot of the printer's output can be addressed. For a non-bit-mapped, character-based printer, a page is organized into lines and columns. A letter or some other character is printed on a specified line in a specified column. Although some character-based printers allow half-spacing, the position of characters is still very restricted, providing only about 5,600 print positions on a printed page (66 lines of 85 characters each). Further, only a predefined set of characters can be printed.

A bit-mapped printer is organized by lines and columns of dots. At a typical density of 300 dots per inch vertically and horizontally, each page has well over 8 million print positions. Each dot on the page can be turned on (printed) or off (not printed). Characters and symbols are formed from groups of dots and can be placed anywhere on the page. They can readily be increased or decreased in size.

Further, with a bit-mapped printer, anything can be printed, including multiple typefaces and sizes, hand-drawn art, digitized photos, graphs, charts, and text. Shading and background halftones (gray blocks) can be used to improve the printout's appearance. The document in Figure 3-14 was produced using a bit-mapped printer.

Figure 3-14 Document Produced on a Bit-Mapped Printer

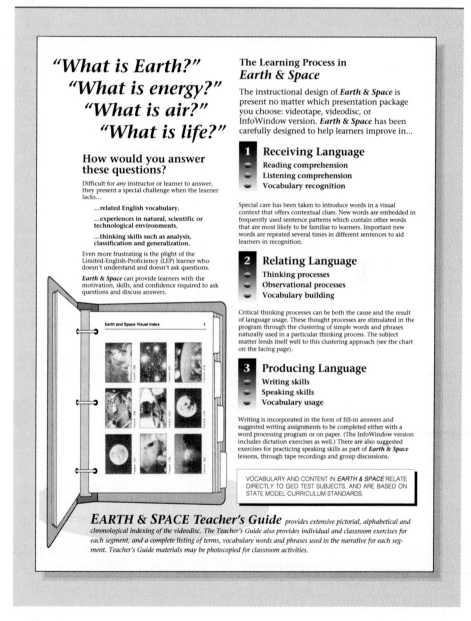

"What is Earth?" "What is energy?" "What is air?" "What is life?"

How would you answer these questions?

Difficult for *any* instructor or learner to answer, they present a special challenge when the learner lacks...

...**related English vocabulary,**

...**experiences in natural, scientific or technological environments,**

...**thinking skills such as analysis, classification and generalization.**

Even more frustrating is the plight of the Limited-English-Proficiency (LEP) learner who doesn't understand and doesn't ask questions.

Earth & Space can provide learners with the motivation, skills, and confidence required to ask questions and discuss answers.

The Learning Process in *Earth & Space*

The instructional design of ***Earth & Space*** is present no matter which presentation package you choose: videotape, videodisc, or InfoWindow version. ***Earth & Space*** has been carefully designed to help learners improve in...

1 Receiving Language

- Reading comprehension
- Listening comprehension
- Vocabulary recognition

Special care has been taken to introduce words in a visual context that offers contextual clues. New words are embedded in frequently used sentence patterns which contain other words that are most likely to be familiar to learners. Important new words are repeated several times in different sentences to aid learners in recognition.

2 Relating Language

- Thinking processes
- Observational processes
- Vocabulary building

Critical thinking processes can be both the cause and the result of language usage. These thought processes are stimulated in the program through the clustering of simple words and phrases naturally used in a particular thinking process. The subject matter lends itself well to this clustering approach (see the chart on the facing page).

3 Producing Language

- Writing skills
- Speaking skills
- Vocabulary usage

Writing is incorporated in the form of fill-in answers and suggested writing assignments to be completed either with a word processing program or on paper. (The InfoWindow version includes dictation exercises as well.) There are also suggested exercises for practicing speaking skills as part of ***Earth & Space*** lessons, through tape recordings and group discussions.

> VOCABULARY AND CONTENT IN *EARTH & SPACE* RELATE DIRECTLY TO GED TEST SUBJECTS, AND ARE BASED ON STATE MODEL CURRICULUM STANDARDS.

Earth and Space Visual Index 1

EARTH & SPACE Teacher's Guide *provides extensive pictorial, alphabetical and chronological indexing of the videodisc. The Teacher's Guide also provides individual and classroom exercises for each segment, and a complete listing of terms, vocabulary words and phrases used in the narrative for each segment. Teacher's Guide materials may be photocopied for classroom activities.*

Used by permission of Media Learning Systems, Pasadena.

The advantages of such printers are that the quality of print and the number of printing options are dramatically improved. The disadvantage is that the computer needs to send many more instructions to the printer—one for each dot on the page instead of one for each character. This means that considerably more data must be processed to construct a bit-mapped page.

Because of the amount of work involved, some bit-mapped printers include their own microprocessors. **PostScript** is a standard language for instructing such microprocessors. When you buy printers, you may hear, "This is a PostScript printer," meaning that the printer is a bit-mapped printer that adheres to the PostScript language standard. The availability of such a standard allows different types and brands of computers, printers, and programs to coordinate their activity in a predefined way. The software publisher, for example, need not produce a different version of its product for every model of bit-mapped printer. This is a great saving to all.

Video Displays   Like printers, video displays may be character-based or dot-addressable. Character-based displays commonly provide 24 rows of 80 characters, for a total of 1920 display positions. Today, dot-addressable, or *graphics,* displays, are more common. The **VGA display** that is currently standard on PCs provides 640 dots horizontally by 480 dots vertically, or more than 300,000 screen dots, each of which can display 256 colors.

The most common video display device is the **cathode ray tube (CRT)**, which uses technology similar to TV picture tubes. Displays based on the CRT are called **monitors**. The technology of **flat panel displays** is developing rapidly, and these devices are used in most portable computers.

Other Output Devices   Other forms of output hardware include plotters for making sophisticated graphs, charts, and maps, and cameras for producing 35-millimeter slides, microfiche, and microfilm. Computers can also produce bar codes and other forms of paper output intended to be read by both humans and computers.

Voice output is used in the telephone information system, where the requested number is reported using a voice output system. Voice output is becoming common in voice messaging systems.

Removable storage media are also sometimes used for output, for example, to transfer data from computer to computer. A tape or removable disk can be produced and physically transferred from one computer to another.

PROGRAMS

Computers are general-purpose devices. To make the computer do one particular task, a program of instructions is loaded into system memory and executed. This section describes the major types of programs and the essential concepts of programming languages that you, as a future business professional, need to know.

Although hundreds of types of computer programs exist, they comprise two major groups: **systems programs** and **application programs**. Systems programs are the closest to the hardware; they control the computer's resources and allocate resources to other programs on request. Systems programs supervise the activity of other programs. They are general purpose and are not tailored to any particular application.

Application programs process data to meet user needs. There are three major categories of application programs. First, **horizontal market applications** provide a generalized capability useful to a wide variety of individuals and organizations. Word processing programs and spreadsheet programs are examples of horizontal market applications. The term *horizontal* is used because the market for these programs cuts horizontally across all industries.

Second, **vertical market applications** satisfy a need that is specific to a particular industry. A program that performs order entry for appliance retailers is an example. The term *vertical* is used because the market for these programs cuts vertically within a specific industry.

Third, **custom application programs** are created specifically for the needs of one organization or department. Custom programs are often developed by the in-house MIS department or by outside consultants or software development vendors. Since custom applications satisfy a need that is particular to a given company, they cannot be licensed to others. A program that tracks operational expenses for the Goodyear blimp is likely to be a custom application program.

This section describes each type of program in more detail. First, however, consider the execution of a program in the CPU.

A Sample Program

Figure 3-15 shows portions of the primary memory contents and the ALU contents of an example generic computer. This computer is processing a program that inputs a value and checks to determine whether that value is 0. If it is, the program

Figure 3-15   Example Processing of Computer Program

Primary Memory Contents   Memory Addresses   Memory Location Values

1000 LOAD 2, 1028	1001 INPUT 1029	1002 LOAD 3, 1029	1003 COMPARE 2,3
1004 IF = GO TO 1011	1005 INPUT 1030	1006 LOAD 4, 1030	1007 COMPARE 3,4
1008 IF > GO TO 1012	1009 PRINT 1032	1010 GOTO 1001	1011 STOP
1012 PRINT 1033	1013 GO TO 1001	1014	1015
1016	1017	1018	1019
1020	1021	1022	1023
1024	1025	1026	1027
1028 0	1029 4221	1030 3756	1031
1032 'NOT GREATER'	1033 'GREATER'	1034	1035
1036	1037	1038	1039

ALU Contents

Current Instruction 'PRINT 1033' at 1012		Address of Next Instruction 1013
Register 2 0	Register 3 4221	Register 4 3756

directs the computer to stop. If it is not, then the program inputs a second value. The two values are compared, and, if the first value is greater, the word *GREATER* is printed; otherwise the words *NOT GREATER* are printed. Then the process is repeated until a 0 is entered.

In Figure 3-15, primary memory is shown as the cells in a table. Each cell has an address, beginning with 1000 and numbering consecutively by 1s. The address of each cell is shown in its upper-left-hand corner.

Primary memory is used to hold both program instructions and program data. In this example, memory locations 1000 through 1013 hold program instructions, and locations 1028, 1029, 1030, 1032, and 1033 hold data. This arrangement is typical.

The first instruction of the program is to load the value of location 1028 into register number 2. This places a 0 in register 2. Then, a number is input from some external device (such as a keyboard) into memory location 1029. The number read happens to be 4221. Then this number is loaded into register 3 and the contents of registers 2 and 3 are compared. If they are equal, control is transferred to location 1011. Otherwise a second value is input into memory location 1030.

You can follow the rest of this program to be sure that it performs as specified. The contents of the ALU are shown when the computer is processing the instruction in location 1012.

This simple example is typical of the processing of a computer program. All programs, no matter how complex, follow a process like this. Of course, the processing may be more involved, since there can often be hundreds of thousands and even millions of instructions in a program.

Systems Programs

Systems programs provide the interface between hardware and application programs. As shown in Figure 3-16, systems programs are the core program component. The most basic systems program is the **operating system (OS)**. This program manages other programs' access to the CPU and to external hardware devices. For example, when a program wants system memory allocated to it, it asks the OS to reserve the space. When a program wants to read data from a disk or a tape, it asks the OS to perform the read on its behalf.

Utility programs are another type of systems program. Utilities provide generalized services, such as formatting a new disk, copying a file, making a backup copy, or editing text. Usually the OS and the utilities are bundled together in an OS package. Such packages are generally licensed by the computer's manufacturer.

Notice the word *license*. Computer programs are not sold to users; rather, they are licensed. In legal terms, *sale* means transfer of ownership, whereas *license* means the right to use something in a specified manner. When people speak of purchasing software, they almost always mean purchasing a license to use the software. A license to use an OS can be purchased for a few hundred dollars. The cost of buying the software itself, if it were for sale, would be in the hundreds of millions of dollars.

The **communications control program (CCP)** is another type of systems program. This program controls telecommunications applications like teller processing at a bank. Chapter 12 considers the CCP. **Database management systems (DBMS)** are also considered systems programs. The DBMS provides

Figure 3-16 Program Layers

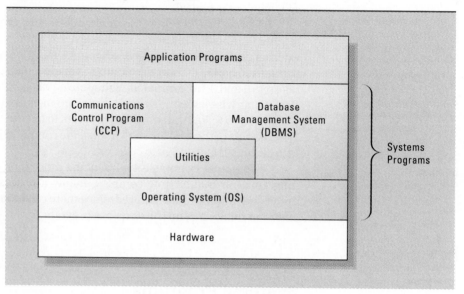

facilities to define, process, and administer the database and its applications. Chapters 5 and 8 will consider database applications in more detail.

Both the CCP and the DBMS can be licensed from the hardware vendor or (more likely) from an independent software publisher. Characteristics of systems programs are summarized in Figure 3-17.

Horizontal Market Application Programs

Horizontal market application programs provide features and functions to solve business problems common to most industries. Horizontal market applications are commonly used in personal computer systems: word processing programs, spreadsheet programs, graphics programs, and others. Although they are less common, horizontal products exist for workgroup systems, such as collaborative-writing word processors, and enterprise systems, such as general ledger accounting packages.

Horizontal application programs are almost always licensed from independent software vendors. Sometimes they are bundled with hardware as an inducement to purchase, but they are seldom developed by the hardware manufacturer itself.

Many horizontal application programs provide incredibly powerful functions and features at a modest price. This is possible because the market for such

Figure 3-17 Characteristics of Types of Programs

Systems Programs
- Liaison between hardware and other software
- Examples: OS, CCP, DBMS, utility programs
- Licensed by manufacturer, independents

Horizontal Market Application Programs
- Appeals to market across industry types
- Examples: Word processing, spreadsheets, desktop publishing
- Licensed by independents

Vertical Market Application Programs
- Appeals to market within industry type
- Examples: Law office time and billing, auto parts inventory management
- Licensed by VARs, some independents

Custom-Developed Application Programs
- Developed by in-house personnel or by contract
- Examples: Applications unique to the company
- No license necessary

programs is so large that development costs can be amortized over hundreds of thousands of units. For example, if a product costs $5 million to produce, and if it can be sold to 500,000 users (a reasonable expectation for a successful horizontal product), then the cost for development is only $10 per unit. Because of these economies, it *never* makes sense for a company to custom-develop horizontal application programs. These programs should always be licensed from outside software vendors.

Vertical Market Application Programs

Vertical market applications satisfy a need that is specific to a particular industry, such as a program to manage time and billing accounting for a law office or a program to manage inventory for auto parts distributors. Vertical market programs address more specific needs than do horizontal market programs; they address a particular need in a particular industry.

Vertical market programs are almost always licensed by independent software companies, often by **value-added resellers (VARs)**. These are companies that acquire hardware and systems software, add vertical application software to it, and sell the combined package as a unit. The term arises because the vertical market software adds value to the computer and the systems software. Most often, VARs also sell training and consulting services that support their products.

The quality of vertical market software and of the VARs that support it varies widely. Although many highly reputable vertical market vendors provide substantial value and service, others have created countless problems for their customers. The barrier to entry for a VAR is low. Anyone can develop programs, advertise them locally as a vertical product, and enlist customers. This differs from systems and horizontal market software, where the financial resources required to develop and market a product make a barrier that is difficult for even the most qualified person to surmount. Thus, when dealing with a VAR, check for a proven record of success with many customers who have needs similar to yours.

Custom-Developed Application Programs

Twenty years ago, all but the most fundamental systems software was developed by in-house staff. It was a rare exception when programs were obtained from outside vendors. Today, in contrast, companies look first to outside sources before they develop their own programs.

Custom program development makes sense only when no other action is possible. The time required and the risk inherent in the process usually make custom development undesirable. Further, the development costs of custom programs must be fully carried by the company; there is no opportunity to amortize development costs with other companies.

Custom-developed application programs are like tailored clothing. They can be created to provide a very accurate fit to unique requirements, but they are also quite expensive. Sometimes the value of the solution justifies the cost. Just as a rock star can justify tailored clothes, so, too, can a trader on the New York Stock Exchange justify a custom-developed stock-analysis program. Most people buy their clothes off the rack, and most professionals should look first to off-the-shelf programs.

Characteristics of applications programs are summarized in Figure 3-17.

Computer Languages

About a thousand computer languages are in active use today. Of these, a few dozen have become commercially important. You need only a limited knowledge of a few.

Computer languages developed in stages that loosely paralleled the generations of computer hardware described earlier in this chapter. For first-generation computers, people wrote programs in **machine language**, the binary code of the computer. In that code, an instruction might be stated: 100100110110110111011101110011100. Can you imagine spending a day writing such programs? Understandably, errors were common and productivity was low.

For second-generation computers, symbolic instructions of **assembly language** were substituted for the binary code of machine language. Typical assembly language statements are as follows:

```
AR      3,4
ST      5178,3
```

The first instruction causes the ALU to add the contents of register 4 to the contents of register 3 and to place the result in register 3. The second instruction says to store the result in memory location number 5178. With assembly language, errors were reduced and productivity increased, but programming was still a very slow and difficult task.

Assembly language is still used in some applications such as systems programs that control computer-to-computer communication. Although such languages are difficult to use and hence result in high program-development costs, they provide the programmer with great flexibility to craft very efficient programs that completely control every detail of processing.

For third-generation computers, **higher-level languages** came into widespread use. Instead of adding register values and storing results in physical memory locations, commands in these languages have more meaning to humans. Here are two commands from a higher-level language called COBOL (COmmon Business-Oriented Language):

```
READ EMPLOYEE-RECORD.
MOVE "0056" TO PAY-CODE.
```

The first instruction directs the computer to read data about one employee into memory (the structure of that data has been predefined as EMPLOYEE-RECORD). Then, in the second instruction, the value 0056 is placed in the memory space that has been labeled PAY-CODE.

Higher-level languages are sometimes called procedural because, to get a particular result, the programmer must specify a procedure for the computer to follow. Most business applications are written in procedural languages.

In the fourth generation, **nonprocedural languages**, such as the query language SQL, became popular. Here is an SQL command:

```
SELECT JOB#, CUST-NAME, PROFIT
FROM CONTRACT
WHERE PROFIT > 400
```

The values of the columns JOB#, CUST-NAME, and PROFIT in a table called CONTRACT are to be displayed. Only the rows in which profit is greater than 400 are to be shown. This statement is nonprocedural in that the user is specifying the result wanted, not how to obtain it. The means of manipulating the table to obtain this result are left to the system.

Today, **object-oriented programming systems (OOPS),** such as C++ and Smalltalk, are increasingly used. These systems manipulate *objects,* containing both data and the actions that can be performed on the data. The promise of OOPS is quicker program development and modification.

What a Business Professional Needs to Know About Languages As a future business professional, you need to remember five important computer languages. First, every computer has an assembly language. Other than for the most performance-critical and difficult programming tasks, however, this language should not be used. Programmers should nearly always use a higher-level language.

Three third-generation languages are widely used in business. One of these is used in most custom-developed applications for your benefit. You, yourself, will probably never use any of these languages.

COBOL is the oldest, most prevalent language and has served many businesses well for three decades. **C** is an excellent language developed at Bell Labs that enjoys considerable use in developing commercial microcomputer software. Beginners All-purpose Symbolic Instruction Code (**BASIC**) was designed to teach the rudiments of programming. Early versions of BASIC were not effective for commercial applications, but recently a number of vendors, most notably Microsoft, have extended BASIC to become a sophisticated and powerful language.

Finally, **SQL** is the American National Standards Institute selection as a fourth-generation language. Of these five languages, this is the one you are most likely to employ in creating ad hoc queries of a database.

DATA

This section introduces the fundamental concepts of data representation. Then it considers file processing and describes two major varieties: sequential and direct access. Finally, it considers database processing.

Data Representation

Computers represent data in the form of binary digits called **bits**. A bit is simply a number that can have one of two values, 0 or 1. Computers use bits for storage because they are easy to represent electronically. A switch is on or off; an electric current is flowing in one direction or another; a spot is magnetized or not.

Bits can be used to represent data in a number of ways. To represent **characters**, a code is used to let a number represent each different character. The code consists of a sequence of bits called a **byte**.

Two **character codes** are common. The first is **ASCII** (pronounced as-key), American Standard Code for Information Interchange. Although ASCII is virtually always stored and used as an 8-bit code, only its 7-bit component has full industry-wide acceptance. The use of the remaining bit (potentially adding up to 128 characters to the code) varies from manufacturer to manufacturer. ASCII is used with all prominent microcomputers, most minicomputers, and many mainframes. The second code is **EBCDIC** (pronounced eb-see-dick), Extended Binary Coded Decimal Interchange Code. It is used on mainframes (especially those manufactured by IBM) and on some minicomputers. EBCDIC is an 8-bit code.

Portions of ASCII and EBCDIC codes are shown in Figure 3-18. For example, in ASCII, the bit pattern 01000001 represents the character *A*. The pattern 01000010 represents *B*. Other characters are represented similarly.

Numbers are represented in several ways. If the numbers are not to be used for arithmetic (as with the numbers in an address, for example), they, too, are

Figure 3-18 ASCII and EBCDIC Character Codes

Character	ASCII	EBCDIC	Character	ASCII	EBCDIC
A	0100 0001	1100 0001	S	0101 0011	1110 0010
B	0100 0010	1100 0010	T	0101 0100	1110 0011
C	0100 0011	1100 0011	U	0101 0101	1110 0100
D	0100 0100	1100 0100	V	0101 0110	1110 0101
E	0100 0101	1100 0101	W	0101 0111	1110 0110
F	0100 0110	1100 0110	X	0101 1000	1110 0111
G	0100 0111	1100 0111	Y	0101 1001	1110 1000
H	0100 1000	1100 1000	Z	0101 1010	1110 1001
I	0100 1001	1100 1001	0	0011 0000	1111 0000
J	0100 1010	1101 0001	1	0011 0001	1111 0001
K	0100 1011	1101 0010	2	0011 0010	1111 0010
L	0100 1100	1101 0011	3	0011 0011	1111 0011
M	0100 1101	1101 0100	4	0011 0100	1111 0100
N	0100 1110	1101 0101	5	0011 0101	1111 0101
O	0100 1111	1101 0110	6	0011 0110	1111 0110
P	0101 0000	1101 0111	7	0011 0111	1111 0111
Q	0101 0001	1101 1000	8	0011 1000	1111 1000
R	0101 0010	1101 1001	9	0011 1001	1111 1001

represented by a code. In this same code, the pattern 00110001 represents a 1, for example. Numbers that are used for arithmetic are represented by translating them into some form of binary (base 2) representation. Usually, one method of translation is used for whole numbers, and a different method is used for numbers that may have fractions. The particulars are beyond the scope of this discussion.

Each byte represents a single character. As detailed in Figure 3-19, bytes are grouped together to form **fields**, or *data items*. In this figure, EmployeeID and EmployeeName are field names. Using the ASCII code, an employee ID with a value of AB11 is represented by the bit pattern 01000001 01000010 00110001 00110001. (The spaces are not part of the code but are placed here for readability.)

A group of logically related fields is called a **record**, and a group of records is called a **file**. Figure 3-20, for example, shows fields comprising an employee record; all of the employee records considered as a group are called the Employee file.

File Processing

Computer data is processed in two fundamental ways: file processing and database processing. With **file processing**, data is stored and processed in a series of separated files. Consider the situation in Figure 3-21. Here, two different programs are processing two separate files. One program processes the Employee file (Employee Data) to produce reports about employees; the second program processes a file about personal computer hardware (PC-Hardware Data), to produce a report about the inventory of hardware. The format of the PC-Hardware file record is shown in Figure 3-22.

The two fundamental ways of organizing files are sequential and direct-access.

Sequential File Organization In **sequential file organization** records are stored and accessed in sequence. Sequential files are processed by batch-processing TPS applications. Records are sorted before they are processed. For example, in Figure 3-23, a batch of employee time slips is being processed against a sequential file of employee records. Records have been previously written on the Employee master file in ascending order of employee number.

Time slip records are also sorted into employee number order. The processing program reads the first time slip and the first record from the old employee master file. If they are for the same employee, the program processes the time slip, produces the check, and writes an updated employee record to the new employee master file.

If the records are not for the same employee, other action is taken. For example, if the number on the time slip is greater than the number on the master employee record, this means that an employee did not work during this time

Figure 3-19 Hierarchy of Data

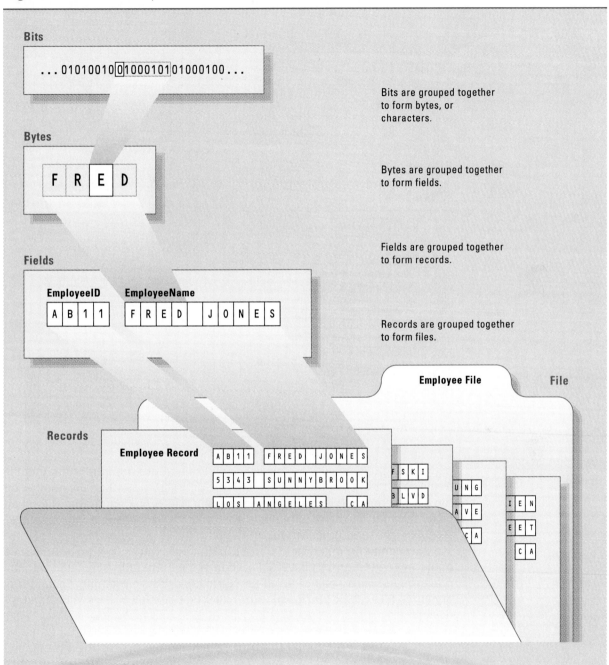

Bits are grouped together to form bytes, or characters.

Bytes are grouped together to form fields.

Fields are grouped together to form records.

Records are grouped together to form files.

Figure 3-20 Employee File Record Format

EMPLOYEE

EmployeeID	EmployeeName	Phone	Dept	PayRate	TotalPay toDate	TotalTax toDate

Figure 3-21 File Processing
In file processing, each application has its own separate data files that are processed by its programs.

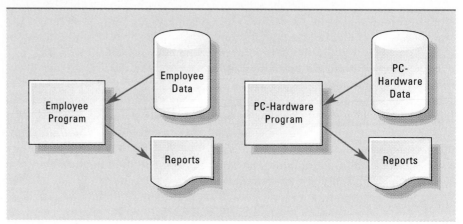

period. The program simply copies the employee record from the old master file to the new master file. If the number on the time slip is less than the number on the master employee record, then the time slip is for a new employee. The action taken depends on the requirements; the program may create a new employee record or take some other action.

Sequential file organization is used in situations where data can be processed in batches and where a substantial portion of the master file is updated with the processing of each batch. Payroll processing is a classic example. Sequentially organized files can be processed using either tape storage devices or disk storage devices.

Direct-Access File Organization When on-line processing systems are needed, **direct-access file organization** is used. Consider a system to authorize credit card purchases. When you make a credit card purchase, the merchant is

Figure 3-22   PC-Hardware File Record Format

PC-HARDWARE

Serial#	Desc	AcqDate	Cost	EmployeeID	EmployeeName	Phone

Figure 3-23   Processing Sequentially Organized File of Time Slips

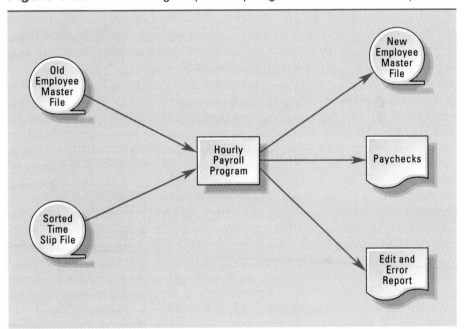

usually required to verify your credit. To do this, the merchant accesses a computer system that maintains a file including credit card number, status (valid, lost, stolen, etc.), and available credit. It is impractical to store this data sequentially. Both you and the merchant would become quite impatient if you had to wait some minutes for the computer system to read the file sequentially down to your record. Clearly, direct access to your record is required.

For direct access, a file must be stored on a direct-access device—that is, a disk—so records need not be processed in sequence. In addition, some means must be used to determine the location of a particular record. **Indexes** are one common means.

Consider the credit card authorization example. Suppose records are stored on a disk in such a way that 1,000 of them reside on each track. Further suppose that the credit card file is stored on 300 tracks so that a total of 300,000 records can be accommodated. Now, if the relative position of a record in the file is known, it is possible to determine its physical location. Record number 2050, for example, resides on track 3 of the file in relative position number 50.

If it were practical to issue credit cards numbered sequentially from 000000 to 300000, then the position of each card's record would be the same as the card number. For a variety of reasons, however, this is seldom practical. What is needed instead is some means of establishing a relationship between the credit card number, or some similar identifying value, and the record's relative location in the file.

Figure 3-24 shows an index that establishes this relationship. Whereas a book index contains topics with page numbers that state where each topic can be found, the credit card index contains credit card numbers with the relative record locations in the file.

Figure 3-24 Index

This index to a direct-access file shows account numbers and the direct-access locations of the corresponding data records.

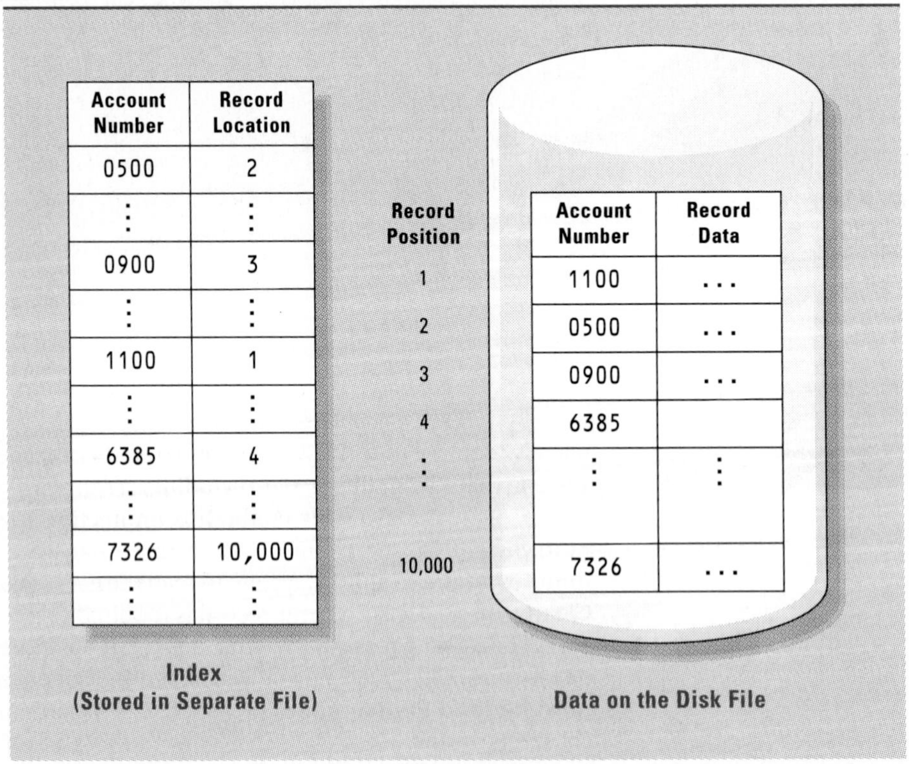

Index
(Stored in Separate File)

Data on the Disk File

Direct-access organization permits on-line access to data. It has the disadvantage, however, that indexes must be created and maintained. Indexes take file space and thus increase the amount of storage required. Processing can only be done on disks or similar devices; tape may not be used.

Direct-access file organization is often used in personal computer applications, though most users are unaware of this. Almost all horizontal market software uses one variation or another of direct-access file organization. A word processing program, for example, stores text and related data in a direct-access file. Spreadsheet programs do the same. The details of processing are taken care of by the horizontal product, however, and the user need not be aware of the indexes or other data structures in use.

Problems with File Processing File processing is adequate for many information systems, and it was the backbone of the computer industry for many years. However, it has disadvantages.

First, data is duplicated. Figure 3-22, for example, shows the format of the PC-Hardware file. Compare it to the Employee file format in Figure 3-20. Note that the EmployeeID, EmployeeName, and Phone fields appear in both files. The duplication wastes file space, but there is an even more serious disadvantage. When data is stored in two or more places, it is likely that the values will come to disagree with one another. If an employee changes her phone number, for example, the value of the Phone field must be changed in two files. If it is changed in one but not in the other, a **data integrity** problem is created.

In this simple case, it may appear easy to prevent integrity problems. In more realistic examples, however, where there are thousands of records and many files, such problems can become difficult to prevent. Further, once data integrity has been lost, it is difficult to regain. Questions like the following become nearly impossible to answer correctly: How many different values exist? Which one is correct? How many reports have been generated with invalid data?

The second disadvantage of file processing is the difficulty of relating records in one file to records in another. Suppose the user wants to be able to produce a report that shows employee ID, employee name, department, phone, and a list of all of the computer equipment assigned to the employee. With file processing, one way to do this is to duplicate several employee file fields in each record of the PC-Hardware file. This approach, however, generates considerable duplicated data.

Another choice is to somehow combine the data from the Employee file with the data from the PC-Hardware file. Since these files are separate, a new program must be written to extract the appropriate data from each file and combine it into a third file. This alternative is time-consuming and costly.

Because of the problems of duplicated data and the need for data integration (and for other reasons), file processing is being replaced by the second type of processing, **database processing**.

Database Processing

So far, we have defined the term *database* in an informal, intuitive manner. A more formal definition is this: a **database** is a self-describing collection of integrated records. It is self-describing because it contains, as part of itself, a directory, or dictionary, of its contents. In this way, a database is like the library at your university. The library contains, as part of its collection, a description of itself in the card catalog. The records are *integrated* because, even though a database can contain multiple files (usually called tables), the records within those tables are processed by relationship to one another.

Figure 3-25 shows how the EMPLOYEE and PC-HARDWARE tables are processed in a database setting. The DBMS acts as an intermediary between the user or application program and the database. The DBMS stores and processes the data so that records can be accessed via their relationship to other records.

Figure 3-26 shows the tables in the Allocation database: EMPLOYEE and PC-HARDWARE, with sample data. (Note that duplicated data that was present in the

Figure 3-25   Database Processing

In database processing, various applications use the DBMS to access data of various kinds stored in a common database.

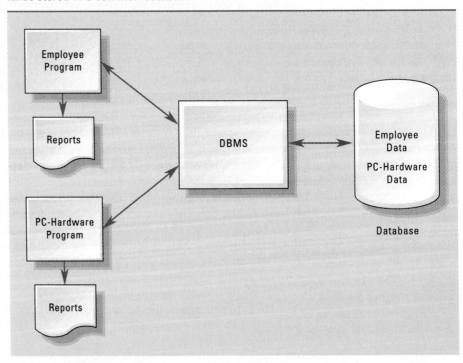

Figure 3-26 Tables in the Allocation Database
(a) Formats of EMPLOYEE table and PC-HARDWARE table in the Allocation database.
(b) Sample data illustrates field contents in each table.

(a) **EMPLOYEE**

EmployeeID	EmployeeName	Phone	Dept	PayRate	TotalPay toDate	TotalTax toDate

Common Data Item

PC-HARDWARE

Serial#	Desc	AcqDate	Cost	EmployeeID

(b)

EMPLOYEE						
EmployeeID	**EmployeeName**	**Phone**	**Dept**	**PayRate**	**TotalPay toDate**	**TotalTax toDate**
100	JONES	33234	ACCT	12.34	11334.00	2156.44
200	SMITH	22345	ACCT	12.34	10778.33	1976.55
300	TAYLOR	44567	SALES	19.84	15778.44	4987.28

PC-HARDWARE				
Serial#	**Description**	**AcqDate**	**Cost**	**EmployeeID**
409011	PS/2 MOD 70	2/27/90	5,667.44	100
321150	L-PRINT III	12/13/90	2,470.19	100
409011	MAC IIE	2/19/90	7,224.21	200
321151	L-PRINT III	12/13/90	2,470.19	200

PC-Hardware file is not included in the PC-HARDWARE database table.) To produce a report about equipment assigned to employees, the user or program first obtains Employee records from the DBMS. Then, it requests the DBMS to provide all PC-Hardware records that are related to each Employee record. For the data in Figure 3-26, the DBMS would obtain the data about employee Jones from the EMPLOYEE table and display it, and then access all rows in the PC-HARDWARE table that have Jones's employee ID number (100). Thus, the first two rows of the PC-HARDWARE table would be obtained.

Similarly, to produce a report about PC-HARDWARE, the user would first obtain the desired PC-Hardware record and then ask the DBMS to provide the Employee record that has the same value of EmployeeID. For example, for the equipment with Serial# value equal to 409011, the data for employee 200 (Smith) would be obtained.

SUMMARY

An information system consists of five components: hardware, programs, data, procedures, and people. Early systems focused on hardware, then programs, then data. Today, organizations, people, and procedures are the focus.

First-generation hardware was based on vacuum tubes; second-generation hardware used transistors. Reliability increased dramatically with the use of transistors. Third-generation hardware employed integrated circuits; and fourth-generation hardware used very large-scale integration (VLSI) of computer circuitry. Today, computer hardware is characterized by explosively rapid change and dramatic improvements in the price/performance ratio.

Hardware can be classified into input, processing, storage, and output categories. Major types of input hardware are keyboard, mouse, scanner, voice input device, handwriting input device, modem, light pen, and bar code and other readers.

Processing hardware includes the central processing unit (CPU) and main memory. The CPU is composed of the control unit and the arithmetic-logic unit (ALU). Processors are classified in terms of speed and word size. Speed can be expressed in terms of cycles, or millions of instructions per second (MIPS).

The two major types of processor memory are read-only memory (ROM) and random-access memory (RAM). The contents of ROM are nonvolatile; they are determined when the chip is manufactured and cannot be changed. Programmable read-only memory (PROM) can be programmed by the manufacturer of devices that use the memory. RAM can be read and written by the user, and it is volatile. Microcomputers contain far more RAM than ROM.

Computers include a data bus, or processor channel, for connecting the processor to external devices. In a microcomputer, channels contain expansion slots that accept cards to drive printers, plotters, disk units, coprocessors, and similar equipment.

Historically, processing hardware was classified as mainframe computers, minicomputers, and microcomputers. In recent years, these categories have been blurred. Today, what are left of these categories are sociological descriptions of the environment in which each type of processor was typically used: enterprise applications, workgroup applications, and personal applications.

Most computers today are complex instruction set computers (CISC), although today's designs make use of higher-performance reduced instruction set computer (RISC) technology, partially or completely. Computers in commercial use today are based on the von Neumann architecture. In the future, parallel computing architectures may become prevalent.

Disks are the most common form of storage in information systems. With disks, data is magnetically recorded in concentric circles called tracks. The same amount of data is recorded on each track. Hard disks can be stacked on top of one another; a cylinder is composed of all of the tracks that can be read while the read/write heads are held in a fixed position. Hard disks can be permanent or removable.

Diskettes, or floppy disks, are single-disk units that come in two common sizes: 5-1/4 inches (flexible) and 3-1/2 inches (hard plastic case). Diskettes are used, primarily, to transfer data from one computer to another or for backups.

A second, common type of storage is magnetic tape. Data is recorded in blocks on the tape, and all data must be processed sequentially. It is not possible to update data in the middle of a tape file. Tape read/write units are expensive, but the marginal cost of storing data on tape is low.

Three types of optical disk exist. CD-ROM provide read-only, high-capacity storage. Write-once/read-many (WORM) devices can be written once and can provide a permanent record of transactions. Erasable optical disks can both read and write, though the technology is still developing. The advantage of optical disks is high capacity; the major disadvantage is speed.

Printers and video displays are the most common form of output hardware. Inexpensive dot matrix impact character printers are commonly used in personal information systems. Line printers are used for printing large volumes of data in enterprise information systems. Nonimpact laser printers are increasingly used in systems of all types. The output of a bit-mapped printer is addressed by bit position and not by character, hence bit-mapped printers can print multiple typefaces and graphics. Many bit-mapped printers require a microprocessor; PostScript is a standard language for instructing such a processor.

Video displays, too, can be character-based or dot-addressable. Today's standard VGA display is a dot-addressable system with graphics capabilities. Common video display devices are CRT monitors and flat panel displays.

There are four types of programs. Systems programs control and allocate the computer's resources; they include operating system (OS), utilities, communications control program (CCP), and database management system (DBMS). Horizontal market application programs solve a general business need and cut across industry types. Examples are word processing and spreadsheet programs. Vertical market application programs meet a need specific to a particular industry, such as time and billing applications for law firms. Value-added resellers (VARs) specialize in the development, sales, and support of vertical market software. Finally, custom-developed programs are developed by and within the company that uses the program. Programs are not purchased; rather, a license to use the program for a specified purpose is purchased.

Computer languages developed in stages that roughly parallel the hardware generations. Machine language was the first generation; assembly language, the second; and high-level languages such as the COBOL, C, and BASIC, the third. The fourth, and current, generation includes nonprocedural languages like SQL.

Data is represented by bits, or binary digits. Bits are grouped into bytes, which are grouped into fields, or data items, which are grouped into records, which are grouped into files. Character data is represented by a code. Numbers used for arithmetic have some form of binary representation.

The two major types of data processing are file processing and database processing. There are two ways of organizing data for file processing. Sequential file organization permits data access only in a predetermined sequence. Direct-access file organization permits data access in random order. File processing has several disadvantages; one problem is data duplication (with the attendant problem of data integrity), and another is the difficulty of relating records to one another.

A database is a self-describing collection of integrated records. Databases contain multiple files (tables); relationships among the records in the tables are represented by data.

KEY TERMS

Charles Babbage	Third-generation computer	Input hardware
ENIAC	Integrated circuit	Source form
First-generation computer	Database management	Machine form
Second-generation computer	Fourth-generation computer	Keyboard
Compiler	VLSI	Terminal
		Mouse
		Point and click interface

Scanner
Voice input
Pen-based system
Handwriting input
Machine data input
Modem
Light pen
Bar code
CPU
Control unit
ALU
Register
I/O
Cycle speed
Megahertz
MIPS
Word size
ROM
RAM
Nonvolatile memory
PROM
Volatile memory
Kilobyte (K)
Megabyte (MB)
Data bus
Processor channel
Port
Expansion slot
Microprocessor
Mainframe computer
Minicomputer
Microcomputer
LAN
RISC
CISC
von Neumann
  architecture

Parallel computing
  architecture
Disk
Track
Read/write heads
Sector
Hard disk
Cylinder
Gigabyte (GB)
Average access time
Diskette, or floppy disk
Magnetic tape
Sequential access
Direct access
Optical disk storage
CD-ROM
WORM
Erasable optical disk
Character printer
Line printer
Page printer
Impact printer
Nonimpact printer
Bit-mapped printer
PostScript
VGA display
CRT
Monitor
Flat panel display
Systems program
Application program
Horizontal market
  application program
Vertical market
  application program
Custom application
  program

OS
Utility program
License
CCP
DBMS
VAR
Machine language
Assembly language
Higher-level language
Nonprocedural
  language
OOPS
COBOL
C
BASIC
SQL
Bit
Character
Byte
Character code
ASCII
EBCDIC
Field
Record
File
File processing
Sequential file
  organization
Direct-access file
  organization
Index
Data integrity
Database processing
Database

REVIEW QUESTIONS

1. List the five components of an information system.

2. Explain how the evolution of information technology moved from left to right across the five components in Figure 3-1.

3. What was the defining characteristic of first-generation computers? What was the primary focus of this generation?

4. What was the defining characteristic of second-generation computers? What was the primary focus of this generation?

5. What was the defining characteristic of third-generation computers? What was the primary focus of this generation?

6. What does VLSI stand for? Why was it important?

7. Characterize the focus of information systems today.

8. Name the basic categories of hardware.

9. Name and describe the function of three types of input hardware.

10. Explain the function of CPU, control unit, ALU, system memory, and registers.

11. Explain the term *cycle* in reference to a processor. Why is the speed in cycles faster than the instruction speed?

12. What does MIPS stand for?

13. What is the difference between a 16-bit microprocessor and a 32-bit microprocessor?

14. Explain how cycle time and word size influence processor performance.

15. Explain the differences among ROM, PROM, and RAM.

16. What type of computer memory is volatile? Nonvolatile?

17. Define kilobyte and megabyte.

18. Explain the purpose of the data bus.

19. Explain the difference between a computer and a processor.

20. Explain the historical significance of the terms *mainframe computer, minicomputer,* and *microcomputer.*

21. Explain the sociological meanings that today correspond to mainframe computers, minicomputers, and microcomputers.

22. Explain the difference between CISC architecture and RISC architecture.

23. How does a parallel computing architecture differ from the von Neumann architecture?

24. Define the terms *disk, track, sector,* and *cylinder.*

25. Why is there the same amount of data on a small, inner track as there is on a large, outer track?

26. Explain the difference between hard disks and diskettes. What applications are common for each?

27. Explain the difference between sequential access and direct access. Which is possible with magnetic tape? Which is possible with disks?

28. Describe the differences among CD-ROM, WORM, and erasable optical disks. Name one advantage and one disadvantage of optical disk units.

29. What are the differences among character printers, line printers, and page printers? Between impact printers and nonimpact printers?

30. How does a bit-mapped printer differ from a character-based printer? Why does it matter?

31. Differentiate between character-based displays and graphics video displays.

32. Name four categories of programs.

33. What is the function of systems programs? Name four types of systems programs.

34. Explain why programs are almost never purchased.

35. Explain the meaning of the term *horizontal market application program.* Name two such programs.

36. Explain the meaning of the term *vertical market application program.* Give examples of two such programs.

37. What is a VAR? What function does a VAR serve?

38. Under what conditions do custom-developed programs make sense?

39. Briefly describe the four generations of computer languages.

40. Name five languages that this chapter says that you, as a future business professional, should know.

41. Explain the purpose of SQL.

42. Describe the relationship of bits, bytes, characters, fields, records, files, tables, and databases.

43. What are two types of file organization? How are they used with personal information systems, if at all?

44. Describe two disadvantages of file processing.

45. Define the term *database*.

46. How does a database reduce data duplication?

DISCUSSION QUESTIONS

1. As computer technology has become more reliable and more easily used, it has been possible for information systems to better address the needs of people and organizations. If this trend continues, there will be less and less need for computer specialists. Discuss what you think are the likely impacts of this phenomenon on organizations. What will happen to MIS departments? What role will line departments take with regard to information systems?

2. The semiconductor industry has outperformed itself every year for the last 10 years. The capabilities of today's computers would have been mind-boggling 10 years ago. There is no end to this trend in sight. Computers very likely will continue to become more and more powerful without cost increases (and possibly with cost decreases). What are we going to do with all of this computing power? What applications seem likely to you? What are the implications of this situation?

PROJECTS

A. Central Illinois State University is considering the establishment of a modern on-line student registration system. To use this system, a student would sit down at any terminal or networked PC on campus at a scheduled time, establish contact with the system, and register into specific classes for the coming term. Envision such a system. What hardware components would be required? What program components? How would the data probably be processed? Be specific in presenting a detailed listing of likely hardware, program, and data components.

B. At Economy Appliance Company, a regional retail chain, large appliances such as refrigerators and washers are sold through retail stores but delivered by truck to customer homes from inventory stored at a central warehouse. Small appliances such as TVs and microwave ovens are sold from inventory at each store. Economy Appliance provides PCs to its salespeople at each point of sale. Salespeople use the PCs to enter data about each sale and print a sales receipt on an attached printer. The PCs are connected by a network within each store to a PC containing that store's database of inventory, customer credit, and other information. Each store's PCs can access the company's centralized information located on a minicomputer at headquarters. Its data includes the central warehouse inventory and the chainwide accounting system. Using this information, provide a detailed listing of the hardware components, the program components, and the data components of Economy Appliance's MIS. In each category, consider what items appear likely to be used, and be prepared to defend your informed guesses.

C. Suppose you are the manager of MIS for Economy Appliance Company (See Project B). Here are some examples of the inquiries that your boss, owner Ed Potrero, has made over the past few months. For each inquiry, (a) classify the topic of Ed's inquiry—hardware (which type?), programs (which type?), or data; and (b) describe at least one specific change that might meet the challenge of Ed's question.

1. "A sales rep for one of our vendors was in yesterday, and she had a little PC with a mouse attached. That mouse sure made her computer easier to use. How come our computers don't use a mouse?"

2. "Down at the grocery store, they just sweep each product over that little spot in the checkout station, and it automatically records the price and prints a receipt. Couldn't we do that?"

3. "Prices are going sky high on our preprinted five-part customer receipt forms. Since we run these things through the printer, why can't we let the printer just print the entire form instead of making it print additional text onto a preprinted form? If we do that, we can just print receipts, form and all, onto blank paper, can't we? It looks like we'd save quite a bit."

4. "I saw an article that claimed most businesses could shift from a bigger old computer to a much smaller and cheaper new computer with no loss in computing power. Why are we still using that big minicomputer for our accounting system? Maintenance costs on that thing are killing us!"

5. "I talked to a sales rep from J&G Software yesterday, who said their retail appliance accounting system could cut our data processing costs by at least 25 percent. Here's the spec sheet. What do you think?"

D. Over the next few days, identify examples of various types of data input. Consider data input methods used by retail stores, fast-food restaurants, telephone answering systems, college registration systems and courses, and other computerized organizations. Briefly describe at least six methods of data input other than the standard keyboard. (Here's one hint: Look carefully at the keyboard used for data entry at your favorite fast-food restaurant. Is it a standard keyboard like the one on a PC? If not, what are the differences?)

M I N I C A S E

"Electronifying" Core Business Operations

With the swipe of a card, the touch of a key, or the push of a button on a fax machine, transaction processing is moving out of the back office and into customers' hands. Call today's core business operations "electronified," says Steven Weissmann, associate director at BIS Strategic Decisions in Norwell, Mass .

One typical case is Electrical Engineering & Equipment Co. (3E) in Des Moines, Iowa. Until about nine months ago, the wholesaler of electrical components handled sales receipts much the same way it had since 1923. Paper order slips from 3E's customers—distributors and retailers—were delivered by hand to the order-entry department and keyed into host computers. Back orders from the company's 2,200 customers took about two weeks to fill, and employees had no way to know if a part was in stock or how much time was needed to get it.

With 3E's sales nudging $50 million, the old system had to go, says IS director Bernice Mohn. "One large customer said we could either get an on-line ordering system or lose their account," she says. 3E decided to develop a new system.

Using an NCR 3550 mainframe with RAID disk arrays and third-party software, 3E created a database containing purchasing information, ordering patterns, and histories for all of its customers. Soon, other customers wanted to transmit their orders via PCs. Today, 35 to 40 remote orders a month are called in by modem, Mohn reports.

"There are definite productivity gains," Mohn says. Specifically, 3E can fill 96% of its back orders in three to five days. Moreover, 3E's customers can place orders or query their accounts 24 hours a day, seven days a week, freeing inside sales staff from administrative work.

Surprisingly, few companies are using the new systems to cut the payroll. Rather than lay off employees, many of these transaction-processing innovations are allowing workers to concentrate on their primary jobs. For example, salespeople freed from paperwork have more time to assist customers with their purchases.

At 3E, IS director Mohn is testing an electronic data interchange (EDI) system that would give customers computer-to-computer access and file transfer with 3E's databases. Distributors will be able to order, check inventory, and extract data for their own forecasts on line with the supplier. Sales staff, in turn, will no longer have to retrieve this information for customers and will be "more dedicated to sales," Mohn says. ■

Paula Klein, excerpted from *InformationWeek*, May 24, 1993, pp. 51, 52.

Discussion Questions

1. Summarize the advantages of letting customers place orders electronically rather than placing them through sales-people. Do you see any potential disadvantages?

2. EDI lets customers directly access the data in a company's database. Describe EDI's advantages.

3. On the one hand, companies implement strict data security measures to keep information out of competitors' hands; on the other, they permit customers to access their databases through EDI. Are these two trends in conflict? What limitations would you place on customer access to your company's database?

4. Give additional examples of "electroni-fication" of core business operations. Consider banking, retail sales (including credit sales), and other areas.

4

The Value Added by Information Systems

WHY DO ORGANIZATIONS CREATE INFORMATION SYSTEMS? The answers to this question are complex and detailed. This chapter concentrates on building a framework for providing answers; the framework will be used throughout the book.

Failing to ask the above question will place you in the vulnerable position of relying on others' beliefs that information systems have value to you. You must be able to assess this question for yourself and for the unique business situations that you will encounter during your career.

Information systems can add value in many ways. They help organizations or individuals improve the products that the organizations produce and the processes they use to produce them. Information systems can also facilitate management, help people make better decisions, and help create a barrier to market entry in order to solidify an organization's competitive advantage. Each of these possibilities are described in this chapter.

INFORMATION SYSTEMS ADD VALUE TO PROCESSES AND TO PRODUCTS

The dimensions of **process** and **product** can help us identify ways in which information systems **add value** to an organization. To understand how this can be done, consider the following conversation at Elliot Bay Nurseries, a mail-order company that sells garden supplies and equipment:

> "This is the third complaint letter in two days! We can't have this! Look at this pile of complaints! What's going on?"

> [Ms. Jamie Richardson, president and owner of Elliot Bay Nurseries, shoves a stack of customer complaint letters into the hands of Chris Sweeney.]

> "The problem, Ms. Richardson, is that most of the time, I can't tell what's really a priority shipment. For instance, Brooke runs into the warehouse demanding a prompt shipment for one of her favorite customers. So we get right on it. Then Colleen does the same. So whose shipment should get first priority?"

> "Chris, just take them as they come. You know how to do that."

> "Sure I do, but look at our order document. Where does it say that this is a priority shipment? There's no place on the document for the order takers to indicate that. Most of the time we don't know about the *real* priority shipments."

> "Chris, that's not the whole picture. Many of these letters say we shipped the wrong goods."

> "Yes, but those are errors in the order documents. Look more closely at them. We're shipping what the order documents say to ship. It's the order takers who write down the wrong item numbers. That's the real problem."

> "Chris, I don't know. Are you sure you're picking the right stuff?"

Reflect for a minute on this conversation. Customers are complaining about the lack of promptness and accuracy of the orders they are receiving. The orders are the products of Elliot Bay Nurseries, and judging from the conversation, there are problems in those products.

Elliot Bay's products are the result of activities, or processes. Calls are received from customers, order documents are filled in, shipments are prepared, and

Figure 4-1 Context Diagram for Order Fulfillment Department

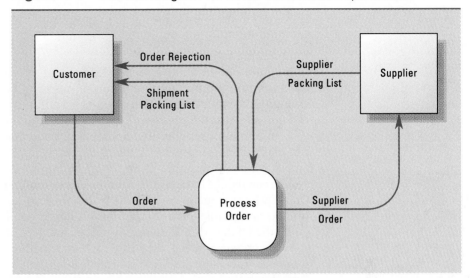

packages are sent. The process transforms input received from customers and suppliers into output wanted by customers. In fact, a business, like an information system, follows the I/P/O structure described in Chapter 1.

Products and processes are related; in general, improving or degrading one affects the other in a like manner. Information systems can influence an organization's products and processes. Consider the words of Porter and Millar, two respected business researchers:

> Information technology is changing the way companies operate. It is affecting the entire *process* by which companies create their *products*. Furthermore, it is reshaping the product itself: the entire package of physical goods, services, and information companies provide to create *value* for their buyers [Italics added][1].

To understand the difference between process and product, consider Figure 4-1. The order fulfillment department receives orders and supplier shipments (represented by supplier packing list) as input and produces shipments (represented by shipment packing list), order rejections, and supplier orders as output.

---

1. Porter, Michael E. and Victor E. Millar, "How Information Gives You Competitive Advantage," *Harvard Business Review*, Vol. 63, No. 4, July/August 1985.

ADDING VALUE TO PROCESSES

A *process* is a system of activities; it is a set of actions coordinated to accomplish some goal. The order fulfillment department follows specific processes that transform the input it receives into the output it is expected to produce. An example is the process by which an order is verified by checking its completeness and ensuring that the customer's payment or credit is acceptable.

Information systems are an important component of many processes and can make processes less labor-intensive, more efficient, faster, more enjoyable, and so forth. For example, in the order fulfillment department, an information system can reduce the amount of manual labor required to check customer credit. Or, an information system can divide the order-verification work among several workers and enable them to accomplish a job more efficiently and enjoyably as a group than if they were individually processing the orders.

To understand the ways in which information systems can add value to processes, this chapter reviews some of the important models of business processes, then shows the relationship of these models to the types of information systems defined in Chapter 2.

Models of Business Processes

A number of researchers have studied business processes and their relationship to information systems. The classic model of organizational process was set out by Simon:

> An organization can be pictured as a three-layered cake. In the bottom layer we have the basic work processes—in the case of a manufacturing organization, the processes that procure raw materials, manufacture the physical product, warehouse it, and ship it. In the middle layer, we have the programmed (structured) decision-making processes, the processes that govern the day-to-day operation of the manufacturing and distribution system. In the top layer, we have the nonprogrammed (unstructured) decision-making processes, the processes that are required to design and redesign the entire system, to provide it with its basic goals and objectives, and to monitor its performance.[2]

These same three levels were later described by Robert Anthony, who defined the levels as **operational control**, "the process of assuring that specific tasks are

2. Simon, Herbert A., *The New Science of Management Decision.* New York: Harper & Row, 1960, p. 40.

carried out";[3] **management control**, "the process by which managers assure that resources are obtained and used effectively";[4] and **strategic planning**, "the process of deciding on objectives of the organization, on changes in these objectives, on the resources used in attaining these objectives."[5]

Gorry and Scott Morton built upon these foundations to establish a two-dimensional framework, which is depicted in Figure 4-2.[6] The columns of this figure show the three layers identified by Simon and Anthony, and the rows identify the degree of structure involved in the processes. Amount of structure means the amount of human judgment and evaluation required in each activity. **Structured activity** requires little judgment, evaluation, or insight. It relies instead on the application of known formulas, in which the values of the key variables are also known. In structured activities, much of the decision making can be automated.

Figure 4-2   Gorry and Scott Morton Systems Classification

	Operational Control	Management Control	Strategic Planning
Structured			
Semistructured			
Unstructured			

3. Anthony, Robert N., *Planning and Control Systems: A Framework for Analysis.* Boston: Harvard University Graduate School of Business Administration, 1965, p. 69.

4. *Ibid.*, p. 27.

5. *Ibid.*, p. 24.

6. Gorry, G. Anthony and Michael S. Scott Morton, "A Framework for Management Information Systems," *Sloan Management Review*, Fall 1971, pp. 55–70.

Unstructured activity requires considerable judgment, evaluation, and human creativity. No known formula can solve the problem, and values of some key variables—sometimes even the identities of key variables—are not known. Unstructured activity is very difficult to automate.

The Simon view and the Gorry and Scott Morton view have an important difference. Simon contended that activity became less structured as it moved from operational to management to planning activities. To Simon, Figure 4-2 should have no rows; activity becomes less structured while moving from left to right across the columns. Gorry and Scott Morton postulated that there are actually two dimensions: type of activity (the columns) and degree of structure (the rows). According to their model, operational control can be structured or unstructured, as can management control and strategic planning.

Both of these points of view have merit. Although decision making at the operational level may be both structured and unstructured, there is no doubt that most of it is structured. Similarly, both types of decision making occur at the strategic planning level, but the most important is unstructured.

Business Processes and the Types of Information Systems

Chapter 2 described five types of information systems. Figure 4-3 uses the Gorry and Scott Morton grid to show the approximate domains of each system type. TPSs are used primarily for structured operational and, to a lesser degree, management control applications. MISs (narrow definition) are used primarily for semistructured management control applications, although MISs overlap into the operational and strategic planning realms as well.

DSSs are used primarily for less-structured decision making, whether that occurs at the operational, management, or strategic planning levels. ESSs are used primarily for structured management and strategic planning applications. Finally, OASs, as facilitators of interpersonal communication, underlie all of this activity.

Each of these types of systems adds value to the process it supports. Each makes the process more efficient, improves process coordination, creates a better working environment, reduces errors and mistakes, or accomplishes some similar service.

Processes at Elliot Bay Nurseries

Processes at Elliot Bay Nurseries (Figure 4-1) involve each of the three levels of decision making. Examples of operational questions are as follows: Is this order valid? Do we have 6 dozen yellow variegated iris bulbs in stock? Have we received

Figure 4-3 Domains of Information System Types

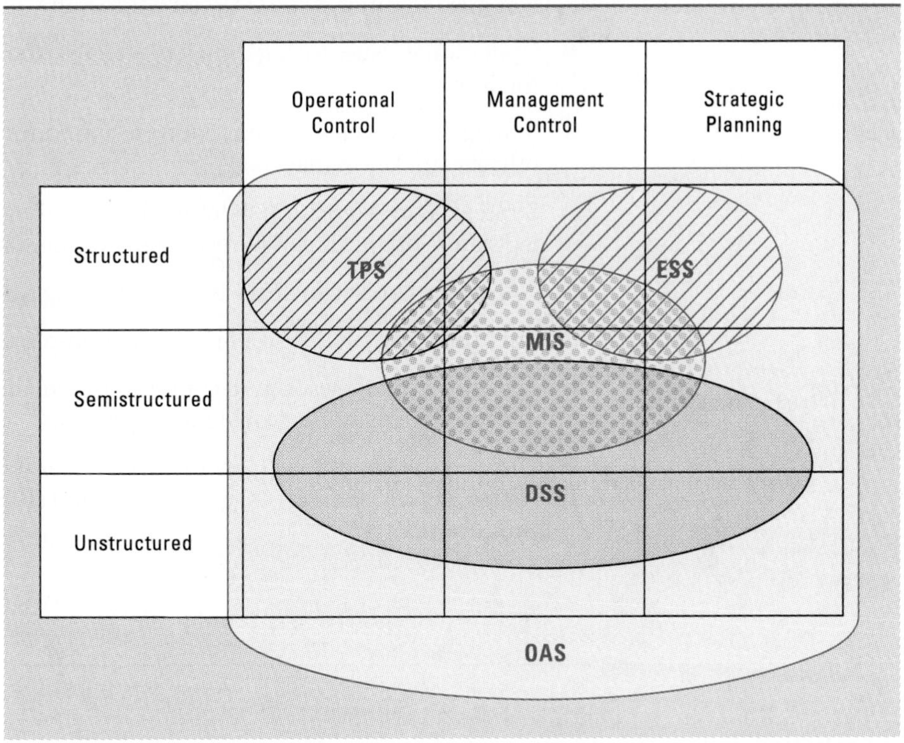

the payment from Customer 12334? Such operational questions are usually answered by TPS applications.

Management decisions involve the allocation and use of resources: Are we getting sufficient yield on our seed crops? Is our inventory too large (or small)? Are we receiving payments fast enough from our customers? Such questions are usually addressed by MIS and, to a lesser extent, DSS applications.

Strategic planning questions involve objectives: Should we add (or remove) a product line? Is our advertising program appropriate? Should we change the terms on customer orders to encourage faster payment? These primarily unstructured questions are best addressed by DSS applications.

ESS applications provide information to support high-level executive management control and planning. They are concerned with questions about the status and activity of the business at a very high level. For example, the CEO may want to know the balance of the company's checking account, not to write a check, but as a measure of organizational success in management and planning. An ESS involves structured questions, but the questions are asked for management and strategic purposes, not for operational purposes.

Finally, OAS applications underlie all of the activities of Elliot Bay Nurseries. Messages created through the OAS can address the following issues:

- Operational issues (using E-mail to let Sales know that a large order is on the way)

- Management issues (disseminating a six-month inventory status report to officers and key managers)

- Strategic issues (creating slides to display during a presentation to state legislators on the effects of recent environmental regulations)

OAS applications can deal with the following types of questions:

- Structured questions (a report on last month's sales volume)

- Semistructured questions (a computerized management conference on whether raising prices would increase profits)

- Unstructured questions (a memo from marketing to President Richardson suggesting the addition of garden tillers and shredders to the company's product mix)

ADDING VALUE TO PRODUCTS

Products are the output of processes; they are things, documents, agreements, services, and the like, that are produced by the business activity. Figure 4-1 shows the dataflows related to the processing of orders at Elliot Bay Nurseries. The order fulfillment department's products are represented by the dataflows created by Process Order: shipment packing lists for shipped orders, order rejections for rejected orders, and supplier orders when needed.

Products differ in their **characteristics**. A shipment might consist of packages of seeds, seeds and general planting instructions, or seeds and planting instructions specific to the climatic conditions at the customer's address. Products also differ in **delivery:** speed of delivery and convenience in the way they are delivered.

Enhancing Product Features and Characteristics

The most obvious way that information systems support products is by enhancing features or adding new characteristics to the product. Consider the customer shipment made by the order fulfillment department. Information systems can be used to add value to the shipment product.

For example, an information system could produce planting and care instructions that are specifically tailored to the products ordered and to the region of the shipment. These instructions could even be adjusted to account for the time of year of the shipment. Imagine the delight of a customer who receives instructions that begin, "You will receive this shipment on 8 October. Because of the light rain in Chicago this past month, we recommend that you plant your tulips. . ."

Or, an information system could be used to examine the particular combination of items that have been ordered: "We recommend that you do not plant the onions next to the potatoes because of the likelihood of attracting green-tinkered slanks." An information system could even combine the current order with order information from prior years: "Last year you ordered bush beans from us. The soil in which you planted those beans would be an ideal location for the beets that you are receiving today."

Figure 4-4 A Product's Information Component
Documentation is an information component of many computer-related products.

The introduction of new product characteristics can add a competitive advantage and change the nature of the industry. If Elliot Bay developed a system that combined order information from several years, it would provide an inducement to customers to order all of their products from Elliot Bay, every year. This creates a barrier to market entry for other companies and changes the structure of the market.

In general, every product has both physical components and **information components**. Even a product as basic as cement has an information component (e.g., how long it will be before the cement sets). Other products have information components that concern their use, maintenance, and repair. As Porter and Millar state,

> Historically, a product's physical component has been more important than its information component. The new technology, however, makes it feasible to supply far more information along with the physical product. For example, General Electric's appliance service data base supports a consumer hotline that helps differentiate GE's service support from its rivals'.[7]

What is a *product*? If you buy a clothes washer, what are you buying? Certainly it includes the machinery that washes your clothes.[8] However, the product also includes documentation about how to use and maintain the machine and how to diagnose problems. In addition, it includes information systems that improve customer support, catalog and identify replacement parts, and facilitate the delivery of parts. Finally, since the product includes service, it also includes the training and knowledge of the repair person. Good information systems add value to each of these components of the product.

Facilitating Product Delivery

Information systems not only enhance product characteristics, they also improve product delivery. For example, to a buyer with a credit card, an airline reservation and a ticket to any destination in the world is no more than a short telephone call away.

There are many other examples: Some companies support in-home computer-based shopping; banks provide automated teller machines (ATMs); and organizations order parts or raw materials through automated organizational purchasing systems. For example, an attendant at a car rental company carries a

---

7. Porter and Millar, "Competitive Advantage."

8. Today, this machinery is likely to contain a microprocessor or some other computer-based device. We will not consider such applications of computer technology in this text. Although it is important, such applications fall outside of the definition of MIS as the development and use of information systems in organizations.

portable computer terminal. When a customer returns a car, the attendant keys in the car's license plate number, and the portable terminal accesses a central computer that computes the amount due. The attendant's unit prints the invoice, and the customer transaction is completed on the spot—with no standing in line.

As with product enhancements, improving the delivery of a product can create new levels of customer expectations and change the nature of the competition. Ten years ago, ATMs were merely a convenient adjunct to banking services. Today, they are required to make a bank competitive. People have come to expect 24-hour ATM service as part of the checking account product.

Up to this point, the discussion has focused on ways in which the incorporation of information systems into processes and products improves them. However, information systems can also be used in the process of change that continuously *improves* processes and products. That is the focus of the next section.

ADDING VALUE BY ENHANCING THE ABILITY TO CHANGE

Information systems can also add value by enhancing our ability to change processes and products for the better. This process of change was recognized many years ago by Edward Deming, a man considered by many to be the father of the quality movement in manufacturing. In his classic book, *Out of the Crisis,*[9] Deming stated that there are four ways an organization can increase its quality: (1) innovating a new process, (2) improving a current process, (3) innovating a new product, or (4) improving a current product. Figure 4-5 provides examples.

Innovation in process or product usually involves dramatic changes—a discontinuity between what has been and what is now. With just-in-time (JIT)

Figure 4-5   Examples of Deming's Four Ways of Increasing Quality

	Innovate	**Improve**
Process	Just-in-time (JIT) inventory management	Reduced flow of forms processing
Product	Electronic spreadsheets	New feature added to an existing spreadsheet program

9.   Deming, Edward, *Out of the Crisis.* Boston, MA: MIT Press, 1986.

inventory management, a supplier delivers goods just as they are needed for manufacturing purposes. This is an example of innovation in process. Electronic spreadsheets are an example of innovation in product; when first introduced, they were completely new and unlike any previous program. The speed, accuracy, and flexibility of financial analyses were dramatically increased with such spreadsheet products.

Improvements involve adjustments rather than dramatic changes. They are minor changes that make the product more usable or the process more productive. Reducing the time it takes a form to flow through the accounts payable department is an improvement in process. Adding a new feature to an existing spreadsheet program is an improvement in product. Information systems can support all four of the example actions in Figure 4-5.

Recently, in part because of the tremendous success of Japanese manufacturing, increased emphasis has been placed on the process of making continuous changes to improve quality in business. The phrase *total quality management* has become a buzzword in many business groups. Throughout this text, you will see how information systems can add value by supporting the process of change to both process and product.

Adding Value by Changing Processes

To change a process for the better, first find out how well the output serves its intended purpose, then use that knowledge to modify your activity. That is, use **feedback**. The role of feedback is shown in Figure 4-6. In general, input is processed to create output, and information about the quality of the output is used to change input or processing. This requires that the quality of the output be measured and compared to some applicable criteria and that information about the results be presented in a form that can be used in changing inputs and processes.

For example, a law firm may obtain feedback from its clients on their perceptions of the quality of the services provided. This feedback is then used to alter the firm's process of providing services.

Information systems play several roles in a feedback system. For one, they can be used to facilitate the provision of feedback information. Examples are the structured and recurring reports provided by an MIS.

Additionally, information systems can be used to facilitate the necessary changes in input and processing. An obvious use of such information occurs in automated manufacturing systems in which the automated process is changed in accordance with information that is fed back to the computer-controlled manufacturing equipment. A less obvious use would be to employ a DSS to predict the impact on output of various changes in input or process.

Figure 4-6 The Role of Feedback in Making Changes

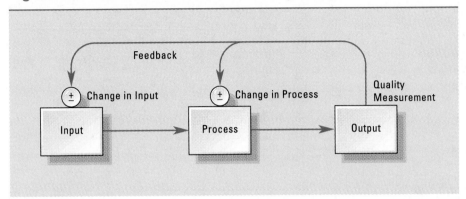

The management control function usually involves process improvements, whereas strategic planning more often involves process innovation. The changes made by managers as a result of information in MIS reports are usually intended as improvements in process. The setting and adjusting of organizational goals and objectives in the course of strategic planning, however, is likely to involve innovation rather than just improvement.

Adding Value by Changing Products

Information systems can also contribute to the process of changing products. Products can be changed either through innovation—new products and new ways to deliver products—or through improvement.

As with process improvement, product improvement requires feedback. The organization must measure the results of its products and compare those results to organizational expectations or other standards. For example, suppose a software vendor publishes a word processing program. To improve this product, the publisher measures the satisfaction of purchasers. These measurements are then fed back so the publisher can decide on product improvements.

As with process improvements, information systems can be used both to gather the feedback and to facilitate the design and development of product improvements. Information systems, such as electronic mail systems or systems for producing newsletters, can also be used to communicate the need for changes to personnel involved in the process. The ways in which information systems add value by increasing quality of products and processes are listed in Figure 4-7.

Figure 4-7 How Information Systems Can
Improve Processes and Products

- Providing feedback
- Adjusting automated processes
- Predicting outcomes of input or process changes
- Facilitating communication about changes

A Model of the Value Added by Information Systems

To summarize, information systems add value to processes and products in three ways (see Figure 4-8). First, they add value by facilitating ongoing business processes—that is, by supporting operations, management, and strategic planning. Second, they add value by being a part of the product characteristics and product-delivery system. Third, they add value by supporting changes in processes and products through improvement and innovation. This framework is used throughout the text to discuss added value.

HOW INFORMATION SYSTEMS ADD VALUE TO MANAGERS

The preceding section discussed ways in which information systems can add value to an organization by enhancing its processes and products and its ability to change. This section focuses on managers and the ways in which information systems can add value to them.

The Nature of Management

The **management** job is a complicated one. Managers live in a world of tensions; they must constantly balance a variety of visions, needs, and constraints. They have their own visions of the organization's future, but they are pulled, too, by the visions, needs, and hopes of others who have vested interests. In trying to balance

Figure 4-8 Three Ways Information Systems Add Value

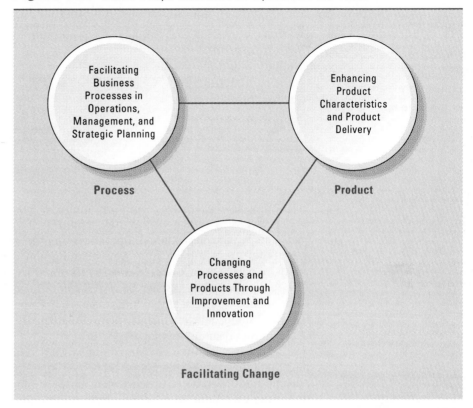

these forces, they face constraints: conflicts among people, irrational acts, unpredictable and sometimes hostile environmental changes, and nonsensical programs forced down their throats by people with power but limited knowledge. All this happens in real time, necessitating decisions and actions on a time scale that the manager does not control. In short, management is one delicate balancing act after another.

How Managers Spend Their Time

A number of researchers have investigated how managers spend their time. The results are surprisingly consistent across time, industry, and level of manager. Mintzberg studied the activities of chief executives,[10] Stewart studied 160 mid-

10. Mintzberg, Henry, *The Nature of Managerial Work*. New York: Harper & Row, 1973.

Figure 4-9   Managers' Use of Time

Activity	Percent of Time
Scheduled meetings	59
Unscheduled meetings	10
Telephone calls	6
Tours	3
Desk work	22

and senior-level executives,[11] Carlson studied 9 Swedish company presidents,[12] Sayles observed and analyzed the activities of 75 lower- and middle-level managers,[13] and Guest studied supervisors on production lines.[14]

From these studies, one overwhelming and consistent conclusion arises about managers at all levels: *Managers talk and listen; the overwhelming majority of management time is spent in verbal communication.* Mintzberg found that CEOs spend 78 percent of their time engaged in verbal activity. Stewart found that mid- and senior-level managers spent 66 percent of their time in verbal activity. Other studies bear out this same conclusion.

Figure 4-9 summarizes Mintzberg's results. The CEOs he studied spent 69 percent of their time in meetings—59 percent in scheduled, preplanned meetings and another 10 percent in unscheduled hallway or pop-in meetings. Six percent of their time was spent on telephone calls, and another 3 percent, on tours. Desk work accounted for only 22 percent of these managers' time.

Adding Value to Management with Information Systems

These data indicate the characteristics of a manager's job (see Figure 4-10). First, managers are social; they spend their time listening and talking. Many choose their careers because they enjoy social activity. Hence, any information system

11. Stewart, Rosemary, *Managers and Their Jobs.* London: Macmillan, 1967.

12. Carlson, Sune, *Executive Behavior: A Study of the Work Load and the Working Methods of Managing Directors.* Stockholm: Strombergs, 1951, p. 52.

13. Sayles, Leonard, *Managerial Behavior: Administration in Complex Organizations.* New York: McGraw Hill, 1964, p. 162.

14. Guest, R. H., "Of Time and Foremen," *Personnel*, Vol. 32, 1956, pp. 478–486.

Figure 4-10 Characteristics of Managers

- Social
- Spend two-thirds of time in meetings
- Have many brief encounters
- Constantly attempt to gain information
- Consider traditional MIS reports as not too important

that takes a manager away from social activity for any length of time will be disliked and probably unused.

Second, since two-thirds of a manager's time is spent in meetings, any way in which information systems can enable the manager to be more productive in meetings will add value. Chapter 5 discusses personal systems applications for producing documents, graphics, and other presentation materials to improve the information content of meetings. Chapter 8 describes electronic mail systems, which can be used to conduct meetings electronically and thus eliminate the need for some face-to-face meetings. Chapter 8 also discusses the use of collaborative systems for improving the productivity of all types of meetings.

Third, a manager's time between meetings consists of many brief encounters. Mintzberg states that half of the managers' activities were completed in less than 9 minutes. Stewart found that, in 4 weeks, managers had an average of nine periods in which they were uninterrupted for 30 minutes or more. Managers seem to be conditioned to short interactions on a fast pace. This indicates that long reports may receive only cursory attention. If you have a lot of information to communicate, the best way to do it appears to be via a meeting.

Fourth, managers are constantly attempting to gain information. In verbal contact, managers spent twice as much time receiving information than giving it. Further, three-fourths of a manager's paperwork is input; one-fourth is output. In seeking information, they are looking for *the difference that makes a difference.* Information systems that help them identify whether or not a difference is significant are likely to add value. Thus, reports that show facts within a context are more likely to be helpful than those that do not. A report of expenses compared to the budget is more helpful than a report of expenses alone. A report that compares current performance to that of some prior period is likely to be judged more helpful than one that just shows current performance.

Finally, managers do not place much value on MIS reports. For Mintzberg's CEOs, the traditional MIS report comprised less than 20 percent of all input paper and less than 15 percent of all paper. Additionally, the reports tended to receive cursory attention, and, of 40 such reports in the time of his study, only 2 elicited a response from a manager. MIS reports are sometimes produced long after the fact; in these cases, their information content is dated. MIS reports also tend to require a concentrated span of time for study—time that managers simply do not have.

Therefore, a system that is judged valuable by a manager must offer useful support in addition to producing reports. Managers appreciate information systems that help them communicate quickly and effectively, especially in meetings. They also value information systems that aid in assimilating and monitoring information, as do electronic mail systems and personal database systems. Finally, information systems that aid the executive processes—particularly decision making—will also be considered valuable.

HOW INFORMATION SYSTEMS ADD VALUE TO PROBLEM SOLVING AND DECISION MAKING

Problem solving and decision making are two of the most important activities in business. The **problem-solving** process involves five activities, undertaken in the order shown in Figure 4-11. First, an investigation is conducted to gather information about the problem. Here, particulars of the problem are identified; the problem is defined; and the constraints, problem scope, and problem environment are described. Next, a number of alternative problem solutions are developed. These alternatives are then evaluated, and, in the next stage, one is selected. In the fourth stage, the selected alternative is implemented. Finally, after implementation, the situation is monitored and the problem solution is modified, as necessary.

Decision making is a subset of problem solving; it consists of the first three stages. Simon, one of the pioneers of decision sciences, called these three stages **intelligence, design,** and **choice.**[15] The third stage, the selection of an alternative, is sometimes considered by itself and is referred to as **choice selection.** Some authors use the term *decision making* to refer to all five of these steps.[16] The model shown in Figure 4-11 is the one we will use. It was first published by Huber, and it distinguishes the differences among the problem-solving, decision-making, and choice-selection processes.[17]

15. Simon, *New Science of Management Decision*, p. 2. (Actually, Simon built on the work by John Dewey in *How We Think*, published in 1910!)

16. Griffin, Ricky W., *Management*. Boston: Houghton Mifflin, 1984, p. 205.

17. Huber, George P., *Managerial Decision Making*. Glenview, IL: Scott, Foresman, 1975, p. 8.

Figure 4-11   Components of Problem-Solving Process

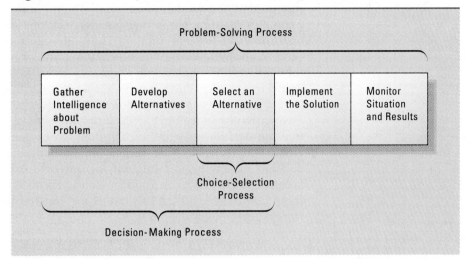

Decision-Making Models

A number of models of the decision-making process agree on the above stages, but differ in their assumptions about the process and the order in which the stages occur. **Classical decision theory** originated in the early 20th century as an outgrowth of classical economic theory. It assumes that managers are always rational, that they have perfect information about the problem and its alternatives, and that they have a complete specification of the objectives to be maximized. Such assumptions are never met, and this theory serves today only to mark an end point of a continuum of decision theories.

Behavioral decision theory relaxes these assumptions. It assumes that the decision makers have imperfect knowledge about the problem and its alternatives and that they are unable or unwilling to make a rational assessment of the best possible decision. Simon used the term ***bounded rationality*** to refer to the behavior of decision makers working within the limits of their knowledge of the problem and their ability or willingness to make rational decisions. He also coined the term ***satisficing***, which refers to the process of identifying an acceptable, workable solution. He stated that, instead of **optimizing** to find the best possible solution, managers *satisfice* to obtain a solution that meets a minimum standard of sufficiency.[18]

18. Simon, Herbert A., *Administrative Behavior*, 3d ed. New York: Free Press, 1976, p. 241.

March expanded on these ideas when he defined the term *contextual rationality.*[19] This model recognizes that people make decisions under pressure in a complex environment involving many decisions and multiple criteria for each, with limited knowledge and time. The model also recognizes that most decisions occur in an ambiguous environment; the specific issues involved may be unclear, the relationship to the solution alternatives may be indirect, and the whole process occurs in a political environment. In short, people make do and muddle through.

A final extension to the loosening of the assumptions of classical decision theory was developed by O'Reilly. Citing the work of many others, O'Reilly stated that the decision-making process often works backwards from that shown in Figure 4-11. Instead of freely identifying alternatives and rationally selecting them, decision makers begin by identifying one or a few outcomes that they deem acceptable. They then constrain the decision process so that it will generate one of these results. We will call this model the **constrained results** decision process. Here is how O'Reilly defines it:

> First, in organizations, participants typically have preferences for outcomes that reflect organizational as well as individual goals. These outcomes act to define a set of constraints which result in the decision process moving from right to left [as portrayed in Figure 4-11].[20]

Additionally, O'Reilly extends his argument to discuss the role of information in this process:

> Second, due to the potential for disagreements among participants, the entire decision process may be one of bargaining and negotiation as various actors pursue their interests. In this political process, information becomes a potentially useful or threatening commodity.... Depending on the nature and importance of the goals sought, decision makers may systematically search for supporting information while ignoring other types.[21]

To summarize, decision theory arose from economic theory at the start of this century. It has evolved from a rather naive and mathematical orientation to a more pragmatic, political orientation. Today, decision makers are understood to balance many factors in a complex political setting, under constraints of limited knowledge and time. They are also understood to be biased in their approach to the decision.

---

19. March, James G., "Bounded Rationality, Ambiguity, and the Engineering of Choice," *Bell Journal of Economics*, Vol. 9, 1978, pp. 587–608.

20. O'Reilly, Charles A., III, "The Use of Information in Organization Decision Making," *Research in Organizational Behavior*, Vol. 5, 1983, p. 108.

21. *Ibid.*, pp. 108, 109.

Adding Value to Decision Making with Information Systems

The goal of information is to improve the quality of decisions and their resulting problem solutions. To do this, information systems facilitate activity in each of the five stages in Figure 4-11. The way in which information is used depends on the process model we adopt. Here, we will consider two of the models: the bounded rationality model and the constrained results model. Keep in mind that these models provide two perspectives on the same process; neither model is right or wrong in all circumstances.

Information Systems and Bounded Rationality Decision Making The primary role for information systems within the context of the bounded rationality model is to expand the boundaries and to increase the rationality of the decision process. Boundaries can be expanded by obtaining greater intelligence on the problem, by developing more alternatives, by considering more criteria in choice making, by reducing the risk and increasing the speed of implementation, and by providing more knowledge about the effectiveness of the implementation. Communication and office automation systems can be employed to improve communication throughout the process. Existing information systems, including TPS or MIS applications, can also provide intelligence about the problem. Both existing and new TPS and MIS applications can be used to facilitate the monitoring of the solution.

Information systems make the decision process more rational in two ways. For one, information via OAS applications is used to improve the communication between the decision maker(s) and those who have knowledge about the problem or its solution. This is especially important in group decision making when effective communication is essential both for an effective decision and for the implementation of that decision. For another, information systems can be used to generate and evaluate mathematical models of alternatives. Spreadsheet programs, statistical packages, and financial management programs can be used for this purpose. Figure 4-12 lists some of the categories of information systems that are used to widen the boundaries of the decision-making process.

Information Systems and Constrained Results Decision Making According to the constrained results model, decision makers identify one or several acceptable solutions and constrain the decision-making process to produce one of those results. In some cases, the constraining is unintentional. In others, the constraints are placed intentionally, for example, to manipulate the problem-solving process to maintain their own power base, to limit the

Figure 4-12   Information Processing and Problem-Solving Stages

Obtaining Intelligence	Developing Alternatives	Making Choices	Implementing Effectively	Monitoring
Communications (OAS)				
Existing Information Systems (TPS, MIS)	■ Expert Systems ■ Engineering Systems ■ Graphics Systems	■ Spreadsheet Programs ■ Statistical Packages ■ Financial Management Programs	■ Project Management Software ■ Personal Database Applications	Existing and New Information Systems

growth of other departments, to protect vital assets, or to increase the size of their staff or influence.

Information systems play a different role for these two cases. When the constraining occurs unintentionally, information systems can be used to make the decision makers aware that they are constraining or distorting the process. O'Reilly cites evidence that memories of past events are selective and tend to be self-serving. For example, project managers may remember that projects went more smoothly and quickly than they did in actuality. Information systems that keep accurate records of the resources required to accomplish tasks can be used to mitigate this tendency.

In cases where the results are intentionally constrained, information systems can be used to manipulate the decision process. Much of this activity at least borders on the unethical. In these circumstances, information systems may be used to increase the power of the manipulator. For example, OAS applications can be used to censor input to the decision makers; or large volumes of supporting data can be generated to overwhelm any negative data. This is sometimes done, for example, by generating many more positive spreadsheet analyses than negative ones. All of the analyses are projections and hence *are fiction*. But the psychological influence of pages and pages of positive analyses and only a few pages of negative ones can make the project's potential seem more positive than it really is.

Similarly, graphics can be used to deceive. Out-of-scale graphics can be drawn to distort the real meaning of the data. Key negative data points can be hidden or not labeled, while favorable aspects of the graph can be attractively labeled. Data can be presented in a graphical, visual context that has little to do with its real context. Monetary amounts can be shown in real, nominal units rather than in comparable, standardized units. Even worse, some data can be shown in nominal dollars while other data is shown in adjusted dollars. Dimensions can be added to the graph that do not exist in the data. Excellent examples of graphics with and without integrity have been developed by Tufte.[22]

The point of the preceding paragraphs is not to tutor you on ways to lie with information systems. Rather, the point is to increase your awareness of such possibilities. You may find yourself so biased by enthusiasm for a project, an alternative, or a group that you unintentionally distort the information that you produce. Be on guard for this possibility. Such deceptions are usually unethical if intentional and seldom bear fruit in the long run.

At the same time, also be aware that others may do the same thing. Memory distortions are natural; when possible, ask for corroborative evidence from historical data records. Keep in mind that all projections are fiction; they are only restricted by the creativity of the person who developed them. Learn to interpret graphical presentations carefully. Information content is not measured by the weight of the paper or by the number of colors in a graph.

Group Decision Making

Much of the theory of decision making assumes that decisions are made by a sole, authoritarian individual. Although that assumption is valid in some settings, such as in the military, in some medical situations, and in other tightly controlled groups, most decision making in business is not done by a single individual. Instead, decisions are made by groups.

There are a number of advantages of a group decision process. Although an individual can readily make a decision, the real business need is to solve a problem, and group action will be required for that. As shown in Figure 4-11, implementation follows selection; if the group is not a party to the decision, it will be less likely to be committed to implementing it.

In addition, if the group is involved in the decision, success is more likely. With involvement, group members will have their egos embedded in the decision and will try harder to make it work. Additionally, the group decision process will improve members' understanding of both the problem and the decision. Members of the decision group will also be able to communicate the decision and its rationale to others in the organization, thus improving the understanding of the decision by the entire organization. Further, if group members have a chance to air their ideas

---

22. Tufte, Edward R., *The Visual Display of Quantitative Information*. Cheshire, CN: Graphics Press, 1983, pp. 53–77.

and alternatives prior to the decision, they will be less likely to engage in destructive activity when implementation begins.

Another advantage of group decision making is that groups consider more facets of the problem. It is very difficult for a sole individual to understand how the decision will impact all departments, individuals, external entities, procedures, policies, and the like. Involving more people provides more background knowledge and reduces the likelihood that an aspect of the problem will go unconsidered.

The advantages of group decision making occur whether we assume the bounded rationality model or the constrained results model. Under the bounded rationality model, involving more people widens the boundaries so that the problem will be better understood, more alternatives will be considered, and the selection criteria will be more comprehensive. Under the constrained results model, group decisions enable a more appropriate set of potential solutions to be identified. Groups also bring out more of the political and environmental issues that will impact both the decision and its implementation.

There are, unfortunately, disadvantages of group decision making as well. First, the group process is more time-consuming and hence more costly. Groups are notoriously inefficient as various members express (sometimes long-winded) opinions and alter, distract, or confuse the direction of meetings. Second, group dynamics can have more of an impact on the decision than is appropriate. A group can be dominated by one or two individuals. Or, factions within a group may use the decision process to act out hostility toward one another: "I don't understand this issue, but if he's in favor of it, then I'm opposed." Perhaps even worse, the group can be so cohesive that it fails to doubt itself. This effect, sometimes called **groupthink,**[23] occurs when the group members so closely identify with one another and the group that they fail to notice that they are out of touch with reality.

A final disadvantage of group decision making is that it sometimes generates ugly, compromise decisions and problem solutions. If the group is not strongly led, then everyone's favorite idea may be worked into the final solution. This can create decisions that are so weak, full of ambiguity, and complicated that, they are, in effect, no decision at all.

In the last few years, *group decision support systems* have been developed to reduce or eliminate some of the disadvantages of group decision making. With such systems, it is more difficult for one person to dominate the group, and the tendency toward groupthink can be reduced. We will consider this subject in greater detail in Chapter 14.

Thus, group decision making can result in better decisions than individual decision making. For this to occur, however, the group dynamics must be carefully managed by the group leader. Thus, with group decisions, the group leader, rather than authoritatively making the decision, instead authoritatively manages the group process, which, in turn, makes the decision. Advantages and disadvantages of group decision making are shown in Figure 4-13.

---

23. Griffin, *Management,* p. 212.

Figure 4-13 Advantages and Disadvantages of
Group Decision-Making Process

Advantages

- Greater group commitment to the decision and its implementation
- Better group understanding of the problem and the rationale for the decision
- Improved communication to implementors
- Reduced likelihood of destructive activity at implementation
- More comprehensive consideration of the problem and related issues

Disadvantages

- More time-consuming
- Greater cost (of the decision, not necessarily of the problem solution)
- Inappropriate influence of group dynamics (domination, rigidity, groupthink)
- Tendency toward compromise solutions of poor quality

INFORMATION SYSTEMS
AND COMPETITIVE ADVANTAGE

In this chapter you have seen a number of different ways that information systems can add value to organizations and to individuals who work in them. Information systems can add value to both processes and products. They can be used for both innovation and improvement in product quality and process quality. They can be used to facilitate management and to enhance problem solving and decision making.

As information systems are used in this way, they change the nature of both the organization and the industry in which it operates. Porter and Millar put it succinctly:

> The information revolution is affecting competition in three vital ways: It changes industry structure and, in so doing, alters the rules of competition. It creates competitive advantage by giving companies new ways to outperform their rivals. It spawns whole new businesses, often from within a company's existing operations.[24]

---

24. Porter and Millar, "Competitive Advantage," p. 150.

Nothing is static in the business environment. As one organization improves or innovates with information systems, other organizations are forced to respond. If they do not respond, market forces will correct for their inaction, and they will lose market share and suffer other dire consequences. Thus, competition must respond to changes caused by the introduction of information systems.

The result of this process is that there is no static solution to the role of information systems in business. The information systems applications that are on the leading edge of innovation in 1994 will become the minimum essential for organizational survival by 1996, and they will be obsolete by the turn of the century. This pattern will hold at least as long as the semiconductor industry continues to make large improvements in price/performance ratios. The new, cheap intelligence will be used as the core of more sophisticated information systems that create competitive advantage.

Thus, you will be mistaken if you look for particular information systems solutions as permanent solutions. Instead, successful business professionals will view the introduction of new information systems as a recurring process. The introduction of new systems that add value in new ways will become a regular part of the business operation.

This completes our study of the foundations of information systems. We will next turn to the subject of personal MIS in the next three chapters.

SUMMARY

Information systems can add value to business processes. A process is a set of actions coordinated to accomplish some goal. Information systems can make processes more efficient, faster, more enjoyable, and so forth. Three dimensions of business process are operational control, management control, and strategic planning. Each of these dimensions involves different levels of structure. Various types of information systems can be used to add value to each of these process dimensions.

Information systems can also add value to business products. Products are the results of processes; they are things, documents, agreements, services, and the like. Products differ in characteristics and delivery. Information systems can impact both of these product aspects. Information systems can enhance characteristics and facilitate delivery. All products have an information component. With information technology, the information components of products are becoming more sophisticated and important. Information systems can make product delivery faster, more convenient, or both. Enhancing products and improving delivery creates a new level of customer expectation and changes the nature of competition.

Finally, information systems can enhance an organization's ability to change processes and products. According to Deming, there are four ways to increase quality: (1) Innovate or (2) improve (3) the process or (4) the product. Innovation involves dramatic changes; improvement involves smaller adjustments. Information systems can add value to an organization by enabling change of all four types.

Management is a social activity. The managers typically spend two-thirds of their time in meetings, so information systems that enhance meeting performance are useful to them. Outside meetings, their time is broken into many brief encounters, so complicated ideas may be best communicated in meetings. Managers are constantly seeking information, so context showing significance should be included with reported information. Since managers see little value in MIS reports, a useful information system should include other facilities.

The best way to communicate a complicated message to a manager may be a meeting. Managers tend more to be information receivers than information givers, and management consists of many brief encounters, many meetings, and very little uninterrupted desk time.

Since managers are social, information systems that remove managers from people for long periods of time will be disliked. Information systems that improve the productivity of meetings add value to managers. Managers are constantly attempting to gain information. Systems that produce information in context and help managers decide which differences make a difference are valued by managers. Managers do not particularly value the traditional MIS report. Systems must do more to add value to managers. Systems that facilitate the roles of management will be judged positively by managers.

The five stages in problem solving are (1) gathering information about the problem, (2) determining alternatives, (3) selecting an alternative, (4) implementing the solution, and (5) monitoring the situation and the results. The first three stages are sometimes called decision making.

Decision-making theory has evolved from classical economic theory that assumed perfect knowledge and rationality, to models that make more realistic assumptions. Two important models are Simon's bounded rationality model and O'Reilly's constrained results model.

Information systems can facilitate decision making and problem solving by expanding the bounds of the decision process (assuming the bounded rationality model). They can also help to reveal unknown mental constraints (assuming the constrained results model). Finally, information systems can intentionally be used to deceive. It is natural for humans to distort data in favor of preferred alternatives, but business professionals must be on guard for biases that cause them to make such unknown distortions in the information they produce.

Most business decisions are made by groups. Although the quality of a group's decision can be better than that for an individual's decision, such decisions take longer. In addition, groups can also deceive themselves. Information systems can be used to improve group decision-making performance.

Information systems create competitive advantage by changing the rules of competition.

KEY TERMS

Process
Product
Added value
Operational control
Management control
Strategic planning
Structured activity
Unstructured activity
Product characteristics
Product delivery
Information component
(of product)

Innovation (of process
or product)
Improvement (of
process or product)
Feedback
Management
Problem solving
Decision making
Intelligence (phase)
Design (phase)
Choice (phase)

Choice selection
Classical decision
theory
Behavioral decision
theory
Bounded rationality
Satisficing
Optimizing
Contextual rationality
Constrained results
Groupthink

REVIEW QUESTIONS

1. Define the term *process*, and give an example of a process at your university.

2. Define the term *product*, and give an example of a product provided by your university.

3. Explain the statement that information technology is changing the ways that companies operate.

4. Describe two ways that information systems, as components of processes, can improve the processes.

5. How is an organization like a three-layered cake?

6. Explain the terms *operational control, management control,* and *strategic planning.* Give an example activity for each.

7. What is the difference between a structured activity and an unstructured activity?

8. Explain the difference between Simon's description of business activity and the Gorry and Scott Morton model.

9. For which types of business activity are TPS applications most suited?

10. For which types of business activity are MIS applications most suited?

11. For which types of business activity are DSS applications most suited?

12. For which types of business activity are ESS applications most suited?

13. For which types of business activity are OAS applications most suited?

14. Name a product that you have used in the last two hours, and describe its physical and information components.

15. Explain how information systems can enhance the features and characteristics of a product.

16. Explain how information systems can facilitate a product's delivery.

17. For the product you named in your answer to question 14, explain how an information system could be used to enhance its features and delivery.

18. According to Deming, what are four ways to increase quality?

19. Explain the difference between innovation and improvement.

20. Define the term *feedback*, and give an example.

21. Explain each of the circles in Figure 4-8.

22. What is the one activity that best characterizes management work?

23. Summarize the nature and relative frequency of CEOs' activities according to Mintzberg.

24. Describe four implications of the Mintzberg study for information systems.

25. Name and briefly describe the five stages in problem solving.

26. What are the stages in decision making? What names did Simon use for these stages?

27. What is choice selection?

28. Briefly explain classical decision theory.

29. Briefly explain behavioral decision theory.

30. Explain the term *bounded rationality.*

31. Explain the term *satisficing.*

32. Briefly explain contextual rationality.

33. Explain the constrained results decision process.

34. Explain how information systems can improve decision making using the bounded rationality decision model; using the constrained-results model.

35. Summarize the advantages and disadvantages of group decision making.

36. Explain how information systems create competitive advantage.

DISCUSSION QUESTIONS

1. Tour your campus and locate an organizational function such as student records processing or procurement, or some function similar in scope. Describe two or three processes involved in that function. Describe two or three products involved in that function. How do you think information systems could add value to the processes you identified? How do you think information systems could add value to the products you identified?

2. Compare and contrast the Simon model of an organization with the Gorry and Scott Morton model. Which do you think is more appropriate? Is there one dimension or two? Why does it matter?

3. The Mintzberg study was done for CEOs and was completed over 15 years ago. During the intervening period, the use of computer technology and information systems in business has dramatically increased. If Mintzberg were to repeat his study today, do you think the results would differ? If so, how? If not, why not? Would the results differ if the study considered a different level of manager? Why or why not?

4. Suppose you are dean of the College of Business. The business faculty are complaining to you that too many underqualified students are being admitted as business majors. Describe how you might use the problem-solving process in Figure 4-11 to solve this problem. After you have completed the descriptions, if possible, ask your dean to come to class and describe how he or she would go about solving such a problem. If your plan is substantially different, ask the dean why your plan would not work. (In larger institutions, this is probably infeasible. Instead, suppose the problem pertains to a department, and ask the department chairperson to respond.)

PROJECTS

A. Consider your role as a student.

1. What are your processes? Consider processes at the operational control, management control, and strategic planning levels. How do information systems add value to your processes? (Consider both manual and computer-based information systems.)

2. What are your products? How do information systems add value by enhancing features and adding new characteristics to your products? How do information systems facilitate delivery of your products? How could additional information systems add further value to your product characteristics or delivery?

3. How do you use information systems to provide feedback and facilitate improvement in your processes and products? How could additional information systems improve your ability to engage in continuous improvement of processes and products?

B. Consider the role of a teacher in a college course. (You may wish to focus on the role of an ideal business course teacher.) Using the model in Figure 4-8, how can information systems add value to that teacher?

C. Over the next few days, track your use of time in college-related activities, using the categories of Figure 4-9. Then compare your use of time with that of managers. What differences, if any, do you find? If there were differences, would your educational experience be enhanced if your courses required you to spend your time more nearly in the proportions experienced by managers? On the other hand, can you see differences between the roles of manager and student that justify the differences, if any, that you found in time usage?

M I N I C A S E

Many and Varied

Customers today demand great variety—even individual customization—in their products and services. But increasing competition dictates that costs keep decreasing as well. Companies that once pursued either low prices or high differentiation are discovering that they can combine the best of both strategies in mass customization.

Just-in-time delivery, lean production techniques, concurrent engineering, time-based competition, cross-functional teams and a host of other advances have increased flexibility and responsiveness, allowing companies to offer variety and customization without accompanying cost increases. Indeed, building variety and customization into processes can actually lower costs.

Information technology is a critical enabler of the shift from mass production to mass customization. Most commonly, it supports or creates an infrastructure that collects information about individual customers and applies that information to the production process. Mass production relies on forecasts of future demand. Mass customization is based on what each customer wants and needs today.

The Philadelphia-based magazine *Farm Journal* provides an interesting illustration. Beginning around 1980, the magazine began customizing its 14 issues for individual readers. Subscribers fill out questionnaires about their farms (information about types of livestock raised, acres devoted to each crop, etc.). Their answers are entered into an online database. *Farm Journal*'s production process uses this information to create a magazine

for each subscriber consisting of a 50-page editorial core combined with articles and advertisements applicable to that subscriber. Each month, hundreds, and sometimes thousands, of different versions of *Farm Journal* are sent to 800,000 subscribers.

When the functions customers desire are extremely well-defined, it is often possible to embed them within the product. Matsushita has introduced a washing machine that automatically personalizes itself—not only to the user, but to each load of wash. The machine uses optical sensors to determine the size and dirtiness of the load and microprocessors with fuzzy logic—an artificial-intelligence technique that can respond to small variations in attributes and learn to provide desired results—to select which of 600 different wash cycles will work best.

Finally, IT allows companies to practice what William Davidson, associate professor at the University of Southern California's School of Business, calls "precision pricing." It is simple economics that a company should charge the most each individual will pay for its products or services. In mass-production firms, however, pricing economics became one of "guestimating" what single price would yield the highest profits. In mass-customization firms, pricing can be done to the individual.

Progressive Corp., of Cleveland, practices both pinpoint marketing and precision pricing, focusing on its "nonstandard pool"—people whose [insurance] policies were canceled or rejected, generally because of previous accidents combined with "poor" demographics. By maintaining an exhaustive database on

customers and analyzing demographics in great detail, Progressive can locate those in the nonstandard pool who are not much higher-risk than normal. For example, while motorcycle ownership alone may be enough to automatically place someone in the nonstandard pool, Progressive knows that middle-aged motorcyclists with young children do not have worse than average accident records. Progressive then calculates the price at which it can lure individuals from their current insurance firms, using one of 14,000 separately priced policies. ■

B. Joseph Pine II, excerpted from *CIO*,
May 15, 1993, pp. 26, 30.

Discussion Questions

1. Summarize the concept of mass customization. Describe its advantages.

2. Describe the relationships of information systems to mass customization.

3. People once feared that computerization would force everyone to be treated alike, with no allowance for individual differences; today, computerization lets everyone be treated differently, as this article describes. What has changed between the first view and the second?

4. How could the concepts of mass customization be applied to higher education? Give at least two examples showing outcomes that you would expect. For each, describe the information systems that would be required to produce that outcome.

Personal Management Information Systems

PART II CONSIDERS THE FIRST OF THREE TYPES OF MISs: personal information systems. This category comprises applications that professionals use to improve their personal productivity.

This part contains three chapters and a module. Chapter 5 surveys personal information systems applications and goals. Chapter 6 describes the five components of a personal information systems application. Chapter 7 discusses a method of building personal information systems, focusing on the role that you, as a future business professional, should play. Finally, Module A illustrates the development of personal database applications.

5

Personal Information Systems: Applications and Goals

PERSONAL INFORMATION SYSTEMS are computer-based systems that help individuals enhance their productivity. They are employed by a wide range of business professionals: managers; technical professionals; attorneys, accountants, and other knowledge workers; politicians; and so forth. They are also used in every business functional area.

Dozens of different **personal information system** applications exist. This chapter describes characteristics of the major types of such applications, and is organized according to the three primary functions the applications perform: communications, analysis, and tracking and monitoring. Also presented are applications that integrate these functions. Finally, the framework developed in Chapter 4 is used to discuss the ways in which personal information systems add value to individuals.

Many students enter an MIS course thinking that the systems discussed here are all there is to business computing. This is not the case. Learning to use a spreadsheet or a DBMS is interesting and useful, but learning why and under what conditions you use one or the other is far more important. Furthermore, personal information systems are only one of the three major categories of information systems that you should know. Therefore, even if you are proficient in using a personal computer, you may not know all you need to know about MISs.

THE NEED FOR PERSONAL INFORMATION SYSTEMS

"That wraps it up. I think everything's in place for a fantastic trade show. You've all got your schedules for booth duty, and you'll receive your itinerary, airline tickets, and hotel reservations this afternoon. I'll be here the rest of today, then I leave for Atlanta tonight. The booth is already there, as is most of the computer equipment. I'll have it set up tomorrow.

"Remember, besides the announcement of the Silverado products, we also want to feature the new releases of the existing products that Jan mentioned. Any questions?"

LuAnne Price is the trade show manager for Legacy Systems, a company that develops and sells microcomputer applications software. As a computer software company, Legacy participates in a half-dozen trade shows every year. The two biggest and most important shows are the **COMDEX** (Computer Dealer's Exhibition) shows—held in Las Vegas in fall and in other cities in spring. In the scenario you just read, LuAnne is briefing all of the Legacy staff who will be attending the show in Atlanta, about 30 people in all.

LuAnne's job requires her to coordinate thousands of details. The shows are popular and crowded, and she must book the booth space and hotel rooms six months in advance. In addition, Legacy demonstrates its products at the shows, which requires about a dozen microcomputer systems of different types. LuAnne must borrow the equipment from Legacy employees, have it shipped to the show, set it up, and, occasionally, have it repaired. When the show is over, she must return each machine to the proper employee at the Legacy home offices.

Legacy usually holds at least one press conference at each of the COMDEX shows. LuAnne must book the space for this and coordinate her activities with the rest of the marketing staff. Finally, Legacy always has a cocktail party for key dealers and distributors, about 700 people in all. For this, she must obtain space, hire catering services, select entertainment, and so forth.

Figure 5-1 shows a portion of the organizational chart at Legacy. LuAnne works for the director of Marketing Communications, who works for the VP of Marketing. Marketing Communications also includes the advertising manager and the manager of Public Relations. The director of Product Marketing, who supervises all of the product managers, also reports to the VP of Marketing.

LuAnne views the work involved with trade shows as falling into three phases: planning, execution, and follow-up. During the planning phase, she works with the rest of Marketing to build the framework of a plan. She needs answers to questions such as: What marketing objectives does Legacy have for the show? What products will be featured? What events will occur? What will the competition do? What is the budget?

Figure 5-1 The Legacy Systems Marketing Organization Chart

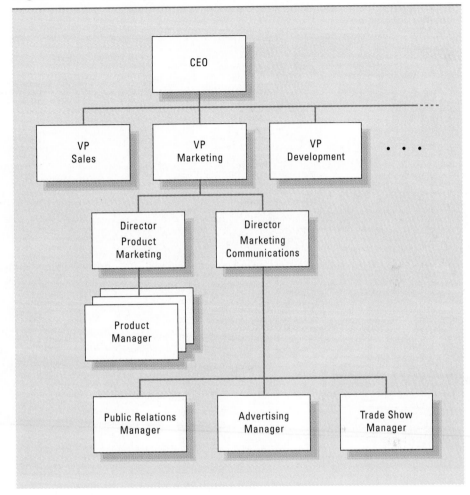

Given this information, she then formulates a specific plan. Her process is iterative. She first assumes a certain booth space and location (size and location determine price), a certain number of employees attending, and a budget for the party and other events. Then she determines the cost of her assumed plan, compares it to the budget, and makes changes as necessary. She makes a number of iterations through this process before presenting it to her boss, then to her boss's boss (the VP of Marketing), and finally to her boss's boss's boss (the CEO). At each level, she makes more adjustments.

Figure 5-2 Trade Show Exhibition
Presenting an exhibition booth at major trade shows is an important part of the marketing program of most computer companies.

LuAnne's plan receives high-level management attention for two reasons. First, trade shows are critically important to Legacy's position in the market. Second, the shows are very expensive; her budget is just under $1 million per year. The shows can be a good investment or a bad one, and there is more than ample opportunity to waste money.

During the execution phase, she is both director of events and chief problem solver. Everyone defers to her, even the CEO. They do this because they know how complicated her job is; she has to balance many factors, and if they override her judgment, they may throw the whole plan out of balance. They also defer to her out of respect; she is incredibly good at her job. For three years, her shows have met their objectives and come in under budget.

As chief problem solver, LuAnne is confronted with a tremendous variety of issues, including the following, which were posed to her on the convention center floor the day prior to opening in Atlanta:

"LuAnne, we shipped 15,000 product summary brochures. I can find only 1,000. Where are the rest?"

"LuAnne, this is Robin. The hotel desk had no reservation for Mr. Franklin's suite. How do you want me to handle this?"

"We shipped the wrong micros. We can't demo all the products without a 4-megabyte machine. Now what?"

"LuAnne, I lost my booth duty schedule. Do you have another copy?"

"There's a storm in Denver that closed the airport. The West Coast salespeople won't be here until Monday, at the earliest. We'd better revise the booth schedule and get it out to everyone."

"Good heavens. Did we forget to bring a vacuum cleaner for the booth?"

"LuAnne, someone just ran a forklift into a corner of our booth. They're real sorry, and they want to know what they can do. What shall I tell them?"

During the follow-up stage, LuAnne makes certain that all of the Legacy equipment is returned and accounted for. She informs operations if any equipment is lost or damaged. She also serves as the focal point for resolving grievances between Legacy and any of its contractors. Most important, LuAnne is a key member of the management team that reviews the show to determine whether objectives were met and whether the financial investment was worthwhile. This team also establishes strategy, policy, and procedure for upcoming trade shows.

As you can see, LuAnne has an important and complicated job. She also has little administrative support. She shares an administrative assistant with the public relations manager, but otherwise, she is on her own. She can and does call on many other Legacy employees for assistance, but none report to her.

LuAnne would be unable to accomplish her job without a number of personal information systems. She uses microcomputer systems for document preparation, for financial planning, control, and analysis, and for tracking equipment and other resources.

There are many categories of personal information systems applications. Of the examples shown in Figure 5-3, a few are tools of such fundamental importance that all businesspeople need to understand them. These are applications to support interpersonal communication, such as word processing, desktop publishing, and presentation graphics programs; applications for analysis, such as spreadsheets and statistical programs; and applications for tracking and monitoring, such as database and project management programs.

Figure 5-3 Examples of Personal Information Systems Applications

Application	Purpose
Accounting	Home and small business accounting
CAD	Engineering drawings
Check Writing	Personal accounting
Data Communications	Remote access through a modem
Desktop Publishing	Producing page layouts for complex documents
Draw	Creating line drawings
Facsimile (Fax)	Sending and receiving documents
Financial Management	Managing personal finances
Graphics	Creating painting-like art
Graphing	Analyzing scientific data
Linear Programming	Optimizing within linear constraints
Mapping	Geographical data analysis
Math	Mathematical analysis
Personal Database	Tracking and monitoring
Presentation Graphics	Preparing graphics and slides for business presentations
Programming Language	Creating custom applications
Project Management	Managing complex projects
Spreadsheet	Calculation and analysis of business data
Statistical Analysis	Performing statistical manipulations
Tax Assistance	Preparing income tax forms
Time Management	Scheduling daily activities
Word Processing	Creating and producing documents

PERSONAL INFORMATION SYSTEMS FOR INTERPERSONAL COMMUNICATION

The first general category of personal information systems are those used to facilitate interpersonal communication. Verbal and written communication is exceedingly important to business professionals. Again and again, business leaders have told business educators to help students develop effective communication skills. Learning how to use information systems technology to improve your communication is part of that task.

Information systems can add value to individual communication by facilitating the preparation, editing, and printing of all types of documents—from simple memos to presentation slides, large reports, catalogs, and even books. The documents can contain straightforward text, or they can include multiple type fonts, type sizes, tables, graphics, pictures, and other document design elements. The foundation of all text processing is word processing.

Word Processing

With **word processing**, documents are often entered via a computer workstation or an individual's personal computer. They can be immediately printed or stored and subsequently printed. Word processing is much more efficient than typing. A mistake can be corrected without rekeying the entire text, missing text can be inserted, text can be copied, and undesired text can be readily removed.

In addition to easy error correction, other advantages of word processing include ability to move and copy large blocks of text; and capability to automatically search a document for particular letters, words, or phrases, and, in some cases, automatically replace one group of characters for another wherever they occur. Many word processing systems also include spelling checkers, which are modules within the word processing program that identify possibly misspelled words and propose corrections.

The keying and printing of word processed documents are separate tasks. Once a document has been entered, it is stored on disk. Later, the user can direct the word processing program to print the document. The document can be sent directly to a printer, or the signals needed to create the printout can be saved on another file and sent to the printer later.

Much of the physical format of a document need not be specified until print time. Width of margins, number of lines per page, line spacing (e.g., single-spaced, double-spaced, etc.), and similar format characteristics can be changed after the document has been keyed. With most word processors, footnotes, page headings, and footings are all automatically adjusted when the physical format of the document is altered.

Because keying is an easy way to draft a document and because the inevitable errors can be corrected before printing, many professionals key their own documents. Once the document has been entered, the professional may give the disk to a secretary, who then formats it according to office standards and practice and prints it. In accounting, consulting, and many types of law, word processing has all but eliminated the use of dictating equipment.

The first successful word processing program was WordStar, which, at one time, had the bulk of the market share. Recently, however, WordPerfect and Microsoft Word are the most widely used programs.

When LuAnne finishes creating a document, she often transmits it by E-mail or **facsimile (fax)** rather than printing it. Many word processing programs can transmit messages through E-mail systems. Fax technology delivers messages by telephone line to a machine that prints them in a form similar to one the computer printer would produce. The transmitted data represents a picture of each document page. The fax process requires that the sender have a modem with fax capability and a fax program, which takes the place of the printer module in the word processing program. The receiver must have a fax machine or a computer/modem combination capable of receiving fax transmissions. Both E-mail and fax provide faster delivery than standard mail for paper documents.

Mail Merge Facilities   It is often useful to send the same basic letter to a number of different individuals or businesses, but with each copy personalized to some degree. For example, salespeople may want to conduct direct-mail sales activity by sending **personalized form letters** to their customers. (The phrase "personalized form letter" may seem contradictory. After all, how can a form letter be personalized? The phrase is an oxymoron, like "jumbo shrimp" and "thunderous silence.") Such letters are written by creating a generic form of the letter, then personalizing each individual copy by filling in addressee's name and address, company name, and other data in appropriate locations. This process is called **mail merge.**

As shown in Figure 5-4, two files are required to produce such letters: one file containing the generic form of the letter and another containing the list of addressees and other data to be inserted. The exact technique used depends on the particular word processing product, but in general, each line of the addressee file is given a label such as T1, T2, and T3. When creating the document, the typist keys a code such as *@@T1* in the location of the document where the characters on line T1 are to be inserted. In this way, the two files are merged. One letter is generated for each set of lines in the addressee file. Figure 5-4 shows the preparation of two letters using this process.

Figure 5-5 shows a schematic of the system used by a salesman to prepare letters for a direct mail sale campaign. First, he identifies the products he wants to promote. Then, he queries his customer data to determine what types of customers are most likely to purchase certain portions of that inventory. On a given occasion, he might identify three types of customers. He then writes three form letters, one for each type. Next, he accesses his customer database using a query language (described below) to produce three different addressee files. Each file includes the customer's name and address and the name of the most expensive item purchased in the last quarter. This data is to be inserted in appropriate places in the form letters. He then runs the mail merge option on his word processor to produce the form letters. In this way, the salesperson makes dozens of highly focused contacts with customers in less than a day.

Figure 5-4   Preparation of a Personalized Form Letter

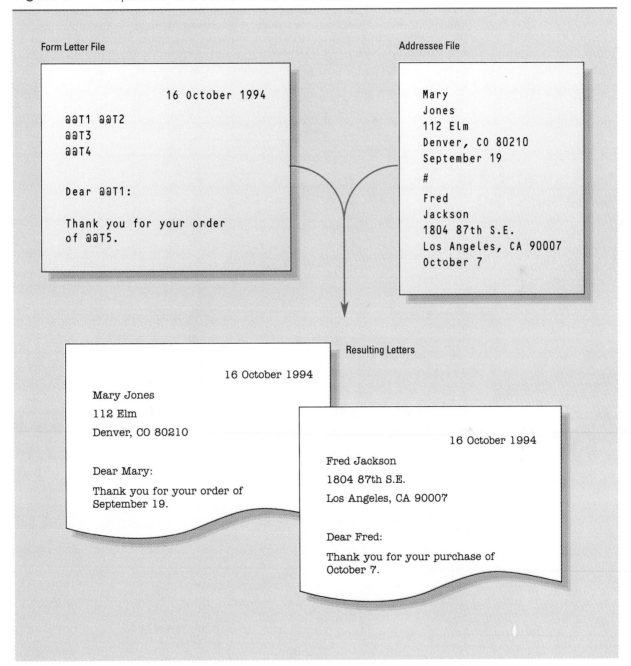

Figure 5-5   Use of Mail Merge for Direct-Mail Sales
By querying the customer database, the marketer produces specialized mailing lists containing addresses of customers likely to purchase certain types of products. Each list is merged with an appropriate advertising letter to promote that type of product.

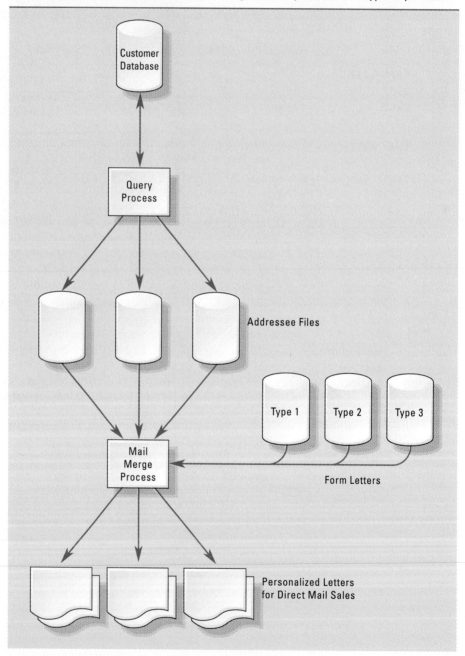

Automated Document Production Another word processing application produces what is known as boilerplate documents. A **boilerplate** is a standard document form into which someone inserts specific data. It is an extension of the personalized form letter concept.

Many insurance documents are boilerplates. An insurance policy consists of many paragraphs of legal language that describe the basic contract between the insurance company and the insured. At various places in the document, an agent or a clerk fills in the appropriate data: name, address, amount of insurance, beneficiary, and so forth. Word processing systems can be used to create such documents in a process similar to that for form letters.

An extension of the boilerplate process automatically creates documents from a list of boilerplate paragraphs. This process is commonly used in the production of wills. An attorney interviews the client and annotates a checklist of paragraphs with data for the boilerplate paragraphs. Later, the attorney (or an assistant) inputs the annotations to a program that selects the appropriate paragraphs, fills in the boilerplate data, and produces the will. In this manner, the attorney obtains a great productivity boost from the personal information system.

For even greater productivity, a record can be kept of the paragraphs in each will. When the law changes with regard to a particular paragraph, a personalized form letter announcing the change can be sent to each client having a will with that paragraph. The boilerplate paragraph can be changed according to the new law, and new wills can be produced very inexpensively. When this process is used, wills and other similar documents generate very large profit margins.

Advanced Word Processing Applications Often, people perform certain document processing tasks repetitively. For example, suppose an attorney needs to keep track of her professional telephone calls. She could do this manually using pen and paper, but most of the time, the attorney is already using her word processing application when she receives a call. Because of this, it is convenient for her to use word processing to keep the log.

The steps the attorney takes to record a call are always the same. First, she opens the telephone log; then she skips past records of previous calls to the end of the document and enters date, time, client name, and comments about the conversation. Then she closes the document.

Performing this sequence is slow, boring, and tiresome. To ease her task, the word processing program she uses allows her to define and use a macro. A **macro** is a sequence of actions that can be stored and later recalled to perform repetitive activity.

Before using the macro, the attorney must first create it. There are several ways to create a macro. One common way is for the attorney to start a macro recorder, which will record any sequence of steps she takes. With the recorder on, she opens the document, skips to its end, and adds the system date and time. Pausing the recorder, she adds the call comments, restarts the recorder, and closes the document. She then stops the recorder and gives the macro a name.

From that point on, whenever she invokes that macro, the same series of steps will be followed.

Creating the macro saves the attorney considerable time and also keeps her from making errors such as neglecting to close the call log document. Macros are often used to produce the automated documents described in the previous section.

Some vendors have extended the concept of a macro to include a complete programming language. With these programs, users do not employ a macro recorder, but instead write programs that process elements of documents. For example, Word for Windows, a word processor licensed by Microsoft, includes a version of BASIC. With this language, users can develop word processing–oriented computer programs that integrate very complex and sophisticated logic into documents.

Consider, for example, the problem of preparing insurance documents. A word processing application program could be written to determine the best type of policy from data entered by an agent using the document program. The program would select the proper paragraphs, fill data into appropriate locations, and then print the required documents. It could also store data for communications to the insurance company's headquarters or take other action.

A word processing program that includes a computer programming language has great potential for improving the productivity of professional workers, and you will likely see increased use in the future. One trend, already emerging, is commercial programs written in a word processor language and marketed as a special-purpose add-on. For example, such programs may store an author's notes or a researcher's source bibliography in a database, or they may automate the process of creating documents in specialized formats such as TV scripts.

Desktop Publishing

Desktop publishing (DTP) is a computer-based application that can be used to integrate text with graphics to produce professional-quality page layouts, pamphlets, and even books. The pages may have multiple columns; many varieties of type styles and sizes; rules, bars, boxes, and other graphical symbols; pictures; and even multiple colors. The most common DTP applications are Aldus PageMaker, Frame Technology FrameMaker, Microsoft Publisher, and Quark Xpress.

The products of DTP can be equivalent in quality to those manually produced by typographers, graphic artists, and graphics professionals. The output of DTP can be printed on paper or directed to a typesetting machine for printing by standard, large-volume printing presses. From the several examples of DTP output shown in Figure 5-6, you can see the quality and variety of output that are possible.

LuAnne Price, as spokesperson for Legacy Systems at the COMDEX show, produces a newsletter (shown in Figure 5-7) each day of the show. This newsletter

Figure 5-6 Examples of DTP Output

These examples illustrate the range of DTP products.

summarizes the Legacy staff's daily activities and major accomplishments. It is used to provide visibility for accomplishments to the show staff and to encourage and reward successes.

The newsletter need not be produced by DTP; it could also be word processed. The primary difference is that a DTP program can provide for multiple flows of text (such as various articles in a magazine), and a word processing program manages only a single flow (such as the single text of a business report). The formatting and output capabilities of today's word processing and DTP programs

Figure 5-7   Sample Legacy Systems COMDEX Newsletter

Legacy Systems   Volume 3, Issue 2

Newsletter

What's New at Comdex

This year's Spring Comdex show has been described as one of the best yet. There are several new products and developments, as well as seminars on what the future holds for the computer industry. There are many exciting displays that give us a hint of what is to come in future years, as well as demonstrations of what is available right now.

Microsoft introduced its new release of PenWindows 2.0 with improved character recognition and a faster, more robust operating system. The system runs on any 386 notebook computer and includes MS Word for PenWindows and NoteTaker. There is

In This Issue

Legacy Update

Legacy Systems is proud to once again be involved in the Comdex show. Mr. Franklin feels that this event is an important part of the business and has a strong impact on our sales. In addition to increased exposure, it is also a chance for us to learn what is happening in the industry.

Mr. Franklin also stressed the importance of all employees attending scheduled staff meetings while at the show. (See Page 4 for the scheduled times for staff meetings.) If we work together, we can make this time as productive as possible.

LuAnne would also like to thank all the dedicated employees that put many hours into making this event a success for Legacy Systems. We expect to get very good publicity and exposure for our name and our products.

One of our products may even be featured in one of the trade journals next month. This is due to the extra effort our employees put

Page 1

---

are otherwise quite similar. LuAnne chose DTP because she needs to manipulate several separate text flows (articles) in each newsletter.

Figure 5-8 summarizes the components of a DTP application. Source files of text and graphics are input to the DTP program. These files are combined, sometimes within the context of document templates, and laid out on the

Figure 5-8 Components of a DTP Application

Files containing text, graphics, and templates are processed to create the final document.

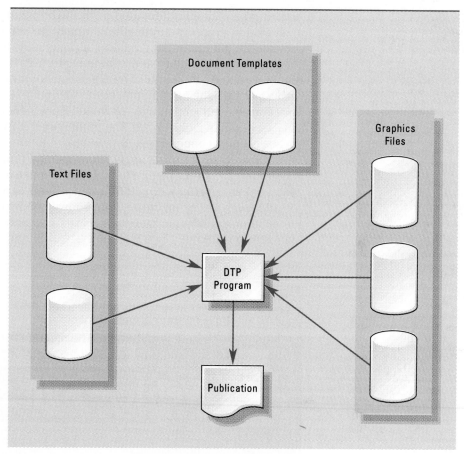

publication according to directions provided by the user. Once the layout is complete, the document is directed to a printer or to printing machinery. Normally, laser-quality printers are required because the output is a graphic, not a character-based, document.

In the last several years, word processing programs have expanded in capabilities. Many of them now include functions that were previously available only with DTP programs. For example, most of today's word processing programs can integrate tables, pictures, and graphic symbols into documents. It is possible that, in the next few years, DTP programs will be less frequently used by nonpublishing professionals. It is also possible that the evolving market for DTP will be comprised exclusively of graphic designers and publishers.

Presentation Graphics

A third type of application used to facilitate communication is composed of **presentation graphics applications**, which are used to prepare graphics and presentation materials. The graphics capability provides output such as pie charts, bar graphs, and line plots, as shown in Figure 5-9. The presentation capability is usually used to create overhead transparencies or presentation slides. When using such a program, the presentation creator defines a master slide that has the basic format of text and graphics, as shown in Figure 5-10a. Then text is added to each slide, as shown in Figure 5-10b. The result is a set of overhead transparencies that have a consistent appearance.

Presentation graphics applications include programs that interface with a wide variety of output media. In addition to a personal computer printer, such programs can interface with sophisticated printing or plotting equipment, produce 35-millimeter slides, or create slide shows for display on computer screens. Presentation graphics packages include SPC Harvard Graphics, Aldus Persuasion, Microsoft PowerPoint, Lotus Freelance Graphics, and WordPerfect Presentations.

Figure 5-9 Graph Produced by a Presentation Graphics Application
Presentation graphics applications provide greater flexibility to customize business graphics than do most spreadsheet programs.

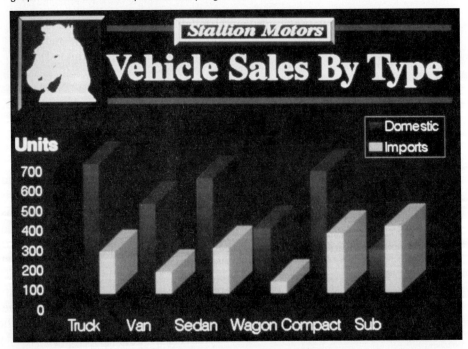

Figure 5-10 Using a Presentation Graphics Application

(a) To prepare a set of slides, the user first creates a master template. **(b)** The user adds specific phrasing to create each slide from the template. The result is a series of slides with a consistent appearance.

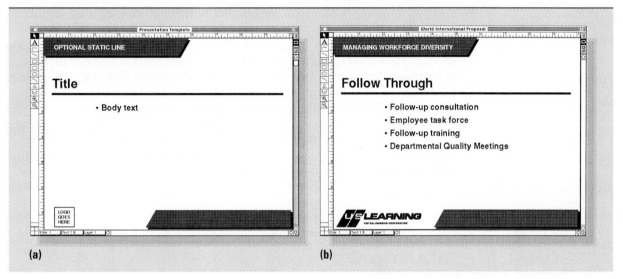

(a)   (b)

Figure 5-11 Uses of Interpersonal Communication Applications

Type of Application	Possible Use by Trade Show Manager
Word Processing	Memos, letters of transmittal, progress reports
Mail Merge	Letters to the COMDEX show staff
Automated Document	Individualized demo instruction letters to staff
DTP	Show newsletter, information pamphlets
Graphics and Presentation	Presentations to management and staff

Interpersonal Communication Applications at Legacy Systems

Figure 5-11 shows uses of communication applications by LuAnne Price in her role as trade show manager at Legacy Systems. She employs word processing for day-to-day communication activity. As the plan for the show progresses, she uses mail merge facilities to send personalized form letters to the show staff. Later, just before the show, LuAnne allocates responsibility for demonstrating specific products to each staff member. Since the products have different demonstration procedures, and since the documentation she sends about each procedure varies according to the experience of the staff member, LuAnne uses a word processing program to determine which paragraphs to include in each staff member's instruction letter.

As stated, she wants to portray a professional image to the staff during the show, so she uses DTP to produce a daily trade show newsletter. Prior to the start of the show, she also develops a pamphlet of useful information (local emergency information, local addresses, a brief restaurant guide, etc.) to give to each member. She also uses DTP to give this pamphlet a professional appearance.

Finally, LuAnne uses graphics and presentation applications to produce overhead transparencies that she uses to report on the development of the show plan to management. Also, she uses these programs to prepare materials to brief the staff both before and during the show.

PERSONAL INFORMATION SYSTEMS FOR ANALYSIS

The second group of personal information systems consists of systems that facilitate analysis. Most such applications involve the analysis of financial data, though analyses of survey results, feedback data, and operational data are also commonly performed. The analyses are often used for planning, budgeting, and forecasting applications.

At a practical level, the most commonly used analytical applications are spreadsheets.

Spreadsheet Applications

Electronic spreadsheet programs are used to perform repetitive calculations that have potentially complicated data interrelationships. Such applications are common among business professionals; in fact, they are the second most frequently used application. (Word processing is first.)

In Chapter 2, we watched Sarah Morris use a spreadsheet application to compute the profit and loss of her seminars and to perform what-if analyses concerning price changes. She used her spreadsheet analysis to represent the relationship of costs and revenue to the number of attendees and costs at various seminar locations.

The primary benefit of spreadsheets is not that they can quickly perform a series of calculations; rather, it is that they can be developed to be driven by a few input parameters. This characteristic allows what-if analysis to be performed easily and quickly. Sarah Morris could readily determine the impact on seminar profitability as the number of attendees changed.

When developing a spreadsheet, it is important to keep that characteristic in mind. Spreadsheet experts not only try to reduce the number of separate input values, but they also try to cluster all the inputs into a particular area. Reducing the amount of input not only makes the spreadsheet easier to use, it also reduces the likelihood of error.

Advanced Spreadsheet Applications   Sarah's spreadsheets were quite simple, involving only a dozen or so variables and a few equations. More complex spreadsheet applications involve multiple spreadsheets which carry over and input the results of one sheet to others, creating a **system of spreadsheets.** Figure 5-12 shows the spreadsheets that LuAnne uses to compute show expenses. Here, the number of people required to perform product demonstrations at the show is computed in one spreadsheet. These computations are input to a second spreadsheet, which computes personnel travel expenses. The computations are also input to other spreadsheets that determine size and cost of booth and equipment expenses, respectively. Finally, the results of all of these separate spreadsheets are combined into an overall trade show expense spreadsheet.

Spreadsheets are often used to model complex business processes. In some of these applications, the data interrelationships can become quite complicated and even circular. Consider, for example, the computation of interest income, which is determined by interest rate and amount of cash invested. Cash is a function of cash flow, which is determined by net income. Net income, in turn, is calculated by subtracting taxes from pretax income. Pretax income, however, is determined, in part, by the amount of interest. Thus, there is a circularity in the calculations. Most commercial spreadsheet programs have a means for handling circumstances like this; they usually make a series of successive approximations that converge into an answer.

Consider, in this last example, the consequences of a change in interest or in tax rates. Prior to electronic spreadsheets, such calculations were a nightmare. With a spreadsheet program, the financial analyst need only change one or two parameters, and the program will perform all of the recalculations.

Spreadsheet programs, like word processing programs, support macros, which allow repetitive series of spreadsheet operations to be stored and re-executed when necessary. The macro capability of spreadsheets is increasingly incorporating programming languages, as has been done with word processing packages.

Spreadsheet Graphics   Lotus Development Corporation set the standard for spreadsheet programs when it introduced Lotus 1-2-3 in the early 1980s. This

Figure 5-12   System of Spreadsheets for Legacy Systems

Demo Requirements Calculation Spreadsheet							
		Silverado			Goldstar		
	Introductory	VAR	Retail	Introductory	VAR	Retail	
	Demos	Demos	Demos	Demos	Demos	Demos	Totals
NumRequired/Day	30	18	22	28	20	40	790
TimeRequired	0:10	0:30	0:15	0:15	1:00	0:30	
Demos/Day/Station	36	12	24	24	6	12	
NumStationsRequired	1	2	1	2	4	4	14
Staff Number Computations							
NumStationsRequired	14						
StaffReq/Station	2						
NumDemoStaff	28						

Equipment Expense Spreadsheet			

Booth Requirements and Expense Spreadsheet			

Staff Travel Expense Calculation Spreadsheet				
	DemoStaff	ShowStaff	Management	Totals
NumStaffRequired	28			
Airfare	$21,700			
Hotel	$9,016			
Food	$6,440			
Miscellaneous	$980			
Total	$38,136			

Trade Show Expense Spreadsheet			

program not only provided support for spreadsheets, it also produced elementary, but very useful, **graphics.** In fact, the program's name, 1-2-3, refers to its spreadsheet, graphics, and database functions.[1]

Today, all successful spreadsheet programs can produce basic graphics, including pie charts, bar graphs, XY-line plots, and similar graphics. Figure 5-13 shows graphs created from some of the data in the system of spreadsheets in Figure 5-12.

Spreadsheet Programs   The first commercially popular electronic spreadsheet program was a program called VisiCalc. In one of the more interesting developments in U.S. business during the 1980s, VisiCalc's enormous lead in market share was overtaken dramatically by Lotus 1-2-3. Today, Lotus 1-2-3 shares the market with Microsoft's Excel and Borland's Quattro Pro. The spreadsheet-like program, Lotus Improv, specializes in financial analysis.

You may use a spreadsheet program as part of your MIS course. If that is not possible, find another way to use a spreadsheet program. Familiarity with electronic spreadsheet processing is mandatory for every business professional today.

External Data Sources

Analysis problems often require data that is not immediately available within an organization. In this situation, many businesspeople use their personal computers as a **communications gateway** to sources of data. There are two ways to do this. The first is to equip the computer with a device called a **modem**, which connects the computer to a telephone line. Then the user activates a communications program, which connects the personal computer with the source of data. The second way is to connect the computer through a local area network into a wider network, such as the worldwide **Internet**. The Internet provides access to many varied sources of data.

There are hundreds of **data utilities** that offer nearly any imaginable type of data service. Examples are bibliographic searches on topics or key words; access to data, including current or past stock quotations; government statistics; marketing data; and so forth. Using the services of a data utility can improve the quality of an analysis by increasing the scope and accuracy of the data considered. It can also reduce the time it takes to gather the data and thus improve the delivery schedule of the results.

---

1. As you will soon see, the claim of database capability in spreadsheet programs is largely marketing hype. Spreadsheets do not store a database by any stretch of the imagination. The so-called database component of a spreadsheet is a facility for storing, searching, and recalling spreadsheets or portions of spreadsheets.

Figure 5-13 Spreadsheet Graphs

These graphs are typical of the output created by today's spreadsheet programs.

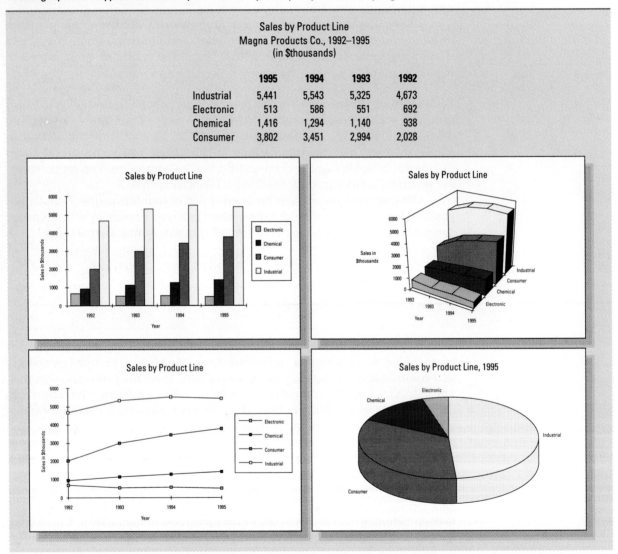

	1995	1994	1993	1992
Industrial	5,441	5,543	5,325	4,673
Electronic	513	586	551	692
Chemical	1,416	1,294	1,140	938
Consumer	3,802	3,451	2,994	2,028

Statistical and Operations Research Applications

A final group of personal information systems for analysis are those that are more mathematically oriented. For example, **statistical applications** analyze data by formal statistical procedures. Programs perform regression analysis,

analysis of variance, statistical tests for the differences between means, and other similar procedures.

The use of statistical procedures has increased in business in recent years, partly because microcomputers have become powerful enough to perform procedures that at one time required mainframe computers. Statistical packages such as SAS and SPSS are now available on personal computers.

Another factor giving rise to increased use of statistics is that businesspeople have become more sophisticated in interpretating data. Today many business managers know that, if an analysis shows that one business policy results in $10.4 million profit and a second, in $10.9 million profit, these policies may, in fact, be no different. Their apparent difference may be statistically insignificant.

Accordingly, it is important for you to understand basic statistical procedures and know how to use statistical applications. You probably will do this in statistics classes if you have not done so already.

Operations research (OR) uses mathematical models to represent business operations. The models are analyzed with the goal of optimizing or at least substantially improving performance against formalized goals. The most common and best known OR technique is called **linear programming,** in which an objective function expressed as a linear equation is optimized subject to linear constraints.

Linear programming programs have long been available on large computers, and recently also on personal computers. One linear programming package named LINDO, for example, is now available in versions for many computers.

PERSONAL INFORMATION SYSTEMS FOR TRACKING AND MONITORING

The third and final major category of personal information systems includes those used for tracking and monitoring. Such systems maintain facts or figures about entities important to the business professional, and they produce reports about status or changes in status of those entities. Such applications are used primarily to keep track of something. Two types of tracking and monitoring systems are database applications and project management applications. We will consider each in turn.

Personal Database Applications

A database application is a computer-based information system that stores data in the format of a database, as described in Chapter 3. A **personal database application** is a database application that has a single user.

Figure 5-14 shows an example of a personal database that LuAnne uses to keep track of the booth duty schedule at the trade show. This database has three tables. The EMPLOYEE table stores the names of employees and their hotels and room numbers while they are at the trade show. LuAnne uses this information to contact personnel when she needs to. The STATION table has data about each demonstration station, including the serial number of the computer and the type of product being demonstrated at that station. Finally, the SCHEDULE table keeps data on who is demonstrating on each station and when they are demonstrating. Sample data from the Booth Duty database is given in Figure 5-14b.

A database contains multiple tables and represents the relationships among the rows of the tables. In Figure 5-14, for example, the relationship between an employee and his or her schedule is carried by the EmployeeName field. Abernathy's assignments, for example, can be determined by accessing all rows in the SCHEDULE table having the value "Abernathy" in the EmployeeName column.

Figure 5-14   Personal Database
(a) An outline of LuAnne's database structure. **(b)** Sample data in LuAnne's three database tables.

(a) Table Name	Column Names
EMPLOYEE	EmployeeName, Hotel, Room
STATION	StationNumber, MachineID, Product
SCHEDULE	Day, Time, StationNumber, EmployeeName

Column names that are underlined are unique identifiers of table rows.

(b)

EMPLOYEE

EmployeeName	Hotel	Room
Abernathy	Hyatt	1722
Johnson	Hyatt	1811
Slovenic	Hilton	789
Turkle	Hyatt	1133
Vines	Hilton	1534

STATION

StationNumber	MachineID	Product
1	386-05	Silverado
2	386-07	Silverado
3	486-01	Goldstar

Figure 5-14 *(continued)*

SCHEDULE			
Day	**Time**	**StationNumber**	**EmployeeName**
Wednesday	8 A.M. – 10 A.M.	1	Slovenic
Wednesday	8 A.M. – 10 A.M.	2	Abernathy
Wednesday	8 A.M. – 10 A.M.	3	Turkle
Wednesday	10 A.M. – 12 P.M.	1	Vines
Wednesday	10 A.M. – 12 P.M.	2	Johnson
Wednesday	10 A.M. – 12 P.M.	3	Turkle
Wednesday	1 P.M. – 3 P.M.	1	Slovenic
Wednesday	1 P.M. – 3 P.M.	2	Abernathy
Wednesday	1 P.M. – 3 P.M.	3	Johnson
Thursday	8 A.M. – 10 A.M.	1	Abernathy
Thursday	8 A.M. – 10 A.M.	2	Slovenic
•			
•			
•			

Figure 5-15 Components of a Personal Database Application

- **Database**—Interrelated tables of data
- **Data-Entry Forms**—Used to add, change, and delete data
- **Reports**—Formatted presentations of data
- **Query Language**—General-purpose data-access language
- **Menus**—Lists of actions to control activity
- **Applications Programs**—Written to support unique requirements

Components of a Database Application For someone like LuAnne to effectively utilize the database, she needs a *database application,* which is a database coupled with other components. As shown in Figure 5-15, a database application includes database, data-entry forms, reports, query language, and a series of processing menus. It may also include a number of application programs. Consider each of these components in turn.

Data-entry forms enable the user to enter and edit data. To add schedule data, for example, LuAnne uses the data-entry form shown in Figure 5-16. This

Figure 5-16 Booth Duty Data-Entry Form

In this data-entry form, the shaded fields are completed automatically by the program, and the unshaded fields are entered by the users.

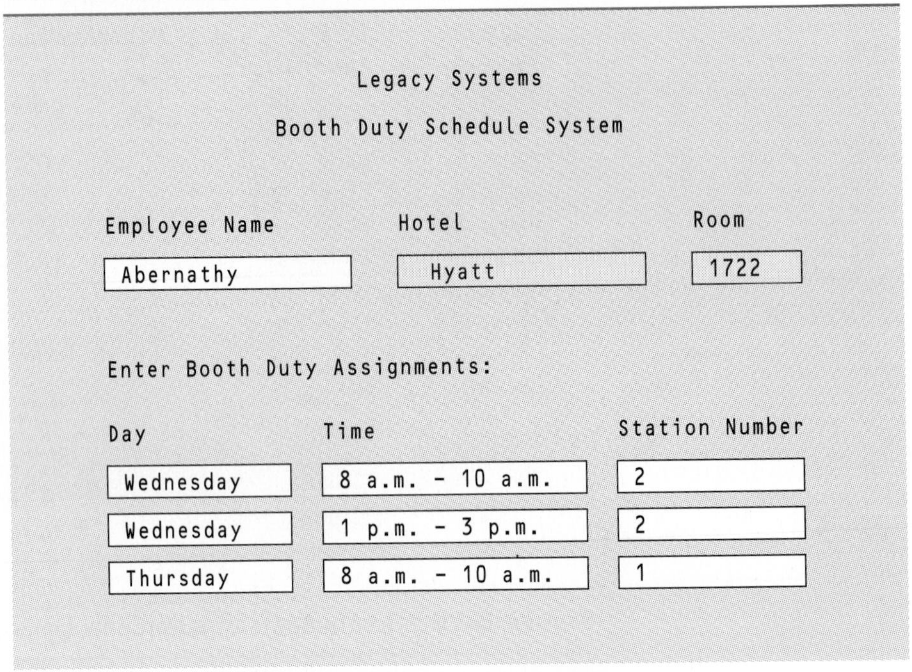

```
                        Legacy Systems
                   Booth Duty Schedule System


      Employee Name           Hotel                    Room

      | Abernathy      |      | Hyatt        |         | 1722    |


      Enter Booth Duty Assignments:

      Day               Time                     Station Number

      | Wednesday |     | 8 a.m. - 10 a.m. |     | 2              |

      | Wednesday |     | 1 p.m. - 3 p.m.  |     | 2              |

      | Thursday  |     | 8 a.m. - 10 a.m. |     | 1              |
```

form contains data stored in both the EMPLOYEE table and the SCHEDULE table. It works as follows: When the user enters data for the EmployeeName field, the Hotel and Room fields are filled in using stored data (unless, of course, the name is not stored in the database, in which case an error message is generated). Once the employee data is displayed, the user can add the schedule data.

Periodically, LuAnne needs to produce reports on the data stored in the database. For example, when she needs to print a schedule of demonstration duties for each employee, she directs the database application to produce the report shown in Figure 5-17. This report contains data from both the EMPLOYEE table and the SCHEDULE table. Other reports can also be produced to print a master duty schedule or to list the schedule of employees for each demonstration station.

A **report** is a formatted presentation of data from the database. Reports are, by far, the most common way of displaying information from a database. Another less frequently used alternative is a **query language,** which is a general-purpose language for obtaining data from the database on an ad hoc basis. SQL is the most popular query language.

Figure 5-17 Booth Duty Schedule Report
A report like this one is produced for each employee each day.

Legacy Systems

Booth Duty Schedule Report

To: Abernathy

       Room 1722

       Hyatt

The schedule for your booth duty on Wednesday, 6 May is:

Time	Station Number
8 a.m. – 10 a.m.	2
1 p.m. – 3 p.m.	2

Please arrive at the booth at least 10 minutes prior to your scheduled time to coordinate with on-duty staff. Call LuAnne at the booth (543-1043) or in Room 1411 at the Hyatt for information.

Most database applications also include menus. A **menu** is a list of options from which the user can choose, thereby directing and controlling processing activity. Sometimes, one menu can invoke a submenu, and so forth, for several levels. An example of a system of menus for the Booth Duty database is shown in Figure 5-18. Finally, the database application can also contain application programs that accomplish functions that cannot be done with the generic features of the personal DBMS.

Personal DBMS   The database is processed by a program called a **database management system (DBMS).** Most DBMS programs include default components created by the DBMS when tables are defined. For example, when the EMPLOYEE table is defined, a default data-entry form is created by the DBMS for entering EMPLOYEE table data. Similarly, a default report is created for listing that data.

The defaults, though convenient, are often rough-cut and difficult to use. Consequently, most DBMS programs provide other tools to customize and tailor

Figure 5-18 Menu System of the Booth Duty Application
To perform work with the application, the user selects an action from
this menu system.

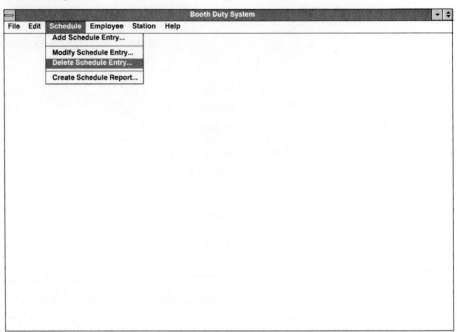

forms, reports, and menus. These customized items are useful for many
applications, but not for all. Most DBMS programs also support a programming
language so that application programs can be written to express unique or rare
processing logic or other needs. The use of these tools and languages, however,
requires programming and other advanced expertise.

Figure 5-19 summarizes the relationship among the types of programs that
may appear in a database application. The DBMS interfaces with the OS to manage
the data. Users access the database using an application consisting of data-entry
forms, reports, and menus. Several alternative applications exist. The default
application includes those forms, reports, and menus that the DBMS automatically
creates. The customized application consists of forms, reports, and menus created
using tools provided with the DBMS program. A programmed application consists
of forms, reports, and menus created and processed by application programs
custom written for the application. Finally, users can access the database using a
general-purpose query language such as SQL.

Popular microcomputer DBMSs include Borland dBASE IV and Paradox,
Microsoft Access and FoxPro, ORACLE, and DataEase. These programs have widely
varied capabilities and features. Most include support for SQL.

Figure 5-19   Relationships Among Programs in a Database Application

The user may interact by using the default application, a customized application using tools provided by the DBMS, a customized application provided through programming, or through a general purpose query language such as SQL. In any case, the user's commands are executed by the DBMS, which accesses the data through the facilities of the OS.

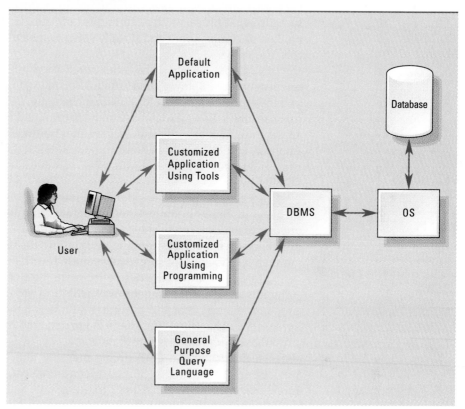

The Choice Between Spreadsheet Applications and Database Applications

Unfortunately, considerable confusion has arisen among businesspeople concerning the appropriate roles for spreadsheet and database applications. In fact, spreadsheets and databases are different types of applications and are intended for different purposes.

Spreadsheet programs process spreadsheets by making repetitive calculations on interrelated variables. The use of the term *database* in conjunction with spreadsheet programs is unfortunate and has introduced confusion into the market. A spreadsheet is not a database; though some similarity in appearance exists between a spreadsheet and a table, their basic functions and interconnections are different.

Some spreadsheet programs offer a very rudimentary set of commands for querying data in the spreadsheet's rows and columns. These facilities encourage unknowing users to attempt to perform database functions with a spreadsheet. This misunderstanding is unfortunate. The program's facilities are crude and cumbersome and usually serve to create more problems for the user than they solve.

DBMS packages, on the other hand, keep track of facts and figures about entities such as employees and schedules. DBMS programs manage tables of data, and they provide a means for creating, changing, deleting, and displaying values in those tables. Rows in database tables are not related to one another by formula as they are in a spreadsheet; rather, they are related by data-item value. For example, an EMPLOYEE table row and a SCHEDULE table row are related if the value of EmployeeName in EMPLOYEE matches the value of EmployeeName in SCHEDULE.

Some DBMS programs offer formula-calculation capabilities that are similar to those available in spreadsheet programs and with which users sometimes attempt to perform spreadsheet work. This, too, is a mistake. The facilities available are generally not robust enough; and, in any case, it takes longer and is more cumbersome to attempt spreadsheet analysis with the DBMS.

Finally, an important difference exists between the way that spreadsheet programs handle data and the way DBMS programs handle it. A spreadsheet program assumes that the computer's RAM is large enough to hold the user's spreadsheet. The user is thus restricted to that amount of data. On the other hand, most DBMS programs assume that databases can involve millions of characters of data, and so they use both active memory and magnetic disk during their processing. This means, in general, that a DBMS can process, at any one time, far more data than can a spreadsheet program.

There are cases in which DBMSs and spreadsheet programs need to interface with one another. For example, a financial analyst may spend a number of weeks developing a budget using a spreadsheet program and then choose, once the budget is finalized and approved, to store the spreadsheet data using the DBMS. At the same time, data maintained by a database application may be used as input for a spreadsheet analysis. Most DBMS and spreadsheet programs have features to facilitate the exchange of data from one program to the other. We will consider these situations under "Integrated Applications" below.

A suggestion to the students then, is to learn to use spreadsheet and DBMS programs for their intended purposes. When both types of processing are required, exchange data between programs. Trying to use a spreadsheet for a database job (or a vice versa) will result in frustration and inefficiency.

Project Management Applications

The second major category of tracking and monitoring systems is **project management applications,** such as Microsoft Project and CA-Project, which keep track of tasks and resources within a project.

With this type of application, the user defines tasks that need to be accomplished for a project and assigns a start date and time and an estimated time to completion. The user can also allocate resources and personnel to the task, then create **Gantt charts, critical path graphs,** and other types of project management displays. Furthermore, as the project progresses, the user can input actual dates and times of task completion, and the application will update the displays.

An important characteristic of project management applications is their ability to assign task dependencies. A given task can be defined so that it cannot be started before a second task is finished. Alternatively, two tasks can be defined to start together, or one task can be defined not to finish until another task is finished.

Figure 5-20 shows a portion of the project management application that LuAnne developed for use in booth setup activities. According to this plan, she

Figure 5-20   A Project Management Work Breakdown Structure
One of the outputs of project management applications is this hierarchical list of tasks and task dependencies.

Legacy Systems
Work Breakdown Structure—Booth Setup Activities

ID	Name	Duration	Scheduled Start		Scheduled Finish		Predecessors
1	1 Set up booth	0.23ed	05/05/95	8:00 A.M.	05/05/95	1:30 P.M.	
2	1.1 Uncrate booth components	1h	05/05/95	8:00 A.M.	05/05/95	9:00 A.M.	
3	1.2 Assemble booth	2h	05/05/95	9:00 A.M.	05/05/95	11:00 A.M.	2
4	1.3 Clean shelves	0.5h	05/05/95	11:00 A.M.	05/05/95	11:30 A.M.	3
5	1.4 Install carpeting	1h	05/05/95	11:30 A.M.	05/05/95	1:30 P.M.	4
6	2 Set up computer station 1	0.14ed	05/05/95	1:30 P.M.	05/05/95	4:45 P.M.	
7	2.1 Set up hardware	0.06ed	05/05/95	1:30 P.M.	05/05/95	3:00 P.M.	
8	2.1.1 Unpack hardware	0.75h	05/05/95	1:30 P.M.	05/05/95	2:15 P.M.	5
9	2.1.2 Connect hardware	0.5h	05/05/95	2:15 P.M.	05/05/95	2:45 P.M.	8
10	2.1.3 Run diagnostic checks	0.25h	05/05/95	2:45 P.M.	05/05/95	3:00 P.M.	9
11	2.2 Set up software	0.07ed	05/05/95	3:00 P.M.	05/05/95	4:45 P.M.	
12	2.2.1 Install OS	0.25h	05/05/95	3:00 P.M.	05/05/95	3:15 P.M.	10
13	2.2.2 Install application software	1h	05/05/95	3:15 P.M.	05/05/95	4:15 P.M.	12
14	2.2.3 Run diagnostic checks	0.5h	05/05/95	4:15 P.M.	05/05/95	4:45 P.M.	13
15	3 Set up computer station 2	0.04ed	05/05/95	2:45 P.M.	05/05/95	3:45 P.M.	
16	3.1 Set up hardware	1h	05/05/95	2:45 P.M.	05/05/95	3:45 P.M.	9

and her staff first need to set up the booth and the hardware for each demonstration station, and then they need to load the required software.

The display in Figure 5-20 is called a **work breakdown structure.** It is a hierarchical list of tasks and task dependencies. The project manager application uses this structure to create the Gantt chart shown in Figure 5-21. Although this feature is not shown in Figure 5-21, the project management application can help LuAnne determine when there are schedule conflicts for resources (e.g., two tasks requiring the same set of tools at the same time) and when there are personnel conflicts (e.g., two tasks requiring LuAnne's attention at the same time).

Figure 5-21   Gantt Chart

Project management applications often show the time frames of tasks in a project in this type of graph, called a Gantt chart.

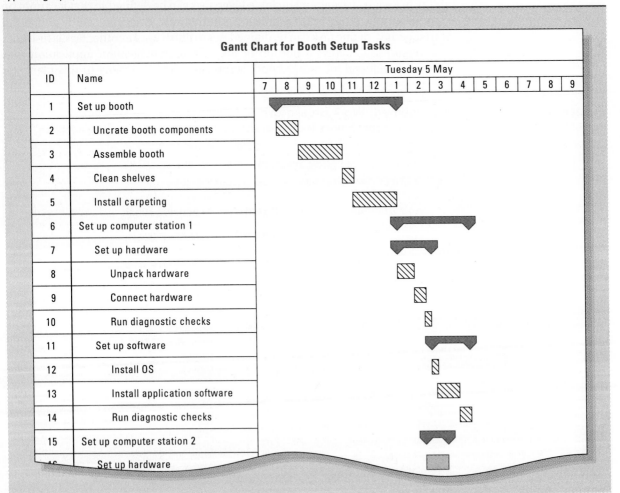

INTEGRATED APPLICATIONS

The microcomputer industry has used the term **integrated application** in two different ways. The term first referred to microcomputer packages that included word processing, spreadsheet, and database capabilities all as a single product, such as First Choice and Microsoft Works. For a variety of reasons, such products had only limited success for business applications, and they appealed more to home computer users. As a result, that use of the term has largely disappeared among business users.

The second meaning of the term refers to a system of several microcomputer applications that share data. Such a system can make the results of one application available to other applications (e.g., database processing results to a DTP program; or spreadsheet results to a word processing program).

For example, suppose that LuAnne uses the Booth Duty database shown in Figure 5-14 to create and maintain the employee work schedule during the trade show. Further suppose that she has designed the show newsletter illustrated in Figure 5-7 to include the day's booth duty schedule as a standard section.

Each day, LuAnne updates the employee schedule using the database application. She would like for the changes she makes in the database to be automatically reflected in the daily newsletter when it is printed, and she can use an integrated application to do this. The day's booth schedule is output from the database application and input to the DTP application; the DTP program integrates the schedule into the newsletter. In this way, LuAnne only needs to update the schedule in the database and then print the newsletter. The DTP program will automatically pick up the input file created by the database application.

There are two types of application integration, static and dynamic. With **static integration,** one application program passes a static file of results to another application. If the data on which that file was produced is subsequently changed, those changes are not reflected in the static file. For example, if the database is changed after LuAnne's schedule file is created, those changes will not be reflected in the shared file. LuAnne will have to instruct the database application to recreate the shared file and import it again before printing the newsletter.

With **dynamic integration**, a linkage is established between the programs that share data so that current data is always available. For example, under dynamic integration, when LuAnne's daily newsletter is printed, the DTP application accesses the database application to obtain the current values of the database. These values are then used to create the booth duty schedule. In this way, LuAnne knows that all changes made to the database will be made available to the DTP program. **Dynamic data exchange (DDE)** and **object linking and embedding (OLE)** are facilities of Microsoft Windows that provide dynamic integration for many personal computer applications.

Dynamic integration is very useful. For example, suppose that, every Monday morning, a sales manager is required to create a sales report describing the prior week's sales. Further, suppose that all sales are recorded in a spreadsheet program that is dynamically linked to a standard sales report document. With such a system, the manager can enter the sales data in the spreadsheet at convenient times throughout the week. On Monday, he then prints the sales report; all of the week's data will automatically be included.

VALUE ADDED BY PERSONAL INFORMATION SYSTEMS

So far, this chapter has surveyed the major types of personal information systems. Although knowledge of the basic features and characteristics of these applications is important, in itself it is not enough.

Suppose for a moment that you have just begun a new job as a buyer for sporting goods in a major department store. You want to excel in your new job, and so consider applying information technology to your work. How do you proceed? The discussion to this point presented different applications and described what they do. However, you want to start from a different vantage point. Given your job, what personal information system might help you to excel?

One way to proceed is to use the model of the value added by information systems that was developed in Chapter 4, which states that all business activity can be broken down into *processes* and *products*. In the case of an individual, the processes are methods and procedures by which that person accomplishes his or her job; the products are things that the individual produces for others. Processes are often not visible to other people; products are.

The model for value added by personal information systems is shown in Figure 5-22. The three value-added groups are personal processes, personal products, and facilitating change.

This model may be useful to you as a business professional, since you can use it to analyze your job according to the activities in Figure 5-22. For each category of added value, consider the types of information system that will facilitate the activities in that category. Proceeding in this manner will help you to identify potential information systems applications in your job. It also puts the horse before the cart: Rather than start with a personal computer product and look for a use, you will start with a business need and look for a product.

Value Added to Personal Processes

The three dimensions of process described in Chapter 4 are operations, management, and strategic planning.

Figure 5-22 Value Added by Personal Information Systems

Value Category	Value Added
PERSONAL PROCESSES	
Operations	Using information systems in taking action to accomplish one's job
Management	Using information systems in acquiring and effectively using the assets needed to accomplish one's job
Strategic Planning	Using information systems in setting and adjusting goals and objectives for one's job
PERSONAL PRODUCTS	
Product Characteristics	Including information components as characteristics of one's product
Product Delivery	Using information systems to increase the speed or ease with which one delivers one's product
FACILITATING CHANGE	
Change in Process Quality	Using information systems to create improvements in the efficiency and effectiveness of one's activities
Change in Product Quality	Using information systems to create improvements in one's product characteristics, such as appearance or accuracy

Operations Personal operations involve the execution of specific tasks to accomplish one's assigned job. For a product manager, it means developing a product plan; for an engineer, creating an engineering drawing or analysis; for a salesperson, making sales calls; and so forth.

Consider personal operations in the context of your new job as a buyer of sporting goods. What are your operations activities? You most likely talk with vendors, decide on products to carry, place orders, and monitor sales.

You could use a number of types of personal information in your job—for instance, a spreadsheet application to assess revenues and costs of different types of sporting goods product lines, or a database system to keep track of orders placed and shipments received. Or, suppose you spend a considerable amount of time preparing order documentation. If so, you might develop a number of word processing macros that facilitate the preparation of order documents.

Figure 5-23   Value Added by LuAnne Price's
Personal Information Systems

Value Category	Example Activity	Personal Application Type
PERSONAL PROCESSES		
Operations	Communication of plan	Word processing
	Verification of equipment delivery	Database
Management	Determining budget requirements	Spreadsheet
	Tracking progress on show plan	Project management
Strategic Planning	Evaluating success of show	Integrated application relating project sales contracts to project expenses
PERSONAL PRODUCTS		
Product Characteristics	Detailed daily schedule	Database
	Product-level budgets	Spreadsheet
	Employee performance goals	Database
Product Delivery	Daily update on schedules in Legacy trade show newsletter	Word processing
		Database
		DTP
FACILITATING CHANGE		
Change in Process Quality	Feedback on time required to execute plan	Project management
Change in Product Quality	Feedback on accuracy of budget	Connection to corporate accounting system

Potential uses of information systems for LuAnne, the trade show manager at Legacy Systems, are shown in Figure 5-23. LuAnne uses a word processing application to facilitate communication of the trade show plan to her managers and to all employees working at the show. She also uses a database application to track the equipment shipped to the show.

Management   In general, management control concerns the acquisition and effective use of resources. Personal management involves the acquisition and use of assets by an individual. Often, the assigned asset is a monetary budget, but it can also be equipment, personnel, or consumable goods. In the case of an engineer, a designer, or an attorney (or some other knowledge worker), the allocated asset is sometimes that person's own time. An attorney, for example, might spend 5 hours in the library to develop the best possible opinion on a legal question.

In your new job as sporting goods buyer, what actions must you take to acquire and utilize assets for your job? Perhaps you need an increased budget to support your activities. If so, what information systems might you use to convince your manager of this necessity? You could use a spreadsheet to demonstrate not only the size and nature of the necessary budget increases, but also the anticipated economic return resulting from the budget expansion. You could also use a presentation application to develop transparencies that illustrate the ways in which the budget increase is justified. Finally, you might use a word processing system to develop a memo delineating your position.

Examples of LuAnne Price's use of personal information systems for management control are listed in the management section of Figure 5-23. She uses a spreadsheet application to determine the budget for the trade show. In fact, she keeps each year's financial plan and uses it as a basis for developing the next year's plan.

LuAnne also uses a project management application for tracking progress on the trade show plan. The program she uses allows her to input the percentage of completion on each task of the plan. She then uses it to print Gantt charts illustrating her progress. The charts' professional appearance helps establish her personal credibility long before the trade show begins.

Strategic Planning   In regard to personal information systems, strategic planning involves setting and adjusting personal objectives, which can and often do overlap with workgroup and enterprise objectives. The concern here, however, is how an individual establishes his or her own opinion about such objectives.

In your job as a sporting goods buyer, what goals and objectives might you have? You probably were given performance goals by your manager when you were hired, such as increasing sales of your product lines by 5 percent, increasing the profitability of the product line by a certain amount, or reducing unsold inventory by some amount. At first such goals will likely be given, but as you gain experience, you will have more voice in setting your own goals.

What types of personal information systems might help you with these tasks? Setting goals and objectives tends to be an unstructured task, so the direct application of personal systems is less likely. However, some useful applications exist. For example, a spreadsheet can help you perform what-if analysis to determine the feasibility of goals you are given or goals that you want to set for yourself. You might use mail merge facilities to communicate with each of your vendors to gather information that you would use to establish your goals. You could also use a presentation application to prepare visual aids describing your goals to management or vendors.

As shown in Figure 5-23, LuAnne Price uses an integrated application to help her evaluate the trade show's success, which enables her to set better goals and objectives for subsequent shows. Her application integrates a database of sales contacts developed during product demonstrations into a spreadsheet managing the trade show costs. She uses the application to allocate related benefits to costs for specific products; this helps her set performance goals for future trade shows.

Value Added to Personal Products

We now turn to the ways in which personal information systems add value to an individual's products. First note the distinction between personal processes and personal products. Processes concern activities that create products. Process activity occurs within the individual's sphere—only the individual sees or knows about it. The product is the entity delivered from the individual to someone else.

As stated in Chapter 4, information systems add value to products by enhancing product characteristics and by improving product delivery. An individual's products are the things that person produces as part of his or her job: The product of an advertising copywriter is advertising copy; of an auditor, an audit; and of a quality control engineer, a controlled product process.

Notice the relationship between an individual's products and an organization's products. The company produces a product, say a clothes dryer, that is assembled from many individuals' products. In some cases, an individual's product relates directly to the organization's product; in other cases, it does not. A clothes dryer engineer's work relates directly to the clothes dryer, but an organizational behaviorist's work (which might be recommending reorganization of the accounting department) does not directly relate. In both cases, however, the individual produces a product.

Product Characteristics   Consider the ways in which information systems enhance personal product characteristics. The product of most business professionals is a knowledge product—for example, a sales plan, a series of commitments, or a recommendation to hire or promote someone.

In your job of sporting goods buyer, the major product is a series of orders for sporting goods items. You can enhance your product by ordering at the last possible moment, thus reducing inventory costs. Or, you can buy from several sources and increase competitive pressure among your vendors. You could also develop a system under which you trade goods with other outlets of the department store.

Suppose one of your responsibilities is to build enthusiasm among the sales staff. You could use DTP to develop a sporting goods newsletter, building motivation by publicizing, among other things, the best sales records among the staff members.

As shown in Figure 5-23, LuAnne adds value to her products by making them more detailed. She breaks the daily schedule into 2-hour increments. Before LuAnne took over the trade show job, the schedules were vague, simply indicating that certain sales regions were responsible for the booth, in general, for half-day periods. The result was a sloppy and slapdash attitude on the part of the trade show staff. With the more detailed schedule, the salespeople have been able to specialize in demonstrating particular products at particular stations. The result is a more professional look throughout the booth.

LuAnne also enhances her product by allocating trade show costs to specific categories of products. Furthermore, she has developed specific performance goals for each member of the trade show staff. Those goals enable the staff members to better measure the effectiveness of their processes at the trade show.

Product Delivery A second way in which personal information systems add value to products is to improve product delivery. With information systems, individuals perform their work faster, which means that information products are provided more frequently and kept more current. Additionally, personal products are made more accessible. Work results are made immediately available to concerned workers via electronic mail, for example. Or, when an engineer identifies a problem with a product, that problem description is disseminated quickly to concerned employees throughout the company.

Such rapid personal product delivery has a downside, however. An individual's error can also be quickly communicated. Imagine the chaos and disruption that could occur if an erroneous description of a product problem was broadcast through the sales and customer support departments, later to be retracted, then changed, and then retracted again.

In your new job as sporting goods buyer, you can improve your product's delivery by speeding up the process of preparing orders. You can also send up-to-date sales information to sales staff and management.

Figure 5-23 shows how LuAnne Price uses information systems to improve the delivery of her product. Throughout the show, Legacy employees schedule appointments with customers, distributors, and other vendors. For a number of valid reasons, the employees need to know who is meeting with whom. To meet this need, LuAnne uses a word processing application to produce a daily meeting schedule, and then she inputs this schedule into the trade show newsletter. Using her database application, she has the newsletter delivered to the rooms of every Legacy employee at the show by 7:00 A.M. each morning. This schedule also contains announcements, summary of news breaking at the show, booth duty schedule, and summary of the competitors' activities.

Value Added by Facilitating Change

One of the ways professional work differs from nonprofessional work is that the professional person is given greater latitude in the use of his or her time. The professional is expected to reflect on his or her processes and products and to make changes when appropriate. Whereas the attitude of a nonprofessional can sometimes be, "They tell me what to do and I do it," the attitude of a professional is expected to be, "There's a better way to do this job, and I'm going to figure it out and do it." When a professional makes changes in the use of resources, often no one else is even aware that a change occurred. A higher output or a better product are the only indication of a change.

Change in Process   Process improvement requires feedback. To know how well you are doing on a job, you need to gather data on the results of your activities. With that data, you can adjust your process and determine the impact of the adjustment. For example, suppose that, in your job of sporting goods buyer, you sense you are not using your time as effectively as possible. Accordingly, you decide to keep a daily activity log over a period of 6 weeks to determine where your time is going. To do so, you use a personal database application to enter the time spent at various tasks.

After the six-week period, you examine your data to determine where the bulk of your time has been spent, and you are surprised at the number of hours you spent with vendor salespeople. You consider the situation and decide to shorten that time by sending the vendor salespeople, prior to their sales calls, a description of your sales goals for the coming period.

You do that while continuing to use the daily activity database application. After some period of time, you measure the amount of time you are spending with vendors, add the amount of additional time spent preparing and sending the goal descriptions, and determine whether your change has been effective. These activities illustrate the ways you can use information systems to improve your process.

LuAnne uses a project management system to assess her productivity. Each year, she develops a project plan for her activities and then records progress on that plan using the project management software. At the end of the show, she compares results on her plan with prior years' results to assess the impact of changes in processes for planning and conducting the trade show.

Change in Product   Information systems can be used to improve the quality of a personal product as well as the product's characteristics and delivery. Quality can be measured in both accuracy and appearance. Using information systems, you, as the sporting goods buyer, can improve the accuracy of the quantities you order. LuAnne can improve the accuracy of the budgets in her plan, the accuracy of her schedules, and so forth.

Information systems can also be used to improve the quality of the product's appearance. To see why this is important, suppose that LuAnne carelessly produces the documentation of the trade show plan and that it is poorly organized and unattractively presented as a set of hard-to-read photocopied pages. A number of

Figure 5-24 Effective Change Based on Feedback
Making worthwhile changes in process or product depends on receiving and
benefiting from feedback.

consequences are likely. For one, employees at the trade show are more likely to
be misinformed and may even miss booth duty or important meetings. Second,
since LuAnne is indirectly communicating little pride in the plan, the employees,
too, will take little pride. They may not take the schedule seriously, and their
feelings about the plan may carry over into their business dealings at the trade
show as well.

Product quality improvement also requires feedback. In the case of your job
as sporting goods buyer, you need to know how accurate your order quantities
are. You need to know the number of stockouts and the amount of goods that went
unsold. You can use a personal DBMS to track this data.

Similarly, LuAnne needs to obtain feedback on the accuracy of her plan. In
Figure 5-23, she uses an information system with a communication connection to
the corporate mainframe to obtain actual expense figures. She uses this data to
improve the accuracy of her budgets for future trade shows.

SUMMARY

Personal information systems are computer-based information systems used by individuals to facilitate their work. Your focus on this topic should be broader than simply learning how to use certain products. Although such learning is useful and interesting, it is more important that you learn the characteristics of different types of personal information systems and the conditions under which to use each type. Furthermore, keep in mind that personal information systems are just one of the three major MIS categories.

The major categories of personal information systems are those that support communications, those that support analysis, and those that support tracking and monitoring. In this chapter, the word *communications* refers to human, not machine, communications.

The communications category of products is concerned with the creation, storage, and display of documents. These documents can be simple text-only documents, or they can include varieties of typefaces, type sizes, and even graphics. Word processing programs are used to manipulate text. Mail merge is an option in most word processing programs that facilitates the production of personalized form letters and similar documents. Boilerplate and automated document production extends mail merge capabilities to create tailored documents with very high productivity. Most word processing programs allow the definition of macros that accomplish repetitive tasks. Some word processing programs even include a programming language.

Desktop publishing (DTP) programs integrate text and graphics to produce high-quality, professional-looking publications. Graphics applications are used to produce high-quality statistical graphics, and presentation applications can produce high-quality presentation materials. Both graphics applications and presentation applications interface not only with printers but also with 35-millimeter cameras and other output devices.

The most popular application for analysis is the electronic spreadsheet. Such spreadsheets are used to perform repetitive calculations of potentially complicated data interrelationships. Electronic spreadsheets replicate manual spreadsheets, but they take away the need to perform manual calculations. Spreadsheets are especially useful for planning, forecasting, and budgeting applications. Systems of spreadsheets can be developed to model complicated business activities. Most spreadsheet programs include graphics and "database" capabilities as well. The use of the term *database* in this context is an unfortunate and misleading exaggeration by spreadsheet publishers' marketing departments. It is more correct to say that spreadsheets and portions of spreadsheets can readily be stored and retrieved.

Applications that provide a (computer) communications gateway are also used for analysis. Such applications enable the user to access data sources provided by data utilities. A final category of analysis programs are statistical packages and programs that support operations research (OR) methods such as linear programming.

Two types of tracking and monitoring applications are personal database applications and project management applications. A personal database application keeps track of data about entities such as vendors and purchases. Such applications have facilities to store, modify, delete, and display facts and figures about those entities. Databases consist of tables interrelated by data-item values. A database application includes database, data-entry forms, reports, menus, and, possibly, application programs. Users interface to a database via default applications, customized applications, programmed applications, or a generalized query language such as SQL.

Spreadsheet and database programs should be used for the purpose for which they were designed. Although spreadsheet programs have some database capabilities and database programs have some spreadsheet capabilities, these should not be misused. Instead, when the need arises, users should exchange data from the spreadsheet to the database or from the database to the spreadsheet.

Project management applications keep track of a project's tasks and resources. They can create work breakdown structures and produce Gantt charts, critical path graphs, and other similar project management displays.

Integrated applications enable several microcomputer applications to share data. With static integration, one application passes a static file of results to another application. With dynamic integration, a linkage is established between the programs so that current data is always available. The model of value added by an information system can be used to help identify potential applications of personal information systems. According to this model, personal information systems can add value to an individual by facilitating the individual's work processes or products. Categories of work process are operations, management, and strategic planning, and process quality. Categories of work product are product characteristics, product delivery, and product quality.

KEY TERMS

Personal information system	Graphics (in spreadsheet)	Query language
COMDEX	Communications gateway	Menu
Word processing	Modem	DBMS
Facsimile (fax)	The Internet	Project management application
Personalized form letter	Data utilities	Gantt chart
Mail merge	Statistical application	Critical path graph
Boilerplate	OR	Work breakdown structure
Macro	Linear programming	Integrated application
DTP	Personal database application	Static integration
Presentation graphics application	Data-entry form	Dynamic integration
Electronic spreadsheet	Report	DDE
System of spreadsheets		OLE

REVIEW QUESTIONS

1. Define personal information system.

2. Who uses personal information systems applications?

3. List the three major functions supported by personal information systems.

4. What is the purpose of applications that support interpersonal communication?

5. What is the function of a word processing application? How does word processing differ from typing?

6. Describe how the fax process works.

7. What are mail merge facilities? What function do they serve?

8. Explain the use of the two files in a mail merge application.

9. What is a boilerplate document? Give an example of boilerplate, other than the examples in this text. What is the advantage of producing boilerplate with word processing applications?

10. What is a macro? Why would an individual choose to use one? Explain how a macro can be created using a macro recorder.

11. Explain the use of a programming language within a word processing application. What functions might the programs written in this language serve?

12. What is the function of DTP applications?

13. What types of files are required for DTP?

14. What is the function of a presentation graphics application? What types of output devices do such applications use?

15. Name two word processing products.

16. Name at least three DTP products.

17. Name at least three presentation graphics products.

18. What is the function of an electronic spreadsheet? What types of applications does it commonly serve?

19. Describe the advantages of electronic spreadsheets over manual spreadsheets.

20. Describe an example in which a system of multiple spreadsheets would be appropriate.

21. Describe a situation in which the computational logic of a spreadsheet is circular.

22. What are the three basic subsystems of a spreadsheet package?

23. Name three spreadsheet products.

24. Explain the role of a communications gateway for analysis applications.

25. Describe two reasons why statistical applications are seeing increased use in business.

26. Name two types of applications used for tracking and monitoring.

27. What is the function of a personal database application?

28. Name at least five basic components of database applications.

29. Explain how tables are interrelated in a database.

30. Give an example of a data-entry form.

31. Give an example of a report.

32. Give an example of a menu.

33. Under what conditions is it necessary to use a database programming language?

34. Name at least four DBMS products.

35. Under what conditions would you choose to use a spreadsheet rather than a database application?

36. Under what conditions would you choose to use a database application rather than a spreadsheet?

37. What is the function of a project management application? Describe the role of a work breakdown structure and a Gantt chart.

38. What is an integrated application? What function does it serve?

39. Name and describe two types of integrated application.

40. Sketch a table that shows the components of each of the three categories of the model of value added by an information system.

41. For each row in your answer to question 40, fill in a microcomputer application that could be used to fulfill that function. Explain how the product would be used.

DISCUSSION QUESTIONS

1. Consider a job in your major area of study that is similar to LuAnne Price's job. The job should involve considerable responsibility, should be visible to the organization's management, and should not involve the supervision of employees. Write a brief job description for that job. Consider the three major categories of personal information systems. How could personal information systems from each of the three categories be used in the job you have described? How could each of the major functions in Figure 5-22 be facilitated by personal information systems in that job?

2. Suppose that you manage the customer support department at Legacy Systems. You have given one of your employees the task of writing a proposal to start a customer support newsletter that will be mailed to all registered customers. The employee asks you what kinds of information systems might be helpful. How do you respond?

3. Describe a situation in which it would be appropriate to use an electronic spreadsheet application. What characteristics of the situation make you believe that a spreadsheet is appropriate? Describe a situation in which it would be appropriate to use a database application. What characteristics of the situation make you believe that a database is

appropriate? How do the two situations differ? Are there any conditions under which it would make sense to exchange data between the two applications? Why or why not?

4. Using the data in Figure 5-14, describe the steps needed to meet the following requests for reports. That is, if you had to create the report yourself, how would you use these tables to find the answers?

   a. There has been a last-minute change in the Goldstar product, and the people who are scheduled to demo Goldstar need to be informed of the change. Create a report of all employees who are scheduled to demo Goldstar.

   b. The distances between hotels are long, and public transportation is overwhelmed by the load of visitors. Someone has suggested that LuAnne set up carpools to get employees from the various hotels to the convention center. Create a report showing the names of employees from each hotel who are scheduled in each time slot.

   c. Machine 386-07 is malfunctioning. The technician needs to talk to employees who have used that machine to try to establish what was happening when it first began to malfunction. Create a report listing the employees who have worked with that machine in order by time period.

5. It is sometimes said that information systems productivity increases arise more often in the form of being able to do new things than in being able to do the same things more efficiently. How does this idea apply to LuAnne Price at Legacy Systems? Compare LuAnne's current working methods to those she would likely have used before PCs: processing by human memory and brain and producing reports mostly by pen and paper. How much of her productivity improvement arises from doing the same jobs more efficiently? How much from being able to do new jobs or provide output at new levels of quality? Give specific examples.

PROJECTS

A. Identify someone who holds a professional job that involves planning and organizing and that is, to a degree, similar to LuAnne Price's job. Set up an interview with that person. Explain that you are studying the use of personal information systems. Does this person use any personal information systems? Why or why not? What are the top two or three issues for that person in each of the categories of Figure 5-22? For each category, think of at least one personal information system that could be used. Is such a system used? If so, what are the advantages and disadvantages of using it? If not, why not? In your report, include examples from the person's experience.

B. Pick a partner. Have one person take the job of learning how to use a spreadsheet program and the other person, the job of learning how to use a personal DBMS. Using the DBMS, develop an application to maintain a transcript of the courses both of you have taken and the grades both of you have received. Using the spreadsheet product, develop an application to maintain a budget for the school year for each of you. After solving the problems, switch the tools you are using. Attempt to solve the transcript problem with the spreadsheet product and the budget problem with the DBMS. Are you able to solve the problems? If so, what are the disadvantages? If not, why not?

C. Use a word processing program to create a personalized form letter addressed to each member of your class and to the teacher. In the letter, explain how the form letter facility of your word processor works. Attach examples of the two files that were merged to create the personalized form letter. Is there any reason why the examples should be produced individually, as the personalized form letters were? If so, what is the reason? If not, is there an alternative production method for the examples that may be more economical in work time and other resources? (Document the comparison.)

D. Identify an employee at your school or elsewhere who uses a project management program on the job. Interview that person. What types of projects does the person manage? What advantages does the program offer over doing the same work by hand? In a typical project, does the schedule ever need to be revised? How is the program helpful in accommodating delays and unexpected problems that may be incurred during the execution of the project? In your report, include examples from the person's experience.

M I N I C A S E

A Really Big Show

It takes a lot more than a little self-confidence and a winning smile to deliver a good presentation. These days, you've got to have high-quality visuals. Dale Carnegie himself would be hard pressed to get a message across without them.

In the last 10 years, computer-generated graphics have raised the standard for presentation materials. In most business environments, hand-drawn charts and graphs are no longer acceptable. Today's audiences expect visuals to look professional. And in many of the best presentations, graphic images don't simply complement the speaker's message; they deliver it and drive it home.

Studies support the common-sense assumption that the use of solid visuals will strengthen any presentation. A study of presentation effectiveness conducted by Douglas Vogel, associate professor of management information systems at the University of Arizona in Tucson, concludes that the judicious use of color and graphic elements or icons, for example, results in increased audience attention, comprehension and retention. Furthermore, high-quality graphics add to a presenter's credibility and increase the likelihood that an audience will act on the information it receives.

The good news is that within the last two years, major improvements in presentation software packages and an evolution in the consumer hardware base have made such software easier to use.

In essence, what users want from their presentation software is a graphic artist in a shrink-wrap, according to William Coggshall, president of Pacific Media Associates in Mountain View, Calif., a market-research firm specializing in presentation graphics and multimedia software. After inputting a few words and numbers, they'd like to see their presentations created automatically.

Speakers who prepare their presentations the night before delivery—which the majority of presentation software users do, experts say—will particularly appreciate the ability to choose from fill-in-the-blank templates or style pages. Most new packages on the market offer users a wide variety of style sheets that they can either customize or use as is. These master pages free the average user from having to match colors, choose appropriate typefaces and sizes, and determine how to lay out text and graphics. When more experienced users or experts in the graphic-arts department create a presentation, they can use the style sheets as a starting point for their own designs.

The capability to view entire presentations at a glance is another recent innovation. Sometimes referred to as a "slide sorter" or "light table," this feature allows users to organize the flow of their presentations by manipulating thumbnail-size visuals on their screens. The only drawback, experts like Coggshall caution, is that it's hard to read the text on the tiny visuals.

A growing number of presenters now display their creations right on their PCs or use projection panels to project the images from their PCs onto larger screens. Running their presentations in this way allows speakers to incorporate transitioning effects such as fades or diagonal wipes between their images. Some vendors have incorporated some very clever and eye-catching transitions in their packages. Users of Lotus's Freelance Graphics can open and close a graphic curtain between images, for example.

Users who choose to display their presentations using PCs and/or projection panels can also employ visual movement effects, called "builds." For example, a user could display bulleted items being added to a bullet chart, grow a bar in a bar chart, or show a light bulb icon becoming illuminated. ■

Lucie Juneau, excerpted from *CIO*, February, 1993, pp. 64-66.

Discussion Questions

1. Why do you think minimum standards of quality for presentation visuals have changed over the past 10 years?

2. Give examples of presentation graphics program capabilities that improve on the old manual drawing techniques.

3. Compare the costs and benefits of using a presentation graphics program yourself and turning the job over to a graphic artist, who prepares graphics for you.

4. How much difference do you think it would make in your ability to learn in the classroom if teachers routinely employed the graphics methods described in this article? Offer specific examples in defending your answer.

6

Components of Personal Information Systems

HARDWARE
- Personal Computers
- Workstations
- Characteristics of Microcomputers
- Personal Computer Specifications
- Input and Output Hardware
- Storage Hardware

PROGRAMS
- Systems Programs
- Horizontal Market Application Programs
- Vertical Market Application Programs
- Custom-Developed Programs

DATA
- File-Processing Data
- Database Data

PEOPLE
- Clientele
- Users
- Operations Personnel
- Systems Development Personnel

PROCEDURES
- Procedures for Normal Processing
- Procedures for Failure Recovery

THIS CHAPTER DISCUSSES THE PARTS OF A PERSONAL INFORMATION SYSTEM by using the five-component model introduced in Chapter 1. According to that model, information systems are composed of hardware, programs, data, procedures, and people. The chapter describes each of those elements as they pertain to personal information systems.

Chapter 3 presented a foundation of technology concepts regarding hardware, programs, and data. This chapter expands that foundation by further describing the technology as it is used in personal information systems.

Before proceeding, recall the symmetry in the five-component model: Programs are instructions for hardware just as procedures are instructions for people. Hardware and people are the active elements of the system. Data is the interface between machine elements and human elements.

HARDWARE

Microcomputers are the basis for hardware in personal information systems. The term *microcomputer* is broader than you might think. Strictly speaking, a microcomputer is any computer based on a microprocessor chip. There are microcomputers in airplanes, ships, delivery vehicles, and some industrial machinery. When we speak of microcomputers within the context of personal information systems, we usually mean something more specific. Most often we mean either a personal computer or a workstation. Let us consider each.

Personal Computers

A **personal computer** is a computer system that includes microcomputer, display unit, keyboard, and disk storage. Personal computers vary in size. The largest are **tower configuration** models, in which the chassis containing microcomputer and disk storage stands as a unit on the floor, as shown in Figure 6-1. This configuration is normally used for more powerful computers having large disk capacities.

Most commonly, personal computers are sized to fit on a desk. Generally, the microcomputer and disk storage are contained in one chassis, and the keyboard and display are separate. Although such **desktop computer** systems can be moved, they are not designed to be portable.

Laptop, notebook, and palmtop computers, on the other hand, are designed for portability. Their small size allows them to be carried home or taken on business trips. **Laptop computers** are small, typically weighing between 7 and 15 pounds, and they can be held on one's lap, as shown in Figure 6-2. Even smaller **notebook computers** weigh less than 5 pounds and can fit within the outlines of a notebook. **Tablet computers**, as shown in Figure 6-3, are pen-based; all data entry is done by writing on the screen with a stylus. These systems, now being introduced, require special versions of OSs and programs.

Laptop and notebook computers have microcomputer, display, keyboard, and disk storage integrated into one unit. They typically include batteries that enable them to be used for a period of hours away from a power source (e.g., on an airplane). A common problem with these smaller computers is readability of the display. Although improvements in this area have been made in recent years, the more readable displays remain relatively expensive. Therefore, laptop and notebook computers are often connected to a normal display screen when one is available.

Two families of personal computer exist. The first was designed and developed by IBM and is now manufactured, not only by IBM, but also by Compaq, Digital Equipment Corporation, Hewlett-Packard, Zenith Data Systems, and others. This family is commonly called the **IBM PC**, or **PC**, or **PC-compatible** family. The

Figure 6-1 Personal Computer with Tower Configuration

A tower PC has ample room for expansion. The large case can accommodate additional disk drives as needed and has many slots for adapter cards.

Figure 6-2 Laptop Personal Computer

The laptop configuration is today's most common type of portable computer, easily carried in a business briefcase yet large enough to provide a comfortable keyboard and screen.

Figure 6-3 Tablet Computer
Pen-based computers like this one use the screen both for display and for data input by stylus.

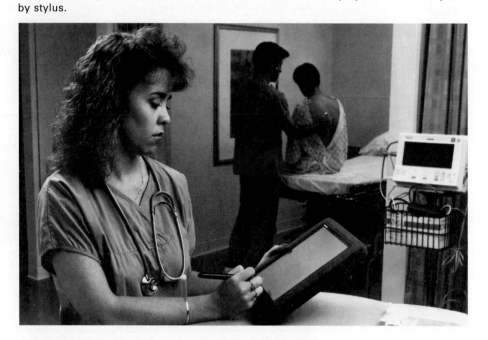

second family, designed, developed, and manufactured by Apple Computer, is the **Macintosh**. Only Apple manufactures and sells these computers.

It is not particularly difficult to manufacture a PC, nor does it require a substantial investment in capital. One can obtain the component parts (microprocessor, memory, data bus, power supply, and disk storage) and assemble them without great knowledge or skill. Therefore, many small manufacturers of PCs, or **PC clones**, exist. Usually, the prices of PC clones are considerably less than prices of PCs from established manufacturers; such clone makers have less overhead because they do no research or development.

Debate rages on about whether buying PC clones is a good idea. The price is right, but quality, support, and vendor viability widely vary from manufacturer to manufacturer.

Workstations

Workstations are high-performance microcomputer systems that are neither PC nor Macintosh. Originally developed for engineering applications such as

Figure 6-4 Engineering Workstation
The large, extremely high-resolution displays on this computer are a good clue that it is a workstation.

computer-aided design (CAD), they are, in fact, sometimes called **engineering workstations.** Such workstations typically are faster than personal computers, have more memory, and almost always have large, very high-quality displays, as shown in Figure 6-4.

Workstations are well suited to engineering applications. Usually priced between $5,000 and $50,000, their cost is declining as the capabilities of PCs are dramatically increasing. As a result, the gap between PCs and workstations is rapidly disappearing.

Characteristics of Microcomputers

A microcomputer consists of microprocessor, RAM and ROM, and data bus, or processor channel, to connect the microprocessor with memory and external devices (printers, disks, and so forth). The microprocessor, the brain of the computer, contains the ALU, a **clock** to synchronize events, **registers** for holding data that the ALU is processing, a **control unit** for decoding and controlling execution of instructions, and other components.

Figure 6-5 Intel and Motorola Families of Microprocessors

Word Size	Intel	Motorola
8 bits	8088	68000
	PC-XT	Mac Classic
	(80186)	(68010)
	(little used)	(little used)
16 bits	80286	68020
	PC-AT	Mac LC
32 bits	80386	68030
	386 PCs	Mac LC III
	80486	68040
	486 PCs	Mac Quadra
	Pentium	68050

Although over a hundred different **microprocessors** have been invented in their short history (since about 1974), only a few have had importance in the commercial world. Early important microprocessors were the Intel 8080, the MOS Technology 6502, and the Zilog Z-80. The 6502 was the basis of the Commodore PET and Apple II computers. The Z-80, which is a variation on the 8080, was the basis for the TRS-80 microcomputer.

Since those early years, two families of microprocessors have dominated the market (see Figure 6-5). The Intel family has been the basis of the IBM PC (and compatible) line of personal computers first introduced in late 1981. **Intel** microprocessors include the **8088** (the commercial version of the 8080), the **80286**, the **80386**, the **80486**, and the **Pentium**. The second line of microprocessors was developed by **Motorola**. The **68000** family has the most important Motorola microprocessors, and these are the basis of Apple's Macintosh family of computers.

Microcomputers can utilize a large variety of different peripheral equipment. All of this equipment, however, needs to be connected to the CPU over the data bus. To allow for such connections, microcomputers have **slots** that accept **adapter boards** as shown in Figure 6-6. These boards contain circuitry that drives equipment like disks, printers, plotters, bar-code scanners, and the like. The slots are connected to the data bus, which is in turn connected to the CPU.

Figure 6-6 Adapter Board

Adapter boards like this one plug into slots in a microcomputer to add capabilities such as special I/O facilities or the controller for additional disk storage.

Personal Computer Specifications

When you buy a personal computer, you must specify certain characteristics. To determine these characteristics, consider your requirements and the personal applications you will need. (A process for accomplishing those tasks is discussed in Chapter 7.)

The basic decision, whether to buy a computer from IBM PC or Macintosh family, is likely to be based on factors such as the need for compatibility with other computers in your company and the type and brand type of applications you want to run.

After deciding on the basic type of personal computer, you need to specify the type of processor and the speed of processor within that type. In general, the bigger the number, the faster the processor. A Pentium is faster than an 80486, which is faster than an 80386, and so forth; there are generally choices within each type. The 80486 processors, for example, can be purchased in 33-, 50-, and 66-megahertz versions, among others. (See Figure 6-7.)

Next, you need to decide on the amount of RAM to purchase. For a graphical user interface such as Windows, 4MB of RAM is often considered minimum,

Figure 6-7   Intel CPUs over Time

CPU	Introduced	Price at Launch	Current Price	MIPS at Launch	Highest MIPS	Number of Transistors
8086	June 1978	$ 360	n/a*	.33	.75	29,000
286	February 1982	$ 360	$8	1.2	2.66	134,000
386	October 1985	$ 299	$91	5	11.4	275,000
486	August 1989	$ 950	$317	20	54	1,200,000
Pentium	March 1993	$ 900**		112		3,100,000

*Discontinued
**Estimated
Source: *Byte,* May 1993, p. 94.

though many experts would say 8MB is barely adequate for today's typical applications. In a character-based system such as MS-DOS (without Windows), 1MB or 2MB will probably do.

Once you have decided these issues, you can select a brand of computer. Most name brand manufacturers supply computers across a wide spectrum of capability. One consideration is the number of slots you might need. For most applications, all personal computers have an adequate number of slots. If, however, your application requires an unusual amount of special hardware (e.g., extra disk drives, plotters, printers, and different types of sensors), then you should ensure that there will be enough slots when you acquire the computer. Different models of computers may have different numbers of slots.

Input and Output Hardware

The most common input and output hardware for personal computers are keyboard, display, and printer. There is little to say about **keyboards**; they all serve the same function, though, unfortunately, the positions of many keys varies from one keyboard to another. If the standard keyboard for the computer you wish to buy has a key layout that you find awkward and inconvenient, you may be able to switch to a different keyboard. Or, you can sometimes redefine the meaning of keys through the OS.

Most keyboards for laptop and notebook computers are somewhat scaled down in size, which may make them hard to use unless you have very small fingers.

Computer Displays Computer **displays** vary in a number of ways. First, they vary in size from small 6-inch displays to very large screens for use in group presentations. Displays also vary in their support for color. Some displays support only one color (typically white on a black or green background), and others support many. Most color displays allow for 256 colors; others support more.

Displays also vary in their **resolution**. Each display consists of a number of spots, called **pixels**, that can be illuminated. A typical display supports 640 by 480 pixels. (The dimensions refer to the number of pixels in the horizontal and vertical dimensions.) More expensive displays, especially those used with workstations, have thousands of pixels in both dimensions.

Questions have been raised whether working near the electromagnetic emissions of a computer display may involve some health risks. Manufacturers have taken steps to reduce these emissions, and research has produced no conclusive evidence of risk. However, the issue remains to be finally resolved.

The question of emissions is one of a series of issues in the **ergonomics** of personal computing—issues related to protecting the health and safety of the computer user. Other issues include the provision of adequate, glare-free lighting; supportive seating; placement of computer equipment for strain-free access; and scheduling of frequent breaks from computer-intensive work. Ergonomic issues become ethical issues when an employer requires an employee to use a computer on the job and thereby accepts responsibility for the employee's safety in using the computer.

Printers Both dot matrix and laser printers are used in personal computer applications. **Dot matrix printers** produce lower-quality documents, and for text-processing applications such as DTP and presentation generation applications, laser printers are required for satisfactory output.

Laser printers, such as the one in Figure 6-8, contain their own microprocessors that can process specialized computer programs without aid from the personal computer microprocessor. This characteristic gave rise to the development of printer languages like **PostScript**. One advantage of such languages is tremendous flexibility in printing multiple fonts in many sizes and in printing graphics.

Another advantage of using a printer language is that the process of building the printed display characters is off-loaded to the printer's CPU. This frees the personal computer's CPU for other work. When such a printer is used, the output is quickly dispatched, which enables the user to resume work while the printer operates independently.

Figure 6-8 Laser Printer

The laser printer is the most widely used type of printer in today's personal information systems.

Printers, like personal computers, have RAM. For some applications with some printers, it is necessary to buy and install additional RAM in the printer.

Storage Hardware

Two types of storage hardware are commonly used with personal computers: magnetic disk and optical disk. Tape is sometimes used for backup purposes, but it is almost never used for active data processing by a personal computer.

Magnetic Disk   Personal computers use both hard disks and floppy disks, or diskettes (the latter in 3½-inch and 5¼-inch sizes). The 3½-inch diskettes use newer technology, and so have higher capacity (up to 1.4MB). Older PCs may have only 5¼-inch diskette drives; newer PCs may have one of each size or only 3½-inch drives. Programs are universally available on 3½-inch diskettes and, usually, also on 5¼-inch diskettes (but sometimes only on special order). Since an important purpose of diskettes is to facilitate the exchange of programs and data among computers, you should equip your PC with the size drives that permit you to exchange diskettes conveniently.

Hard disks are usually mounted within the chassis of the personal computer. They range in capacity from 40 megabytes to over 1 gigabyte (1 billion bytes). Hard disks consist of a tower of disk surfaces mounted on a spindle.

Disk technology has evolved dramatically in recent years and will most likely continue to do so. Today, even laptop computers have 100MB to 200MB hard disks. This is amazing, considering that such disks must operate on battery power and are subjected to the knocks and abuses of taxi rides, air travel, and so on. Diskette technology is also evolving; 20MB and 30MB diskettes are in the foreseeable future.

Optical Disk The major advantage of optical disks is very high storage capacity. Optical disks are often used in multimedia applications, combining motion video, high-resolution bit-mapped graphics, and sound. Both technology and applications are currently under development. The move toward a set of standards for multimedia hardware, programs, and data structures for motion video, graphics, and sound is well under way. For example, one standard specifies a way to transmit information about musical sounds; this technology is called **Musical Instruments Digital Interface** (MIDI). Using the MIDI standard, programs and computerized audio **synthesizers**, or sound-generating devices, can communicate in predictable ways.

Currently, the move toward multimedia is led by companies marketing computer games, but Microsoft Corporation and other mainstream business program vendors are actively pursuing multimedia applications, too. For example, Microsoft has recently purchased a large share of the Dorling Kindersley Publishing House. This publisher has 600 leading titles of illustrated books that Microsoft apparently intends to put into multimedia format on optical disk. Since Microsoft, the world's largest software publisher, has stated a goal of revolutionizing the presentation of information using multimedia products, it is likely that such applications will become important in the future.

PROGRAMS

This section describes characteristics of the basic types of programs used with personal information systems: systems programs, horizontal market programs, vertical market programs, and custom-developed programs.

Systems Programs

The most important systems program is the OS. There are several personal computer OSs, and we will discuss the basic characteristics of each. In addition, we will consider the use of a **graphical user interface (GUI)**, which may require additional systems programs.[1]

MS-DOS   The most popular microcomputer OS, **MS-DOS**, is developed and licensed by Microsoft. Although it is used in more than 70 million personal computers, worldwide, this popular and successful program has very humble roots.

In the early 1980s, IBM wanted an OS to support its soon-to-be-announced 16-bit personal computer. At the time, the most popular microcomputer OS was CP/M from the Digital Research Corporation. CP/M would support only 8-bit microprocessors, and IBM wanted a new version that would support its processor. Digital Research agreed but encountered a number of delays.

Meanwhile, the success of two people working in a small company, Seattle Computer, was also being hampered by the lack of a 16-bit OS. So, in a matter of 2 months, they developed a simple 16-bit OS that they named QDOS, for "quick and dirty operating system." At the time, Microsoft, which also needed a 16-bit OS, acquired the rights to QDOS. When IBM lost patience waiting for Digital Research, Microsoft licensed QDOS to IBM. The product was renamed MS-DOS, Version 1.1. In order to have ownership of its trademark, IBM called its version **PC-DOS.**

Microsoft retained the rights to license MS-DOS to other companies, and soon versions of MS-DOS were available with microcomputers from Digital Equipment Corporation, Compaq, Hewlett-Packard, and Zenith Data Systems, to name a few. MS-DOS quickly became the standard OS, and it remains so today.

The current version of MS-DOS is 6.0, with capabilities that greatly exceed those in Version 1.1. MS-DOS grew with the industry.

MS-DOS Memory Terminology   For a variety of reasons, one important characteristic of MS-DOS could not be changed. As it was developed, QDOS represented main memory addresses in such a way that no more than 640KB of memory could be utilized. This seemed entirely reasonable for the memory sizes prevalent in the early 1980s. (A 256K memory was then considered big.)

As the years went by, however, the semiconductor industry found ways to produce memory less and less expensively, and soon 1 megabyte of memory was relatively inexpensive. This memory could not be utilized, however, because of the addressing limit in MS-DOS.

---

1.   The word *may* is used here because GUI environments are sometimes built into the OS. In particular, both the Macintosh OS and the OS/2 include the GUI. Neither MS-DOS nor UNIX includes a GUI, and to have one, they require the use of additional systems programs.

Application software developers, especially spreadsheet vendors, needed more memory. (Remember that all of a spreadsheet resides in memory at one time.) Two approaches were taken. The first, called **expanded memory**, required special hardware and software to make memory addresses between 640KB and 1MB available for processing. The second, called **extended memory**, added memory beyond the 1MB limitation. It also required special hardware and software. Such memory is generally not available to applications, but it can be accessed and used by other systems software.

These distinctions are losing importance today, however. Microsoft Windows, Version 3.0, which runs on top of MS-DOS, is able to provide virtually unlimited memory addressing to applications that run under it. As a consequence, only applications that run under MS-DOS and that do not run under Windows are subject to these limitations today.

Macintosh OS In 1984, Apple Computer announced an exceedingly innovative personal computer called the Macintosh. This computer provided the first commercially successful GUI. To understand why this event was important, examine Figure 6-9, which shows the MS-DOS interface next to a GUI interface. The user of MS-DOS is offered a blank line and command prompt that looks like *C:/>*. The user of the GUI is offered a rich and interesting visual environment that is exceptionally easy to use.

The user of a Macintosh can manipulate programs and files through the use of **icons**, which are graphical symbols. To delete a file, for example, the user

Figure 6-9 Character-Based User Interface and GUI

The character-based user interface requires the user to remember and type commands to perform tasks. The GUI provides a much more visually interesting environment, with a point and click interface.

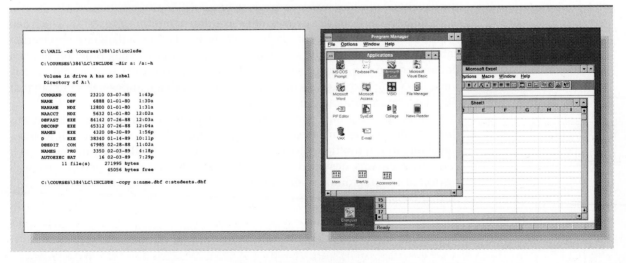

touches the file's icon with the mouse pointer, holds the mouse button down, and drags the file icon to a trash can icon. At that point, the trash icon balloons up to show that there is garbage in it. This method of input is called a **point and click interface**.

Such a system was a tremendous contrast to the character-and-command-oriented nature of MS-DOS. The MS-DOS user had to remember the format of many different commands to accomplish the work, but the Macintosh user simply manipulated icons. This capability enabled many people who had little interest in computing to be able to use a personal computer. For reasons that go beyond the scope of this text, the **Macintosh OS** was also innovative in its structure and in its programming interface.

Many of the ideas for the Macintosh OS originated among employees of Xerox working at Xerox PARC (Palo Alto Research Center) in Silicon Valley. The use of mice and point and click interfaces and the notion of multiple windows were pioneered at PARC. Unfortunately, Xerox has enjoyed little commercial benefit from the product of its own research and development activities.

Although the Macintosh was innovative in 1984, few features were added until the recently released System 7, which provides innovative and new capabilities, especially for workgroup applications.

OS/2 In 1987, IBM announced a new family of personal computers, the PS/2 family. At the same time, it announced a new OS that it had codeveloped with Microsoft: **OS/2.**

OS/2 was written to accomplish several important goals. First, it overcomes the 640KB memory limitation in MS-DOS. Additionally, it takes advantage of memory protection hardware that was engineered into the 80286 (and above) microprocessors in a way that MS-DOS could not do. With this feature, application programs are much less likely to interfere with one another's memory, and thus the likelihood of catastrophic errors is reduced. OS/2 also includes a GUI.

Finally, OS/2 enables concurrent execution of multiple programs, which can share the CPU in round-robin fashion. With this feature, a database application can sort a large table at the same time that a word processing program prints a document and the user processes a spreadsheet. The CPU is allocated among these tasks for short intervals of time in such a way that it appears to a human that they are being simultaneously processed.

Although OS/2 has experienced growing pains, as did Windows when it was first introduced, the current version is well respected and competitive. It features the ability to run multiple programs simultaneously in different windows, and it can run programs designed for DOS and Windows. OS/2 is particularly well respected by programmers developing workgroup applications. Chapter 9 will further consider this subject.

UNIX   A fourth OS used with personal information systems is **UNIX,** initially developed at Bell Labs in the 1970s. For most of its history, UNIX has been utilized by scientists and engineers for mathematically oriented work. It is the most commonly used OS on workstations.

Although UNIX might have been more popular with business users, it was not, due to its relatively complicated and unfriendly user interface. This interface was acceptable to technically oriented engineers, but the typical user of a word processing or spreadsheet package found it threatening and confusing.

Recently, a set of standards for a UNIX GUI have come into use, and with this interface, UNIX may see increased use in commercial applications. Characteristics of OS for personal information systems are summarized in Figure 6-10.

GUI Environments   The Macintosh and OS/2 OS integrate a GUI as part and parcel of the OS. With MS-DOS and UNIX, however, the GUI environment is provided by another product. Windows is used for MS-DOS, and another product, X-Windows, is used for UNIX.

Windows, which runs on top of MS-DOS, provides both a GUI environment and a method of overcoming the 640KB memory limitation. Windows effectively permits the use of very large memories under MS-DOS. It has become one of the most successful products in the history of personal computing. X-Windows has not had the same success, but it is growing in popularity.

Figure 6-10   Characteristics of PC OSs

OS Name	Date Introduced	Characteristics
MS-DOS or PC-DOS	1981	World's most popular OS Character based 640KB memory limitation
Macintosh OS	1984	Very innovative in 1984 First commercially successful GUI environment Innovative structure and programming interface
OS/2	1987	Multiple applications open simultaneously GUI Provides well-respected programming environment
UNIX	1971	Primarily used for engineering and scientific applications Most popular OS on workstations May become more popular in business with GUI

Today's GUI environments have a number of significant advantages. First, multiple applications can be open at the same time. For example, the Windows or Macintosh user can open a spreadsheet application in one window and a word processing application in a second and can nearly instantly switch from one to the other.

A second advantage is that the GUI user can highlight an item in an application and copy it to a temporary holding area called the **clipboard**. The transferred item can then be copied into a second application. In this way, tables and graphs from spreadsheets can be inserted into business reports, as can reports created by DBMSs.

A third advantage is that GUI environments provide an easy-to-use interface. In addition to the use of icons and a common point and click action, all such environments provide pull-down menus at the top of the screen. In nearly every program's menu, the left-most entry is *File*, with standardized entries for such actions as creating a new data file, opening an existing file, saving the current file, and exiting from the program. Similarly, in nearly every program, the second entry is *Edit*, with standardized entries for selecting items for manipulation and cutting and pasting. Other entries, such as *View* and *Format*, often appear with somewhat standardized contents. When the user clicks on an entry, the menus expand to show submenu choices in a standardized way. Also, communication with the user is facilitated with standardized graphical displays such as dialog boxes, option buttons, check boxes, and list boxes, as shown in Figure 6-11.

A fourth advantage is that most GUI application programs are written to use both the graphical interface and the keyboard consistently. Thus, for example, in Windows, the F5 key is used for the GO TO function in most applications. In a word processor, it means "go to a page"; in a spreadsheet, "go to a particular cell"; in a project manager, "go to a particular task." Consistent use of the help facility is another example of standard interfaces.

There are incredible savings to users of such standard interfaces. When a user familiar with one GUI program acquires a new program in the GUI family, he or she already knows much about how to operate the new application. Thus, the time required to learn a new product is much reduced. Also, the operation of programs that have a standard user interface results in fewer errors.

A fifth advantage of applications designed to run under GUI environments is that nontext graphics can be processed with them. The user can employ the mouse to draw lines and figures and to make graphical annotations. This capability is essential for applications like DTP and more sophisticated word processing programs.

A final advantage of GUI environments is that they are attractive. This may seem silly, but to the person who sits in front of a computer all day, a visually appealing interface is a great boon. Again, compare and contrast the two interfaces in Figure 6-9. Advantages of a GUI interface are summarized in Figure 6-12.

Figure 6-11 Facilities Provided by the GUI

Every element of this screen display is provided by program instructions that are modules of the GUI. As a result, program user interfaces are highly standardized, each programmer does not have to create the displays all over again, and the user faces a very consistent environment from one program to another.

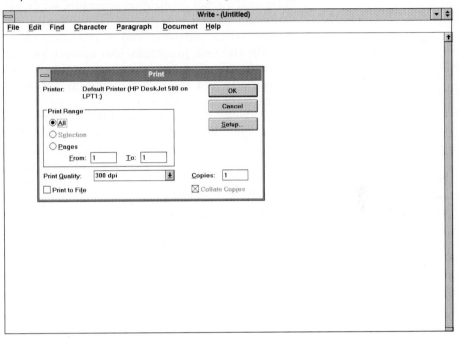

Figure 6-12 Advantages of Today's GUI Applications

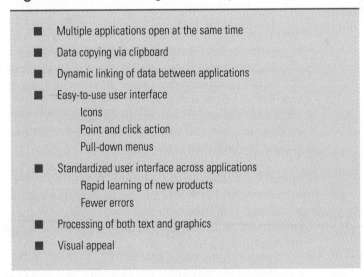

- Multiple applications open at the same time
- Data copying via clipboard
- Dynamic linking of data between applications
- Easy-to-use user interface
  - Icons
  - Point and click action
  - Pull-down menus
- Standardized user interface across applications
  - Rapid learning of new products
  - Fewer errors
- Processing of both text and graphics
- Visual appeal

Horizontal Market Application Programs

The second category of programs used in personal information systems is **horizontal market application programs**, which cut horizontally across industry types and include programs for communications such as word processing programs, DTP programs, and graphics and presentation programs. They also include analysis programs like spreadsheet applications and statistical and operations research programs. Finally, they include programs used for tracking and monitoring, such as database management and project management applications.

Although the capabilities of these programs are not further described here, several general observations are appropriate. First, with the success of GUI environments, most vendors of non-GUI products are adapting their programs to this environment as quickly as they can. The days of non-GUI applications appear to be numbered. If you have a choice in products in your environment between a non-GUI program and a GUI program, the latter is the better bet if all other things are equal.

Second, when you decide to buy (meaning *license*, as you recall) a horizontal market program, adopt a long-term perspective. Your commitment extends far beyond the price you pay for the product. Over time, you will develop skills in using a particular product that will have definite value to you. If you have to change to another product, those skills may become useless, and you will need to take time to retrain yourself. And, as you use a product, you will develop a library of data files that will also have value to you. If you have to switch to another product, converting those files may be time-consuming, if, indeed, it is even possible.

Over time, program vendors continually upgrade programs, often offering the **upgrades** to registered users at a fraction of the full retail cost. Some upgrades are relatively minor, offering correction of problems that arise only rarely and compatibility with specific new hardware products. Others are relatively major, offering new capabilities and features that nearly every user may want. Minor upgrades are usually designated by a small increment in version number; for example, the difference between Windows Versions 2.0 and 2.03 was small to most users. Major upgrades are usually designated by a change in the integer part of the version number; the upgrade from Windows Version 2.03 to Version 3.0 was extremely significant to users.

Do not assume, however, that if the change in version number is small, you do not need to make the upgrade. Producing a new release is very expensive; a software publisher would not go through the expense for a small upgrade if the problems being fixed were not severe. You may make an exception, of course, if you know that the problem being fixed involves a function or feature that you do not need and will never use.

Major product upgrades (e.g., a change from version 2.x to 3.x) often involve a change in the product's file structure. For example, the file structure used by

PageMaker, Version 4.0, is different from that used by Version 3.0. Whenever you load a document created under Version 3.0 into Version 4.0, the program converts the document to the new format and saves it under a new name. This is fine as long as you realize that, once converted, the new file can no longer be read by Version 3.0.

In general, a personal information system user should budget for regular upgrades to key software packages. Most major packages are upgraded once a year or so. Unless you are in a hurry to obtain the specific features and functions of a major upgrade, it is generally a good idea to wait for several months before making the change. In the interim, watch the computer industry press to determine whether the new release has many bugs, errors, or problems. If so, save yourself trouble and wait for the subsequent minor correcting upgrade before making the conversion.

Sometimes you will hear that a particular version of a product is in **beta release.** This means that the new version has passed the vendor's internal testing and has been sent to selected customers for customer testing prior to release. During the beta phase, customers report problems they identify and the problems are corrected. The length of time between beta release and product release varies, depending on the number and severity of problems that the customers find.

Vertical Market Application Programs

Vertical market application programs are sold to a particular type of business or for a particular type of business function. For example, a program that specializes in marketing analysis for publicly owned hospitals is a vertical market program. The features and characteristics of such programs depend on the industry and the function they serve, and it is not possible to make general comments about their functionality.

There are general guidelines about licensing such programs, however. For one, vertical market programs are generally created by smaller companies that have less to invest in their development. When Lotus, WordPerfect, or Microsoft develop a product, you can be certain that it has received considerable resources and attention. It is also likely to be well tested before it is released.

The situation is very different for vertical market programs. Such a program may have been developed by an underfinanced company that is anxious to generate revenue as soon as possible. In such a case, the program may be released long before it is ready. Many, many users have found themselves having to help the vendor debug such programs, which is frustrating and time-consuming. It can also be embarrassing to be unable to complete a business task or a project because of the failure of a program.

Additionally, the long-term survival of many vertical market vendors is questionable. When dealing with such a vendor, ask for its history and size and for the number of users of its product. If the company is small, recognize that it may go out of business. If so, you may have to provide your own support or pay to correct errors in the product.

Custom-Developed Programs

The term *programming* is used in a restricted sense in most personal information systems. With the exception of database applications, few personal systems require that programs be developed in the traditional sense of hiring professional programmers to build an application. More often, the user is creating macros or using application languages embedded within an application, such as a word processing programming language.

Macros Consider macros first. In Chapter 5, we described one way to create a macro, by using a macro recorder. Another way to create a macro is to write it by using a macro command language. An example of such a macro for a spreadsheet is shown in Figure 6-13. The left-hand column contains macro commands, and the right-hand column has comments about the macro instructions.[2]

Figure 6-13 Spreadsheet Macro
This macro averages a series of numbers entered by the user.

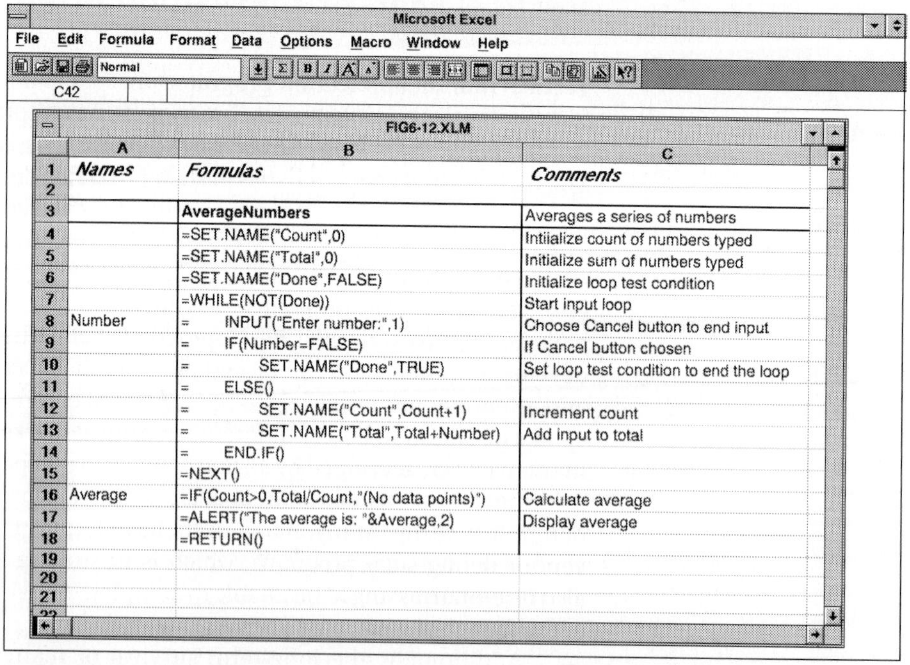

	A	B	C
1	*Names*	*Formulas*	*Comments*
2			
3		**AverageNumbers**	Averages a series of numbers
4		=SET.NAME("Count",0)	Intiialize count of numbers typed
5		=SET.NAME("Total",0)	Initialize sum of numbers typed
6		=SET.NAME("Done",FALSE)	Initialize loop test condition
7		=WHILE(NOT(Done))	Start input loop
8	Number	= INPUT("Enter number:",1)	Choose Cancel button to end input
9		= IF(Number=FALSE)	If Cancel button chosen
10		= SET.NAME("Done",TRUE)	Set loop test condition to end the loop
11		= ELSE()	
12		= SET.NAME("Count",Count+1)	Increment count
13		= SET.NAME("Total",Total+Number)	Add input to total
14		= END.IF()	
15		=NEXT()	
16	Average	=IF(Count>0,Total/Count,"(No data points)")	Calculate average
17		=ALERT("The average is: "&Average,2)	Display average
18		=RETURN()	
19			
20			
21			

2. See *Microsoft Excel Ver. 4.0: User's Guide 2.* Redmond, WA: Microsoft Corporation, 1992.

To write a macro, the user must know the macro language of the product that is used and must also be familiar with elementary programming concepts. General principles of programming apply to macros as well as to more traditional computer programs.

Personal Application Languages   Some word processing applications now include complete programming **application languages.** Figure 6-14 shows a WordBasic program to ask the user whether an author's name should be included in the footer at the bottom of each document page, and, if so, to create such a footer. The first part of the program prepares and displays a dialog box (MsgBox) in the standard style of Windows. The dialog box asks the user to respond with Yes (which will be represented as –1 by the program) or No (which will be represented as 0). If the answer is Yes (–1), then the program accesses the storage place for footer text and enters the author's name (previously defined). Otherwise, the program reassures the user that no author-name footer has been entered.[3]

Versions of the BASIC programming language are increasingly provided as application languages with horizontal market programs.

Figure 6-14   WordBasic Program
This program is written in the programming language supplied with Microsoft Word for Windows.

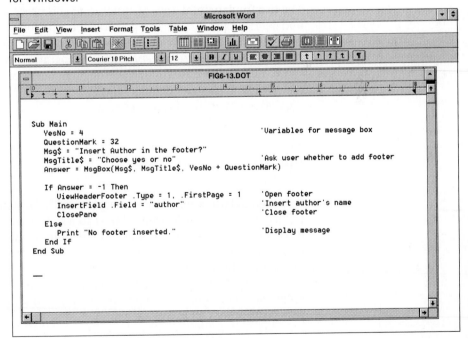

---

3. See *Microsoft WordBasic: Using WordBasic.* Redmond, WA: Microsoft Corporation, 1991.

Database Application Programs The final type of custom-developed programs that occur with personal information systems is comprised of application programs that process a database. These programs require the most knowledge and skill of any type, and they typically are not written by the end user, but by professional programmers.

Most personal DBMS products allow for three types of programming languages. First, the DBMS typically provides a language of its own. Borland's Paradox, for example, includes a language called Paradox Application Language (PAL). Second, many DBMSs can process the SQL language. Finally, DBMS products usually provide interfaces for programs written in standard programming languages such as BASIC, C, or COBOL.

In any case, programs require the skills of a professional. If the users' needs can be met by using the DBMS's normal commands without programming or by licensing vertical market programs, then no additional application programs will be necessary. Needless to say, this is quicker and cheaper.

DATA

The two fundamental ways of structuring and processing data are file processing and database processing. In a personal information system, the data processed by the OS and many horizontal market programs is processed in files. Thus, word processors, DTP programs, spreadsheet programs, project managers, and the like all process data in files. DBMSs, on the other hand, process data in databases.

Vertical market programs vary. Some include a DBMS and store their data as databases. Others use file processing.

File-Processing Data

For nondatabase applications, the personal information systems user has little influence over, and little need to know about, the structure of the applications files he or she uses. It is, for example, entirely unimportant to a DTP program user to know how the documents and text are stored in files. All the user needs to know is the name of the file and where it is located.

Several principles of data administration are important to the user. The following sections illustrate these principles with MS-DOS; the principles pertain to users of other OSs as well.

File Names and Extensions In MS-DOS, **file names** consist of a series of up to 8 characters followed by a period, then a **file extension** of 1 to 3 characters. The general format is NNNNNNNN.EEE, where *N* represents a character in the file's name and *EEE* represents the file's extension.

To identify the program that created a file, many horizontal applications provide standard file extensions. PageMaker, for example, applies the file extension *pm4* to all document files created by PageMaker, Version 4.0, and it applies the file extension *pm3* to all such files created by Version 3.0. Thus, if you encounter a file with the name *M122591.pm4,* you know that the file probably was created by PageMaker 4.0.[4] Figure 6-15 shows some standard file extensions used by applications running under MS-DOS and Windows.

Some applications do not provide such file extensions. For example, XyWrite does not append any extension to the files it saves. For such programs, it is good practice to develop a standard extension of your own so that you know which program created the file. Also, observe in Figure 6-15 that the extensions are not unique. For example, the extension *.doc* is used by both MultiMate and Word for Windows. If you were using both products, it would be good practice to consistently substitute a different extension for one of them.

The first 8 characters of the file name are usually left for the user to determine. It is good practice to develop your own standards for this part of the file name. For example, you might decide to prefix all word processing letters with the letter *L* followed by the date of the letter. The file name L121192.doc would then represent the letter you saved on 11 December 1992 using either Word for Windows or MultiMate. Similarly, you could decide to prefix all memos with the letter *M,* and so forth.

File Directories All OSs discussed in this chapter support hierarchical **file directories.** This means that files can be grouped in clusters arranged hierarchically, like a family tree. For example, Figure 6-16 shows a hierarchy used by LuAnne Price at Legacy Systems for one of her disk volumes—*E:.*

LuAnne has four major directories. As shown from left to right, they contain Lotus 1-2-3 programs, text-processing programs, trade show plan data files, and trade show newsletter data files, respectively. Two of these directories have subdirectories. The first, E:\TEXT, contains the subdirectory E:\TEXT\WP—which holds LuAnne's word processing programs—and the subdirectory E:\TEXT\PM— which holds her DTP programs. The second, E:\TSPLAN, contains the subdirectories E:\TSPLAN\PLAN92 and E:\TSPLAN\PLAN93 that have, respectively, the 1992 plan data and the 1993 plan data.

---

4. The word *probably* is used because nothing prevents a user from giving a non-PageMaker file the extension *.pm4.* This would be bad practice, however. Most horizontal market products append the standard extension by default, but the user can override the default, usually creating confusion later.

Figure 6-15 Typical File Extensions for MS-DOS and Windows Applications

Extension	Product	Description
bmp	Paintbrush	Bitmap
cal	Calendar	Data
cbt	Many products	Computer-based training data file
crd	Cardfile	Data
db	Paradox	Database file
dbf	dBASE	Database file
doc	Word for Windows	Document
doc	MultiMate	Document
dot	Word for Windows	Document template
dll	Windows 3.0	Dynamic link library
pcx	Paintbrush	Data
pm3	PageMaker 3.0	Data for version 3.0
pt3	PageMaker 3.0	Template for version 3.0
pm4	PageMaker 4.0	Data for version 4.0
pt4	PageMaker 4.0	Template for version 4.0
rbf	R:base	Database file
txt	Notepad	Data
wk1	Lotus 1-2-3	Spreadsheet
wri	Write	Document
xls	Excel	Spreadsheet
xlc	Excel	Chart
xlm	Excel	Macro

LuAnne has separated her program files from her data files. In general, this is a good idea. If she does not do this and if the data files are intermingled with program files, the directories will soon become very confused. In LuAnne's case, every spreadsheet file, for every project with which she has been involved, would be intermingled with her Lotus 1-2-3 files. This would be difficult to administer.

As LuAnne has arranged her directories, all of the files for the 1994 trade show plan will be found in one directory. LuAnne will use the extensions to the files to determine which program created them. Thus, if she finds a file *P121191.wk1*

Figure 6-16 File Directory Arrangement

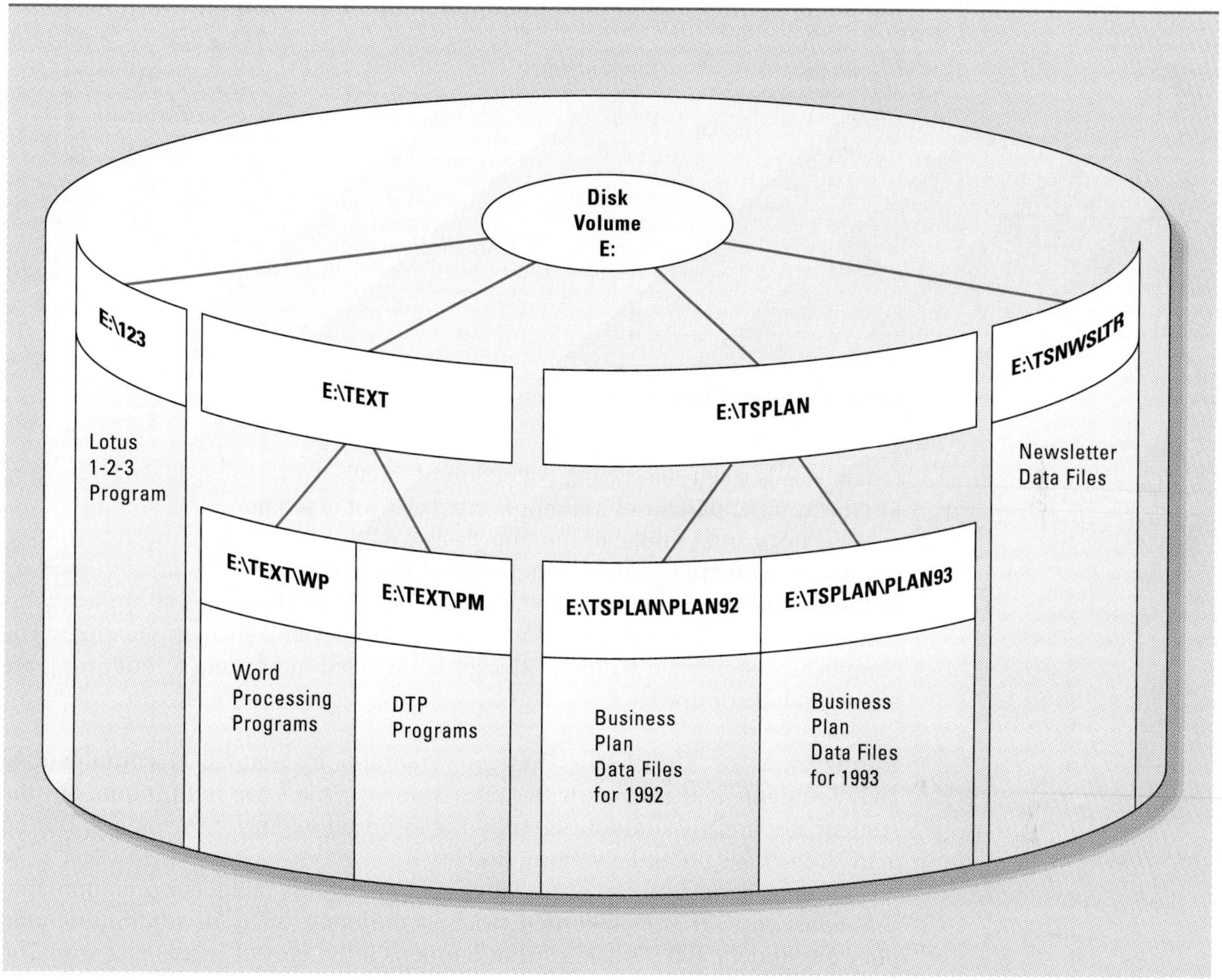

in the directory E:\TSPLAN\PLAN94, she will know that it is a Lotus 1-2-3 spreadsheet she created on 11 December 1993. The fact that it appears in the PLAN94 directory tells her it is associated with that plan.

Careful planning of directories saves considerable confusion, errors, and reworking. It may not seem too important to you as a student, but if you become a frequent user of personal information systems in your job, you will find that quickly generating many files can become a confusing morass. The easiest way to solve this problem is to avoid it by careful planning at the onset.

Figure 6-17   Sample Data for the STUACT Table

StudentID	StudentName	ActivityName	ActivityCost
100	Baker	Skiing	$ 700
200	Charles	Scuba	$ 500
300	Jones	Tennis	$ 150
400	Baker	Tennis	$ 150

Database Data

A database is a self-describing collection of integrated records, as we have seen. Microcomputer databases are represented as a set of tables.

In horizontal applications, the design of the files is fixed by the vendor, but in database applications, the design of the tables and other structures is up to the user or developer. This means that, for all but the simplest applications, database design skill and expertise is required to develop such applications. The complicated subject of database design is surveyed in Module A. Following are a few general comments.

Importance of Database Design   The table in Figure 6-17 contains data about students and their activities. The student names are not unique, but the student IDs are. In addition, a student can enroll in only one activity, but an activity can have potentially many students.

Several problems can occur when processing this table. For one, note that the tennis cost, $150, is recorded twice in the table: once for student 300 and once for student 400. Consider what happens if the cost of tennis changes. The application will have to find every row in which tennis occurs and change its cost value appropriately. Also, suppose that student 200 decides to drop out of school. If you remove this row from the table, you will lose the fact that scuba costs $500. Finally, for this table, how would you enter the cost for a new activity, say volleyball? Until a student actually enrolls in the activity, you have no way of recording its cost.

A better database design would result if you divide this single table into two tables, as shown in Figure 6-18. The two new tables avoid the preceding problems. If the cost for tennis changes, simply change the tennis row in the ACTIVITY table. If student 200 drops out of school, you do not lose the cost of scuba; and when a new activity is defined, you can enter its cost directly into the ACTIVITY table.

In general, in good database design, a table should have a single theme. The problem with the STUACT table in Figure 6-17 is that it contains data about two

Figure 6-18 Student Activities as Two Tables

STUDENT		
StudentID	**StudentName**	**StudentActivity**
100	Baker	Skiing
200	Charles	Scuba
300	Jones	Tennis
400	Baker	Tennis

ACTIVITY	
ActivityName	**ActivityCost**
Skiing	$ 700
Scuba	$ 500
Tennis	$ 150

themes: students and activities. Fewer problems will result if the table is broken into two tables, one about students and one about activities, as shown in Figure 6-18.

The process just described, called **normalization**, is important in the design of databases. You will learn more about this process in Module A. You may also take a database course after you complete your MIS course. For now, just be aware that the developer of a database application has important tasks in database design.

Database Files DBMS products manage their OS files in two ways. In one, each table is carried in a separate OS file. In the other, all of the database tables are carried within one or two files, making for easier data administration.

For example, the R:base DBMS creates three OS files for every database: one containing the description of the database; another containing the user's data; and still another containing indexes and other overhead structures. If the database contains 1 table, there will still be 3 OS files. If the database contains 100 tables, there will still be 3 OS files.

In the dBase DBMS, each table is carried in a separate MS-DOS file. Thus, if there is only 1 table, there will be only 1 OS file for that table. (Other files probably exist, but that discussion is beyond the scope of this text.) If there are 100 tables, then there will be 100 OS files.

The danger in the second approach is that files from separate databases may become intermingled. For example, suppose that files from three large databases are all stored in the same directory. If the user wants to move one of the databases to another directory, or even to another computer, it will be laborious to identify and copy all of the files. With the former approach, only nine files will exist in the directory for the three databases, and it will be easy to identify the appropriate files.

PEOPLE

So far this chapter has considered three of the five components of a personal information system: *computers* follow instructions in *programs* to process *data.* These components exist because they add value to an individual. On the individual's side of the information system are *people* who follow instructions in *procedures* to obtain the value they want.

People, like hardware, are active members of the information system. People take actions to cause the system to process input data, produce results, or respond in some other way. This section defines the classic roles of people in an information system and then shows how those roles pertain to a personal information system. We will also present basic categories of procedures.

Clientele

Systems **clientele** are the ultimate beneficiaries of the system. Although the system exists to serve them, they are not generally part of the operation of the system. The salespeople at the trade show are the clientele of LuAnne's scheduling system. In the long run, however, the clientele dictate the character of the information system, even though in the short run, they do not influence its behavior other than to make requests for service.

Users

Users employ the information system during the course of their officially designated work. Users key in data, make requests for system action, and serve as the liaison between the system and its clientele. LuAnne is the user of all her information systems.

In some cases, particularly with personal computer applications, one person plays the role of both clientele and user. LuAnne, for example, uses her system to prepare a roster of attendees. (In this task, she is in the user role, since preparing the roster is one of her duties as trade show manager.) She also checks the roster when she wants to communicate with someone. (Here she is in the clientele role; she is using the product of the trade show manager.)

The distinction between clientele and user becomes more important with larger enterprise applications. For instance, consider an airline reservation system whose clientele include people who want to reserve space on certain flights. The users are employees of the airlines or the travel agencies who interface with the reservation system. The clientele speak with the users; the users interact with the system via their computer terminals. The users interpret the output from the system on behalf of the clientele.

Operations Personnel

The duties of **operations personnel** are running the computer hardware, starting and stopping programs, and managing removable data storage. Operations personnel also perform certain types of routine equipment maintenance. The knowledge and experience of operations personnel vary across a wide spectrum. At one end of the spectrum are the professionally trained staff that support an enterprise computer center. These people typically have some college education but not necessarily a four-year degree. They also have additional training specific to the equipment they are operating and to the systems they run.

At the other end of the spectrum are personal information systems, where end users serve as their own operations personnel. These people generally have little or no operations training and usually are professionals in a discipline far removed from data processing. Workgroup computing systems fall between these extremes. Often one or two members of the workgroup receive some training in computer operations, and those members perform as operators as an official part of their job description.

Consider LuAnne Price again. At the trade show, she serves as her own computer operator. She sets up the equipment, ensures that it is operating correctly, installs any necessary programs and data, and runs her applications. She may also perform routine maintenance such as changing the printer's toner cartridge.

Systems Development Personnel

Systems development personnel build the information system. The two common job descriptions within this category are systems analyst and programmer. **Systems analysts** are concerned with the development of all five components of the information system. They work with users and clientele to determine the features and functions required of the system. They evaluate alternatives and participate in designing and constructing all parts of the system.

Programmers design, develop, and test computer programs. They also participate in designing and developing the data component. Programmers are less concerned with the development of system requirements.

The job of a systems analyst is like that of a consultant and includes substantial interaction with people in the user community. Programming tends to be more of a technical job having far more interaction with computers than with people. In some organizations, the two jobs are combined into the position of a programmer/analyst, who is concerned with all five components.

Typically, the users of personal information systems come into contact with systems development personnel in one of several ways. For example, at the time a system is purchased, the computer dealer may provide certain development services or a number of labor hours of system development time as part of the purchase agreement. Similarly, VARs provide technical expertise, either as part of their package or at extra cost. In addition, many personal information system users also employ consultants from time to time. Finally, in a larger organization, the MIS department often dedicates certain employees as technical consultants to assist personal information system users.

As with the clientele and operations roles, users can also serve as systems developers themselves. This role, however, requires considerable expertise, and the user who embarks upon it should have a burning interest in computer technology and a lot of time. As a general rule, it is better to leave systems development to those who make it their profession.

PROCEDURES

The final component of an information system is procedures. Procedures are instructions for people, just as programs are instructions for computers. Unfortunately, procedures have often been the poor stepchild of information systems, sometimes overlooked entirely until confusion, inefficiency, or disaster occur. Other times they are an afterthought: "Oh, by the way, we'd better write up some instructions for the users."

Procedures should be considered throughout the systems development process. Although the creation of procedures may not require as much time as the development of programs, this fact should not cause them to receive less priority. The actions of the humans in the system are at least as important as (if not more important than) the actions of the computer hardware.

Figure 6-19 summarizes the categories of procedures that need to be developed for all types of MISs—personal, workgroup, and enterprise. As shown

Figure 6-19 Categories of Procedures

	Normal Processing	Failure-Recovery Processing
Use		
Operations		

in the columns of this figure, there must be procedures for both normal operations and failure-recovery operations. Additionally, there must be procedures both for users and for system operators.

Since, in personal information systems, users serve as their own operators, the two types of procedures overlap. Thus, in this chapter, we consider just the procedures for normal processing and procedures for failure-recovery processing.

Procedures for Normal Processing

Users must have **procedures for normal processing** that direct them on how to obtain the results they need to succeed in their jobs in a timely, controlled fashion. Users must know how to start their computer and related hardware, how to initiate programs and submit requests for work, how to interact with computer programs, and how to interpret error messages that are generated.

All computer programs today should be accompanied by thorough, well-written, and easy-to-understand documentation. Most horizontal application programs have at least three types of such documentation. **Tutorials** gradually lead the new user through examples of the program's capabilities. A well-written tutorial usually involves demonstration programs as well. A **user manual** documents how to accomplish common tasks, such as how to produce a report in a word processing program or how to create a graph in a spreadsheet. A user manual is task oriented. A **reference manual** provides more in-depth and technical descriptions of the program's commands, capabilities, functions, and the like. Example entries may include how to use the Save As command or what entries you must make to use the Zoom feature. A reference manual is feature oriented. High-quality documentation is crucial and should be one of the criteria for selecting programs.

In addition to information about the programs, users need procedures for operations activities. Such procedures concern the maintenance of system components. They include instructions for setting up of the hardware, installing programs and data files, and performing basic equipment maintenance such as changing printer ribbons, cleaning in and around equipment, and so forth. Procedures should also describe how to manage data files on disk devices.

One of the most important user procedures is that concerning **security**. Users need to know how to protect their data from accidental or intentional loss or theft. They also need to be informed about the security facilities of their system, which may include physical keys for locking the computer, passwords, and account numbers. There are a number of other alternatives, depending on the application in use.

Procedures for Failure Recovery

No matter how well designed and well constructed they are, all information systems fail at one time or another. Any of the five components can fail: The hardware can malfunction; programs may have bugs, or errors; data can be lost; procedures can be misunderstood and misapplied; and people can make mistakes. The time to consider such possibilities is well before the failure, not when the failure has just occurred. **Procedures for failure-recovery processing** specify what to do when the system fails and how to proceed once the system is recovered.

First, users must know how to detect that a failure has occurred. Obviously, if the computer screen goes blank and the keyboard is dead, a problem has occurred. Other types of problems are less obvious. Users need to be able to identify both normal behavior and abnormal behavior for the system.

When a failure does occur, a user needs to know, first, how to bring activity to a halt. For example, if a user accidentally deletes a file, it is possible to recover that file, *providing that no other file processing is done prior to the recovery attempt.* Thus, the user of a personal computer system needs a procedure stipulating that the user should either cease processing when he or she accidentally deletes a file and call whomever supports him or her for assistance or initiate file recovery for him- or herself.

Next, the user needs to know how to proceed in order to identify and fix the problem. In many cases, this is a matter of knowing whom to call. Users should have lists of specialists' names and telephone numbers. Furthermore, users need to know what are fair expectations in terms of response time and costs. Depending on the circumstances, considerable money may be saved by taking the microcomputer to the repair facility rather than requesting on-site service.

In operations, users need to anticipate failure. Backups of the data need to be made regularly. Additionally, some record of the work load processed since a backup must be kept so that, during recovery, the files can be restored from the backup data and then the work load can be reprocessed (or recovered in an equivalent way).

Procedures must exist not only for making the backup copies, but also for performing the recovery. During a failure, time is critical and the pressure may be intense (as with LuAnne Price on the floor of the trade show). It is important that the recovery be done once and done correctly. An actual failure is hardly the time to begin thinking about what to do.

SUMMARY

The five components of an information system are hardware, programs, data, procedures, and people. Personal information systems use either personal computers or workstations as the basis for the hardware component. Personal computer types are tower configuration, desktop, laptop, and pen-based tablet models. Two families of personal computers are common: the IBM PC and PC-compatible family and the Apple Macintosh family. Workstations are higher-performance microcomputer systems than either of the two families, with larger, higher-quality displays. They are commonly used in engineering.

Personal computers contain a microprocessor chip. The Intel family of 8088, 80286, 80386, 80486, and Pentium is used for the IBM PC and PC-compatible personal computers. The Motorola family of 68000 microprocessors is used for the Macintosh family. When buying a personal computer, you need to specify the family of computer, the type and speed of processor, the amount of memory, and the brand of computer. You also need to consider the number of slots, if you will have much special-purpose equipment.

Input and output equipment for most personal information systems consists of keyboard, display, and printer. Computer displays vary in size, color, and resolution. Both dot matrix printers and laser printers are used in personal information systems. Laser printers can print a variety of fonts and font sizes, and they can also produce graphics. PostScript is a powerful printer language used by the microprocessors found in laser printers.

Both diskettes and hard disks are used in personal computer systems. Diskettes hold up to 1.4 megabytes of data. Hard disks store up to 1 gigabyte of data or more. Disk technology is rapidly evolving, and these numbers are likely to increase dramatically.

Optical disks are used in multimedia applications, for which vendors are currently developing standards.

Programs used in personal information systems include systems, horizontal market, vertical market, and custom-developed programs. Four major OSs are used in personal systems: MS-DOS (by far the most popular), Macintosh OS, OS/2, and UNIX. MS-DOS can address up to only 640KB of memory; this limitation gave rise to expanded and extended memory.

At the time of its introduction, the Macintosh OS was exceedingly innovative, providing the first commercially successful GUI environment. That OS was also innovative in its structure and programming interface. OS/2 developed in popularity only slowly, but its current version has been quite successful. UNIX, developed at Bell Labs, has been used mostly by scientists and engineers and is the most popular OS on workstations. Since a new, easy-to-use GUI interface has been developed for UNIX, this OS may become more popular with business users.

Windows, an add-on program that runs with MS-DOS, provides a GUI for DOS. X-Windows is a set of standards for a UNIX GUI.

Today's GUI environments provide a number of advantages. Multiple applications can be open at the same time; data can be shared across applications via the clipboard; and the interface is easy to use, with icons, pull-down menus, and point and click capability. Also, applications written under a GUI environment can have a standard user interface, which reduces learning time and errors. Other advantages are that GUI systems allow for the processing of graphical data, and the systems themselves are visually appealing. They are likely to become the standard interface to personal computers.

Among horizontal market applications, GUI applications are preferred. You should adopt a long-term perspective when acquiring a horizontal market product. It is a good idea to license upgrades as they become available.

Vertical market application programs are usually provided by smaller companies, and the buyer should beware. The product may not be very well tested, and the economic viability of many vertical market vendors is questionable.

Custom-developed programs for personal systems do not usually involve the hiring of a professional programmer. Usually, this term refers to the generation of macros or programs within applications. Macros can be created using a macro recorder, or they can be programmed.

Database application programs are the one case in which a personal information system may require the services of a professional programmer. Such programs can be written in languages specific to the DBMS product, in SQL, or in standard programming languages such as BASIC, C, or COBOL.

The two fundamental ways of processing data are file processing and database processing. The OS and all horizontal market programs use file processing. Vertical market programs can use either file processing or database processing.

For nondatabase applications, the personal information system user has little influence over or need to know about the internal structure of the files. The user should observe and follow file-naming conventions established by vendors. Also, the user should develop personal naming conventions to be able to quickly identify file contents.

The user should establish some specific pattern for hard disk file directories. In general, it is best to group programs into directories of their own and data files into directories for specific projects. By following the file-naming conventions, the identity of the program that created the file can be determined from the file name.

A database is a self-describing collection of integrated records. The design of the database is determined by the users or the database developer. In general, in a well-designed database, each table has a single theme. Tables that have more than one theme should be broken up in a process called normalization. DBMS products vary in the way they store files. Some products store each table in an OS file of its own. Others store all of the tables in a few OS files, which provides easier data administration.

Four basic roles are played by people in information systems. Clientele are the ultimate beneficiaries of the system. Users directly employ the system to accomplish tasks in their job. Operations personnel run the equipment and related facilities. Systems development personnel create and maintain information systems. For personal information systems, one person often fulfills the roles of clientele, user, and operations personnel. Sometimes users also act as their own systems developers.

Procedures are instructions for people and are as important as programs are to hardware. The four categories of procedures are: normal procedures for users, normal procedures for operations personnel, failure-recovery procedures for users, and failure-recovery procedures for operations personnel. Since most personal MIS users serve as their own operators, procedures for such systems can be divided into normal and failure-recovery procedures.

KEY TERMS

Microcomputer	Slot	Upgrade
Personal computer	Adapter board	Beta release
Tower configuration	Keyboard	Vertical market
Desktop computer	Display	application program
Laptop computer	Resolution	Application language
Notebook computer	Pixel	File name
Tablet computer	Ergonomics	File extension
IBM PC, or PC	Dot matrix printer	File directory
PC-compatible	Laser printer	Normalization
Macintosh	PostScript	Clientele
PC clone	MIDI	User
Workstation	Synthesizer	Operations personnel
Engineering	GUI	Systems development
workstation	MS-DOS	personnel
Clock	PC-DOS	Systems analyst
Register	Expanded memory	Programmer
Control unit	Extended memory	Procedures for normal
Microprocessor	Icon	processing
Intel 8088, 80286,	Point and click interface	Tutorial
80386, 80486 and	Macintosh OS	User manual
Pentium	OS/2	Reference manual
microprocessor	UNIX	Security
family	Windows	Procedures for failure-
Motorola 68000	Clipboard	recovery processing
microprocessor	Horizontal market	
family	application program	

REVIEW QUESTIONS

1. Explain the differences among microcomputers, personal computers, and workstations.

2. Describe the characteristics of tower configuration, desktop, laptop, and tablet personal computers.

3. What are the two families of personal computers?

4. Define the terms *IBM PC, PC-compatible,* and *PC clone.*

5. What is a workstation?

6. Name the two major families of microprocessors.

7. What is an adapter board, and what is its purpose?

8. List the characteristics you need to specify when buying a personal computer.

9. What are the three most common types of personal computer input and output hardware?

10. What is a pixel, and how does it relate to display resolution?

11. List advantages of a printer programming language such as PostScript.

12. Name the two types of magnetic disk used with personal computer systems. What are the capacities of each?

13. What is an optical disk? What is its chief advantage?

14. What is a leading application for optical disk technology?

15. List the four major OS used with personal information systems.

16. Briefly summarize the origins of MS-DOS.

17. Describe the 640KB limitation of MS-DOS, and explain how expanded and extended memory relate to this limitation.

18. Explain why the Apple Macintosh OS was innovative when it was introduced.

19. Explain the use of icons and mice in the point and click interface.

20. What are the characteristics of OS/2?

21. Who have been the primary users of UNIX? What has been the major impediment for using UNIX in the business environment?

22. Summarize the advantages of today's GUIs.

23. Why is a standardized user interface advantageous?

24. Why should you adopt a long-term perspective when acquiring a horizontal market application?

25. Explain the difference between a product upgrade from release 3.01 to release 3.03 and a product upgrade from release 3.0 to release 4.0. What posture should you take with regard to each of these types of upgrade?

26. Explain why users should be cautious when acquiring vertical market application programs.

27. Explain how the term *programming* is used with regard to personal information systems.

28. Describe two ways of creating a macro.

29. Explain the role of a programming language provided as a feature of an application such as a word processor. What benefits does such a language provide?

30. Describe the three types of language that can be used with many DBMS products.

31. Explain how many applications use the file extension portion of a file name.

32. Why is it important for users to develop standards for naming their files?

33. Explain the technique recommended in this text for allocating files to file directories.

34. Describe three problems with the table shown in Figure 6-17.

35. Explain the process of normalization, and show an example other than the one in this chapter.

36. Why is it more convenient for the user if the DBMS product allocates all tables to a small number of OS files?

37. Describe four categories of information systems personnel. What are the functions of each? Which of these categories are combined in a personal information system?

38. Defend the assertion that procedures are more important than programs in information systems.

39. Name four fundamental types of procedures. How do these types pertain to procedures for personal information systems?

DISCUSSION QUESTIONS

1. A common misconception among businesspeople is that an information system consists of computers and programs only. Suppose someone who has this misconception embarks on a project to develop a personal database application. What problems and pitfalls are they likely to encounter? What important issues will they fail to address? When will they become aware of their misconception?

2. It has been said that the purpose of a personal information system is to transfer work from a human to a computer so that a job that a human accomplishes following procedures becomes a job that a computer accomplishes following programs. How does this statement pertain to LuAnne Price in Chapter 5? Do you think this is an accurate statement for her? Do you think it is an accurate statement in general?

3. Suppose you have a job that involves use of a spreadsheet program to prepare profit and loss statements for projects (similar to those that Sarah Morris prepared in Chapter 2). Your supervisor tells you that you are about to be promoted into a new job (which you have been seeking), but that, before the promotion will take effect, you will need to write good documentation of the procedures you follow. What topics should your documentation cover? How complete should it be? Outline that documentation. In general, when do you think such documentation should be written?

4. You have been working for weeks developing a set of spreadsheets for the annual departmental budget. You have developed a very sophisticated model and a number of exceptionally complete budgets. You have shown early versions of them to your boss, and she is delighted. As you begin to print the first page of the final output, you hear a screeching sound that seems to be coming from your hard disk drive. What do you do?

PROJECTS

A. Interview a business professional who uses a personal information system. Describe the hardware, programs, data, procedures, and people involved in the system. How was the system created? How successful has the system been? If the user could change the system in some way, how would she or he change it?

B. Define a specific need for a personal information system; for example, you might set out requirements for a system for your own use as a student or for your use in a work setting you describe. Specify the hardware components needed to meet that system's requirements. Consider both a system that would minimally meet requirements (and whose development is restricted by a tight budget) and a system that would better meet the requirements (due to a somewhat larger budget). Describe the difference in value and cost of the two systems.

C. For a particular personal information system that you specify, gather information to compare MS-DOS, MS-DOS with Windows, OS/2, Macintosh OS, and UNIX as possible OSs. What criteria should be applied, and what weight should be given to each? Investigate published information, and gather information from computer stores and users. Based on your criteria, explain the advantages and disadvantages of each potential OS.

D. Interview a salesperson at a local computer dealer. What kinds of personal information systems does that person sell? Which systems generate the most problems for the dealer? What kinds of problems are they? Do the problems relate to any of the five components in particular? If the salesperson could have three wishes regarding a change in customers' behavior, what would those three wishes be?

E. Using a personal DBMS, create STUDENT and ACTIVITY tables based on the sample data in Figure 6-18. Add at least 25 sample records to the STUDENT table, and add at least 5 sample records to the ACTIVITY table. At least one of the added activities should be selected by no students. When the tables are complete with sample data, generate sample reports. First, create a report showing the list of names of students who have selected each activity. (Also, for each activity, show a count of students selecting it.) Second, create a report showing the total income for each activity. (Also show the total income for all activities.) Specify and create samples of at least two additional reports that a user might find helpful.

M I N I C A S E

The Software Wars

The PC software industry is in the midst of a price war that has altered not only how software is valued but also how it is marketed, distributed, and supported—some say permanently.

The most obvious implication of the price war is that software programs, particularly business applications such as spreadsheets and word processors, have become commodities, subject to the same market pressures as cigarettes and compact discs. This means users, especially corporations and other volume purchasers, can negotiate wide-ranging, enterprise licensing deals at very attractive terms. Indeed, some wily users have licensed popular applications for as little as one-twentieth of the list price.

Microsoft fired The Shot Heard 'Round The Software Industry. Last fall, the software giant introduced a relational database product called Access at a limited-time introductory price of $99, compared with the industry-standard $700 price tag. When the offer expired and the dust had settled three months later, Microsoft had shipped more than 750,000 discounted copies of Access to resellers—a number roughly equivalent to the entire desktop database market up to that point, according to Kathleen Schoenfelder, Microsoft's Windows applications manager.

Other vendors were quick to react. Lotus announced that the Windows version of its next-generation spreadsheet product, Improv, would cost just $99. Asymmetrix Corp. introduced a new presentation graphics package called Compel, also for $99. Computer Associates International Inc. offered the upgrade for a new version of its desktop database technology, Clipper, at $149. And Borland reacted with a limited-time price of $199 for a bundle of its Quattro Pro spreadsheet and Paradox database.

Even though the suggested retail price of Microsoft's Access has returned to $495, some say the software landscape is permanently altered. "What we're rapidly coming to is a price point that says every application is going to be $99 on the desktop," says Matthew Cain, a software analyst with the Meta Group Inc. in Westport, Conn.

Confused? So are a lot of customers. Suggested retail prices "can bear little or no resemblance to actual selling price," says Eileen Rudden, VP of product marketing at Lotus. Tactics such as competitive upgrades, suite selling, and volume licensing are all ways to carry on a price war without lowering the list price—a fine line to tread. "Vendors are trying to dance around the price point without upsetting the apple cart of customers who pay full price," says Stephen Dukker, president of the Compudyne division of CompuUSA, a reseller in Addison, Texas.

The price war has been waged most aggressively in the corporate arena. PC software vendors have been pursuing corporate customers willing to standardize on their products with volume prices as low as 80% off the suggested retail price. ■

John Soat with Rob Kelly and Anthony Vecchione, excerpted from *InformationWeek*, May 3, 1993, pp. 38–44.

Discussion Questions

1. Summarize the results of the recent software price war, as described in this article.

2. As a software purchaser, what kinds of special pricing offers should you seek to obtain software as economically as possible?

3. Describe the advantages and disadvantages to software vendors of reduced software prices.

4. What categories of software are included in the price wars, and what categories are not included?

7

Developing Personal Information Systems

THIS CHAPTER INTRODUCES INFORMATION SYSTEMS DEVELOPMENT, beginning with a comparison of three different development processes. The text describes and discusses all three of these processes, but this chapter focuses on the first process, prototyping, the process most often used for developing personal information systems.

The chapter also describes the nature of the prototyping process, then defines and illustrates the activities undertaken to develop information systems with this process. Finally, it applies prototyping techniques to the development of communication and spreadsheet applications. Module A, which follows this chapter, illustrates the use of prototyping in the development of a personal database application.

SYSTEMS DEVELOPMENT PROCESSES

Suppose you held the job of LuAnne Price (the trade show manager for Legacy Systems whose work was discussed in Chapter 5) but had no personal information systems. Suppose you knew that personal information systems could add value to your job. How would you proceed?

A time in your career probably will come when you will need to answer this question. You will know that you could do your job better if you were using an information system, but you will not necessarily know how to proceed. How would you go about building your own personal information systems?

Styles of Systems Development

Over the years, a number of styles of successful systems development have evolved, which fall into the three major patterns summarized in Figure 7-1. Each style is a variation on the general problem-solving process described in Chapter 3 and summarized in Figure 7-1a.

Not all of the styles in Figure 7-1 are appropriate for developing personal information systems. They are introduced here and their domain of use is described. Then the focus will turn to one of the styles, prototyping, that is used when developing personal information systems.

Custom Programming   Figure 7-1b shows the problem-solving stages as they have been adapted to systems development in the classical **systems development life cycle (SDLC)**. This SDLC has been used for many years to develop systems that involve the creation of custom-developed programs. Observe that the implementation stage of the problem-solving process has been broken into three phases: design, programming, and installation.

The classical SDLC places most attention and priority on the program component of a system. In fact, as you can see, one stage of the process is named programming. This orientation to the programming component occurred because custom programming is so expensive, time-consuming, and risky that considerable attention needs to be devoted to it.

When developing custom programs, programmers must pay great attention to defining complete and accurate requirements. It is so expensive to change custom programs that the requirements must be known in as much detail as possible before programming begins. In fact, programmers adapted the carpenters' adage: measure twice and cut once.

Licensed Programs   Figure 7-1c shows a second version of the SDLC, which assumes that programs are *licensed* rather than custom-developed. Here,

Figure 7-1 Systems Development Processes

(a) Stages in general problem-solving process; **(b)** classical SDLC (in-house custom program development); **(c)** SDLC (licensed programs); **(d)** SDLC (prototyping)

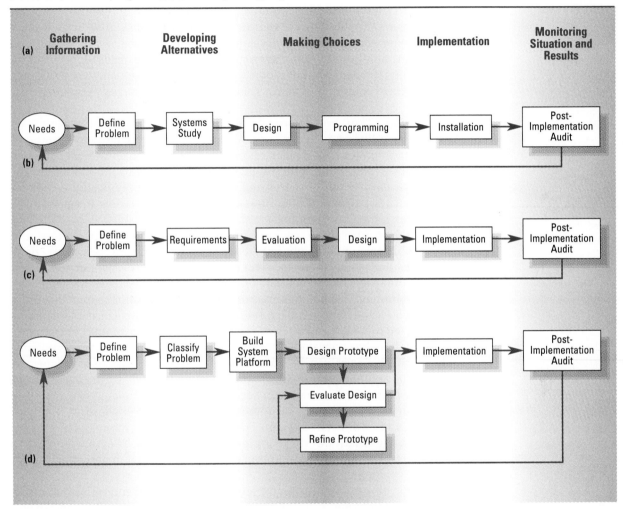

programming is not a separate stage; programming is included as one of the five components to be addressed in the design and implementation stages. Also, as shown in Figure 7-1c, a separate evaluation stage has been added.

This style of systems development emerged as program packages became prevalent and businesses could license application programs from vendors and adapt them to their needs. Because the cost of programming was amortized over all the customers of the package, such alternatives were much cheaper. Systems with licensed programs can also be developed more quickly since they need not be programmed from scratch.

When such licensed programs are used, requirements only need to be specified to a level that will allow an effective comparison and evaluation of the program package alternatives. Less detail is required here than with custom programming. Also, the focus in developing systems with licensed programs is on determining how best to adapt the programs to the unique needs of the business. One technique, called dataflow modeling, is particularly useful in this regard with workgroup and enterprise systems. This technique is considered in Chapter 10.

Prototyping   The third version of the SDLC process is summarized in Figure 7-1d. This version, called **prototyping**,[1] uses modern technology to develop a prototype of the application (or critical elements of it) very quickly. The prototypes are used and evaluated, and, in the process, additional requirements are identified. The prototype is then refined or redesigned, and the process is repeated until no new requirements are discovered and no further refinement seems necessary. The final version is then implemented.

As shown in Figure 7-1d, with prototyping, the problem is defined and classified. Then a system platform consisting of hardware, programs, data, procedures, and people is created. This platform is used to design the prototypes, which are evaluated, redesigned, and refined until the final system is implemented.

With prototyping, no attempt is made to obtain a complete and final list of requirements at the front end of the development process. Instead, it is understood and expected that many requirements will not become known until one or more prototypes have been developed and evaluated. Note that this strategy is possible only when prototypes can be quickly developed—which means developed by some method other than traditional programming.

Prototyping evolved naturally because, for most personal applications, the easiest way to determine the requirements is to use the application itself. For example, suppose you have the job of developing the Legacy Systems trade show newsletter. The easiest way to determine the requirements is not to write them in words, but rather to develop an example newsletter, show it to potential readers, and invite comments.

Prototyping can be used for personal, workgroup, and enterprise systems. In workgroup systems and enterprise systems, prototyping is typically used as a way of representing complex system requirements. A prototype in that setting is often a substitute for a long, detailed, sometimes rather boring narrative explaining the requirements. Rather than read the narrative, those responsible can actually

---

1. This term has been used in a number of different ways in the information systems industry. All of the different meanings, however, share the concept that part or all of the application is developed quickly, usually using tools other than traditional programming languages like COBOL. The meaning of the term *prototyping* developed in this chapter is consistent with the mainstream understanding of the term.

interact with the prototype as a way of understanding and improving the requirements definition.

Systems Development Processes in This Text

Figure 7-2 summarizes the use of these three styles of systems development today. Prototyping is the most frequent way of developing personal information systems. It is also used to help specify requirements for workgroup and enterprise information systems as just described. Since in personal systems prototyping is the primary method of development, we consider it in detail in this chapter. The case in Module A illustrates the importance of this process in developing database designs and applications.

The SDLC process for licensed programs is sometimes used for developing personal information systems. This usually occurs in developing systems that use vertical market applications. A stockbroker, for example, might have a choice of several different commercial packages for managing the portfolios of his or her customers. In this case, the broker would not use prototyping, but would use SDLC in its licensed program version.

SDLC for licensed programs is the most frequently used process for developing workgroup applications, and so we will discuss it in detail in Chapter 10. It is also frequently used in developing enterprise systems.

As shown in Figure 7-2, the classical, program-oriented SDLC is almost never used in developing personal applications. It is sometimes used for workgroup applications, especially in situations where custom-developed programs need to be written to integrate programs licensed from vendors. This third process is most frequently used for developing enterprise systems, and, again, most commonly for

Figure 7-2   Uses of the Three Styles of Systems Development

	Prototyping (Chapter 7)	SDLC for Licensed Programs (Chapter 10)	Classical SDLC (Chapter 13)
Personal MIS	Most frequently used	Sometimes used	Very rare
Workgroup MIS	Sometimes used to specify requirements	Most frequently used	Sometimes used for component integration
Enterprise MIS	Sometimes used to specify requirements	Frequently used	Frequently used for component integration

developing programs that integrate other program components. We will consider such systems development in Chapter 13.

The goal of all of these chapters is to teach you how to proceed when you see an opportunity to use information technology. Knowledge of each of these processes will help you know what to do, whether the opportunity is for a personal, workgroup, or enterprise system.

Your Role in Personal Information Systems Development

The role you play in the development of a personal information system can vary. You will most certainly be the primary, if not the only, user. You will probably also be part of the clientele and, likely, the sole operator. In addition, depending on both the complexity of the system to be developed and the personnel available to you, you may also be the developer. You may be the one to build the prototypes and revise the designs. Then again, you may have the assistance of personnel from your corporation's MIS department or that of a paid consultant.

Some user departments have one or more individuals who are knowledgeable about both the business domain and the information technology. You may receive assistance from this type of person as well.

This chapter assumes that you will be the primary developer. This is not always recommended. Certainly, if you have professionals you can call upon, do so. On the other hand, there are many types of systems that you should be able to develop yourself. One of your lessons from this chapter should be a sense of when to develop the system yourself and when to call in a professional.

PERSONAL INFORMATION SYSTEM DEVELOPMENT WITH PROTOTYPING

Figure 7-3 lists the stages to be accomplished when using prototyping to develop a personal information system. First, the problem needs to be defined. As you will see, the goal here is to be certain that the problem is correctly understood and that a computer-based information system is a feasible alternative. A plan is also created in this stage.

Next, the problem solution is classified. The type of application and its size, constraints, and future use all need to be determined. This information is then used in the third stage, in which the systems platform is created. The platform will

Figure 7-3 Stages in Developing Personal
Information Systems with Prototyping

1. **Define Problem**
   Define problem statement
   Assess feasibility
   Create a project plan

2. **Classify Solution**
   Determine type
   Determine size
   Determine constraints
   Determine future use

3. **Create Systems Platform**
   Specify programs
   Specify hardware
   Specify data
   Describe procedures
   Identify people

4. **Design Application**
   Develop initial design
   Evaluate design
   Redesign

5. **Implement System**
   Produce results
   Document system

be used first to build the prototypes. Later, for personal information systems, it will become the basis for the operational information system.

With the system development platform in place, the application design is created. As stated, this will be an iterative process, in which an initial set of requirements is used to develop the first design. That design is then evaluated, refinements and additional requirements are suggested, and a second design is developed. This process is repeated until no more refinements or requirements are obtained.

In the last stage, the system is implemented. The meaning of implementation for prototyping is considerably different from its meaning for other types of systems development. In many ways, especially when users are their own developers, the system has been already implemented. The final result, or last prototype, is produced and documented.

This section summarizes each of these stages, then illustrates the use of the SDLC process in developing communication and spreadsheet applications. Database applications are discussed in Module A.

Defining the Problem

Figure 7-4 summarizes the major tasks during the first stage of systems development—*problem definition*. First, you need to define the problem. This may sound innocuous and obvious, yet, time after time, people either forget to do it or think they can pinpoint the problem when, in fact, they are pinpointing a symptom of the problem.

Problem Statement Definition   One useful definition of the word *problem* is: a perceived difference between what is and what ought to be. There are three parts to this definition. First, a problem is a perception, something that one or

Figure 7-4   Major Tasks in the Problem Definition Stage

- **Define Problem Statement**
    A distinction between
        what is and
        what should be

- **Assess Feasibility**
    Cost
    Schedule
    Technology
    Political environment

- **Create a Project Plan**
    Stages and tasks
    Personnel required
    Costs
    Schedule

more people believe to be true. Since it is a perception, however, the danger always exists that what one person perceives is entirely different from what another person perceives. Many times an information system has been developed to solve a problem that was perceived by one person involved but not by others. The developer waits for applause, but gets criticism instead.

For example, before the next trade show, LuAnne Price's boss says: "LuAnne, we've got to get coordinated at the show. Nobody knows what's going on. Last year, if Frank had known about my meeting with Ajax, he would have countered its plan to buy from two vendors, and we could have had another $30,000 in sales. Somehow, we've got to get our act together."

The boss has just described his perception of the problem. It is tempting to conclude that his perception is the problem, but it may not be. Perhaps the problem is not that Frank did not know about the meeting. It may have been

Figure 7-5 An Important Part of Problem Definition Is Gathering Information
Since various individuals perceive a problem differently, it is often useful to get several viewpoints before settling on a final problem definition.

that Frank was too busy to attend it or that he missed it for some other reason. LuAnne could spend a lot of time developing a system to keep people better informed, only to find out that no change in process occurs because the people were already informed.

Knowledge of information technology is important, but it comes with a risk. When we know how to use and develop a certain type of information system, we become biased toward perceiving problems that can be solved by that type of system. In other words, a person who knows how to use a hammer may begin to see every problem as a nail that needs pounding. Realizing that tendency, we must be careful in the problem definition stage. We need to take time to fully understand the problem before leaping into the technology solutions that immediately come to mind.

A problem is a perceived difference between what is and what ought to be. LuAnne has heard her boss's description of his perception of the problem. Before doing anything, LuAnne would be wise to check with other members of the trade show staff to determine how they perceive the problem. She may (1) receive confirmation of her boss's statements, (2) learn more about the problem described by her boss, or (3) learn about some entirely different problem.

The second element of problem definition concerns *what is*. To define the problem, we must know the current situation. It is so tempting to assume that we already know the current situation; after all, LuAnne was at last year's trade show, too. As the center of the trade show staff, however, LuAnne had an entirely different experience from other members. She always knew what was happening because she was the primary coordinator. Her experience of what is varies considerably from other people's.

Finally, a problem concerns *what should be*. Here it is tempting to provide vague statements using phrases like "improved communication" and "better coordination," but what do these phrases mean? We must be more specific. Ask yourself the following questions: How will I know when I have it? What measures of success will there be? If you cannot answer those questions, then stop. You do not yet know what should be.

In short, when defining the problem, state what is and what should be, and realize that many perspectives need to be considered. In your statements, use concrete examples as much as possible. Then verify your problem statement with the important people in your business life. If the assignment came from your boss, check it out with him or her. If colleagues, co-workers, or subordinates are important to the problem, check it out with them.

You may think that such an attitude borders on insubordination. Certainly, if carried to an extreme, it might. In some measure, however, your boss expects you to do some of his or her thinking. Bosses often give incomplete, vague, and imprecise assignments. The important point is for you to understand the problem before going very far. Admiral Grace Hopper, a pioneer in information systems, has warned us that we should do nothing until we know what it is we are supposed to do.

The Legacy Trade Show Communication Problem   LuAnne considered the problem her boss had described and decided to investigate further. She spoke with others, including Frank, the one who had not known about the boss's meeting with Ajax. She found that there were several dimensions to the trade show communication problem. The major issues were as follows:

The booth duty schedule changes often as staff members trade responsi–bilities. For example, as the recent show progressed and the Legacy employees made appointments with employees of other companies, they traded booth duties. Over time, the official schedule became out of date and no one knew for certain who would be working and at what time. In the confusion, the booth was actually overstaffed, unnecessarily keeping people from other activities.

Communication about meetings set up at the show is poor. People do find out, after the fact, that they missed meetings they should have attended.

The staff would like to see important and newsworthy exhibits by customers and competitors, but they have little time to find them. One common comment was, "I wish I had known about the 3/M exhibit. I didn't know they were showing their new product, and I would like to have seen it." A clearinghouse of exhibit information would greatly help.

Every show has a morale problem as the staff becomes worn out by long hours. Disseminating good news for Legacy during the show would help dispel the low morale.

Feasibility Assessment   Assessing feasibility is a process of determining whether or not an information system can reasonably be expected to provide an effective solution to the identified problem. To assess feasibility, you must first know the type of system that will be developed to solve the problem. Then you can assess the four dimensions of feasibility: cost, schedule, technology, and political environment, as listed in Figure 7-4.

LuAnne knows she has a communications problem, so she decides to consider either a word processing application or a DTP application. Since she does not yet know the requirements, this is a guess on her part. She might be wrong, but making such a guess enables her to get started.

Cost feasibility addresses the question, Is an information system within the appropriate realm of cost? At this early stage, precise measures of costs and values of benefits are impossible to obtain, so the question is answered with ballpark estimates. The goal here is to determine whether the project makes reasonable sense from a financial standpoint. If the system is likely to cost $500,000 and its value is under $100,000, then the proposed system is cost infeasible.

The following scenario illustrates an example of LuAnne's thinking:

> My microcomputer system cost $12,000, and I might use it for 1/12 of the year to develop and support some type of application that improves show communications. So, roughly, that's $1,000 for hardware.

Next, for software, I may need to buy two new microcomputer applications. So, I'll add another $500 for programs. That may be high, but I'll start there.

Now, what about my time? Let's say it takes me 2 weeks to develop the applications and another week to get set up for the show. I'll probably also need a half-time assistant at the show to help produce the newsletter. That's 5 labor weeks—say $5,000 for labor.

All together, that's $6,500 to develop this system and use it the first year. I know it will cost less in subsequent years.

At this point, LuAnne is clearly making approximations. Her microcomputer will probably last more than a year, so the hardware cost is estimated too high. Also, the cost of two new application programs may vary from $300 to $1,200 or more, depending on the applications. Her labor costs are also approximate. At this point, she simply wants a reasonable measure of the system's cost.

As you can see, the reasoning at this stage is an estimate. LuAnne is attempting to ensure that she is not developing a $100,000 system to solve a $5,000 problem. Her estimates of costs are approximate. She does not consider the costs of paper for printing the newsletter or the cost of distributing it to the staff during the show. She is aware there are such costs, but here, she simply wants to pin down the biggest items of cost.

Similarly, her estimates of value are also approximate. Because they are so vague, she looks at the problem from several vantage points, and if those perspectives provide roughly comparable results, she will feel more comfortable about her analysis.

To understand the importance of cost feasibility, suppose LuAnne had decided that, in order to solve the problem, she needed to put a microcomputer in every person's hotel room and link the computers together over the telephone lines. A cost estimate of such a system would likely be in the range of $100,000, and the benefits would probably not support such an expensive system; the proposed solution would be cost infeasible.

These sorts of back-of-the-envelope estimates are crude. It is important, however, to make them in order to avoid spending time and resources building a system that cannot make economic sense.

Schedule feasibility concerns whether or not the system will be available in time. LuAnne needs to decide whether she can develop the system on time. If she has 3 or 4 months before the show, she can probably find the necessary 2 or so weeks to develop the system. If, however, she has only 1 month before the show, then, considering all of her duties, she probably cannot develop it in time. If the latter case is valid, the system is considered schedule infeasible.

Schedule feasibility problems often involve external agencies. For example, a system that produces information for the annual audit is schedule infeasible if it is finished 2 months after the auditors need it. A system that produces information for the stockholders' report is infeasible if it cannot be available before the stockholders' meeting.

Technical feasibility is the third dimension of feasibility assessment. Here the question is, Can existing technology provide a solution to the problem? In the case of the Legacy trade show communications problem, there is no question that existing information systems technology will be adequate. Producing reports or a newsletter to communicate schedules and events is well within the capabilities of today's technology.

What are examples of technically infeasible solutions? Suppose Legacy invites its European and Asian salespeople to the trade show. If LuAnne needs a system to automatically translate a report or newsletter into French, German, Japanese, and Mandarin Chinese, then her system would be technically infeasible, at least today. Systems that necessitate 50 gigabytes of data in a personal computer or that require the solution of large linear programming models in less than a second on a personal computer are also currently infeasible.

Most business-oriented personal information processing solutions that you will consider are technically feasible today. Setting aside such special requirements as natural language translation, today's technology will support most personal information needs. This is not always true for workgroup and enterprise systems, however. In a large corporation, we often encounter the need for solutions that are not yet within technology's reach. You will see examples later in this book.

Organizational feasibility, the final component of feasibility, concerns the political environment. Does the proposed solution fit within the cultural, social, and policy constraints of the department or the company? For example, the senior partners of a large, traditional law partnership may believe it is unseemly for them to use a computer keyboard. An information system that requires them to key in requests for reports is organizationally infeasible: These partners would probably not be caught dead at a keyboard. (Considering the competitive advantage of information systems, this attitude may turn out to be quite expensive to the partners, however.)

A more realistic example concerns constraints that exist for reasons of control or security. A bank, for example, may be concerned that no customer data be removed from the bank premises. At the same time, the bank may want its employees to access customer data with a personal computer. The danger is that, with personal computers, employees could make unauthorized copies of data. A "normal" personal computer would be organizationally infeasible in this environment. Personal computers without diskette drives, however, would be organizationally feasible.

The various types of feasibility are often linked. For example, a project to develop a certain system using MS-DOS may be organizationally infeasible because the users insist on a GUI platform. When Windows is added to the platform, the project may be technically infeasible because the hardware is inadequate. When adequate hardware is specified, the project becomes cost infeasible. In fact, nothing has changed except the name of the category.

The goal of feasibility assessment is to determine whether or not the proposed system makes sense. The next stages of systems development are time-consuming and expensive. If the proposed system is infeasible, it is better to find out earlier than later. This may seem to go without saying, but more than one company—in fact, probably thousands—have installed $100,000 systems for $30,000 problems.

Project Plan Creation   Once the problem has been defined and the feasibility assessed, the last task in the definition stage is to build a **project plan**. How will the project be conducted? What personnel will be required? What tasks will be necessary? Who will carry those tasks out? What schedule will be followed? What money will be needed? When will the money be needed?

The remaining four stages should be used as a framework for building a project plan. First, the problem solution must be classified; then the system platform, created; the prototypes, created and evaluated; and the system, implemented. Depending on the size, scale, and expense of this system, some number of levels of management need to be involved. If you are building a small spreadsheet application for yourself, you probably only need to keep your boss appraised informally. Developing large enterprise systems requires reporting on an extensive and formal basis.

Figure 7-6 shows a Gantt chart of a project plan for developing the Legacy trade show newsletter. In this plan, major tasks are identified and approxi–mate times are given for each task. As shown, the tasks could be accomplished more quickly, but LuAnne cannot work on this project full time because she has other duties.

Classifying the Solution

Once the problem has been defined, the next step (as described in Figure 7-3) is to classify the solution. This step produces information necessary for creating the system platform. It also serves to establish guidelines for the development activity. For example, if it is known that the system will be needed only to solve a particular problem and that it will be discarded once it has been used, then otherwise unwise shortcuts and abbreviations can be taken. On the other hand, if the system will be used for years by individuals other than the initial system developer, then time should be taken to organize the application clearly and consistently.

Application Type   The first task is to determine the *application type* that will solve the problem. The categories listed in Figure 7-7 include communications, analysis, tracking and monitoring, and integrated applications. The problem statement should give clear guidance as to which type of system is appropriate.

For example, for the Legacy Systems trade show problem, a communications application will be needed. Considering the need to maintain and publish the

Figure 7-6 Project Plan for the Development of the Legacy Trade Show Communication System

Trade Show Communication System Development Project Plan

ID	Name	Duration	5 January (3–11)	12 January (12–18)
1	Define the Problem			
2	Problem Statement	1d		
3	Feasibility	2d		
4	Plan	4h		
5	Classify Solution	2h		
6	Create System Platform			
7	Buy Software	1d		
8	Install Software	1d		
9	Learn Advanced Features	3d		
10	Design			
11	Initial Design	1d		
12	Review and Rework	4d		
13	Implementation			
14	Document Procedures	1d		
15	Train Assistant	1d		

booth duty schedule, however, the communications application will need to be integrated with a tracking and monitoring application.

The category of application largely determines the nature, size, and cost of the system platform, so it is important to be as accurate as possible at this stage. If the problem is overestimated, money will be wasted on a system that is larger than necessary; if it is underestimated, the problem will not be successfully solved.

Next consider the problem against the application types in each category and pick the application that seems most appropriate for the problem. The communications category includes word processing, DTP, graphics, presentation,

Figure 7-6   *(continued)*

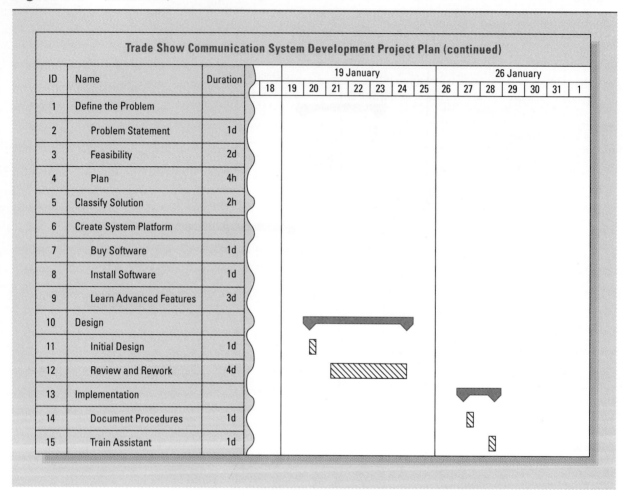

ID	Name	Duration		19 January							26 January						
			18	19	20	21	22	23	24	25	26	27	28	29	30	31	1
1	Define the Problem																
2	Problem Statement	1d															
3	Feasibility	2d															
4	Plan	4h															
5	Classify Solution	2h															
6	Create System Platform																
7	Buy Software	1d															
8	Install Software	1d															
9	Learn Advanced Features	3d															
10	Design																
11	Initial Design	1d															
12	Review and Rework	4d															
13	Implementation																
14	Document Procedures	1d															
15	Train Assistant	1d															

Trade Show Communication System Development Project Plan (continued)

and electronic communication applications. The analysis category includes spreadsheet, statistical, OR, and decision support applications. The tracking and monitoring category includes database and project management applications.

The Legacy trade show communications problem could be solved with either a word processing program or a DTP program. LuAnne feels that it is important to produce a very professional-looking publication, but in the busy show setting, minimizing complexity is more important. Therefore, she decides to use a high-end GUI word processing program capable of handling some graphics material.

Figure 7-7 Types of Personal
Information Systems

■ **Communications**
Word processing
DTP
Graphics
Presentation
Electronic communication

■ **Analysis**
Spreadsheet
Statistical
Operations research (OR)
Decision support

■ **Tracking and Monitoring**
Database
Project management

■ **Integrated**
Combination of two or more applications

She also knows that she needs a database management application to track the booth duty schedule. The word processing and database applications will need to be integrated.

Application Size   The next task is to determine the size of the application. Major considerations are the amount of data to be stored and the volume and frequency of input and output. When developing size estimates, it is also important to estimate application growth. The size estimates developed here will be used later to determine specifications for the system platform.

Figure 7-8 shows LuAnne's estimates of data storage and report-generation frequency for both the communications application and the database application. For the database, she calculates the number of rows of each type and multiplies that number by the length of the row. For example, consider the booth duty records. There are 15 stations, times the 5 days of the show, times 4 booth duty

Figure 7-8   Estimates of Processing Scale for the Legacy Trade Show Communication System

■ **Data Storage Requirements**
Daily Newsletters:

Without graphics, 7 reports at 25,000 bytes each	=	175,000 bytes
With graphics, 7 reports at 100,000 bytes each	=	700,000 bytes
Storage for newsletter documents	=	875,000 bytes

Booth Duty Database:

30 employee rows at 200 bytes each	=	6,000 bytes
15 station rows at 100 bytes each	=	1,500 bytes
$15 \times 5 \times 4$ duty rows at 50 bytes each	=	15,000 bytes
Storage for database	=	21,500 bytes
Approximate total data storage required	=	**900,000 bytes**

■ **Report Generation Requirements**

Produce daily reports twice before show and each day of show	7 reports
Print 50 copies of each report	
Print booth duty schedule for review	5 times for review for each newsletter

■ **Application Data Growth**
The application will not grow, but one copy of each newsletter and the final booth duty schedule will be kept indefinitely

periods each day, for a total of 300 rows. Each row is 50 bytes long, for a total of 15,000 bytes of booth duty schedule data.

Constraints   The development of a personal information system is sometimes subject to constraints. It is important to consider this possibility before further proceeding with application development.

Constraints can arise from the needs of the application, the user, or the organization. For example, LuAnne's time at the trade show is limited. She may know that she will have, at most, 1 hour to produce the trade show newsletter. If so, she may need to restrict applications to those that can accomplish the task within this limit.

Other examples of constraints are that the application should not be too complicated, should involve programs the user already knows, and should use hardware the user already possesses. Some people insist on GUI applications;

others insist that an application reside on a laptop computer; still others insist that the application not be run on a laptop (because of the generally less-clear visual presentation of laptops).

Other constraints involve hardware. Some organizations have standardized by using particular products and require that all employees follow those standards. The most common example of this type of standard is the use of either an Apple Macintosh computer or an IBM PC or PC-compatible computer. Other similar standards are possible.

Future Use A final consideration in classifying the solution is expected future use of the application. Some applications will only be used to solve a particular problem. When the problem is solved, the application will be thrown away.

An example is a spreadsheet application that will be used to develop a profit and loss statement for a one-time project. Once the project is planned, the spreadsheet will no longer be needed. In this case, the spreadsheet developer can omit steps that would ordinarily be required. Spreadsheet documentation, for example, can be brief.

The danger in throw-away applications is that they are not truly thrown away. The application might be saved "just in case," and sure enough, some months later, a need for the application arises. In this situation, savings obtained by skipping work will probably be lost through lack of clarity or some other problem. In short, if you develop a throw-away application, be sure to throw it away. If you do not intend to delete the application later, then do not take shortcuts.

Another consideration is whether the system being developed will be used only by the developer or whether it will be used by others. If it will be used by others, then it needs to be better organized and documented, which can mean considerably more work. In fact, Fred Brooks, in his classic book, *The Mythical Man-Month*,[2] states that it takes three times longer to develop a system that will be used by others than it does to develop a system that will be used only by the developer.

The developer can create the system platform once the system type has been determined; the size, estimated; the constraints, defined; and the future of the system, assessed.

Creating the System Platform

The purpose of this stage is to create a system platform that can be used to generate the prototypes, and, eventually, to serve as the basis of the operational

2. Brooks, Frederick P., *The Mythical Man-Month.* Reading, MA: Addison-Wesley, 1975.

system. The platform itself is an information system, with each of the five components that were previously discussed.

Programs   It is generally wise to select application programs first. In the previous stage, you classified the solution, and this classification indicated the type of application programs needed. With a knowledge of the general application type, you can approach co-workers, consultants, computer retailers, or other sources to learn about particular products that fall into that type.

Unless you already have computer hardware, select programs first: The programs will dictate the type and amount of hardware you need. For example, some products are available only on the Macintosh, others only on the IBM PC-compatible family. In addition, some products require more memory or disk space than others.

So many choices of application programs are available today that the selection process can become mind-boggling. To help you through the process, publications such as *PC Magazine* and *MacUser* perform product tests and publish their results. Many books about particular applications have also been published. Examples are *Roger Black's Desktop Design Power* and *The Spreadsheet Style Manual.*[3] Such books do not generally rate or review products, but they normally illustrate the use of the most popular products in a particular category.

In general, unless you have substantial expertise in an area, choose an established, mainstream product with substantial aftermarket support, including authorized training centers, effective customer support, a large pool of experienced consultants, and so forth. Unless you are a seasoned user, stay on the beaten path.

Today, on IBM PC-compatible machines, a dichotomy exists concerning applications programs: Some programs use the features and functions of Windows and some do not. Products that do use Windows have the advantage of a consistent GUI, but Windows requires a more powerful computer with more main memory. Other products each have their own interface. Many excellent products are available in both types. Windows products are most likely the products of the future, and, all other things being equal, you would be wise to pick a Windows product over a non-Windows product. This problem does not exist on the Macintosh; all Macintosh programs are GUI programs.

After determining the application program(s) you need, select systems software. You will need at least an OS and possibly Windows. Unless the application you purchase indicates otherwise, select the most recent version of the systems software. A reputable vendor can help here.

Hardware   The basic decision for personal computer information systems hardware is which type of personal computer you will need: Macintosh or IBM

---

3.   Black, Roger, *Roger Black's Desktop Design Power.* New York: Bantam, 1991. Harrison, David, and John W. Yu, *The Spreadsheet Style Manual.* Homewood, IL: Dow Jones-Irwin, 1990.

PC-compatible. Your organization may have a constraint that dictates which machine you use. If it does not, but most people in your department or your other co-workers have one type of machine, then use that same type. Or, it might be that you want to use a particular program product that is only available on one type or the other. In any case, you need to decide on the personal computer type. If you choose the IBM PC family, then you must decide whether you want a brand name computer or a clone.

Within a type, the programs you select will largely determine the speed of the processor and the amount of memory you need. The specifications provided by the software vendors for their products are usually the very minimum. Although Windows can run on an 80286 computer with 2MB of memory, realistically, at least an 80386 with 4MB is required, and an 80486 with 8MB would significantly enhance productivity.

You also need to specify the amount of disk space. The calculations made during the classification stage will help you estimate data storage requirements. In addition, you will need space for programs. Most application programs occupy between 1MB and 15MB of storage. Check with the retailer for specific information.

In general, buy at least two to four times as much disk storage memory as you think you will need. Additional storage is not that expensive, and you probably will find applications for your computer that you cannot anticipate at the time you purchase it. Further, as vendors bring out new products, the need for disk storage continues to rise rapidly.

Two other hardware considerations include display resolution and peripheral equipment. Higher-resolution displays are required for GUI applications. Finally, you may need to select peripheral equipment. A mouse is required for GUI applications; you may want to acquire a scanner if you will be using graphics extensively.

Once you have your computer, you will need to set it up. Follow the instructions that come with the computer. Most are clear and straightforward. Be certain to perform all of the diagnostic checks suggested in the instructions; if any problems arise, return the computer to the vendor.

Data   Once your computer is assembled and running, you will need to format the hard disk and install the systems programs. (Or, it may be that the computer vendor has preinstalled the systems programs for you.) Next you will need to install application programs, but before doing so, plan your directory structure. If you follow the guidelines in Chapter 6, you will maintain a different directory for each major application program and for each major project.

Since application-program installation is straightforward, just follow the directions. During installation, the vendor's install program will normally suggest a default directory for the programs. For example, the install program for Excel suggests the directory EXCEL, and the install program for Paradox, Version 3.5, suggests the directory PDOX35. The installation of future releases of your products will be simpler if you allow the install program to use the directory it suggests; do so unless you are experienced and have a definite reason for overriding the suggested directory.

Procedures   At this stage of the project, two major types of procedures must be considered. First, you must learn to use the applications programs. You can take classes, but this is often unnecessary. As part of every major product today, vendors provide computer-based training (CBT) tutorials for learning to use the product. Before enrolling in a class, spend time with the tutorial. You may find that it is sufficient.

Also, all contemporary applications products have sophisticated help facilities, into which vendors have invested substantial resources. Take time to learn how to use your product's help functions. Many products provide **context-sensitive help**, with which you can ask for help messages specific to the function or action in which you are engaged (see Figure 7-9).

The second category of procedures concerns those that you will follow to develop the system. Since you are using prototyping, you know that you will develop prototypes of your application, then add to and revise those prototypes. At this point, you may want to make that process more explicit.

Figure 7-9   On-Line Help

Microsoft's Visual Basic provides context-sensitive on-line help based on the user's most recent actions.

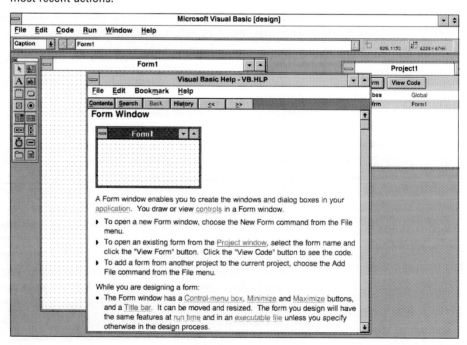

Consider LuAnne's situation in developing the trade show newsletter. She knows that she will need to develop both a database application and a word processing application and that the two applications will then need to be integrated. LuAnne might decide to begin with the database application since that application feeds data to the word processing application. In this case, she establishes a plan to create the database application, then creates the word processing application.

Upon reflection, however, LuAnne realizes that, if she develops the word processing application first, she can show samples of the newsletter to Legacy employees and thereby gain the benefit of feedback. In that process, she will learn what booth duty data is most needed by the employees. Thus, the word processing prototypes will help develop requirements for the database application. Consequently, LuAnne decides to develop the word processing prototype first.

It is important to engage in this type of thinking before proceeding. Preplanning can save extra work later.

People   The last component of the system platform is people. The developer is most likely you; in addition, you will probably need access to experts. Before starting your project, identify people who can help you.

One source of help is the other employees in your department. At least some of them may be knowledgeable about your application type. Your company's MIS department may also have experts available as internal consultants, and, for specific problems about products, you can contact a vendor's customer support line. Articles about innovative ways to use products often appear in popular magazines such as *PC World*. Finally, you can hire a consultant to assist you in developing your application.

Before proceeding, identify the people who will help you evaluate your prototypes. Consider the clientele for the system you are developing, and locate people who typify that clientele. LuAnne, for example, decided to involve a manager, two salespeople, a departmental secretary, and her boss in evaluating prototypes for her newsletter.

With all five components in place, you are ready to create the design.

Designing the Application with Prototypes

Designing with prototypes is an iterative process. First create an initial design, given your knowledge of the requirements at that point. Then place this design before several people and ask for feedback. With the feedback, revise your design and keep revising it until you are satisfied.

This process is described firsthand by Roger Black, a designer of many prominent magazines, in his excellent book, *Roger Black's Desktop Design Power*. Here, Black describes the process of selecting type for the publication *Desktop Communications*.

A caveat about body type that is worth repeating: it is impossible to generalize much about legibility for body type…. The best way to decide is to try a number of alternatives, both in typefaces and in size-leading combinations. If possible, get some samples produced and printed using the exact technology and system that the publication is going to use. Show the samples to a few typical readers. Then decide.[4]

The iterative process of design allows many more alternatives to be considered and evaluated than do the traditional one-time-only descriptions of requirements. The appearance of a design alternative will, in fact, suggest alternatives that would not normally occur.

This process is effective not only for word processing, but for all types of information systems. For a spreadsheet application, for example, the results of one analysis may generate the idea of changing the model to produce another type of analysis. The synergistic pattern—of requirements feeding design feeding requirements feeding design—results in an effective design.

For database applications, a prototype of the database is created and reports and forms are created to enter, change, and display database data. As the clientele review forms and reports, they may think of additional data that they need to see or better ways in which the existing information could be presented.

We will see examples of this iterative process in the next section.

Implementing the System

In the classical SDLC, and to some extent, the licensed program SDLC, implementation is the stage in which the system is created, tested, and made operational. Hardware is installed in the users' work areas; training is conducted, and so forth. Then development team, users, and management evaluate the system, test the results, and decide that the system is ready for the users. Finally, there is a **cutover** point in which the old system (or some portion of it) is disconnected, and the new system, installed. Chapter 10 describes this type of process.

With prototyping, however, this style of implementation does not make sense. For one, the system platform has already been installed in the user's work area, and the user has been actively involved in the development of prototypes. If you are developing the system for yourself, you are the user; you have trained yourself as you have constructed the prototypes.

Furthermore, with prototyping, while the user is building the prototype of the output, he or she is, perhaps unknowingly, also building the prototype of the system. By the time the developer is satisfied with the last prototype, the system has, in the process, been constructed, and it has already been implemented. The evolving prototype platform has become the information system!

---

4. Black, *op. cit.*, p. 270.

Suppose you, as a product manager, are responsible for developing a profit and loss statement on a new line of sporting goods. If you follow the prototyping process, you define your problem, classify it, create a system platform, and then produce an evolving series of profit and loss statements. You may show those statements to your boss or co-workers. When you are satisfied with the results, you report your findings. Meanwhile, as you develop the prototypes of the profit and loss statements, you also develop an underlying system for producing profit and loss statements.

When LuAnne develops a database application for tracking the booth duty schedule, she develops a series of prototypes of forms and reports. When she is satisfied with them, she will have developed a completed, working database application.

With prototyping, when users are doing their own development, the traditional implementation activities occur throughout the development process. The meaning of implementation thus changes: The implementation stage for prototyping is really more of a point at which the developers generate their final output and then take stock of the system.

If the system is a throw-away system, then the users-developers throw it away at that point. If the system will be used again, they document it for future use. If the system is going to be used immediately (say for another profit and loss statement), then it serves as the system platform for the next series of prototypes and designs.

Examine Figure 7-1 again. With prototyping, the system that produced the last prototype (final product) is documented. The cycle is then repeated for the next similar problem. The system that produced the final product of one cycle serves as the initial development platform for the next cycle.

PERSONAL COMMUNICATION APPLICATION DEVELOPMENT

Personal communication applications enable professionals like Roger Black (quoted earlier) to design and develop entire magazines using microcomputers. However, if the only users of such applications were such professionals, the subject would be of less concern to us here. In actuality, communication applications can add substantial value to nonprofessional designers with much smaller needs than those of magazine publishing.

The Challenge (and Opportunity) of Personal Communication Applications

Suppose you are a volunteer for a nonprofit organization that advocates the development of housing alternatives for the homeless. Your group writes to the legislature, creates press releases, produces reports, and makes public presentations. Because these activities are so diverse, you know that it may be difficult to develop momentum for your organization.

A personal communication application can be used to your advantage in this situation. With such an application, you can develop a consistent design for your organization, then use that design in all of your activities. Figure 7-10 shows an example of a consistent design for letterhead, reports, and overhead transparencies. A consistent design will help you build momentum for your group.

The possible obstacle in this case is that most people know little about publication design. Few of us know or understand the number and complexity of designs and layout issues of a publication as common as our daily newspaper. In fact, there is much to consider. The following discussion first introduces fundamental concepts of three aspects of message design—type, graphics, and layout—then considers some of the decisions that LuAnne made in developing the Legacy Systems newsletter.

Because of the complexity of this process in its entirety, for important publications, you may want to hire a professional to develop a design. Or, you might use some of the document templates that are usually provided with communication applications programs. Another alternative is to use one of the ready-made designs published in DTP design books. As you will see, LuAnne chose this last alternative for her publication.

Hardware Platform Description

Advanced word processing requires a GUI interface, which means that either a Macintosh or an IBM PC or PC-compatible with Windows is required. In 1993, the minimum IBM PC system for this purpose is an 80386 processor with 4MB of memory. Realistically, these applications require at least an 80486 with 8MB of memory. As new versions of word processing programs are developed, they are likely to require even more hardware.

To obtain attractive output from advanced word processing programs, a laser printer is required. Further, for printing large volumes and producing color, sophisticated commercial printers such as a Linotype L-300 are sometimes necessary. Although laser printers are within the budget of most personal computer

Figure 7-10 Consistent Design

A personal communication application can provide consistent design over a wide variety of messages.

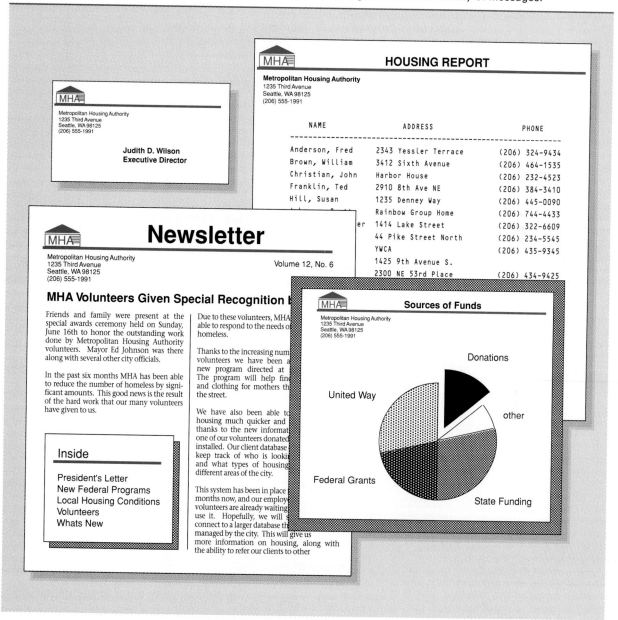

users, professional-quality printers are not. Consequently, for documents that need mass printing or color printing, most users take their document files to a professional who can accept document files in the format of the common word processing programs (e.g., WordPerfect and Microsoft Word).

Advanced Word Processing Concepts

Using prototyping, you create the system platform, then begin developing publication prototypes. There are a number of concepts that you should know about before you proceed.

Type   The creation and use of type is an art form. Although almost everyone reads type every day, most people are unaware of the large number of variations in type. Several important type characteristics should be considered.

The term *typeface* refers to the general style and appearance of type. Examples of several different typefaces are shown in Figure 7-11. There are two general categories of typefaces. **Serif** typefaces have curves, flourishes, and cross-strokes, and they have a classical and traditional look. Common serif typefaces are Times and Palatino. **Sans serif** typefaces (*sans* is the French word for *without*) do not have flourishes, and they provide a cleaner, more contemporary appearance. In general, serif typefaces are considered easier to read, although the degree to which this is true depends on the particular typeface. Common sans serif typefaces are Helvetica and Avant Garde.

Type varies in **size**, which is measured in **points**. One point equals 1/72 of an inch. Thus, 6-point type is 1/8-inch high and very small; 72-point type is 1-inch high and quite large. Letters and other characters vary in height; thus, not all characters in 72-point type are 1-inch high. Consider the size in points as a relative

Figure 7-11   Typefaces

This is an example of Times

This is an example of Helvetica

This is an example of Palatino

This is an example of Courier

Figure 7-12 Serif and Sans Serif Typefaces

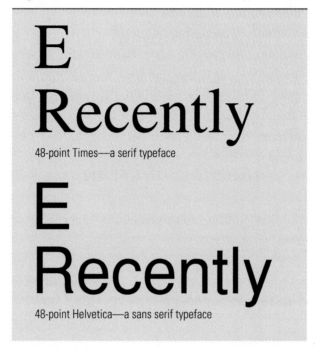

E

Recently

48-point Times—a serif typeface

E

Recently

48-point Helvetica—a sans serif typeface

indicator of type size. Most books, magazines, and newspapers are set in 9- or 10-point type. Newsletters are often set with 11-point type. Figure 7-12 shows examples of 48-point Times and Helvetica.

Type also varies in **style** and **weight**. Examples of style are Roman, italic, bold, and small capitals as shown in Figure 7-13. The weight of the type refers, in general, to the appearance of thickness. Bold type is heavier and is available with standard typefaces. Additionally, many typefaces are designed in several weight versions. For example, Helvetica is available in regular, medium, and heavy weights.

All of the size, style, and weight variations of a particular typeface are referred to as a **type family.** Common type families are *Helvetica, Times, Palatino, Avant Garde,* and *New Century Schoolbook.*

Figure 7-14 presents a number of recommendations for type usage published by the Aldus Corporation.[5] Consider these recommendations when you select your publication type. Also, many professional designers believe that beginners use too many different variations in typefaces and type styles, and they recommend that type be used conservatively, especially by the inexperienced.

―――――――――――――――

5. Vick, Nichoel J., Audrey Thompson, and Anne Milkovich, *Designs for Business Communications.* Seattle, WA: Aldus Corporation, 1988, p. 102.

Figure 7-13   Type Styles

Palatino Roman

Palatino Bold

Palatino Italic

Palatino Bold Italic

PALATINO SMALL CAPITALS

Figure 7-14   Recommendations for Type

- Match typeface to application. (For example, don't use a thin and light typeface for a heavy equipment manufacturer.)
- Choose serif typefaces when presenting a lot of text, since these typefaces are generally easier to read.
- Do not use too many typefaces. In most publications, two will do.
- Use compatible and distinctly different typefaces together. (Helvetica and Times are a good combination.)
- Reserve italics, bold, other styles for titles, captions, and headings.
- Use small capitals for acronyms.

Art and Graphics   Much of the interest created by advanced word processing applications arises because text can be intermixed with art, pictures, and **graphics**. The subjects of art and photography are beyond the scope of this text. However, several rules for using business graphics are summarized in Figure 7-15. Again, these guidelines are adapted from guidelines published by Aldus.[6] Use graphics to

---

6.   *Ibid.,* p. 122.

Figure 7-15   Recommendations for Graphics

- Use graphs to show trends, movements, distributions, cycles.
- Use sans serif typefaces in graph labels.
- Use pie charts for showing parts of a whole.
- Use bar charts to show quantities of a single item.
- Use a pictogram to make a more interesting bar graph.
- Use stack- or multiple-bar charts to show quantities of several items. The units, however, should be comparable.
- Show data relationships with line plot, or XY graph. Use appropriate ranges on data.

show trends, movements, distributions, and cycles of data. Different types of graphs should be used for different purposes as listed.

When combining data in multiple-bar charts or stacked-bar charts, as illustrated in Figures 7-16a and 7-16b, be sure that the data is comparable. The stacked-bar graph in Figure 7-16b is deceiving because it stacks incomparable measures. Sales in units are far different from costs in dollars. Such a graph is never appropriate.

Graphs are communication devices, so their structure should be determined by your communication needs and goals. For example, the line plot in Figure 7-17a is appropriate if your goal is to show the absolute rate of growth in expenses from one period to another; since the Y-axis starts at 0, the height of the line is absolutely proportional to the growth. Thus, we see that there was some increase in expenses during the period. Figure 7-17b foreshortens the Y-axis by not starting it at zero. As a result, it shows much more clearly *how much* increase there was, but it exaggerates the proportionate amount—making it look like expenses roughly tripled during the period. Both graphs tell the truth, but each serves some goals better than others. The lesson is to select graphic devices to serve your communication goals.

Page Layout   **Page layout** is an artistic process. Most professional designers start with unusual, native artistic talent, and they hone that talent over many years of experience. Most of us will have more humble abilities, goals, and objectives, and our results will likely be less dramatic. Still, it is possible to learn the basics of a good layout, even if only for the purpose of selecting an appropriate one from a book of designs.

The design layout should match the purpose of the application. For some publications, the goal is to invite the reader to delve into a topic in which he or she would normally not be interested. In magazines, the purpose is sometimes to

Figure 7-16 Bar Charts

(a) The multiple-bar chart shows revenue and expenses in dollars; **(b)** the stacked-bar chart shows sales in units and expenses in dollars, creating a misleading result.

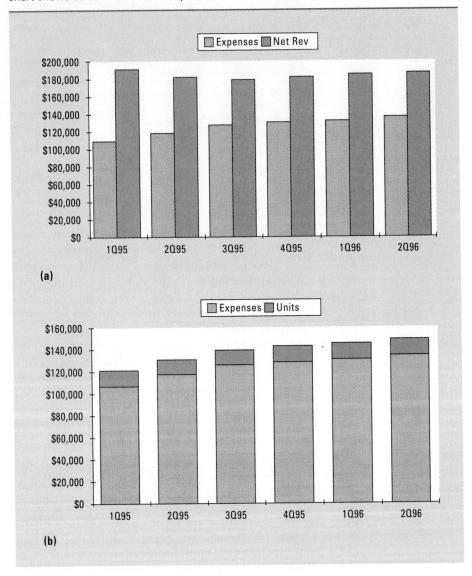

(a)

(b)

Figure 7-17 Line Graphs

(a) A line graph with a zero-origin Y-axis correctly conveys the impression that expenses have increased about 15 percent during the period; **(b)** a line graph with its non–zero-origin Y-axis portrays the dollar amount of the increase more clearly, but it may give the incorrect impression that expenses have roughly tripled.

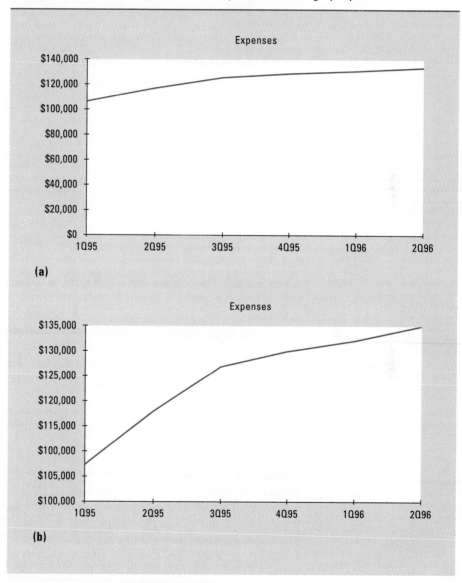

(a)

(b)

Figure 7-18   Recommendations for Page Layout

- Layout should match purpose of the publication.
- For multicolumn layout, select type and column width to allow about 40 characters per column.
- Use plenty of white space—too much is better than too little.
- Balance the design for a one- or two-page layout.
- Use contrast of white space and graphics to achieve balance.
- When locating graphics, the edges of graphics should line up with each other or with something else (e.g., a headline).
- Outline graphics with thin, not thick, lines.
- Justify text for formal traditional look; use aligned-left text for informal or contemporary look.
- Eliminate widows and orphans.

create space for large amounts of advertising without appearing to do so. Some layouts prominently feature text, and they appear literary. Others feature pictures, and they appear approachable and easy to assimilate.

Basic page layout guidelines are summarized in Figure 7-18. Many publications have multicolumn formats. Space can be reserved for pictures, art, and graphics so that text will flow around these areas. According to Aldus, for multicolumn publications, lines of about 40 characters are the easiest to read. The type size and column width should be adjusted to fit this goal.

It is never appropriate to change type size on a particular story just to make it fit the space. Edit the text, change the size of graphics, or add white space instead.

Templates   As you can tell from this discussion, a good design involves the complex interplay of many different factors. Unless you have a natural bent for design or plenty of time to experiment, you might want to use a **design template.** Such a template is a sample design that has been created for a particular use. There are, for example, newsletter templates and report templates. Generally, a template specifies typefaces and type sizes and styles to be used for various elements of the design such as title, headings, and text body. The template also shows where to place art and graphics for a balanced look.

Templates are available from several sources. All DTP program vendors provide or sell templates for various common kinds of publications. Also, many books provide sample designs. (See the References for this chapter.)

Legacy Systems Newsletter

LuAnne Price developed the Legacy Systems newsletter by using prototyping. She already had a computer and the Windows software, and so she only needed to acquire an advanced word processing program in order to build her system platform. She evaluated both WordPerfect and Microsoft Word and could not tell that one would be much better than the other for her publication. Since several people in her office were already using Word, she decided to use it as well. Once it was installed, LuAnne taught herself how to use it, and she learned the rudiments of publication design.

She made two attempts at developing her own design, which are shown in Figure 7-19a and 7-19b. She showed these designs to co-workers, and after receiving

Figure 7-19 Early Prototypes of Legacy Systems Newsletter
(a) First prototype; **(b)** Second prototype.

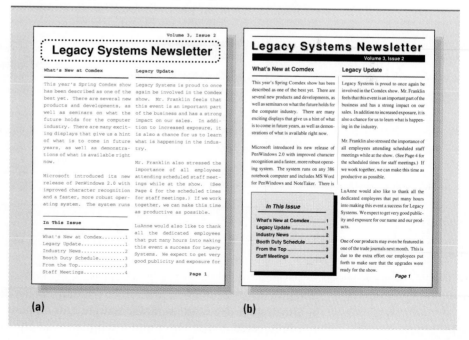

(a) (b)

Figure 7-20 Final Version of Legacy Systems Newsletter

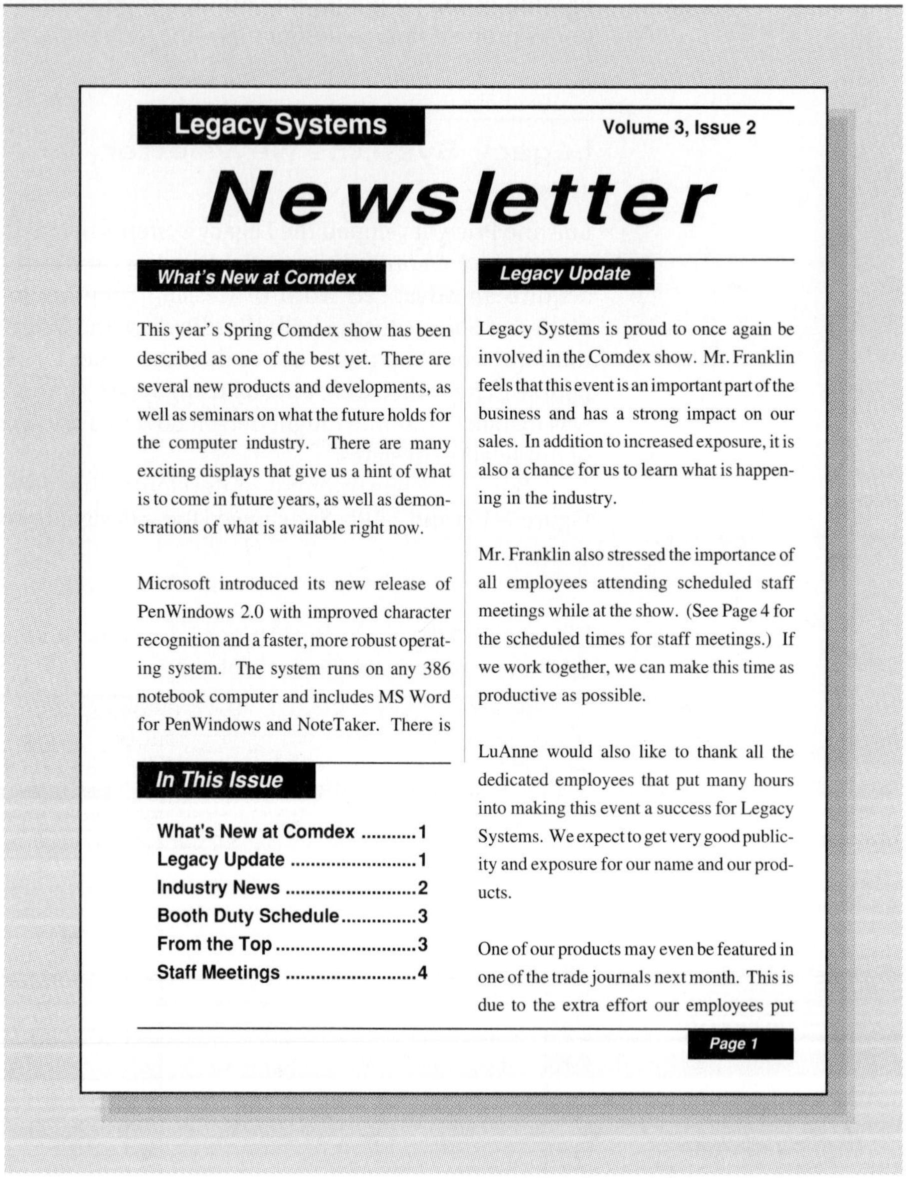

Legacy Systems

Volume 3, Issue 2

Newsletter

What's New at Comdex

This year's Spring Comdex show has been described as one of the best yet. There are several new products and developments, as well as seminars on what the future holds for the computer industry. There are many exciting displays that give us a hint of what is to come in future years, as well as demonstrations of what is available right now.

Microsoft introduced its new release of PenWindows 2.0 with improved character recognition and a faster, more robust operating system. The system runs on any 386 notebook computer and includes MS Word for PenWindows and NoteTaker. There is

In This Issue

Legacy Update

Legacy Systems is proud to once again be involved in the Comdex show. Mr. Franklin feels that this event is an important part of the business and has a strong impact on our sales. In addition to increased exposure, it is also a chance for us to learn what is happening in the industry.

Mr. Franklin also stressed the importance of all employees attending scheduled staff meetings while at the show. (See Page 4 for the scheduled times for staff meetings.) If we work together, we can make this time as productive as possible.

LuAnne would also like to thank all the dedicated employees that put many hours into making this event a success for Legacy Systems. We expect to get very good publicity and exposure for our name and our products.

One of our products may even be featured in one of the trade journals next month. This is due to the extra effort our employees put

Page 1

constructive feedback from them, concluded that her designs were too amateurish. She decided to consult a graphic artist in the company's publications department, who created a style sheet and a template that she could use in producing her newsletter. The result is shown in Figure 7-20.

SPREADSHEET APPLICATION DEVELOPMENT

Prototyping applies to the development of spreadsheet applications just as much as it does to personal communication applications. The basic pattern is the same: Define and classify the application, build the system platform, and create prototypes. Obtain feedback on the prototypes, and refine and redesign as necessary. When no new requirements or refinements are found, implement the system by producing the output necessary to solve the problem. Document the system if it will be used again.

Purposes of Spreadsheets

Spreadsheet applications are used for a number of different purposes, as listed in Figure 7-21. First, they are used for record keeping. A typical example is spreadsheets that record accounting data and produce financial statements. Second, spreadsheets are also used for what-if analysis, as we have seen.

Third, spreadsheets are used for sensitivity analysis. Here we determine the impact of changes in a single variable on output results. An example is a spreadsheet that determines the net worth of an investment, given changes in interest rates.

What-if analysis and sensitivity analysis are different. What-if analysis involves changes in business scenarios. In Chapter 2, Sarah Morris changed her prices, made assumptions about the price change's impact on demand, and calculated various levels of profitability. Sensitivity analysis, on the other hand, involves changes in only a single variable, and their impact is determined only by the model and not by assumptions about the underlying scenario. An example is the present value of an investment for variations of interest rate.

Finally, spreadsheets are used for goal-seeking applications, which use a financial model to work backwards from a desired result to determine the input required to generate it. For example, if a product manager knows that her product

Figure 7-21 Uses of Spreadsheet Applications

- Record Keeping
- What-If Analysis
- Sensitivity Analysis
- Goal Seeking

line is expected to produce an overall 10 percent growth in profit within the next year, she would use a goal-seeking spreadsheet application to determine ways to achieve this goal.

Spreadsheet Criteria

Although the process for developing spreadsheet applications is the same as that for communication applications, the evaluation criteria are different. Criteria for evaluating spreadsheet applications are listed in Figure 7-22. First, an effective spreadsheet is accurate. The results are based on an appropriate model that is accurately implemented in the spreadsheet. Additionally, using a spreadsheet should be easy, which should not only make work more enjoyable, but also increase productivity and reduce the likelihood of errors.

In some cases, the model to be used for the analysis is given. In other cases, with prototyping, the model is part of the systems development process of designing, evaluating, and redesigning. If the model is given, the spreadsheet should be easy to change by structuring the spreadsheet so that critical aspects are readily visible. This means that important input variables are easily changed or removed, formulas can be rapidly identified and changed, and so forth.

Finally, a well-structured spreadsheet application is standardized and consistent. For example, if one percentage value is entered as a whole number—such as 8, for 8 percent—then all percentages are entered in that same way. The application does not require that some percentages be entered as whole numbers and others as decimals. Similarly, if some sales numbers are entered in current dollars, then all sales figures are entered as current dollars. The application does not require that some values be entered as current and others, adjusted for inflation.

Furthermore, if a particular cell is labeled GROWTH_RATE, then all formulas involving the growth rate use this variable in their calculations. It is an invitation to disaster to have one formula with the expression "=C4 * GROWTH_RATE" and a second formula that includes a specific value like 1.08

Figure 7-22   Criteria for Evaluating Spreadsheet Applications

- Accuracy
- Ease of Use
- Ease of Changing
- Standardization and Consistency

for growth rate, such as "=C4 * 1.08". If you do this, then at some point, you or someone else might change the value of GROWTH_RATE without changing the value built in to the second formula.

Spreadsheet System Platform

Spreadsheets are the second most popular microcomputer application. (Word processing is first.) Consequently, spreadsheet applications are available for almost every computer. For IBM PC-compatible computers, there are spreadsheet products for both GUI environments and non-GUI environments. Lotus 1-2-3, the product with the largest installed base, is available in versions for MS-DOS (non-GUI), Windows, OS/2, and Macintosh. Borland's Quattro Pro has Windows and MS-DOS versions. Microsoft Excel requires Windows or the Macintosh OS.

Spreadsheet programs assume that all user data resides in main memory. Large spreadsheets, therefore, may require more memory than the 640KB available in MS-DOS. In fact, spreadsheet applications provided the reason for the development of expanded and extended memory. Today, however, such technology is dated; if your spreadsheet requires more than 640KB, switch to Windows, OS/2, or the Macintosh, where more memory can be used.

The minimum hardware for effectively running a Windows spreadsheet is an 80386 processor with 4MB of memory; realistically, an 80486 with 8MB may enhance your spreadsheet productivity.

Spreadsheet Organization

The spreadsheets that you develop will be easier to use and change if you follow a consistent pattern of organization. When creating a spreadsheet, take a few minutes before turning on your computer to reflect on the spreadsheet's purpose and future use, and on the characteristics of the problem you intend to solve. With this knowledge, plan the spreadsheet's structure and organization.

Often, it is desirable to organize your spreadsheet around a **block design**. One typical block design is shown in Figure 7-23. Documentation about the spreadsheet appears first, in the upper left-hand corner. Immediately to the right of the documentation is the table of contents, which describes the sections within the spreadsheet.

The remainder of the block design reflects the input/process/output (I/P/O) cycle discussed previously. One area of the spreadsheet is used to establish values for variables that change from one analysis to the next. Below that block is a section used for calculations, where formulas for processing are located. Finally, output is collected in the block adjacent to the input block. Locating output in a single section makes it easier to see, print, and graph results.

Figure 7-23 Block Design for Spreadsheet Application

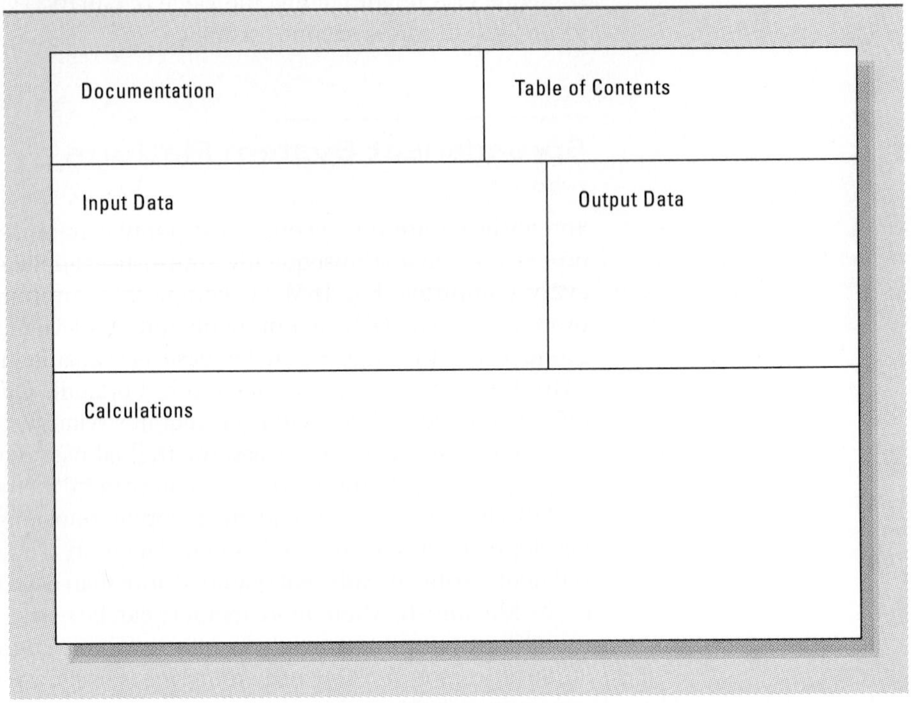

Documentation	Table of Contents
Input Data	Output Data
Calculations	

An example spreadsheet following this block design is shown in Figure 7-24. The documentation section contains the title of the spreadsheet, its purpose, and its developer's name. Some analysts also store the date the spreadsheet was last changed or used.

The table of contents names each block (by block cells), gives the boundaries, and documents any special considerations for that block. Assumptions and warnings appear at the end of this section. The documentation shown here may seem overdone and superfluous, but the comments will prove quite helpful in the future—especially if a large period of time expires between uses of the spreadsheet.

The user enters input data in the input block. Notice that clear labeling ensures that the user knows the type and purpose of input data. Output is gathered in the output section as shown.

Figure 7-24 shows a general-purpose block design, but a number of other possibilities exist. Harrison and Yu describe several others in *The Spreadsheet Style Manual*.[7]

---

7. Harrison and Yu, *op. cit.*, pp. 25–29.

Figure 7-24   Spreadsheet Based on Block Design of Figure 7-23

Documentation

Title:	Product Line Revenue Projections
Purpose:	Calculate revenue net marketing expenses for unit growth rates
Name of Developer:	R. M. Jones

Table of Contents

Input Data Section:	A7 through H18
Calculation Section:	A24 through H46
Output Data Section:	J7 through L22

Input Data

Product Input Data

	A	B	C
Baseline Unit Sales	7220	1770	4390
Price	$18	$35	$25
Unit Sales Growth per Quarter	1.10%	2.75%	1.70%

Marketing Expense Data

Quarter	Amount
1Q95	$107,500
2Q95	$118,000
3Q95	$127,000
4Q95	$130,000
1Q96	$132,000
2Q96	$135,000

Output Data

Results

Quarter	Expenses	Net Rev
1Q95	$107,500	$189,580
2Q95	$118,000	$184,017
3Q95	$127,000	$180,048
4Q95	$130,000	$182,173
1Q96	$132,000	$185,397
2Q96	$135,000	$187,719

Assumed Quarterly Unit Growth

A	B	C
1.10%	2.75%	1.70%

Calculations

	1Q95	2Q95	3Q95	4Q95	1Q96	2Q96
Product						
A						
Units	7220	7299	7380	7461	7543	7626
Dollars	$126,350	$127,740	$129,145	$130,566	$132,002	$133,454
B						
Units	1770	1819	1869	1920	1973	2027
Dollars	$61,419	$63,108	$64,843	$66,627	$68,459	$70,342
C						
Units	4390	4465	4541	4618	4696	4776
Dollars	$109,311	$111,169	$113,059	$114,981	$116,936	$118,924
Total Revenue	$297,080	$302,017	$307,048	$312,173	$317,397	$322,719
Marketing Expense	$107,500	$118,000	$127,000	$130,000	$132,000	$135,000
Revenue Net Marketing Expense	$189,580	$184,017	$180,048	$182,173	$185,397	$187,719

Spreadsheet Testing

In some ways, the use of a spreadsheet can be dangerous: The spreadsheet's output appears so professional that the user can be lulled into a sense of complacency and a belief that the underlying model or analysis contains no errors. The spreadsheet program does not generate warnings or error messages; everything appears perfect, whether or not it really is.

The first criterion for a spreadsheet is accuracy, and that accuracy must be verified by you, the developer. The spreadsheet program cannot ensure that your model appropriately represents your situation; it cannot even verify that your model is consistent and correct. The burden for verifying accuracy belongs to you. Whenever you develop a spreadsheet, remember that you must follow a number of guidelines for tests before disseminating the results to anyone; these guidelines are listed in Figure 7-25.

First, examine your output. This is so obvious that you might wonder why it is stated. However, people often forget this step. Suppose, for example, that you are performing a sensitivity analysis on customer return rates, using the same model and inputting 10 different values for return rate. Suppose your output is an XY-line plot of profitability versus return rate.

When you use this model, your output will be a professional-appearing graph, produced entirely by the spreadsheet application. Look at the graph. Think about it. Verify that you entered the 10 values of return rate correctly. Do not wait until you are explaining the graph to your boss to ask, "What does this break in the curve mean?"

Next, verify input values. If you have organized your spreadsheet to have an input block, this will be easier than if you have placed input values all over your spreadsheet. If you change your model equations from run to run, verify that those changes are correct. Errors in input are easy to make.

Figure 7-25 Guidelines for Testing Spreadsheet Applications

- Examine output
- Verify input
- Check for reasonableness
- Stress-test the spreadsheet
- Involve others

While you are looking at your output, ask yourself if the results seem reasonable. Are the minimum and maximum values within the appropriate range? Do changes from one set of input data to another seem reasonable? Are there any surprises in the output data? If so, what explains them? When you find odd characteristics in your output, examine the input that generated them. Consider possible odd interactions between equations.

To test your model, consider stress testing. Input data values at the very extremes of reasonableness. For example, enter an interest rate of 0 percent, and see if your model generates the correct output. In a profit and loss spreadsheet, enter 0 values for variable costs, and see if your model correctly computes the fixed costs. Check all odd or inexplicable results.

Finally, involve others in your testing process. Explain your output to a disinterested party. Often in the process of explaining something, errors, inconsistencies, or omissions will occur to you. Explaining your results to someone else will force you to take the time to carefully examine your output.

SUMMARY

Processes for developing information systems are adaptations of the problem-solving process described earlier. The classical systems development life cycle (SDLC) emphasizes programming; it is most appropriate when systems involve custom programming. A second version of the SDLC assumes that programs are licensed. Here, there is less emphasis on program design and development. An evaluation stage is added for selecting among licensed program alternatives.

The third style of the SDLC process is called prototyping. With this style, prototypes are constructed, evaluated, and redesigned. No attempt is made to obtain a comprehensive statement of requirements in the beginning; instead, requirements evolve as the prototypes are evaluated and redesigned.

All three processes are appropriate for information systems development. Prototyping is used most frequently for personal information systems, and this chapter considers it in detail. SDLC with licensed programs is frequently used for workgroup systems development. SDLC for custom programming can be used for both workgroup systems development and enterprise systems development.

Using the prototyping process, the problem is first defined. A problem statement is developed; cost, schedule, technical, and organizational feasibility are assessed; and a project plan is developed. Next, the solution to the problem is classified. Basic types of solutions include communications, analysis, tracking and monitoring, and integrated applications. The solution is also classified according to size, constraints, and future use.

The third stage of the prototyping process consists of creating the system platform with hardware, programs, data, procedures, and people. It is usually best to begin with programs since the type of program selected will determine, to a large degree, the hardware requirements.

Once the platform exists, the initial prototype is constructed. It is evaluated, revised, reevaluated, rerevised, and so forth, until no new requirements are determined and no refinements seem necessary. Finally, the system is implemented; it is used to produce the needed results, and the system is documented.

When developing prototypes of personal communication applications, it is important to consider type, graphics, and page layout. Using prototyping, the structure and design of documents to be produced is created using the word processing program. These are evaluated and improved. Often, the information system required evolves as the prototypes evolve.

Spreadsheet applications are also developed using prototyping. Spreadsheets should be structured according to an overall plan. The block structure is often successful. Spreadsheet results should be carefully tested before implementation.

KEY TERMS

SDLC	Context-sensitive help	Type weight
Prototyping	Cutover	Type family
Cost feasibility	Typeface	Graphics
Schedule feasibility	Serif typeface	Page layout
Technical feasibility	Sans serif typeface	Design template
Organizational feasibility	Type size	Spreadsheet block design
Project plan	Point	
	Type style	

REVIEW QUESTIONS

1. Why do you need to know a process for developing a personal information system?

2. Name the three styles of SDLC identified in this chapter, and briefly describe the role of each.

3. Explain the difference between the SDLC and the systems development process.

4. What roles are you likely to take with regard to personal information systems?

5. List the major stages of the rapid prototype style of systems development.

6. Describe the three major activities of the problem definition stage.

7. Define the word *problem*. Explain the importance of the three major components of this definition.

8. Name and describe the four dimensions of feasibility assessment.

9. Why is it important to assess feasibility?

10. How are the various types of feasibility sometimes linked?

11. Name four aspects of problem solution classification.

12. What are the three major categories of solution type? Name two applications in each category.

13. Why is it necessary to make estimates regarding the size of the application?

14. Describe a constraint that might reasonably occur in the use of a personal information system.

15. Describe three possible futures for a personal information system.

16. List five components of a system platform.

17. Why is it appropriate to begin with the program component when building the system platform?

18. Briefly describe a process you could use to select programs for a database application.

19. Describe the major decisions that must be made when acquiring hardware.

20. What general guidelines does the text recommend for designing directories?

21. Describe the two activities to be accomplished for procedures in creating the system platform.

22. What kinds of people might you contact for help in developing a personal information system?

23. Describe the nature of the design stage for systems development using prototyping.

24. Explain the meaning of the text's statement "The synergistic pattern—of requirements feeding design feeding requirements feeding design—results in an effective design."

25. What activities need to be undertaken during the implementation stage of the prototyping systems development process?

26. Explain the meaning of the text's statement "By the time the developer is satisfied with the last prototype, the system has, in the process, been constructed, and it has already been implemented."

27. Explain a situation, other than the one in this chapter, in which it would be beneficial to use a personal communication application to create documents with a consistent design.

28. Describe the typical platform required for an advanced word processing application.

29. Define the following terms: typeface; serif and sans serif typefaces; type size (points); type style; type weight; and type family.

30. Summarize five of the recommendations for type usage.

31. Briefly explain the appropriate application of pie charts, bar charts, and line plots (XY graph).

32. Give two examples showing how a user's communication goals determine the structure of a graph.

33. Summarize five of the recommendations for page layout.

34. List and briefly explain the four purposes of spreadsheets.

35. List and briefly explain the four criteria for evaluating spreadsheets.

36. Summarize the platform required for a spreadsheet application.

37. Sketch the block organization discussed in this text. Why is such an organization recommended?

38. List and briefly explain the five guidelines for spreadsheet testing.

DISCUSSION QUESTIONS

1. Suppose you are an assistant to the director of marketing at a local travel agency. Your boss informs you that she does not believe they are reaching the student population at your college. She wants you to develop marketing materials for this purpose. Suppose you decide to use an information system for this purpose. Describe how you would apply the concepts from this chapter to that problem.

2. The text does not explicitly show how LuAnne integrated the word processing application with the database application. Suppose that LuAnne hires you and informs you that the database application is finished. She has not had time to develop the word processing application. She wants you to do so and then to integrate the two. Describe how you would use the process defined in this chapter to solve the problem.

PROJECTS

A. Suppose a chemistry professor hires you to develop an information system to keep track of course grades. The professor is in charge of the entire introductory chemistry course, with about 1,200 students per semester. She wants a system to keep track of scores on three unit exams and the final exam, plus weekly quizzes for each student. The system will be operated by her graduate assistant, who is an accomplished computer user but who does not have time to develop this system himself.

Because such a large volume of data must be entered, efficiency of data entry is an important consideration. (And since some level of errors is bound to arise, ease of error correction should be a consideration.)

The system should produce a weekly report using code numbers to identify students for posting on the bulletin board. In addition, it should produce a corresponding report with names that the professor and the GA can use in counseling with students.

Apply the prototyping process to solve this problem. For each stage of the process, identify the tasks you must complete, and describe how you would accomplish that task. Assume that the GA has been allocated no computer equipment and no software, but that the university has allocated a budget of up to $5,000. Make other assumptions as necessary, but justify any assumptions you make.

B. Locate a business professional who has recently developed a personal information system. Interview that person, and determine how he or she went about developing the system. How does that process compare with the process described in this chapter? What problems was the system intended to solve? Does it solve those problems? What activities required the most time during development? What activities were the most trouble? What does the person view as the two or three most important successful actions? What were the two or three most important mistakes? What would the person do differently in the future? After your interview, reflect on what you learned. Is the system a success? Was the process used effective? What mistakes were made? What would you do differently?

C. Suppose that, as a field salesperson, you must send a letter each week to your boss describing your sales contacts. The format of the letter is always the same: You write a general summary of activities for the week and then list all of your sales calls. Assume that you keep a record of your mileage for tax purposes in a spreadsheet application. This spreadsheet includes date, time, customer, contact, and mileage.

Design an integrated application to automatically generate the letter to your boss. Assume that you have dynamic data integration. Using a spreadsheet and word processing product, implement your design. Enter sample data into your spreadsheet, and print sales contact letters.

D. Using a spreadsheet program, create the spreadsheet shown in Figure 7-24. Make any necessary assumptions to get the results shown. Use the spreadsheet to consider these questions:

1. If we raise prices 20 percent, sales may drop. What level of sales would we need to maintain at a 20 percent price increase in order to yield an increase in net revenue?

2. Marketing has come up with a plan that may reduce marketing expenses by 11 percent. The result may be some drop in sales. What level of sales would we need to maintain at an 11 percent drop in marketing expenses to yield an increase in net revenue?

3. The parent company has given us the goal of $200,000 in net revenue for the third quarter of 1995. Describe several combinations of changes in the values of this spreadsheet, each of which would achieve that result. Consider at least changes in sales, marketing expenses, unit pricing, and growth rates.

M I N I C A S E

Forget the Rows and Columns

When Lotus Development Corp. announced Improv for Windows last November, it claimed to have defined "a new approach to solving business problems." While perhaps not quite the business process revolution Lotus described, multidimensional spreadsheets such as Improv and CA-Compete from Computer Associates International Inc. and Spreadbase from Objective Software Inc. have given users a new view of the spreadsheet's possibilities.

Multidimensional spreadsheets have a superficial similarity to more traditional spreadsheets, such as Lotus 1-2-3, Microsoft Excel, Borland Quattro Pro, or CA's Supercalc. As in a standard spreadsheet, an array of cells containing data fill the center of the sheet with what appear to be horizontal rows and vertical columns, and a title is given for each item.

But the similarities end there. Multidimensional spreadsheets aren't locked into strict rows and columns. Instead, data is grouped by categories, such as year, region, or department. Items are roughly equivalent to cell labels of spreadsheets. For example, inside a "Regions" category, there may be the items North, South, East, West; a "Products" category may contain the items Hardware, Software, and Peripherals. Items can be grouped together, and categories can be easily added.

Multidimensional spreadsheets "throw away the conventional wisdom in terms of formula development," says John Dunkle, president of Workgroup Technologies Inc. in Hampton, N.H. Formulas are created using real language rather than cell notation. In Improv, "everything is in plain English—the product is user literate rather than spreadsheet literate," he explains. When new items are added to a multidimensional spreadsheet, existing formulas are automatically applied to them.

With multidimensional spreadsheets, users can view data in different ways by simply moving the position of the category in relation to other categories. That flexibility appeals to Margaret Murrin, corporate budget accountant at Underwriters Laboratories in Northbrook, Ill., a user of CA-Compete. "It's neat how you can flip very easily from one view to another," says Murrin. Also, she remarks, the multidimensional spreadsheet's ability to move around columns or rows is a useful feature.

"Improv is very good at not only letting you look at your data but also providing the tools to look at data in many ways at one time," says Workgroup Technologies' Dunkle. "We're using Improv as more than just a spreadsheet. It lets us modify our cuts on very large files quickly and easily."

Tim Bajarin, president of Creative Strategies Research International in Santa Clara, says multidimensional spreadsheets are well-suited for financial analysts. "The guys doing financial modeling absolutely love it," says Bajarin. "It's

easier to use in the context of being more visually oriented." ■

Mark Brownstein, *InformationWeek*, May 17, 1993, p. 57.

Discussion Questions

1. In what ways does Improv differ from conventional spreadsheets?

2. Using multidimensional spreadsheets such as Improv, CA-Compete, and Spreadbase, formulas are typically entered in a form like "Profit = Sales – Costs" rather than by using row and column addresses. When values are entered into columns labeled Sales and Costs, the formula automatically supplies values for a column labeled Profit. How would this change your approach to using spreadsheets?

3. Give an example showing how a user can "flip very easily from one view to another," as described in the article. Show the configuration of row and column labels before and after the change.

4. Describe the advantages and disadvantages of permitting some users in an enterprise to switch to Improv, while other users continue to use conventional spreadsheets. Should an organization standardize on a single spreadsheet package, or should it let users select tools for themselves?

MODULE A

Developing Personal Database Applications

PERSONAL DATABASE APPLICATIONS can be developed by using the process described in Chapter 7, but the activities are somewhat more complicated. Before describing the development of a database application, this module first describes how to build and use a **data model**, which is a statement of data requirements for the database and its applications. The module then details the use of the prototyping process described in Chapter 7 to develop a database application.

BUILDING A DATA MODEL

A database application is used to track things that are important to the user, so to develop the database, you must first determine what those things are—that is, determine the database's contents. You must also determine what facts the user wants to record about those things. Two general approaches exist for making such determinations: top-down data modeling and bottom-up data modeling.

Top-Down Data Modeling

The **top-down data modeling** technique proceeds from the general to the specific, or from the top, down. Using this technique, consider the user environment and imagine or otherwise ascertain the things, or **entities,** that are important to the user. An entity is a person, place, thing, or event such as a customer, a warehouse, a piece of equipment, an order, and so on. Once you have determined the entities themselves, then determine what characteristics, or **properties**, of those entities are important to the user. For example, properties of the customer entity that might be used in a database are customer number, customer name, and customer phone number.

Using top-down modeling, identify the entities and their properties, and then assess **relationships** among those entities. You might determine, for example, that a customer entity is related to an order entity. More specifically, you would determine that each customer is potentially related to many orders.

Once you have determined an initial set of entities, properties, and relationships, document those findings using an **entity-relationship (E-R) diagram**. An E-R diagram for customer and order entities is shown in Figure A-1. In this figure, the entities are listed in rectangles with properties listed below the entity

Figure A-1   E-R Diagram

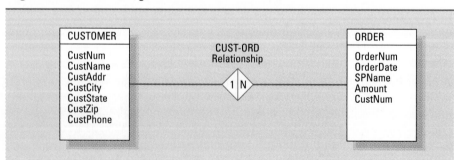

Figure A-2   Tables for the E-R Diagram in Figure A-1

CUSTOMER

CustNum	CustName	CustAddr	CustCity	CustState	CustZip	CustPhone
100	Ajax	124 113th	LosAngeles	CA	98004	332-5578
200	Beemis	34 Elm	Culver City	CA	98055	221-4455
300	Zypher	2245 99th	Torrance	CA	98334	213-4456

ORDER

OrderNum	OrderDate	SPName	Amount	CustNum
1000	05/05/95	Jones	$345.88	100
1010	05/05/95	Parks	$122.45	300
1030	05/06/95	Jones	$224.56	100
1040	05/07/95	Jones	$335.44	100

name. Relationships are shown in diamonds; the relationship 1:N inside the diamond means that one customer entity is related to potentially many order entities. The name of the relationship is shown above the diamond.

Once you have created the E-R diagram, transform it into a set of tables—the CUSTOMER and ORDER tables—to be stored in the database. Tables for the E-R diagram in Figure A-1 are listed in Figure A-2. The process for obtaining the tables is discussed below.

Bottom-Up Data Modeling

The **bottom-up data modeling** technique proceeds from the specific to the general, or from the bottom, up. With this technique, you must first obtain specific examples from the users and the clientele about what they need. To do so, gather documents such as reports and forms that they currently use (or want to have) and analyze those documents to determine what the content of the database should be. The form and report shown in Figure A-3 are examples.

There are several ways of analyzing these documents to perform bottom-up data modeling. The simplest and most appropriate method for personal database applications is to make a list of all of the data items that appear in these two reports. Such a list is shown in Figure A-4a.

Figure A-3 Example Form and Report for the Employee Database

DEPARTMENTAL LISTING			
Department	**Location**	**Phone**	**Manager**
Accounts Payable	R-115	33456	A. M. Franklin
Accounts Receivable	R-119	33678	R. J. Jackson
Customer Relations	J-223	54467	E. R. Coohey
Production	SRJ	55338	F. P. Jason

EMPLOYEE DATA FORM	
Employee Name: Wilson, Kathy D.	Social Security Number: 001-22-3456
Department: Accounts Payable	Pay Code: AR-558
Department Manager: A. M. Franklin	Skill Level: 7
Department Mail Stop: DJ-10	Last Review: 05/09/95

To determine which tables should exist in the database, examine this list and group together data items that appear to be related to one another by a common theme. The data items in Figure A-4a have two themes—departments and employees—and are grouped around these themes, as shown in Figure A-4b. Also observe in this list that two different names exist for the same data item. Manager and department manager represent the same data item.

At this point, transform the list of items into an E-R diagram and proceed as just described. Figure A-5 shows an E-R diagram for the data in Figure A-4. The E-R diagram is then transformed into tables. As you will learn in the next section, the E-R diagram in Figure A-5 would be transformed into the following tables that contain the listed data items:

```
DEPARTMENT  (DeptName, Location, Phone, Manager, MailStop)
EMPLOYEE    (EmpName, SocSecNum, PayCode, SkillLevel, LastReview, DeptName)
```

Sometimes you can use both data modeling approaches. Proceed from the top and move down until you no longer know what to do. Then gather forms and reports and proceed from the bottom and move up. Integrate the designs from the two approaches.[1]

---

1. For a more detailed discussion of these two processes, see David Kroenke's *Database Processing,* 4th ed. (New York: Macmillan, 1992).

Figure A-4 Grouping Database Data Items
(a) List of data items; **(b)** data items grouped by theme.

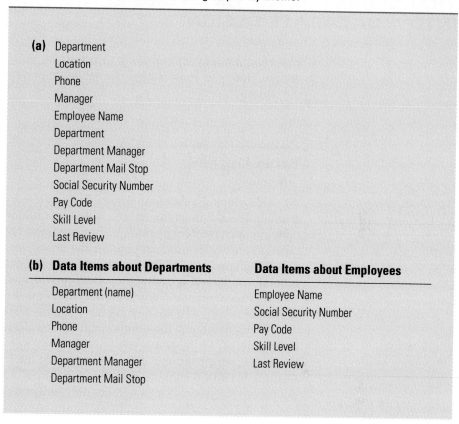

(a) Department
Location
Phone
Manager
Employee Name
Department
Department Manager
Department Mail Stop
Social Security Number
Pay Code
Skill Level
Last Review

(b)

Data Items about Departments	Data Items about Employees
Department (name)	Employee Name
Location	Social Security Number
Phone	Pay Code
Manager	Skill Level
Department Manager	Last Review
Department Mail Stop	

Figure A-5 DEPT-EMP E-R Diagram

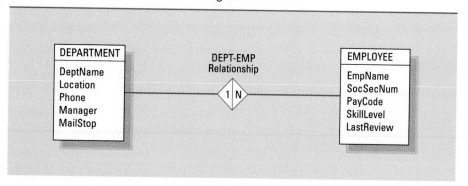

TRANSFORMING THE DATA MODEL INTO A DATABASE DESIGN

You must accomplish two tasks to transform an E-R diagram into a database design. First, you must design the tables, then represent relationships among the tables.

Table Design

When developing a database design from an E-R model, create a table for each entity in the E-R diagram. As stated earlier, to minimize duplicated data, every table should have a single theme. After creating a table for each entity, check the tables to see whether they do contain just one theme.

If you constructed the entities by grouping data items with the bottom-up process, it is likely that each table you create will have only a single theme because such themes were used to group the data items in the first place. Still, it is important to check.

If you developed the entities with the top-down process, then it is possible that some of the resulting tables will have more than one theme. Consider Figure A-6, which shows a different version of the E-R diagram in Figure A-1. In Figure A-6, ORDER contains data about the order, but it also contains additional data about the salesperson's number (SPNum) and commission percentage

Figure A-6   Modified CUST-ORD E-R Diagram

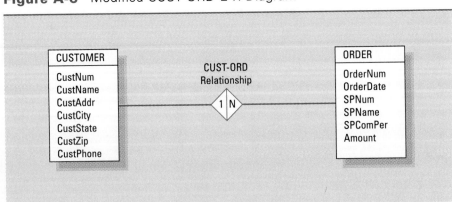

(SPComPer) for the order. Now, if you create a single table from the ORDER entity, it will have the following format:

```
ORDER  (OrderNum, OrderDate, SPNum, SPName, SPComPer, Amount, CustNum)
```

This table contains two themes: One theme is about orders, and the other is about a salesperson and his or her commission rate. To properly represent this ORDER entity, two tables are required as shown in Figure A-7. Observe that the two tables are linked by the common column SPNum.

A **key** is a column (or group of columns) that identifies a unique row in a table. The key of the ORDER table above is OrderNum since a value of OrderNum will determine a unique row in the ORDER table. The key of SALESPERSON in Figure A-7 is SPNum.

Sometimes, when documenting table structure, the key of the table is underlined. Thus, the structure of the two tables in Figure A-7 would be written as follows:

```
ORDER          (OrderNum, OrderDate, SPNum, Amount, CustNum)
SALESPERSON    (SPNum, SPName, SPComPer)
```

For these tables, the column SPNum in the ORDER table is called a **foreign key**, because SPNum is the key of the table SALESPERSON. SPNum, when contained in the table ORDER is a key of a **foreign table**. This terminology is used below.

Figure A-7 Tables Required for the ORDER Entity in Figure A-6

ORDER

OrderNum	OrderDate	SPNum	Amount
1000	05/05/95	10	$345.88
1010	05/05/95	20	$122.45
1030	05/06/95	10	$224.56
1040	05/07/95	20	$335.44

SALESPERSON

SPNum	SPName	SPComPer
10	Jones	0.12
20	Parks	0.10

Relationship Representation

E-R diagrams show both entities and relationships. We define tables to represent the entities as just described. Once those tables have been defined, however, we must then modify them to represent relationships. For example, in Figure A-6, the CUST-ORD relationship must be represented in the CUSTOMER and ORDER tables. The way in which relationships are represented depends on the type of relationship.

In general, there are three types of relationships between two entities: **1:1** (one to one), **1:N** (one to many), and **N:M** (many to many). These relationship types are sometimes called the relationship's **cardinality**.

Figure A-8 shows an example of each of these types of cardinality. In Figure A-8a, one EMPLOYEE entity corresponds to one AUTO entity; this means

Figure A-8   Types of Relationship
(a) 1:1 (one to one); **(b)** 1:N (one to many); **(c)** N:M (many to many).

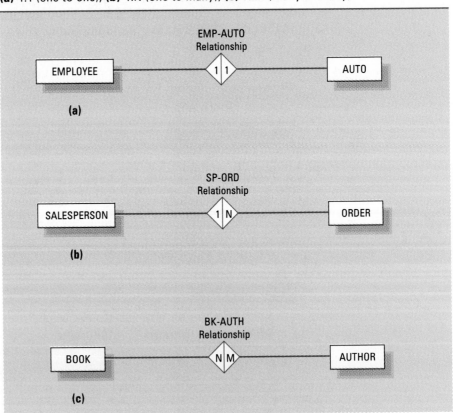

an employee is assigned, at most, one auto and that an auto is assigned to, at most, one employee. In Figure A-8b, one SALESPERSON entity corresponds to many ORDER entities; this means that one salesperson can relate to many orders but that an order is placed by only one salesperson.

In Figure A-8c, one BOOK entity relates to many AUTHOR entities and one AUTHOR entity relates to many BOOK entities. This means that a book can be written by several authors and that an author can write several books. Each of these types is represented differently in a database design.

In the following discussion, assume that each entity is represented by a single table. For the entities in Figure A-8, then, there are EMPLOYEE, AUTO, SALESPERSON, ORDER, BOOK, and AUTHOR tables.

1:1 Relationships   To represent 1:1 relationships, place the key of one of the tables into the other table. Assume that the following two tables represent the entities in Figure A-8a:

```
EMPLOYEE    (EmpNum, EmpName, EmpPhone)
AUTO        (LicenseNum, Type, Color, Year)
```

To represent the relationship between rows of these tables, you can place the key of EMPLOYEE in AUTO or the key of AUTO in EMPLOYEE. Either of the following two constructions will work:

```
EMPLOYEE    (EmpNum, EmpName, EmpPhone, LicenseNum)
AUTO        (LicenseNum, Type, Color, Year)
```

or

```
EMPLOYEE    (EmpNum, EmpName, EmpPhone)
AUTO        (LicenseNum, Type, Color, Year, EmpNum)
```

Consider the first example. If you have an employee and want the auto that he or she is assigned, you can look up the employee's row in the EMPLOYEE table and obtain LicenseNum. With this number, you can look up the correct row in the AUTO table. Similarly, if you have an auto license number and want the data for the employee who is assigned that auto, you can look up the EMPLOYEE row that has the given value of LicenseNum. Analogous processes work for the second alternative.

1:N Relationships   Consider the 1:N relationship between SALESPERSON and ORDER in Figure A-8b. Assume that the following tables represent these entities:

```
SALESPERSON   (SPNum, SPName, SPComPer)
ORDER         (OrderNum, OrderDate, Amount)
```

There are two choices: to place the key of SALESPERSON into ORDER or to place the key of ORDER into SALESPERSON. Unlike 1:1 relationships, both alternatives will not work. To see why, consider the data in Figure A-9. Suppose you try to place the key of ORDER into SALESPERSON. As shown at the bottom of

Figure A-9 Sample ORDER and SALESPERSON Data

ORDER		
OrderNum	**OrderDate**	**Amount**
1000	05/05/95	$345.88
1010	05/05/95	$122.45
1030	05/06/95	$224.56
1040	05/07/95	$335.44

SALESPERSON		
SPNum	**SPName**	**SPComPer**
10	Jones	0.12
20	Parks	0.10

Relationship facts:
Orders 1000 and 1030 were sold by Jones (SPNum 10)
Orders 1010 and 1040 were placed by Parks (SPNum 20)

the figure, salesperson 10 has placed two orders. If you put the key of ORDER into her row in SALESPERSON, you have a problem: There is only space enough for one value in each cell of the table. You cannot place just OrderNum 1000 into the cell or just OrderNum 1030 into this cell; you need to place both. Hence, we cannot put the key of ORDER into SALESPERSON.

Consider the second alternative: placing the key of SALESPERSON into ORDER. Since each row in ORDER corresponds to only one row in SALESPERSON, this alternative successfully results in the tables used in Figure A-7's example. SPNum is contained within ORDER.

In general, for a 1:N relationship, place the key of the table from the "one" side of the relationship into the key of the table on the "many" side of the relationship. Thus, the key of SALESPERSON (SPNum, from the "one" side of the relationship) goes into ORDER (on the "many" side).

N:M Relationships Consider the N:M relationship between BOOK and AUTHOR in Figure A-8c. To understand the meaning of an N:M relationship, consider the sample relationships shown in Figure A-10. Each line in this figure

Figure A-10   BOOK and AUTHOR Relationships

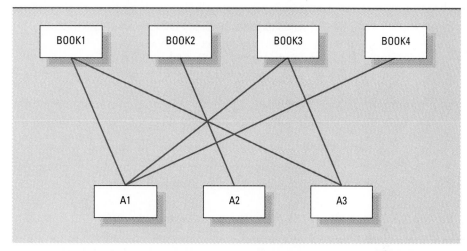

represents a relationship between a book and an author. According to this figure, the book BOOK1 was coauthored by authors A1 and A3. Similarly, author A1 wrote or coauthored books BOOK1, BOOK3, and BOOK4.

Assume that the following tables represent the BOOK and AUTHOR entities:

```
BOOK      (BookID, other data)
AUTHOR    (AuthorName, other data)
```

Nonkey data is not shown here, since it is not needed to describe relationships. Example data for these tables is shown in Figure A-11.

For N:M relationships, placing the key of one table into the other will not work. For instance, Figure A-12 illustrates an attempt to place the key of AUTHOR into BOOK. For the example data shown in Figure A-10, BOOK1 was written by two authors, A1 and A3. Both authors' names cannot be placed in the AuthorName column, since only one value is allowed per cell. For the same reason, the key of BOOK cannot be placed into AUTHOR.

To represent an N:M relationship, create a third table, as shown in Figure A-13. The rows of this new table, called BOOK-AUTH, represent each line in Figure A-10. The first row—BOOK1, A1—represents the first line in Figure A-10. Other rows represent the other lines.

Now you can determine who wrote a book by looking up the book's key in the BOOK-AUTH table. For example, to find the authors of BOOK3, look up that value in BOOK-AUTH and find AuthorNames A1 and A3. Similarly, to find the books written by a given author, look up the author's name in BOOK-AUTH and find the IDs of the books that he or she has written. Thus, to find the books written by A3, look up that value in BOOK-AUTH and find BookIDs BOOK1 and BOOK3.

Figure A-11 BOOK and AUTHOR Tables

BOOK	
BookID	**Other Book Data**
BOOK1	. . .
BOOK2	. . .
BOOK3	. . .
BOOK4	. . .

AUTHOR	
AuthorName	**Other Author Data**
A1	. . .
A2	. . .
A3	. . .

Figure A-12 Unworkable Attempt to Place the Key of the AUTHOR Table into the BOOK Table

BOOK		
BookID	**AuthorName**	**Other Book Data**
BOOK1	A1 but ???	. . .
BOOK2		. . .
BOOK3		. . .
BOOK4		. . .

AUTHOR	
AuthorName	**Other Author Data**
A1	. . .
A2	. . .
A3	. . .

Figure A-13 BOOK, AUTHOR, and BOOK-AUTH Tables

BOOK	
BookID	**Other Book Data**
BOOK1	. . .
BOOK2	. . .
BOOK3	. . .
BOOK4	. . .

AUTHOR	
AuthorName	**Other Author Data**
A1	. . .
A2	. . .
A3	. . .

BOOK-AUTH	
BookID	**AuthorName**
BOOK1	A1
BOOK1	A3
BOOK2	A2
BOOK3	A1
BOOK3	A3
BOOK4	A1

DEVELOPING DATABASES USING PROTOTYPING

Now that you know how to create a data model and transform that data model into tables, you can consider how to apply the prototyping process described in Chapter 7 to the development of personal database systems. To do this, consider a case situation.

Suppose that you work at Elliot Bay Nurseries, the mail-order garden supply company introduced in Chapter 4. One day your boss approaches you and states that the company is concerned about returns. They believe that some customers have been abusing Elliot Bay's liberal return policy, and they want to be able to identify all customers who have returned merchandise. Furthermore, they want to list each return shipment for every customer.

To develop a database application for this problem, you would proceed as described in Chapter 7. First define the problem, then classify it, and, finally, build the system platform. Then build the system by developing a series of prototypes. In this case, since the problem is a tracking problem, you classify the solution as a database solution.

Database Application System Platform

The platform for a personal database application consists of a personal computer with OS (and GUI, if needed in addition) and DBMS. Once the platform has been created, you build a data model, create the database for it, and generate prototypes of forms, reports, and possibly menus. Then you adjust those prototypes until you have an acceptable solution and implement that solution.

Developing Database Prototypes

To develop a prototype for the returns problem at Elliot Bay, you can use either top-down data modeling or bottom-up data modeling. Consider top-down modeling. In this case, you first need to identify the entities involved. Consider the statements your boss made. What are the significant nouns in those statements? Such nouns will suggest the entities to be tracked. Important nouns, and possible entities here, are customer and return shipment, or return, as it will be called here.

Now, think for a minute about the relationship between these two entities. A customer can have many returns, but a return pertains to exactly one customer. Hence, the relationship between a customer and a return is 1:N. An E-R diagram for these two entities is shown in Figure A-14.

To develop the prototype database, assume that each entity can be represented by a single table—in this case, a CUSTOMER table and a RETURN table. What data should those tables contain? You can guess (from the top down) and correct your guesses as you show your prototypes to the users. Or, you can obtain documents and reports and extract the data items from them (from the bottom up).

Suppose you use your knowledge of the Elliot Bay business and make your best guesses. You decide on the following table data:

Figure A-14 CUST-RETURN E-R Diagram

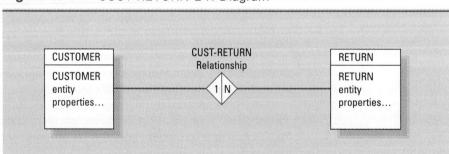

```
CUSTOMER  (CustNum, CustName, CustPhone)
RETURN    (ReturnNum, ReturnDate, CreditAmount)
```

Now consider normalization. Does each table contain a single theme? They do, and so the tables are normalized.

Next consider the relationship between these tables. For a 1:N relationship, place the key of the table on the "one" side into the table on the "many" side. Since one CUSTOMER row relates to many RETURN rows, place the key of CUSTOMER into the RETURN table. The result is as follows:

```
CUSTOMER  (CustNum, CustName, CustPhone)
RETURN    (ReturnNum, ReturnDate, CreditAmount, CustNum)
```

These tables are sufficient to produce your first prototype. To do so, you would input the database design to your DBMS product. At that point, you would also develop prototype reports and forms. The process you would use depends very much on the DBMS product you have; its particulars are not discussed here.

An example prototype report for this database design is shown in Figure A-15. Suppose you show this report to your boss and co-workers and obtain feedback. You may find that you need to add more data to these tables or that you need to add additional tables.

Figure A-15   Prototype of Report for the Returns Tracking Database Application

CUSTOMER RETURN REPORT

Report Date: 03/01/95   Page 1

Customer Name: Frederick P. Abernathy   Customer Number: 12344
Phone: 203-555-0275

Return Date	Credit Amount
01/15/95	$100.75
02/27/95	234.08
Total for Customer 12344	$334.83

Customer Name: Mary James   Customer Number: 34556
Phone: 203-555-2372

Return Date	Credit Amount
01/22/95	$400.00
02/14/95	117.50
02/17/95	237.25
Total for Customer 34556	$754.75

Figure A-16 CUST-RETURN E-R Diagram

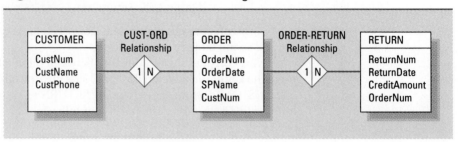

Design Refinement

Suppose that, when you show the report in Figure A-15 to your co-workers, they tell you that it is important to be able to track returns back to originating orders. Given a return, they want to be able to determine the date and the salesperson of the order.

With this feedback, you reexamine your design. A new entity, ORDER, has been identified, and so you need to revise your design. After further conversation and analysis, you develop the revised design in Figure A-16, in which each customer has (potentially) many orders and each order has (potentially) many returns.

The following tables can be used to express the E-R diagram in Figure A-16:

```
CUSTOMER      (CustNum, CustName, CustPhone)
ORDER         (OrderNum, OrderDate, SPName, CustNum)
RETURN        (ReturnNum, ReturnDate, CreditAmount, OrderNum)
```

CustNum in ORDER and OrderNum in RETURN are foreign keys. Now you use the DBMS product to process these tables and produce a report shown in Figure A-17. You again obtain feedback on this report, make revisions, add requirements, and so forth, in an iterative fashion. When no further requirements or refinements are needed, you implement the system.

Database Application Implementation

Implementing a database application follows the same general process described for other types of personal MIS applications. One difference is that you might need to take time to enter appreciable amounts of data before getting started.

Also, you may wish to document procedures for using your database application. Over time, you may forget the instructions, commands, or menus that are used to process the database. If the database application will be used by others, such documentation will be even more important.

Figure A-17   Revised Prototype Report for the Returns Tracking Database Application

CUSTOMER RETURN REPORT

Report Date: 03/01/95   Page 1

Customer Name: Frederick P. Abernathy   Customer Number: 12344
Phone: 203-555-0275

Return Date	Order Number	Order Date	Salesperson	Credit Amount
01/15/95	91-2456	12/17/94	Smythe	$100.75
02/27/95	92-0559	01/07/95	Smythe	234.08
	Total for Customer 12344			$334.83

Customer Name: Mary James   Customer Number: 34556
Phone: 203-555-2372

Return Date	Order Number	Order Date	Salesperson	Credit Amount
1/22/95	92-0772	01/09/95	Smythe	$400.00
2/14/95	92-0772	01/09/95	Smythe	117.50
2/17/95	92-1255	02/03/95	Turkle	237.25
	Total for Customer 34556			$754.75

SUMMARY

A data model is a statement of data requirements for the database and its applications. Data models can be constructed from the general to the specific in top-down fashion, or they can be constructed from the specific to the general in bottom-up fashion. Or, both approaches can be used.

When the top-down modeling process is used, the entities important to the user are identified. Important properties of the entities are determined, and the relationships among the entities are specified. The result is documented in an entity-relationship (E-R) diagram.

Several techniques for bottom-up modeling exist. The one recommended here is to obtain forms and reports and to list the data items contained on them. The list is then organized by theme; each group of data items identifies an entity. Relationships among the entities are identified and documented in an E-R diagram.

Each entity in an E-R diagram is transformed into a table. The tables are then examined to determine whether they each contain a single theme. If not, they are divided into tables that do have a single theme. A key is one or more columns that identifies a unique row. A foreign key is a column that is a key of a table other than the one in which the column appears.

There are three types of relationship cardinality: 1:1 (one to one), 1:N (one to many), and N:M (many to many). The 1:1 relationships are represented by placing the key of one of the tables into the other table. The 1:N relationships are represented by placing the key of the table on the "one" side into the table on the "many" side. The N:M relationships are represented by creating a third table that has the keys of each instance of the N:M relationship.

Developing a database using prototypes involves the same process as described in Chapter 7. First define the problem, next classify it, then build a system platform. Such a platform must include a DBMS product. Then develop the database by constructing a data model, creating a database design, and implementing prototype forms and reports. Adjust the prototypes and the design as needed. Finally, implement the system.

KEY TERMS

Personal database application	Properties	Foreign key
Data model	Relationships	Foreign table
Top-down data modeling	E-R diagram	1:1 relationship
Entities	Bottom-up data modeling	1:N relationship
	Key	N:M relationship
		Cardinality

REVIEW QUESTIONS

1. What is the purpose of data modeling?

2. Give an example, other than the ones in this text, of two entities and a relationship. Diagram your example with an E-R diagram.

3. Summarize the difference between top-down and bottom-up data modeling. Explain the conditions under which you would use one or the other.

4. List the three kinds of cardinality relationships.

5. Give an example of two entities having a 1:1 relationship. Diagram the entities.

6. Show two tables that could represent your example in question 5. Explain how your tables represent the 1:1 relationship.

7. Give an example of two entities having a 1:N relationship. Diagram the entities.

8. Show two tables that could represent your example in question 7. Explain how your tables represent the 1:N relationship.

9. Give an example of two entities having an N:M relationship. Diagram the entities.

10. Show tables that could represent your example in question 9. Explain how your tables represent the N:M relationship.

PROJECTS

A. Use a DBMS to implement the CUSTOMER/RETURN database for Elliot Bay Nurseries as illustrated by the E-R diagram in Figure A-16 and the prototype report in Figure A-17. Add sample data to permit testing of report forms. Create a report showing the customers who have had the largest number of returns. Create a second report showing the customers who have had the largest dollar amounts of returns. Order both lists from highest to lowest returns. For each customer in each of the reports, create a listing like the ones in Figure A-15.

B. Consider the following case: Elizabeth Merrill is a fine artist who paints murals and other artistic designs on the walls of homes and, occasionally, businesses. Elizabeth obtains job leads and referrals from interior designers and past customers. Many of her customers like her work so much that they ask her to produce several paintings in their homes. Sometimes she does this in one visit; other times, several months or even years may go by before the customers ask for additional work.

Elizabeth would like to track the jobs that she has done on each home. Often, a customer will call and say that she painted in their home, and, to her embarrassment, Elizabeth cannot remember who they are or what she did for them in the past. She would also like to track which designers and past customers have referred work to her so that she can thank them.

Build a data model for Elizabeth's business. In your model, show entities and relationships. Make up properties that seem reasonable to you.

Transform your data model into table designs. Sketch the format of a prototype form and report for Elizabeth's business.

C. Use a DBMS to implement the database you designed in project B. Use the DBMS to create the forms and reports you sketched in project B.

D. River Madness is a travel agency that specializes in arranging rafting and kayaking trips all over the world. The company arranges travel, accommodations, equipment, and instruction for all of their trips. They obtain customers from advertising, and they also do substantial repeat business.

River Madness wants to project the image of remembering every customer. Hence, when a customer calls, they want to be able to immediately access the customer's record and determine which trips the customer has taken. They then weave that information into the conversation and make a sales pitch for other, similar trips.

Build a data model for River Madness's business. In your model, show entities and relationships. Make up properties that seem reasonable to you. Transform your data model into table designs. Sketch the format of a prototype form, and report for this business.

E. Use a DBMS to implement the database you designed in project D. Use the DBMS to create the forms and reports you sketched in project D.

Workgroup Management Information Systems

PART III CONSIDERS INFORMATION SYSTEMS that facilitate the activities of workgroups. Chapter 8 discusses workgroup applications and then shows how those applications can add value to workgroup processes, products, and the ability to innovate and improve. Chapter 9 describes the five components of workgroup information systems. Finally, Chapter 10 discusses the development of workgroup information systems. You will learn to apply a five-step process for the development of workgroup systems. You will also learn about two important system tools: dataflow diagrams and the data dictionary.

As you read and review this material, remember that the structure of this part is the same as the structure of Part II. Chapter 8 surveys goals and applications; Chapter 9 describes the five components of information systems; and Chapter 10 discusses development methods.

8

Workgroup Information Systems: Applications and Goals

IN 1980, **VIRTUALLY ALL CORPORATE COMPUTING POWER** resided in centralized mainframe computer systems. Today, at least 95 percent of corporate computing power is in personal computers, most of which have been linked to share data, E-mail, and expensive printers.

In the early days of PCs, they were used primarily to increase the productivity of workers acting individually. Their word processing, spreadsheet, and database programs helped workers to produce more work of higher quality.

Recently, however, PCs have become an important resource to make workers more productive in workgroups. This chapter surveys workgroup information systems. First we define workgroups and discuss several important workgroup characteristics. Then workgroup applications are surveyed, using the same categories used in Chapter 5: communications, analysis, and tracking and monitoring. Finally, this chapter explains how workgroup information systems add value to workgroup process, product, and responsiveness to changing conditions.

WHAT IS A WORKGROUP?

A **workgroup** is a collection of, usually, 2 to 25 people who work together to achieve a common goal.[1] Workgroups are commonly given names like team, task force, department, group, office, and so forth. Usually, members of a workgroup know one another, and most often work side by side in the same location. Members of the group identify with the group and with each other, and, typically, meet together periodically. Examples of workgroups are a customer support group at a software publisher, a team assembled from company personnel to respond to a disaster on company property, and a planning and budgeting office at a major manufacturing corporation.

Although there are several ways of defining workgroups, we will consider the structural definition.[2] A workgroup is "an organized system of two or more individuals who are interrelated so that the system performs some function, has a standard set of role relationships among its members, and has a set of norms that regulate the function of the group and each of its members."[3]

Observe the three components of this definition: function, role, and norm. The **workgroup function**, the purpose for which the group exists, generally is explicitly established in organizational descriptions and tacitly established in organizational budgets. There are two basic types of **workgroup roles**—homogeneous and heterogeneous—and the character of the information systems varies between systems. Finally, **workgroup norms** have an important influence over systems use, as you will learn.

Homogeneous Workgroups

In **homogeneous workgroups**, everyone in the workgroup (except management) fulfills the same role. Within a warehouse shipping group, for example, everyone may work in the role of warehouse operator and have the same job functions of selecting and packing merchandise. All employees may have the same level of training and skills (or, at least, be viewed that way). Work is assigned on a first-person-available, first-person-assigned basis.

---

1. This is an approximate number. Some workgroups can be considerably larger than 25. The point is that the members all perceive that they belong to this group—they identify with the group.

2. Daft, Richard L. and Richard M. Steers, *Organizations, A Micro/Macro Approach.* Glenview, IL: Scott, Foresman, 1986, p. 186.

3. McDavid, J. and M. Harari, *Social Psychology: Individuals, Groups, Societies.* New York: Harper & Row, 1968, p. 237.

Figure 8-1 Warehouse Operations Organization Chart
Warehouse operators comprise a homogeneous workgroup.

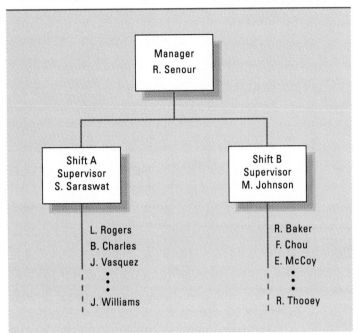

Figure 8-1 shows the organization chart of the warehouse group at Legacy Systems, a computer software publisher. The group works a two-shift, seven-day-a-week schedule. The group manager has two shift supervisors; everyone else has the title Warehouse Operator. As more employees are added to a homogeneous workgroup, productivity increases at a near-linear rate. The second, third, and fourth warehouse operators add about the same amount of productivity as do the tenth, eleventh, and twelfth warehouse operators.

Information systems tend to be easier to build and support for homogeneous workgroups than for heterogeneous workgroups. Since everyone does the same job, attention is focused on information systems to support that single job. Further, a productivity improvement that helps one worker generally helps all workers.

Heterogeneous Workgroups

Heterogeneous workgroups involve several or many different roles and job descriptions. In a customer support group, for example, there are people who specialize in particular products and people whose advanced knowledge and

Figure 8-2 Customer Support Organization Chart
Customer support is a heterogeneous workgroup.

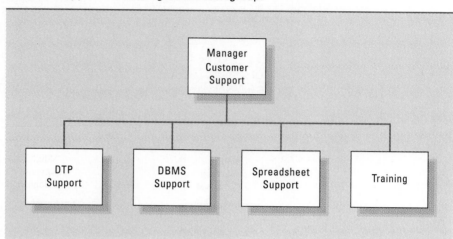

expertise qualify them to handle only certain difficult questions or key customers. Other specialties exist as well.

Figure 8-2 shows the organization chart of the Customer Support group at Legacy Systems. Customer support representatives are assigned to one of four groups, depending on their expertise. Three groups provide support for the DTP products, the DBMS products, and the spreadsheet products. The fourth group trains the members of the Customer Support staff.

When personnel are added to a heterogeneous workgroup, productive capacity does not rise at a linear rate. The first person who knows a great deal about a particular role adds much more productive capacity than does the tenth person. At Legacy, one customer representative in the DBMS group is an outstanding communicator who can quickly detect a customer's level of techni– cal knowledge and effectively adapt explanations. She adds much more productive capacity to the group than another person whose explanatory skills are less fully developed.

This phenomenon makes personnel hiring more difficult. When the work load increases, it is not possible to simply hire another trained person to fill an open position. The manager of Customer Support cannot hire another good communicator as easily as the manager of the warehouse can hire another good operator. For Customer Support, a person must be a good communicator and must also possess the specialized knowledge needed to fill his or her role in the workgroup.

Two important challenges to heterogeneous workgroups concern communication and training. Since the group involves multiple roles, it tends to splinter into subgroups, which not only reduces productivity, but also can result in cliques and other forms of exclusivity that dampen morale. Training is another problem if the workgroup must expand or contract its size. When Legacy announces a new product, for example, the Customer Support group will be inundated with calls about the new product for the first month or two. Some Legacy personnel will need to learn the new product and its features and quirks.

It is more difficult to develop information systems for heterogeneous groups than for homogeneous groups. Since there are many different jobs, a variety of systems are often needed. Instead of 24 people using one system, 6 people may be using four different systems, which means development costs are higher. Further, the development cost of four systems must be amortized by the work of 6 people, instead of the development cost of one system amortized by the work of 24 people.

Additionally, since roles are specialized, information systems must be specialized. At Legacy Customer Support, the needs of a support representative are far different from those of the newsletter's producer. This means that different information systems technologies and, hence, expertise will be required to support the group.

Workgroup Norms

A workgroup norm is an expectation shared among workgroup members that regulates member behavior. For example, norms determine the pace at which members are expected to work, the hours they are expected to keep, and the values they are expected to hold. Norms are powerful influences, and groups find many overt and covert ways to enforce them.

One of the most important ways norms influence information systems concerns the group's attitude about the role of computer systems. If the workgroup norm is that everyone is expected to gainfully utilize computer systems, then, if necessary, group members find ways to overcome computer phobia or other resistance. The group provides support and assistance to new members to adapt to the systems. A typical statement to a new group member might be, "When I first came here, I didn't know how to use a computer, either. But it really isn't so hard. Let me show you how I did it."

On the other hand, if the workgroup norms are opposed to the use of computer systems, then such systems may never succeed. Whoever wants the system to be used must first address the changing of workgroup norms before proceeding with systems implementation. Computer systems seldom succeed if group norms oppose their use.

Figure 8-3 Four Types of Workgroups

	Permanent	**Temporary**
Single-Site	Customer Support group	Proposal Development team
Distributed	Human Resources department	Product Launch team

Types of Workgroups

Figure 8-3 shows four types of workgroups arranged in two dimensions. As shown, workgroups are permanent or temporary, and they have a single site or distributed locations. **Permanent workgroups** are formal departments or offices in the organization, such as Legacy's Customer Support group. **Temporary workgroups** are convened to solve a particular problem or to address a unique opportunity. The examples of temporary workgroups shown in Figure 8-3 involve teams of people formed to develop a proposal and to launch a new product.

Most workgroups are located in a **single site**. However, some permanent workgroups and temporary workgroups are **distributed** at many sites, in which case information systems are particularly helpful to them.

For example, consider the case of a multinational company that has human resources personnel distributed in offices throughout the world. These personnel belong to the corporate human resources workgroup, but they reside with the divisions of the company they support and feel isolated from their profession. In the remote sites, where there are few people with whom they can discuss human resources issues, electronic mail and other types of communication systems help such distributed personnel feel more a part of the human resources workgroup that is distributed throughout the enterprise.

A product launch team is an example of a temporary, distributed workgroup. Launching a product requires that personnel from sales, marketing, advertising, public relations, and other departments come together to perform activities in a consistent and coordinated fashion. A communications system can help the individuals in a group such as a product launch team to stay synchronized in the face of changing conditions.

WORKGROUP INFORMATION SYSTEMS

The purpose of a workgroup information system is to facilitate **workgroup effectiveness**. Nadler, Hackman, and Lawler define such workgroup effectiveness in three dimensions. Workgroups should (1) produce output that meets or exceeds expectations, (2) provide for the personal need satisfaction of group members, and (3) function so as to facilitate the group's capacity for future cooperation.[4]

By the same model, these dimensions of effectiveness are determined by three workgroup effectiveness factors: (1) group effort, (2) group knowledge and skill, and (3) the approach and strategy used to perform work. While information systems influence all three factors, they are particularly important with regard to the last two. Workgroup information systems facilitate workgroup communications and thus improve the group's knowledge and skills. Additionally, workgroup information systems enable both the discovery and the implementation of new approaches and strategies.

Primary Characteristic of Workgroup Information Systems

The primary difference between workgroup information systems and personal information systems is that workgroup systems must support the controlled sharing of data, information, knowledge, and other resources. To accomplish the workgroup's objectives of increasing its productive output through increased effort and knowledge and to provide for better work strategies, members must be allowed access to each other's and to the workgroup's resources.

Controlled sharing enables workgroup members to access the same resources, but this must be done without interfering with each other's work. For example, in a software documentation group, one technical writer may create a document that is clarified by a second writer the following week and updated to reflect changes in the product by a third writer 2 months later. To make this possible, all three writers must share access to the pool of current documentation. But if two writers modify the same document simultaneously, trouble will result. Thus, the information systems must allow the writers to access from a shared pool, but it must do so carefully.

Additionally, controlled sharing involves **security**. Often, not every member of the group needs or should have access to all of the group's information resources.

---

4.   Nadler, David A., J. Richard Hackman, and Edward E. Lawler, III. *Managing Organizational Behavior*. Boston: Little, Brown, 1979, pp. 140–143.

In these cases, the information systems must provide passwords, account numbers, and other forms of security to restrict access and activity.

Granularity refers to the size of the units of data or information that is shared. For example, if the granularity of a shared documentation system is a document, then the entire document is checked out to an individual for processing. The granularity might be larger or smaller than this. For example, a system might be designed to allocate an entire floppy disk to a writer, in which case the level of granularity is the collection of documents on that disk. For another example, if the level of granularity is major sections within a document, then only a portion of a document is checked out to a particular user.

The level of granularity influences the throughput of the shared system. The larger the level of granularity, the greater the chance of delays due to contention, but the easier it is to administer the system. On the other hand, the smaller the level of granularity, the less chance of contention, but the greater the cost of administering the shared resources. You will see the role of granularity in some of the examples that follow.

Hardware Sharing

Although most workgroup information systems involve the sharing of information and knowledge, there is one exception. **Hardware-sharing** applications allow members of a workgroup to share access to expensive computer hardware devices that they could not justify for their own applications alone.

For example, each workgroup member may operate one or more personal information systems. Some applications may require the occasional use of a laser printer, but perhaps none can justify the expense of such a printer by itself. If, however, several applications can use the printer, those applications can justify the expense jointly. Expensive printers, plotters, cameras, and other output hardware are often shared this way.

In addition, fast, large-capacity disks can be shared. The disk is divided into separate parts, and each user has unlimited access to one part of the disk. This differs from data-sharing applications (described below), in which users share access to the entire contents of the disk.

Disk sharing allows for **diskless workstations**, which are cheaper. The absence of a disk reduces the likelihood that data will be stolen or otherwise compromised by copying it via local disks.

Figure 8-4 shows two ways that hardware can be shared. The system in Figure 8-4a is primitive; here, users copy data onto floppy diskettes and carry it to the printer or disk. This is sometimes called **sneaker net**. Figure 8-4b shows a more sophisticated system; here, computers are connected via a **local area network (LAN),** which allows the computers to communicate with one another and with the shared hardware. A LAN consists of cables and processor cards inserted into

Figure 8-4 Hardware-Sharing Alternatives

(a) *Sneaker net* involves carrying data on floppy disks to computers that include the shared hardware. **(b)** The LAN alternative provides full-time sharing.

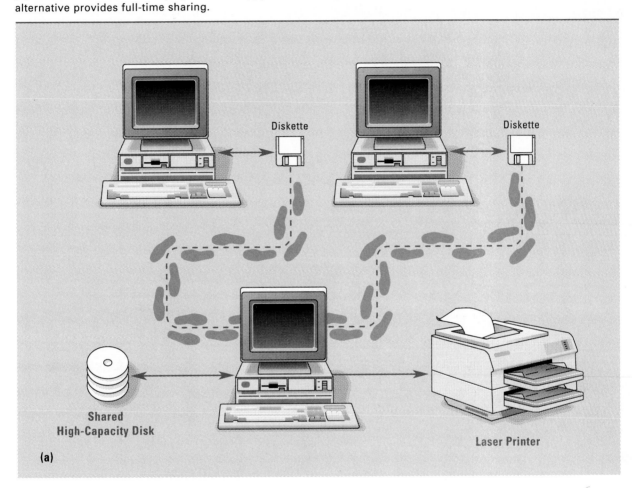

Diskette

Diskette

Shared
High-Capacity Disk

Laser Printer

(a)

the expansion slots of the microcomputers, along with programs to make them work. You will learn more about LANs in the next chapter.

Hardware-sharing systems are, in many ways, the simplest type of workgroup computer system. There is minimal need for coordination and cooperation. Users need only coordinate their use of the hardware, just as they coordinate their use of a copier or other machines. In fact, with some devices, the hardware itself will **queue** (line up) user requests and perform the coordination. Again, the major goal of such systems is to enable workers to share access to expensive hardware that they could not cost-justify on their own.

Figure 8-4   *(continued)*

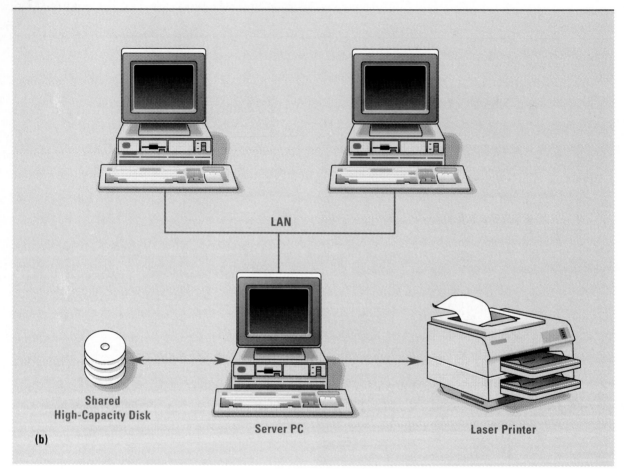

(b)

Data Sharing

So many types of data-sharing information systems are used by workgroups, even the vendors sometimes have difficulty explaining what a product can do. To help sort things out, Briggs and Nunamaker have categorized group information systems in a three-by-three grid (see Figure 8-5).[5] They distinguish systems that focus on (1) improving individual productivity, (2) coordinating the group's operational

5. Adapted from Briggs, Robert O. and Jay F. Nunamaker, Jr., "Getting a Grip on Groupware," University of Arizona Center for Management of Information Working Paper Series 93-06.

Figure 8-5 Group Information Systems

	Communication	Analysis	Information Retrieval
Group Problem Solving and Decision Making	Group conferencing	GDSS	Group memory
Group Coordination	E-mail Group conferencing Collaborative writing	Shared spreadsheets	Shared databases Workflow automation Group scheduling Group project management Shared textbases
Individual Productivity	Word processing Graphics DTP	Spreadsheets	Personal databases Project management

work, and (3) group problem solving and decision making. Systems that focus on individual productivity also enhance group output to the degree that group output includes each individual's output. These systems have been discussed previously and will not be considered further here.

Systems that focus on coordination are designed to support the day-to-day operations of the group. Some are TPSs; others are designed to computerize operations other than transaction processing.

Systems that focus on group problem solving and decision making deal with problems in group dynamics that arise when people face important decisions together. One problem is that in a single meeting, each person can speak only a short time. Obviously, the more participants, the shorter time each can speak. Some information systems for group decision making let all participants enter ideas at the same time by keyboard, giving a larger base of ideas for consideration.

Another aspect of group dynamics is **evaluation apprehension**: the reluctance of some people to contribute ideas when they risk looking bad before superiors. Allowing participants to contribute anonymously may overcome this and other problems.

Finally, distributed groups present special problems of decision-making dynamics, since participants lack the behavior cues present in face-to-face meetings. Shifts in the discussion are often signaled by behaviors that are undetectable through a computer link, often even when the link includes audio and motion video. Study of these distributed group dynamics is in its early stages, yet progress has already begun.

The columns of the Briggs and Nunamaker grid in Figure 8-5 involve the familiar distinction among communication systems, analysis systems, and tracking and monitoring systems, now expanded to include all information retrieval activities. Group information retrieval systems may involve databases like those used in personal systems, or they may involve providing access to large amounts of text information.

The next part of this chapter uses the Briggs and Nunamaker grid to sort out the many types of workgroup information systems.

WORKGROUP INFORMATION SYSTEMS FACILITATE COMMUNICATION

Many types of information systems facilitate workgroup communications. This section discusses three common types of workgroup communications applications: electronic mail systems, group conferencing systems, and collaborative writing systems. Because technology is developing rapidly in this field, during the course of your career, many new forms of computer-based workgroup communication systems probably will evolve.

Electronic Mail

One of the most common workgroup communications applications is **electronic mail (E-mail).** In workgroups, E-mail systems provides an electronic means for creating, editing, and disseminating intragroup communications. Its focus is group coordination.

With E-mail, each person connected to the system is allocated a **mailbox** and a set of programs for creating and reading mail. The mailbox is simply a file into which the E-mail system deposits electronic correspondence.

Figure 8-6 shows a schematic of a typical E-mail application. This system consists of a group of microcomputers connected via communications lines in a LAN. Less commonly, E-mail resides on concurrently accessed minicomputer and mainframe computers. For the system in Figure 8-6, each computer owns a mailbox on a centralized disk where the E-mail system deposits mail. Users periodically examine their mailboxes (via the LAN) to see if they have mail.

Figure 8-6 An E-Mail System

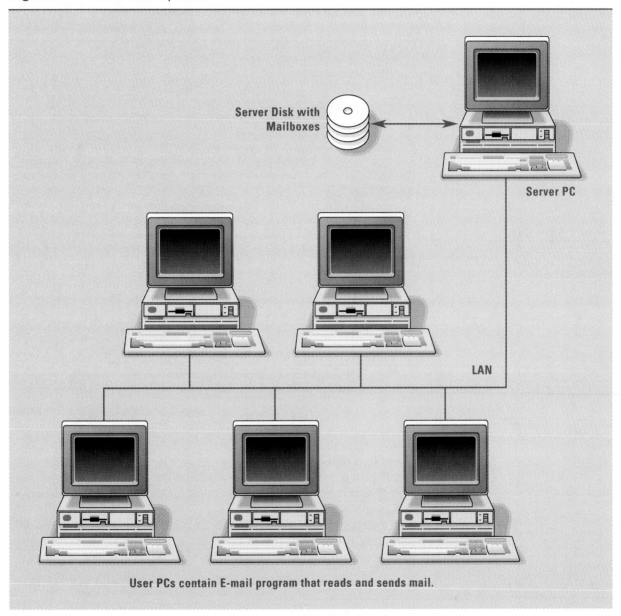

Server Disk with Mailboxes

Server PC

LAN

User PCs contain E-mail program that reads and sends mail.

Figure 8-7 shows a screen that is typical of those used in mail systems. The originator specifies his or her identity and the identities of those to whom the mail is to be directed. The originator of the mail then keys in the message and directs

Figure 8-7 An E-Mail Screen

When the E-mail message load is heavy, the user can select
particular messages to read first.

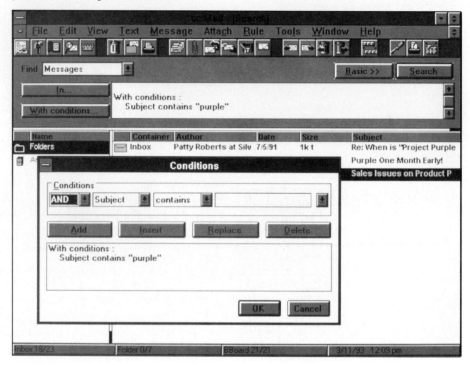

the system to send the mail. Addressees can be specified by name or distribution
list. For example, a user could direct that a message be sent to all employees in a
particular workgroup, to all employees connected to the E-mail system, or to some
other group of users. An address book function maintains a user's address list,
including the various distribution lists.

E-mail systems can be active or passive. An **active** system informs the user
when mail arrives. A **passive** system just deposits the mail and expects the user to
periodically open the mailbox to check for new mail.

Group Conferencing

Group conferencing applications are so widely varied that the title itself means
different things to different people, depending on their personal experiences with

Figure 8-8 A Notes Screen

Lotus Notes has been configured to provide access to many types of information in this company.

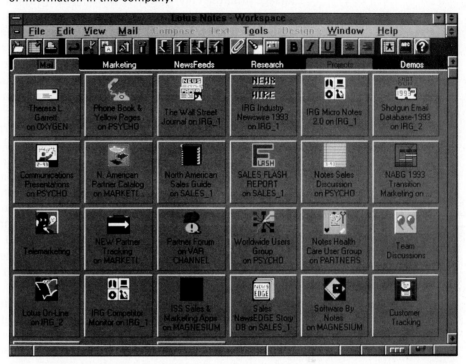

particular products. This section surveys the range of group conferencing applications.

The simplest type of group conferencing is an **electronic bulletin board**, which enables members to exchange information in a meeting-like format. An electronic bulletin board is informal, like the group assembling at break time around the coffee machine. A common file stores messages of interest to the entire group. An example is shown in Figure 8-8. Electronic bulletin boards focus on group coordination.

Another group conferencing facility is an **asynchronous meeting**. As we have seen, managers and executives spend much of their time in meetings. Face-to-face meetings were the only practical means of focusing a group's attention on a particular topic until electronic media appeared. However, the number of meetings that many managers must attend can be overwhelming, and, for distributed groups, the travel time and cost is burdensome. When participants need not meet face-to-face, but only need to focus on a topic and exchange information, the asynchronous meeting may serve the purpose.

An asynchronous meeting is like an electronic bulletin board focused on a single topic that operates for a limited time period. Attendees each receive a message from the chairperson describing the purpose of the meeting, the people involved, and the time frame. Attendees then contribute comments to a shared text file, and their comments are read by other attendees. The time frame, typically from several days to a week, allows members time to respond to each other's comments. If the purpose of the meeting is a decision, consensus may emerge from the dialogue, or a vote may be taken after the comments have been considered. When the meeting is over, the chairperson writes a summary statement and sends it to each member.

Some asynchronous meeting tools are primarily oriented toward group coordination—sharing information—whereas others include resources to support group dynamics and decision making. For example, a tool may treat all comments anonymously, reducing the problem of evaluation apprehension. Another tool may provide facilities to let members brainstorm potential solutions to a problem, then, in a subsequent step, invite members to build on the best ideas generated.

A **group network** is an extension to an asynchronous meeting. Here, the meeting is held over a communications facility like E-mail, but it is held in real time and is interactive.[6] Members all meet at the same time, as with a traditional meeting, but they may not be in the same location. If members are in their own offices, they may access data, reports, graphs, and other forms of information on their PCs. They can present any of this information to the other meeting attendees via the group network facility. Such a facility also provides tools for the chairperson to control the order of activity and voting when necessary.

Group networks typically provide tools to deal with group decision-making dynamics. For example, one system includes a **shared drawing tool**, letting members create diagrams and drawings on the computer screen that are shared by other members. This tool functions much the same as the flip charts or white boards and pens used in face-to-face meetings. Sometimes, one member controls the drawing to sketch an idea, and at other times, each member controls part of the drawing. This tool is often used in a group network room, where members are all in the same place. If members are dispersed, the shared drawing tool is often accompanied by an audio link that lets the presenter simultaneously show a drawing and talk about it.

In **video conferencing**, meetings are conducted among people who are dispersed, using a television link. The earliest versions connected a group in one location with a group or an individual in another location by a television link, enabling members at both locations to see and hear each other. More recent versions use computer links to carry TV-like audio and motion video, along with computerized graphics, reports, screen images, and other shared data. For example,

---

6. Kraemer, Kenneth L. and John Leslie King, "Computer-Based Systems for Cooperative Work and Group Decision Making," *Computing Surveys*, Vol. 20, No. 2, June 1988, p. 125.

computer hardware and program vendors use such systems to introduce important new products to major customers in many cities simultaneously. Video conferencing may be used in ways that focus on coordination or, at other times, on group dynamics and decision making.

Collaborative Writing

Collaborative writing systems let groups work together through a LAN to create important documents (see Figure 8-9). At one small company, for example, major proposals are created over a weekend by a team of key company leaders. In preparation, members spend several days developing facts and figures, themes, and competitive arguments. During that period, members meet and agree on an outline.

Then the team comes together on a Friday evening in a roomful of networked computers. Each member takes a section of the proposal and drafts it. By 8:30 or 9:00 P.M., the first draft is completed. At that point, everyone can see the shape of the document—and the fact that the different sections are not completely consistent. The remainder of Friday evening and Saturday morning are devoted to discovering all the issues raised by these inconsistencies and hammering out solutions.

About noon on Saturday, the revision process begins. At 2:00 P.M., two technical writers and two graphic artists join the group. As each section is redrafted, a tech writer begins editing it, and an artist begins creating its graphics. As they work, members are carefully reading through the entire document on their screens and noting areas that need further work. Their comments are made on the electronic equivalent of paper stick-on notes; a computerized tool attaches each note where it applies in the document file. Each section may go through several cycles of redrafting, editing, reviewing, and further redrafting before the group is satisfied. By late evening, only a few key issues remain to be ironed out, and the group returns on Sunday morning to tackle these. By Sunday noon, the text is in final form, and the graphics have been accepted.

At this point, while the authors take a break, the editorial team uses a DTP program to combine text and graphics into a rough document, using a design template they created in advance. By the end of the afternoon, the document has been finalized and printed, and everyone goes home. One result of this team effort is that the company can respond extremely quickly to changing conditions.

Typical collaborative writing projects are much less dramatic, but just as useful. Large reports, information systems documentation, project plans, brochures, annual reports, and many other types of documents are often written collaboratively. Group members share the task of drafting, then review and revise each other's work. Specialists can be added to the group as needed for graphics support or final production.

Figure 8-9 Collaborative Writing System Hardware

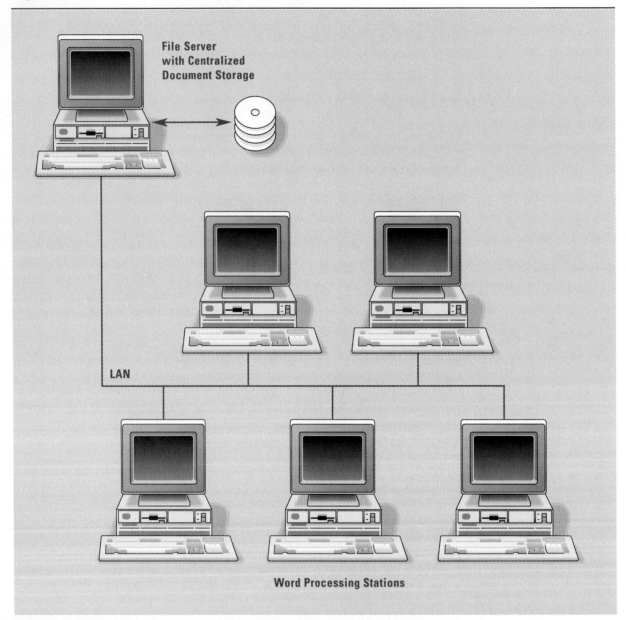

File Server
with Centralized
Document Storage

LAN

Word Processing Stations

When documents are shared, steps must be taken to ensure that one person's work does not interfere with another's. The administration of shared documents and other text is usually accomplished by a combination of programs and procedures. Programs that support group word processing normally include features and functions to check out or otherwise allocate documents to individuals. In most offices, however, these features and functions are augmented by manual sharing procedures. Such augmentation is required to implement control and security provisions that go beyond the capabilities of the product.

Collaborative writing applications focus primarily on workgroup coordination, although some packages also provide limited tools for dealing with the group dynamics of document creation—particularly in resolving the policy questions that often emerge as agreements in principle are expressed in written form.

WORKGROUP INFORMATION SYSTEMS AID IN ANALYSIS

Information systems also facilitate workgroup analysis. The workgroup can coordinate efforts to produce a formal, quantitative analysis such as with a group spreadsheet, or it can work together to solve less structured problems using group decision support systems.

Workgroup Spreadsheets

Some workgroups share spreadsheet data. A group of budget analysts, for example, might share the fundamental format, or **template**, for the corporate budget. A template is to a spreadsheet application what boilerplate is to a word processing application. The template contains the structure of the spreadsheet, independent and dependent variables, formulas, and other parts of the spreadsheet structure. For example, if a company recognizes only food, lodging, transportation, and miscellaneous travel expenses in its budget, then the budget template will contain just those items as part of the travel expense formula.

Large, complicated spreadsheet applications become unmanageable in a single spreadsheet. As described earlier, in this case, the total spreadsheet is divided into subsidiary spreadsheets, which are then combined into higher-level spreadsheets. In some applications, a single individual can manage these subsidiary spreadsheets. But when the additional work and complexity are more than one person can handle, then the spreadsheets are allocated to several workers on different computers and integrated into **workgroup spreadsheets.**

For example, at Specialty Chemicals, a large multidivision corporation, a workgroup spreadsheet application is used in the centralized corporate Plans and Budgets department. In this department, three levels of spreadsheets exist. Individuals work on spreadsheets for functions and for departments within a division. The departmental spreadsheets are combined into total division spreadsheets, which are then rolled into the total corporate spreadsheet. To ensure compatibility, all of these spreadsheets are developed from a common set of templates.

The Plans and Budgets department shares spreadsheet templates and other standard data via a workgroup information system. Additionally, when a subgroup within the department finishes a portion of the budget, it shares this portion with other analysts via the workgroup system. These capabilities are supplemented by an E-mail system and a scheduling application, described below.

Shared spreadsheets are implemented in several ways. For one, a spreadsheet program resides on multiple microcomputers connected via a LAN. For another, a single spreadsheet program resides on a minicomputer or mainframe computer, and multiple users access shared data through a multiuser interface to that program. With a third alternative, personal computer spreadsheet programs transfer data to and from a shared minicomputer or mainframe computer spreadsheet. For example, Microsoft's personal computer spreadsheet program, Excel, interfaces directly with Access Technology's shared minicomputer spreadsheet program, 20/20.

Documentation is critically important in such shared spreadsheets. Without thorough documentation, templates often do more harm than good, since the users seldom recognize the incorrect assumptions and understandings they bring to the task. As a result, incorrect or inappropriate data may be entered, and no one may realize that there is a problem.

Shared spreadsheets focus on group coordination in support of operational activities.

Group Decision Support Systems

Group decision support systems (GDSSs) facilitate group decision making. According to DeSanctis and Gallupe, a GDSS is "an interactive computer-based system that facilitates the solution of unstructured problems by a set of decision makers working together as a group."[7]

---

7. DeSanctis, G. and R. B. Gallupe, "Group Decision Support Systems, A New Frontier," *Data Base,* Vol. 16, Winter 1985, pp. 3–10.

Two important goals of a GDSS are to ensure that group members have the necessary information to make decisions and to eliminate or reduce losses in productivity due to inappropriate group dynamics (e.g., domination by a single, strong personality). GDSSs facilitate the development and dissemination of critical information, including problem definition, specification of alternatives, criteria for choice making, business models, and financial analysis techniques. GDSSs support group dynamics by providing a nonthreatening way for all members to participate.

A typical GDSS allows each team member to have his or her own microcomputer with communications and database access capabilities. Additionally, each computer has access to a group communications workboard and other media such as computer-controlled slide shows, graphics generators, and video projectors.

A successful GDSS facility developed at the University of Arizona consists of a set of group process tools for facilitating group meetings (see Figure 8-10). The system includes tools for various stages of the group decision process—tools for brainstorming, for exploring issues, for gaining a consensus, and so forth.

A key concept of the University of Arizona GDSS is that meetings are organized and managed by a **group facilitator**, who is trained both in the social dynamics of group processes and in the use of the GDSS tools. The facilitator, who is usually

Figure 8-10 A GDSS Facility
The University of Arizona's Decision Planning Lab is an example of a GDSS.

not part of the group, meets with selected group members prior to the meeting to determine the purposes of the meeting and to establish an agenda. The facilitator then chooses the tools to be used throughout the meeting.

For example, in a typical meeting, the group may want to first explore an issue, then brainstorm to obtain a list of potential alternative approaches for solving problems that are identified, and then form a consensus on which alternative should be considered first. In such a case, the facilitator starts the meeting and explains the agenda. Then he or she starts and stops meeting stages, instructs participants on the purpose of each meeting stage, and shows participants how to use the information system tools to accomplish the stated purpose of each stage.

A number of organizations have used this system with considerable success. For example, IBM has used this package to facilitate meetings among its own personnel and to facilitate meetings with customers. It reports that higher-quality decisions are made in less time than with other meeting strategies and systems.[8]

As we have seen, many decision-making processes are controlled by factors other than a straightforward analysis of rational alternatives. The University of Arizona system has succeeded, in part, because it coordinates and facilitates issues as described and understood by the participants. No attempt is made to force the meeting's issues into a mathematical or other formal model. The goal of the system is to facilitate the group's process by keeping the meeting on track, reducing the potential for domination by one or a few individuals, and providing a forum for all participants to contribute equally.

The field of GDSS is only now being fully explored, and more work needs to be done in understanding how groups make decisions before the full potential of GDSS will be realized. Today many exciting opportunities exist both for research and for the application of technology to group decision making. Group decision support systems focus on the group dynamics of decision making.

WORKGROUP INFORMATION SYSTEMS SUPPORT INFORMATION STORAGE AND RETRIEVAL

Workgroup information retrieval applications include five groups: group database management systems, workflow automation systems, group scheduling systems, group project management systems, and shared textbase systems.

8. McGoff, Chris, Ann Hunt, Doug Vogel, and Jay Nunamaker, "IBM's Experience with GroupSystems," *Interfaces,* Vol. 20, No. 6, November/December, 1990, pp. 39–52.

Workgroup Database Management Systems

As you recall, a database contains a group of tables of data related by common values. A row in the CUSTOMER table, for example, is related to a row in the ORDER table if the value of the Customer# column in CUSTOMER matches the value of the Customer# column in ORDER. A database application consists of menus, forms, and reports for processing the database.

Thus, the elements of a **workgroup database** application are the same as the elements of a personal database application. The difference is that these components must support controlled sharing of data.

To understand this concept further, consider the four types of databases as summarized in Figure 8-11. Databases can support one or many users and one or many different applications. One example of a multiapplication database contains customer, salesperson, and order data and is used for order-entry, customer relations, and sales commission applications.

Personal database applications fall in the first column of Figure 8-11, since they support a single user. Further, most personal database applications support only one application, although multiple applications are possible. Workgroup database applications support multiple users and can be used for either single or multiple applications. Workgroup database applications focus on workgroup coordination.

An example of a workgroup database application follows.

Figure 8-11 Database Types and Levels of Database Applications

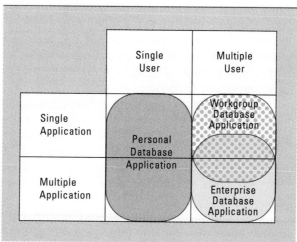

Hack 'n Sack Video Rentals

Hack 'n Sack Corporation is a national retailer of low-cost sundry merchandise. Several years ago, as video recording equipment became more prevalent, Hack 'n Sack decided to enter the video rental business.

The goal in offering rentals was to bring customers into the stores. Rental movies were located in a back corner so that customers, especially parents and children, would be forced to walk through or around the toy and miscellaneous food sections. On average, Hack 'n Sack expects to sell $15 of merchandise for every video rented. To accomplish this purpose, they price rentals as low as possible, intending to operate the video department on a break-even basis only.

A key to keeping the video rental price low is to keep administration costs low. To do this, Hack 'n Sack developed a rental processing database application for the video rental department that operates as follows: When renting the first video, a customer fills out an application form and is assigned a customer number and given a uniform price code (UPC) code strip containing that number. Customers are asked to place the strip on the back of one of their credit cards. A similar code strip, containing a video ID, is placed on the slipcover case of each video. When a customer rents a video, both bar codes are read by a light pen. The system allocates the video to the customer, computes the rental charge, and prints an invoice. The money is collected when the videos are returned; late charges are made for overdue returns. Depending on store volume, from one to seven video checkout stations are installed at each store. These stations share a common pool of customer and video data.

This TPS not only tracks customers and movies but, while processing transactions, gathers data that can be used to manage the video rental department.

Figure 8-12 summarizes the management application of the video rental data. First, a report is generated that shows rental volume by time, day of week, and date. This information is used not only to staff the rental department but also to estimate the number of people drawn into the store and the projected incremental revenue. (The term *estimate* is used because some video customers would have come to the store anyway.)

A second report shows the utilization rate at each checkout station. From this report, the manager decides whether there are too many or too few such stations. Additionally, other data is used to manage the video library inventory. The system computes the checkout rate for each video and also identifies both popular and unpopular titles. This data is used to sell or otherwise dispose of unwanted video inventory and to decide whether to buy additional copies of popular videos.

Still another report summarizes revenues, costs, and contributions to profit and overhead. This report shows the amount of revenue generated per pay period, the cost of labor, and the estimated cost of carrying the inventory. Revenue minus these estimated costs yields the contribution to profit and overhead.

Figure 8-12 Management Application of Video Rental Data

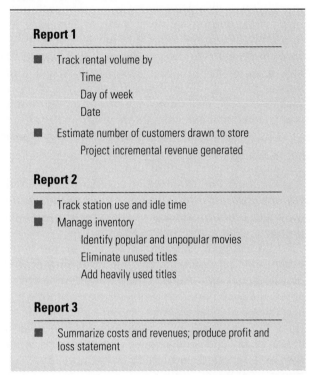

Report 1

- Track rental volume by
    Time
    Day of week
    Date
- Estimate number of customers drawn to store
    Project incremental revenue generated

Report 2

- Track station use and idle time
- Manage inventory
    Identify popular and unpopular movies
    Eliminate unused titles
    Add heavily used titles

Report 3

- Summarize costs and revenues; produce profit and loss statement

Observe that the operation of the video checkout system generates data that Hack 'n Sack can use to better manage the video department. This is typical. Often, the operation of a TPS application generates data that can be used to produce information to better manage the operation—a phenomenon so common that Zuboff gave it the name **informating**.[9] In the long run, it may be that greater value is added to the workgroup by informating than by providing direct support for operations.

Workflow Automation Systems

Using a system much like E-mail, it is possible to automate the flow of paperwork required by many office tasks. For example, if an expense account form requires

9. Zuboff, Shosana, *In the Age of the Smart Machine*. New York: Basic Books, 1988, p. 10.

approval by five persons, then a **workflow automation** system could be devised to ensure that the document is passed along through the sequence of people correctly. In addition, it may be designed to provide each person with the supplementary information needed to process the form. For example, if company policy specifies maximum expense amounts per day in certain categories, the automated form could be designed to check these totals and flag any that exceed the allowance. (In fact, it could do this when the person first fills in the amounts, offering an opportunity to justify amounts exceeding the allowance.) Finally, the system may include tracking facilities to let a supervisor determine exactly where a given form is at any moment and compile summary statistics.

By using E-mail instead of the company's internal paper mail system and by ensuring that each form is routed correctly at each step, a workflow automation system often dramatically cuts the time required to process transactions. For example, a company might reduce the expense account approval process from 2 weeks or more to 2 days or less. In other areas, such as customer order processing, reductions of this magnitude represent significant improvements in a company's service.

The implementation of an automated workflow system provides an opportunity to reexamine company workflow procedures. When a procedure is first designed, extra steps may be included just in case problems arise in those areas. But when no such problems arise, no one may remember to remove the extra steps. In other cases, procedures may include steps that were needed at one time, but not currently. Procedures bloated with such unnecessary steps are common. Beyond simply removing excess steps, however, analysts often find that they can redesign and streamline a procedure with improved effectiveness. Workflow automation systems focus on workgroup coordination.

Workgroup Scheduling Systems

A **group scheduling** system simplifies the scheduling of meetings among group members. Members each put their daily schedules into a shared database, and a scheduling program accesses that database to find, for example, the next available 2-hour meeting time for Chen, Jenson, Gutierrez, and Washington. Anyone who has ever tried to schedule such a meeting knows the frustration of finally reaching each person (after several tries) to find open times, tentatively identifying a meeting time, finding that one person cannot actually meet at that time, and so on.

Shared scheduling systems may be resisted in some organizations because they expose each user's daily schedule to inspection by others. Most commercial systems provide some degree of privacy, but even in those, a determined snoop— or boss—can find out more about a person's time usage than when each worker keeps a separate calendar. In many groups, the ability to schedule meetings conveniently soon overcomes the resistance.

Workgroup Project Management Systems

Workgroup project management is another information retrieval application. This section considers the activities of the Plans and Budgets department at Specialty Chemicals, the group that developed the workgroup spreadsheet application.

As you recall, Plans and Budgets is responsible for producing an integrated corporate budget. To do this, the 11 financial analysts in this department use personal spreadsheet products on microcomputers and integrate their activities with a workgroup, multiuser spreadsheet program on a minicomputer. As described, by using this program, all analysts are able to work from the same spreadsheet templates and to view each other's completed work against their own for consistency.

The multiuser spreadsheet program is a great help to this workgroup, but, unfortunately, is not enough. Various subgroups within the office depend on each other. One particular subgroup can only go so far until it needs the results of another subgroup's efforts. Friction develops when one subgroup is held up by unexpected delays from another subgroup.

This problem is compounded because the work load of the office has sharp peaks and valleys. Two drafts of the budget are produced—a preliminary draft in November and a final draft in May—and each is reviewed by management. Changes on the final draft are received on 1 June and must be incorporated into a consistent budget by the third week in June to be disseminated in time to take effect on 1 July. This schedule means that the work load during the months of October, April, and June is exceptionally heavy. No subgroup wants to be forced to wait due to unexpected delays in the work of other subgroups.

To improve the group's throughput and reduce wasted time due to such delays, the manager of this office instigated the development of a work scheduling system, which was then developed by personnel from the information systems department.

This system tracks the progress of each subgroup's work. The process of developing a budget is broken into tasks and subtasks, and dependencies among these activities are determined and documented. A portion of such task definition is shown in Figures 8-13a and 8-13b. When a subgroup falls behind on an activity, the system calculates the impact of this delay on other subgroups' work. Other groups are forewarned of schedule delays, and they adjust their work plans accordingly.

The scheduling system has enabled this office to better plan and coordinate its work. In addition, two unanticipated benefits have accrued. First, the process of describing tasks, subtasks, and dependencies has made everyone aware of how dependent they are on each other. Quite a few subgroups were unaware of the consequences of delays in their work. As a result, there have been fewer delays. Second, this system makes subgroup performances visible. Since any delays are quickly evident to the group, the subgroups have been more timely since the system was installed.

Figure 8-13 Budget Preparation Task Descriptions and Dependencies
(a) Task descriptions. **(b)** Schematic of task dependencies.

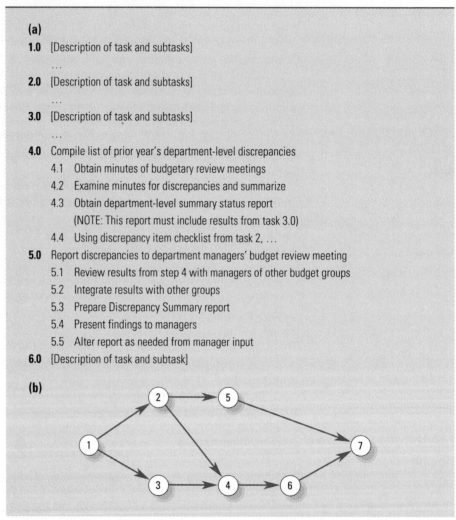

(a)

1.0 [Description of task and subtasks]

...

2.0 [Description of task and subtasks]

...

3.0 [Description of task and subtasks]

...

4.0 Compile list of prior year's department-level discrepancies
    4.1 Obtain minutes of budgetary review meetings
    4.2 Examine minutes for discrepancies and summarize
    4.3 Obtain department-level summary status report
        (NOTE: This report must include results from task 3.0)
    4.4 Using discrepancy item checklist from task 2, ...

5.0 Report discrepancies to department managers' budget review meeting
    5.1 Review results from step 4 with managers of other budget groups
    5.2 Integrate results with other groups
    5.3 Prepare Discrepancy Summary report
    5.4 Present findings to managers
    5.5 Alter report as needed from manager input

6.0 [Description of task and subtask]

(b)

Workgroup Shared Textbase Systems

The structured data used in TPSs and MISs is an important resource for workgroups, but the mountain of text arising from E-mail, bulletin boards, group conferencing systems, and other sources is the group's collective memory, another important resource. To make this resource useful, an efficient information retrieval system is needed. Shared **textbase** systems provide that capability.

In such systems, a user specifies words or phrases and receives a listing of all documents containing them. For example, when a Legacy Systems customer support representative answers the telephone, a textbase system provides access to the shared problem-solving experience of the whole group. If the representative cannot answer a question from memory, then she enters keywords specifying the problem and sees a listing of previously solved problems of that type. For example, if a customer complains that his Legacy DTP package began giving a scrambled display after he installed a new XJ-9 Robo Graphics display card, the representative can key in *DTP* and *XJ-9* and see what solutions have worked before.

The first time a particular customer problem arises, a technician may spend several days figuring out a solution. After communicating with that customer, the technician then describes the problem and solution to a technical writer, who creates an entry about it in the textbase. Once there, the document is available to all the representatives from then on. If the problem is very important or often raised, a note about the new document is entered into the shared bulletin board to let everyone know it exists.

MIS ADDS VALUE TO WORKGROUP PROCESS

So far, we have discussed the basic types of workgroup information systems. Now we consider the ways in which these applications can add value to workgroups, using the model developed in Chapter 4 and set out in Figure 4-7. In this model, information systems add value to **workgroup processes** by facilitating operations, management, and strategic planning. They also add value to **workgroup products** by enhancing product characteristics and delivery. Finally, they help to facilitate change through improvement and innovation.

Legacy Systems' Workgroups

To illustrate the ways information systems add value to workgroups, let's consider the situations of two workgroups at Legacy Systems: the Customer Support group and the Documentation group. As you recall, this company produces and sells microcomputer software.

Legacy Systems operates a Customer Support group that advises and assists customers in the use of its products. Customers call this group when a product appears not to work correctly or when they are confused about how to accomplish a particular task with a Legacy product. The Customer Support group consists of 32 employees.

A second workgroup example is Legacy's Documentation group, which produces the written documentation (small reports and manuals) accompanying each software package. The reports instruct users on how to install the application software, and they summarize important commands and features of the products. Legacy's manuals are several-hundred-page documents that explain each product in detail and illustrate its use.

The Documentation workgroup consists of 20 professional writers who operate in teams of 4 or 5. Each team is assigned the task of developing documentation for a particular product. The teams meet to determine the number and type of documents to be written, and then allocate the writing tasks to team members. Usually several writers are assigned to each document.

Legacy believes it is very important that the documents appear consistent, both physically and logically. Physically, a single design and the same typeface, layout, graphic symbols, and so forth are used for all the documents. Logical consistency is developed by using terms consistently and by illustrating all features using the same set of examples in all documentation.

This section considers the ways in which MISs add value to processes. We begin with workgroup operations.

Workgroup Operations

Workgroup operations involve the execution of specific tasks to accomplish group objectives and functions. Operations for Customer Support consist of providing advice and assistance to customers authorized to receive it. Operations for the Documentation group include conceptualizing, designing, writing, and checking documentation.

Although any of the types of systems described in this chapter can support workgroup operations, collaborative writing, textbase, and database applications are most commonly used. Collaborative writing applications are used in groups that produce documents, either a service group that produces documents written by others or a professional group, say a group of consultants, who author and then produce their own documents.

The Documentation group at Legacy Systems uses a collaborative writing application to plan and develop product documentation. To begin, members of the team create and store a draft outline. They review and comment on this outline, and modify it as the official working outline. Next, team members develop storyboards about the significant sections of the document. A **storyboard** is a summary of a section, a case, an example, a graphic, or some other component of the documentation. Team members review the storyboards and use the comments

Figure 8-14 Value Added to Workgroup Processes

Process Level	Example of Information Systems Use
Operations	Collaborative Writing in Documentation Group: ■ Create draft outline ■ Review and comment on draft outline ■ Develop storyboards ■ Write draft documentation ■ Review drafts ■ Find and correct inconsistencies and mistakes
Management	Management Control: ■ Reports from database application on employee performance enhance management leadership power Information Dissemination: ■ E-mail used to disseminate information Resource Allocation: ■ Allocate resources to most productive workers ■ Allocate tasks to most appropriate workers
Strategic Planning	Issues Addressed by GDSS: ■ Should we use in-house writers or outside contractors? ■ Should we produce on-line or printed documentation? ■ What quality standard is acceptable for us?

to develop a detailed outline. Then they begin writing the documentation by using the outline; as they finish sections of the document, they release the material for review by other team members. In this way, sections of the document receive early review—and mistakes can be caught more readily and with less expense and agony. The team finds the collaborative writing system invaluable in facilitating these operational tasks. The tasks are summarized in Figure 8-14.

Workgroup textbase applications provide group memory in several areas, especially customer support, as described earlier.

Workgroup database applications keep track of entities involved in operations. For Customer Support, this includes the names and registration numbers of customers who have paid for support, plus a summary of prior calls. Other examples include a sales recording system for a regional sales office and a late-payment tracking system for an accounts receivable department.

Workgroup Management

In general, management control concerns the acquisition and effective use of resources. **Workgroup management** involves the acquisition and use of assets by the workgroup. Typically, the workgroup manager is most directly involved with these issues. If the manager has a consensus style, however, some or all of the workgroup may also participate in management issues. Examples of typical management applications are listed in the second section of Figure 8-14.

Management Control   First, workgroup information systems applications can track who is working, how much work they do, and when they do it. This data helps the manager assess the performance of the group as a whole and of its members individually. Consider Figure 8-15, which shows a report produced by an information system that tracks Customer Support representative performance. This report lists the calls handled by a representative and lists total amount of time on the telephones, total average time per call, and, for each operator, number of calls taken, total telephone time, and average time per call. From this data, the

Figure 8-15   Customer Support Representative Performance Report

Customer Support
Representative Peformance Report

Operator Initials: EAF   Date 02/27/94

Customer Name	Call Type	Start Time	End Time	Length
Ajax	10	8:01	8:07	0:06
Gennie Door	20	8:29	8:47	0:18
Devonshire Foods	10	9:11	9:57	0:46
•				
•				
•				

Summary of Activity for EAF:
Total telephone time: 4:18
Total calls taken: 47
Average time per call: 5.5 minutes

manager evaluates the overall group performance and determines the best and worst performances over some time period.

Information like this increases the manager's reward and coercive power. He or she uses knowledge of the group's performance to identify and reward the best performers and to identify, counsel, correct, train, and otherwise coerce the worst performers. Additionally, the manager who possesses information about the group's performance is the expert about how the company is doing and about who should be doing what next.

Information Dissemination   An important function of workgroup systems is information dissemination. Managers can use applications such as E-mail and bulletin boards to quickly disseminate information to employees. The information is conveyed in text form such as memos and letters, in graphical form such as pie charts or bar charts, or in tabular, report form. Quick transmission of information to all workgroup employees simultaneously can stop the spread of harmful rumors, reduce the impact of bad news, and increase the impact of good news.

In addition to facilitating communications, the workgroup system can help develop the information to be transmitted. For example, if the system produces information about the workgroup's performance, the manager can then feed it back to the group. In this way, the group knows how it is doing as compared to yesterday, last year, or some other time frame.

The use of such information varies, depending on the manager's leadership style. Whereas an authoritarian manager takes direct action in response to the data, a more consensus-oriented manager simply provides the data to the group and facilitates the group's actions to improve its own performance. Such a manager lets the group use this data to monitor its own performance and encourages the group through experience and training to improve its performance. Or, the group may increase motivation by sponsoring contests among teams of workers for appropriate rewards.

Resource Allocation   Workgroup information systems can also be used for two types of resource allocation: the allocation of work to the group's resources and the allocation of special resources to group members. An example of the first allocation occurs in a documentation workgroup when the manager uses an information system to decide which writers to assign to certain projects. A similar use could be made in a customer support workgroup to route an incoming call to a particular representative.

An example of the second type of allocation occurs when a new computer is assigned to the most productive writer or a laser printer is allocated to the writer who produces the most graphical output. In another example, the manager of the customer support workgroup allocates training classes to the operators who handle the most calls of a particular type or to those who have the longest service time with certain types of calls.

In all of these cases, workgroup applications systems are used to develop the information needed to make the managerial decision. In order to assign the new computer to the most productive writer, the manager must have a system that creates information about writer performance. Such information will be important to the writers as well.

Workgroup Disturbance Handling   A workgroup information system keeps records about the workgroup's activities, such as who accomplished what tasks and when they did them. An attorney, for example, might query the office manager to learn the identity of an assistant who made a particularly serious mistake (or who produced particularly effective work). A customer might want to know which support representative provided a particular service, and so forth. The workgroup information system can provide information to the manager so that he or she can respond to these queries.

A workgroup information system can help the manager respond to disturbances by identifying the source of the disturbance and by documenting some of the particulars. When responding to a disturbance, the manager's role can be like that of a parent settling an argument between children. He or she does not know what really happened, who is responsible, or what action to take. Information systems applications provide data to facilitate the manager's actions.

Disturbances arise from conditions as well as from complaints. For example, a production line may produce too many defective products, a strike may prevent the delivery of needed components, or an international situation may prevent the sale of certain products to certain countries. In these cases, the manager can use the workgroup information system to assess the condition and to develop possible responses.

Workgroup Strategic Planning

As described in Chapter 4, strategic planning involves setting and adjusting objectives. Since we are concerned here with workgroup information systems, this phrase refers to the setting and adjusting of workgroup objectives.

The last section of Figure 8-14 lists several strategic planning questions for the Documentation group at Legacy Systems. All of these questions are unstructured and involve both tangible and intangible elements. The first question concerns whether Legacy should have an in-house writing staff or use outside contractors.

The first question is answered using a variety of techniques. Spreadsheet programs project costs of either alternative, but the benefits probably involve intangibles that are difficult to represent quantitatively. To perform a financial analysis, someone has to judge the value of the intangible benefits.

The situation is similar for the other two strategic questions. Deciding whether to have on-line or printed documentation involves both tangible and intangible costs and benefits. Setting a quality standard concerns those things as well.

For all of these questions, analysis of quantitative data using either spreadsheet or financial analysis programs is helpful. These questions, however, all involve subjective matters that go beyond a strict financial analysis. For example, the question about whether to use contract writers involves subjective issues of control and responsibility for which quantitative analysis is insufficient.

In addressing these strategic questions, the Documentation group probably would find that a group discussion of the issues using a GDSS would be most helpful. Such a GDSS would enable the members of the group to address imprecise and nonquantitative aspects of these questions. Additionally, workgroup information systems could be most useful for communicating the results.

MIS ADDS VALUE TO WORKGROUP PRODUCT

All the uses of information systems described in Figure 8-14 support processes, or activities, within the workgroup. Information systems can also be used, however, to add value to the workgroup's products.

The product of a workgroup has value to someone outside the workgroup. The product need not be directed to a customer, though such products often are. A workgroup product could be a report to another department or to a manager. For example, Legacy Systems' Customer Support group might send a report to the Documentation group describing the most common misunderstandings in the documentation. This product is an interdepartmental product that is never delivered to a customer.

As with personal information systems, workgroup information systems enable the workgroup to enhance the characteristics and features of its products, or they enable the workgroup to improve its product delivery.

Enhancing Features and Characteristics of Workgroup Products

The Customer Support group at Legacy Systems produces several products, the most obvious being the advice and assistance given to customers. Another product is the report about misunderstandings in the documentation that is given to the

Documentation group. A third product is a list of missing product features that is produced for the marketing department.

Customer Support uses information systems to improve these products in many ways. Several possibilities are summarized in Figure 8-16. Customer Support uses an E-mail system with which support representatives communicate with one another regarding difficult problems and questions. They post unresolved problems on an electronic bulletin board so that the entire group's expertise can be brought to bear on questions when necessary. Using an electronic bulletin board enables members of the group to address questions at their convenience.

Customer Support also uses an information system to track queries made by customers and suggested remedies. In this way, if a customer calls back to report a suggestion that did not work, the support representatives avoid giving the same advice. Service is personalized so that support representatives can ask about the resolution of problems stated in prior calls.

With regard to the product that is delivered to the Documentation group, Customer Support uses an information system to track details of problems reported by customers. For example, instead of reporting that customers have a problem with the DBMS report writer, Customer Support might state: "Seventeen percent of our calls concerned the report writer. Sixty percent of those calls had to do with control breaks, 20 percent concerned the placement of fields, and the remainder

Figure 8-16   Value Added to Workgroup Products

Enhancing Product Features and Characteristics

Customer Support Group Assistance to Customers:

- ■ Use E-mail to address difficult problems
- ■ Track customer problems and provide personalized service

Customer Support Reports to Documentation Group:

- ■ Provide greater detail on problem descriptions
- ■ Track documentation problems by customer type

Improving Product Delivery

Documentation Group Capabilities:

- ■ Deliver documentation on disk
- ■ Provide on-line tutorials and other computer-based training materials
- ■ Connect directly to printers, possibly self-publish documentation

were miscellaneous questions." A more detailed report will have far more usefulness (hence value) to the Documentation group. Another possibility is to report documentation problems by customer type. It may be that most problems are reported by first-time buyers, by customers in the insurance industry, or by sophisticated users. Detailed feedback by customer type enables the Documentation group to determine how best to correct the problem.

The uses of MISs summarized in Figure 8-16 are only a few of the many possibilities for enhancing workgroup products. Again, keep in mind that such products may or may not be delivered to the customer. Often the most important products of a workgroup are intended only for internal company use.

Improving Workgroup Product Delivery

Workgroup information systems can serve to improve the delivery of the workgroup product by developing the product in a more readily usable format or by integrating it with other components of a delivery system.

Consider the product of the Documentation group; typical product delivery issues are shown in the second section of Figure 8-16. Documentation is delivered in hard copy form or on disk. The latter is preferable in some situations, such as when a customer wants to customize the documentation.

Another example concerns on-line access to products. Tutorials, for example, are easier and more interesting to use if they involve on-line use of the product. With such computer-based training, instead of reading about an action, the user performs that action based on directions from the on-line tutorial; and the tutorial also provides help and guidance if the user makes a mistake.

Information systems can also improve product delivery by providing a better integration with other parts of the delivery system. For the Documentation group, word processed and DTP output is transmitted electronically to printing presses and similar devices, which reduces costs, speeds printing, and gives the Documentation group greater control. The members of Documentation may, in fact, be able to publish the documents themselves.

MIS ADDS VALUE THROUGH FACILITATING CHANGE

As stated in Chapter 4, information systems add value by facilitating improvement and innovation. Several possibilities for change in Documentation group processes and products at Legacy Systems are listed in Figure 8-17.

Figure 8-17 Value Added Through Facilitating Change

	Innovation	Improvement
Process	Encourage customers to use a Legacy-sponsored electronic bulletin board to create additions and supplements to the documentation	Use E-mail to send drafts of sections of documentation for customer review prior to publishing
Product	Use animation in computer-based training materials	Track errors in documentation and determine causes, produce more accurate documentation in the future

For example, the Documentation group could innovate the process of developing documentation by allowing customers to contribute additions and supplements to the documentation. To encourage this process, Legacy could pay for an electronic bulletin board that customers could use. The Documentation group could also innovate by adding animation to computer-based training, which would make the documentation easier to use or more interesting to read.

Process and product improvement could be facilitated by obtaining more feedback from the customers. Legacy could use E-mail to send customers sections of documentation as it is being written, and authors could gain near-immediate feedback on their ideas. Further, by using records in their collaborative writing system, the Documentation group could isolate the causes of errors in documentation, correct them, and hence produce higher-quality documentation in the future.

SUMMARY

A workgroup is a collection of people who work together to achieve a common goal. Usually, members of a workgroup know one another and most often work side by side in the same location. More formally, according to the structural definition, a workgroup is "an organized system of two or more individuals who are interrelated so that the system performs some function, has a standard set of role relationships among its members, and has a set of norms that regulate the function of the group and each of its members."

In homogeneous workgroups, everyone in the group fulfills the same role. In such groups, productive capacity rises at a near-linear rate as employees are added to the group. Information systems tend to be cheaper and easier to build in such groups because everyone does the same job.

In heterogeneous workgroups, there are several or many different roles and job descriptions. Productive capacity often does not rise at a linear rate, but varies, depending on the expertise of the first added person and on the needs of the group. Important challenges in heterogeneous groups concern communication and training. Since there are a multitude of job roles and jobs in a heterogeneous group, many different information systems may need to be developed, which may increase the cost of systems development and necessitate more types of expertise.

Workgroup norms are expectations about acceptable behavior. Norms can greatly encourage the use of information systems or substantially hinder it. Information systems cannot succeed if workgroup norms oppose their use.

Workgroups are permanent or temporary, and they have a single site or distributed locations. Information systems can add value to each of these four types.

Workgroup effectiveness can be measured by output, by personal satisfaction of group members, and by group capacity for future cooperation. Effectiveness is determined by group effort, by group knowledge and skill, and by approaches and strategies used to perform work.

The major difference between personal information systems and workgroup information systems is that workgroup systems must support controlled sharing of resources. Controlled sharing enables users to access the same resources without interfering with one another's work. It also enforces security. Granularity refers to the size of the data or information that are shared. Systems with large granularity have high contention, but are easy to administer. Systems with small granularity have low contention, but are difficult to administer.

The major categories of workgroup information systems are hardware-sharing applications and data-sharing applications. Hardware-sharing applications enable members of a workgroup to share an expensive hardware device such as a laser printer or a large-capacity disk. Data-sharing applications are divided into applications that focus on communication, systems that focus on analysis, and systems that focus on information retrieval. Within each category, applications are further divided into systems that focus on improving individual productivity (not considered further here), systems that focus on coordinating the operational work of the group, and systems that focus on the group dynamics of problem solving and decision making.

Workgroup applications that focus on communication include E-mail systems, group conferencing systems, and collaborative writing systems. Additional applications are likely to develop.

E-mail systems provide each user an electronic mailbox into which mail messages can be placed. In an active system, the user is notified when messages arrive. In passive systems, the user must periodically open the mailbox and check for messages. E-mail systems focus on group coordination.

Group conferencing systems include electronic bulletin boards, asynchronous meetings, group networks, and video conferencing. All of these systems can be used in group coordination; in addition, some have facilities to support group dynamics in problem-solving settings.

Collaborative writing systems let users share in the creation of documents. The systems manage the necessary coordination to keep users from interfering with each other's work and to allow collaboration. Such systems focus on coordination, although some include facilities to support problem solving.

Systems that focus on analysis include workgroup spreadsheets and GDSSs. Shared spreadsheets are often based on a common template. In many applications, a system of coordinated workgroup spreadsheets is used. To make such system work, documentation is critically important.

GDSSs often let each group member work from his or her own computer, using its resources in addition to the group's shared workboard and other media. Meetings are managed by a group facilitator, who may choose various computerized tools to use during the meeting. Tools are designed to support group dynamics in problem-solving settings.

Workgroup information retrieval applications include group database management systems, workflow automation systems, group scheduling systems, group project management systems, and shared textbase systems. Group database management systems have the characteristics of personal database systems except that they tend to be more complex. In addition to having more than a single user, they may support a single application or multiple applications. They focus almost entirely on workgroup coordination.

Workflow automation applications provide automatic routing of forms used in routine work processing, along with tracking of the disposition of each form. In addition to reducing processing time, the implementation of workflow automation systems often provides an opportunity to redesign work procedures. These systems serve to coordinate workgroups.

Workgroup project management systems provide resources similar to those used in personal project management except that they provide for increased complexity. Their goal is improved group coordination.

Group textbase systems provide a group memory. Stored documents are indexed for quick, simple retrieval. The primary focus of such systems is coordination.

Workgroup information systems add value to process, to product, and through facilitating change. Workgroup process refers to activities within the group. Workgroup product refers to the output the group produces—whether to customers or to other departments in the organization.

MISs can facilitate workgroup operations, management, and strategic planning. They can also enhance features and functions of workgroup products. Workgroup MISs can improve or innovate either processes or products.

KEY TERMS

Workgroup (two definitions)	Granularity	Template
Workgroup function	Hardware sharing	Workgroup spreadsheet
Workgroup role	Diskless workstation	GDSS
Workgroup norm	Sneaker net	Group facilitator
Homogeneous workgroup	LAN	Workgroup database
Heterogeneous workgroup	Queue	Informating
Permanent versus temporary workgroup	Evaluation apprehension	Workflow automation
	E-mail	Group scheduling
	Mailbox	Workgroup project management
Single-site versus distributed workgroup	Active E-mail	Textbase
	Passive E-mail	Workgroup process
	Electronic bulletin board	Workgroup product
Workgroup effectiveness	Asynchronous meeting	Workgroup operation
	Group network	Storyboard
Controlled sharing	Shared drawing tool	Workgroup management
Security	Video conferencing	
	Collaborative writing	

REVIEW QUESTIONS

1. Give two definitions of *workgroup*.

2. What are the three components of the structural definition of a workgroup?

3. Define *homogeneous workgroup*.

4. Explain why productive capacity increases at a near-linear rate when personnel are added to a homogeneous workgroup.

5. Why are information systems easier to develop for homogeneous workgroups than for heterogeneous workgroups?

6. Define *heterogeneous workgroup*.

7. Explain why productive capacity does not usually increase at a near-linear rate when personnel are added to a heterogeneous workgroup.

8. Describe two challenges for heterogeneous workgroups.

9. Describe ways in which workgroup norms facilitate or interfere with the use of information systems.

10. Name four types of workgroups and give an example, other than ones in this text, of each.

11. List the three dimensions of workgroup effectiveness according to the Nadler, Hackman, and Lawler model.

12. What three factors influence workgroup effectiveness?

13. Describe the essential difference between personal information systems and workgroup information systems.

14. Explain the meaning of *controlled sharing*.

15. Define *granularity*. Explain how the level of granularity influences throughput in a workgroup system.

16. Describe the nature and purpose of hardware-sharing systems. Give an example.

17. Name the rows and columns of the Briggs and Nunamaker grid describing various types of workgroup data-sharing systems.

18. Differentiate between the focus on group coordination and the focus on the group dynamics of problem solving and decision making.

19. Describe three sets of group dynamics problems that arise when groups engage in problem-solving activities.

20. What is the purpose of an E-mail application?

21. What is an electronic mailbox?

22. Explain the differences among an electronic bulletin board, an asynchronous meeting, a group network, and video conferencing.

23. What is the purpose of a collaborative writing system?

24. Explain how a workgroup spreadsheet application differs from a personal spreadsheet application.

25. Define *group decision support system (GDSS)*.

26. What are two important goals of a GDSS?

27. What are the functions of a group facilitator?

28. What are the types of workgroup information retrieval applications?

29. Define four types of databases.

30. Explain the meaning of *informate*.

31. Explain what a workflow automation system does.

32. Describe the advantages and disadvantages of an automated group scheduling system as compared to manual scheduling.

33. Name at least three benefits of the use of group project management systems.

34. Describe the functioning of a workgroup textbase system.

35. Explain how workgroup information systems can be used to support workgroup management.

36. Name at least four ways in which workgroup information systems facilitate workgroup management. Give an example of each way other than those in the chapter.

37. Explain how workgroup information systems facilitate workgroup strategic planning.

38. Explain the difference between workgroup process and workgroup product.

39. Explain how workgroup information systems enhance workgroup product features and characteristics. Describe an example other than the ones in this text.

40. Explain how workgroup information systems facilitate workgroup product delivery. Describe an example other than the ones in this text.

41. Describe at least two ways that workgroup information systems facilitate change. Give an example of each other than the ones in this text.

DISCUSSION QUESTIONS

1. A university department such as accounting or finance can be thought of as a workgroup. Consider the department of your major. Who are the members of that workgroup? Describe the functions, roles, and norms of that workgroup. Is it a homogeneous or heterogeneous workgroup? This

chapter defines three dimensions of effectiveness. Explain how those measures pertain to your major department. Describe one information system used by that workgroup. (If possible, use a computer-based information system.) What type of information system is it? Does that system support sharing of data or other information resources? If so, how? Describe the department's strategic planning, management, and operations activities. What are the department's products in addition to teaching? How are the products delivered? Think of one information system that is currently not in use that your major department could use. Describe the functions served and the benefits of that system.

2. Think of an example of a workgroup in your college or university, such as a group involved with administration, athletics, academics, or some other aspect of college life. Describe the functions of this group. What types of job descriptions do the members of that group fulfill? Is it a homogeneous or heterogeneous group? What type of workgroup is it? Give an example of strategic planning, management, operations, product quality, and product delivery activity for that group.

3. The text states that productive capacity rises at a near-linear rate for homogeneous workgroups, but at a nonlinear rate for heterogeneous workgroups. This position can clearly be justified for workgroups that involve piecemeal work such as warehouse operations. Consider a plans and budgets office at a major manufacturer, however. Suppose the office is staffed only by CPAs who perform basically the same type of financial analyses. This group fits the definition of a homogeneous workgroup, yet it seems less likely that productive capacity will rise at a linear rate as personnel are hired. Explain why this is so. Is it therefore incorrect to maintain that productive capacity rises at a near-linear rate for such groups? How does this issue impact the design and implementation of information systems?

4. Suppose that you have the job of introducing a badly needed information system into an office in which the workgroup norms oppose the use of computers. How would you proceed? Explain and justify the actions you would take, and describe how you would determine whether the actions were effective.

PROJECTS

A. Collect information about the various uses of Lotus Notes or another major groupware program product. Seek advertising material, reviews in computer publications such as *PC Magazine*, and other published sources.

If possible, interview a person who has used Notes in the workplace. Summarize the functions performed by the program. Describe at least five specific potential applications for the program.

B. Identify a workgroup in a local business. Interview the manager and, if possible, one or two workgroup members. Explain that you are learning about the use of information systems in workgroups and you want to determine how such systems are used in a real business. What is the function of the workgroup? What are the roles and important norms? How does the group measure its effectiveness? If the group uses any computer-based information systems, what are their functions? What data or other resources are shared? What is the granularity of the sharing? Determine at least one example of workgroup strategic planning, management, and operations. What are the workgroup's products, and how are they delivered? What information systems, if any, are used to facilitate these functions? Are they successful? If the group has ever installed information systems that were unsuccessful, why were they unsuccessful? What advice would the workgroup have for you in thinking about installing information systems to support a workgroup?

C. Identify at least four textbase products. Collect information from published reviews, advertising, and other sources describing the function of each product. If possible, interview a person who has actually used at least one of these products in the workplace. Describe the specific features and capabilities of each product. How are documents entered into a system? What methods of retrieval are used? Give several examples of inquiries that would be processed successfully by each, and discuss the disadvantages of each. Describe in detail a specific business workgroup application for a textbase program.

D. Interview a VAR or computer dealer who specializes in sales and support of workgroup systems. What types of systems does that person sell? At what price range? What is a typical development process? How long does it take? What activities are involved? What would the VAR or dealer say is his or her most successful installation? What is the least successful installation? Why was one better than the other? What are the most important factors in a successful implementation? Technology? Customer knowledge? Dealer knowledge? System design? Something else? How did the person obtain his or her job? What education, training, and experience does he or she have? What advice would the person have for someone who wanted to perform a similar job?

What's Workgroup Computing?

Everyone has a different definition for workgroup computing. Some say it's a new category of applications called groupware. Others say workgroup computing requires new systems infrastructures or radically different user environments. Still others claim customers need to adopt new databases and data structures to develop workgroup computing solutions. A consistent theme is that workgroup computing is revolutionary new technology.

I've always believed that any definition of workgroup computing should be based on an understanding of people and how they work together. Using information technology and computers to help people work together more productively is what workgroup computing is all about. Although most people today use personal computer applications to carry out individual work and responsibilities, their work almost always is part of a larger organizational process. Virtually any process that involves a group of people collaborating on work is by definition a workgroup activity.

Workgroup computing should be a natural and easily understood extension of the applications and tools customers already have, rather than a separate product category. What they're missing is a strategy to put their resources together in customized workgroup computing solutions. What customers, application developers and solution providers need is an open development platform on which to build optimal, customized workgroup computing solutions.

Microsoft's workgroup computing strategy is based on an open, evolutionary and solutions-based approach to making it easier for people to work together. We are investing in Microsoft Windows, applications and services to provide workgroup and enterprise solutions to customers.

The key components of our workgroup computing strategy are: extending the operating system to provide an open workgroup computing foundation; providing extensive open APIs; incorporating workgroup capabilities in key application; providing general-purpose database technology to leverage existing data and build powerful customized solutions; delivering products that address common problems; and providing development tools and investing in an infrastructure to help customers develop and implement workgroup computing solutions.

Operating systems will evolve in the 1990s to incorporate fundamental workgroup services, which will make all applications "workgroup applications." There are several reasons that the operating system is the best place to address fundamental workgroup computing problems, rather than the application environment.

First, it does not make sense from a practical or customer investment standpoint to have a separate class of applications for users to work with other people. The only way to ensure that all applications can evolve and become workgroup-enabled is to make basic services, such as file sharing and messaging, a part of the operating system.

Second, customers want and need freedom of choice. When the operating system incorporates basic workgroup services and supports abstraction layers and open APIs, customers can separate their client and server decisions and choose applications that best suit their needs while leveraging their existing investments in their infrastructure. The freedom of choice created by open interfaces in the operating system also will drive the development of new, innovative applications and solutions.

Microsoft's workgroup computing strategy encompasses technology from all our product groups. We believe customers want the flexibility to mix and match the best components in developing their workgroup computing solutions. We are investing in Windows, applications and services to make it easier for users to work together and for customers to build custom workgroup and enterprise solutions. Our strategy has three fundamental objectives:

- Enable solutions for real customer problems and workgroup activities.

- Provide an open architecture and development platform for customers, application developers and solution providers.

- Evolve the operating system and applications to include workgroup capability.

Embedding fundamental workgroup services in the operating system and providing a truly open development platform will ensure that customers can protect themselves from getting locked into a single vendor's proprietary application environment. ■

By Bill Gates, co-founder and chairman of Microsoft Corporation, publisher of DOS, Windows, and many application programs.

Excerpted from *Network Computing*, November 1, 1992, pp. 67, 68.

Discussion Questions

1. How does Bill Gates define workgroup computing?

2. Explain how operating system features provide a foundation for Gates's view of workgroup computing.

3. Gates proposes that the workgroup computing platform should include the same applications that the user already uses for personal purposes. Evaluate this proposal. What are the pros and cons of this approach as compared to having separate programs for group work?

4. This discussion of workgroup computing doesn't mention meeting support. Why do you think Gates omitted this topic?

Copyright© 1992 by **CMP Publications, Inc.,** 600 Community Drive, Manhasset, NY 11030. Reprinted from NETWORK COMPUTING with permission.

9

Components of Workgroup Information Systems

A WORKGROUP INFORMATION SYSTEM has the same five components as all information systems: hardware, programs, data, procedures, and people. The significant difference between workgroup information systems and personal information systems is that workgroup systems share data or other resources, which means that the users' computers must be connected to each other and, possibly, to central sources of data. Further, the processing of one user must be coordinated with that of other users so that potential data or other resource conflicts can be avoided or otherwise resolved.

The need for controlled sharing places a burden on each of the five components. Hardware must enable users to communicate; programs must coordinate the actions of both the hardware and the independently acting users; data must be structured to support shared processing; procedures need to coordinate sharing and to provide for backup and recovery in the shared environment; and user and operations roles need to be expanded. This chapter explores these and other issues.

We begin with a discussion of the three fundamental alternatives of multiuser systems, including major advantages and disadvantages of each type. Then we consider one of these alternatives, distributed systems, in detail. Each of the five components of a LAN-based distributed system will be discussed.

In this chapter, strive to learn the terms and functions of the important components of workgroup information systems. In Chapter 10, we will build on this knowledge when we investigate processes of workgroup information systems development.

Because computer communications technology is complicated, we have divided this subject into two parts. This chapter considers computer communications that pertain only to workgroups, and we are primarily concerned with communications via LANs. Chapter 12 will consider computer communications as it pertains to enterprise systems. There we will address mainframe communications, microcomputer to mainframe computer links, and wide area networks.

MULTIUSER SYSTEM ALTERNATIVES

Three fundamental alternatives are used for multiuser processing: centralized, distributed, and hybrid systems.

Centralized Systems

The first, and oldest, multiuser system is the **centralized system**, in which a centralized computer is connected to a number of terminals, as shown in Figure 9-1. The terminals do not contain microcomputers and are sometimes referred to as **dumb terminals.** The centralized computer contains all of the system intelligence. In some cases, if users need microcomputers for other purposes (e.g., for personal information systems), the PCs emulate, or perform like, dumb terminals, which reduces the costs of duplicating a terminal and a microcomputer and diminishes the amount of space required for computer equipment on the user's desktop.

In centralized systems, all the processing is conducted at a distance from the user. The terminals may be connected directly to a nearby computer, or they may be connected via telephone or other communications lines to a computer that is hundreds or even thousands of miles away.

Since all processing occurs at one site, the single computer maintains tight control over processing. It carefully manages access and changes to data, dictates the order of processing, and provides extensive security. All changes to data are known or can be known by monitoring programs.

Centralized systems are most commonly used for enterprise TPS applications. At one time, centralized systems were used for workgroup TPSs, but such systems are being replaced by LAN-based systems, which are much cheaper. Accordingly, we will defer further consideration of centralized systems to Chapter 12. Characteristics, control philosophy, and primary application of centralized systems are summarized in the first column of Figure 9-2.

Figure 9-1 Centralized Processing System

In a centralized processing system, a central computer is connected to user terminals; the central computer does all the processing.

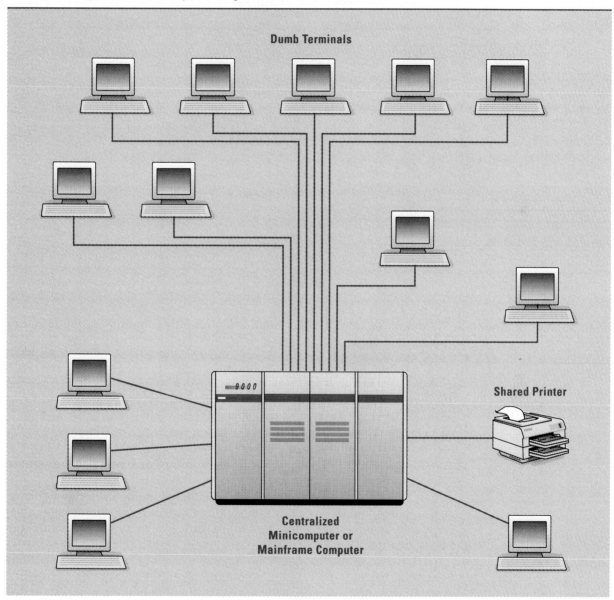

Figure 9-2 Characteristics of Multiuser Alternatives

	Centralized	Distributed	Hybrid
Characteristics	Centralized intelligence on a single computer Dumb terminals or micros that emulate dumb terminals	Independent microcomputers communicate via LAN Server provides network services for micros	Mixture of LANs, micro-computers, minicomputers, and mainframes Connected in a WAN
Control Philosophy	Centralized control of all activities	Independent processing on microcomputers Central control of shared data on server	Hybrid control
Primary Application	Enterprise TPS Too expensive for most workgroup applications	Workgroup MIS and enterprise MIS	Integrated workgroup

Distributed Systems

The second type of multiuser system is the **distributed system** using a **local area network (LAN).** A LAN is a federation of microcomputers directly connected to one another. Although the exact meaning of the term *local* changes as LAN technology becomes more powerful, a good rule of thumb is that the microcomputers must reside within a mile or two of each other, though typical distances are much shorter than a mile.

A LAN connects independent microcomputers using cables and adapter cards inserted into the expansion slots of the PCs. For some systems, the cables are telephone-type wire; others use coaxial cable (like that used for cable TV) or fiber optic cable.

The LAN shown in Figure 9-3 supports hardware sharing, E-mail, and workgroup database processing. It connects five user microcomputers with a special microcomputer called a **file server**, which contains the database on its disk and processes that database in accordance with requests from the other microcomputers. The file server also processes electronic mail and schedules and supervises the processing of requests for the shared printer.

Figure 9-3 Example of a LAN

This LAN interconnects five user microcomputers and a file server with a shared disk drive and printer. E-mailboxes reside on the shared disk drive.

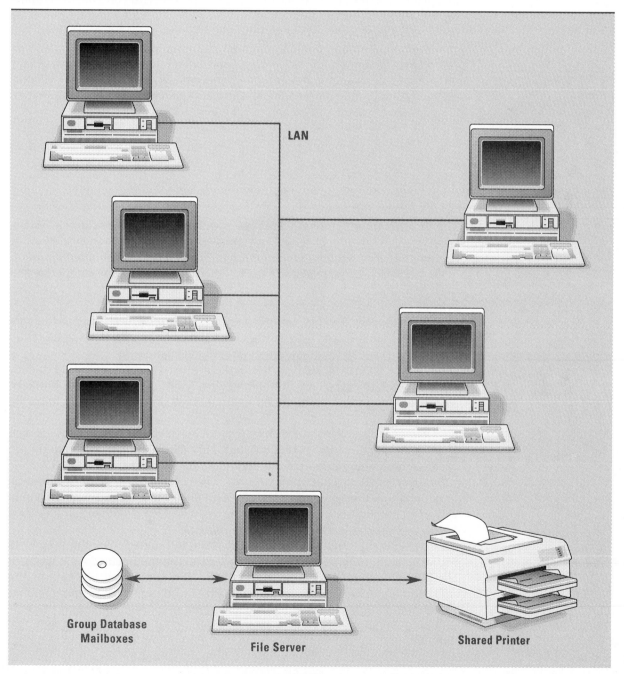

Group Database
Mailboxes

File Server

Shared Printer

LAN

LAN-based systems distribute control throughout the network. Since each microcomputer has its own processing power, it does its own processing independent of the file server and the other computers. A user on a microcomputer can run a spreadsheet application against an out-of-date file it received from the file server 2 or 3 weeks prior, and the file server will not be aware of it. This characteristic is an advantage in that users have more independence and more control over their own processing. It is a disadvantage, however, in that processing on several microcomputers can quickly become uncoordinated and chaotic. Characteristics, control philosophy, and primary application of distributed systems are summarized in the second column of Figure 9-2.

Hybrid Systems

The third multiuser system alternative is the **hybrid communications system**, which is a combination of centralized and distributed systems (see Figure 9-4). In the example of a hybrid system shown in Figure 9-4a, a LAN-based system is connected via a communications line to other LANs, mainframe computers that do centralized processing, and other communication devices. Networks that provide such links are called **backbone networks**.

In the hybrid example shown in Figure 9-4b, several local area networks are interconnected; this type of system is called **linked LANs.** Any of these LANs can also be connected to a mainframe computer as in Figure 9-4a.

In the system in Figure 9-4b, the micros that need to communicate frequently are attached to the same LAN. The independent LANs can communicate, however, so that it is possible for a micro on one LAN to communicate with a micro on another LAN.

Suppose a company maintains three warehouses in geographically separated locations (see Figure 9-4c). A LAN is installed in each warehouse, and all the PCs in each warehouse are connected to its LAN. Most of the time, the users in one warehouse need to communicate only with users in the same warehouse. Occasionally, however, it is necessary for a micro to communicate with a micro in a different warehouse. The interconnection between such geographically dispersed LANs is provided by a **wide area network (WAN)**.

The hybrid system entails hybrid forms of control. For the system in Figure 9-4a, for example, the mainframe controls all the interactions it has with the dumb terminals and may also control the processing of some of the microcomputers that want services from the mainframe. The mainframe does

Figure 9-4 Hybrid Communications Systems

(a) In some hybrid systems, LANs, central processing computers, and other devices are interconnected via a backbone network. **(b)** In others, several LANs are linked. **(c)** Where geographically separated LANs must be interconnected, they often share access to a WAN.

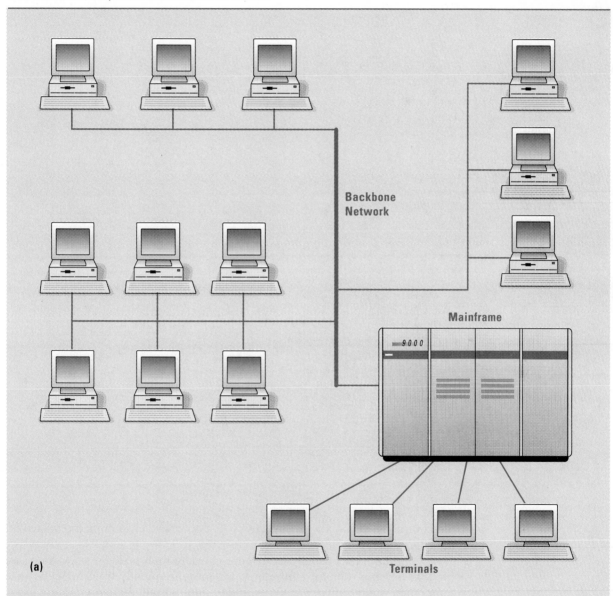

Figure 9-4 *(continued)*

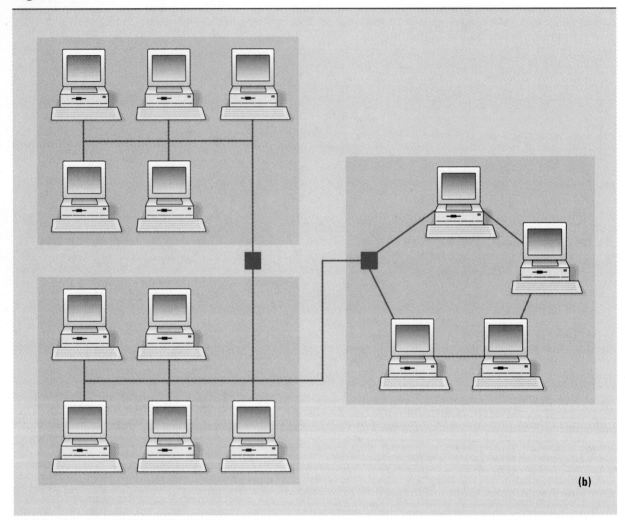

(b)

not control, however, any of the activity that occurs solely among the micros on the LAN.

Hybrid systems usually have more capacity than a single workgroup can productively use. Consequently, they are more frequently used for enterprise rather than workgroup applications, and Chapter 12 will therefore discuss them. Characteristics, control philosophy, and primary application of hybrid systems are summarized in the third column of Figure 9-2.

Figure 9-4 *(continued)*

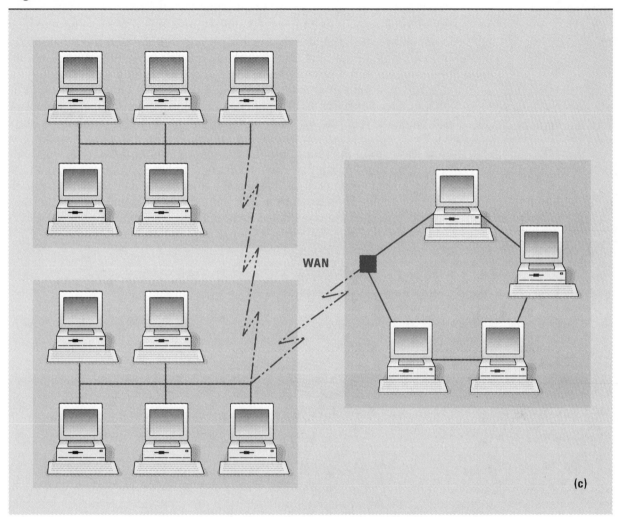

(c)

Comparing System Alternatives

Figure 9-5 summarizes the relative advantages and disadvantages of the three multiuser system alternatives. The major advantages of centralized systems are that they provide centralized control using established technology and vendors and, consequently, involve less technical risk. In addition, they are maintained by information systems professionals, who provide highly reliable operation. On the other hand, centralized systems entail a high initial cost, and the information systems professionals who install and operate them are expensive. These systems do not allow local, independent processing, and they are only as reliable as the CPU is reliable. If the CPU fails, the entire system is inoperable. Because of the high cost, centralized systems are seldom used for workgroup applications.

The major advantages of distributed systems using LANs are low start-up costs, greater flexibility in tailoring and scaling a system to meet processing requirements, ability to support local processing, and higher reliability since multiple computers are involved. If one computer fails, the others can still carry out at least part of their function. The disadvantages of distributed systems are a lack of centralized control, problems due to multiple vendors (typically the LAN, the LAN OS, and the micro hardware come from different vendors), and rapidly changing technology that can quickly make the equipment obsolete. Further, LANs are operated and maintained by workgroup members, who are seldom as highly skilled as the computer professionals who operate centralized systems.

Figure 9-5 Advantages and Disadvantages of Multiuser System Alternatives

	Centralized	**Distributed**	**Hybrid**
Advantages	Centralized control	Low start-up costs	Greatest capacity
	Established vendors and technology	Tailorable, scalable	Hybrid control
	Low technical risk	Local computing possible	Most tailorable and scalable
	High capacity for TPS	Reliability of many computers	
Disadvantages	High cost	Lack of centralized control	Complicated
	Highly trained personnel required for development and, to a lesser extent, for operations	Multiple-vendor problems	Expensive
		Rapidly changing technology	Difficult to set up
	No local computing	Performance cap	High technical risk
	Vulnerable to loss of the single CPU		Some technical problems unsolved, to date

Finally, a LAN can have a sharp performance cap. For example, a certain LAN may support 20 microcomputers well and 30, marginally, and it may not support more than 40 at all. If the work load expands so that 45 microcomputers are required, major changes, such as dividing it into two linked LANs, may be required. Centralized systems also have performance caps, but they tend to peak out more gradually.

Hybrid systems have the greatest capacity and allow for both centralized and distributed control. They are the most flexible and tailorable to an organization's requirements. On the other hand, hybrid systems are the most complicated and expensive to develop and operate. They can be difficult to set up and involve considerable technical risk. In fact, some of the problems of more sophisticated hybrid systems do not yet have technical solutions.

COMMUNICATIONS STANDARDS

Reflect for a moment on the wide variety of equipment and processing methods involved with the alternatives shown in Figures 9-3 and 9-4. There are many problems to consider and many different ways of solving those problems. As a typical example, some computers represent data using the ASCII code, and some use EBCDIC. A file sent from one computer to another may need to be translated from one code to another. Or, as another example, consider what happens when an error occurs on a data transmission—say, a power surge causes 1,000 bits to be lost. How are such errors to be detected and corrected?

Many hardware products and programs exist to solve these and similar problems but they do so in different ways. To further complicate the situation, each vendor has a proprietary interest in its own methods and standards and has little short-term incentive to conform to an industrywide standard. Even more complication occurs because the technology has changed so rapidly. Communications products and approaches initiated in the 1970s had to be later modified to incorporate microcomputers and LANs as they became available. The result of all of these factors is an exceedingly complex array of communications technology, concepts, terms, products, and standards.

This section introduces the basic technical information that you need to understand and use workgroup information systems. The goal is not to make you a telecommunications specialist. Rather, it is to present the big picture so that you can mentally organize major techniques and products. If you are the manager of a workgroup, you will need to know the meaning of the terms in this chapter when you hire others to build a LAN.

Figure 9-6   Communication Standards
Enable Global Computing
Users all over the world can share common data
because standardized data communications channels
provide access.

Data Communication Protocols

Consider a simple command like sending a message from a user on one computer to a user on a second computer. Suppose you, as user A, want to send a message to a coworker, user B. Suppose your coworker is a member of your workgroup and both of you utilize microcomputers on the same LAN. Even though your two computers are directly connected to each other, many problems must be overcome. How do the computers access the shared line? How do they get one another's attention? What happens if your coworker's computer is too busy to accept the data at the present time?

Now consider what happens when the two computers are connected on a backbone network or some other type of communications network. Suppose your office is in Memphis and your coworker works for a division located in Hong Kong. In this situation, even more issues must be resolved. What is the best data pathway from Memphis to Hong Kong? What happens when international processing methods change (as they often do with international systems)? Suppose the data is sent by satellite. How is this to be done? What happens if the data is lost? Suppose your message is proprietary. How is it to be protected from interception by unauthorized people?

In the 1970s, corporations began to see the problems caused by the lack of communications standards, and major manufacturers developed their own standard **protocols**, or sets of rules for conducting data communications. IBM, for example, developed **Systems Network Architecture (SNA),** which is a standard set of strategies, concepts, and facilities for designing and managing a network of computers and related equipment. At the same time, Digital Equipment Corporation developed **Digital Network Architecture (DNA),** its own protocol for the same purpose. Meanwhile, the U.S. military, not wanting to be committed to any particular vendor's standard, developed **Terminal Control Program/Internet Protocol (TCP/IP),** as a vendor-independent standard of connecting terminals to mainframes.

At this point, the microcomputer appeared on the scene, and LANs were developed. New technologies evolved: Xerox, Intel, DEC, and others developed the Ethernet protocol; IBM developed its PC LAN; Novell produced its first version of Netware network operating system; and so forth. In addition, all the then-existing vendors' standards had to be modified to account for this new technology.

In the mid-1970s, the **Open Systems Interconnection (OSI) model** was defined by the International Standards Organization (ISO). OSI is not a specific protocol; it does not specify a single set of rules by which data is to be communicated. Rather, it specifies the set of problems that must be solved by any particular protocol. It is a comprehensive standard that has been robust enough to incorporate new technology as it has developed: LANs, WANs, teleprocessing, and other technologies as well. We will use the OSI model as a framework to organize the discussion of the technology and products for LANs. Today it is the accepted way of defining the functions and relationships of communications products.

The OSI Model

The OSI model consists of seven layers of functionality, each representing a set of tasks that must be accomplished and embodying a set of rules about how one aspect of the transmission is to be conducted.

7. The **application layer** contains rules about how an application program requests data transmission and supplies the data to be transmitted in the proper format.

6. The **presentation layer** contains rules about how the data is to be displayed on the screen, how it may be encrypted or compressed for efficient transmission, and whether it is translated between ASCII code and EBCDIC code.

5. The **session layer** contains rules about how a communications session between two devices is established, what special signals are used to indicate the progress of the dialogue, and how a session is to be reestablished if the connection fails.

4. The **transport layer** contains rules about how the address of the recipient is to be expressed, how large volumes of data are to be broken up into blocks for transmission, and how received blocks are to be reassembled into the complete message.

3. The **network layer** contains rules about how to determine the routing of messages from sender to receiver and how to maintain records of messages transmitted.

2. The **data-link layer** contains rules about resolving competing requests for the use of the channel, defining the beginning and end of data blocks, and detecting and correcting errors.

1. The **physical layer** contains rules about the shape of connectors used to plug the system together, the speed and direction of the transmission, and how the bits are to be represented electrically (or by light pulses, or whatever).

Think of the processing as a production line; each layer represents a production station. Suppose a user in Memphis must communicate a message to a user in Hong Kong (see Figure 9-7). Data is moved from the Memphis user (above layer 7) down through each of the corresponding layers. At each layer (station), the data is prepared for transmission. At layer 1, the data is encoded in a physical signal and transmitted as a stream of encoded bits. At the Hong Kong end, the data is passed back up the series of layers. At each layer, the processing done at the corresponding layer of the sending system is stripped off, and step by step, the data is put into a form that is useful to the receiver.

As it is prepared for transmission, the data is passed down from layer 7 to layer 1, with some processing by each layer. Only layer 1, the physical layer, transmits and receives data directly. When the data is received, it is passed up from layer 1 to layer 7 in the receiver system. However, in another sense, each layer of the transmitting system is speaking directly to the corresponding layer of the receiving system. For example, the processing done by layer 4, say, of the transmitting system must correspond to the processing done by layer 4 of the

Figure 9-7 The OSI Model

To communicate from a user in Memphis to a user in Hong Kong, the data passes through each layer in turn in both systems.

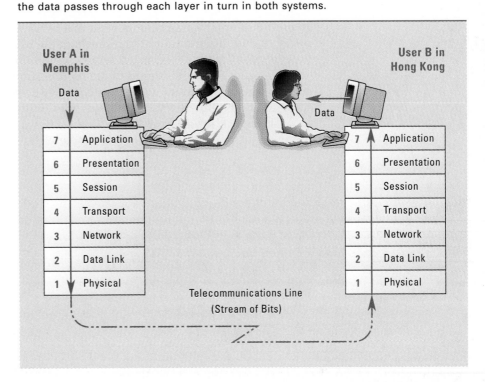

transmitting system must correspond to the processing done by layer 4 of the receiving system for the whole process to work. In addition, the session layer may create session control messages for interpretation by the receiver's session layer (but it transmits them by passing them downward through the lower layers). Therefore, corresponding layers at both ends of a link must reflect the same basic rules of processing.

Note that the objective of the communication is not necessarily to deliver to the receiver an exact duplicate of the data sent by the transmitter. If that were the objective, the process could be simplified considerably. In fact, the data as sent by the transmitter may be EBCDIC-coded data stored in a database using one method of representing its numeric values, and the data required by the receiver may be ASCII-coded data stored in a data file using a completely different method of representing numeric values. As a result, the processing done at each corresponding layer often is not simply designed to return the data to its original form, but rather to translate the data into the form needed.

LAN Protocols

Figure 9-8 shows the major components of a LAN system as each fits into the OSI model. We will discuss Figure 9-8 throughout the balance of this chapter. Do not worry about all of the details in the figure at this point.

In Figure 9-8, the functions of the bottom two layers of the OSI model are accomplished by network-access protocols. Two typical protocols are shown: CSMA/CD and token ring. We will discuss these further in the following section.

The LAN OS resides above the network-access protocols. This system provides the functionality of OSI layers 3 to 6. Finally, application programs sit on top of the

Figure 9-8 The OSI Model and LAN Components

In a LAN, most functions at the physical and data link layers are implemented in hardware, and most functions at the remaining levels are implemented in a network OS.

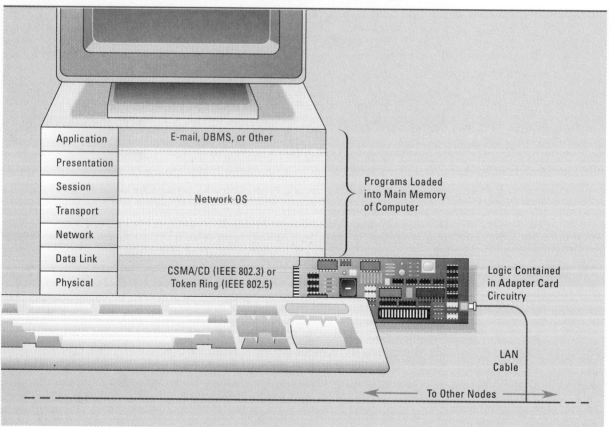

network OS. We will discuss the features and functions of the network OS and LAN-based applications in more detail later in this chapter.

Figure 9-8 illustrates the components of the OSI model that are most important to you when building or buying a LAN. You will need to: select some type of adapter card to implement the network-access protocol in layers 1 and 2; choose a LAN OS; and select applications. When you choose each of these components, watch for compatibility. Not all OSs work with all applications or with all network-access adapter cards.

We now discuss each of the five components of a workgroup information system.

HARDWARE

LAN hardware consists of microcomputers, communications lines, network-access expansion cards, and peripheral equipment. As shown in Figure 9-8, a LAN adapter card is placed in one of the expansion slots of each microcomputer in the network. The communications lines are then attached to the adapter card. (Note: Some *network-ready* microcomputers have built-in LAN adapter circuitry. Also, some wireless LANs use radio transmission as their communications lines.)

The LAN adapter card connects a microcomputer to the LAN and implements the functionality at levels 1 and 2 of the OSI model. Such cards code and decode line signals, and they process a network-access protocol, as described below.

Peripheral equipment is connected to the LAN so that it can be shared among the microcomputers. The equipment can be connected to a computer that is connected to the LAN, or, in some cases, the equipment is directly connected to the LAN. In the latter case, the equipment must also have a network-adapter card. Usually such equipment is expensive, special-purpose hardware like a graphics plotter or a fast, high-quality laser printer.

In a typical LAN, one (or more) of the microcomputers is designated as a server. This microcomputer stores the data that will be shared on the LAN. A **dedicated server** serves the needs of the network only. No user processing is done on a dedicated server. A **concurrent server** both serves the network and performs processing for a user.

LAN Topology

Figure 9-9 shows three of the most common configurations of computers (called **LAN topologies**) used with LANs: bus, ring, and star. With **bus topology**, the computers are connected to a cable like clothes strung out along a clothesline. The

Figure 9-9   LAN Topologies

The common LAN topologies are the **(a)** bus topology, **(b)** ring topology, and **(c)** star topology.

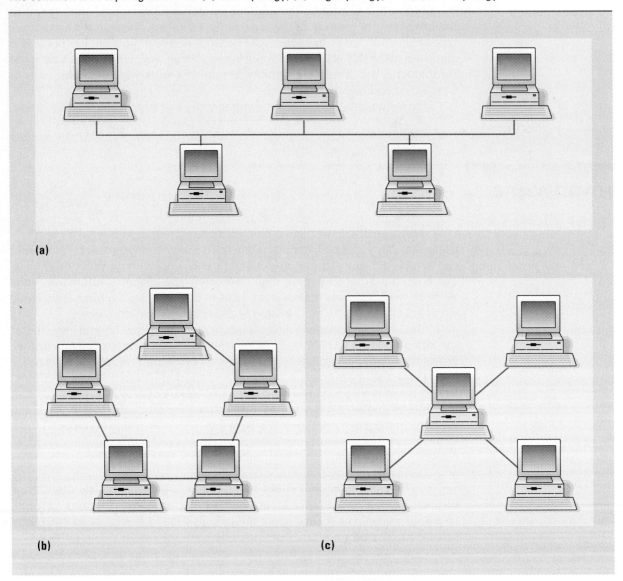

advantages of this topology are that it is easy to install and that it is cheap. One line is run through the workgroup, and the microcomputers are dropped off the line where needed. Adding new computers is also easy; the new computer need only clip into the line. The cost of a bus connection can be less than $500 per computer, or **node**, as the computers in a network are sometimes called.

With **ring** topology, the computers are connected to a line that is closed in a circle or loop. A continuous path exists from one computer through other computers and back to itself. The advantage of a ring is performance; a continuous flow of data can pass around the ring at a very high rate. The disadvantage is dependency among the computers. If one computer is inoperable, the LAN is inoperable.[1] If one computer is slow, all will be slow. Further, due to the need to have a closed loop, more line cable is required than with bus topology.

With **star** topology, one microcomputer is placed in the center of the others, and lines run out from it like arms of a star. The central computer operates as clearinghouse for LAN traffic, receiving messages from a sending node and directing them to the receiving node.

Do not confuse star topology with the centralized processing system. The essential difference is that, with star topology, the nodes are microcomputers; with the centralized system, the nodes are typically dumb terminals. Also, with the centralized system, the central computer controls all processing; with star topology LANs, the central computer simply acts as a message switcher.

The advantage of the star configuration is ease of installation and cabling. The disadvantage is dependence on the central computer. It can become a performance bottleneck, and, if it fails, the network will fail as well.

While bus topology is used in many commercial applications, the ring and the star are rarely used in pure form. Instead, a combination of ring and star topologies has become popular. With this combination, the ring resides within the central node of a star, and the arms of the star are connected to this ring, as shown in Figure 9-10. A continuous flow of data circulates through the ring, and data to and from the micros is transmitted along the arms of the star. This structure has the advantage of a ring without having the expense of longer cabling.

IBM and other manufacturers have published a standard cabling configuration guide that implements this hybrid topology. When publishing this guide, IBM made a commitment to its customers that this standard would be supported for some time and told them that they would be safe to follow this guideline when wiring their new or reconstructed buildings.

---

1. However, it is typically easy to remove an inoperable computer from the ring. (Easy, that is, if the developer has written procedures that explain how to do it!)

Figure 9-10   Combination of Star and Ring Topology
The star and ring topology are commonly used in combination.

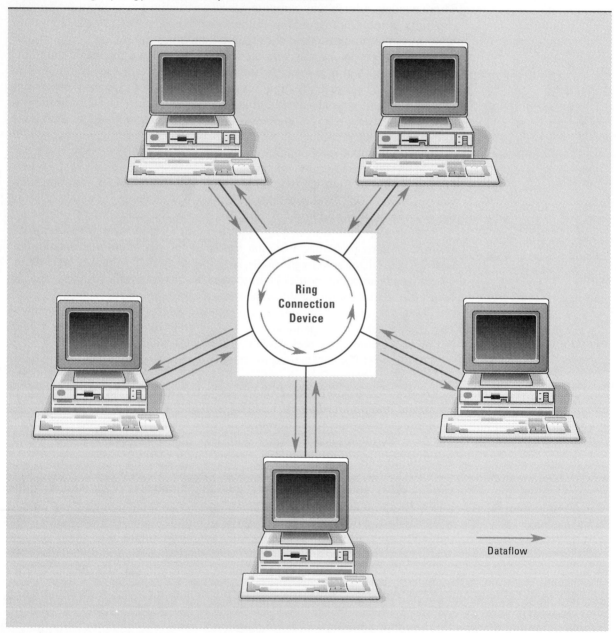

LAN Communications Media and Transmission

Three types of **communications,** or **transmission, media**, or cables, are used on a LAN: twisted pair, coaxial cable, and optical fiber. **Twisted pair** is cheap but has the lowest capacity, and example being the wires typically used for telephone lines. **Coaxial cable** is more expensive but has greater capacity than twisted pair. It also has greater reliability, since it is better insulated. **Optical fiber** is very expensive but has exceptionally high transmission capacity. Since optical fiber uses light for transmission, it is immune to electromagnetic interference and, hence, has very high reliability.

The speed of the LAN depends on the line type and the style of transmission. Optical fiber lines have capacities of up to 50 megabits or more per second. Twisted pair lines are slower, typically 10 megabits per second.

Two strategies are employed with the transmission media: baseband and broadband. With **baseband** transmission, every signal uses the entire capacity of the medium; baseband hardware is simpler and cheaper. With **broadband** transmission, the medium is divided into several subchannels, like the various frequencies on a radio dial, and each signal is assigned to one of the subchannels. This means that many signals may be carried simultaneously on a broadband network. Also, with broadband, both voice and data signals may be carried on the same line. Broadband is the system used for cable TV transmission.

Data-Link Protocols

Topology and cabling have to do with the physical aspects of the network and, hence, fall into level 1 of the OSI model. Level 2, *data link*, concerns the way that the system controls access to the transmission medium. To enable two or more microcomputers to use baseband transmission on the same medium, controlled sharing of the medium is provided by logic built into the network-access cards.

The two most common data-link protocols are contention and token passing.

Contention   With **contention protocol**, each message is addressed with the identities of the sender and the receiver and sent to all nodes on the LAN. Nodes listen to the line; when they detect a message directed to them, they accept it. They ignore all other messages. When a node wants to transmit a message, it first listens to the line and, if the line is not in use, sends its message. If the line is in use, the node waits a period of time and listens again. It follows this procedure until the line becomes available.

With this strategy it is possible for two nodes to decide to use the line at the same time, a situation called a **collision**. When a collision occurs, both nodes follow a standard procedure that is similar to the way a polite conversation is managed. They stop sending, wait a period of time, and then again attempt to transmit their messages. Obviously, if each node doesn't wait a different period of time, they will be in perpetual deadlock.

The advantage of contention is that it is simple and easy to implement. The disadvantage is that considerable excess capacity must exist on the line. Otherwise, nodes wait inordinate amounts of time to send their messages.

The contention protocol has been formalized into a standard by the Institute for Electronic and Electrical Engineers (IEEE). The standard, labeled **IEEE 802.3,** refers to the contention protocol as carrier sense multiple access with collision detection, or **CSMA/CD.** The first commercially successful system that used the contention protocol was **Ethernet.** All three of these terms, IEEE 802.3, CSMA/CD, and Ethernet, describe products that implement this protocol. Contention is almost always implemented on a bus network, although it can be implemented on a ring and its variants.

Token Passing   An alternative to contention protocol is **token passing,** which has also been standardized by the IEEE. Token passing on a ring is called **IEEE 802.5,** and token passing on a bus is called **IEEE 802.4.** The ring version is more common and will be described here. See Madron for information about IEEE 802.4.[2]

Consider the example in Figure 9-11. There are three microcomputers in the LAN, labeled node A, node B, and node C. In the figure, each micro is represented by its adapter card, which performs all the processing described here. In this example, data circulates counterclockwise around the ring. As a bit arrives at an adapter card, the card immediately copies the bit back onto the ring for the next card downstream. In Figure 9-11, node A copies the bit back onto the network for node B. Then the card examines the bit for processing.

Messages consist of three parts: a token heading, the message body, and a token end. (This is a simplified discussion of 802.5.) The token heading (or the **token**) is a special pattern of bits that is recognized as the start of a message. The token can be marked as in use or as not in use. If it is in use, then the card examines the address in the token heading to see if the message is addressed for this node. If so, the card sends the message to the network OS (level 3). If not, the card just passes the message along. The token end terminates the message.

If the token is not in use, then the card can use it to send a message. To do so, the token is marked as in use, and the message is placed on the ring. An end token is generated after the message. So that more than one message can be on the ring at a time, messages are limited in length. When the message comes back to the node that generated it, that node marks the token as not in use. Thus, originators of messages are responsible for removing the messages from the ring.

---

2.   Madron, Thomas W., *Local Area Networks,* 2nd ed. New York: John Wiley & Sons, 1990, pp. 202–222.

Figure 9-11 Token Passing Protocol
A message is passed from node C to node B through node A.

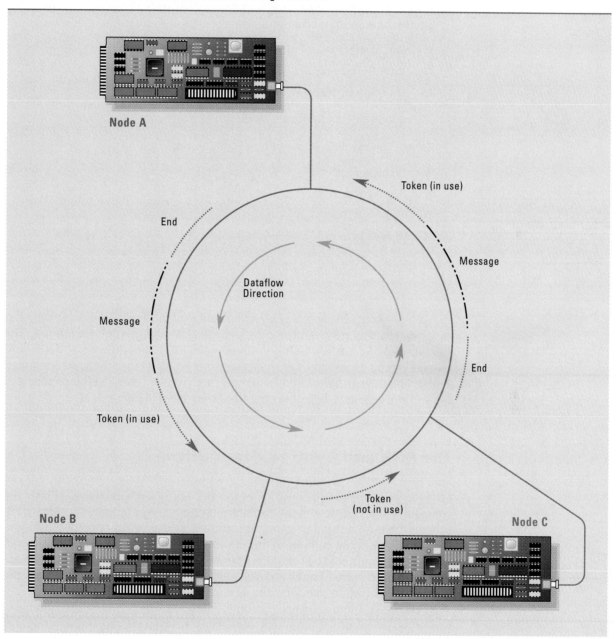

Figure 9-12   Data-Link Protocols Compared

Contention (IEEE 802.3) Ethernet

- ■ Nodes listen to line
- ■ Transmit when line is idle
- ■ Stop when collisions occur
- ■ Almost always implemented on bus

Token Passing (IEEE 802.4 — bus;   IEEE 802.5 — ring)

- ■ Continuous stream of data on network
- ■ Token indicates whether node can transmit
- ■ Addresses in token indicate destination address of message
- ■ Messages removed by nodes that generate them

With token passing, a very high percentage of the available line capacity can be used. There is no need for excess capacity as there is for contention. The disadvantage of token passing is its complexity. Examining each token and assembling and disassembling messages are more difficult than the actions required for the contention protocol. Still, both protocols have seen considerable commercial application. LAN data-link protocols are summarized in Figure 9-12.

The PBX and Centrex Alternatives

An alternative to LAN technology is the **private branch exchange (PBX)**, the company's internal telephone switching system (see Figure 9-13). Most PBX systems today allow for data communication as well as for voice communication. Thus, computers can connect to one another across the PBX without any special wiring being required. The computers can be connected into the telephone system so that an office wired for telephones is also wired for computers. This is not the case with LANs, where special wiring is required.

Most PBX applications operate in serial mode, which is slow, in the range of 56,000 bits per second. Computers interfaced on such a PBX are thus restricted to relatively low-volume applications such as E-mail.

Figure 9-13 PBX System
A PBX can link devices that communicate data as well as providing voice communication.

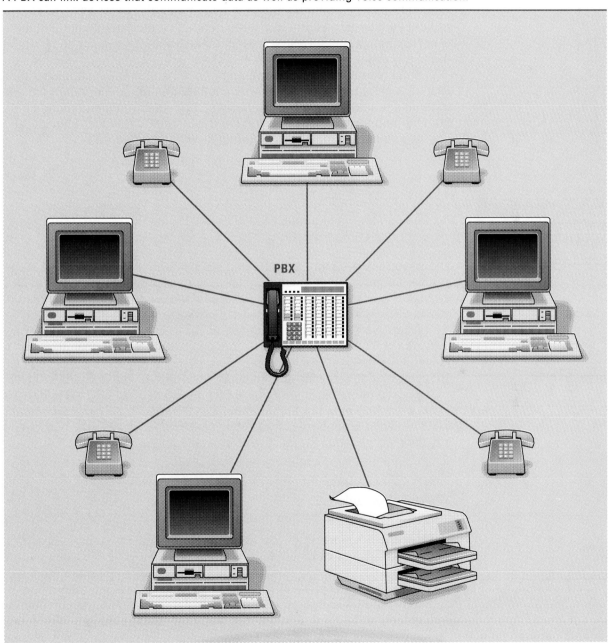

Recently, some vendors have announced systems that can run a token ring network on a PBX system. Since there is no special cabling, however, the communications speed is restricted. A typical token ring on a PBX runs in the range of 4 to 8 megabytes per second. If there is not too much traffic, the advantages of not having to install special wiring may more than make up for any deficiencies due to processing speed.

Some companies use **Centrex** telephone service leased from the local telephone company rather than owning a PBX. Centrex systems allow for data transmission as well as voice transmission. The primary difference between the PBX and Centrex service is that Centrex switching is done at the telephone company, and the telephone company maintains the switching equipment.

PROGRAMS

The basic categories of programs for workgroup information systems are the same as those for personal information systems: systems programs, including the OS, the utilities, and the DBMS, and applications programs for horizontal and vertical markets, as well as custom-developed application programs.

Figure 9-8 shows the relationship of the network-adapter card and the **network OS**. The relationship between the network OS and other programs is shown in Figure 9-14. The relationships shown here are typical for a user computer. The configuration of the file server computer will be different, as described below.

Each computer must have a local OS program (labeled DOS in Figure 9-14) and a network OS program. For the example in Figure 9-14, the computer also has a DBMS, database applications, and other types of applications. The nonsystems programs are not required and are shown as an example only.

The Network OS

The network OS supports LAN processing and must match the processing style of the network-adapter cards in use. If the LAN is a ring using the token passing protocol, then the network OS must support a token passing interface. If the LAN is based on CSMA/CD protocol, then the network OS must support this interface.

Network OSs can be licensed from a variety of sources. The two most popular such systems are Netware 386 from Novell and LAN Manager from Microsoft.

Figure 9-14 Programs in a LAN Environment

The LAN OS provides the link between application programs, the OS, and the LAN hardware.

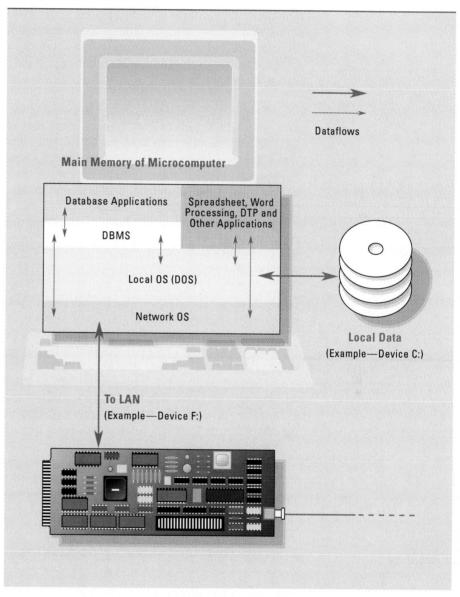

Network Request Processing

The network OS fulfills all the functions in the OSI model levels 3 through 6 on behalf of the application program. Consider an example. Suppose that the user of the computer in Figure 9-14 wants to transfer the file CH9.DOC from a local device C: to the network server device F: and place it in the directory TEXT. To do so, she issues the following:

```
COPY C:\CH9.DOC F:\TEXT
```

This command is sent to DOS. A piece of the network OS has been inserted into DOS, however, and it intercepts the COPY command. If the command involves a network device, as this one does, the network OS keeps the command and processes it on behalf of DOS. If the command does not involve a network device, such as a command to copy a file from one directory to another on device C:, then the network OS gives the command back to DOS for processing.

After the command has been intercepted, the network OS fulfills the OSI levels 3 through 6 functions. It encrypts the file, if necessary, it sets up a session by breaking up the copy request into a series of smaller copies, and it formats each smaller copy request so that transmission errors can be detected. On a LAN, routing (OSI layer 3) is done in a simple way. All messages are transmitted to all nodes. Each node reads the message's address and either ignores the remainder of the message or continues reading, as appropriate. Finally, the network OS passes each formatted data block to the network-adapter card for transmission on the network. All of these processes are performed in reverse order on the receiving node as shown in Figure 9-7. In this case, the receiving node is the file server.

Similar actions are undertaken for all the applications on the user's computer. If the user wants to open a Lotus 1-2-3 spreadsheet file, she runs 1-2-3 as she always does. She can open a directory on device F: just as she can on device C: (the local device). She can open spreadsheets on device F: and save to this device as well.

In Figure 9-14, arrows that stop within the boundary of DOS represent data processed on the local device. Arrows that extend through DOS represent data processed on the network.

Distributed Database Processing

Database processing on a LAN involves additional complications. Databases are processed on a LAN-based system in two different architectures: resource-sharing and client/server.

Figure 9-15 shows the relationships of programs in a **resource-sharing** database architecture. Observe that the DBMS is located on each user computer.

Figure 9-15   Resource-Sharing Database Processing

In resource sharing, all the processing is done on the user computer, and the server only provides complete tables of data.

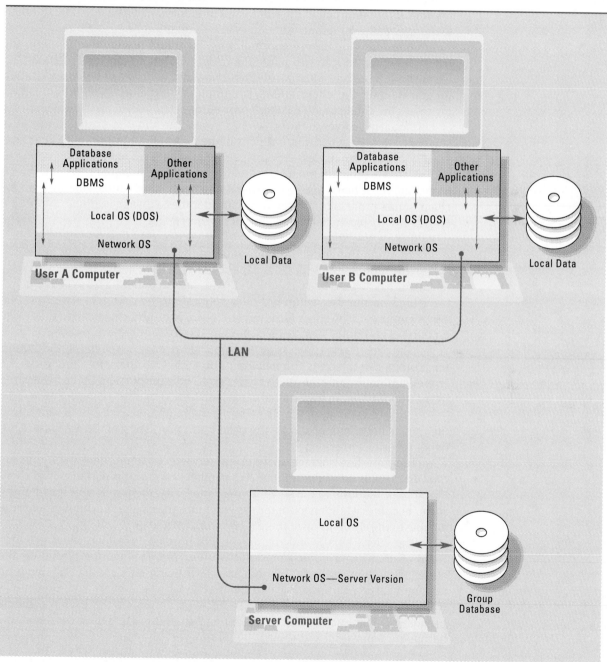

Database application programs make requests for database service to the DBMS, which, in turn, makes requests from the file server for processing against the group database. These requests are transmitted over the network by the network OS. Results are returned to the DBMS and processed; a response is then returned to the application program.

Client/server database processing is illustrated in Figure 9-16. Here, the DBMS is separated into two parts: the client DBMS and the server DBMS. The client DBMS interfaces with the user. When requests are transmitted by application programs, then the client DBMS is completely bypassed. The server DBMS processes the database. All database processing is conducted on the server.

The client/server architecture has several advantages over the resource-sharing alternative. First, only one copy of the server DBMS is required. (The client DBMS can be a simpler, less expensive program.) With resource sharing, copies of the full DBMS program must be located on every user computer. Second, much more data must be transmitted across the network for resource sharing than for client/server processing. To see why, consider the following example. Suppose a database contains the following table of customer data:

CUSTOMER (Cust#, CustName, CustAddress, CustCity, CustState, CustZip)

Now suppose that a database application needs to access every row of data for customers located in zip code 46041. With resource sharing (as in Figure 9-15), the DBMS on the user computer must request all the customer data from the server computer. The entire file is transmitted across the LAN, and then the DBMS on the user computer locates the customers having the desired zip code.

With client/server processing, the application program sends only the request for customer data across the network. The DBMS on the server processes the request and sends only the answer back. Thus, only the portions of the file desired by the application are transmitted across the LAN.

A third advantage of the client/server alternative is that a DBMS centralized on a single node better controls the concurrent processing of the database. Also, better security is provided.

There are disadvantages to the client/server architecture, however. By placing the DBMS on the server computer, less parallel processing is possible. If 20 client PCs submit requests to the server at the same time, the processing speed of the server becomes a bottleneck in the system. Since the client PC cannot process the database entirely on its own, there is less work for it to do.

The client DBMS and the server DBMS need to be the same product. A DBMS that has a particularly effective user interface can be placed on the client computers, and a DBMS that has particularly effective security, control, and multiuser performance can be placed on the server. For example, a workgroup might choose to place Paradox or Access on the user computers because of their easy-to-use interfaces and to place SQL Server on the server because it is powerful and robust.

Figure 9-16 Client/Server Database Processing

In client/server processing, the client DBMS on the user's computer contains the user interface. The server DBMS on the server computer does all the database processing in response to requests from the client DBMS.

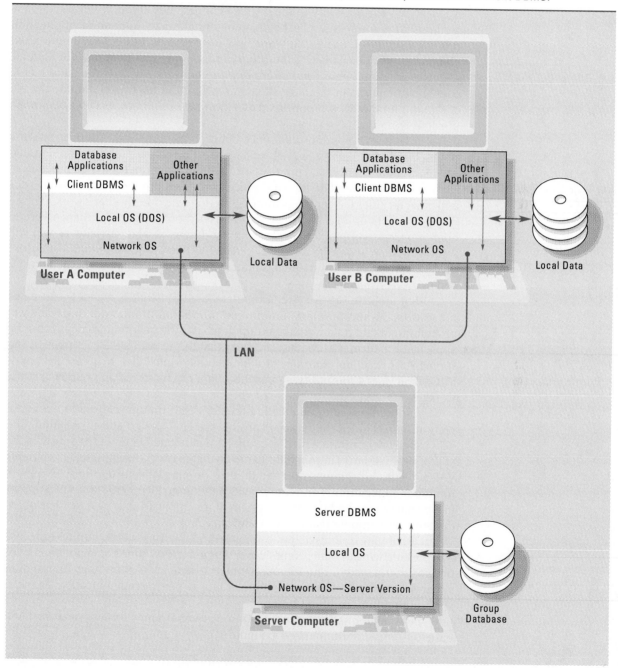

Application Programs in a Distributed System

Application programs vary in the degree to which they are aware of and use the facilities of the network. To begin, most single-user horizontal application products, such as Lotus 1-2-3, Word, and WordPerfect, can run on a networked computer without change. If the program uses only the local disk for storage, then the program is not even aware that the network exists. If the file server is used for storage, then the only difference is that the user must employ the file designator for the file server instead of a local file designator, as described in the previous section.

There is an important difference between using a single-user version of a product to access data on a LAN server and using a true multiuser version of a product. A multiuser version provides features and functions for shared processing, such as shared boilerplate for word processing. Such products also provide locks and other facilities to keep users from interfering with one another's work. Using a single-user version of a product for multiuser processing leaves the workgroup open to errors and problems due to uncoordinated update activity, as you will soon see. When acquiring multiuser versions of such products, you must ensure that the version of the horizontal product you are licensing matches the network OS you have installed.

With a client/server system, nondatabase application products can make requests of the server DBMS. For a word processing program or a spreadsheet program to obtain data from the group database, the only requirement is for the application to format its requests in a way that the server DBMS can process. The spreadsheet Excel, for example, provides a utility called Q+E to access data from SQL Server. Using this utility, spreadsheet data can be stored and retrieved in the workgroup's database.

In most cases, the value-added reseller (VAR) that develops and markets a vertical market software package controls the LAN design and installation. The VAR usually determines which network hardware and OS to use and installs the appropriate version of its programs to run on that network. A high-quality, reputable VAR provides all the expertise required to develop and install the LAN-based, multiuser applications—and also provides training, documentation, and support for the operations and use of the system. If the application is custom developed, then the development team plays a similar role.

Developing multiuser applications on LAN-based systems requires expertise and the balancing of many complicated design factors. You should not attempt to develop such a system yourself, unless you contemplate a career as an information systems specialist and your company is willing to pay for your education. For such applications, hire a professional!

Considerations for the acquisition of various types of programs for LAN-based systems are summarized in Figure 9-17.

Figure 9-17   Application Programs in the LAN Environment

Type of Application Program	Characteristics
Database Application Programs	Resource sharing: Access DBMS on local computer
	Client/server: Access user DBMS on local computer
	User DBMS accesses server DBMS on server computer
Horizontal Application Products	Access local data without change
(Word Processing,	Access files on server data using server device name
Spreadsheet, DTP)	For multiuser control, use multiuser version of the product
	Can access group database data using server DBMS
Vertical Application Products	Specifically designed for LAN environment
Custom Applications	Developers establish LAN specifications

DATA

Workgroup information systems differ from personal information systems in that at least some data is shared. Some types of data sharing are easy to accomplish. An E-mail system, for example, follows the originator's instructions to send a copy of a memo to everyone on a distribution list. The memo is shared in a way that presents no data management problems.

Other types of data sharing do create data management problems. Two workers who are making different changes to the same boilerplate paragraph can cause havoc with each other. To see why, suppose that each worker obtains a copy of the same paragraph at 8:00 A.M. They both begin keying their changes, and, say, at 8:15 A.M. the first worker stores his changes. At 8:20 A.M. the second worker stores her changes. Changes made by the first worker will be overwritten by the changes of the second. To prevent problems such as this, data updates must be coordinated.

To coordinate the processing of shared data, data must be properly organized and appropriate procedures developed. This section considers the organization of data, and the next section will discuss procedures.

Data can be shared without being processed simultaneously, as you have seen. Two users might agree that one will process data in the morning and the other, in the afternoon. They share the same data, but not concurrently. In such **nonconcurrent data sharing**, users must return all the data they have been processing at the end of the agreed-on time period; otherwise, update problems can occur.

In a LAN-based environment, **concurrent data sharing** occurs when two users read the same data from the file or database server and process it on their local computers during the same period of time.

When designing a shared-data application, the developers must first decide whether data is to be concurrently shared. If not, the data must be organized so as to allow sharing but not to allow concurrency. If concurrency is allowed, the data and the procedures must be developed; otherwise, chaos will result.

Nonconcurrent Data Sharing

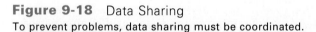

Nonconcurrent data sharing can be done by **data partitioning** or **processing partitioning**. If the data is partitioned, then it is divided into groups, each of which is processed by a single user. For example, when the accounts receivable department processes past due accounts, it could partition these accounts into groups by company name. One account representative could be assigned companies with names beginning with *A* through *J*, another, with *K* through *S*, and

Figure 9-18   Data Sharing
To prevent problems, data sharing must be coordinated.

a third, with *T* through *Z.* In this way, the accounts receivable data is shared, but it is shared in such a way that one user's actions cannot interfere with another's.

Preventing concurrency by data partitioning is not always feasible. If, for example, a workgroup enters orders from telephone calls, then data partitioning of the inventory file is infeasible. Such partitioning would assign certain products to one operator, other products to a second, and so forth. A customer who wants to place a multiple-item order could conceivably be transferred to a different operator for each item. This, clearly, is impractical.

A second way of accomplishing nonconcurrent sharing is to partition the processing. With this mode, all the data is assigned to a single person for processing, but only for certain periods of time. Thus, one user might be authorized access to all the data in the morning, and a second user in the afternoon. Both data and processing partitioning allow data to be shared without concurrency. In some circumstances, neither mode is acceptable, and data must be processed concurrently.

Concurrent Data Sharing

As stated, concurrent data sharing occurs when two or more users process the same data during the same time period. The nature of the shared system depends largely on the level of granularity. Historically, database and file processing applications share data at the record (or table row) level of granularity. Other applications share at the file level. We first discuss record-, or row-, level sharing.

Record-Level Sharing   Three fundamental situations arise with **record-level sharing**: (1) read/read, where two users concurrently read the same record; (2) read/update, where one user reads records while a second user updates records; and (3) update/update, where both users update records.

No problems will arise in the first case. Both users can concurrently read the same record without causing each other any problems. The second case may or may not create problems, depending on the needs of the applications. No problem will arise as long as the user who is reading understands and accepts that the data he or she is viewing may be inconsistent.

For example, in Legacy Systems Customer Support, suppose that one user is producing a report about the number of calls handled by each operator during the past week, while the rest of Customer Support continues normal operations against the database. Calls are taken, and the customer call data is updated concurrently with the report generation. In this case, the user of the report must realize that the report is based on changing data. An operator whose last name starts with *A* may have fewer calls than an operator whose last name starts with some other letter whose data was collected a few moments later. The difference may be due to the fact that new calls were reported as the report was in preparation. Under these circumstances, the report is not a fair basis for comparison among operators, but that may not matter in some cases.

If, however, the user needs an exact report of the number of calls at a particular point in time, then the concurrent changes do present a problem. If the report is used to compute bonuses for support representatives, then the report must be based on consistent data; updates must be disallowed while the report is being produced.

Consider another problem of read/update concurrency. The actions of two users are summarized in Figure 9-19. User A wants to count the number of refrigerators in Warehouses 1, 2, and 3. User B, concurrently, is transferring three refrigerators from Warehouse 1 to Warehouse 2. Because of the order in which the file server processes the reads and writes, user A concludes there are three fewer refrigerators in inventory than there actually are. This is sometimes called the **inconsistent read problem**. Before discussing means of preventing this problem, consider the final type of concurrency.

Update/update concurrency occurs when two users are updating the same data concurrently. Such concurrency is always a problem. Figure 9-20 shows an example of the **lost update problem** in which two users read and change the same data. There are four units in inventory at the start of the two transactions. Three units are removed by user A, and two units are removed by user B. The final count, however, shows two units in inventory. This result occurs because changes made by the first user are lost due to the update made by the second user.

In general, the solution to concurrency problems is for each user to use **record locking**, which locks data that is read with the intent to update. Thus, in both Figures 9-19 and 9-20, reads for update must be preceded by lock requests. If a user tries to obtain a lock on a record that is already locked, then that second lock

Figure 9-19 Inconsistent Read Problem

User A attempts to get a total of refrigerators in all three warehouses while user B is transferring three refrigerators from Warehouse 1 to Warehouse 2. Follow the steps in order and see how user A gets the wrong total of refrigerators.

| User A | DATA | | | User B |
	W_1	W_2	W_3	
1. Read count for Warehouse 1 (4)	4	10	7	2. Read count for Warehouse 2 (10)
	4	7	7	3. Decrement count by 3 (7)
				4. Write count for Warehouse 2 (7)
5. Read count for Warehouse 2 (7)				6. Read count for Warehouse 1 (4)
7. Read count for Warehouse 3 (7)				8. Add 3 to Warehouse 1 count (7)
9. Total 18 (shoud be 21)	7	7	7	10. Write count for Warehouse 1 (7)

is refused. In this way, locks prevent the concurrency problems because no record can be read until the update is complete.

Locking solves one problem but introduces another. Suppose two users are running application programs to process orders (see Figure 9-21). Suppose user A's program obtains a lock on the record for diamond necklaces, while user B's program obtains a lock on the record for plush black velvet boxes. Now, when user A attempts to lock the record for a plush black velvet box, this lock request is refused, because user B already has it locked. User A is thus made to wait. Next, however, user B requests a lock on the record for diamond necklaces. This lock

Figure 9-20 Lost Update Problem

Follow the steps in order and see how user A's update is lost through a problem in concurrent processing.

User A (Remove 3 units from inventory)	DATA			User B (Remove 2 units from inventory)
	W_1	W_2	W_3	
1. Read count for Warehouse 1 (4)	4	10	7	2. Read count for Warehouse 1(4)
3. Decrement by 3 (1)				
5. Write count for Warehouse 1 (1)	1	10	7	4. Decrement by 2 (2)
	2	10	7	6. Write count Warehouse 1 (2)

Figure 9-21 Deadlock Problem

User A and user B are each processing orders for a diamond necklace and a plush black velvet box. Follow the steps in order and see how user A and user B have each blocked the other from completing their processing.

User A	DATA		User B
	Necklace	Box	
1. Accesss necklace record for update	Lock		
		Lock	2. Access box record for update
3. Request box record for update			
			4. Request necklace record for update
(Awaiting access)			(Awaiting access)

may not be granted either because user A has it locked. User B is thus made to wait as well. This situation is called **deadlock,** or *the deadly embrace.*

A deadlock can be overcome only by canceling one of the order transactions and starting it over after the conflicting order is completed. Multiuser application programs that require concurrent update access to shared data use a *commit/rollback* technique in which all the data necessary to complete a transaction is accessed and locked before the transaction is committed and data is updated. If a deadlock occurs (or necessary data cannot be accessed for other reasons), then the transaction is rolled back without any update. At that point, it can be safely restarted.

The locking and unlocking of data, along with the resolution of deadlocks, is done by the application program or by the DBMS. Users are not asked (nor trusted to remember) to place locks before accessing data and are not bothered with the task of resolving deadlocks. You should know, however, that such locks are being placed.

File-Level Sharing   The second major type of concurrent data sharing, **file-level sharing,** is at the file level of granularity. This occurs in workgroup information systems in which **monolithic files** such as word processing documents, spreadsheets, publications, and graphic images are shared across the workgroup.

These files are monolithic because they are not structured into records as databases are. Such files, including word processing documents and graphics files, must be processed as one unit. A user or an application is granted authorization to modify any or all of the file. A user of a file that contains a graphic image, for example, is granted the authority to change all of the file, as a unit. No attempt is made to coordinate processing of a piece of the image.

The concurrent sharing of monolithic files is not as regimented as is such sharing of database data. Control tends to be spotty and is determined as much by the adequacy of manual procedures as by controls in programs.

To begin, most network OSs do provide facilities to control shared files. When first accessing a file, the application program or the user stipulates whether or not the file is to be shared with others. If the file is not to be shared, the network OS will not allow any other entity to open the file while it is being processed.

Multiuser horizontal application programs usually take advantage of these features. A shared word processor, for example, locks a document file as nonshareable when someone is editing the document. For other products, it is less certain. A paint and draw program, for example, may not pay attention to these issues. In this case, it is up to the user, following manual procedures, to ensure that the file is locked.

This is an undesirable state that probably will change as more and more shared-use products are developed. For now, be aware of the need to control the sharing of monolithic files. Also be aware that manual procedures may need to be developed to fill in for the deficiencies of some products.

PROCEDURES

A workgroup information system resides in a community of users. Where programs do not provide facilities for coordinated access, procedures need to be developed to coordinate the processing of workgroup members and ensure that one user's actions do not interfere with another's. To understand the need for **coordination procedures**, consider several examples:

■ In a law firm, several attorneys are making changes to different sections of the same document. They submit work to three different assistants, who must access the same document from a file server on a LAN (see Figure 9-22).

■ In the Plans and Budgets office at Specialty Chemicals, several financial analysts combine their individual work into a common, corporate spreadsheet. The analysts share this spreadsheet via a LAN.

■ In the publications department of a major manufacturer, product repair manuals are produced using a shared DTP system. One group within this department is responsible for creating drawings, a second, for writing text, and a third, for integrating text and graphics to form documents. A number of different versions of specifications exist for each product; these versions correspond to versions of the product. When changes are made to text or graphics, they must be incorporated into the appropriate documents.

The first two examples illustrate the need for control over concurrent data access. The principle here is the same as that for record locking. Users must lock

Figure 9-22 Lost Update Problem with Documents
User A's editing changes to the document are lost.

Action	CONTENTS		
	User A Memory	**User B Memory**	**Disk Storage**
User A calls up document for edit	Original document		Original document
User B calls up document for edit	User A edited version of document	Original document	Original document
User A saves edited document	User A edited version of document	User B edited version of document	User A edited version of document
User B saves edited document	(Other work)	User B edited version of document	User B edited version of document

data before they change it. Unfortunately, few LAN-based products provide this level of locking. Therefore, workgroups must institute manual procedures to prevent the inconsistent read and lost update problems on monolithic files.

In the law firm situation, for example, the assistants must have a procedure for "checking out" a document for the purpose of changing it. Other assistants who attempt to access the document while it is checked out must be informed of its status. The assistants can then coordinate their activities. It is essential that they be informed, however, that others are working on the same document. Without this knowledge, they will not know of the need to coordinate work.

The third example illustrates a different type of shared-data problem. Here, the workgroup is coordinating its efforts to create product repair manuals. They need to ensure that the correct version of a drawing, for example, is matched with the correct text and placed in the appropriate publication. This workgroup needs a system to track the relationship of drawings, text, and documents. If the group's DTP program does not have such features the group needs to create a database application to track the documents and their components.

As we have seen, the four categories of procedures are user and operations procedures for normal processing and for failure recovery. We will consider these four categories as they pertain to workgroup information systems. Keep in mind that procedures must not only be developed but also be clearly and completely documented and users must be trained on both their importance and their use.

User Procedures for Normal Processing

The important types of user procedures for normal processing are listed in Figure 9-23a. First, users need to know how to initiate access to the LAN, typically, by issuing a series of commands. With systems in which those commands are gathered together into a stored program procedure, the user need only invoke that procedure to access the LAN.

Additionally, for shared hardware systems, there must be procedures that explain how to use the shared hardware. These include ways to make requests for service, to cancel requests, to change scheduling priorities, and the like.

Next, users need procedures for accomplishing their work, the specific nature of which depends on the type of application. Procedures for an E-mail application differ from those for a shared database application; procedures for both need to be developed and documented, however. Another important component of procedures is a description of the constraints on processing. Users are more likely to comply with the constraints if their rationale is included.

Another important type of procedure concerns security and control. With a shared system, all users have a responsibility to ensure that data and other resources are appropriately protected against mistakes in processing, inadvertent losses,

Figure 9-23 Procedures for Workgroup Information Systems
Examples are shown of procedures for **(a)** normal processing and **(b)** failure recovery.

(a)

User Procedures for Normal Processing

- Initiating access to LAN (network)
- Using shared hardware
- Accomplishing work
- Placing constraints on processing (with rationale)
- Maintaining security and control
- Maintaining backup

Operations Procedures for Normal Processing

- Starting hardware and programs
- Monitoring and tuning system
- Periodically maintaining hardware, programs, data
- Maintaining security and control
- Maintaining activity log and other record keeping

(b)

User Procedures for Failure Recovery

- Correcting errors and detecting failures
- Maintaining business operations during failure
- Implementing post-recovery measures

Operations Procedures for Failure Recovery

- Detecting failures
- Resolving problems
- Initiating recovery activities
- Maintaining failure logs and other record keeping

and purposeful misuse. Chapter 12 summarizes control procedures in detail. Finally, users need procedures to back up their data for protection against hardware or other systems failure.

Operations Procedures for Normal Processing

Procedures for operations in normal processing are also listed in Figure 9-23a. First, operations personnel, even more than users, need procedures for starting the system, including those for starting the file server and related hardware as well as for initiating the OS, the DBMS, and other programs. Next, most LANs and other networks have a number of adjustable features that are set depending on the work to be done. The adjustment is sometimes called tuning the system. Most systems produce performance statistics to facilitate such tuning. Operations personnel need procedures to obtain and interpret such statistics and procedures for making specific adjustments.

Networks sometimes require periodic maintenance. While such maintenance can be required for hardware (e.g., cleaning a printer or changing the printer's toner cartridge), maintenance is sometimes also required for programs and data. Periodically, it may be necessary to reload data, to adjust files in directories, to clean up unused space, and so forth. Operations personnel need procedures for such activities.

Operations personnel also need control and security procedures that specify when the system is to be operational, who is authorized access to the physical network facilities, how the network is to be shared, and so forth. Additionally, most file servers maintain a log of activity that should be examined periodically for unauthorized or suspicious activity. A separate manual log may need to be kept as well.

Finally, operations personnel need procedures for backup activity. Periodically, the shared disk space should be backed up and the backups stored in an off-premise facility.

User Procedures for Failure Recovery

User procedures for failure recovery are summarized in Figure 9-23b. First, procedures are needed for correcting errors and detecting system failures so that, when unexpected system behavior occurs, users have criteria for determining whether the problem was caused by user error or system failure.

Next, users need procedures that specify what to do while the system is down. For example, in Customer Support, customers will continue to call for service even though the LAN-based system that processes the customer database has failed. How should the representatives proceed? What customers should they serve? What data should they gather? What restrictions should they place on their operations? All of these questions need to be answered long before any system failure occurs.

Finally, users need procedures to follow after the system has been recovered. They need to know how to determine how much of their work load needs to be reprocessed, and they need to know how to reprocess it. They also need procedures to help them validate that the reprocessed work has been correctly entered into the system. Other procedural needs depend on the particular type of application.

Operations Procedures for Failure Recovery

Operations personnel also need procedures for failure recovery, as listed in Figure 9-23b. As with users, they need to know how to detect that failure has occurred. In some cases, the nature of the failure is obvious, but in others, it is difficult to determine whether the problem was caused by user action, power variances, or other factors. Given that a failure has occurred, operations personnel need procedures that specify recovery activities. What should the operator do? Whom should he or she call for assistance? What users need to be contacted? What should they be told?

Additionally, operations personnel need procedures that stipulate actions to take once the system problem has been resolved. Files may need to be recovered from backups, saved work loads may need to be reprocessed, and other actions will need to be taken. Such procedures need to be carefully thought out well in advance.

Finally, operations personnel need a standard procedure and format for keeping records of failure and recovery activities. These records serve a number of purposes, including documentation for complaints to vendors and even for potential litigation.

This has been a brief survey of the types of procedures that need to be developed and documented for workgroup information systems. It is by no means comprehensive. When you work in or manage a workgroup, realize the importance of procedures in shared information systems. Do not fall into the mistaken belief that information systems eliminate the need for manual procedures. Instead, such systems make the presence of complete procedures, consistently applied, even more important.

PEOPLE

The final component of workgroup information systems is people. As with other information systems, there are users, operations people, and development people. With the exception of operators, the jobs and their descriptions are similar to those discussed previously.

Workgroup Operations People

With personal information systems, every user serves as his or her own operator. With workgroup information systems, however, this is often not the case. As indicated in the preceding section, there are too many activities for users to perform on their own. Some group of people needs to be identified as the group that operates the system.

Normally, in most workgroups, a few members of the workgroup are specially trained to become **user/operators**. These people learn how to operate the LAN and associated equipment, and are trained in the procedures listed in Figures 9-23a and 9-23b. They know how to start and stop the system, how to respond to routine problems, and whom to call in case of nonroutine problems or failures.

Several people within the workgroup do need to be trained to accomplish the operations job. Often, people are given operations responsibility as a part-time job. A likely candidate for such a job is the group's administrative assistant. Some groups find that one or two of their members have a special interest in or bent for operations work.

In some applications, someone in the workgroup is designated as the **network**, or **LAN, manager**. This person maintains the hardware and the network systems programs. Typical tasks include adding new computers to the network, extending the network to new rooms or buildings, upgrading the network's file server, installing new versions of network software, and the like. Considerable training and experience are necessary to perform this job well. If the workgroup is small, most likely these tasks are accomplished by an outside consultant on a part-time basis. For a larger group, however, it can be more cost-effective to hire an in-house network manager.

The need for workgroup members to develop expertise in LAN management is a cost of LAN-based systems and a point of potential vulnerability. Carefully selected group members pressed into LAN management and properly trained may enjoy parts of the job, but they may ignore less interesting parts. They may make technical errors that would not be made by the information systems professionals who operate centralized systems.

Data Administration People

Additionally, the fact that data is shared creates the need for a new job type, that of **data administrator**. The functions of this job are to guard and protect the data. Without this position, the shared data has no owner other than the group. Consequently, no one may consider it his or her responsibility to protect the data. When a problem occurs, members of the group will accuse one another: "I thought YOU were going to make the backup!" Additionally, from time to time, group members disagree about how the data should be processed, who has the right to perform what actions on the data, and when they should perform those actions.

The data administrator ensures that backup and recovery procedures exist and are followed. This person also provides a focus for discussions about the use (and meaning) of the data. The administrator is the single person to whom group members can come with questions, problems, and concerns. Without an administrator, issues about the care, control, and processing of the data go unaddressed. Assigning a person to these tasks increases the usefulness and reliability of the data.

Data administration is not necessarily a full-time job. Often, a group member has this job in conjunction with other duties. To be effective, the data administrator needs strong diplomacy skills. He or she also needs to have the respect of group members and the full support of the group manager. We will say more about data administration when we discuss enterprise system components.

SUMMARY

A workgroup information system, like other business computer systems, has five components: hardware, programs, data, procedures, and people. Workgroup systems involve the controlled sharing of data or other resources; this need places special requirements on each component.

There are three fundamental types of multiuser information systems. A centralized system, the oldest type, involves a central computer that communicates with users situated at dumb terminals. Centralized systems maintain tight control over processing and are used primarily for enterprise TPSs.

The second type of multiuser system, the distributed system based on a LAN, involves multiple, independent computers that communicate with one another via a communications line. With distributed systems, control is distributed throughout the network, which allows users great independence but can create coordination problems. This alternative is most often used for workgroup computing.

The hybrid system, the third type of multiuser system, combines centralized processing with network processing. Examples are linked LANs, LAN-based systems connected through a backbone network to other LANs and mainframe computers, and geographically dispersed LANs connected through a WAN. Providing a hybrid form of control, such systems have great capacity and are most frequently used for enterprise applications. The advantages and disadvantages of each system are summarized in Figure 9-5.

A protocol is a set of agreements that permit the communication of data. Examples are SNA, DNA, and TCP/IP. OSI is a seven-layer framework for protocols that is sufficiently robust to be applied to nearly all current data communication technologies. In the transmitting device, data is passed from the application down through the layers to layer 1 where it is physically transmitted to the receiving device, where it is passed back up through the levels until it becomes available to the application.

In LANs, the bottom two OSI layers are accomplished in hardware by network-access protocols. The hardware consists of micros, communication lines, network-adapter cards, and, possibly, peripheral equipment. One or more microcomputers are designated as the file server, which can be either a dedicated server or a concurrent server.

Three LAN topologies are the bus, the ring, and the star. The bus is cheap and easy to install but has the least performance. A ring involves more cabling but has greater performance. Stars are infrequently used, except when the center of the star hosts a ring within it.

Communication, or transmission, lines include twisted pair wire (such as telephone wires), coaxial cable (as with cable TV), and optical fiber (which has very high capacity). Twisted pair and coaxial cables are most frequently used with LANs. Baseband transmission allows for the transmission of a single signal; broadband supports many signals and is the same type of transmission as is used for cable TV.

Topology and cabling concern level 1 of the OSI model. Data link, the level 2 OSI component, concerns the way that the computers access the transmission media. A data-link protocol is a method for packaging messages and placing them on the transmission media.

Two common data-link protocols are contention and token passing, which are implemented in the logic of network-access cards inserted into the expansion slots of the computers.

With contention protocol, the line is managed as is a polite conversation. Contention protocol has been formalized into a standard by the Institute for Electronic and Electrical Engineers (IEEE). The standard, IEEE 802.3, or carrier sense multiple access with collision detection, is sometimes called Ethernet, since Ethernet was the first commercially successful version of this protocol.

Token passing is the second common data-link protocol. IEEE 802.4 and 802.5 define standard protocols for token passing. With token passing, a continuous stream of data is passed from computer to computer. The token is a special pattern of bits that heads a communications message. If the token is in use, the adapter card examines the data to see if the message is for that card, and, if so, it sends the message to the network OS program for processing. If the token is not in use, then the adapter card can use the token to send a message. To do so, the network-access card marks the token as in use and adds the message after the token. When the token returns to the originating node, the token is marked as not in use.

Alternatives to the LAN for local-area data communications are the PBX and Centrex service from the local telephone company. These systems use existing telephone lines for communication, but current systems have less capacity than LANs.

The categories of programs for workgroup information systems are the same as for other information systems. A LAN requires a network OS which fulfills the functions of levels 3 through 7 of the OSI model. If the workgroup processes a database, then a multiuser DBMS is required. With resource-sharing architecture, the DBMS is placed on the user nodes and the file server operates as a disk manager. With the client/server architecture, the DBMS is divided into two parts. The server DBMS, which does all the processing of data, is placed on the server. Application programs access it from the client computers, as do the client DBMSs, which contain the user interface of the DBMS. The client/server architecture requires only a single copy of the complex server DBMS, requires less transfer of data over the LAN, and provides better control of concurrent processing, but it permits less parallel processing.

Most single-user application programs run as-is on a network, although storing and retrieving files from the file server may require special commands on the user's part. Many horizontal programs also exist in multiuser versions; these products take advantage of the file management capabilities of the network OS. Vertical market and in-house custom-developed programs on networks can be specifically designed for shared processing on the network.

Data for workgroup applications is usually shared, either nonconcurrently or concurrently. Nonconcurrent data sharing can be done by data partitioning or processing partitioning. Concurrent processing permits multiple users to process the same data on their computers during the same time period.

Concurrent data sharing is of two types, depending on the level of granularity. Record-level sharing occurs most often in database and file processing applications. Records must be locked before they can be read for the purpose of update. Record locking solves both the inconsistent read and lost update problems, but introduces the problem of deadlock. Resolving deadlocks requires the commit/rollback technique.

The second type of data sharing occurs at the file level of granularity. Such sharing, the sharing of monolithic files, occurs most often with noncoded and nonstructured data, although spreadsheet data is also shared in this way. Sharing facilities tend to be spotty; there are facilities for controlling such sharing in the network OS, and in most multiuser products. Still, some products have no such capabilities. Users must often supplement program controls for sharing with manual procedures.

A workgroup information system resides in a community. Procedures must be developed to coordinate workgroup processing. Such procedures augment the procedures needed for user and operations normal processing and user and operations failure recovery processing.

Workgroup information systems require more sophisticated operations than do personal information systems. Consequently, some users need to be specially trained. These users then serve as (possibly part-time) operations staff. Data administration is a new job type needed for shared systems. The data administrator guards and protects the shared workgroup resources.

KEY TERMS

Centralized system	LAN topology	Resource-sharing
Dumb terminal	Bus topology	architecture
Distributed system	Node	Client/server
LAN	Ring topology	architecture
File server	Star topology	Nonconcurrent data
Hybrid communications	Communications media	sharing
system	Twisted pair	Concurrent data
Backbone network	Coaxial cable	sharing
Linked LANs	Optical fiber	Data partitioning
WAN	Baseband transmission	Processing partitioning
Protocol	Broadband	Record-level sharing
SNA	transmission	Inconsistent read
DNA	Contention protocol	problem
TCP/IP	Collision	Lost update problem
OSI model	IEEE 802.3	Record locking
Application layer	CSMA/CD	Deadlock
Presentation layer	Ethernet	File-level sharing
Session layer	Token passing	Monolithic files
Transport layer	IEEE 802.5	Coordination
Network layer	IEEE 802.4	procedures
Data-link layer	Token	User/operator
Physical layer	PBX	Network, or LAN,
Dedicated server	Centrex	manager
Concurrent server	Network OS	Data administrator

REVIEW QUESTIONS

1. List the five components of an information system.

2. What burden does the need for controlled sharing place on each of the five components?

3. List the three fundamental types of multiuser information systems.

4. Describe the characteristics, control philosophy, and primary application of centralized systems.

5. Describe the characteristics, control philosophy, and primary application of distributed systems.

6. Sketch a hybrid system with a backbone network, another with linked LANs, and another with a WAN.

7. Describe the advantages and disadvantages of centralized systems.

8. Describe the advantages and disadvantages of distributed systems.

9. Explain why communications standards are needed.

10. What is a data communications protocol? Give at least three examples of protocols.

11. What is the purpose of the OSI model? Explain how each level is like a production station.

12. In the OSI model, explain why, when a message is received, the levels are processed in the opposite direction from the direction in which a message is sent.

13. In a LAN, which layers of the OSI model are processed by network-adapter cards? Which layers are processed by the network OS?

14. What are the main hardware components of a LAN?

15. What is the function of a file server? Explain the difference between a dedicated server and a concurrent server.

16. Describe and illustrate bus topology, ring topology, and star topology.

17. Describe the three types of communications media. What is the relative speed of each?

18. Explain the function of a data-link protocol. What level of the OSI model does such a protocol represent?

19. What is contention? How does it relate to CSMA/CD, IEEE 802.3, and Ethernet?

20. Describe the contention protocol. How does it handle conflict on the LAN?

21. Describe the token passing protocol. How does it handle conflict on the LAN?

22. What does token passing have to do with IEEE 802.4 and IEEE 802.5?

23. Describe the PBX and Centrex alternatives to the LAN. Differentiate between the PBX and Centrex.

24. Name the categories of programs involved in workgroup information systems.

25. What are the functions of a network OS?

26. Sketch the resource-sharing LAN architecture.

27. Sketch the client/server LAN architecture.

28. Explain why it might be desirable to have one server DBMS product and a different client DBMS product on a LAN.

29. How do application programs for workgroup information systems differ from those for personal information systems?

30. Explain *nonconcurrent data sharing*. Give an example.

31. Explain *concurrent data sharing*. Give an example.

32. Give an example of nonconcurrent data sharing by data partitioning.

33. Give an example of nonconcurrent data sharing by processing partitioning.

34. Describe three situations for concurrent data sharing at the record level. Which cases raise problems?

35. Give an example of the inconsistent read problem.

36. Give an example of the lost update problem.

37. Explain how record locks prevent inconsistent read and lost update problems.

38. Give an example of the deadlock, or deadly embrace.

39. What technique do application programs use to resolve deadlocks?

40. What is a monolithic file?

41. Summarize the needs and issues for file-level locking.

42. Summarize user procedures for normal processing.

43. Summarize operations procedures for normal processing.

44. Summarize user procedures for failure recovery.

45. Summarize operations procedures for failure recovery.

46. Explain why workgroup information systems need operations personnel. Who usually fulfills this function?

47. Summarize the duties of the workgroup data administrator.

DISCUSSION QUESTIONS

1. Suppose you manage Customer Support for Legacy Systems. You want to develop an information system to track customers who are authorized to receive service and to maintain a record of the services your department has provided. Make a list of the five most important functions this system would serve. These functions should include, at least, TPS and MIS (narrow definition) services. Suppose you receive two proposals from two different vendors. One proposal is for a LAN-based system using contention-oriented network-access cards, and the other is for a LAN-based system using token passing network-access cards. List the criteria you would use in choosing between these alternatives. How would you go about obtaining the information you need to evaluate these criteria? Under what circumstances do you think contention would be better than token passing? Under what circumstances would the reverse be true?

2. Suppose you manage Customer Support at Legacy Systems and you have installed a LAN of microcomputers to meet the needs described in question 1. The support representatives are complaining that the system loses the data they enter. List three potential causes of this problem. How would you isolate the cause? Suppose it turns out that the network OS is incapable of providing record-locking services for the DBMS and application programs. Describe three alternatives you could pursue to solve this problem.

3. Suppose you are a member of a student team that is jointly writing a major term report for your marketing research class. Members work at various times using individual computers connected by a LAN. Devise two procedures to let group members safely access the text of the paper, one to implement concurrent access and one to implement nonconcurrent access. The programs you use have no special resources to support your procedures. Mentally check your procedures carefully, and revise until you are convinced that each would work. Finally, document your procedures, and compare advantages and disadvantages of each. Which procedure would you use?

PROJECTS

A. Find a published comparative review of various LAN OS products. (Check back issues of *PC Magazine*, if available, or other publications.) Based on the material in the article, describe three hypothetical workgroup information systems, each of which would be best served by a different LAN OS. Explain why you selected the LAN OS for each system. What differences among the three systems are most important in determining which LAN OS would work best? Is there any justification for using the same LAN OS on all the LANs in a company? If so, which LAN OS would you select? If not, why not?

B. Locate a workgroup in an organization that has installed a LAN-based system. What functions is that system supposed to serve? How well does it serve them? What types of hardware and programs are in use? How is the data shared? What is the level of granularity? If more than one system is used, do the levels of granularity differ? What user procedures exist? Are they documented? If so, how well? What training do the users receive? What operations procedures exist? Are they documented? Are some personnel identified as operators? If so, what training did they receive? Is there a data administrator? If so, what does that person do? If not, why not? After your interview, reflect on the systems in use. If you were the manager of that workgroup, what would you do differently?

C. Contact a computer dealer who specializes in LANs. What brands of hardware does that dealer sell? What network OS products does the dealer carry? In the dealer's opinion, what is the best network OS? What are the principal changes the dealer has noticed in the market in the past 3 years? How are customers changing? How are their needs changing? How has the technology changed? How does the dealer expect LANs to be used in the future? What will be the key success factors for dealers in the future?

M I N I C A S E

Workgroup Computing

The personal computer revolution of the last decade brought freedom for individual users and perhaps even gains in personal productivity. But it was also unsettling for many organizations. Individual empowerment did not necessarily further group goals. It was difficult to translate individual gains into measurable gains for organizations. The adherents of centralized computing might even argue there was a net loss as their world spun out of control.

The great promise of workgroup computing is that it will bring reintegration with little or no loss in freedom for individual users. It will mean that individual users will be able to work more closely together and to serve organizational goals better. Since groups working together tend to be the source of economic value, this will bring tangible gains in organizational productivity.

The bright future of workgroup computing lies as much in its economic as its technological possibilities. In fact, its rapid growth over the next two years and beyond will be driven mainly by its ability to deliver real, tangible gains in organizational productivity. Money tends to be the best motivation in every organization outside the federal government.

But there are other factors at work too. Perhaps the most important is the allied growth in local and wide area networks. It's been estimated that about 30,000 PCs are connected to networks every day. By the end of 1993, more than half the world's 100 million PCs will be connected. These are obviously dramatic numbers for an industry struggling with much slower growth in terms of the number of new standalone PCs sold.

Networks, of course, are not synonymous with workgroup computing. They are a necessary condition—kind of like plumbing. So what is important is the evidence that networks are being used for more than just simple file-sharing or connections to peripherals. LAN-based electronic mail, for example, has become the fastest growing application, and that includes all applications—for PCs, mainframes, minicomputers and workstations, and for standalone as well as networked computers.

Meetings may be necessary for doing business but the notion of a perpetual meeting or even more meetings is not likely to win many adherents. What groupware can do is help structure meetings, make them more productive, and perhaps even make some of them unnecessary.

An early Notes customer, for example, found Notes useful to what it called "unmeetings." Initially, Notes was used to help prepare for meetings by making sure everyone had the latest information and by holding discussions beforehand to sharpen the agenda. It was also an invaluable tool for follow-up, making sure agreements stuck and people did what they said they would. In other words, it assumed the vital organizational function of information sharing and coordination.

Eventually the groups using Notes found that, in many instances, the premeeting discussions and the post-meeting coordination were all that was required, and they were able to dispense with the formal, physical manifestation of the meeting.

If there is one single concept that will guide the future of workgroup computing, it surely is communications—not the concept of the meeting, or connectivity, or even information. For by itself, information has no value. It has value only if it can be communicated and if that communication leads to the production of goods and services. ∎

By Jim Manzi, president, chairman, and chief executive officer of Lotus Development Corporation, publisher of Lotus Notes and other application programs.

Excerpted from Network Computing, November 1, 1992, pp. 79–81.

Discussion Questions

1. How does Jim Manzi define workgroup computing?

2. Describe the contribution of Lotus Notes to business meetings, as described by Manzi.

3. Explain the relationship between networks and workgroup computing, as described here.

4. Manzi implies that the workgroup computing platform should include different programs from the personal computing platform. Evaluate this suggestion. What are the pros and cons of separate workgroup programs as compared to the applications that the user already uses for personal purposes?

Copyright© 1992 by **CMP Publications, Inc.,** 600 Community Drive, Manhasset, NY 11030. Reprinted from NETWORK COMPUTING with permission.

10

Developing Workgroup Information Systems

THIS CHAPTER CONSIDERS THE DEVELOPMENT of workgroup information systems. It provides a different perspective on systems development from that taken in Chapter 7 on developing personal information systems. Here, we discuss the use of the classical systems development life cycle (SDLC). The first part of this chapter considers the five stages of the SDLC and applies them to the development of workgroup information systems. The second part explains the fundamentals of dataflow modeling, an important tool for understanding and modeling information requirements. Dataflow diagrams are exceedingly useful, not only in developing information systems, but in general, for documenting the flow of activity in a department or an office. Module B, which follows this chapter, illustrates the development of a workgroup information system for Customer Support at Legacy Systems, the software publisher.

As you read this chapter, place yourself in the role of the workgroup manager or of some other key participant in the development activity. Assume that someday you will participate in developing a workgroup information system. Continually ask yourself, How would I do that? How would I proceed?

As with the discussion of personal information systems development, this chapter sets out one possible process for developing workgroup information systems. It is not necessarily the single best one but is simply one process that works. Later in your career, you can consider this process as a basis from which you may, at times, make excursions.

THE WORKGROUP SYSTEMS DEVELOPMENT PROCESS

The fundamental difference between workgroup information systems and personal information systems is that workgroup systems involve the sharing of data, information, and other intellectual assets among many people. Because many people are involved, the systems development process is more complicated, takes longer, and involves more risk.

It is sometimes possible to develop workgroup information systems using the prototyping process described in Chapter 7. To do this, the workgroup forms a project team, defines the problem, classifies the solution, and develops the system through iterative prototypes.

For workgroups, though, there are dangers in following this prototyping process. For one, the systems platform may be larger and more expensive; without detailed knowledge of requirements and work load, it is difficult to know what type of platform to create. Further, the cost of correcting a mistake can be high. For example, if a group builds a platform using network-access cards for a baseband network on IEEE 802.3 and later finds that this system has insufficient capacity, upgrading the network can involve considerable expense and wastage.

Additionally, because workgroup information systems involve multiple users, they are more complicated. Without focused attention on requirements specification, important requirements may not be noticed until after implementation. This is especially true since some requirements for workgroup information systems arise from peculiarities having to do with data sharing. These requirements most likely will not become apparent from prototyping.

Finally, most workgroup development projects involve personnel from outside the workgroup, such as people from the organization's MIS department or independent VARs. Such external personnel are unlikely to commit to a process as vague as development by prototyping, in which we continue to construct prototypes until we're satisfied.

For all of these reasons, prototyping is usually used for *parts* of workgroup information systems rather than for full systems. In developing personal information systems, we prototype a complete application as a way of defining its requirements. There, prototyping is fundamental to the systems development process. By contrast, in developing more complex workgroup information systems, we prototype forms, reports, menus, and other components to test whether they meet the predefined requirements effectively. Prototyping is reduced to the level of one useful tool among many.

Figure 10-1 summarizes the SDLC process we will use. Briefly, we define the problem, specify the requirements, evaluate alternatives, and then design and implement the system. We will consider each of these stages in turn.

Figure 10-1 Workgroup SDLC Stages

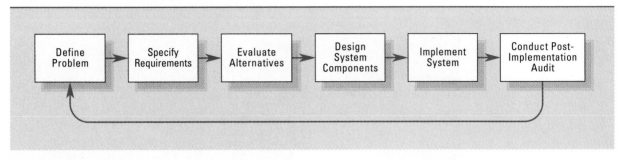

PROBLEM DEFINITION STAGE

The purpose of the **problem definition stage** for workgroup systems development is to perform preliminary work to ensure that the problem to be solved is understood, to assess feasibility, and then to develop a plan of action. These are the same problem definition stage tasks as for personal information systems development. (In fact, many workgroup applications grow out of prior personal information systems.) The only difference in problem definition for workgroup systems development is the greater complexity.

Problem Definition

The problem definition is harder to formulate in a workgroup information systems setting than in a personal information systems setting for two reasons. First, recall that a problem is a perceived difference between what is and what ought to be. Since there are many people in a workgroup setting, there can be many perceptions. In most cases, at the onset of the project, there will be at least several different perceptions of the problem. Only rarely does a system designed to solve one perceived problem automatically solve the other perceived problems.

Thus, when developing workgroup information systems, it is important to obtain the workgroup's **consensus** on the problem to be solved. We have consensus on a problem when all workgroup members (or at least all influential members) *agree* with the problem statement, *accept* that the problem as defined is the one to be solved, and are willing to *support* efforts to solve that problem.

Consensus does not imply agreement. In fact, we may never get all the workgroup members to *agree* on a definition of the problem. We can, however,

Figure 10-2 Group Problem Definition
The goal of the problem definition stage in group systems development is consensus.

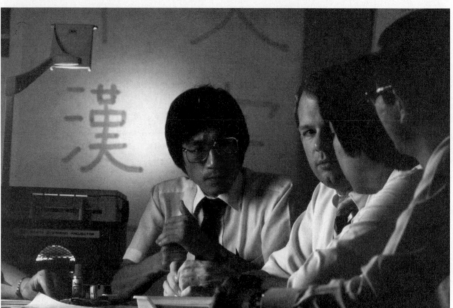

often get the team members to accept a problem statement as one that the group wants to work on. To accept the problem statement, the workgroup must first *understand* it, and, for the acceptance to mean anything, they must be willing to *support* the solution to the problem statement they have accepted.

In order to obtain consensus, the problem definition needs to be documented, presented to key people, and then adjusted in accordance with their feedback. If this is not done, the entire development effort may be directed to the wrong goal, or group resistance to the system may become strong enough that the system may fail.

If achieving consensus on the problem definition is impossible, as it is in some cases, do not proceed with the project. It is vital to have consensus on the problem definition before proceeding.

The second reason problem definition is more difficult for workgroup systems than for personal systems is that the underlying business systems are more complicated. There are more people involved and more activities, and there is typically more data, not just in volume but also in kind. This complexity means that it will be more difficult and more time-consuming to determine both what is and what should be.

Dataflow diagrams are one way of expressing the fundamental nature of a business system in a readily comprehensible manner. They can be used to express both what is and what should be. Examples are given later in this chapter.

One of the most important functions of problem definition is to set reasonable expectations. The members of the group may tend to think that the new system will solve more of their problems than it actually will. If so, when the new system is installed, these people will be disappointed, even though the system improves their work in many ways. Sometimes it is wise to document the problems that the new system will *not* solve.

Feasibility Assessment

The second task in the definition stage is **feasibility assessment**. The four dimensions of feasibility—cost, schedule, technology, and political environment—apply to workgroup information systems development just as much as they apply to personal information systems development.

Cost, **schedule**, and **technical feasibility** may be more difficult to assess for workgroups because there are more cost factors to consider and more people and activities to coordinate. Still, the fundamental activities are the same as presented in Chapter 7. It is easier to establish costs than benefits, but it is essential to establish benefits, even if they are intangible and difficult to quantify, such as improved service or enhanced internal communication.

In a workgroup information system, the assessment of **political feasibility** must address the social dynamics of the group. Influential members of the group must endorse the project. If the system is positively regarded by the group, people will tend to make it work. If it is negatively regarded, the system will likely fail no matter how well designed it is.

As you have seen, workgroup norms often dictate members' responses to the new system. Developers need to work within such norms as much as possible. In conflicts between system use and workgroup norms, the norms always win, sooner or later.

Further, an information system that takes away important responsibilities from key members of the group is bound to fail. Suppose, for example, that one of the key perks, or benefits, of being a shift supervisor of a work crew is the assigning of projects to people. A system that automatically assigns work will eliminate that perk. If the shift supervisors are not given some reason to endorse the new system despite the loss of this benefit, they will most likely sabotage it, unconsciously or consciously. Therefore, such a system should be considered politically infeasible.

Do not assume that a system judged politically feasible by management is politically feasible to employees. Often management does not understand important dynamics of the group. The best way to assess political feasibility among group members is to ask them.

Project Plan Building

The third task in the definition stage is to build a **project plan**. Here again, the work is not different from that for personal information systems, just more complicated, with more people involved and more activities to coordinate.

Part of the project plan is to create the project development team. For workgroup systems, the team consists of key workgroup members possibly augmented by outside experts. Especially during the design and implementation stages, personnel from the MIS department or an outside vendor will be added to the team. When the plan is created, the important task is to identify which personnel from the workgroup will be involved and what their tasks will be.

In constructing the plan, far more time must be allowed for review, discussion, and possible rework than for personal systems development. To be successful, the system itself must be understood, accepted, and supported, which means that key people need to be given a chance to comment on and influence the development of the system. Such activity should be built into the schedule and plan. Considerations for the problem definition stage in the development of a workgroup information system are summarized in Figure 10-3.

Figure 10-3   Problem Definition Stage in Workgroup Systems Development

- Define problem
    - Perception of what is and what should be
    - Many perceptions
    - Consensus
        - Understanding
        - Acceptance
        - Support
    - Realistic expectations

- Assess Feasibility
    - Cost, schedule, and technology
    - Political feasibility must address social dynamics of the group

- Build Project Plan
    - More complicated than with personal systems because of greater complexity and scale
    - Build project development team—identify workgroup members who will participate in the systems development
    - Allow time for review, discussion, and rework

REQUIREMENTS STAGE

The purpose of the requirements stage is to identify and document the requirements for the information system. Since the requirements are used in subsequent stages to build the system, they must be written or otherwise documented in prototypes and sketches. This documentation is sometimes used in soliciting bids from potential vendors on the systems development project.

For a successful system to be developed, the requirements must be accurate. If they are not accurate, either the system as developed will be abandoned or the group will need to invest additional resources to rework the system.

General Strategy

To understand the general strategy of requirements determination, consider the analogy of cooking. When cooking, we work backward: We begin with what we want, consider the ingredients we need, and then consider the amount we want to make and the constraints we have to work around or surmount. As summarized in Figure 10-4, this is roughly what we do when developing information system requirements. First we determine what information results we need, then we decide what data is needed to produce those results, and then we consider the scale of the system and any constraints in equipment, software, processing, or personnel. For systems development, we also need to document our findings.

In many kitchens, in reality, what we often do is to start with the ingredients on hand and figure out how to combine them into a palatable meal. If we have leftover turkey, then we figure out something to make with it. However, in information systems, this is a recipe for disaster. For example, if group members know how to use Lotus 1-2-3, they may be tempted to seek a way to do every new task by using 1-2-3, whether or not it is suited to the task. Such preferences should be considered in developing requirements, but they should not be promoted to the level of constraints that must absolutely be met.

Output Requirements

The specific statement of **output requirements** depends on the type of application to be developed. For OA applications, for example, we need to determine the nature of the communication to be facilitated. For example, a requirement might be to provide E-mail capability or to support a workgroup bulletin board. If specific message formats or contents are known, then they should be documented as well.

Figure 10-4 Requirements Stage in Workgroup Systems Development

Task	Example
Determine Output to Be Produced	*For communication applications:* Nature of communications, communications format and content *For analysis applications:* Type of analysis; ways in which members will share data and results; means by which work load will be divided *For tracking and monitoring applications:* Format of reports, screen displays, and menus; nature of ad hoc query requests Be aware of inconsistent terminology and differences between form and content Use prototypes for clarity
Determine Necessary Input	Examine output requirements and work backward to determine input necessary to produce that output *or* Examine existing workgroup forms, collect data from them, consider additional requirements suggested by forms Use DFDs to learn of existence of both input and output requirements
Estimate Processing Scale	Amount of data Growth of data Frequency of data changes Frequency of report production Amount of concurrent work load Growth in concurrent work load Response time requirements
Determine Constraints	Hardware Programs Data Procedures—especially controls People
Document Requirements	Need for consensus on requirements Requirements document Prototypes Request for proposal

Output requirements are different for analysis applications and for tracking and monitoring applications. For analysis, we need to know the type of analysis that will be performed (e.g., financial, statistical, OR), the ways in which members will share data and results, and the means by which the work load will be divided among group members.

For tracking and monitoring systems, we need to know the format of reports, screen displays, menus, and the nature of any ad hoc query requests that may be made. This data is important because we will use it to determine the content and structure of the files or database to be processed in a manner similar to that described in Module A.

Since these users of workgroup information systems will have differing needs and objectives, they all (or at least a large representative sample) need to be interviewed. When interviewing many people, consider these points.

Inconsistent Terminology   First, different users may use the same terms in different ways, which may be confusing to both the workgroup and the development team. In a technical writing group, the word *editing* may have a significantly different meaning to every member of the group. Do not assume consistency in terminology, even in a small workgroup.

Form Versus Content Differences   Second, users' requests vary in both form and content. Sometimes the users' different requests are simply format variations on the same theme. One user may want, for example, a list of all the work done by technical writers to be sorted by writer. Another may want the list sorted by time of completion, and a third may want it sorted by project. All three of these reports, as shown by the examples in Figure 10-5, are compatible. They are essentially the same report, but entries are formatted and sorted differently.

Contrast these similar reports with the two reports shown in Figure 10-6 that are about different aspects of the technical writing work load. One report involves data about the client and project coordinator, and the other involves the equipment used in document production. The difference between the reports in Figures 10-5 and 10-6 is that those in the first figure are different views of the same entity. Those in Figure 10-6 are, however, views of different entities.

The handling of such differences will be discussed in the next section. For now, just be aware that, while it is important to document all requirements, it is especially important to obtain requirements of output that concern different entities (like those in Figure 10-6). Adding a new report by changing the sorting order is easy; adding a new report by adding data about additional entities is more difficult.

Prototypes of Requirements   Finally, the best way for users to comment on the content or format of some kinds of requirements may be for them to evaluate **prototypes** of these items.

Figure 10-5 Three Similar Reports

TECHNICAL WRITING WORK LOAD REPORT BY OPERATOR

Writer	Job #	Date	Start	Complete	Project
AEL	1010	27 Feb 95	9:20 a.m.	11:40 a.m.	917-4200
AEL	1027	27 Feb 95	12:14 p.m.	7:44 p.m.	804-1700
DLB	1007	27 Feb 95	8:20 a.m.	1:22 p.m.	401-1800

TECHNICAL WRITING WORK LOAD REPORT BY TIME OF COMPLETION

Complete	Writer	Job #	Date	Start	Project
11:40 a.m.	AEL	1010	27 Feb 95	9:20 a.m.	917-4200
1:22 p.m.	DLB	1007	27 Feb 95	8:20 a.m.	401-1800
7:44 p.m.	AEL	1027	27 Feb 95	12:14 p.m.	804-1700

TECHNICAL WRITING WORK LOAD REPORT BY PROJECT

Project	Writer	Job #	Date	Start	Complete
401-1800	DLB	1007	27 Feb 95	8:20 a.m.	1:22 p.m.
804-1700	AEL	1027	27 Feb 95	12:14 p.m.	7:44 p.m.
917-4200	AEL	1010	27 Feb 95	9:20 a.m.	11:40 a.m.

Note that these prototypes are used differently from the prototypes in personal systems development. There, the prototype became the system. Here, prototypes are used to illustrate parts of the system. Often, in fact, they are fake— nonworking static screen displays, for example, that simply show how something will look. Such prototypes, sometimes called **rapid prototypes,** are important because most people can relate better to an example or illustration than to a written description of complicated structures. Consider the following description:

> An icon of a file drawer appears in the upper left-hand corner of the screen display. To the right of that icon is a grey bar that extends across the top of the screen. The name of the program appears in reverse characters within the grey bar. Underneath the grey bar is a clear bar containing the words File, Edit, View, Insert, Format, Utilities, Macro, Windows, and Help. A single letter of each of these words is underlined. Text appears in the center of the screen.

Figure 10-6 Two Dissimilar Reports

TECHNICAL WRITING JOB REPORT WITH CLIENT DATA

Job #	Date	Writer	Client	Coordinator
1007	27 Feb 95	DLB	AGLIT	KJD
1010	27 Feb 95	AEL	FQGC	MES
1027	27 Feb 95	AEL	DBLIT	HFB

TECHNICAL WRITING JOB REPORT WITH EQUIPMENT DATA

Job #	Date	Writer	Client	Equipment
1007	27 Feb 95	DLB	AGLIT	WPG-36
				Graphics
				FAX
				Integrated WP
				macro library
1010	27 Feb 95	AEL	FQGC	WPG-36
				FAX
1027	27 Feb 95	AEL	DBLIT	WPG-36
				PC-C80486
				Scanner-45

Suppose you were asked to comment on the screen display just described. Most likely, you have no more than a vague sense of what it looks like and you would find it difficult to provide any useful response to this description. The prototype of this display, shown in Figure 10-7, provides a clearer, more realistic notion of the system than does the text description.

This prototype is even better if you can actually use the display. If you had the prototype on a computer and could move the mouse pointer around and click on the various words in the menu across the top of the screen, you would obtain a much better sense of its nature and would be able to critique it more accurately.

A prototype is even more useful if users can try to use it to do real work. Are there better ways of presenting the information? You will be amazed how much more input users can provide if they are presented such prototypes and asked to work with them.

Figure 10-7 Prototype of Screen Display

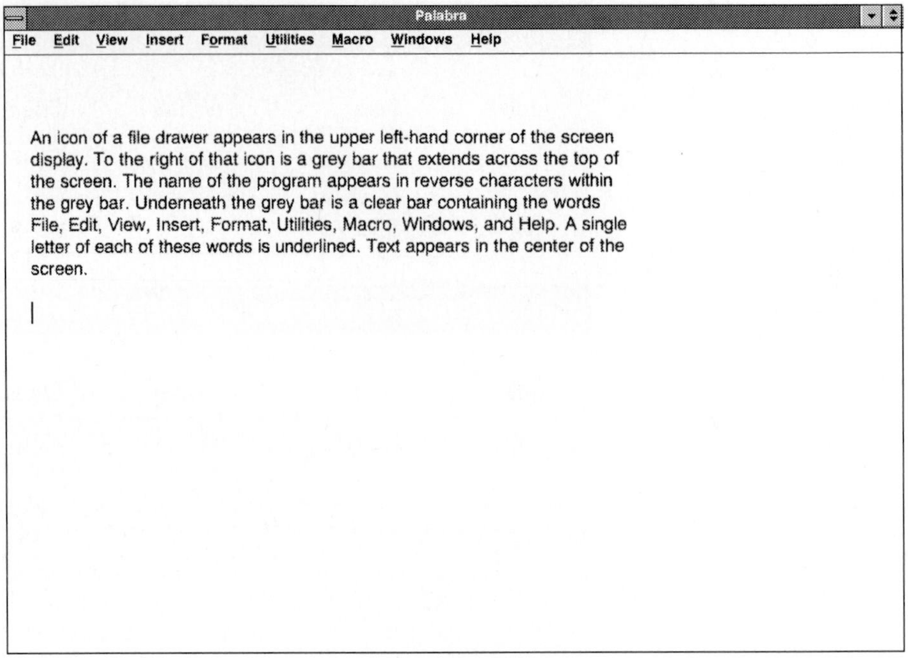

For these reasons, prototypes are often used in specifying requirements for workgroup systems. Again, observe that, when used this way, prototypes augment the SDLC process, allowing a more complete and accurate statement of systems requirements.

Input Requirements

The next step is to determine what **input requirements** are needed to produce the desired output. Using the previous cooking analogy, once we know we want to make blueberry pancakes, we then need to determine the ingredients required.

There are two ways to proceed; often both are used. First, the developer can examine the output requirements and work backward to determine what data is needed to produce those requirements. Following this method, the developer builds a list of data items and searches the business for sources of this data.

The second method involves locating **standard forms** that are already being used to organize and record work. The data in these forms is examined to determine whether the output can be produced from them. If so, a requirement is developed

Figure 10-8 Technical Writing Work Request Form
When a technical writing task is identified, this form is filled out.

Job#:	Requested By:
Date:	
Time Submitted:	Phone:
Related Job Numbers:	
Time Needed By:	Time Completed:
Job Description:	
Writer:	Special Equipment:
Number of Pages:	Number of Copies:
Special Request Approval Code:	Project Coordinator:

to capture the form data (or at least part of it). Sometimes such forms contain data that suggests additions to output requirements.

In the case where both methods are used, the developer may begin searching for data to be used to produce the output and then encounter a manual form. The form may contain data that suggests changes to the reports and so forth, in an iterative manner.

Consider the form in Figure 10-8, which is filled out whenever a problem is recognized in a software manual that needs correction by a technical writer. Whoever designed this form believed that, for some reason, each data item on the form is important. Thus, standard forms can be used to develop a list of candidate data items to store.

Standard forms can also be used to check the completeness of output requirements. If, on a manual form, the group collects data that does not show up on any of the output requirements, then some output was missed or the data is needed for purposes other than those being addressed by the workgroup information system being developed.

Sources of input documents and forms can be identified in several ways. We will use dataflow diagrams to identify them later in this chapter.

Processing Scale Estimates

Our basic approach to requirements determination, as Figure 10-4 shows, is to determine output requirements and then input requirements. The output requirements document the information that is to be produced. The input

Figure 10-9 Concurrent Processing
In estimating processing scale, it is important to estimate the concurrent work load.

requirements indicate the data to be entered and stored in the system. In addition, the requirements must include **estimates of processing scale**, which include the amount and growth of data, the frequency with which data is changed, and the frequency with which reports are to be produced.

Additionally, it is necessary to make estimates of the amount of **concurrent work load**. In order to determine the type and capacity of processing hardware, questions like the following need to be answered: How many concurrent users will there be? How long will their sessions last? Over which hours of the day? On which days of the week? What will be the average number of users? What will be the maximum? The answers to these questions will be used to select system components such as transmission media, data-link protocol, network OS, and size and speed of client and server computers.

It is important to be as accurate as possible in answering these questions. If the work load is underestimated, too little processing power will be obtained and performance will be poor. The system may have to be replaced with more powerful hardware at potentially considerable expense. If the work load is overestimated, too much processing power will be obtained and money wasted.

Because of the importance of these estimates, it is also appropriate to estimate the growth in concurrent work load. How many users will be added per quarter? Per year? What sort of processing will the new users perform? What programs will the new users invoke? If a high rate of growth is anticipated, then it is often appropriate to acquire excessively powerful hardware at the onset. The cost in wasted capacity is more than compensated by the savings in not having to upgrade the computer as the work load grows. Further, in this case, a premium is attached to those alternatives that provide an easy growth and expansion path. By the same token, if little growth is anticipated, then it is wasteful to acquire excess capacity.

One more estimate—the response time required for different types of processing—is a key factor in determining the amount of processing power required. How quickly must the screen be displayed? How quickly must the data be processed? How many orders per hour need to be entered? Will there be a customer on the telephone line waiting for a response? A system in which several hours can elapse between the time a report is requested and the time it is printed obviously requires less powerful hardware than one in which report printing must occur while the customer waits.

Constraints Determination

In addition to requirements about what the information system is to produce, it is often necessary to develop requirements about **constraints**, conditions or situations that will limit the system. In developing these requirements, consider the five components of an information system individually.

First consider hardware. If members of the group already have microcomputers, they probably will want to continue using them. In this case, there will be a constraint stating that the new system must utilize that type of computer, if at all possible. (Bear in mind, though, that replacing all those computers may sometimes be the most cost-effective solution and should not be discarded out of hand.) As with personal systems, another type of hardware constraint can arise from a corporate policy or standard. The MIS staff of the company may have decided that all information systems are to utilize a particular make or model of computer. Such standards are usually established to ensure that the workgroup's computers are compatible for communication to other computers in the enterprise.

Constraints on programs can arise for the same reasons as can constraints on hardware. If the workgroup or individual already has particular horizontal market programs that can be used in the new system, then the users' investment in learning these programs has already been made. Additionally, the enterprise may have established a standard, say, that all spreadsheet applications will use a particular product such as Quattro Pro. In the case of programs, compliance with the standard is important because most of the organization's support and training effort will be devoted to the standard set of products.

Hardware and programs may also impose constraints on each other. For example, suppose the workgroup determines that there is a vertical market application system that meets most of its requirements. Considerable savings can be realized by licensing this program rather than attempting to build a custom program for the application. In this case, only hardware capable of executing the vertical market application can be considered.

Data constraints arise differently than do constraints on hardware and programs. Data constraints typically exist because of a need for data security, control, or coordination. For example, a workgroup information system may require a data file from the corporate mainframe. If, for scheduling and coordination reasons, this data is available only on the second and fourth Tuesday of the month, then the schedule becomes a data constraint. Other examples are that certain data may not be changed or that, if an employee number is changed in one file, it must also be changed in another.

Procedural constraints are restrictions on human activity. For example, it may be that sensitive data can be viewed only by particular people or that the results of an analysis cannot be made widely available until after a certain date.

Restrictions on duties and authorities are other examples of such constraints. In a workgroup that produces negotiable instruments (like checks), the usual procedure is to separate the authorizing of payments from the production of the checks. If a single employee were allowed both to authorize payments and to generate checks, a control weakness would exist. The employee would be able, for example, to authorize and generate payments to fictitious people. Thus, to strengthen control, duties and authorities are separated. We will discuss such controls further in Chapter 12.

When such procedural restrictions are in place, the workgroup information system must support or at least not countervail them. Consequently, such constraints need to be made part of the requirements.

Finally, examples of constraints on people are that only a department manager can authorize a certain analysis or that the primary users of the system will be clerical personnel with minimum training, and so forth.

The output, input, and processing requirements are positive requirements stipulating what the system is to do. Constraints are negative requirements stipulating what the system is not to do.

Requirements Documentation

As we have seen, to be successful, a workgroup information system must have the understanding, acceptance, and support of the group members. To gain these, the influential members of the group must be allowed to participate in the development and final acceptance of the requirements. If such users are involved in this way, then not only will the requirements be more accurate, but the users will also be more committed to the project.

Thus, once the requirements have been determined, they must be documented and reviewed. The form of **requirements documentation** varies, depending on the size of the project, the intended mode of development, and the nature of the project. Normally, a text document summarizes the requirements. Sometimes such documents also include a detailed written description of each requirement that is often augmented by sketches, report layouts, and screen form designs.

In addition to the requirements document, many development projects include prototypes of menus and forms that simulate the appearance and action of the user's interface. The advantage of such prototypes is that future users get a more realistic notion of the system than they would obtain from written descriptions. This enables the users to provide more accurate feedback to the developers.

The requirements review can take several formats. For one, users can be asked to review and comment on the requirements documentation. Or requirements can be presented in meetings and reviewed by representatives of the group en masse. Prototype examples can be placed in the work environment for users to review and comment on.

Generally, the review generates more useful information if, at some point, group sessions are held. The comments of one member of the group often stimulate the thinking and questions of other members. The problem with such meetings is that they are time-consuming (and thus expensive), and, if not carefully controlled, can degenerate into unproductive discussions. Guidelines for conducting such review sessions are listed in Figure 10-10.

Figure 10-10   Guidelines for an Effective Requirements Review Meeting

- Publish an agenda before meeting that sets out the following:
    Starting time
    Ending time
    Purpose
    Place
- Distribute requirements document before meeting
- Require that participants read requirements document before meeting
- Have a meeting moderator to keep the discussion on track
- Start and stop meeting on time; hold more meetings if not finished
- Clarify that purpose of meeting is to define *requirements* not *solutions*
- Do not use meeting to air grievances or conduct departmental business
- Give respectful consideration to all suggestions
- Keep minutes and distribute them afterward

EVALUATION STAGE

The purpose of the **evaluation stage** is to build a general strategy for developing a workgroup system to meet the requirements defined in the prior stage. During this evaluation, the requirements are first reconsidered, and, if necessary, some are removed. Then the requirements are communicated to potential vendors, bids are received, and a vendor is selected. During the evaluation stage, your role with regard to the project will probably change in that you will become more of a manager or overseer and less of a doer.

Transition in the Users' Role

To this point, the discussion has assumed that you will have a key role in developing the workgroup information system. This is probably the case in the definition and requirements stages. Even if you, personally, do not do the work of these stages, then your employee or someone close to you will undoubtedly do it. And, in any case, you will be wise to stay abreast of the project in these critical stages.

Beyond the definition and requirements stages, however, most non-information systems professionals have neither the time nor the expertise to continue to develop the workgroup information system. Once the project enters the design and implementation stages, the system will begin to involve expertise that is probably not worth your while to obtain or that requires more time to obtain than you have, even if you think that attaining it might be worthwhile.

Consequently, most users do not work directly in designing and implementing a workgroup information system. Instead, they manage that activity by providing guidance and direction and by approving the initiation of work and the disbursement of funds.

This fact is a key difference between the development of a personal information system and the development of a workgroup information system. With a personal information system, you may perform your own design and implementation. For a spreadsheet application, for example, you would select the hardware and software yourself, learn how to use the software, design your own file directories, and build and implement your own spreadsheet applications.

For any but the simplest workgroup information systems, this is too much to expect of yourself. Attempting to build such a system yourself changes your job expectations to those of an information systems professional instead of those of a business professional in some non-MIS discipline.

Thus, when developing a workgroup information system, you most likely will employ some person or group from outside your workgroup to design and implement your system. This group might be composed of employees from the MIS department of your own organization, an outside contractor, or both.

It is during the evaluation stage that you make this key transition. Up to this stage, you and your group possess the expertise—and know the problem, what output you need, what data is available, and so forth. No one from outside your group has this expertise.

Once you have defined the problem and its requirements, however, you (and your group) change roles. You become the consumer of someone else's expertise. Up to this point, *you* are expected to have the answers. Beyond this point, *they* are expected to have the answers. At this same time, you also become dependent on the expertise (and competency) of an outside agency, and you lose a degree of control.

Requirements Evaluation

Once the requirements have been documented, they are reconsidered during the first part of the evaluation stage. Sometimes one, two, or even several requirements have been developed that, on reflection, make the system far more complex or costly than is appropriate. A typical example is that users may say they need on-line access to several years of sales data. When confronted by the magnitude of the data storage required, they may decide instead that on-line access to the last year's data will be sufficient.

This task is where, as one user put it, "reality sets in." Each requirement is considered in light of (1) the overall needs of the system and (2) the potential cost. Be aware that, in this sense, cost refers not only to direct dollar cost but also to performance cost, administration cost, operations cost, and the like.

The culmination of this task is a final list of approved requirements that will be used as a blueprint for the system and for developing criteria for system test and acceptance. Most workgroup information systems involve the assembly of off-the-shelf hardware and programs, along with some level of customization to meet specific group requirements. Therefore, the next development step is to identify information systems professionals who have the expertise to specify components and do the customization.

Alternative Vendor Identification

Assuming that neither you nor your company's MIS department will perform the design and implementation work (which is often the case for workgroup systems development), you must identify sources, or **vendors,** who can. There are several possibilities. Depending on your company's policy, you may be required to use the expertise of the in-house MIS department. Or your MIS department may be willing to provide consulting expertise to help you select a vendor. Or your company may be so small that it has no such department. Or you may decide to take the project outside the purview of your MIS department.

Unless you know that you will never need to integrate your system with any of the enterprise systems (and it is doubtful you can ever be certain of this), it is generally best to involve your MIS department with your project. This department may have standards or constraints that you need to consider. They also may have considerable expertise working with the vendors whom you will contact, and they may provide invaluable assistance in dealing with those vendors. They can also evaluate your RFP and other documentation and improve your chances of getting what you want.

There are a number of additional sources for identifying vendors. For one, talk with people in your profession at trade shows and professional meetings. How do groups like yours handle the problem in their company? Which vendors and what products have they used? How did it work out? Find out which companies seem to have the best reputation.

Other sources for identifying vendors are hardware companies and dealers. If you are considering a major hardware acquisition, the hardware vendors can assist you in finding the right programs, service, and support. If your needs are

Figure 10-11   Sources of Vendor Contacts

- Your company's MIS department
- Consultants
- Professional colleagues
- Departments with similar needs in other companies
- Professional organizations
- Professional meetings
- Hardware dealers
- Local chapters of professional associations like Data Processing Management Association (DPMA) and Association of Computing Machinery (ACM)
- Local computer clubs
- Advertising in your trade's publications

more modest, local microcomputer dealers can provide assistance in locating VARs, consultants, and other potential vendors. Again, as much as possible, speak with individuals who have direct experience with the sources and with their services and products. Sources of vendor contacts are summarized in Figure 10-11.

Once you have assembled a list of potential vendors, the next step is to communicate your needs to them.

Vendor Communication

Your goal is to obtain a solution to your problem. You want to select a vendor who will provide the system and the services that will meet your requirements. You also want to pay no more than a fair price.

To communicate your requirements to potential vendors and solicit bids on the project, you put your approved and accepted requirements into a **request for proposal (RFP)**. The RFP asks the vendor to propose a solution to your problem and indicate how much it will cost to implement that solution. It sets out background of the project, specific requirements (output, input, processing scale, and constraints), overall schedule and dates, vendor selection criteria, and other

Figure 10-12 Characteristics of a Good RFP

- Clearly written
- Consistent
- Complete
- Descriptions of:
    Background, context, and processing environment
    Specfic requirements
    Constraints on system
    Constraints on procurement process
    Needs *not* solutions (unless a particular solution is required)
    General description of evaluation criteria
    Response dates
    Single point of contact for questions

information that will help a vendor prepare a proposal. Depending on the size and nature of the project, it is sometimes appropriate to have the corporation's legal counsel review the RFP. Characteristics of a good RFP are summarized in Figure 10-12.

Since this is not a text on negotiating, purchasing, or commercial law, we will not address the negotiating process except to state a few rules of thumb that pertain directly to information systems. First, coordinate your activity with your organization's purchasing department, which may have established policies that you should follow. They may also want to review your RFP and, possibly, to have one of their staff members involved in the negotiation.

Second, there is almost never any reason to withhold information about your problems, needs, and requirements from potential vendors. In general, the more the vendors know about your needs, the better the job they can do in responding to your RFP.

Third, while it is often beneficial to let the vendors know that you are conducting a competitive process, it is best to keep the identity of the particular vendors confidential, at least until you have received the proposals. At that point, it may make sense to discuss the merits of one approach with a vendor who suggested a different approach. But describing one vendor's proposal in detail to another vendor may be unethical and even illegal.

Finally, realize that vendors know the strengths and weaknesses of their products much better than you do. While reputable vendors will not bid unworkable solutions, salespeople are trained to sell the products they do have. Thus, for example, a vendor who has no LAN product will bid a minicomputer solution to your problem, and will do so even if he or she *knows* that a LAN product might provide a cheaper solution. Unless the salesperson is unethical, exceedingly hard pressed, or downright foolish, he or she will not bid an infeasible solution. At the same time, if another vendor has the best solution, the burden lies with you to find that out.

With these guidelines, invite vendors to your group, discuss your situation in general terms, and present the vendor with the RFP. To protect your business confidentiality, make it clear that you want all copies of the RFP returned to you at the end of the selection process. While government agencies are sometimes required to have open meetings with all bidders at the same time, you will likely learn more from these meetings if you meet with the vendors singly.

At your meeting, make your schedule clear. Set realistic dates for responses, and keep to them. Let the vendor know whom to contact if there are questions or if there is a need for further information.

Sometimes negotiations can evolve into gamesmanship, power plays, personality conflicts, and so forth. Avoid all of this to the greatest extent possible. You have one objective: to obtain a long-term solution to your problem at a fair price. Focus on that objective.

Alternative Selection

Many different techniques can be used to select one of the alternatives. In your finance courses, you are learning how to perform cost-benefit analyses in which estimates of costs are compared to estimates of the dollar value of benefits. Usually, the timing of the costs and benefits is considered to develop an estimate of the rate of return on the capital investment.

Where reasonably sound estimates of the value of the benefits can be determined, such cost-benefit analyses are an excellent way to choose among alternatives. Unfortunately, information systems often have many intangible benefits and factors. For example, although there is no *dollar* benefit of having workgroup information for input to the shareholders' report available a month before the shareholders' meeting instead of 2 weeks before, clearly, there *is* a benefit. If senior management is able to take a week to prepare for the meeting, they can present the affairs of the corporation more professionally.

Because of the intangible nature of system benefits, a pure cost-benefit analysis is seldom used to select among alternatives. Sometimes a rate of return is computed using just the tangible benefits, and then the intangible benefits and factors are considered subjectively alongside the results of the cost-benefit analysis. Figure 10-13 lists typical intangible factors.

Figure 10-13 Intangible Factors in Alternative Selection

- Ease of system expansion
- Vendor reputation or position in the marketplace
- Simplicity or other beauty of design
- Anticipation of future technology
- Especially effective vendor personnel or management
- Local support office

Proposal Evaluation

You should begin your evaluation process before you receive the proposals. While the RFP is out, check on the reputation of the vendors and on the reputation of the products they are likely to bid. Obtain a list of existing users from the vendors. Call those users, and from them, obtain the names of other users, especially any who are known to be dissatisfied. Try to accomplish all of this background work before the proposals are received.

One pundit once remarked that the worst thing that can happen to a great restaurant is to receive an outstanding newspaper review. Suddenly the public pours in and service suffers. A similar phenomenon can occur with information systems vendors. A vendor that provided fantastic service installing 20 systems last year will be hard pressed to provide the same level of service for 100 systems this year. Ideally, the vendors you select will be growing, but at a manageable rate. (This comment pertains to vendors that are providing service as part of their bid. If you are just buying products, then all you need to know is that sufficient quantities of the product exist in inventory.)

Once the proposals are received, evaluate them. Some groups use a quantitative process. They develop a list of criteria, assign so many points to each criteria, and then rate each proposal on those criteria. Other groups use a more subjective approach. Both approaches can work.

Either way, there are a number of criteria to check. First, has the vendor's sales team been responsive? Was the proposal submitted on time? If necessary, did the vendor ask the appropriate questions? Does the proposal appear to be the work of a professional team and company? Appearance counts. Carelessness here is potential evidence of carelessness in systems development.

Second, did the vendor take the time to understand your problem and your requirements? Does the proposal address your needs, or did the vendor submit what appears to be a standard bid? Further, is the proposed solution a sensible one? Does it respond to each of your requirements? You now can reap the benefit of the work you did in documenting your requirements. Use those requirements as a checklist for evaluating the proposals.

Third, examine the vendors' costs. Did the vendor understand the problem and include all the costs? Compare the costs of the proposals. Costs that are considerably less than those of the competition are suspect.

Sometimes it makes sense not to pick the lowest cost proposal. For one, that proposal may not meet all of your requirements. Even if it did, reputation, responsiveness, and professionalism can sometimes offset additional cost.

Further, consider the lifetime cost of an information system. Suppose that you have 15 people using a system 30 percent of their time. Over a year, a total of 4.5 labor years are spent using the system. The cost of that labor may be $200,000 or more. Considering that cost, does it make sense to select a proposal that is $15,000 cheaper if the user interface of that proposal is more difficult to use? Often, the differential in proposed costs is unimportant when considering the long-term system costs.

Another consideration is schedule. Has the vendor responded to your schedule requirements? Does the schedule, as proposed, seem realistic? Has ample time been allowed for installation, testing, and training? Are payments tied to progress so that the vendor has a financial incentive to meet the schedule? Is the vendor willing to back up the schedule estimates with cost penalties if the schedule is not met?

Finally, keep in mind the imbalance of knowledge. The vendors have submitted dozens or hundreds of bids; this is your first proposal. They know far more than you do about the negotiating process. If you hampered by a lack of knowledge or that you run a substantial risk because of your inexperience, hire a consultant or other outside source of expertise. Find someone who has been through a similar process many times, and take advantage of that person's knowledge.

The Contract

The vendor will submit a **"standard" contract** for you to sign. Do not assume there is anything at all *standard* in a standard contract. Do not sign this contract. Instead, hire an attorney experienced in information systems procurement.

Here is an example of the kinds of problems you can encounter. Your vendor will attempt to write the contract to sell you products "as is." The only warranty the vendor will provide is a warranty on hardware functioning and error-free disks. How are you protected if there are substantial errors in the product's programs? As a minimum, have your RFP included as part of the contract, but this must be done in special ways. Again, hire an attorney experienced in information systems procurement. There are too many considerations for you to attempt to do your own legal work.

It is a good idea to build task accomplishments and review dates into your contract. It is even better to tie vendor payments to the successful completion of these reviews. It is during these reviews that you have an opportunity to verify that the project is on track and on schedule. Again, *do not sign the standard contract!* Considerations for the evaluation stage are summarized in Figure 10-14.

Figure 10-14 Evaluation Stage in Workgroup Systems Development

- Transition Stage

- Requirements Evaluation

- Vendor Sources
  - Involve your organization's MIS department
  - See sources in Figure 10-11

- Vendor Communication
  - Coordinate with your corporation's purchasing department
  - Make full disclosure of your problem, needs, and requirements
  - Meet with vendors singly, if possible
  - Specify that all copies of the RFP are to be returned

- Proposal Evaluation
  - Check for vendor and product reputation
  - Formal, quantitative, or subject evaluation can work
  - Other criteria:
    - Responsive to RFP?
    - Understand problem and requirements?
    - All costs included?
    - Schedule realistic and acceptable?
  - Get help evaluating, if necessary

- Contract
  - Do not sign "standard" contract
  - Get legal help for all but the smallest and simplest contracts

DESIGN STAGE

The purpose of the **design stage** is to develop specifications for each of the five components of the information system. The requirements and the general approach from prior stages are input to the design process; the results are specific statements about the structure of the components needed to meet the requirements with the chosen approach.

You will not develop the design; only information systems professionals have the expertise to design systems as complex as most workgroup systems. In fact, when considering hardware, programs, and portions of the data components, there will be aspects of the design that you need not even understand. It is crucial, however, that your vendor understand them. Therefore, you should manage this activity as you manage the activity of any other technical effort. Assess people and their competency. When you suspect problems are developing, follow your intuition. If necessary, involve someone who does understand the technical details.

Hardware Specifications

The term *design* may seem to be a misnomer for the hardware component. Few applications necessitate the design of new hardware. The design and construction of special-purpose computing equipment is almost never necessary or cost-justifiable for business computer systems. Instead, off-the-shelf hardware components are selected and integrated to form the system's hardware. During the design stage, specifications for such hardware are developed.

In many cases, a good portion of the hardware design task has been done by the vendor in developing the bid. If so, then, at this point, these specifications are simply refined, and the level of detail is increased.

Program Specifications

When programs are acquired off the shelf or licensed from VARs, the tasks for program design are similar to those for hardware: The developer needs to determine the specifications of the programs to be licensed.

Although workgroup systems are seldom constructed around totally custom-developed programs, some customization is often required to mold off-the-shelf programs to a workgroup's specific needs. When programs are custom developed or off-the-shelf programs are customized, the structure and logic of the customized portion is created during this stage. This work, which is accomplished by the vendor, is complicated, and understanding it requires more expertise than the typical business manager or user has. Unfortunately, there is not much you can do to influence this stage of the project, which is one reason why selecting a vendor with a proven track record is important. Also, do not let this stage extend for any lengthy period of time. If the vendor says that a long design phase is required (more than, say, a month), then break up the project into subphases in which visible results are produced more quickly.

Data Design

Tasks in data design vary, depending on the type of system. In the case of nondatabase applications (e.g., spreadsheet, word processing, and DTP), most of the work involves developing data standards. During this stage, standards are established for naming files, for creating directories and allocating files to them, and for formatting screen forms, reports, and other output. Standards are a great aid for data administration and can save many labor hours in the long run. Such standards need to be established during design so that they can be followed from the start of the implementation stage.

For database applications, there is more to be done. The vendor will examine the forms, reports, and menus and produce a data model using a process similar to that described in Module A. That data model will then be transformed into a database design. As with programs, there is not much that the business manager or user can do at this point. Again, do not let the time in this phase expand into large increments.

Representatives of the workgroup should be given an opportunity to review and approve the final design of the user interface. This includes menus, data-entry forms, report layouts, and command sequences. While some of these components will have been established during requirements definition, it is important to verify that the developer has understood and incorporated these requirements. New elements of the user interface should receive thorough review.

Procedure Design

As we have seen, the four types of information systems procedures are user procedures for normal processing and for failure recovery and operations procedures for normal processing and for failure recovery. Usually in workgroup information systems, workgroup operations procedures are accomplished by specially trained workgroup members on a part-time basis. Therefore, user and operations procedures are documented separately.

User Procedures   For normal processing, users need procedures for logging onto the network, starting the applications, entering and editing data, producing reports, and ending user sessions. They also need procedures for periodically making backup copies of the data.

For failure recovery, users need to know what to do when the system fails. The business will not stop because the network is down, and users will need to know what to do at such times. Users need procedures that will help them answer the following questions: What activities can they continue to perform? What data should be saved? How should the data be saved? Once the system is repaired, how are users to proceed? How can users determine if any of their prior work was lost?

Operator Procedures   Operators will likely be group members who perform the operations function on a part-time basis. They will need procedures for both normal conditions and failure recovery. In regard to the former, procedures need to be designed for starting and stopping the network, adding new users to the network, and removing users from the network. Backup procedures need to be documented. Routine maintenance procedures (e.g., printer cleaning) also need to be documented.

For failure recovery, the operators need procedures for identifying and correcting the problem. Such procedures often include the name and telephone number of someone who can help diagnose and fix such problems. Data-recovery procedures need to be documented. Procedures for documenting problems for systems developers also need to be created.

In addition to the procedures described here, procedures for reducing the possibility of unauthorized processing also need to be developed. Such procedures, often called controls, will be discussed at length in Chapter 12.

Job Descriptions

The last design task concerns the development of those portions of job descriptions that pertain to the use or operation of the application. For example, suppose that, with a new system, a manager and her assistant regularly use a graphics application that displays data stored on the workgroup's database server computer. The application requires that these people have different knowledge and skills than they currently possess. During the design stage, the specific skills and proficiency levels for all users need to be determined. This information is then used to establish their training requirements and to modify their job descriptions.

Pay close attention to the procedure and personnel design components. Ask for an outline of procedures, and if it is not comprehensive, ensure that changes are made. Also, review a draft of the user job descriptions and the plans for personnel

Figure 10-15 Design Stage in Workgroup Systems Development

- Manage as for any technical project
  - Assess people
  - Follow intuition
  - Get help when necessary
- Hardware
  - Develop specifications
- Programs
  - Develop specifications
  - Design structure and logic of custom programs (if any)
- Data
  - Develop data standards
  - Create data model and transform it into database design
- Procedures
  - Develop for both user and operations procedures
  - Develop for normal and failure recovery procedures
  - Check for completeness and feasibility
  - Ensure that data-entry and conversion procedures are appropriate
- People
  - Review draft of new or altered job descriptions
  - Prepare for personnel training

training. The vendor may tend to view procedural and personnel issues as *your* problem. Manage this activity so that the vendor comes to view them as *our* problem.

Considerations for the activities during the design of a workgroup information system are listed in Figure 10-15.

IMPLEMENTATION STAGE

As with design, during the **implementation stage**, you manage others' activities. During this stage, the five components are acquired, installed, and tested. Generally, each component is tested by itself and then an integrated test is conducted. Finally, the system is installed in the operational environment, and operations are cut over to the new system.

Hardware Acquisition, Installation, and Testing

At this stage, the hardware is purchased, installed, and tested. For most workgroup information systems, the lead time on the purchase of hardware is not too long. Unless the order is unusually large, microcomputers and related equipment are usually available within a week of their order. This is usually true as well for network equipment, unless there are peculiar requirements.

Once the hardware is received, it needs to be unpacked, assembled, connected, and tested. The vendor or developer performs these actions on behalf of the workgroup. Unless the vendor is working with a new type of equipment, installation of a LAN should not take too long—half a day for each user station and up to 2 days for the server.

Program Acquisition, Installation, and Testing

Once the hardware is installed, programs are the next component to be installed. Again, the vendor performs these tasks. Off-the-shelf programs such as the network OS, other systems software, and horizontal market applications should be readily available. Installing all of this software and making it work together can be time-consuming and problematic. Many types of unexpected errors can occur.

If the vendor has experience working with the software and the hardware, there should not be many delays. If the vendor is integrating new software and hardware or integrating components that he or she has not worked with before, appreciable delays are possible.

If schedule delays develop, do not allow test procedures to be abbreviated to make up lost time. Better to be late than to accept defective components that will cause operational problems once your group has become dependent on the system. Also, if delays occur, do not allow the vendor to catch up by skimping on procedure documentation or user training. It is better to plan on a certain amount of delay from the official schedule and to allow the vendor to take the time to perform quality work.

Data Conversion and Verification

Once the hardware and programs have been installed, the next step is to convert the data to magnetic form and to verify its correctness. Specific steps depend on the nature of the application. In general, it is necessary to obtain the data from sources, key it into the application, and then painstakingly review the data for correctness. This review is very important. Bad input data will produce incorrect results, and it is deadly to the reputation of the application to produce bad reports at the start.

Do not depend on the source data being complete and free from errors. In many cases, the source data is incomplete, hard to find, and full of errors and omissions—even if the developers have been assured that all the data is available and correct. Experienced developers investigate such possibilities ahead of time and plan on delays due to problems with source data.

During implementation, data is entered and verified. Here again, manage this activity to ensure that it occurs on a timely basis and that verification procedures are not abbreviated.

Procedure Documentation

Procedures are documented during this stage. As this occurs, review the procedures yourself and with key members of your staff. Ensure that the procedures are realistic and that sufficient training has been scheduled for users to be able to follow the procedures.

Once the procedures are written, users should be asked to follow them. The developers should then modify procedures in accordance with the problems discovered.

The testing of procedures is vital for two reasons. First, the mind-set of a user is quite different from that of the developer. By this stage in the process, the developer will take many esoteric facts about the system for granted. The user will, perfectly reasonably, say "Why would I do that?" and the developer will be thinking "Wow, I thought that was obvious."

Second, procedures can have errors, just as programs can. Until all the processes have been worked through, there is always the possibility that the procedures will ask someone to use data that has not yet been entered, that the product will not work quite the way it is expected to work, or that it will take users far longer to do something than was anticipated.

It is vital that the users' first experiences with the system be successful. This can be assured only by carefully testing procedures prior to installation.

Personnel

During the implementation stage, personnel are hired (if required) and trained. Training may include outside training on the hardware and the programs, and it may also include in-house training on the system and its procedures. The amount of training depends on the nature of the application, the experience of the users, and the amount of frustration that users are willing to put up with. (Less training means more user frustration as the users begin to work with the system.)

By the way, users are not a homogeneous group in their attitude toward technology. Some are willing to invest considerable time in learning the system and its operation. They want to explore all the facets of the system. Others only want to know the minimum essentials they need to accomplish their jobs. As much as possible, the training program should accommodate these differences.

Check that the quality of the training is appropriate. If not, take corrective action. Follow up on these items while the system is in development. Do not wait for problems to develop after installation. The best way to solve a problem is not to have it at all!

System Integration and Testing

Once the five components have been obtained, installed, and tested, the final task is to integrate the components and test the system as a unit. This activity is the system's dress rehearsal. Before the system is installed in the operational environment, it is taken on a shakedown cruise. All the major components of the system (including backup and recovery) are invoked and the response, measured. Discrepancies are documented and fixed or scheduled to be fixed.

Your job as manager is to make certain that the rehearsal occurs on schedule and that adequate time is allocated to it and then to evaluate the results. From this evaluation, you make the decision either to implement the system or to rework some of the components. Once you are satisfied with the results of the dress rehearsal(s), you can initiate your systems installation. These tasks are summarized in Figure 10-16.

Installation

The four major styles of systems installation are parallel, phased, pilot, and plunge. For **parallel installation**, the new system is run in parallel with the old system until the new one has proven effective and reliable. This is often difficult to do, since components of the old system and the new one often conflict. In on-line systems, for example, running the two systems may mean asking users to enter all data twice.

Phased installation occurs when a portion of the system is installed on the entire operation. If all goes well, additional portions of the system are installed until either a problem is encountered or all of the system is installed. For example, in installing a new accounting system, the order-entry module may be installed

Figure 10-16 Implementation Stage in Workgroup Systems Development

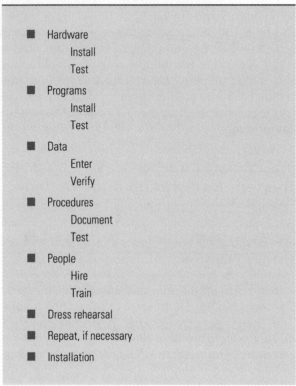

- Hardware
    - Install
    - Test
- Programs
    - Install
    - Test
- Data
    - Enter
    - Verify
- Procedures
    - Document
    - Test
- People
    - Hire
    - Train
- Dress rehearsal
- Repeat, if necessary
- Installation

first and used until all the problems seem to be worked out. Then the accounts receivable module may be added, and so on. In this way, the organization's vulnerability to problems in the new system is limited.

Pilot installation is done by implementing all of the system in just a part of the organization. If several groups are to share a system, then it may be installed for a single group at a time and operated until all the problems appear to be solved. As with phased installation, such a strategy limits damages of a defective system.

Finally, **plunge installation** involves stopping the old system and starting up the new system in a single step. With the plunge method, a group may shut down the old system on Friday evening, tear out the old hardware and install the new over the weekend, then start up the new system on Monday morning. This strategy is exceedingly dangerous and should be avoided if at all possible. If the new system does not work perfectly right out of the box, and few do, the workgroup can be placed in a very precarious position.

As the system is installed, its reliability and performance should be assessed and problems identified and fixed. Ultimately, there is a point at which the system is accepted and backup systems can be removed. At this point, known as the **cutover point**, the workgroup commits to the new system. This decision should be made only after extensive successful experience with the system. It is wise, also, to schedule the final vendor payment after this point.

DATAFLOW DIAGRAMS

Information systems professionals use a wide variety of conceptual tools in analyzing and designing systems: analytical frameworks, diagramming methods, checklists, and so on. Of these, **dataflow diagrams (DFDs)** are very useful to nonprofessionals and simple to learn. You can use DFDs to document business activity and interaction among employees who work together to accomplish tasks. Obviously these diagrams do not make complicated systems any less complex, but they do provide a way to deal with this complexity.

In this section, you will learn how to create DFDs. This modeling skill will benefit you in developing workgroup information systems applications and in any other activity that requires you to understand and model the flow of data within an office.

Purpose

The purpose of a DFD is to identify and record the essence of office processing by representing the flow of data among processes. A DFD is a snapshot of the data movement in an organization or in a workgroup within an organization.

DFDs do not show logic. They are unlike flowcharts, pseudocode, and other tools used for documenting program logic. To understand this, imagine a snapshot of the trains and subways in Manhattan Island. Suppose the picture shows two trains emerging from a tunnel. The snapshot shows the trains emerging, but it does not show why. DFDs are like this snapshot, but they show the movement of data rather than trains.

Elements of DFDs

Four basic elements are shown on DFDs, as illustrated in Figure 10-17.

Figure 10-17 DFD Symbols

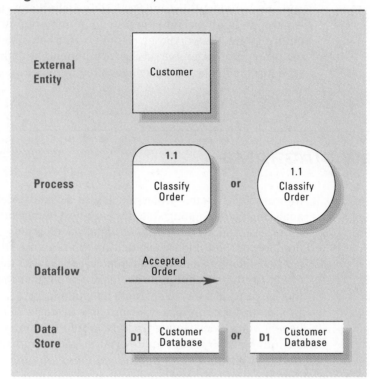

External Entities First, **external entities**, shown by squares or rectangles, can be offices, departments, companies, people, or other agencies outside the scope of the system being modeled. The name of the external entity is written within the rectangle. Sometimes such rectangles are called sources and sinks. A **source** is an external entity that produces a dataflow. A **sink** is an external entity that absorbs a dataflow. Nothing is documented about sources and sinks except their names and the dataflows they produce or absorb.

Processes The second element shown on a DFD is a **process**. Processes, which are shown in rectangles with rounded corners or in circles, are normally given a number and a name. The numeric coding system that is most often used will be explained below.

　　The name of the process, consisting of an imperative verb followed by an object, is written inside the box. In Figure 10-17, the name of the process is Classify Order. Examples of other acceptable process names are Create Shipment, Validate Order, and Accept Return.

Neither people's names nor departments' names should be shown in a process symbol. The reason is that names are ambiguous identifiers of processes. Writing a person's name or department's name in a process box does not specifically indicate which of that person's many processes is being followed in the DFD.

Dataflows   A **dataflow**, the third element of DFDs, is represented by a labeled, directed arrow. The dataflow in Figure 10-17 represents the flow of the data aggregation called Accepted Order. Sometimes, dataflows are single data items like a registration number. Others are composites such as Accepted Order. Still others are forms, reports, or other documents. The content of dataflows is normally documented separately from the DFD in a data dictionary, as described later.

The medium of the dataflow is not shown.[1] The order could be in electronic form, or it could be provided verbally over the telephone, in writing on an order form, or in some other manner.

In some situations, it is tempting to place physical items on dataflows. Resist this temptation. The purpose of a DFD is to show the flow of data; placing a physical entity on a dataflow can mask underlying data. Thus, instead of having a dataflow called Shipment, find out how the shipment is represented in data and document that dataflow. Shipping Invoice, Packing List, or some other term is likely a better description of the flow of data than Shipment.

Data Stores   The fourth and last element of a DFD is a **data store**. Like processes, data stores often have a number and a name. Data stores are represented by a rectangle with one side missing or as two horizontal lines with the data store name between them, as shown in Figure 10-17.

Data stores do not indicate the storage medium. The storage could be in a cardboard box, a filing cabinet, or a computer file, or it could be inside some person's mind. The point of a data store is to document data at rest.

The four elements used in DFDs—external entities, processes, dataflows, and data stores—can be used to model many different offices, activities, and situations.

Example DFD   Examine Figure 10-18, which shows a portion of a DFD. The process Classify Order accepts a dataflow called Order from the external entity called Customer. It sends the dataflow Rejected Order back to the Customer entity and sends the dataflow Accepted Order to a second process called Process Order. (Note: Both dataflows may not be generated in response to every order, and the DFD does not attempt to document which cases generate which dataflow.) Both Classify Order and Process Order use the Customer and Order Data data store. The Classify Order process obtains the dataflow Customer Payment Data from

---

1. A second type of DFD called a *physical DFD* does show the medium. This section focuses on the more commonly used *logical DFD*.

Figure 10-18   Portion of a DFD

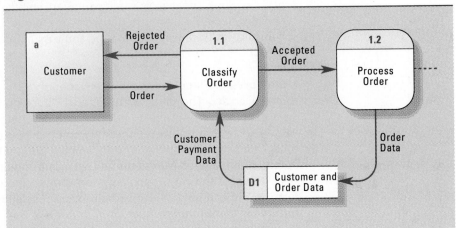

the data store, and the Process Order process places Order Data dataflow into the data store.

Multiple-Level DFDs

The processing of most workgroups and organizations is too complicated to fit on a single DFD. Consequently, DFDs are usually produced in groups at several levels. Each level of diagram represents a finer level of detail in the workgroup's process.

Context Diagrams   The highest-level DFD is called a **context diagram**. This diagram, which shows the scope of the activity to be modeled, has only one process symbol. The name of the function to be modeled is shown in this process symbol. The context diagram is the only diagram in which the name of the process is not an imperative verb followed by an object. The external entities are arranged around the process symbol. Dataflows show the data received from and sent to the external entities.

Figure 10-19 shows an example context diagram for the Customer Support workgroup at Legacy Systems. According to this diagram, Customer Support interfaces with Customer, Sales Training, Sales, Steering Committee, and Documentation external entities.

As shown, Customers provide their registration numbers and a question to be answered. Customer Support responds with a refusal or an answer to the

Figure 10-19 Context DFD for Customer Support

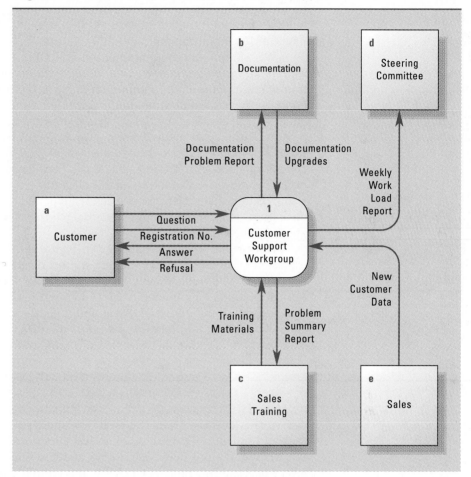

question. (The refusal is sent when the registration number is invalid, but that logic is not shown in a DFD.) Periodically, Customer Support sends reports to Documentation and Sales Training and to the Steering Committee, as shown. Documentation provides Documentation upgrades; Sales Training provides training materials. Sales provides new customer data for customers who have purchased the customer support package.

This context diagram shows scope, boundaries, and overall environment for Customer Support. It is considered a level 0 DFD. To show the processing that occurs within Customer Support, a DFD of the next level is prepared by exploding the central process into a level 1 DFD.

Level 1 DFDs   Figure 10-20 shows the **level 1 DFD** for Customer Support. According to this diagram, there are five major processes within Customer Support: Answer Question, Prepare Reports, Review Reports, Add New Customers, and Remove Unpaid Customers.

We will not discuss every item in this DFD. There are, however, several aspects that you should note. First, observe the names of entities or processes from the next higher level. Customer, for example, represents the Customer external entity on the context diagram. In the upper left-hand corner of Figure 10-20, the dataflow Question is shown as an input from Customer to the Answer Question process. The purpose of this dataflow is to show which of the five processes within Customer Support receive the dataflow Question, which was documented in the context diagram. All the other dataflows between Customer Support and the external entities are also shown on this diagram.

It is important to ensure that all the input and output to and from a process on one level is accounted for by diagrams on the next level. When it is, the diagrams are said to be **balanced**.

Notice the process numbering in Figure 10-20. All the processes are an explosion of process number 1 on the context diagram, and so they all carry the number 1.n. The n identifies a subprocess within process 1. Thus, for example, Answer Question is numbered 1.1 and Add New Customers is labeled 1.4. A similar numbering technique is used for data stores. The data store Customer and Request is numbered 1/D1 for process 1, data store number 1. If there were a second data store on this DFD, it would be labeled 1/D2, and so forth.

Level 2 DFDs   Figure 10-21 shows a **level 2 DFD**. This diagram is an explosion of process 1.1 (Answer Question) on the level 1 DFD. Observe that each process is numbered 1.1.n because it is a process within process 1.1. Similarly, note that the data store is labeled 1.1/D1. This DFD is balanced with the level 1 DFD because all the input and output to process 1.1 at level 1 is shown here at level 2. Observe, too, that a new data store, Reference Library, appears. This data store did not appear at level 1 because only process 1.1 uses it. It is entirely contained within process 1.1 and hence is not visible until process 1.1 is exploded. Finally, note the names of external entities and data stores that share dataflows with these processes.

Building DFDs

Creating a DFD is an artistic process. We cannot specify a set of rules by which you can create an accurate and communicative diagram every time. Instead, what we can do is discuss a number of principles and illustrate them with examples. From these you will gain a sense of how to proceed.

First, building a DFD is an iterative process. Start with a lot of paper, or use a computer-aided systems engineering (CASE) tool, such as DEFT (discussed further

Figure 10-20 Level 1 DFD for Customer Support

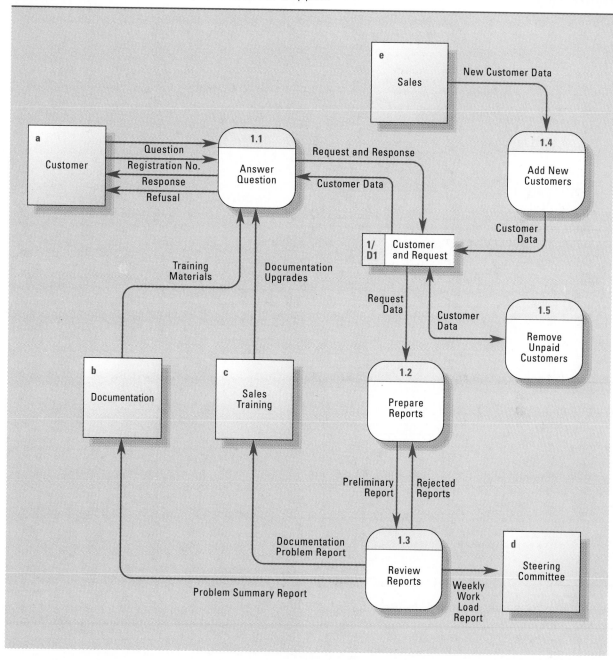

Figure 10-21 Level 2 DFD for Answer Question Process

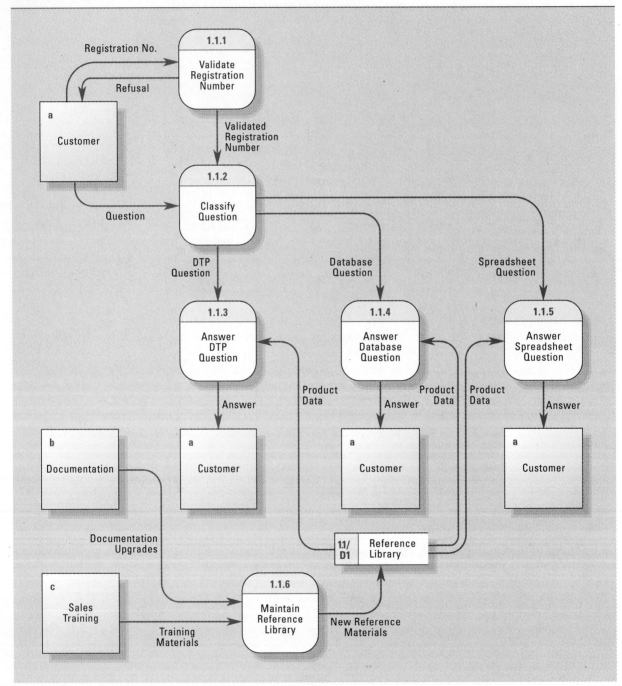

in Chapter 13), to draw DFDs—and expect to make mistakes. Plan on doing four, five, or six different versions of the same diagram. The human mind is iterative in its processing, and you will not know exactly what to do until you have learned what not to do. Be patient with yourself.

Second, start anywhere. Work until you do not know what to do next, and then start again someplace else. Keep working until you have connected all of your different starts. Work from the top down (i.e., from the big picture to the detail level) or from the bottom up (i.e., from the detail level to the big picture), or use both methods and alternate them.

Third, do not expect to get everything into a single diagram—it will not fit. Use leveling, as shown in Figures 10-19 through 10-21. In general, no more than seven processes should be shown at any given level. If you perceive a need to have more than this, then combine some of the processes into a single process and explode (open up) that process on another level.

Figure 10-22 shows a number of common mistakes to avoid. Do not document dataflows between external entities. While such flows may occur, they do not concern the system being modeled. Also, dataflows should not occur between an external entity and a data store (or the reverse). A process is required to receive the dataflow and place it in the store. Similarly, dataflows cannot occur between data stores. A process is required to remove the data from the first store and place it in the second.

At this point, You have enough knowledge to make your own DFDs. Take an example that is close to you—say, the recording of grades—and work through it. The best way to learn how to make a DFD is to do it. The discussion questions and projects at the end of this chapter provide a number of suggestions.

Dataflow modeling is useful in situations beyond just developing information systems. Whenever you want to understand the flow of work in a complicated office situation, consider developing DFDs. They are useful both for developing your own understanding and for communicating that understanding to others.

Documenting Dataflows with the Data Dictionary

Although we have chosen names for dataflows in these diagrams that suggest the meaning of the data items, this is often not enough. In Figure 10-19, for example, what exactly is a Weekly Work Load Report? How does it differ from a Problem Summary Report?

DFDs can often be given more meaning if they are accompanied by a description of the dataflows. Such a description, sometimes called a **data dictionary**, is a file or a database that documents data requirements and explains, in detail, the meaning of each dataflow. There should be one entry in the data dictionary for every dataflow on every DFD.

Figure 10-22 Incorrect Dataflows

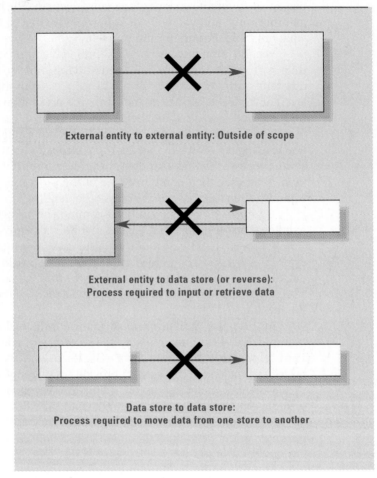

External entity to external entity: Outside of scope

External entity to data store (or reverse):
Process required to input or retrieve data

Data store to data store:
Process required to move data from one store to another

Several entries from the data dictionary that would accompany the DFDs in Figures 10-19 through 10-21 are shown in Figure 10-23. Observe that name, description, type, and format are recorded for each dataflow. The name is the name of the dataflow on the DFD. The description explains the meaning of the item and its function. The type specifies whether the item is a paper form, a screen form, a report, a verbal message, a simple data item, a file or database, and so on. The format specifies the physical format of the data item or lists the data items it contains.

In addition to these descriptors, certain rules may govern values that data items can or cannot have. Rules for the data item Registration Number are included in the description in Figure 10-23.

Figure 10-23   Data Dictionary Entries

Name	Description	Type	Format
Registration Number	A number assigned to a particular copy of a product. The number is assigned to a customer when the customer registers the product. The number is valid if the customer's name matches the one provided with the product and if customer support payments are up to date.	Data item	Nine characters starting with the letters *LGS* as follows: LGSnnnnnn
Weekly Work Load Report	A report of Customer Support's weekly activity. It contains the following: ■ Date printed ■ Number of calls received this week ■ Average length of call ■ Average customer wait time ■ Number of calls by question type ■ Number of calls by product type ■ Number of calls by document ID	Report	Composite
Number of Calls Received	The number of calls received over the Customer Support line in a given period of time. These calls are counted by the Customer Support voice mail system	Data item	Positive integer
• • •	• • •	• • •	• • •

Some CASE systems that facilitate the development of DFDs also contain programs for creating and maintaining the data dictionary. Further examples appear in the CASE section of Chapter 13. Such products would provide reports similar to that in Figure 10-23 and many other reports as well.

Observe that some of the dataflows are **elementary**, and others are **composites** of other dataflows. The dataflow Registration Number is elementary—it cannot be further decomposed. The dataflow Weekly Work Load Report, however, contains many other data items. In general, every composite dataflow should be reduced to elementary items in the data dictionary. Each data item in the Weekly Work Load Report, for example, is defined in the data dictionary, even though none show up as independent items on any DFD.

Documenting Process Logic with Procedure Specifications

In addition to the data dictionary, DFDs are also sometimes accompanied by descriptions of the logic within the processes. Such descriptions, sometimes called **procedure specifications**, explain how the process transforms the inputs it receives into the output it produces.

Consider Figure 10-24, which shows the logic of Validate Registration Number (process 1.1.1 in Figure 10-21). This process, which is documented in a semiformal manner called **structured English**, shows the logic used to accept or reject a registration number. This format is not necessary; any unambiguous statement of the logic of the process will do.

Figure 10-24   Procedure Specification
This procedure describes the process Validate Registration Number (1.1.1) in Figure 10-21.

```
Obtain Registration Number from Customer
Access the Customer data in the Customer and Request data store
IF Registration Number exists
      THEN
              IF Account is paid
                  THEN   Send Validated Registration Number
                                    to Classify Question process
                  ELSE   Attempt to obtain credit card payment
                          IF can obtain payment
                              THEN   Send Validated Registration Number
                                            to Classify Question process
                              ELSE   Send Refusal to Customer
                          END-IF
      END-IF
      ELSE Send Refusal to Customer
END-IF
```

SUMMARY

Workgroup information systems involve the sharing of data, information, and other intellectual assets among many people. Because many people are involved, the systems development process is more complicated, longer, and involves more risk than for personal information systems.

The prototyping development process described in Chapter 7 is seldom used for workgroups. The workgroup platform is larger and more expensive, and more detailed knowledge of requirements is needed to build it. Correcting mistakes can be expensive. Requirements having to do with sharing may be missed with prototyping development. Finally, outside personnel are not likely to commit to development via prototypes.

The development process used with workgroup systems has five stages: define the problem, specify the requirements, evaluate the alternatives, design the system components, and implement the system. During the first phase, the problem is defined, feasibility is assessed, and a plan is constructed. Problem definition can be difficult for workgroup systems because there will often be several different perceptions of the problem and the business functions being computerized are often more complicated. An important goal is to achieve a consensus of the problem definition among key members of the workgroup.

The dimensions of feasibility are the same as those for personal information systems: cost, schedule, technology, and political environment. The last dimension, political environment, is especially important to assess for workgroup systems, since workgroup norms and attitudes have a major influence on systems' acceptance and success. The project plan should include a definition of the members of the project team. For workgroup systems, the plan should allow extra time review, discussion, and rework during the development project.

The purpose of the requirements stage is to identify and document the requirements for the system. To develop requirements, we work backward, from output to input to size, constraints, and documentation. Requirements differ by type of application. When developing workgroup requirements, many people will be interviewed. Some users will employ inconsistent terminology; it will be important to identify form versus content differences. Prototypes of parts of the system can help clarify requirements statements. To determine input requirements, the developers can seek data that will enable them to fulfill the output requirements, they can examine existing workgroup forms, or they can use both methods.

Processing scale estimates of the application need to include not just the amount and growth of data and the frequency of report product, but also the amount and growth of concurrent work load. Constraints on processing also need to be identified.

Workgroup requirements need to be documented, then reviewed, understood, accepted, and supported by key group members.

During evaluation, requirements are reconsidered and possibly removed. Then, most often, professional developers are selected. An RFP is developed and delivered to users, bids are received, and one is selected.

During the evaluation stage, the users make the transition from taking the lead on development to being managers of others' work. Users are the experts on the problems and the requirements. Professional developers take the lead in design and implementation.

Users are typically not involved in the systems design activity, especially as it involves hardware, programs, and, to a large degree, data components. Users should be given an opportunity to review and approve the design of the user interface. Additionally, the design of procedures, job activities, and training should be reviewed.

During the implementation stage, systems components are acquired, installed, and tested individually. Then an integrated test, or dress rehearsal, is conducted. There are four styles of installation: parallel, phased, pilot, and plunge. The plunge style should be avoided.

Workgroup information systems involve the interaction of many people in complicated relationships. Dataflow diagrams (DFDs) are important tools for understanding and documenting these relationships. A DFD is a snapshot of the data movement in an organization or in a workgroup within an organization.

The four basic DFD symbols represent external entities, processes, dataflows, and data stores. A context diagram shows the boundaries and scope of the system. It contains one process symbol that names the activity being documented. The context diagram is exploded into one or several layers of a DFD. At each level, all of the input and output at the higher level should be accounted for.

To be meaningful, DFDs should be accompanied by a data dictionary that defines the dataflows. The format of the data dictionary varies, but, at the minimum, it should include the name, description, type, and format of each dataflow on each DFD. Some dataflows will be composites of others. The composite items should be decomposed into elementary data items, and each elementary item should be included in the data dictionary as well.

A procedure specification is a description of the logic within a process. It describes how input dataflows are transformed into output dataflows. While structured English is often used to express policy statements, any unambiguous statement of logic is acceptable.

KEY TERMS

Problem definition stage	Concurrent work load	External entity
Consensus	Constraint	Source
Feasibility assessment	Requirements documentation	Sink
Cost feasibility	Evaluation stage	Process
Schedule feasibility	Vendor	Dataflow
Technical feasibility	RFP	Data store
Political feasibility	"Standard" contract	Context diagram
Project plan	Design stage	Level 1 DFD
Output requirements	Implementation stage	Balanced diagram
Prototype	Parallel installation	Level 2 DFD
Rapid prototypes	Phased installation	Data dictionary
Input requirements	Pilot installation	Elementary dataflow
Standard forms	Plunge installation	Composite dataflow
Estimates of processing scale	Cutover point	Procedure specification
	DFD	Structured English

REVIEW QUESTIONS

1. What is the fundamental difference between a personal information system and a workgroup information system?

2. Explain why the prototyping development process described in Chapter 7 is not used for workgroup systems development.

3. List the five stages in workgroup systems development.

4. List the three major tasks in the definition stage.

5. Why is problem definition more difficult for workgroup systems than for personal systems?

6. Define *consensus*, and explain how it differs from agreement.

7. What is the recommended course of action when achieving group consensus is not possible?

8. Name the four dimensions of feasibility.

9. Briefly describe important considerations in assessing political environment organizational feasibility for workgroup systems development.

10. In a project plan, why should more time be allowed for review in workgroup systems development than for personal systems development?

11. Explain why it is important to obtain a clear definition of terms from users when identifying requirements.

12. Explain how the reports in Figure 10-5 differ from the reports in Figure 10-6 in terms of the amount of work required of the developer.

13. Explain the role for prototypes in workgroup systems development. How does this role differ from that described for personal systems development?

14. What is a rapid prototype?

15. How do standard forms ease the specification of input requirements?

16. Explain how the need for concurrent processing influences the estimation of processing scale.

17. Why is it important to estimate the growth of concurrent work load? What can happen if the growth is considerably underestimated? Overestimated?

18. Give an example of a procedural restriction for a workgroup information system.

19. Summarize the ways in which requirements can be documented. Why are group sessions recommended in the review of requirements?

20. Explain how the users' role changes during the evaluation stage. How do users' responsibilities differ in the definition and requirements stages from those in the design and implementation stages?

21. What is the key difference in the users' roles between the development of a personal information system and the development of a workgroup information system?

22. Name three sources for identifying vendors.

23. Why is it good policy to involve your company's MIS department with your development project?

24. What is an RFP, and when should one be used?

25. Summarize four considerations to use when communicating with vendors prior to the award of your contract.

26. Who has the burden for identifying the best solution to your problem?

27. What vendor evaluation activities can you perform prior to receiving the responses to a proposal?

28. Summarize criteria for evaluating proposals.

29. Explain how knowledge is unbalanced in the vendors' favor.

30. Why should you not sign the standard contract? What should you do instead?

31. Summarize activities for users in the design stage of workgroup systems development.

32. Summarize implementation activities for each of the five components of a workgroup information system.

33. What is the purpose of a DFD?

34. Explain why Figure 10-20 does not show logic. What does it show instead?

35. Name the four dataflow symbols, and describe the function of each.

36. What is an external entity?

37. Does a dataflow show the medium of the flow?

38. Explain the differences among an office, a person, and a process. Which should be shown in the process symbol? Why?

39. Does a DFD show the medium of a data store?

40. What is the purpose of a context diagram?

41. What are balanced DFDs?

42. When should you decide to create another level in a DFD?

43. What is a data dictionary? What is its role? Name four descriptors that should exist for every dataflow.

44. What is an elementary dataflow? Give an example.

45. What is a composite dataflow? Give an example.

46. What is a procedure specification? What is its role?

DISCUSSION QUESTIONS

1. You are a member of a workgroup that is in the process of developing an information system. The manager of the workgroup does not have a particularly strong personality or management style nor does he understand the problem to be solved. Three of the more outspoken members of the group have different interpretations of the problem; they each lead a subgroup within the workgroup that supports their position. A $100,000 contract has been awarded to a consulting company to develop the information system. You have been with the group for about 18 months and have the respect of most of the workgroup members. You have not joined any of the three factions. What do you do?

2. You are a member of a workgroup that is in the process of developing an information system. The manager of the workgroup has a very strong and domineering management style. The manager has, almost single-handedly, defined the problem and requirements and selected a vendor. You believe that a significant issue has been left out of the problem definition and that a number of critical requirements have been omitted. Further, you believe that a number of influential members of the group intend to subvert the development activity. A $100,000 contract has been awarded for the development effort, and the vendor is scheduled to begin work in a week. What do you do?

3. You manage a workgroup that is about to begin developing an information system. You are talking with a manager who runs a workgroup in a different functional area and who has just completed a development effort. That manager advises you to hide your project from the corporate MIS department. That group, she says, will only slow you down with meetings, paperwork, and endless requests for justification. You believe that your workgroup information system will require data from the corporate database. How should you proceed?

4. You are in charge of the development of a proposal for a $37 million bid for a government project. Your corporation has just purchased a collaborative writing system and installed it in a suite of offices with 20 microcomputers connected on a LAN. Your manager tells you to use this new system for developing your proposal. You know that the proposal development effort will involve very high pressure with critical time constraints. No one in your company has used the system for anything other than prototype projects, but those projects indicate that substantial productivity gains are possible. How do you proceed?

PROJECTS

A. Suppose you own and manage a small pottery shop. You sell your product over the counter for cash or check, and you accept VISA and MasterCard. You deposit money and charge card receipts with your bank. You purchase clay, paint, glazes, and equipment from a number of different vendors. Occasionally you must have kilns and pottery wheels repaired. You pay two part-time helpers an hourly wage. Draw a context diagram of your business.

B. Interview the officer or administrator at your college who is responsible for the course registration system. Gather information about at least these topics: What procedure is used to determine which courses are to be offered, which faculty members are to staff each one, what room is to be used, and what time slot is to be assigned? How is the course schedule published? What procedures are followed by students in the process of registering? What procedures, if any, are followed in evaluating the progress of the registration process during the course of the registration and afterward? Collect enough information to create a context diagram and at least two level 1 DFDs.

C. You manage the purchasing department for a $10 million sales business. Your staff consists of three purchasing agents plus yourself. Your department receives purchase orders (POs) from other departments in the company. The agents check the POs for completeness and accuracy and then check the corporate budget to determine whether sufficient unencumbered funds exist to purchase the items. If the funds exist, the agents choose, from departmental records, the appropriate vendors, and then the agents order the items. When items are received in the shipping department, the shipping personnel generate a receiver document and send a copy of that document to your department. When all items have been received, the agent closes the PO. Periodically, you review open POs to ensure that work is being completed on time. Generate a context diagram and at least one DFD for this department.

D. Gather information from your course instructor, then create a context diagram and at least one level 1 DFD describing the process of assigning course grades to students in your course.

E. Interview a workgroup in an actual business. Pick a function that is large enough to require a context diagram and two levels of DFD, but one that is not so large or complicated that you cannot understand its basic flow in a matter of an hour or two. Develop a DFD. If possible, obtain copies of paper forms used in this business. Develop entries for a data dictionary to describe that form. Create a procedure specification for one of the processes in your chart. Use structured English (as in Figure 10-24) for this specification. Review your work with a member of the department for accuracy, and make changes as necessary. Describe any errors or misconceptions that you had.

M I N I C A S E

LAN Security: Protecting Corporate Assets

Whether it's medical records, financial statements, legal documents about customers, or the home phone numbers of congressmen on your payroll, the confidentiality and validity of corporate information is paramount. The risk of a lawsuit or damage from mishandled proprietary information, whether accidentally or intentionally disclosed, is significant. In well-reported incidents earlier this year, hackers broke into Equifax, an Atlanta-based credit bureau, and used the credit card information they obtained to make fraudulent purchases.

Don't think that can't happen to you. Any company that keeps information about its customers is vulnerable to this kind of intrusion. But how does a company secure the data that needs protection when that same data is needed by workers to process orders, answer questions, and make decisions?

The key is to distinguish between authorized and unauthorized use. From a systems standpoint, it's easy to control and monitor who uses what data, which is an effective deterrent to mischief.

However, there is little an IS manager can do to prevent someone from peering over the shoulder of an authorized user or making a copy of a printout. Unfortunately many users don't think much about the value of the information with which they work.

It's important to encourage responsible use of corporate information, says Larry Seibel, information security manager at The Huntington National Bank of Columbus, Ohio. "The outside threat can be easily controlled,"

he adds, but the internal threat that comes from misuse and human error is much greater.

Accidental destruction of data is the biggest threat to enterprise computing, asserts John Worthen, president of Pyramid Technologies, a Rocky Hill, Conn., publisher of security software. He estimates that at least one of every 500 PCs suffers some kind of data loss every day. A comprehensive security plan can play an important role in reducing these incidents, he says.

After months of complaints from customers, a network administrator for an East Coast metallurgy company, who insisted his name not be used, discovered that a disgruntled employee had altered records so the system would generate delinquency letters even when accounts were current. No money was stolen, but the loss of goodwill among the company's customers was immeasurable. Like so many other hacking incidents, no criminal charges were ever filed.

How do unauthorized users gain access to sensitive areas of computer networks? The No. 1 way, say security analysts and IS managers, is through compromised passwords. Despite all the scolding by IS folks, users continue to thwart security efforts by sharing passwords, leaving log-on information in their desks, using the same password for every system, or picking obvious passwords.

Once users start thinking about security and the value of corporate data, a real security program can be implemented. The ACM publishes a free brochure: *300 Ways to*

Develop Your Computer Security and Contingency Planning. (Contact ACM at P.O. Box 39110, Washington, DC 20016.) The brochure breaks down security risk areas and gives numerous tips. Among them: Change passwords frequently, make backups, use encryption on sensitive data, and record violations and attempts at unauthorized access.

IS managers agree that it's crucial to disable the account of anyone who leaves an organization or takes an extended vacation, but they say that personnel departments frequently don't inform IS of staffing changes. LAN administrators should immediately change all supervisory passwords whenever someone leaves the department. ■

Doug van Kirk, excerpted from *Infoworld*, November 23, 1992, pp. 43, 46.

Discussion Questions

1. Summarize the major threats to network security.

2. Why is the internal threat more difficult to manage than the external threat?

3. According to the article, "Many users don't think much about the value of the information with which they work." Suggest at least three steps that a company could take to improve this situation.

4. Describe at least three categories of procedures for network security that typical companies should adopt.

678

MODULE B

Developing an MIS for Legacy Systems' Customer Support

THIS MODULE REVIEWS THE DEVELOPMENT OF A WORKGROUP MIS for Customer Support at Legacy Systems. Although we consider each of the five stages of development, there is insufficient space here to discuss each stage comprehensively. Instead, we focus on concepts and procedures that will be important to you as a business professional.

CASE BACKGROUND

Legacy Systems develops microcomputer applications; its principal products are DTP, DBMS, and spreadsheet applications. Like most such vendors, Legacy maintains a Customer Support group that answers customer questions about the use of these products. According to Legacy policy, when a customer registers a product, he or she receives 30 days of customer support for free. After that, customers must pay an annual fee to receive customer support services. The Customer Support group validates registration numbers and ensures that customer support has been purchased before assisting customers.

Recently, Legacy experienced explosive growth, and the Customer Support group had difficulty keeping up with the work load. The staff underwent tremendous turnover. Charlie Parks, the manager, convinced his management to increase the staff to 25 people, enabling him to staff 20 customer support positions for a 10-hour period. Work loads were reduced, and turnover fell, although there were still long hours and much frustration in the department.

Customer Support was organized in accordance with the DFDs shown in Figures 10-19 through 10-21. In truth, these figures appear to document a more sophisticated system than actually existed. The Customer and Request data store, in fact, consisted of a printed list of authorized customers, and the Request and Response data was simply a large collection of manually prepared forms. A Customer Support representative filled out one form for each call processed.

The Customer data was updated by processes 1.4 and 1.5 in Figure 10-20 once each week. Then the customer requests were collected and stored in boxes. Some of the data on these documents was entered into a computer-supported database in Prepare Reports process (1.2 in Figure 10-20), which was used to produce the reports in Figure 10-19.

This was the situation when Frank Stravelko, Legacy's vice president of Sales, barged into Charlie Parks's office one morning:

"Look, Charlie, what did you do with all those people you hired? Can't they return their phone calls? This is a major crisis!"

"Now, Frank, take it easy. Just tell me in words. What is the problem?"

"Universal Industries, our biggest account. Nobody here in Customer Support will return their calls. Now, Universal is under the impression that $100,000 of business a quarter entitles them to some support. Crazy, huh? Well, actually, Charlie, I'll tell you, I'm under that impression, too! In fact, I'm under the impression that everybody in this company ought to drop everything they're doing and return those people's phone calls! Now!"

"OK, Frank, OK. Just give me the names, and I'll get back to them."

"Charlie, some of these people have been waiting three weeks! Three weeks! I mean, I can understand that not everybody in your department knows everything about every product. And now and then, I can understand that we need to look into something and get back to them. But that's the key phrase here: Get back to them!

"Also, they've been complaining that, when we do give them advice, it often doesn't work. Then when they call back the next day, they get a different person who gives them the same bad advice. Why can't we keep track of what we tell them so that, at least, we can give them a *different* wrong answer each time!"

Thus, even though Customer Support had added employees, there were still problems, many of which involved the representatives not knowing the answer to questions and having to look into the matter further and call the customer back (referred to as a *callback*). Unfortunately, there was seldom enough time to make the callbacks on a timely basis.

Charlie responded to Frank in two ways. First, he solved the particular problem involving their number one customer by asking his top support representative to take care of it. Second, he decided to investigate building an information system that would prevent or minimize the callback problems and that would track both customer problems and recommended solutions.

DEFINITION STAGE

Since Charlie believed in the process that you have studied in this course, he began with the definition stage and with problem definition in particular. He met with several of his senior representatives and created a team to solve the problems. They began by defining the problem.

Problem Definition

After discussions with many support representatives, the team decided that there were two major problems: First, nobody was tracking the number of open callbacks (callbacks that had not been made). Although the representatives had each kept track of the names of people to whom to return calls, their methods were too informal to be satisfactory. Charlie had no way of monitoring overdue callbacks.

Charlie and the representatives needed to know how many items were open, which representatives had taken the callbacks, who the customers were, and how long the callbacks had been open. He wanted to be on top of callbacks that had remained open too long, and he wanted every callback to be made in less than three working days.

Second, the representatives had no way of knowing what advice had been given to customers on their problems. When customers called back because prior advice had not worked, the support representatives did, in fact, often repeat the prior recommendation.

The support representatives needed a way to record both the customers' problems and the advice that had been given. Then, if a customer had to call again because the advice did not work, the next representative could find out what had already been recommended.

Feasibility

The team members continued to meet over the next month. After defining the problem, they turned to the issue of how feasible it would be to build an information system to track the customers, their queries, the support representatives' responses, and the open callbacks. They wanted each customer support station to have a computer that accessed a central database of customer data while the customer was on the phone. This clearly was a tracking problem that would involve some type of database.

The team members were uncertain about the cost and technical feasibility of this type of system, so they asked a systems analyst from their company's MIS department to assist them. After listening to them and reviewing the situation, this person informed them that what they wanted was technically feasible and that they should be able to develop, install, and implement such a system for under $100,000. The team was stunned that it might cost this much.

Still, they considered the cost benefit of such a system. If they could quickly obtain a customer's history and know immediately what problems the customer had been experiencing and what had been done so far, they were certain that they could avoid hiring at least three new people in the next year—a labor savings of more than $100,000 in one year. Thus they could pay for the system in the first year, and subsequent years would be gravy. Hence, the team concluded that the system would be cost feasible. Schedule and political feasibility also seemed likely.

Creating the Project Plan

When it came time to develop a project plan, the team members realized that, while they had defined *what is*, they had not really defined *what should be*. The information system they had identified would, in fact, solve the second problem, but it did not directly address the first one. How were they to account for open callbacks?

Defining What Should Be At first, the team members thought that they would assign all callbacks to a separate, special team for resolution. If a representative could not answer a question, then the matter would be referred to someone on the special team. However, they soon realized that resolving callbacks was an important way that representatives learned. If the callbacks were taken away from the representatives, they wouldn't be able to add to their knowledge, and the need for callbacks was unlikely to decrease.

Instead, the team members decided to allow support representatives to process callbacks, but only under a strong system of controls: Representatives would be given 2 days to resolve a problem and to call the customer back. If the customer was not called back by that time, then the callback would be labeled as overdue and given to a special team to address the problem. Charlie wanted to track all such callbacks so that he could provide management direction and feedback to representatives who generated too many overdue callbacks.

The team summarized its conclusions in the DFD presented in Figures B-1 through B-4. First, as shown in Figure B-1, the team corrected a misleading dataflow from its earlier context diagram (Figure 10-19). The support representatives did not necessarily provide an *answer* to customers, but they did provide a *response*. Sometimes the response was an answer, and sometimes a callback. They documented this meaning for the dataflow Response in the data dictionary (not shown).

The team adjusted the level 1 Customer Support dataflow (Figure 10-20) to allow for the processing of overdue callbacks. The adjustment is shown in the shaded area of Figure B-2. Callbacks would be stored in the new, computer-based version of the Customer and Request database as one type of response.

Figure B-3 shows the revised level 2 DFD for the Answer Question process. In this DFD, the dataflow Response replaces the dataflow Answer.

The processing of overdue callbacks is shown in Figure B-4. Each day, a process would search the Customer and Request database for callbacks that were more than 2 days old. Any such callback would be retrieved and then processed as shown. If some time would be required to answer the callback, the customer would be called and given an apology, along with an estimate regarding how soon the question could be answered. In parallel, members of the special team would

Figure B-1 Revised Customer Support Context DFD

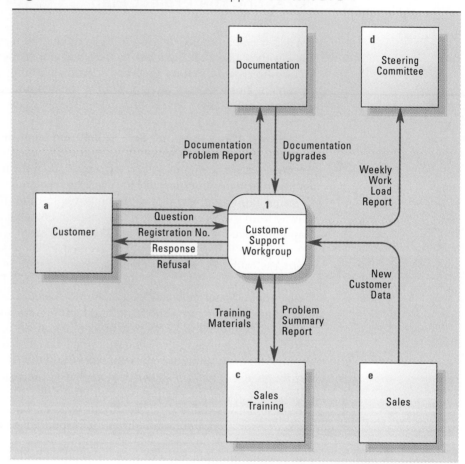

determine the answer and call the customer as soon as possible. If the problem could be immediately resolved, then the customer would be called with the solution. All overdue callbacks and their results would be stored in a new data store called Overdue Callback.

Project Plan Given these findings, the team then built a plan and allowed extra time for review and feedback from other experienced Customer Support representatives. Also, it concluded that the development of the system would require an outside vendor. No one in Customer Support had the expertise or the time to develop the system; and the corporation's MIS department was far too busy for the task.

Figure B-2 Revised Level 1 DFD for Customer Support

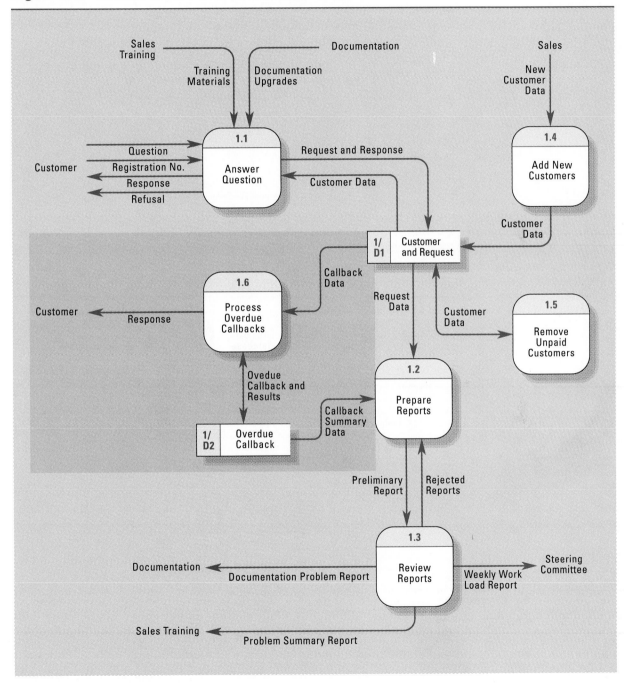

Figure B-3   Revised Level 2 DFD for Answer Question Process

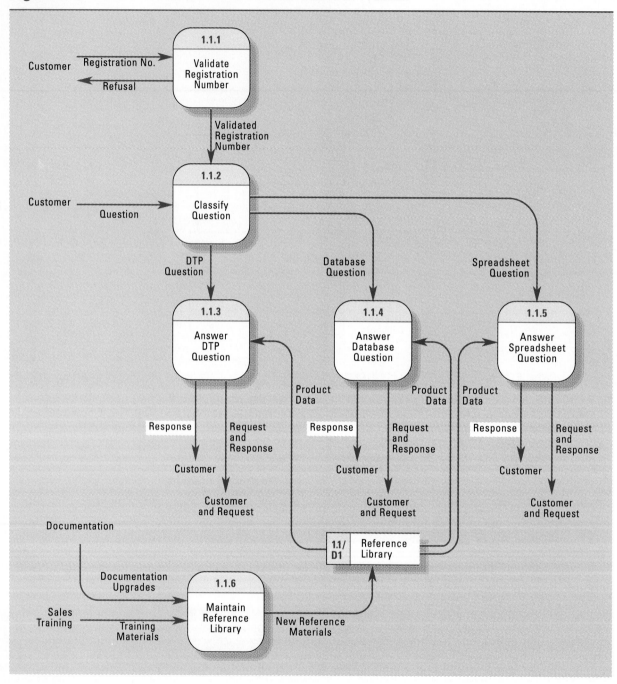

Figure B-4 Level 2 DFD for Processing Overdue Callbacks

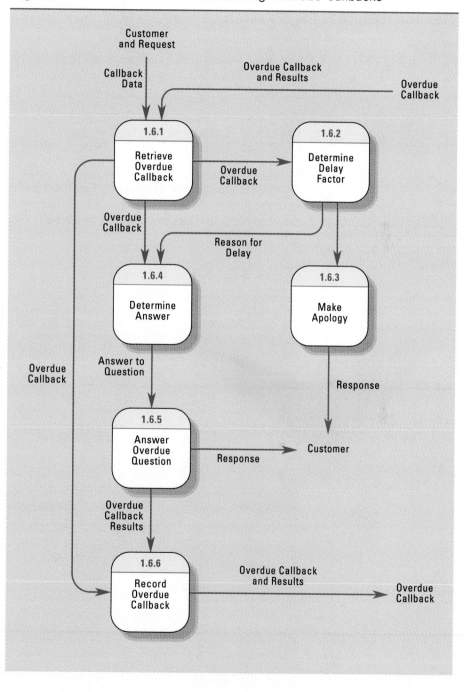

REQUIREMENTS STAGE

The team next turned its attention to the four types of requirements we have previously identified: output, input, scale, and constraints.

Output Requirements

Output requirements can be identified by examining the dataflows shown in Figures B-1 through B-4. They are summarized in Figure B-5. The Documentation Problem Report and the Problem Summary Report were identical to the reports of the same name in the current system. The Weekly Work Load Report, summarizing

Figure B-5 Output Requirements

Output	Frequency	Description
REPORTS		
Documentation Problem Report	Monthly, quarterly	Frequency of questions by section of documentation
Problem Summary Report	Monthly, quarterly, on demand	Frequency of questions by topic
Weekly Work Load Report	Weekly	Summary of Customer Support accomplishments
SCREEN DISPLAYS		
Customer Data	Per call	Display of customer data, prior questions, and recommendations
Callback Data	Daily	Display of pending, overdue Callback Responses
Overdue Callback and Results	As needed throughout day	Data about overdue callbacks that are in the Process Overdue Callbacks Process. Stored in the Overdue Callback data store.
Callback Summary Data	Weekly	Open callback data used to prepare the Weekly Summary Report

Figure B-6 Customer Data Input Form

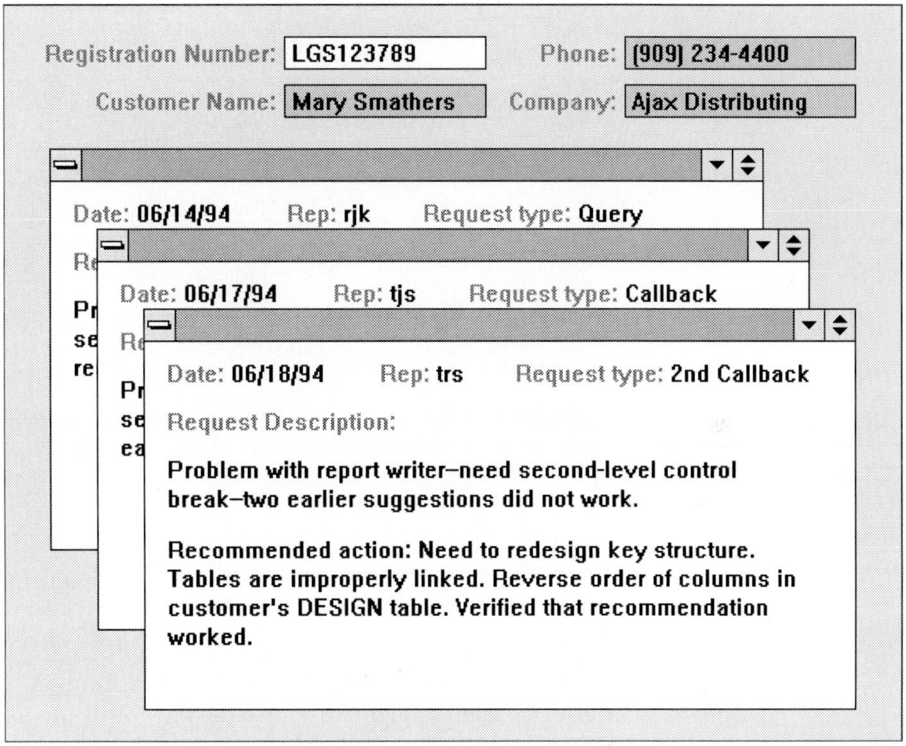

work accomplished by the Customer Support department, was to be modified to include a section on the number of callbacks processed on time, the number processed late, and the number still open.

The remaining outputs are screen displays. Customer Data is used for both output and input. It is used for output when displaying customer data at the start of a call. The representative enters the customer number (or name and other data), and the system responds with customer data in the format of Figure B-6. From that point on, the form is used for input. It is also used for entering new customers.

The other screen displays in Figure B-5 concern the processing of callbacks. Data about overdue callbacks is output in the Callback Data display. The status and results of each overdue callback are both input to and output from the Overdue Callback data store with the Overdue Callback and Results form. Finally, Callback Summary Data is output to the Prepare Reports process and is used to create the callback data on the Weekly Summary Report.

Figure B-7 Input Requirements

Input	Description
Customer Data	Display form used to enter and change: Product registration data Payment data Call requests Response data Callbacks
Overdue Callback and Results	Used to enter data for tracking overdue callbacks that are being processed. It is used to enter both the status of open overdue callbacks and the final results of processing.
Menus	Used to control application and request production of reports

Input Requirements

Input requirements can also be identified from dataflows in Figures B-1 through B-4. As listed in Figure B-7, two display forms are used for data input: Customer Data and Overdue Callback and Results. The Customer Data display form is used both to enter and to change product registration, payment, call requests, and response data. Callbacks are also entered using this form. A second form, Overdue Callback and Results, is needed to enter the results from the processing of overdue callbacks. Both of these forms are also output forms and were listed in Figure B-5 as well. Finally, menus are needed for the users to control the application and request the production of reports.

Estimates of Processing Scale

The processing scale estimates are summarized in Figure B-8. The team estimated both the current requirements and the requirements as projected in 18 months, the size of the database, the number of concurrent system users, the number of users of the Customer application (assuming that some users would use the system for nonapplications such as the sharing of hardware), and the required response time.

Figure B-8 Estimates of Processing Scale

	Current Processing Requirements	**Estimated Requirements in 18 months**
Database Size	75,000 customers at 500 bytes each = 37.5 million bytes	150,000 customers at 500 bytes each = 90 million bytes
Concurrent Users	22 concurrent system users, maximum 17 concurrent system users, average	37 concurrent system users, maximum 33 concurrent system users, average
	20 concurrent Customer application users, maximum	35 concurrent Customer application users, maximum
	16 concurrent Customer application users, average	31 concurrent Customer application users, average
Response Time	Less than 2 seconds, average Less than 10 seconds, maximum	Less than 2 seconds, average Less than 10 seconds, maximum

Figure B-9 Constraints

1. Installation cannot disrupt Customer Support for more than one weekend.

2. The system can be inoperative no longer than one-half day, maximum; no more than one-half hour is expected.

3. System must fail not more frequently than once per month, maximum; less than once per quarter is expected.

Constraints

Finally, the team considered constraints, summarized in Figure B-9. One constraint concerned the installation of the system; Customer Support could be disrupted for, at most, one weekend. Other constraints concerned reliability. The system could not be inoperative for any extended period of time (certainly less than half a day, and, hopefully, less than half an hour), and it must fail infrequently (certainly less than once per month, and, hopefully, less than once per quarter).

The Requirements Document

The team summarized the requirements in an RFP. It also developed an internal document describing its plans and intentions for dealing with vendors.

EVALUATION

To identify sources of vendors, the team contacted its in-house purchasing department, the corporation's MIS department, and a number of Customer Support departments in other companies in the industry. The team also visited several reputedly high-quality local computer dealers. It selected dealers who were known to sell software development services and systems support as well as products.

After settling on five potential vendors, the team invited each of them in for a tour and a presentation of its needs. Each prospective vendor was given a copy of the RFP. One vendor declined to bid on the project due to an overcommitted schedule. Charlie asked one of the remaining four vendors not to bid once he had met the personnel his staff would be involved with: "For some reason, I don't trust those people, and I don't want to work with them." He did not say more.

The Bids

The three bids are summarized in Figure B-10. The first alternative proposed by a computer manufacturer, involved a minicomputer and a teleprocessing system architecture. It was the highest-cost bid. The company had an excellent reputation for quality, service, and support. This alternative was used by several other companies that were similar to Legacy.

The remaining two alternatives both involved microcomputers connected on a LAN. The second alternative involved a bus architecture using an IEEE 802.3 LAN, while the third involved a token ring network with IEEE 802.5 network-access cards. The second alternative was considerably less expensive than the third.

Bid Evaluation

Concerned that it did not have enough technical expertise to adequately evaluate the proposals, the team asked a professional from the MIS department for

Figure B-10   Summary of Three Alternative Bids

Alternative 1

- Minicomputer with 25 terminals
- Hardware provided by manufacturer
- Programs included in the Customer application
    E- mail
    Minicomputer spreadsheet and word processing available
- **Total package cost, $89,000**

Alternative 2

- LAN using bus architecture with IEEE 802.3
- File server plus 12 microcomputers
- Proposed to develop Customer application
- Questionable understanding of problem
- **Total package cost, $46,000**

Alternative 3

- LAN using IEEE 802.5 token ring architecture
- File server plus 12 microcomputers
- Proposed to develop Customer application by adapting a similar program developed for other reasons
- Cost breakout:

12 microcomputers	$24,000
LAN cards and other hardware	23,000
File server	12,000
Program development	20,000
Total package cost	**$79,000**

assistance. That person worked with the team members for 3 days as they evaluated the proposals.

The extended team decided against the first alternative because it did not want to employ a minicomputer. The team felt that using microcomputers on a LAN would provide greater flexibility. When not needed for the Customer application, the micros could be used for other purposes such as word processing, spreadsheets, and DTP.

After considering the second and third alternatives at great length, the team decided that the third alternative was better for several reasons. First, it suspected that the vendor of the second alternative had not fully appreciated its problem. It also feared that the bus architecture would not be able to handle performance requirements. Also, this vendor did not have experience that directly related to the development of programs for Customer Support.

The third vendor's proposal seemed to meet the team's immediate needs and could also be expanded. Further, the MIS professional stated that he thought the token ring architecture would predominate in the future. This meant that there would be more options for expansion with that alternative.

Once the team had decided on a vendor, it worked with the corporation's purchasing and legal departments to finalize a contract. After considerable discussion, the vendor reluctantly agreed to include the RFP as part of the contract.

DESIGN

The essence of the design activities is summarized in Figure B-11. The team was not directly involved in designing the hardware, the programs, or the database. It did, however, approve the format of all screens, menus, and reports. It also approved the procedures that would be used to start and stop the system, to make backups of the data, and to restore the system.

Charlie asked a number of experienced representatives to work with the vendor to develop the user procedures for normal operations. He worked with some of these same people to revise the job descriptions for support representatives. The revision reflected the specialization that would now occur. Three different job descriptions were prepared, one for each major process shown in Figure B-2. Training requirements for each of these three groups were established, and training classes were created.

IMPLEMENTATION

The implementation took place in three major phases. First, the vendor acquired the hardware, developed the programs, and then created the database and filled it with data. Each component was tested individually. Procedures were finalized

Figure B-11 The Design Stage of the Customer
Support Information System

Hardware

- Specify memory size, configuration of micros
- Specify type, characteristics of LAN cards
- Specify CPU, memory size, configuration of server
- Design layout of hardware in Customer Support
- Determine cabling routes
- Build test plan

Programs

- Determine type and version of LAN OS
- Set up operational characteristics of micro OS (CONFIG and similar files)
- Select DBMS product
- Design application programs
- Design test plans and facilities

Data

- Design database
- Design forms, reports, and menus
- Determine data conversion methodology
- Determine verification plan

Procedures

- Design startup and processing procedures for support representatives
- Design administration procedures and report preparation
- Design procedures for monitoring callbacks and processing overdue callbacks
- Design backup and recovery procedures, including what representatives should do when system is inoperative
- Plan for conducting dress rehearsal

People

- Design job descriptions for new categories of support representatives
- Determine training requirements
- Design training plan
- Design means for feedback from users

and documented, and a group of 10 users was trained. A system with 10 microcomputers on the LAN was assembled in a corner of one of Legacy's warehouses (so as to not disrupt the Customer Support group's daily operation). One evening, the first group of representatives tested all the components of the system in the warehouse. Several problems were identified and corrected, and the system was tested again.

The second phase began when the system was installed in Customer Support and run in parallel with the existing system. The installation took place between 4:00 p.m. one Friday and 2:30 a.m. the following Monday. All the cabling, furniture, and micros and the LAN server were assembled during that time. Some work needed to be done during part of the next week, but it was accomplished during nonbusiness hours.

The old and new systems were run in parallel for 2 weeks. Users checked the customer registration numbers against the customer list while entering customer data into the computer system. Manual call sheets were also filled out in conjunction with the keying of data. This required considerable extra work by the representatives, but they endured with good humor. Charlie had made it clear how important it was to have the parallel test.

During the 2 weeks, the system performed quite well. It did fail once, in the middle of the third day of use; the problem turned out to be a defective card in one of the microcomputers, and it was readily fixed. During the parallel test period, a number of minor problems were identified and corrected. In fact, such problems continued to be found for several months after the installation. None of them was severe, however.

At the end of the 2-week parallel test, Charlie asked the staff to perform a recovery operation. A number of procedural glitches were discovered, but the recovery otherwise was successful.

The Customer Support group, together, made the decision to cut off the old system the next week. Charlie wanted to have a consensus of the group so that, if any problems did develop, all employees would feel a personal responsibility to fix them. Figure B-12 summarizes the essence of the implementation activities.

EPILOGUE

Over time, the number of callbacks was substantially reduced and a callback was rarely more than 3 days old. Further, Charlie always knew about the older callbacks and was able to take corrective action where necessary. When nothing could be done to speed up the callback (e.g., Product Development couldn't locate the source of a particular problem), Charlie was also able to warn Frank and the sales staff so that they could provide customer support in other ways.

Figure B-12   The Implementation Stage of the Customer Support Information System

Hardware

Prior to Dress Rehearsal

- Obtain micros, install LAN cards
- Configure file server
- Build test facility of 10 micros in warehouse
- Test; test facility

After Dress Rehearsal

- Disassemble test facility
- Move micros to Customer Support
- Install cabling
- Locate micros in work setting and connect
- Test

Programs

Prior to Dress Rehearsal

- Install OS on test facility micros
- Test each computer individually
- Install LAN programs on server
- Integrate test micros into LAN
- Test LAN
- Install DBMS on server
- Install DBMS portion on micros
- Test DBMS functioning in LAN
- Build and test application programs
- Install application programs on micros
- Install test database
- Run test sets on application against test database

After Dress Rehearsal

- Modify and test application programs as required
- Install application programs on remaining 10 micros
- Run test sets on application against test database
- Convert application to run against operational database

Data

Prior to Dress Rehearsal

- Create database structure
- Build test database
- Create menu structures
- Create form structures
- Create reports
- Test menus, forms, and reports against test database
- Build operational database
- Verify operation data completeness and quality

After Dress Rehearsal

- Modify database structure and data as required
- Modify menus, forms, and reports as required
- Verify changes

Procedures

Prior to Dress Rehearsal

- Document procedures
- Run all procedures in dress rehearsal

After dress rehearsal, modify procedures as necessary

People

Prior to Dress Rehearsal

- Train personnel
- Test procedures and training in dress rehearsal
- After dress rehearsal, adjust personnel assignments as necessary

After dress rehearsal, adjust training as necessary

At the end of a year, Customer Support was able to handle 43 percent more calls than they had prior to having the new system. They were also able to reduce overtime to a manageable level. The best news was that only 2 people had left the department in that year, compared to 17 departures the year before. Charlie estimated that the labor savings alone were more than $225,000, and this did not include the savings in recruiting and training. All in all, the system was judged a tremendous success.

DISCUSSION QUESTIONS

1. Put on your skeptic's hat. Suppose you are an investor in Legacy Systems and question this system as a business investment. Was it really necessary? Weren't most of the benefits due to the manager's finally getting on top of the callbacks? Did the group really need the information system to do this? Shouldn't Charlie have made these changes without the $100,000 investment? Isn't that a lot of money to pay for a few reports about how late a callback is? Wouldn't a yellow pad of paper and a bunch of number 2 pencils have done just as well? List five critical and pointed questions you would ask Charlie about this investment at the annual shareholders' meeting. Substantiate these questions with opinions indicating that Charlie and Legacy made a poor investment.

2. Suppose you are Charlie, and, in advance of the annual shareholders' meeting, you have been told that a hostile investor is going to question the wisdom of the $100,000 investment in this system. (See question 1.) Prepare a written justification for this system for the CEO to read and use during the meeting, if necessary. In the justification, explain why the system was necessary, what its benefits are, what alternatives were considered, and so forth. Prepare notes to use to back up the CEO in case you are called on during the meeting.

3. Suppose Charlie asked you to build the project plan during the definition stage. List the tasks that need to be accomplished. For each task, estimate the person hours required. Make a schedule of the tasks.

4. List and describe the nature of procedures that should be developed for this system. Include user and operations procedures for both normal processing and failure recovery.

5. Chapter 10 mentioned the need for data administration of shared-data resources. In the case described here, no one on the development team paid attention to such issues. What problems are likely to occur due to this omission? What will happen when there is a need to store more data about customers? When Legacy decides to offer new forms of customer support? When the recovery process does not work? What should Charlie do about these issues?

6. The application programs for this system were developed by the vendor. From time to time, errors may be discovered or Customer Support may need to expand or alter the nature of the programs' processing. Should the same vendor be used for this? What are the advantages and disadvantages? Who owns the programs? Where are they physically located? What if the vendor physically controls the programs and refuses to let Charlie or anyone else have access to them? Suppose the vendor provides excellent support service for a number of years, so much so, that no one ever thinks about the location or ownership of the programs. The vendor, however, is acquired by another company that subsequently is forced into Chapter 11 bankruptcy. All the company's assets are frozen. What should Charlie do? In general, who should own the programs? Where should they be stored? Who should maintain them? What should the contract between Legacy and the vendor say about these issues?

PART IV

Enterprise Management Information Systems

PART IV CONSIDERS INFORMATION SYSTEMS that support enterprise-wide activities. Such systems typically integrate activities of several departments, facilitating the information flow from department to department. As enterprise information systems are assimilated into the organization, they may instigate change in underlying business processes and even in the nature of the business.

The structure of Part IV mirrors the structure of Parts II and III. Chapter 11 discusses the application of management information systems to enterprise functions and activities. It describes the ways in which such systems add value and benefit the enterprise. Chapter 12 describes the five components of enterprise information systems. It pays particular attention to the data and procedure components, since these are the components with which you, as a business professional, will be most involved.

Finally, Chapter 13 discusses the development of enterprise information systems. It reviews the five stages of the systems development process and shows the broad role of prototyping in that process. It also considers the role of computer-aided systems engineering in developing enterprise information systems. Normally, users are the consumers of others' services in developing enterprise information systems, so in Chapter 13, you should strive to learn what services you can expect and how to obtain them. Finally, Module C considers the experience of one enterprise in developing an enterprise information system.

11

Enterprise Information Systems: Applications and Goals

THIS CHAPTER INTRODUCES ENTERPRISE INFORMATION SYSTEMS. Of the hundreds of such systems, we will define and illustrate five fundamental types. One type, the localized application, consists of personal and workgroup information systems. Since these systems have been discussed in prior chapters, they will not be further described here.

The second type, the interdepartmental application, consists of systems that integrate departmental activities. Just as workgroup applications integrate the activities of many people, interdepartmental applications integrate the activities of many departments.

The remaining three types of enterprise systems offer the greatest potential benefit, but, unfortunately, they also require substantial, even radical, change in the enterprise processes, networks, and scope. These categories are relatively new, but, as you will learn, they are most likely to be the most successful types of enterprise systems in the future.

This chapter will conclude with a discussion of the ways in which enterprise information systems add value. We will use the same value-added model used in Chapters 5 and 8.

ENTERPRISE INFORMATION SYSTEMS

An **enterprise** is a system of people, equipment, material, data, policies, and procedures that provides a product or a service, often with the goal of making a profit. The term *enterprise* encompasses a broad range of organizations, including corporations, partnerships, sole proprietorships, governmental agencies, or nonprofit groups.

An enterprise has owners or sponsors who invest money in the organization with the expectation of future financial reward or some other benefit.[1] To protect their investments, the owners or sponsors select representatives as members of a board of directors. The owners and sponsors and the board appoint officers of the enterprise to manage its day-to-day affairs.

The application of MIS and related technology to the enterprise is a broad subject. Considering the variety of enterprises and the tremendous array of information systems technology that supports them, there are myriad possible applications. To bring order to this discussion, we will address applications in five categories, as shown in Figure 11-1. These categories were developed as part of a collaborative study between MIT's Sloan School of Management and 12 major enterprises.[2]

The categories are arranged on a two-dimensional axis showing potential benefit versus the degree of business transformation required to develop the category of application. **Localized applications** include personal and workgroup information systems. Since we considered these systems in prior chapters, we will not consider them further here.

Interdepartmental systems extend workgroup information systems to provide integrated support for departments across the enterprise—both integration of the technology platform and integration of the underlying business processes. At Elliot Bay Nurseries (first discussed in Chapter 4), an example of an interdepartmental system is an order-entry system that supports order processing through the sales, operations, and accounting departments.

Neither workgroup information systems nor interdepartmental information systems require radical changes to the business organization. When such systems are developed, there may be changes in business procedures, but such changes tend to be small and evolutionary. The sales and operations departments may, for example, exchange information in a different format using a different media, but the basic processes and organization of the enterprise remain the same.

---

1. The term *sponsor* is used for nonprofit and governmental agencies. It refers to people such as legislators or philanthropists who provide money for the enterprise.

2. Venkatraman, N., "IT-Induced Business Reconfiguration," in *The Corporation of the 1990s*, Michael S. Scott Morton, ed. New York: Oxford University Press, 1991, pp. 122–158.

Figure 11-1 Enterprise MIS Application Categories

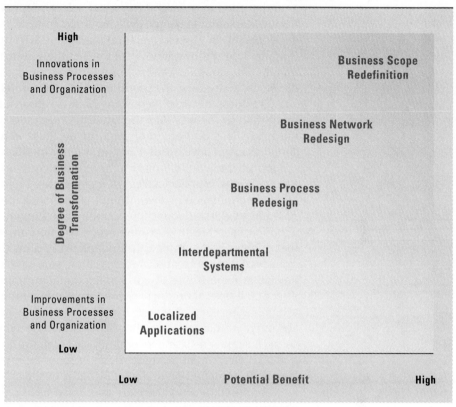

The remaining three categories in Figure 11-1 involve radical and revolutionary changes in business processes and organization. **Business process redesign** involves information systems that induce a fundamental change in the way the business conducts its internal processes.

To understand business process redesign, consider the process that Elliot Bay undertakes to select the plants, seeds, and garden equipment it will carry. Suppose that, with the current system, Product Marketing makes product selection decisions on its own and simply informs the rest of the enterprise on what products will be carried. This system at times creates problems for the other departments. For example, Product Marketing sometimes selects products that are difficult to package and ship. Also, it may select products that are difficult to grow, thus resulting in high levels of customer dissatisfaction and in many returns. Even Advertising has requirements; it needs certain products to be carried so as to create an attractive and exciting catalog. These requirements are often overlooked by Product Marketing.

An information system that induces business process redesign would involve a fundamental change in the product-selection process. For example, instead of having Marketing make the decision on its own, an information system could be developed to allow personnel from Marketing, Advertising, Sales, Operations, and Product Support to collaboratively select the product line. To do this, the group might use a group DSS to integrate the separate opinions into joint product line decisions. In this case, the product-selection process is radically changed.

Business network redesign refers to information systems that involve innovation in the way that the enterprise interacts with other enterprises in its business network. For example, with business network redesign, Elliot Bay's suppliers might develop information systems in which its employees directly enter orders into the supplier's order-entry system. Another example would be for Elliot Bay to give its suppliers access to its inventory information so that the supplier could determine, on its own, when to ship goods to Elliot Bay. Still more radical possibilities exist, as you will see later in this chapter.

The final category, **business scope redefinition**, refers to information systems that enable the enterprise to fundamentally alter the products and services it provides. Such information systems change the basic nature of the business. Elliot Bay might, for example, discover that its customer database has great value for the direct-mail sales of products beyond garden plants and supplies. Elliot Bay might expand its business to include the sales of clothing, holiday gifts and decorations, and other products. Or it might discover that other companies are willing to pay to use its customer lists, and, over time, the company might evolve into a data utility that sells direct-mail customer data. In these examples, the information system leads to the redefinition of the scope of the business.

As stated, we have already addressed localized information systems. This chapter addresses the four other categories of enterprise MIS applications. We begin with interdepartmental information systems.

INTERDEPARTMENTAL INFORMATION SYSTEMS

The products and services produced by an enterprise are seldom created by a single department acting alone. Instead, most enterprise action is the result of the coordinated activity of several different departments. Consider, for example, the purchasing of supplies. A department, say Engineering, is allocated a supply budget from Finance. When supplies are needed, Engineering orders those supplies from Purchasing. Purchasing verifies authority and funds availability with Accounting and issues a purchase order to a vendor. The Receiving department accepts the goods and delivers them to Engineering. Accounts Payable sends a payment to the

Figure 11-2 Using an Interdepartmental Information System

The purpose of an interdepartmental information system is to provide coordinated information to people in various positions so that they can deal consistently with customers and others.

vendor. Observe, in this process, that the activities of one department must be coordinated with those of other departments.

Interdepartmental information systems integrate the activities of different departments into a single business system that produces coordinated, appropriate responses to the enterprise's environment. The information system provides infrastructure so that the activity can be done faster, more cheaply, or more accurately, or in some other improved manner.

In producing a response, each department uses an information system to retrieve information about the prior actions of other departments. It also uses the information system to store information about the department's own actions for use by other departments. An interdepartmental information system is the ribbon that ties departments together so that they can produce a coordinated and appropriate response to the outside world.

An Interdepartmental Information System for Revenue Generation

To better understand interdepartmental systems, consider the information system that supports a typical revenue-generation process. Figure 11-3 shows a DFD of that process. Sales material is generated by Marketing and given to Sales. Sales are generated through solicitations of customers; orders are received. A sales report is sent to Marketing so that Marketing can judge the effectiveness of its marketing

Figure 11-3 DFD of Revenue-Generation Process

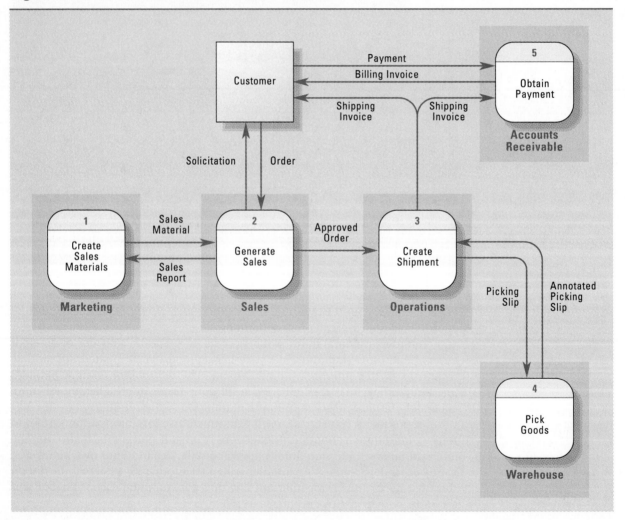

programs. Approved orders (Figure 11-4a) are sent to Operations, where the shipment is created. Goods are picked (Figure 11-4b) at the warehouse, and a shipping invoice is sent with the shipment to the customer. A billing invoice (Figure 11-4c) is subsequently sent to the customer by Accounts Receivable, and a payment is received.

Figure 11-4   Sample Report Forms for Order-Entry System
(a) Approved order. **(b)** Picking slip. **(c)** Billing invoice.

(a)

EB Electronic
Approved Order

Customer Number:	1	Sold to:	Video Discount City
Our Order Number:	4		2947 E. Riverside
Order Date: 2 June 94 Time: 11:33			Balboa, CA 94235
Customer PO number:	12399		
Sold by:	D. Johnston	Terms:	Net 30 discount (5%)

Item Number	Item Description	Quantity Ordered	Unit of Measure	Unit Price	Total Amount
100	13-inch Color TV	1	ea	$ 292.99	$ 292.99
200	Video Camera	1	ea	$ 985.05	$ 985.05
300	T90 Videotape	12	ea	$ 7.67	$ 92.04
			Subtotal		$ 1,370.08
			State Tax @ 7.5%		$ 102.76
			Freight		$ 13.62
			Order Total		$ 1,486.46

(b)

EB Electronic
Picking Slip for 2 June 1994

Picking Slip Number: 3		Page: 1	
Customer: Video Discount City		Customer PO Number: 12399	

Order Number	Item Number	Item Description	Number Ordered	Bin Number	Number Shipped
4	100	13-inch Color TV	1	1	
4	200	Video Camera	1	5	
4	300	T90 Videotape	12	10	

Figure 11-4   *(continued)*

(c)

**EB Electronic
Invoice**

Invoice Number:	2		Invoice date:	2 June 1994	Page: 1
Sold to:	Video Discount City		Terms:	Net 30	
Attention:	Robert Anderson		Your Order Number:	12399	
	2947 E. Riverside		Our Order Number:	4	
	Balboa, CA 94235				

Item Number	Item Description	Quantity Shipped	Unit of Measure	Unit Price	Total Amount
100	13-inch Color TV	1	ea	$ 292.99	$ 292.99
200	Video Camera	1	ea	$ 985.05	$ 985.05
300	T90 Videotape	12	ea	$ 7.67	$ 92.04
			Subtotal		$ 1,370.08
			State Tax @ 7.5%		$ 102.76
			Freight		$ 13.62
			Order Total		$ 1,486.46

Observe that the departments need to coordinate their activities. The warehouse needs to know what goods to pick; Accounts Receivable needs to know what has been shipped in order to generate a correct billing invoice. Realize, too, that the company is processing many orders, not just one. Each department must balance the needs of one order with the needs of all other orders in the system.

Figure 11-5 depicts the integrative function of the order-processing information system. This system connects all the departments involved in obtaining, recording, fulfilling, and billing an order. The shaded circle in this figure represents a system that integrates the activities of the various departments. This system is potentially composed of the five components: hardware, programs, data, procedures, and people.

In some cases, this circle represents a system that has all five components. In other cases, the circle represents people following procedures to manually process the system's data (e.g., hand-carrying manually prepared picking slips to the warehouse). The fact that a department is shown within the circle just means that the employees of the department have access to some (unspecified) form of the system's data.

Figure 11-5   Integration Provided by Interdepartmental Information Systems

With interdepartmental information systems, the customer receives consistent, coordinated responses from all departments.

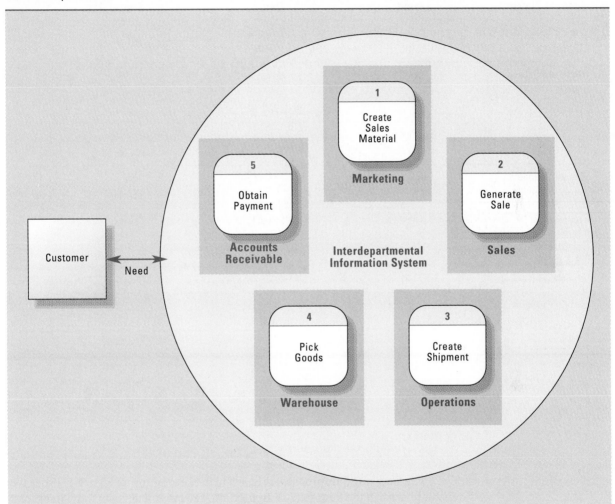

Need for Shared Data   To understand the ways in which departments depend on one another for data, consider Figure 11-6, which summarizes input, output, and stored data required by each process in Figure 11-3. As shown in the first row, the Create Sales Material process (in Marketing) receives a sales report and creates sales material as its output. In order to decide what materials are most effective, employees in this department need to examine not only the sales report but also records of past orders created by other processes (not shown).

Figure 11-6 Summary of Process Inputs, Outputs, and Stored Data

Process Name	Input	Output	Stored Data
Create Sales Material (Marketing)	Sales Report	Sales Material	Order
Generate Sale (Sales)	Sales Material	Solicitation	Customer Order Sales Call
	Order	Approved Order	Customer Payment
Create Shipment (Operations)	Approved Order	Picking Slip	Order Inventory
	Annotated Picking Slip	Shipping Invoice	Customer Order
Pick Goods (Warehouse)	Picking Slip	Annotated Picking Slip	Inventory Order
Obtain Payment (Accounts Receivable)	Shipping Invoice	Billing Invoice	Customer Order Payment
	Payment		Customer Order Payment

The Generate Sale process (in Sales) in the second row of Figure 11-6 has two major phases. In the first, the sales material is used to solicit customers. In order to determine which customers to solicit, the department consults past Customer, Order, and Sales Call data. In the second phase, once an order is received from a customer, the Generate Sale process consults past Customer and Payment data to determine whether or not the order can be approved. This data will have been created or modified by the Obtain Payment process.

There are also two phases of activity in the Create Shipment process (in Operations). In the first phase, the process receives an approved order and produces a picking slip. In the second phase, it receives the annotated picking slip and sends a shipping invoice (along with the shipment) to the customer. A copy of the shipping invoice is sent to Accounts Receivable.

To produce the picking slip, the Create Shipment process must have access to both the Order data and the Inventory data. Similarly, to produce the shipping invoice, the Create Shipment process needs access to Customer and Order data.

Finally, the Obtain Payment process receives a copy of the shipping invoice so that it knows what has been shipped. It accesses Customer, Order, and Payment data to create a billing invoice. Finally, a customer payment is received, and Customer, Order, and Payment data is updated.

In these processes, departments create data for their own use and also for the use of other departments. By storing data, the information system provides the infrastructure for departments to conduct a consistent and coordinated series of actions with the customer.

Each process in this table can have its own separate repository of data and its own information system to process that data. Such an arrangement was the rule prior to the advent of computer-based systems, when companies processed six- and eight-part order forms (forms with five or seven carbon copies attached) and each department kept its own file copy of the form (e.g., the pink copy, the goldenrod copy, etc.). In fact, the very need for **multipart forms** indicates that departments need to share the same data.

Different Views of Shared Data   While the users in this process share data, they do not always have the same view of this shared data. Figure 11-7 shows examples of different views of Customer data for the Generate Sale (Sales), Create Shipment (Operations), and Obtain Payment (Accounts Receivable) processes. Sales cares most about the name of the person to call. Operations is most concerned with the shipping address and other shipping data. Accounts Receivable is most concerned with billing data. A list of data views is shown in Figure 11-8.

The need for different views of the same data is typical in enterprise systems. It also makes their development difficult. For example, an enterprise database must contain data sufficient to support all the users' views. The applications must be able to access this data and to materialize it in the format needed by the users. This requires considerable forethought in designing the database and its applications.

Characteristics of Interdepartmental Information Systems

Interdepartmental information systems must be standardized. To produce a consistent response, every similar transaction must be processed similarly. Otherwise, havoc results.

Because interdepartmental information systems serve so many different people, changes must be carefully controlled. One of the many users of a given report, for example, cannot unilaterally decide to change the format of that report—

Figure 11-7   Three Views of Customer Data
(a) Sales view of customer. **(b)** Operations view of customer. **(c)** Accounts Receivable view of customer.

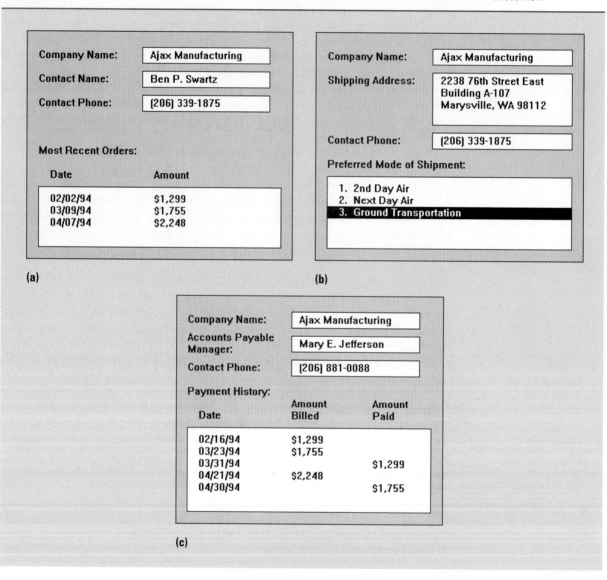

Figure 11-8   Various Views of Data

Department	Views
Sales	Orders by salesperson
	Orders by region
	Orders by customer
Operations	Orders processed
	Orders to be processed
	Back orders
Warehouse	Picking slips
	Item locations
	Item use
Accounting	Receivables by customer
	Receivables by date
	Invoice

that could cause havoc with the other users. Similarly, the order of activities in systems processing cannot be changed without careful consideration, coordination, and management. All departments that employ the system depend on a certain specified order of action; changes to this order can also cause havoc.

Since interdepartmental information systems must be standardized and changes to them carefully controlled, there is a greater need for systems management. Interdepartmental information systems require a person or a group to maintain them and to manage change. As we move from personal to workgroup to interdepartmental information systems, the size of the system increases, thus giving rise to the need for management.

Finally, an interdepartmental information system supports several or even many different applications. The workgroup information system at Legacy Systems (discussed in Module B) facilitated only Customer Support activity. In that system, there is one kind of data (Customer Call data) and one kind of process (Customer Support). Compare this system to the revenue-generation information system in Figure 11-3. Order processing supports (or at least dramatically impacts) order processing, shipping, warehousing, manufacturing, and accounting applications. The data within an interdepartmental information system is heterogeneous; many different types of data must be stored for many different purposes. The characteristics of interdepartmental information systems are listed in Figure 11-9.

Figure 11-9 Characteristics of Enterprise IS

- ■ Standardized
- ■ Carefully controlled changes
- ■ Needs systems management
- ■ Supports many users and applications
- ■ Has heterogeneous data

Comparison of Workgroup and Interdepartmental Information Systems

Some students find it difficult to distinguish between workgroup information systems and interdepartmental information systems. Since you will take a different posture in developing these two types of systems, you must be able to make this distinction. Figure 11-10 lists important distinguishing characteristics.

First, with a workgroup information system, the users know and work with each other. They share a community; incompetency or irresponsible actions by one member is quickly evident to all. Consequently, there is considerable group pressure to behave responsibly toward the system. With interdepartmental information systems, however, most users are strangers to one another. Mistakes that cause havoc to other users are not directly evident. It happens to "the other people" who work in a different group. There is less group pressure for responsibility to the system overall. In fact, no group of people is considered the "system overall."

Second, a typical workgroup information system has, at most, several dozen users, whereas an interdepartmental information system may have several hundred or even thousands of users. Therefore, change is much easier to accomplish in a workgroup system. The workgroup can accomplish in one or two group meetings the same change that requires months of communication, publication, and training for the interdepartmental system. Consider the difficulty in changing an airline reservations system as compared to the difficulty of changing Legacy System's Customer Support application.

Another difference between the two types of information systems is the amount of data to be processed. A workgroup system may process up to about a billion bytes of data, whereas an interdepartmental system may process several hundred billion bytes of data. With proper data, tools, and procedures, a workgroup database can be totally recovered, from scratch, within an hour or two. An interdepartmental database may require days or weeks to recover from catastrophic

Figure 11-10 Differences Between Workgroup IS and Enterprise IS

Workgroup	Enterprise
Users know and work with one another	Users strangers to one another
At most, several dozen users	Several hundreds or even thousands of users
At most, 1 billion bytes of data	Several hundred billion bytes of data or more
A few entities	Dozens of entities
One or a few applications	Many different applications
Peripheral system; subfunction of company	Central business function

failure, or it may never be recovered completely. The structure of a workgroup database can be drastically altered and the data reloaded in a weekend. Changes to the structure of an interdepartmental database may require months of planning and weeks of piecemeal alteration to be completed.

Interdepartmental systems require not only more data but also more complicated data. With a workgroup database, typically only a few types of entities are involved. For the Legacy Customer Support database, for example, there were customers, support representatives, and call entities. For an interdepartmental database, there are usually dozens of different entities and dozens of different views of each entity.

Another difference concerns the number of applications. A workgroup system usually has one or a few applications. Legacy's Customer Support was concerned only with the management of customer calls. Many different business functions are involved in an interdepartmental system. Order processing, for example, is concerned with the management of orders, inventories, manufacturing, shipments, and accounts receivable.

Finally, a workgroup information system typically involves one subfunction of the company, for example, customer support, product marketing planning, or engineering design. When a dysfunction or failure occurs in a workgroup information system, that subfunction is dramatically impacted, but the rest of the organization carries on. An interdepartmental information system, on the other hand, by definition, involves a major function of the company. Revenue generation, for example, is a central and critical function. Failures in interdepartmental information systems paralyze the entire organization and must be infrequent and brief.

INTERDEPARTMENTAL INFORMATION SYSTEMS AND ENTERPRISE FUNCTIONS

Figure 11-3 illustrates how a single enterprise information system can integrate the processing of many departments to create a coordinated response for revenue generation. A similar figure can be developed for all the basic activities of an enterprise.

Although every enterprise is unique, the activities of most enterprises follow the set of generic functions listed in Figure 11-11. While the particulars of these functions vary from enterprise to enterprise, every enterprise has them in one form or another. The preceding section discussed an interdepartmental information system to support the **revenue-generation function**. Other types of interdepartmental systems support purchasing, personnel and payroll, asset control, manufacturing, planning and budgeting, and accounting functions. This section describes the general format of three of these functions: purchasing, personnel and payroll, and manufacturing.

The Purchasing Function

The **purchasing function** consists of those activities necessary to acquire goods and services from outside vendors, to account for the expenses, and to make payments on a timely and cost-effective basis. Figure 11-12 depicts the principal processes and dataflows for the purchasing function. This figure addresses only the purchasing of goods. Purchasing of services is somewhat different and is discussed later.

Figure 11-11   Generic Functions of an Enterprise

- Revenue generation
- Purchasing
- Personnel and payroll
- Asset control
- Product development and planning
- Manufacturing
- Accounting

Figure 11-12 Processes and Dataflows for the Purchasing Function

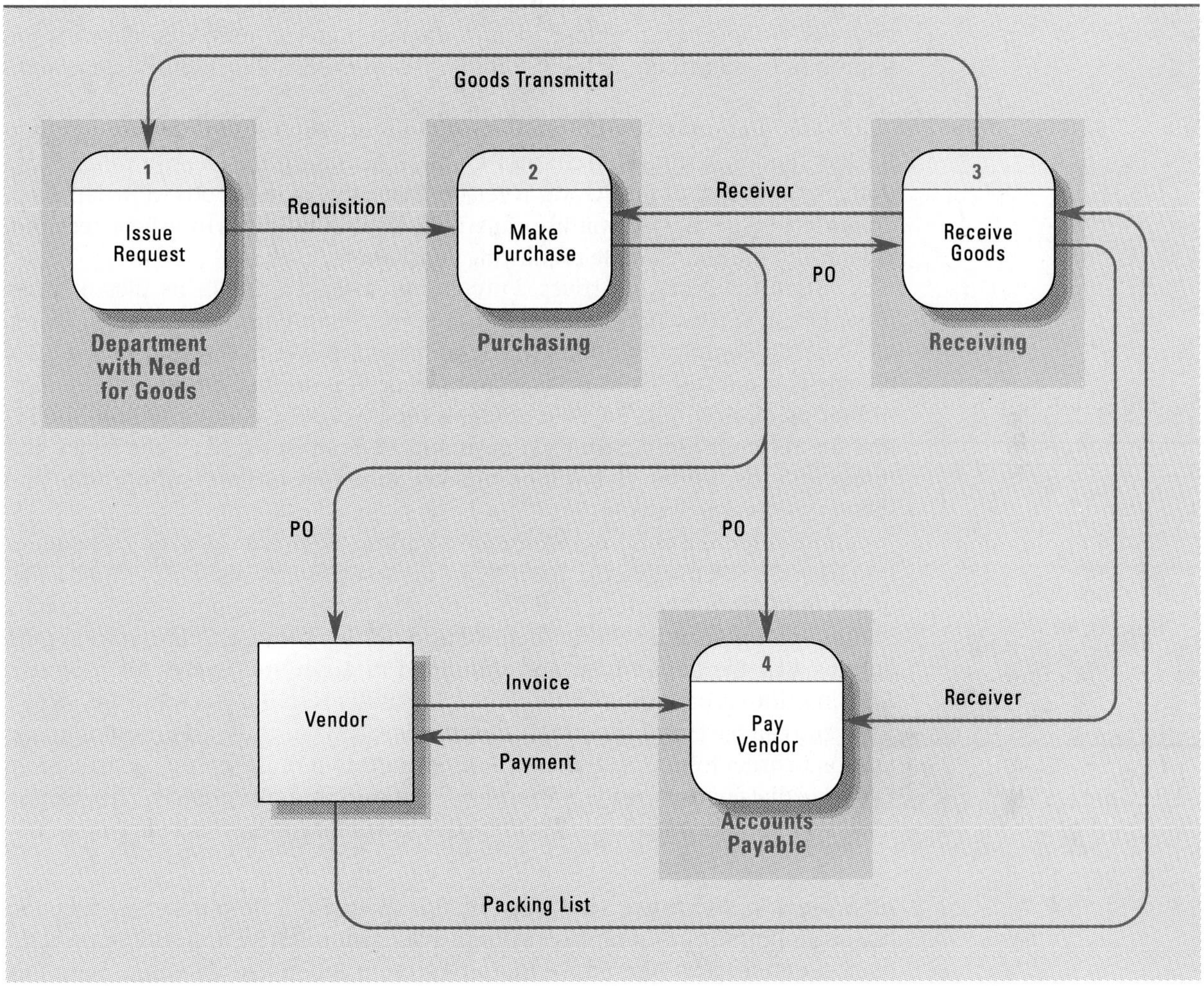

Purchasing Activity Flow A department issues a request for supplies, raw materials, finished goods, or some other good in the form of a requisition. To make the purchase, Purchasing validates the requisition, checking for necessary authorization signatures, valid expense codes, and the like. Purchasing then generates a purchase order (PO) and sends it to a vendor. A copy of the PO is sent to the Receive Goods process in Receiving and to the Pay Vendor process in Accounts Payable.

In response to the PO, the vendor creates a shipment that includes a packing list. The shipment with packing list is accepted by Receiving. Receiving compares the packing slip to the PO and to the goods received and creates a document called a receiver that associates the shipment with its PO and indicates what goods were received. If there is a problem such as damaged goods, Receiving contacts the appropriate department or the vendor and takes exception actions (not shown in Figure 11-12).

Once the goods have been accepted, the receiver is sent to Purchasing and to the Pay Vendor process in Accounts Payable. If necessary, the receiver will indicate that only a portion of the PO was received, that some of the goods were damaged, and so forth. A goods transmittal form, which shows what goods have been received, is sent with the goods to the requesting department.

When the receiver arrives, Purchasing closes the PO in its files or takes other action (follow-up on goods not received, etc.). When the receiver arrives in Accounts Payable, that department adds the receiver to the copy of the PO it already has and stores this package until it receives an invoice from the vendor. At that point, Accounts Payable validates the invoice by comparing it to the PO and the receiver and schedules a payment. Depending on payment policy and terms with the vendor, this will occur some time between the current time and the next several months.

In the case of services, the process varies somewhat. In most companies, Purchasing is still involved in that a department sends a requisition to Purchasing, which then sends a contract to the vendor. The vendor provides services directly to the department and submits an invoice to the department. This invoice is then approved by the department and submitted to Accounts Payable for payment. Also, in some cases, a copy of the vendor's contract is sent to Accounts Payable.

You can see from Figure 11-12 how the departments must act in a coordinated fashion in order to make purchases. Each department must serve a particular role to ensure that goods are ordered, received, and paid for appropriately. The purpose of an information system is to facilitate this interdepartmental activity.

Information Systems to Support Purchasing The purchasing function can be supported by a number of different information system designs. Figure 11-13 depicts one feasible alternative that involves an integrated database. With this system, Purchasing, Receiving, and Accounts Payable store their data in a common database, PO Data, which obviates the need for open PO files and open payables files. POs are stored in the database by Purchasing. When Receiving accepts a shipment, it consults the database to extract the PO that generated the shipment. It then creates a receiver in the database and modifies the PO to show that the goods have been received. Unless there is a problem, Receiving need not notify either Purchasing or Accounts Payable of the arrival of the goods.

When Purchasing needs to know what POs are open, it simply examines the database. Further, when Purchasing needs to know vendor lead times, it computes them by subtracting PO dates from receiver dates.

Additionally, Accounts Payable need not create an open payables file. The presence of a PO without a receiver in the database signifies that a payable is open.

Figure 11-13 Purchasing System Supported by an Integrated Database

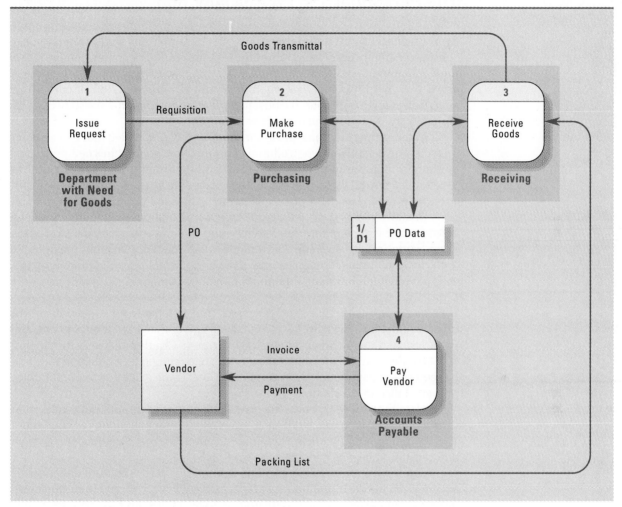

(Also, the presence of a PO without a receiver indicates a need to encumber funds, even though the payables file is not open.) When the vendor invoice arrives, Purchasing needs only to consult the database to validate the invoice. It then schedules the payment.

Observe how the information system provides infrastructure for the interdepartmental activities. It reduces the documents in the organization and allows departments to more quickly determine the status of particular purchases. It also creates information that can be used to better manage the purchasing process, through the process of informating.

The Personnel and Payroll Function

Every business has a **personnel and payroll function** to hire, pay, account for, and administer employees. The nature of the function varies, depending on the size of the company, the industry, the nature and culture of the company, the ratio of salaried to hourly personnel, whether or not the organization is part of the government (or does substantial business with the government), the state in which the company operates, and other factors.

In many organizations, personnel and payroll are divided into two separate systems. The personnel system administers personnel policy, hires new personnel, evaluates employee performance, creates compensation plans, and so on. The function of payroll is to pay employees according to their contracts with the enterprise and the work they have performed. This section considers only payroll.

In many businesses, several different payroll systems exist, perhaps one for hourly employees, one for professionals, and one for organizational executives. Large, substantially diversified companies may maintain separate payrolls for each division. Small companies may have an informal personnel function, and their payroll functions may be performed by their banks.

Payroll Activity Flow   The processes and dataflows for a generic payroll function are shown in Figure 11-14. To collect pay, employees submit work records to the Manage Payroll process in their department. Hourly employees turn in time sheets or time cards. Salaried employees will need not do this, although they may be required to complete time sheets so that their time can be accounted for and properly billed to the client.

The department approves the time sheet and possibly adds data concerning vacation time, sick leave, and time off, thereby creating an approved time sheet. The Pay Employee process in Payroll then computes pay, accounts for sick leave and vacation time, and generates the paycheck.

Enterprises are required to make deductions from employee pay for taxes and FICA payments. In addition, most enterprises allow employees to automatically deduct other payments such as insurance, investments, and so forth, from their checks. Personnel manages these deductions.

Payroll pays external agencies on behalf of the employee, usually sending one check to each agency accompanied by a report detailing the amounts to be applied to the accounts of all employees. Often these reports are sent in computer-sensible form such as magnetic tape so that the receiving agency need not rekey hundreds or thousands of employee contributions. The external agencies periodically send reports to the enterprise and to the employees, detailing the employee's contributions, which provides a control on the accuracy of Payroll's work.

Figure 11-14 Processes and Dataflows for Payroll Function

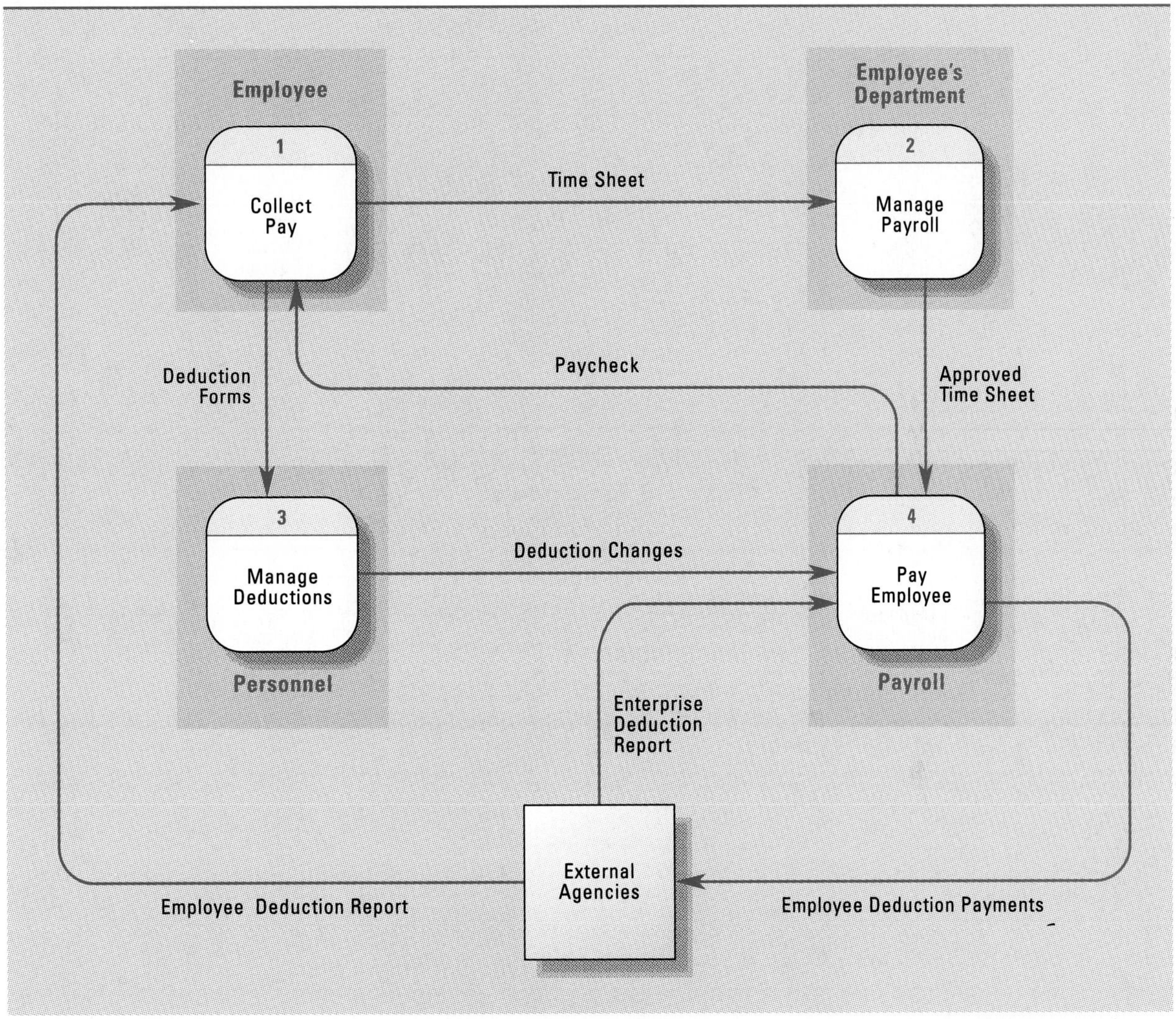

At the time they are hired, employees fill out deduction forms, which are sent to Payroll. Additional or changed forms can be sent by the employee to Payroll at any time.

Information Systems to Support Payroll Figure 11-15 illustrates the interdepartmental sharing of payroll data. In this figure, several departments share

Figure 11-15 Payroll with Employee Database

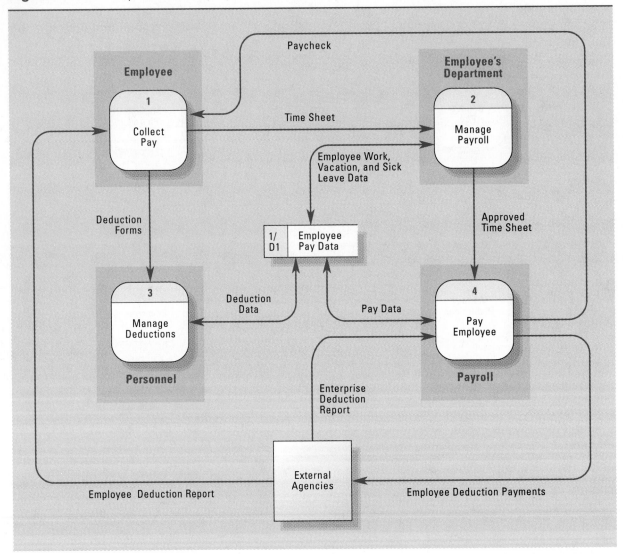

a centralized store of employee data. The employee's department uses this data store, in part, to determine the amount of vacation days, sick leave, and other benefits due the employee. The Manage Deductions process stores deduction data in this data store, and the Pay Employee process obtains pay data for computing the employee's paycheck from this data store. Since there are many commercial packages for computing payroll, it seldom makes sense for an organization to develop its own system.

Operating a payroll system can be a great hassle. Since the system processes employee finances, it is always possible that an employee will make unauthorized changes to his or her pay rates, accrued retirement, and so forth. The system must be carefully controlled to prevent such unauthorized changes. (We will discuss controls in the next chapter.) Consider the problems of a computer operator processing his or her own paycheck.

Most companies prefer that salaries and pay rates be kept confidential. If the company produces its own payroll, the system users and operators will be privy to this sensitive data. As a general rule, the more people who know something, the greater the chance that it will become public knowledge. Thus, confidentiality is difficult to maintain. Consider the problems of the computer operator processing her boss's paycheck.

Because of these difficulties, many companies, even substantially large ones, have their payroll processed by an outside vendor. Control is improved because employees are not processing their own checks. Confidentiality is maintained because the vendor's employees do not normally know the company's employees.

Often, too, economies of scale can be gained by having payroll processed by a specialized vendor. That vendor knows all the rules and regulations for federal and state tax reporting, for example, and can ensure that the company files the appropriate reports on time. Similarly, a specialized vendor maintains professional contacts with local medical insurance companies, financial institutions, and so forth. Unless you work for a very large company, it makes sense for your payroll to be processed out of house.

The Manufacturing Function

The **manufacturing function** is a broad and complicated subject. Obviously, the process used to manufacture, say, toothpicks differs substantially from that of building computers, which differs substantially from building jet engines. Further, many activities are involved in manufacturing, including inventory management, machine scheduling, labor management, robotics and factory automation, quality control, and other subjects. This section just touches on the issues that consider the role of information systems in manufacturing.

Manufacturing Activity Flow Figure 11-16 summarizes the manufacturing process from a very high-level and generic view. In this figure, processes that are part of the Manufacturing department are within the light area. Other processes reside in other departments, as labeled in the diagram.

Engineering designs products and sends product specifications to the Schedule Production process. Marketing analyzes the product line, the competition,

Figure 11-16 Processes and Dataflows for Manufacturing

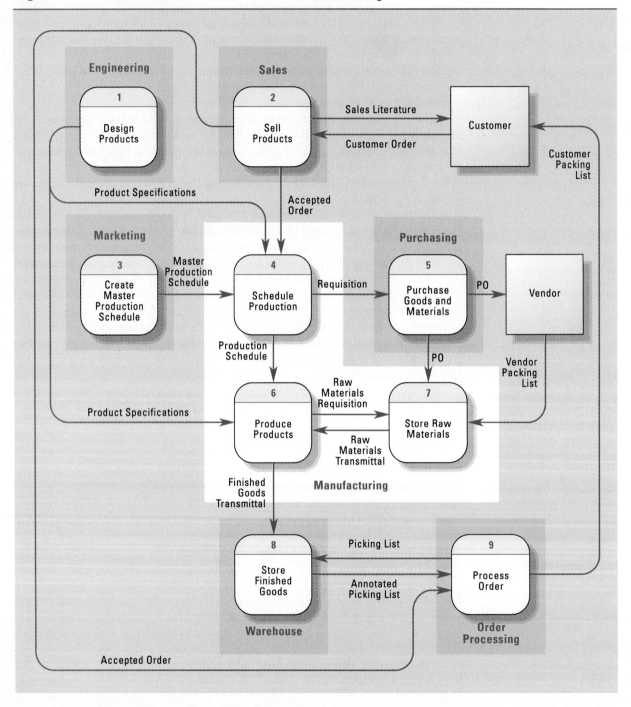

the economy, and other factors and creates a master production schedule that sets outs the types of products to be sold and the amounts and approximate dates of expected sales. The Schedule Production process uses this document to plan production, including the production facilities required, inventory levels needed, and necessary labor.

To determine raw material requirements, the Schedule Production process uses a bill of materials or a list of material components for each product. This list is either provided by Engineering as part of product specifications or produced by the Schedule Production process. Raw materials cannot be obtained instantaneously; delay between the time they are ordered and the time they are received is called the **lead time**. Therefore, the Schedule Production process must order raw materials in advance of the need.

Sales sells products to customers. Accepted orders are input to the Schedule Production process which integrates the arrival of accepted orders with the expectations of sales in the master production schedule. In concert with Marketing, the Schedule Production process modifies the production schedule if customer demand seems significantly different from that which has been planned.

If the order requires custom production, the Schedule Production process places the order on the production schedule. Companies vary in the ratio of stock to custom production. In some companies, only orders for stock items are accepted; in others, all items are custom manufactured, and in still others, a mixture of stock and custom production is supported.

The production process uses the product specifications from Engineering to manufacture goods according to the production schedule. Raw materials are removed from inventory, the goods are manufactured, and finished goods are placed in the warehouse. In companies that manufacture their own components, data about the manufactured components is stored by the Store Raw Materials process (not shown).

Observe in Figure 11-16 how the manufacturing process touches the other processes we have discussed. The purchase of goods and materials is part of the purchasing process, and sales, storage of finished goods, and processing of orders are part of the revenue-generation process. This is typical. Enterprise systems are highly integrated in this way; no process stands alone, but rather each sends and receives input from one another.

Figure 11-16 is a high-level abstraction of a complicated process. In a large manufacturer, many different sites are involved, with many different production lines. Hundreds of products and subassemblies are brought together. It may require years for any single person to understand the entire production process. In some companies, it is possible that no single individual understands the entire production process.

Information Systems to Support Manufacturing   A number of important information systems support manufacturing. For example, **manufacturing resource planning** (MRP II) facilitates the purchasing of raw materials and

Figure 11-17 Shop-Floor Control
MRP II and JIT provide different approaches to materials inventories and the handling
of work in progress on the shop floor.

automates production scheduling and shop-floor control. MRP II is used to process products in large batches. When each batch is finished, it is moved along to the next production station. MRP II is better suited to the production of discrete products like cars and computers than to the continuous processing of bulk products used in petroleum refineries and chemical processing plants.

Alternatively, the **just in time (JIT)** system moves products in small batches from station to station as soon as they are ready. Materials arrive "just in time" from suppliers, reducing inventory holding costs. A JIT system requires nearly perfect cooperation from suppliers to pace deliveries to the fluctuating demands of manufacturing processes. An important advantage of JIT manufacturing is that it meets customers' needs for very reliable deliveries on rapidly fluctuating schedules. Today, most MRP II systems include resources to support JIT.

In **computer-aided design/computer-aided manufacturing (CAD/CAM)**, another information system used in production, designs from engineering are transformed by an information system into **numerical control** instructions for machines and robots. Thus, a design can be transformed from a drawing into commands to direct a drill press to make certain holes in certain locations or to direct a saw to cut material in certain ways. Robots can be directed in a similar way.

Finally, some information systems facilitate optimized production scheduling. There may be dozens or hundreds of different ways of scheduling the production of certain quantities of certain goods within a specified time frame. Some schedules are better than others in that they require fewer machine changes and tool setups. Information systems have been developed to compute the best or, at least, a good schedule for producing the required items.

All of these systems address individual components of the process in Figure 11-16. There are benefits of integrating these systems, just as there are benefits of integration in other business areas. **Computer-integrated manufacturing (CIM)** attempts to bring together the disparate manufacturing information systems, including MRP, JIT, CAD/CAM, and production scheduling, into a single system. CIM systems are under development now and probably will come into widespread use during your career.

BUSINESS PROCESS REDESIGN

Both localized and interdepartmental systems involve small, evolutionary changes in the underlying business processes. They exist primarily to support the organization and the processes already in place. Such systems help businesses do what they are already doing more efficiently. It is becoming increasingly apparent that this is often not the best way to apply such technology.

As summarized in Figure 11-1, greater benefit can accrue to organizations that are willing to make revolutionary changes in their organizations and processes. Information systems and technology improve communication and coordination and can serve as an infrastructure to support collaborative and concurrent business operations that were not possible in the past:

> Currently, the design of business processes is based on a set of principles of organization developed to exploit the capabilities offered by the Industrial Revolution. Concepts such as centralization versus decentralization, span of control, line versus staff, and balancing authority versus responsibility, as well as mechanisms for coordination and control, are derived from this general set of principles. Although these are generally valid even today, it appears that the IT (information technology) revolution could significantly alter some of these principles—thus rendering some modes of organizing relatively inefficient....
>
> In the few selected cases where we have observed business process redesign, a common feature is an unmistakable recognition that revolutionary changes in the design of organizational processes are necessary to best exploit the emerging technological capabilities.[3]

---

3. Venkatraman, "IT-Induced Business Reconfiguration," p. 138.

To better understand this phenomenon, consider the product development process at Legacy Systems.

Legacy Systems' Product Development

Legacy Systems develops and sells microcomputer software applications, including spreadsheet, DBMS, and DTP. At one time, when Legacy Systems was organized according to the chart shown in Figure 11-18, products were developed using the process shown in Figure 11-19. With this process, the characteristics of a new product (or a major new release) were developed by Marketing and given to Development, which then built the product according to the specifications provided by Marketing. The product was tested by Quality Assurance, and, after bugs were removed, the product was sold by Sales. Finally, Customer Support provided customers with advice and assistance on the product.

Legacy had a number of problems with this business process. For one, only the product manager (in Marketing) took overall responsibility for the product. The allegiance of the other employees was to the department in which they worked. Software engineers, for example, identified with other engineers in Development. Their allegiance was to their group and to technology; they did not take ownership for the product.

Another problem concerned the serial nature of the development process. The needs of the customers were best known by Customer Support, but it was the last department in the development process; by the time Customer Support provided input, it was too late. By then, the product had been sold and shipped to thousands of customers. Customer Support blamed Sales for overselling the product, Sales blamed Development, and Development blamed Marketing for specifying a product that could not be developed in the first place.

Figure 11-18 Traditional Organization for Legacy Systems

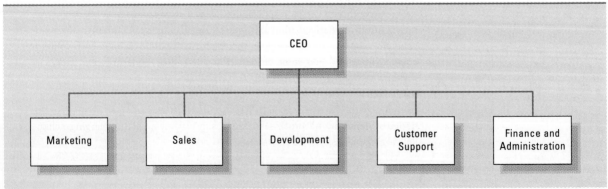

Figure 11-19 Sequential Product Development at Legacy Systems

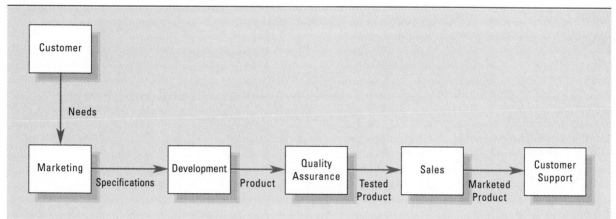

Because of these problems, Legacy Systems radically redesigned its development process. It changed its organizational structure to the product-oriented one shown in Figure 11-20. Simultaneously, it changed the development process to be more concurrent, as shown in Figure 11-21.

With the new organization process, all employees, regardless of their specialties, identified with their assigned product. They worked as a team to develop the specifications, to build the product and its documentation, and to support the customers. Marketing and development personnel were required to spend time in Customer Support on a regular basis and became far more aware of the customers' needs.

To make this radical change, Legacy relied heavily on information systems and technology. Legacy has an enterprise E-mail system through which anyone in the firm can communicate with anyone else. The most junior Customer Support representative can readily send messages to the product manager. Further, each product division has developed a number of interdepartmental systems that support the development of its particular product. This enables each product line to operate as a small company within the broader context of Legacy Systems.

When Legacy instituted this radical change, there were a number of problems. For one, some management jobs were eliminated. The duties and authorities of some people were changed, and not everyone was happy with their new circumstances. Some people, in fact, openly fought the change. Finally, the revised organization required people to view their jobs differently. While most people appreciated the newly attained accountability for their product, some did not. A number of employees left the firm as a result.

Overall, however, the change was exceedingly successful. Far higher quality products are being produced that better meet the customers' needs. Further, when problems do develop, the staff responds more quickly and more consistently.

Figure 11-20   Product-Oriented Organization for Legacy Systems

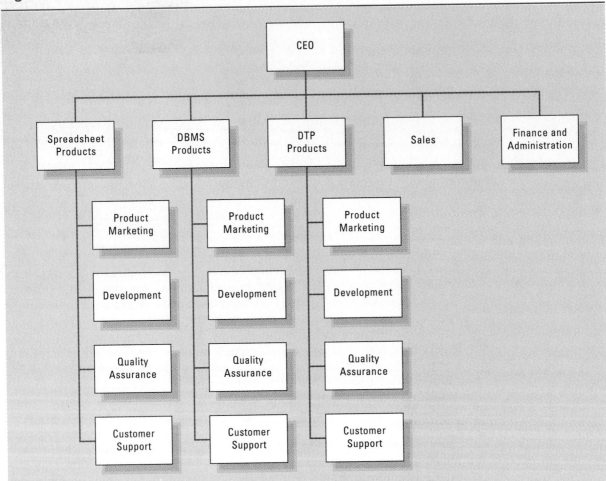

Organizational Consequences of Process Redesign

As you can see from the experience of Legacy Systems, the nature of information systems development is different when organizations engage in business process redesign. Instead of taking the existing organization and business processes as requirements and constraints, the developers consider the organization and its processes to be part of the system to be designed. Rather than automating processes

Figure 11-21 Concurrent Product Development at Legacy Systems

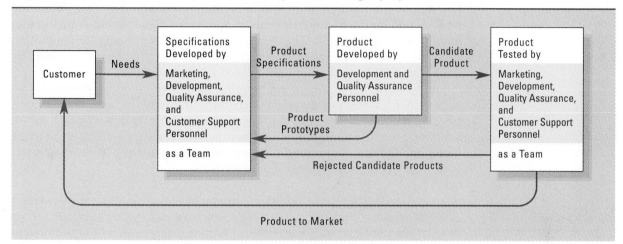

because they exist, the developers strive to improve business processes in conjunction with the systems development. According to an article in the *New York Times*, "The most savvy technology managers now speak of re-engineering company operations, not just computerizing antiquated processes."[4]

Business process redesign causes a number of organizational changes.

Reduced Need for Management and Staff   Enterprise information systems can reduce the need for management and staff personnel. For one, communications applications can increase the manager's span of control and reduce the levels of management required. According to Peter Drucker, when an organization focuses on new roles for information, the organizational structure changes:

> Almost immediately, it becomes clear that both the number of management levels and the number of managers can be sharply cut. It turns out that whole layers of management neither make decisions nor lead. Instead, their main, if not their only, function is to serve as "relays"—human boosters for the faint, unfocused signals that pass for communication in the traditional preinformation organization.[5]

Thus, organizations in which business processes have been redesigned to take the fullest advantage of technology tend to be flatter. They have fewer levels of management, and managers have greater spans of control.

4. Rifkin, Glenn, "The Rise, and Often Fall, of Computer Managers," *New York Times*, May 14, 1991, p. C7.

5. Drucker, Peter F., *The New Realities*. New York: Harper & Row, 1989, p. 209.

This reduction in personnel requirements extends beyond managers, however. When business processes are redesigned, technology can reduce the need for all types of staff personnel. Examples are document-processing information systems that reduce the need for filing clerks; presentation application products that eliminate the need for graphic artists; and bibliographic data on CD-ROM that reduces requirements for reference librarians.

Thus, part of the savings and benefit from business process redesign is that large numbers of staff jobs become unnecessary. In Drucker's words, "Information-based organizations need central operating work such as legal counsel, public relations, human resources, and labor relations as much as ever. But the need for service staffs—that is, for people without operating responsibilities who advise, counsel, or coordinate—shrinks drastically."[6]

Increased Concurrency Another consequence of business process redesign is the possibility of greater concurrency. When Legacy Systems switched to its product-oriented structure, it was able to include people with more specialties in developing product specifications. In this way, the product team could benefit, early in the development process, from the knowledge and experience of personnel from Sales, Engineering, and Customer Support. The team worked *concurrently*.

In many cases, the ability to work concurrently is brought about solely by the use of new information technology. For example, in the publishing industry, concurrent DTP enables writers, editors, and graphic designers to work side by side in heretofore impossible ways:

> Traditional publishing took so long that layouts could only emerge as series of iterations—proofs…. The new tools allow editors and designers to truly collaborate…. Two designers can work together, or a designer and an editor can sit down and start pushing things around on the screen until they're happy. Sometimes, against all precedent, you will see the chief editor sitting at the keyboard adjusting a layout with the startled designer looking on…. Magazines are a team endeavor.[7]

In other cases, concurrent activity is the result of organizational, contractual, and technological change. In the building trades, concurrent engineering has been used to design, engineer, and build better, safer, and cheaper buildings. Bringing the perspectives of several disciplines together early in the process increases the quality of design and construction decisions. Doing so, however, requires not only changes in information systems support and organizational structure, but also changes in the contractual arrangements among the companies.

---

6. *Ibid.*, p. 210.

7. Black, Roger, *Roger Black's Desktop Design Power*. New York: Bantam, 1991, p. 203.

Organizational Resistance to Process Redesign

Business process redesign can involve radical changes in organizational structure, personnel responsibilities, reporting relationships, and the like. Such changes are seldom accomplished gracefully; often they are painful: "People look at glitzy examples of technology implementation, and they overlook how complex it is to drive these processes through."[8]

Consider, for example, some of the problems Legacy Systems faced when changing to its product-oriented organization. Traditionally, all the software engineers reported to the VP of Development. With the change, those engineers reported to the business unit manager of their assigned product line. Prior to the change, the VP of Development had 49 software engineers reporting to him. After the change, there were 7. Further, these 7 people were given specialized tasks to develop tools and investigate emerging technology. The VP of Development lost control over the development of Legacy's bread and butter products. He was taken out of the mainstream of Legacy's business and, ultimately, left the company.

Similar comments pertain to other functional managers. The Customer Support group was broken up; and all the support representatives were assigned to a product team and began reporting to the team's business unit manager. The manager of Customer Support had no employees left to supervise and was asked to manage one of the three teams. The number of personnel he directly supervised fell from 55 to 17.

As you can imagine, these changes were resisted. In fact, if the CEO had not taken a strong leadership role in forcing these changes, the changes never would have occurred. Legacy had been locked in what one engineer called "the embrace of the dead": The managers who had the power to make the change were the very managers who would suffer the brunt of the consequences. These managers were reluctant, to say the least, and predicted dire consequences for the future of the company. The CEO kept on track and forced the changes through.

In the final analysis, Legacy was able to produce higher-quality products for less money. Customer satisfaction rose. Employees who had far greater responsibility and accountability to a product found their jobs far more rewarding.

As systems developers become involved in business process redesign, they become increasingly involved in the design and in the dramatic changes. Considerable work has been done on this subject in the discipline of organizational behavior. In fact, in many ways, systems development at the enterprise level is merging with that discipline, and systems development teams often involve both

---

8. McFarlan, F. Warren, as quoted in Rifkin, "The Rise, and Often Fall, of Computer Managers," p. C7. See footnote 4.

Figure 11-22 Consequences of Business Process Redesign

■ Fewer management levels
(Drucker's relay managers eliminated)

■ Reduced need for staff
(Librarians, research assistants, graphic artists)

■ Higher degree of concurrency
(engineering, product management)

■ Radical and revolutionary redesign of processes

technologists and organizational behaviorists. The consequences of business process redesign are summarized in Figure 11-22.

BUSINESS NETWORK REDESIGN

Business network redesign refers to the use of information systems to enable enterprises to interact more productively. The MIT study identified the four types of network redesign listed in Figure 11-23.[9] These alternatives are listed in increasing order of enterprise coupling. We now consider each in turn.

Electronic Data Interchange

The simplest way organizations can use information systems to redesign their interrelationships is to define **electronic data interchange** (EDI) standards. With such standards, the enterprises can transmit data to and from each other without human intervention.

A well-known example of EDI involves the Internal Revenue Service (IRS). The IRS defined a data interchange standard so that both individuals and businesses

---

9. Venkatraman, "IT-Induced Business Reconfiguration," p. 143.

Figure 11-23 Alternatives for Business Network Redesign

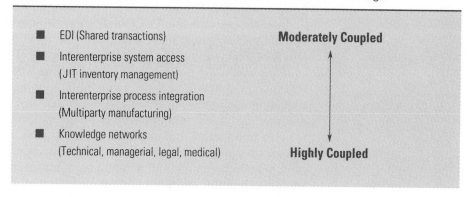

can file their taxes electronically, which saves the taxpayer time and reduces IRS paperwork processing and data entry.

To develop this system, the IRS first needed to define and publish the data interchange standard. Then vendors of tax preparation programs could add features and functions to their products to produce tax returns in this standard format.

The banking industry was an early adopter of EDI standards. Banks agreed on standard formats of banking transactions so that they could exchange data in computer-sensible format. This sped the processing of bank transfers and other activities. Automated teller machines (ATMs) would be impossible without an EDI standard.

EDI involves a low degree of enterprise coupling. The standard is defined, and organizations can use it if appropriate. Other types of network redesign require a higher degree of coupling.

Interenterprise System Access

With **interenterprise system access**, two or more enterprises open their information systems to each other so that they can share and process transactions on each other's information systems. Whereas EDI is concerned with sharing data in a standardized format, interenterprise systems access allows enterprises to execute transactions on each other's information systems. With such access, each organization becomes a direct user of the other organizations' information systems.

Interenterprise system access enables enterprises to more efficiently conduct transactions with one another. With the JIT inventory method, for example, the manufacturer and the supplier tap into each other's information systems. An information system that resides with a manufacturer can access an information system that resides with the supplier in order to trigger the shipment of goods from the supplier. The systems are open to one another.

Airline reservations are another example of interenterprise system access. Travel agents access airline reservation information systems to obtain inventories of available seats and to purchase tickets on behalf of their clients. The employees of airline reservations companies thus become users of the airline companies' information systems. In some cases, airline employees are allowed access to competing airlines' reservations systems. In this way, the airlines can reserve seats and purchase tickets using each other's information systems.

To understand the benefit of interenterprise system access, suppose that you are on a business trip and your flight from New York to Los Angeles has just been canceled. You need to obtain a reservation on another flight. You do not know which airline has the best alternative for you, so you simply pick an airline, say United Airlines, and stand in its line. Upon reaching the agent at the counter, you find that only some other airline, say American Airlines, has a flight that meets your needs. Without interenterprise systems access, you will need to contact American to book the reservation. With the system, however, the United Airlines reservation agent can access American's reservation system and obtain the reservation for you.

Interenterprise System Integration

With **interenterprise system integration**, a business system is shared among two or more enterprises so as to allow a single process to be distributed across several enterprises. Just as interdepartmental systems integrate the activities of several departments so that the departments provide a coordinated and consistent response to their environment, interenterprise systems integrate the activities of several enterprises so that they can provide a coordinated and consistent response.

In fact, the business activities shown in the DFDs in Figures 11-12 through 11-16 can pertain to interenterprise systems just as much as they pertain to interdepartmental systems. In this case, the processes shown are undertaken by departments in different companies.

For example, consider the manufacturing processes shown in Figure 11-16. Suppose that several organizations decide to manufacture and sell products as a consortium. Suppose that company A is especially strong in sales, marketing, and order fulfillment. Another company, say company B, is especially adept at product engineering. Finally, suppose company C is strong in manufacturing.

With these relative strengths, the companies can be more competitive operating as a unit than they can on their own. To obtain the benefit of cooperation, company A is given responsibility for processes 2, 3, 8, and 9; company B, for process 1; and company C, for processes 4, 5, 6, and 7.

Such widely distributed manufacturing activities are difficult to manage. To ease the burden of interenterprise management and thus better realize the benefits of collaboration, the companies might build an information system that integrates their activities into a coordinated process.

Such a system is a step beyond interenterprise systems access. Here, a single system is spread across and integrated into three enterprises. It is not that there are three separate companies sharing each other's information systems. Rather, the three companies, together, share a single information system that integrates the activities of processes in all three companies.

Knowledge Networks

The fourth type of network redesign identified by the MIT study is the integration of expertise into **knowledge networks**. Here, the expertise of several experts and organizations is integrated into a single system. Knowledge networks do not process transactions; rather, they provide better interpretation and understanding of complex phenomena.

An example of the use of a knowledge network involves the treatment of patients with complicated injuries. In such cases, the treatment of one medical specialty sometimes interferes with the treatment provided by a different medical specialty. Drugs used, for example, to reduce the likelihood of a blood clot closing an artery in the heart may inhibit the healing of damaged tissues and bones. The goals and objectives of each medical specialty must be considered, and a treatment program must be devised that will be most effective for the overall health and healing of the patient.

The integration of knowledge and expertise is important in other disciplines as well. Groups of investors might integrate their expertise in developing a portfolio; attorneys could integrate their expertise in a complicated lawsuit; and physicists and nuclear engineers could integrate their expertise to decide how best to respond to an emergency in a nuclear power plant.

There is nothing revolutionary about professional people combining their expertise to jointly address a problem. What is new is that information systems enable professionals to do this more easily and frequently since, using information systems technology, the experts need not all reside in the same location. Further, information systems can provide better analytical support. Using group DSS, for example, all the experts in a discussion can access the same large database, images, or graphics.

Further, information systems can provide business infrastructure so that independent contractors can have many of the benefits normally associated with larger organizations. Two hundred and fifty independent attorneys, for example, could use information systems to pool their expertise in flexible groups according to the needs of a particular client or case. In this way, the overhead of a permanent partnership could be avoided.

BUSINESS SCOPE REDEFINITION

The final category of enterprise information systems application is business scope redefinition, which includes information systems that enable enterprises to expand the scope of their activities. The MIT study identified four major ways in which business scope can be redefined; these are listed in Figure 11-24.

Entry to New Market

Information systems can allow an organization to redefine its scope by facilitating entry to a new market. Elliot Bay, for example, might decide to use its information systems to expand sales into Canada. To do this, Elliot Bay could purchase mailing lists of customers in Canada and enter that data into its existing direct-mail information systems. The presence of the information systems greatly eases the transition to a new market.

Information technology provides a new alternative for companies to expand to new markets. In the past, when an enterprise wanted to expand to a new market, its choices were either to spend considerable time, money, and effort to develop a presence in the new market or to acquire another company that already had a presence in that market. With information technology, market presence can be gained by acquiring customer data in the new market and by using

Figure 11-24 Alternatives for Business Scope Redefinition

■ Entry to new market
(Elliot Bay expands to Canadian market)

■ Entry to new product category
(Elliot Bay adds clothing to its product line)

■ Technology-induced definition of new product category
(Elliot Bay develops and sells multimedia landscape design products)

■ Technology-induced market changes
(Elliot Bay changes market expectations with regard to product support)

information systems to quickly and inexpensively create a presence to the customers in that market.

Entry to New Product Category

Information systems can also help companies develop new products. Elliot Bay, for example, could use its existing customer database to expand from the sale of garden supplies and equipment to the sale of holiday gifts, garden furniture, or clothing. The information systems developed to process direct-mail sales can be readily applied to the new product category.

Technology-Induced Products

In some cases, products and markets are induced by information technology. Multimedia products, for example, provide flexible access to vast stores of information in the form of text, illustrations, graphics, and audio. The presence of this emerging technology creates new product opportunities.

At Elliot Bay, for example, a multimedia product could be developed that would show customers the best ways to plant and care for the stock they purchase. Elliot Bay could gain a competitive edge over its competitors by tailoring the presentation to the Elliot Bay product line.

Technology-induced products need not be as dramatic as this, however. On a more modest scale, Elliot Bay could use the information it has on customers and their purchases to develop new products. It could use an information system to create fertilizer and pesticide products tailored to each customer. By processing information about past purchases and climatic regions in which customers live, Elliot Bay could create specific lawn and garden-care packages. It could develop a product similar to the books sold by book-of-the-month clubs; for a fixed fee (set depending on the size of a customer's lawn and garden), Elliot Bay would ship the appropriate fertilizers and pesticides for a customer's purchases and region.

For the customers to gain the most benefit, they would need to have all of their stock registered in the Elliot Bay computer system. This would provide an incentive for customers to purchase products only from Elliot Bay.

Technology-Induced Market Changes

As you have seen, technology creates opportunities for new products and markets. In doing so, the technology sets new competitive standards and changes customer expectations and preferences. While this is an advantage for new, small, and strategically aggressive enterprises, it is a danger to existing businesses, especially those in which change is slow and difficult.

To succeed into the next century, businesses will need to foster flexibility and adaptability. A solid core technology can be made obsolete by rapidly developing technology. Businesses will need to constantly monitor changes in products and markets so as to remain competitive. They will also need to proactively consider the ways they can use technology to redefine their business activities.

VALUE ADDED BY ENTERPRISE INFORMATION SYSTEMS

Chapter 4 introduced a model of the value added by information systems that has three components: process, product, and change. Chapter 5 discussed some ways personal information systems add value to each of these components. Chapter 8 described the ways workgroup information systems add value to these components. This section summarizes the ways in which the types of applications listed in Figure 11-1 add value to enterprise process, product, and quality.

Value Added to Processes

The three levels of process discussed in this text are operational control, management control, and strategic planning. Interdepartmental systems have the greatest impact on operational control. Given that a system exists, we can use interdepartmental systems to enable separate departments to respond to operational needs in a consistent and coordinated fashion.

Management control, defined in Chapter 4 as the acquisition and use of assets, is influenced by enterprise information systems applications in both the interdepartmental and business process redesign categories. For existing business systems, interdepartmental information systems create data from day-to-day transactions that can be processed to provide management control. Such applications fall under the narrow definition of MIS applications first discussed in Chapter 2.

As you have seen, in some cases, information technology induces changes in process structure. A management team can use business process redesign to manage its allocated assets in a new way. Successful managers in the future will come to regard business process redesign as an important part of managerial activity.

Strategic planning processes are most involved with information systems that facilitate business network redesign and business scope redefinition. The use of information systems to create new networks among enterprises should become a standard consideration in developing business strategy. Similarly, changes in business scope allowed information systems to support the company's entry to new markets, and products will also become an important part of strategic planning.

Value Added to Products

Enterprise information systems can add value to products by enhancing product features and characteristics and by improving product delivery. Here, the term *product* means the result of a coordinated process within the enterprise. Thus, products can mean not only the products that are sold (such as nursery stock or microcomputer applications software), but also the services that support the products (such as customer support) and even output like orders to suppliers.

Interdepartmental systems can improve enterprise products by increasing the rapidity with which the enterprise departments can produce a coordinated response. Consider the purchasing function. If each department in Figure 11-12 maintains its own file of open POs, then making a change to a PO will be difficult and time-consuming. If, as in Figure 11-13, the departments share an integrated PO file, then a change will be much more readily accommodated.

Information systems that facilitate business process redesign, business network redesign, and business scope redefinition can all add value to products. Business processes can be redesigned to provide greater flexibility in creating and supporting product changes.

Business networks can be redesigned to enable enterprises to gain from a collaboration that enables each enterprise to specialize in the activities for which it has the greatest relative strength. Such networks allow products to be created, developed, manufactured, and supported by a consortium of enterprises. Enterprises can compensate for their weaknesses by tapping into the strengths of other enterprises. Information systems that facilitate business scope redefinition allow not only for the definition of new product characteristics, but also for delivery to new markets and even the creation of entirely new products.

Value Added Through Facilitating Change

In considering the factors that affect an organization's ability to change, we are most concerned with facilitating business process redesign, business network redesign, and business scope redefinition. These areas enable people and departments to interact with one another and with the environment in new and radical ways, further facilitating experimentation and change.

A company's ability to redesign depends on the flexibility of its MIS. Where systems are inflexible, redesign is nearly impossible to implement, and consideration of redesign seldom arises because it is impractical. Where systems are flexible, the ability to change is enhanced, and managers are encouraged to consider such changes.

A major factor today in increasing the flexibility of MIS is **computer-aided systems engineering (CASE)** in constructing new systems. As Chapter 13 explains, CASE involves using information systems to build information systems, along with new methodologies of systems development that add flexibility and adaptability. As CASE tools improve and CASE methodologies are more widely used, two results can be expected. First, process and network redesign and business scope redefinition become more practical as potential solutions to problems. Second, positive experiences with such fundamental changes will attune managers to consider further change in these areas as additional opportunities emerge.

SUMMARY

An enterprise is a system of people, equipment, material, data, policies, and procedures that provides a product or a service, often with the goal of making a profit. The applications of MIS to enterprises fall into five categories: localized applications (considered previously), interdepartmental systems, business process redesign, business network redesign, and business scope redefinition.

Interdepartmental information systems integrate the activities of different departments into a single business system that produces coordinated, appropriate responses to the enterprise's environment. Both localized and interdepartmental systems involve little redesign of the underlying business processes; they support business activities as they exist.

Business process redesign refers to applications in which the underlying process is redesigned as the system is developed. Business network redesign refers to systems that involve the ways in which multiple enterprises work together. Business scope redefinition consists of applications that change the nature of the business.

Interdepartmental information systems allow integration of the activities of separate departments so that the departments respond in a consistent and coordinated way. Often, interdepartmental systems involve shared, centralized databases that enable each department to record the results of the work it has done. With interdepartmental systems, users will have different views of the same data. Because such systems must be standardized, and changes to them carefully controlled, there is a need for enterprise systems management. They involve many applications and heterogeneous data.

Interdepartmental information systems differ from workgroup systems in several ways. First, whereas the users of a workgroup information system know each other personally, the users of an interdepartmental information system are often separated, both physically and organizationally. Further, workgroup systems normally involve, at most, a few dozen users, whereas interdepartmental systems can have hundreds or even thousands of users. Still another difference is that interdepartmental systems manage hundreds of times more data than do workgroup systems. Further, this data is far more complicated and heterogeneous than is workgroup data. Finally, while workgroup systems typically involve just one subfunction of a company, interdepartmental systems cross many departmental boundaries and involve a major enterprise function.

Four examples of interdepartmental systems are illustrated in this chapter: revenue generation, purchasing, personnel and payroll, and manufacturing. The interdepartmental activities for these examples are illustrated with DFDs. A variety of information systems could be developed to support each diagrammed activity.

Business process redesign is emerging as a necessary step to optimize the use of information technology. Rather than simply automating existing processes, the underlying business processes are redesigned to take advantage of the opportunities provided by technology. Consequences of business process redesign include a reduced need for management and staff, increased concurrency of activity, and organizational resistance.

Business network redesign refers to the use of information systems to enable groups of enterprises to interact more productively. Four types of network redesign occur: electronic data interchange (EDI), in which organizations agree on common data standards; interenterprise system access, in which organizations use one another's information systems; interenterprise system integration, in which enterprises develop shared information systems; and knowledge networks, in which enterprises use information technology to share expertise.

Applications that involve business scope redefinition change the nature of the enterprise's activities. Technology can enable a business to enter a new market, to develop products for a new product category, and to develop new products induced by technology.

All five categories of enterprise MIS add value in the same way that personal and workgroup information systems add value. They add value to process by facilitating operational control, management control, and strategic planning. They add value to products by enhancing product features and characteristics and by improving product delivery. Finally, enterprise information systems can facilitate flexibility in an organization's ability to respond to environmental changes.

KEY TERMS

Enterprise
Localized application
Interdepartmental
    system
Business process
    redesign
Business network
    redesign
Business scope
    redefinition

Multipart form
Revenue-generation
    function
Purchasing function
Personnel and payroll
    function
Manufacturing function
Lead time
MRP II
JIT

CAD/CAM
Numerical control
CIM
EDI
Interenterprise system
    access
Interenterprise system
    integration
Knowledge networks
CASE

REVIEW QUESTIONS

1. What is an enterprise?

2. List the five categories of enterprise MIS application.

3. Describe an example of an interdepartmental information system.

4. Describe an example of an information system that involves business process redesign.

5. Describe an example of an information system that involves business network redesign.

6. Describe an example of an information system that involves business scope redefinition.

7. In regard to Figure 11-5, explain three ways in which the various departments need to coordinate their activities. How can an information system help departments do this?

8. Give an example, other than one in this text, in which two departments would need to have two different views of the same data.

9. Summarize the characteristics of interdepartmental information systems.

10. Compare and contrast workgroup and interdepartmental information systems.

11. What departments are involved in the revenue-generation function? Briefly, what does each department do with respect to revenue generation?

12. Explain the function of each dataflow in Figure 11-12.

13. What departments and external agencies are involved in the purchasing activity in Figure 11-12?

14. In Figure 11-13, explain the role of the requisition and the PO.

15. Describe the role of the PO data store in Figure 11-13.

16. What is the purpose of the personnel and payroll function? What departments and external agencies are involved?

17. Explain the function of each dataflow in Figure 11-14.

18. Why do many companies choose to have their payrolls processed by outside vendors?

19. What is the function of the manufacturing theme? What departments and external agencies are involved?

20. Explain the function of each dataflow in Figure 11-16 that directly involves manufacturing activities (i.e., processes 4, 6, and 7).

21. What is the production schedule? What is its purpose?

22. Explain the purpose of MRP II.

23. What is the JIT inventory management strategy?

24. What is CIM? What is its focus?

25. Describe the need for business process redesign.

26. Describe the changes that Legacy Systems made to its product development process.

27. Summarize the benefits that Legacy Systems obtained from redesigning its product development process.

28. Explain how the use of information systems that involve business process redesign can reduce the need for management and staff.

29. Explain how Legacy Systems obtained greater concurrency of activity when it changed its product development process.

30. Summarize the reasons why there may be organizational resistance to business process redesign.

31. Describe EDI, and give an example other than one in this text.

32. Describe interenterprise system access, and give an example other than one in this text.

33. Describe interenterprise system integration, and give an example other than one in this text.

34. Describe knowledge networks, and give an example other than one in this text.

35. Give an example, other than one in this text, of a way in which information technology can provide entry to a new market.

36. Give an example, other than one in this text, of a way in which information technology can provide entry to a new product category.

37. Give an example, other than one in this text, of a way in which information technology can induce new products.

38. Give an example, other than one in this text, of a way in which information technology can induce market changes.

39. Summarize the ways in which enterprise information systems add value to processes. Which categories of applications most influence operational control? Management control? Strategic planning?

40. Summarize the ways in which enterprise information systems add value to products.

41. Summarize the ways in which enterprise information systems can facilitate change.

DISCUSSION QUESTIONS

1. Redraw Figure 11-3 showing a shared data store containing customer, order, inventory, and payment data. Use Figure 11-6 as a guide in defining dataflows.

2. Figure 11-13 shows a purchasing system that shares a PO data store. Develop an alternative system for supporting purchasing that does not involve such shared data. What are the advantages and disadvantages of the two alternatives? Describe enterprises in which one of the two alternatives is clearly superior to the other.

3. Develop a DFD for the personnel function.

4. The chapter describes several types of organizational resistance to business process redesign. Describe how you think such resistance can be overcome. What consequences are likely if such resistance is not overcome?

5. Suppose that you are in charge of strategic planning for an enterprise. (Pick any enterprise in which you are interested.) Explain how you think information technology could redefine the scope of that enterprise. In your answer, consider the categories listed in Figure 11-24.

PROJECTS

A. Interview a senior manager from a local company. Reach to the highest-level manager that you can. Explain to this person that you are studying enterprise information systems and that you would like to gain a firsthand perspective on business systems and the information systems that support them. During the interview, find out which of the five types of information systems applications are used in that enterprise. For each type, how successful has the system been? What problems have occurred? How have those problems been overcome?

B. Obtain information about the enterprise information systems used at your college. What functions are included? What data stores are shared? What major groups of users are involved? Diagram the dataflows of at least one major set of functions, such as course registration and student billing. Include the major external sources and sinks, the major processes, and the major data stores. Describe the procedure that an officer of the college follows to obtain a list of students enrolled in a course or a list of current courses for a particular student.

C. Locate a business that uses an interdepartmental information system. Draw a DFD of that system. Create an input/output/storage table for the major processes of the system (similar to the one in Figure 11-6). What problems were encountered in the development of the system? To what degree has the system been accepted by the users? What changes would the company make to the systems if it could? In general, how successful has the system been?

D. Locate a business that has attempted business process redesign. Interview managers in that business. Describe the nature of the business before the change and after the change. What benefits have accrued? What costs? What types of resistance were encountered in making the change? How were the resistances overcome? Is the overall effort of the change judged to have been worthwhile?

M I N I C A S E

Roadway Finds Electronic Highway Paved with Gold

When a customer entrusts a package to a common carrier, there's often a lot more at stake than whether or not the parcel actually gets to its destination. Reputations and repeat business ride on the carrier's capability to deliver the right parcel to the right place at the right time.

So it stands to reason that the more information a transportation company can provide to its customers, the more likely they are to remain customers.

Roadway Express Inc. was one of the first trucking companies to recognize just how hungry its customers were for up-to-the-second data. After all, knowing exactly when a shipment will arrive can help businesses manage inventories, allocate warehouse personnel, and even plan marketing and promotional activities. Roadway understood that instantaneous access to customer information could be a tremendous asset.

It quickly became clear that the only viable solution was a total replacement of existing systems with a distributed client/server architecture using SQL database technology.

The goal of the new system was to provide remote field offices with real-time access to sales, delivery, and freight records via a dedicated network and give Roadway customers access to the same data using a choice of access methods.

But Roadway didn't stop with making information pathways within Roadway flow more smoothly. Instead, senior executives decided to use the new systems to help Roadway customers with their just-in-time (JIT) inventory efforts. JIT requires extremely close and cooperative relationships among customers, their suppliers, and the transportation firm.

Here's how it works: When a Roadway truck is loaded, the dock worker scans a bar code imprinted on a manifest, or individual shipping document, attached to that customer's shipment. That data is transmitted via radio to the Informix database on the local Unix server, which in turn transmits it to Akron headquarters via the SNA network. An electronic data interchange (EDI) message is subsequently sent to the customer notifying it that the shipment is on its way and when it will arrive.

Roadway also built a PC-based database and communications program, called EZ-Bill, that lets customers access Roadway databases as well as create and maintain their own shipping records.

When Roadway programmers first wrote EZ-Bill using Informix and provided EDI links to its own Informix and DB2 databases, they thought as many as 500 Roadway customers would be interested.

"We'd targeted small to midsized customers because we thought that larger customers with more sophisticated IS departments wouldn't need it," Long says. "But we were astonished when more than 3,000 of our customers asked for the program." Roadway didn't charge its customers for software and support services. "This is a value-added service for our customers," he says.

Customers can also access Roadway's host databases using a Touch-Tone phone. By dialing a toll-free number, customers dial into AT&T Conversant communication servers linked to the DB2 databases. So even customers who choose not to go the PC route can check on shipments, invoices, or schedules. This access method is enormously popular.

"We're averaging about 209,000 telephone calls a month, which tells us our customers needed technology options in order to access information," Long says. ■

Alice LaPlante, excerpted from *Infoworld*, March 8, 1993, p. 54.

Discussion Questions

1. Describe how information technology has added value to Roadway Corporation.

2. How has Roadway redesigned its business, as described here?

3. Why doesn't Roadway charge customers for the use of its database access and programs?

4. Using the information in this article and your own information systems knowledge, describe the five components of Roadway's information system.

12

Components of Enterprise Information Systems

ENTERPRISE INFORMATION SYSTEMS, like personal and workgroup information systems, consist of five components: hardware, programs, data, procedures, and people. Since enterprise information systems support more users, the hardware component is usually more comprehensive and expensive than that for personal or workgroup information systems. There are also many more hardware alternatives, and they are more complex. Enterprise information systems involve the same categories of programs as do personal and workgroup information systems, but those programs must be designed to manage very large numbers of concurrent transactions and other processing requests.

Enterprise information systems not only involve far more data than do personal and workgroup information systems, but that data is also more complicated and there are more different user views of the data. Furthermore, because enterprise information systems involve multiple departments, conflict often exists over where the data should be physically located.

Since enterprise data is crucial to the operation of the company, procedures need to be developed that protect data against accidental, malicious, or criminal loss. Procedures must also be developed to organize and control processing and to deal with failure and recovery. Finally, enterprise information systems require an in-house staff of professionals to develop, monitor, and maintain them. We will discuss the types of personnel required and the organization of the people in an MIS department.

HARDWARE

Since enterprise information systems often involve hundreds or even thousands of users dispersed over a wide geographic area, they are far more complicated and complex than are personal and workgroup systems. At one time, all enterprise systems were supported by teleprocessing. Today, however, a number of additional hardware configurations are in use. This section considers four typical enterprise hardware configurations: LANs, teleprocessing, internets, and backbone networks.

LANs

In Chapter 9, we described how LANs are used for workgroup information systems. LANs can also be used for enterprise information systems but are subject to two critical limitations. Normally, the computers in a LAN must reside within a mile or two of each other, and most LANs can effectively support fewer than 50 or so microcomputers. Because of these limitations, LANs can be used as the basis only for small enterprise systems.

To understand how a LAN might be used in an enterprise setting, consider Figure 12-1, which is a copy of the DFD of the purchasing function shown in Figure 11-13. Suppose that the data store in Figure 12-1 is implemented as a database of purchasing data that will be processed according to the client/server architecture described in Chapter 9. Users in Purchasing, Receiving, and Accounts Payable process this database.

Figure 12-2 shows how a LAN could be used to support this purchasing system. According to this figure, client computers are located in Purchasing, Receiving, and Accounts Payable. The LAN connects all of these computers to a database server that processes the Purchasing database. As shown, a bus topology is used. Each client computer processes application programs that issue requests for database service from the server.

One advantage of the LAN is that the client microcomputers can be used for work besides purchasing, including E-mail and personal computer applications such as word processing or spreadsheet analysis.

A summary of the characteristics of LANs is shown in the first row of Figure 12-3. Recall from Chapter 9 that both bus topology and ring topology can be used for a LAN. Also, access to the LAN is normally controlled by either contention (IEEE 802.3) protocol or token passing (IEEE 802.4) bus and (IEEE 802.5) ring protocols.

For a small enterprise, this alternative would be adequate. If, however, there are more than 50 users or if the users are geographically distant, then the LAN cannot be used. One of the alternatives described below would be required.

Figure 12-1 Dataflows for the Enterprise Purchasing Function

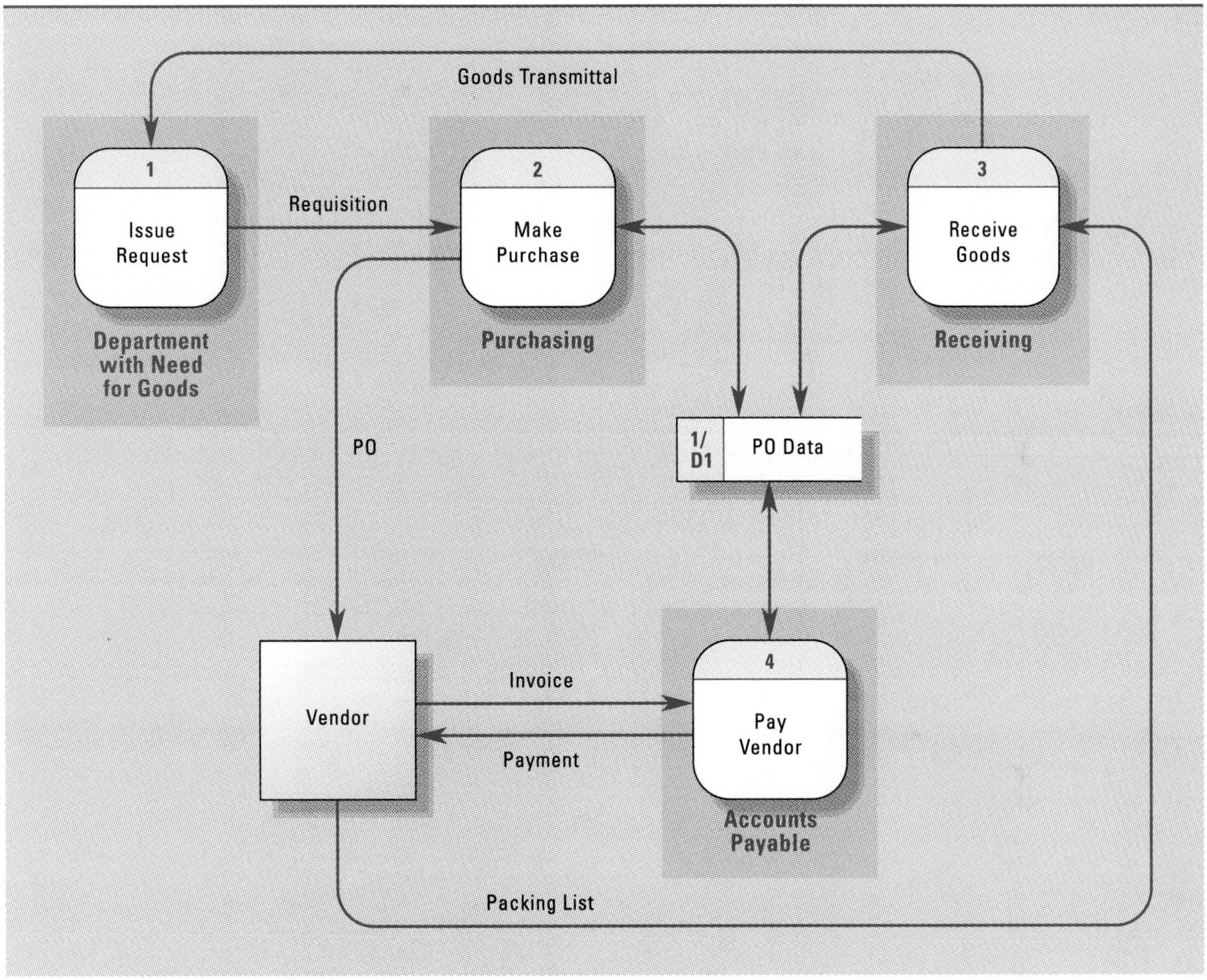

Teleprocessing Systems

The classical approach for supporting enterprise information systems is **teleprocessing**. With this approach, all applications processing occurs on a centralized computer, which is almost always a mainframe computer or a minicomputer. The centralized computer controls the order and priority of processing. There is little need for intelligence at the user stations, and dumb terminals or microcomputers that emulate dumb terminals are used.

Figure 12-2 A LAN Alternative for the Purchasing Function

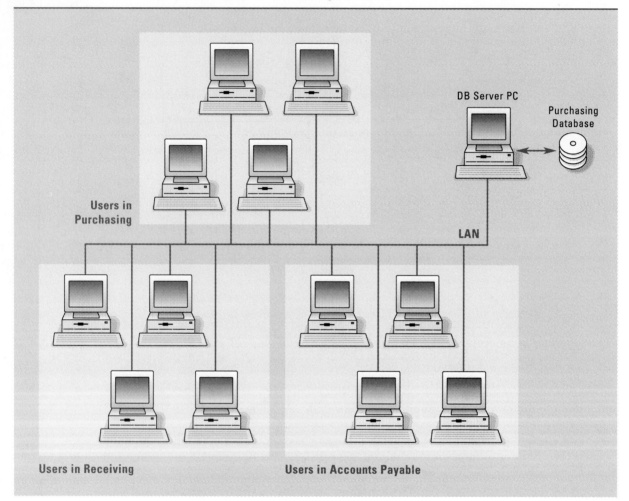

Figure 12-4 shows an example of the use of teleprocessing for enterprise purchasing. Terminals are located in each of the three departments that process the purchasing database. Each terminal sends to the centralized computer transactions that are processed by the appropriate application program.

Unlike LANs, teleprocessing systems can be expanded to accommodate many users over large geographic distances. The ellipses (...) shown in Figure 12-4 indicate that many terminals are not shown. In fact, a large teleprocessing system could support hundreds or even thousands of users dispersed geographically across North America or the world.

Figure 12-3 Enterprise Information System Hardware Alternatives

System Type	Characteristics	Examples
LAN	Multiple microcomputers connected together One or more file, database, or other servers Bus and ring topologies are common Computers within a mile or two of each other Generally fewer than 50 computers	Contention (IEEE 802.3) Token passing (IEEE 802.4 and 802.5)
Teleprocessing	Processing performed by centralized computer Users access applications via dumb terminals or micros emulating dumb terminals	Terminal emulation with IBM 3278/79 and VT100 Polling Multiplexing
Internets	Multiple LANs interconnected Requires bridges, gateways, and routers	Routing functions between LANs
Backbone Networks	Network supports communications among computers of any type Hundreds or thousands of computers and terminals possible Wide geographic distribution possible via WAN	TCP/IP SNA DEC DNA

Because teleprocessing is so prevalent, we will consider the components of a teleprocessing system in detail. Examine Figure 12-4, which shows the three basic components: user or (as it is sometimes called) end-user hardware, transmission media, and the centralized, processing computer.

End-User Hardware With teleprocessing, since all applications processing occurs on the centralized computer, little intelligence is required in end-user hardware. Thus, the user can access the teleprocessing system from either a **dumb terminal** (a device with keyboard and screen, but no CPU) or a microcomputer with **terminal emulation**. Microcomputers are not necessary and probably would not be used for this purpose at all except that the users already have them on their desks. Further, even if they do not, a microcomputer costs only somewhat more than a dumb terminal.

Considering the connection to the communications line, if a dumb terminal is used, a **port,** or **line connector,** will be built into the terminal. If a microcomputer is used, then a terminal emulation communications card must be installed in one of the micro's expansion slots. These cards are similar to those used for LAN connections.

Figure 12-4 A Teleprocessing Alternative for the Purchasing Function

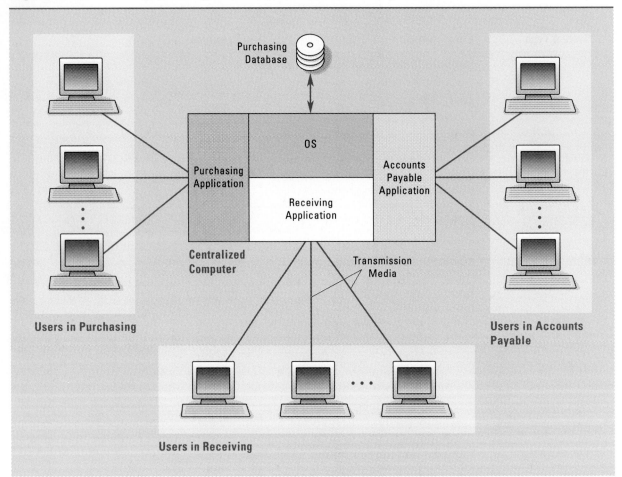

The type of terminal emulation card required depends on the brand of centralized computer. For connecting to IBM mainframes, an IBM 3278/79 terminal emulation card is required. For connecting to Digital Equipment Corporation (DEC) hardware, a VT100 protocol card is required. These two cards serve as a de facto standard; work-alike substitutes are marketed by many manufacturers besides IBM and DEC.

In some cases, where LANs reside in a user department, only one microcomputer on the LAN is equipped with a terminal emulation card, shown for Receiving in Figure 12-5. Observe that the terminal emulation micro serves as a **network server** for the LAN, sharing its access to the teleprocessing system among clients in the LAN. Clients send transmissions intended for the centralized

Figure 12-5 A Teleprocessing Alternative with a LAN for the Purchasing Function

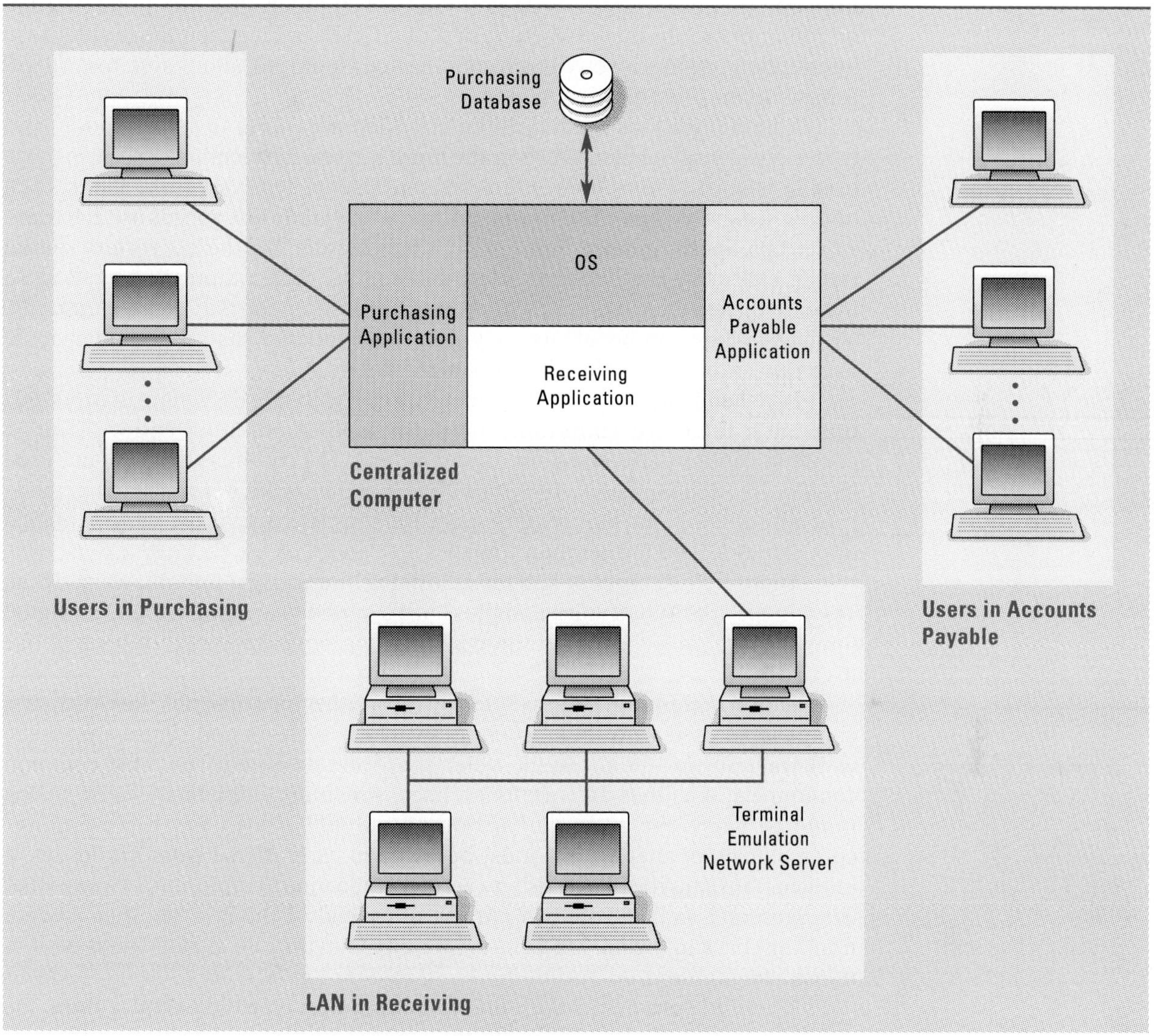

computer across the LAN to the network server micro, which in turn relays the transmission to the centralized computer. Responses from the centralized computer are processed in reverse.

The advantage of using the LAN in this way is that only one micro need be equipped with a terminal emulation card. The disadvantage is performance; in Figure 12-5, all transmissions from Receiving must pass through a single server. If there is not too much traffic, however, this may not be a substantial problem.

Communications Media   Communications media are used to transfer signals from one communicating device (terminal or computer) to another. We touched on communications media when we described LANs in Chapter 9. Since enterprise information systems involve more complicated communications systems, we will expand on the prior discussion here.

Communications media can be classified according to speed, mode, and type. Consider speed first. **Voice-grade lines**[1] are communications lines like those used in telephone lines (hence their name). Their speeds vary from 300 to 9,600 bits per second, or **bps**.[2] The most common voice-grade line speeds are 2,400 and 14,400 bps. Speeds greater than 9,600 bps may require that the line receive special tuning, called **line conditioning**. Some modems use data compression methods to increase the effective communication rate by recoding the data more compactly, so that the same number of bits carry more information. A matching modem must decompress the data at the other end of the line.

Wideband lines have much greater capacity, with speeds of more than 500,000 bps. Such lines are commonly used in satellite communications and in communications between or among computers. The communications lines used in LANs are wideband lines. In general, wideband lines are not restricted to the 1-mile limit of LANs, but they require special cabling such as coaxial cable or optical fiber, if they extend farther than 1 mile.

There are two types of line mode. **Analog lines** carry a smooth, wavy signal. The sounds of a human voice and those of a symphony are analog signals. **Digital lines** carry an off/on signal of the type used inside computers to represent bits (0s and 1s).

Although communications lines can carry either type of signal, the electronics components used with them, such as switching systems and signal amplifiers, work well only for the mode for which they were designed. The most common communications lines are telephone lines, which are implemented for analog mode to carry the sound of a human voice. To be used for computer communication, analog lines must be made to carry digital data. To do this, a **modem** translates the bits by using a certain audio tone to represent 0 and another to represent 1 as in Figure 12-6. At the other end of the line, another modem translates back to digital. Modems are required anytime an analog line is used to transmit digital data.

The third communications line classification is type. **Full-duplex lines**, the most common, allow traffic to be transmitted on the line in both directions

---

1. The terms *communications media* and *communications lines* are used interchangeably in practice. In theory, the term *communications media* is broader because it encompasses electromagnetic signals that are transmitted without a physical line. Most people use the term *communications lines* to include such transmissions and ignore the fact that, in such cases, there really are no physical lines.

2. You will sometimes hear the term *baud* as a measure of line speed. Baud refers to the rate at which a line can change state. The speed of the line in bits per second is often greater than the speed of the line in baud. Thus, *bits per second* is a better term to use.

Figure 12-6 Analog and Digital Line Modes
Digital signals are translated into analog equivalents by a modem.

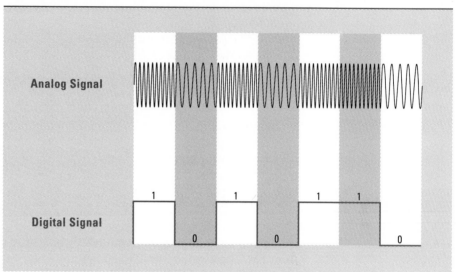

simultaneously. One way to do this is to reserve the frequencies above a certain level for traffic in one direction and the frequencies below that level for traffic in the other direction.

Half-duplex lines, which are rare, allow traffic to be transmitted in both directions, but not simultaneously. **Simplex lines** allow only one-way transmission. They are mostly used today to carry signals from remote sensors to computers, and most likely you will never encounter one. Line classifications are summarized in Figure 12-7.

WANs and MANs When communications lines must cross public roadways or property owned by others, access rights must be negotiated with each landowner. Since this is impractical, companies usually lease such communications services from **common carriers,** companies that have been granted special access rights to install communications lines across private property in return for providing communications services at goverment-regulated rates.

A **wide-area network (WAN)** is usually operated by a common carrier that provides data communications interconnections among geographically dispersed nodes. For example, if a company has major offices in Omaha, San Francisco, Lagos, Hong Kong, and Antwerp, it would lease WAN services to provide teleprocessing access to personnel in these offices.

A **metropolitan-area network (MAN)** provides similar interconnection within a large city or region. For example, if a company has five separated plants located

Figure 12-7 Communications Line Classifications

- Line Speed
  - Voice-grade (300–9,600 bits per second)
  - Wideband (500,000 bits per second or more)
- Line Mode
  - Analog
  - Digital
- Line Type
  - Full-duplex
  - Half-duplex
  - Simplex

within a 20- to 30-mile radius, it probably would lease telecommunications services from a MAN operating within that region.

Connections to Communications Lines As stated, if the user employs a dumb terminal, the line connection is built into the terminal. If the user employs a microcomputer, the connection is usually made via an adapter card inserted into an expansion slot in the case of a microcomputer.

At the other end of the line, the attachment to the processing computer is made via a **communications port**, which is the processing computer's equivalent to an adapter card; it is simply a physical connection to the line. Large mainframes have dozens or even hundreds of communications ports.

When the data transmitted over the communications line consists of the characters typed by the user and straight text transmitted in response by the computer, the line capacity is very lightly used. The fastest human typists can barely sustain speeds of 100 words per minute, which translates to about 10 characters per second, or 80 bps. Few humans can read computer output faster than 1,000 words per minute, which corresponds to about 120 characters per second, or about 950 bps.

Thus, most users cannot keep a communications line consistently busy. For short periods of time, such as during the transmission of a graphic image, a user may keep the line very busy. But during most periods, when the user is contemplating what to do next or entering data, the costly line will be nearly idle.

Therefore, businesses often connect several or even dozens of users to the same line. When this is done, some means must be created to keep the traffic from one user from being confounded with the traffic from another. This problem is similar to the contention problem described for LANs. The difference here is that the terminals on the users' ends probably have little intelligence. Two teleprocessing contention-management alternatives are used: polling and multiplexing.

Figure 12-8 Multiplexing

The characters shown on the screens of the terminals are transmitted one after the other to the main computer. Some have arrived; others are still in the transmission line. Characters from each terminal are interleaved by the multiplexer.

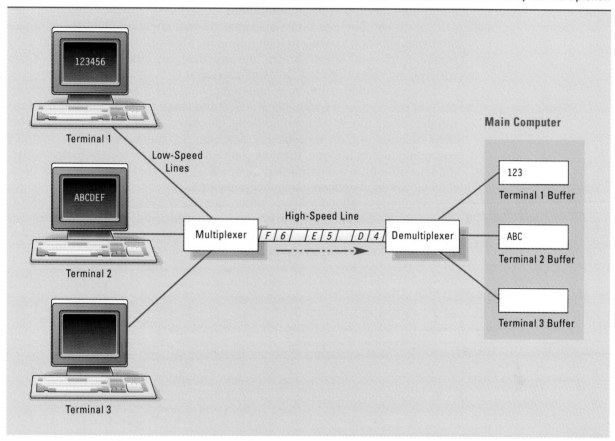

Polling In **polling**, the centralized processing computer asks each terminal, in round-robin fashion, if it has anything to send. If so, the message is sent. If not, the computer asks the next terminal, and so forth. Periodically, the processing computer sends messages back to the terminals, again in round-robin fashion.

The advantage of polling is that no intelligence is required in the end user's hardware. The disadvantage is that CPU time on the centralized computer (which is already probably very busy) is required to perform polling. Because of this, some mainframe computers are assisted by **front-end processors**, auxiliary computers that perform this and other communications services.

Multiplexing With **multiplexing**, the messages from terminals are interleaved. As shown in Figure 12-8, a time slot is granted to each terminal. If the terminal has something to send, it fills the time slot with data. If not, that slot remains empty. An advanced type of multiplexer increases the effective communication rate by **buffering** (storing up) data that arrives too quickly to be sent and using it to fill the empty time slots left by inactive terminals.

At the computer end, the signal must be demultiplexed. Here, the messages are separated out according to their time slots. This function is performed by the front-end processor, which also provides error detection (and correction), character conversions, data encryption, and other services.

Observe a critical difference between polling and multiplexing. With polling, the line that carries the signal operates at the same speed as the line from the terminal or computer. With multiplexing, the communications line is much faster than the lines from the terminals or computer. In fact, if n computers are to be connected to a multiplexer, then the communications line must be n times faster than the lines from the terminal or computer. (If buffered multiplexers are used, then the line may not need this much capacity.)

Figure 12-9 shows yet one other alternative, which involves a PBX. As previously described, a PBX is a privately owned, computer-based telephone exchange. In Figure 12-9, the PBX lets relatively slow user stations (connected to telephone jacks) share a high-speed line. As with other types of line-sharing devices,

Figure 12-9   The PBX as a Line-Sharing Device
The PBX can be used to let low-speed terminals share a high-speed communications line.

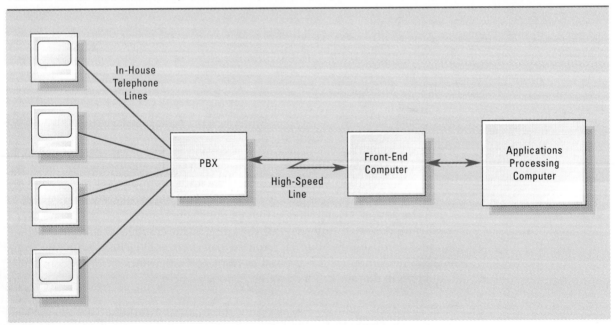

the PBX combines the slower speeds of lines to the end users into a single signal for the higher-speed line.

Processing Hardware The third hardware component consists of the computers that process the applications and the databases. The type and use of these computers depends on the system architecture. In a teleprocessing system, all applications processing is done on a single processing computer. While there may be other CPUs (in a front-end processor or PBX), these CPUs do no applications processing. In Figure 12-10, for example, the mainframe and the

Figure 12-10 A Bank Teleprocessing System

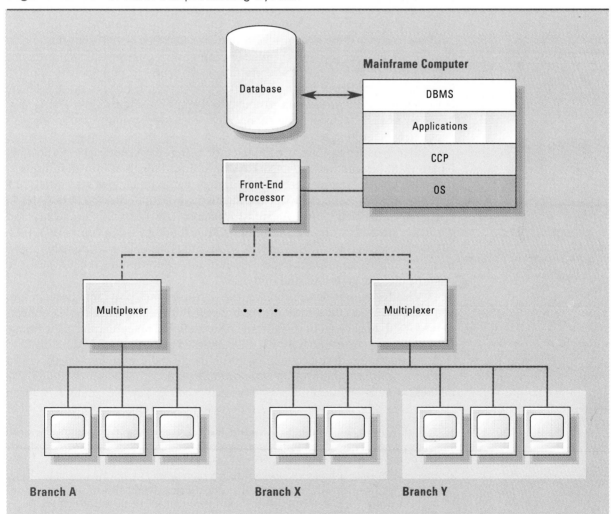

front-end processor both possess CPUs. Only the mainframe, however, does applications processing.

Historically, mainframe computers were used as the center of teleprocessing systems. As minicomputers gained power, however, they came to be used as well. Today, since microcomputers are rivaling the power of mainframes, even they can be used for teleprocessing, though newly developed systems using microprocessors usually are LAN-based.

The second row of Figure 12-3 summarizes characteristics and protocols for teleprocessing systems.

Internets

Suppose you work for an enterprise that has installed a LAN like the one in Figure 12-2. Further suppose that you have outgrown this network; performance may be degrading because there are too many users, or perhaps you want to incorporate distant users into the network. To solve these problems, one possibility is to develop a teleprocessing system like the one in Figure 12-4. Doing this, however, involves considerable change; teleprocessing requires you to install a completely different type of technology.

An alternative to converting to teleprocessing is **internetworking**, shown in Figure 12-11.[3] Here, multiple LANs have been linked together into an **internet**, a collection of LANs interconnected into a single communications system[4]. As one LAN is outgrown, others are added. In this figure, there are separate LANs in Purchasing, Receiving, and Accounts Payable. The LANs in Purchasing and Receiving are both structured according to bus topology using contention (IEEE 802.3) network-access cards. The LAN in Accounts Payable is a ring using token passing (IEEE 802.5) network-access cards. Connections among the networks are made by bridges, gateways, and routers.

A **bridge** is a device containing the hardware and programs necessary to connect two LANs of the same type. The bridge in Purchasing, for example, connects to the LAN in Receiving. Both of these LANs are based on contention. The bridge passes messages from one LAN that are addressed to a computer in the other.

A **gateway** is a device containing the hardware and the programs necessary to connect a LAN to another LAN (or other minicomputer or mainframe computer) of a different type. In Figure 12-11, the gateway in Accounts Payable connects its token

---

3. The field of data communications and internetworking is changing very rapidly. For a recent summary, see: Fitzgerald, Jerry, *Business Data Communications: Basic Concepts, Security, and Design*, 4th ed. New York: John Wiley & Sons, 1993, pp. 507–562.

4. Note the difference between *an internet*, which is composed of LANs within a company, and *the Internet*, a specific worldwide confederation of regional communication networks interconnecting universities, research institutes, governmental agencies, and companies. The Internet is a major E-mail carrier between organizations.

Figure 12-11 An Internet

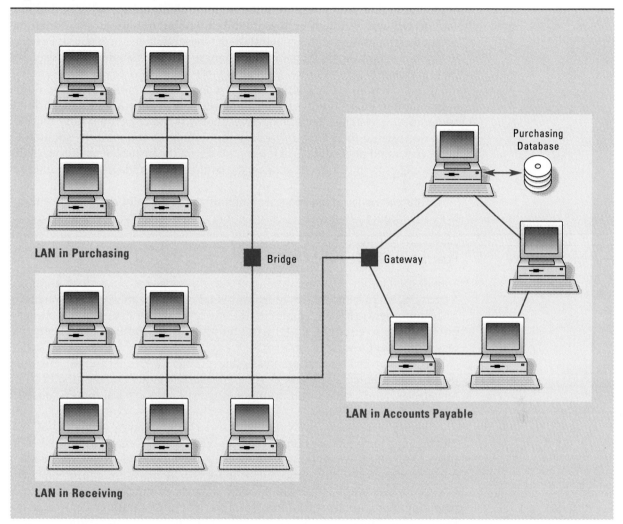

LAN in Purchasing

Bridge

Gateway

Purchasing Database

LAN in Accounts Payable

LAN in Receiving

passing LAN to Receiving's contention LAN. One of the personal computers in Receiving serves as both a bridge (to Purchasing) and a gateway (to Accounts Payable).

A **router** is a device used to connect dissimilar LANs in a complex internet where there may be multiple pathways connecting one computer to another. The router contains data about the various pathways in the internet and can optimize the routine of messages to balance the load of traffic on the various parts of the internet. Since this is a complex task, the router is a more expensive device than the bridge or gateway.

In Figure 12-11, the Purchasing database is processed by a database server in Accounts Payable. We do not have sufficient information to know why the database was located here. It might be that the token passing network is faster than the others, or perhaps most activity against the database originates in Accounts Payable. In any case, all transactions against the database are routed to the database server for processing.

The internetworking alternative is new and just now emerging. Some organizations have found that internets are a cheaper alternative to large teleprocessing systems. Because of the economy, some companies have recently been **downsizing** their large teleprocessing systems to internets. In addition to lower cost, another advantage of internets is flexibility. Instead of acquiring all the processing capability it needs at once, the company can add LANs to the internet as needed.

Characteristics of internets are summarized in the third row of Figure 12-3.

Backbone Networks

A fourth alternative hardware configuration for enterprise information systems is a **backbone network (BN)**, a large central network to which all the computers in an enterprise are connected. It provides the infrastructure for enterprise telecommunications.

A BN may include mainframes, minicomputers, LANs, terminals, and other devices. If the enterprise includes geographically separated offices, the BN may include WAN links leased from common carriers. Gateways and routers are used to connect LANs to a BN.

Figure 12-12 shows a BN that links three geographically separated offices. The separate locations are connected by a WAN, which forms part of the BN. In the St. Louis office, a mainframe with terminals, two LANs, and several independent microcomputers are interconnected to the LANs in Montreal and the independent PCs in the San Diego office. The result is a single complex network capable of providing approximately the same level of service as if all these devices were in the same room. Thus, the BN removes the penalty of distance from the data communications service.

Communications backbones support at least three basic functions: They provide some form of message passing or E-mail between users; they allow for file transfer among computers; and they support terminal emulation. The first two functions allow users to communicate and share data with one another. The third function allows the backbone to be used as a communications medium for teleprocessing. In Figure 12-12, for example, a user on a LAN can use the backbone's terminal-emulation capabilities to access an application on the mainframe. Services on the communications backbone will cause transmissions from the

Figure 12-12 A Backbone Network

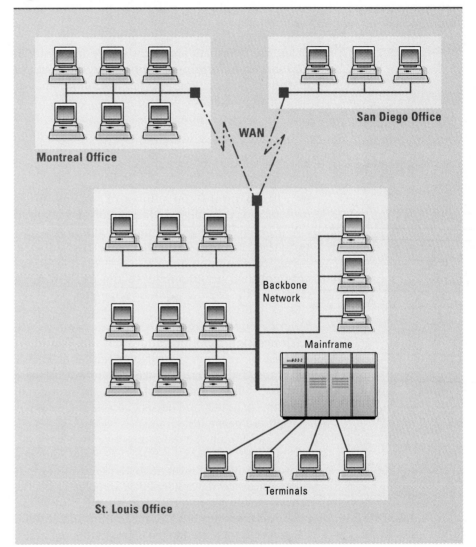

microcomputer on the LAN to appear to the mainframe as if they had originated on a terminal.

TCP/IP, a communications protocol specifically developed for BNs, will be considered further in the next section on programs. Characteristics of BNs are summarized in the fourth row of Figure 12-3.

PROGRAMS

Enterprise information systems utilize the same four types of programs as do personal and workgroup information systems: systems programs, horizontal market application programs, vertical market application programs, and custom-developed programs.

Systems Programs

As with hardware, the subject of systems programs for communications processing is exceedingly complicated and involved. As systems software, they are acquired from the CPU manufacturer, from the vendor of the OS (possibly as part of the OS), or from a specialty software house. The subject is so complicated that most MIS departments allocate their most technically accomplished programmers to the tasks of maintaining and, occasionally, modifying the communications programs.

Teleprocessing Communications Control   To understand the need for **teleprocessing communications control**, consider the system in Figure 12-10. Suppose the computer shown here resides at a bank and that over 200 terminals are connected to over a dozen communications lines. Further suppose that terminals submit transactions that are processed by one of seven different programs (e.g., demand deposit accounting, loan payment, line of credit activity, MasterCard payment).

Now assume that the communications hardware operates correctly and that messages are accepted from the terminals, combined and transmitted over the high-speed lines, delivered to the central computer site, deconcentrated or otherwise processed as necessary, and correctly deposited in the main memory of the processing computer. The question is, Now what?

Each message is a transaction for one of the seven application programs. Each must be delivered to the appropriate program. That in itself is tricky enough, but consider this: Each of those programs is processing many other transactions concurrently. Not only will the program most likely be busy when the new message arrives, but a line or queue of messages might already be waiting for it. The new message needs to be placed in line with all the others and processed in turn. And all of this activity must occur fast enough that the customer notices no appreciable delay.

The necessary coordination tasks are handled by a computer program called the **communications control program (CCP)**. This program keeps order among the TPS programs, their input, and their output. For example, Customer

Information and Control System (CICS), licensed by IBM, is a widely used CCP that also provides transaction processing services.

Curiously, with mainframe computers, the CCP is an add-on product. It must be licensed (and paid for) in addition to the OS. With minicomputers, the CCP is built into the OS. This anomaly arose because, historically, teleprocessing was an add-on to the batch processing typical of most mainframes. Minicomputers, however, were designed to perform teleprocessing from their onset. Be aware that, in both cases, the functions of the CCP must be performed; such functions are simply included in the OS of most minicomputers.

Network Communications Control Network communications control protocols concern the packaging and processing of messages across a communications network. As you have seen, the ISO developed a seven-layer network communications standard called the OSI reference model. This OSI model, discussed earlier in the context of LANs, applies to protocols for any of the communications alternatives described in this text. Figure 12-13 summarizes the seven layers of the OSI model.

Figure 12-13 The OSI Model

Layer 7 — **Application**	rules about how an application program requests data transmission and supplies the data to be transmitted in the proper format
Layer 6 — **Presentation**	rules about how the data is to be displayed on the screen, how it may be encrypted or compressed for efficient transmission, and whether it is translated between ASCII code and EBCDIC code
Layer 5 — **Session**	rules about how a communications session between two devices is established, what special signals are used to indicate the progress of the dialogue, and how a session is to be reestablished if the connection fails
Layer 4 — **Transport**	rules about how the address of the recipient is to be expressed, how large volumes of data are to be broken up into blocks for transmission, and how received blocks are to be reassembled into the complete message
Layer 3 — **Network**	rules about how to determine the routing of messages from sender to receiver and how to maintain records of messages transmitted
Layer 2 — **Data link**	rules about resolving competing requests for the use of the channel, defining the beginning and end of data blocks, and detecting and correcting errors
Layer 1 — **Physical**	rules about the shape of connectors used to plug the system together, the speed and direction of the transmission, and how the bits are to be represented electrically (or by light pulses, or whatever)

In the late 1970s, the U.S. military wanted to develop a vendor-independent protocol for network communications. The OSI model was at that time under development, and it was not clear how important that model would become. Therefore, the military developed its own communications protocol called **Terminal Control Program/Internet Protocol (TCP/IP)**. Since vendors who wanted to sell communications and computer hardware to the military had to develop products that conformed to this standard, many companies conformed to this standard. Today, TCP/IP is commonly available.

The relationship of OSI to TCP/IP is shown in Figure 12-14. At the OSI application layer, TCP/IP provides terminal emulation capability (TELNET), a file transfer protocol (FTP), and a rudimentary E-mail application called Simple Mail Transfer Protocol (SMTP). The next TCP/IP layer, the TCP service layer, accomplishes the functions of the presentation, session, and transport layers of the OSI. The OSI network layer, which routes messages across the network, is handled by the Internet Protocol (IP). The data-link and physical layers are assumed to be Ethernet (IEEE 802.3) or other types of data-link control.

Some capabilities described in the OSI model are omitted from TCP/IP. Consequently, the U.S. government is urging vendors to develop products to a version of the OSI model called **Government OSI Protocol (GOSIP)**. If the

Figure 12-14 The Relationship of OSI to TCP/IP

OSI	TCP/IP
Application	TELNET FTP SMTP
Presentation	
Session	TCP Service
Transport	
Network	IP – Routing
Data Link	IEEE 802.3 and other
Physical	

government is successful, there probably will be a wide range of products that adhere directly to the OSI model. In the meantime, most communications-oriented products for communications backbones and WANs support TCP/IP.

During the 1970s, IBM, DEC, and other mainframe vendors were also developing communications standards. IBM developed **Systems Network Architecture (SNA)**, a set of processing concepts that document IBM's data communications strategy to enable its major customers to develop strategic information systems plans. More than a protocol, SNA includes proprietary IBM protocols and also includes rules, procedures, structures, and statements of strategic direction.[5]

Because SNA was initially developed prior to the widespread use of minicomputers and prior to the invention of microcomputers, it has been forced to undergo a number of dramatic changes as technology has changed. For example, the concepts of LANs were added on to SNA after its inception.

SNA is important to large IBM users because it specifies the standards to which IBM will develop its data communications technology and products. Since it is a proprietary standard, the U.S. government and many large organizations have avoided products based on SNA. These organizations did not want to become locked into products that were available from just one vendor.

Regardless of their type, protocols are implemented in hardware and in systems programs. In addition to these programs, enterprise information systems need horizontal market, vertical market, and custom-developed application programs.

Horizontal Market Application Programs

Horizontal market application programs meet needs that cut horizontally across industry types. Some network systems software provides horizontal application programs. TCP/IP, for example, provides for a rudimentary E-mail. Beyond such rudimentary capabilities, however, horizontal programs must be acquired in addition to the systems software. An enterprise that wants more sophisticated E-mail, for example, would need to license an E-mail application.

Horizontal market programs such as word processing and spreadsheet packages are rare for enterprise information systems. Most such packages are used instead in personal and workgroup information systems settings.

The most popular horizontal application for enterprise applications is accounting systems. There are standard packages for general ledger, accounts payable, accounts receivable, payroll, and other, similar accounting and accounting-related applications.

5.   Madron, Thomas W., *Local Area Networks,* 2nd ed. New York: John Wiley & Sons, 1990, pp. 74-75.

Horizontal packages in other business areas tend to be standardized across a number of industries. Most notable are horizontal manufacturing applications for MRP, CAD/CAM, inventory management, machine scheduling, and related applications.

Vertical Market Application Programs

Vertical market application programs, a large component of most enterprise information systems, are developed by independent vendors for application within specific industries. There are vertical market application programs for all types of interdepartmental activities. For example, in the revenue-generation processes, there are order-entry applications for parts distributors, appliance retailers, and computer dealers. Similarly, for purchasing, there are applications to facilitate specific purchasing activities. Specialized applications are also available for personnel and payroll applications, asset control, product development and planning, manufacturing, and accounting.

Vertical market applications are developed and often supported by VARs. The degree of support depends on the posture taken by the organization's MIS department. If that department is staffed to support such applications, then support is brought in-house. Otherwise, the VAR is paid for support. The choice between these two alternatives depends on enterprise policy, the work load of the MIS department, the capability and quality of the VAR, and the price of the service. Some organizations choose external support for some vertical market packages and in-house support for other packages.

Custom-Developed Application Programs

Historically, almost all enterprise application programs were custom developed. It was assumed that, when an organization acquired a computer, it would also need to hire a staff of programmers and other systems development personnel. Today, that is not the case, for several reasons.

First, when programs are custom developed, the organization must pay the entire development expense. On the other hand, if programs are purchased, then development expense can be spread across all the purchasers. And, as new needs arise, with purchased programs, the cost of adaptation is spread across all the using organizations.

Additionally, developing custom applications requires considerable time. The systems development staff must first acquire the subject matter expertise to

Figure 12-15 Custom-Developed Application Programs
Custom-developed application programs, once common, are now the exception.

develop the application, and then they must design, program, and test it, all of which can take a year or more. Then, too, during this period the requirements may change. On the other hand, if the applications are acquired from an outside vendor, they can often be installed and operational within 30 to 60 days.

Third, developing applications is risky. There is no guarantee that the requirements will be correct or understood; if they are, there is no guarantee that the programs will be correctly written and tested. On the other hand, when acquiring developed programs, an organization can evaluate what it is buying. Such evaluations are themselves risky, but less so than investing in a new development effort.

For these reasons, most organizations today avoid developing custom programs if at all possible. In fact, many companies are converting the custom programs they do have into vertical or horizontal packages. The exception to this is applications with unique requirements for which no suitable package exists. These include unique applications on the cutting edge of MIS, which may be developed by large companies with the resources to make such investments. Most applications in most companies are no longer custom programs.

DATA

Enterprise data is stored and processed to enable the business to maintain successful relationships among both internal departments and employees and external agencies. Data is used to organize the activities of the business to generate appropriate and consistent responses to conditions, situations, problems, and opportunities.

There are several important dimensions to the data component for enterprise information systems. For one, as discussed in the previous chapter, users have different views of data. The sales department wants to keep different data about customers than does the accounts receivable department. An enterprise information system must be developed so that all users can obtain the views of the data they need.

Another consideration for enterprise data is that different departments and processes depend on one another. Changes made by one department impact the processing of a second department. To keep users from interfering with one another, the processing rights and responsibilities of users must be specified in detail. Finally, the location and degree of duplication of data must be determined.

Departmental Data Interdependencies

Enterprise information systems are developed to help personnel produce appropriate and consistent responses to situations that arise. We do not want to call on customers who have asked to be left alone, nor do we want to agree on one price and bill with a higher (or lower) one. The chief advantage of integrating data is that it increases the chances of appropriate and consistent responses.

In the previous chapter, when we discussed the revenue-generation function, we observed that Marketing, Sales, Operations, and Accounts Receivable all process customer data. This statement puts the cart before the horse. More accurately, department interacts with the customer, and, to produce appropriate, consistent behavior, each must refer to (and maintain) data about the customer.

From this vantage point, the problems with duplicated data become even more clear. If each department maintains its own customer data, then each will have its own view of what is appropriate behavior with regard to that customer. When the data varies, the company risks having two departments deal with the customer in inconsistent ways. For example, Sales may be taking orders from customers that Accounts Receivable will not approve. Integrating data reduces the likelihood of this inconsistent behavior.

One benefit of integrating data is that the dependency among departments becomes evident. When one department's interaction with the customer depends on actions taken by another department, the two departments will need to share integrated data. Accounts Receivable, for example, must collect the exact amount of money that Sales has said will be due. Sales, therefore, must accurately key the prices and terms of the order. In this case, Sales is creating data that it does not use. If Sales makes an error, the problem will not manifest itself in Sales but rather in Accounts Receivable.

This dependency exists whether data is integrated or not. Integrating the data simply makes it more evident. When an enterprise information system is first installed, this characteristic may appear to be a disadvantage of data integration. In point of fact, the problem existed before the data was integrated. Integration just brings it to the surface. In the long run, this characteristic is an advantage.

Data-Distribution Alternatives

In a company with several central processing computers, suppose that you are responsible for determining where to place customer data. If you put all of it on one computer, then substantial communications costs to access that data may occur for the users who are not near that computer. You could break up the data and try to place customer records close to the users who need them the most. You could also replicate the data and duplicate it on several computers.

So far we have described the disadvantages of duplicating data. There are times, however, when data duplication is desirable—but it should be done only with the knowledge of possible data-integrity problems. Features must be created in the information system to prohibit inconsistent data from developing.

The four fundamental alternatives for locating data are summarized on a continuum in Figure 12-16. On the one end of this continuum, all of the database can be placed on a single computer. On the other end, the database can be **partitioned**, or split into pieces, and the database can be **replicated** so that some partitions are stored on two or more computers. In between these extremes is a database that is partitioned but nonreplicated and a database that is nonpartitioned, with each entire database replicated on two or more computers.

These alternatives are illustrated in Figure 12-17. For this example, suppose the database consists of four pieces, W, X, Y, and Z. Figure 12-17a illustrates the first (leftmost in Figure 12-16) alternative. There is one database, all of which is stored on one computer; hence there is no replication. Figure 12-17b shows the next alternative. Here, the database has been partitioned into two pieces; pieces W and X are stored on computer 1 and pieces Y and Z are stored on computer 2. In Figure 12-17c, the entire database has been replicated on two computers. Finally,

Figure 12-16   Database Distribution Alternatives

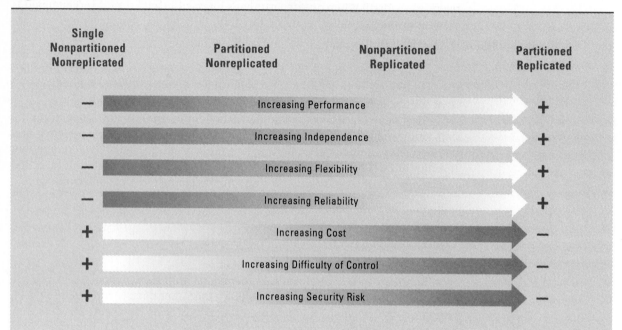

in Figure 12-17d, the database has been partitioned and a portion (Y) has been replicated.

Characteristics of these alternatives are listed in Figure 12-16. Alternatives toward the right provide an increase in performance, independence, flexibility, and reliability. On the other hand, those alternatives also involve greater expense, greater difficulty of control, and greater risk to security.

Of these advantages, one is particularly significant to future business managers. Alternatives on the right of Figure 12-16 provide increased flexibility and hence can be better tailored to the enterprise structure and the enterprise process. A highly decentralized manufacturing company, for example, in which plant managers have wide latitude in their planning, can never be well satisfied by an enterprise information system with the structure of Figure 12-17a. The structure of the organization and the structure of the company fight with one another. Thus, alternatives on the right-hand side can provide a better and more appropriate fit to the organization than can those on the left-hand side.

The greatest disadvantage is difficulty of control and the resulting potential loss of data integrity. Consider the database architecture in Figure 12-17d. A user connected to computer 1 can read and update a data item in partition Y on computer 1 at the same time a different user connected to computer 2 can read

Figure 12-17 Database Distribution Alternatives
(a) Nonpartitioned, nonreplicated data. **(b)** Partitioned, nonreplicated data. **(c)** Nonpartitioned, replicated data. **(d)** Partitioned, replicated data.

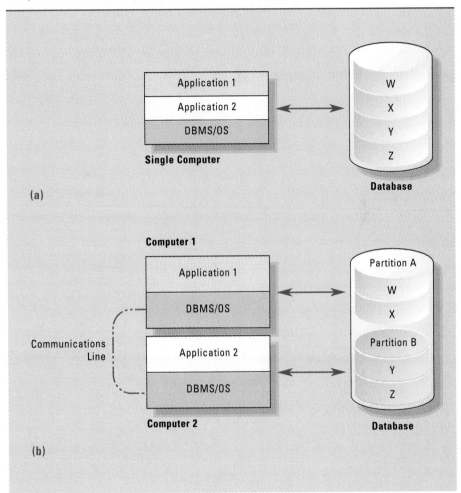

and update that data item in partition Y on computer 2. For reasons beyond the scope of this text, the strategies used to control concurrent processing for a database on one computer do not work, generally, for those on multiple computers.

In time, new algorithms and technology may be developed, but for now, it is not possible to allow unrestricted concurrent processing of a partitioned, replicated database. Instead, if this architecture is to be used, restrictions must be placed on processing. We will consider an example in the next section.

Figure 12-17 *(continued)*

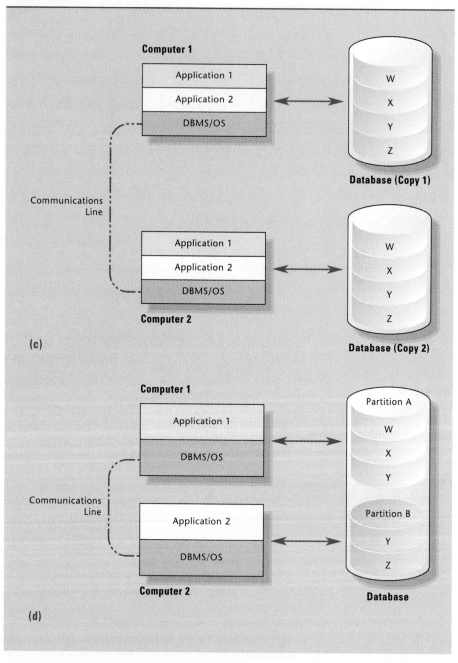

Distributed Database System at Legacy Systems

Legacy Systems operates information systems to support revenue generation. These systems integrate the activities of Marketing, Sales, Order Processing, Warehouse, and Accounts Receivable, as discussed in the previous chapter. We will consider a portion of this system to illustrate both the need for distributed database processing and the restrictions that must be placed to achieve appropriate control.

Figure 12-18 shows a portion of the revenue-generation system that involves Order Processing and Product Marketing. In Order Processing, order-entry clerks

Figure 12-18 Partitioned, Replicated Database at Legacy Systems

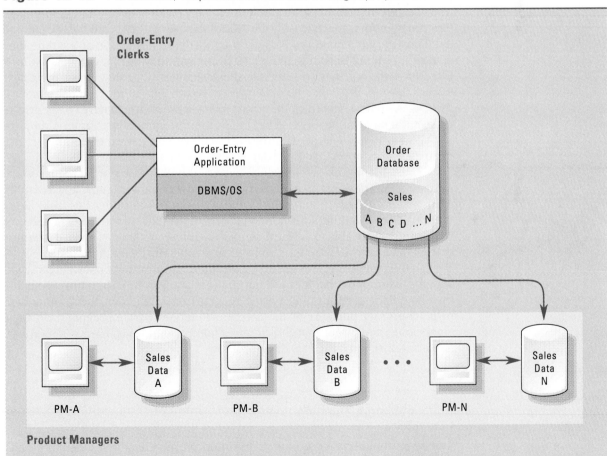

utilize an order-entry application to process the order database. This database is then used by the warehouse and later by Accounts Receivable, but that is not shown in Figure 12-18.

Product Marketing is staffed by product managers (PMs), who have responsibility for the development, sales, and support of product groups. As part of their job function, the PMs regularly report sales of their products to their managers and to other Legacy personnel. In addition, once each month they produce a revised sales schedule, which is used by Finance for cash planning and by Production for production planning.

To perform these functions, the product managers need current sales data. As shown in Figure 12-18, they extract this data for the products they manage from the operational Order database. In doing this, they create a partitioned, replicated database. It is partitioned because they take only a portion of the Order database; it is replicated because there are two copies of the portion they take: their copy plus the copy that remains on the Order database.

To prevent data-integrity problems, Legacy makes two limiting assumptions. First, no attempt is made to keep the PMs' databases current with the operational database. By agreement, the PMs get the most current data, as of the time they extract it. Two milliseconds later, massive changes may be made to the data they just extracted, but they will not see these changes until they make their next extract. Second, the PMs are not allowed to return data to the Order database. If they believe data is incorrect, they must follow a procedure to have someone else change the data via the order-entry application program. Furthermore, they are not allowed to change the data they extract, even on their own computer. The organization assumes that the Order database is the sole official version of orders.

These limitations are workable because the PMs do not need the most up-to-date data. The most frequent changes involve new sales, and the PMs can accomplish their job function by saying, "This data was current as of Monday morning," or something similar. All the users of the PMs' reports understand that limitation and are able to perform their jobs within it. If the PMs needed the most current data, then this database architecture would not be feasible.

In this system, the PMs are part of an enterprise information system designed with the assumption that they will not change data. For the PMs to be responsible members of their organization, once they agree to this limitation, they must adhere to it. The other portions of the revenue-generation system depend on their compliance, and errors, inaccuracies, and misconceptions can result somewhere in the organization if the PMs do not comply.

International Data Communications

Among multinational corporations, additional concerns about data communi–cations arise from the problems associated with **transborder data flow**—sharing data across national boundaries. International data sharing raises an important new set of business factors. Consider the following examples:

- Currency exchange fluctuations may change the cost-effectiveness of a data center in one country as compared to another.

- Local differences in time zones, working hours, and holidays affect the timing of data needs.

- Language differences affect not only interpersonal communication, but also language requirements for data entry screens, output reports, and system documentation.

- The use of locally manufactured equipment may be required that is not consistent with equipment elsewhere in the company.

- Stringent privacy regulations may restrict the transmission of data about individuals across national borders.

Although the common carriers that provide data communications service in the United States are private companies, in most other countries they are operated by government-owned **postal, telephone, and telegraph (PTT)** monopolies. That is, the only data communications providers are government agencies. In some cases, the requirements of PTT agencies are designed to support infant national computer industries by requiring the use of locally manufactured equipment in any system that is connected to data communications services.

Privacy Another important factor in transborder data flow is the stringent regulations that have been established in some countries to protect individual privacy. Within many countries, access to databases containing information about individuals, such as payroll and performance data, is closely regulated to prevent the data's use for purposes other than those specifically authorized. Such countries prohibit the transmission of personal data to destinations outside their national borders, where they lose the ability to regulate its use.

Three main strategies have been adopted by multinational corporations to respond to these challenges. The first strategy is to educate corporate executives about the special factors that apply to international information systems. Thus, the planning of corporate information systems can take these factors into account. The second strategy is to increase local processing of data within foreign countries to reduce the volume of raw data that must cross borders. Reducing the volume of data to be communicated reduces the company's vulnerability to changes in PTT fees and regulations. The third strategy, which is closely related, is to process personal data within the country where it originated (for example, by processing payroll data and producing paychecks there), to avoid problems with privacy regulations. In this way, data is processed locally where privacy regulations can be enforced, and only summary information not identifiable to any individual is transmitted across the national border.

PROCEDURES

By now you are familiar with the four standard types of procedures: normal and failure recovery procedures for both users and operators. These procedures are required for enterprise information systems just as they are required for personal or workgroup information systems.

Because of the large number of users and large amount of data, procedures for enterprise information systems tend to be more standardized and formalized than for other types of systems. The bank that uses the system shown in Figure 12-10 has more than 200 tellers, all of whom must follow the same procedure. If not, chaos will result, and there will be little control over operations. This means that procedures must be well documented and users well trained.

Similar comments apply to the operations activity of enterprise information systems. Critical enterprise activities depend on the proper initiation and execution of TPSs and other systems. Jobs must be started on time and according to expected procedure, and problems that develop must be dealt with promptly and correctly.

Enterprise operations activity is crucial not only because it supports the flow of business activity, but also because operations is responsible for one of the organization's most critical resources: data. There are often several hundred billion bytes of data in an enterprise information system. If a mistake is made in processing that data, say the operator mounts the wrong disk unit, the consequences can be disastrous. In fact, it may take weeks to recover from the damage—with great inconvenience to enterprise activities. For these reasons, operations procedures must be well designed and documented and the operations staff, thoroughly trained.

Controls Over Enterprise Information Systems Processing

Because enterprise information systems are so critical and frequently involve the control and accounting of the organization's assets (e.g., accounts payable), much thought has gone into procedural controls of enterprise information systems processing.

Over the years, accountants and auditors have established ground rules for appropriate controls. In fact, auditors are required by the American Institute of Certified Public Accountants (AICPA) to evaluate the controls against these ground rules for any information system on which they rely in an audit. In this section, after demonstrating the need for enterprise information systems controls, we will briefly review these ground rules, or categories, of these controls.

The Need for Controls

To understand the need for controls over computer processing, consider the following three scenarios.

Fictitious Sales   John Smith works in Accounts Payable for a large organization. John's brother-in-law sells paint. The company John works for buys paint; sometimes the paint goes to a supply locker, and sometimes it is delivered directly to the site at which the paint will be used. Since paint is consumable, it is difficult to determine whether or not it was actually used.

One day John decides to create fictitious deliveries of paint. John forges requisitions and POs. He creates artificial receiving documents, which cause payables to be created. Every month, his brother-in-law receives a check for paint he never delivers. After 6 months of this, John buys a 1958 Corvette and buys gold jewelry for his friends. His company's profit margin is reduced, but not enough for anyone to notice.

Illegal Funds Transfer   Consider another scenario. As a computer programmer at a bank, John writes and maintains programs that process deposits and withdrawals and compute interest payments on savings accounts. One day, he notices that the only transaction on some accounts is the payment of interest. As he looks, John determines that these accounts are owned by elderly and possibly deceased people. On a day off, John drives to a remote branch of his bank and creates a savings account under a fictitious name, say Elmo Cratchet.

One day, while John is working on the savings information systems programs, he adds program statements to move the money from three large, inactive savings accounts into Elmo's account. At the end of the month, the program instructions move the funds back. John writes the programs so that these transfers will not appear on the savings account statements. Meanwhile, his account earns the interest on $700,000 of other people's money. After 18 months, he quits his job, removes the changes from the programs, and takes a delightful trip through Europe on the misappropriated interest of $100,000.

Theft of Equipment   In a third scenario, John is walking through the production area one day and notices a large number of used computers in a storage room. On inquiry, he learns that this equipment is accumulated through each quarter and sold at the end of the quarter to a used-equipment dealer. John works in Accounting, where one of his duties is to maintain a list of used equipment.

Through discreet inquiries, he learns that one of the warehouse employees has an expensive drug habit. He approaches this person and enlists her support. Each week, John deletes certain records of used computer equipment from the inventory list. He gives the serial numbers to his accomplice, who steals the equipment and sells it on the black market. The two split the proceeds.

Figure 12-19 Types of Computer Crime

- Manipulating computer input
- Changing computer programs
- Stealing data
- Stealing computer time
- Stealing computer programs

Figure 12-19 summarizes the basic types of computer crime. The first and third scenarios are examples of a crime committed by manipulating computer input. The second example involves changing computer programs. Other types of crime are stealing data, stealing computer time, and stealing programs. We will not consider all of these types here. For further description of these and other types of crime, see *Crime by Computer* and the *Criminal Justice Resource Manual.*[6]

EDP Controls

As mentioned, accountants and auditors, along with information systems professionals, have developed ground rules for appropriate control over information systems processing. These people introduced the term **EDP controls**. EDP, an accounting term, stands for electronic data processing. Today, EDP auditing is a separate profession with its own EDP Auditors' Association.

EDP controls are features of information systems that reduce the likelihood of accidental losses, unauthorized activities, and computer crime. Although such controls involve all five components of an information system, we consider them in this section because your involvement with them as a business professional will occur most frequently in procedures. Categories of EDP controls are listed in Figure 12-20.

Management Controls

Managers have an important **management control** responsibility with regard to enterprise information systems. They need to take an active role in the

---

6. Parker, Donn B., *Crime by Computer.* New York: Scribners, 1976. Bureau of Justice Statistics, *Criminal Justice Resource Manual.* Washington, DC: U.S. Dept. of Justice, 1979.

Figure 12-20 Categories of EDP Controls

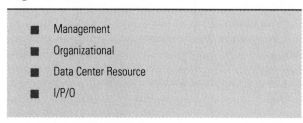

- Management
- Organizational
- Data Center Resource
- I/P/O

development, management, and use of such information systems. It is most important for managers to take seriously the development roles that we have described in Chapters 7 and 10 and that we will further describe in the next chapter.

If managers do not take an active role in the information systems involved in the activities they manage, they will leave a vacuum. The people who do work with the information system will begin to feel ignored and unappreciated. They may begin to think that no one cares about the work they do or that their work is judged unimportant by management. They may be tempted to misuse the system just to see if they can do it. As time goes on, this misuse can grow until it reaches the stage of computer crime.

There are a number of specific measures for managers to take. First, management must let people know that it views information systems as important, by discussing systems at departmental meetings, by recognizing them when they have been especially useful, and by making the resolution of systems problems an important priority. Managers should take whatever other actions they can to communicate to their employees that information systems are an integral part of the business and that such systems are important. Among other benefits, such an interest increases the belief that potential unauthorized or criminal activity will be caught.

Second, managers who have responsibility for the use or operation of information systems should manage those systems as they would manage other activities. They should request periodic reports on the operation of these information systems that include the number of transactions (or other unit of measure) processed, the number of hours logged on the system, the percent of time the system was available and unavailable, and the number of hours of processing without failure. Further, managers should take steps to determine how effectively the information system accomplishes its function. Are the users satisfied? Does the system serve its intended purpose? Can users accomplish their work effectively and efficiently? All of these monitoring actions contribute to the employees' sense of importance about the information systems.

Additionally, when problems occur, managers must follow up on them immediately. They must find out what caused the problem and take steps to fix it.

Figure 12-21   Types of Management Controls

- Attend to MIS applications
- Manage MIS activity
- Follow up on problems
- Take control procedures seriously

Failures that occur regularly are especially suspicious. If, as a manager, you suspect any unauthorized or criminal activity, contact your MIS department for assistance.

Finally, management should consider control procedures important and ensure that employees view them the same way. If the department is supposed to count the number of invoice forms and balance this number against a number printed on a computer report, then management should ensure that this is done. Management controls are summarized in Figure 12-21.

Organizational Controls

Organizational controls concern the company's organizational structure. The fundamental principle is that organizations should be structured so that the authority to control an asset is separated from the duty to act on the asset. For example, in writing checks for accounts payable, one person should have the authority to approve an expenditure and a different person have the duty of writing the check. This is called the **separation of duties and authorities**.

In the first computer crime scenario, concerning fictitious sales, one problem was that John had both the authority and the duty of creating requisitions, POs, and receiving documents. A better system of controls would involve six people. One person would create a requisition and another person would approve it. A third person would create the PO, and a fourth person would approve it. A fifth person would create the receiving document, and a sixth person would generate the check. With such a system, six different people would need to be in collusion to be able to perpetrate a crime. An illegal activity with this many people would be difficult to orchestrate and keep hidden.

Separation of duties and authorities should be accomplished for all valuable assets, not just money. No programmer should be able to make changes to a program and place that changed program into the operational library by himself or herself. Instead, at least two people should be involved. One person should make the changes, and a second person should install the changed program into the official program library. Unfortunately, in many companies, programmers have far too much latitude. An employee known to be a superior programmer often has the freedom to change programs. This is particularly true in companies in which there have been problems with computer systems.

The separation of duties and authorities has value only if someone consistently checks transaction records against approval documents. In the case of accounts payable, for example, someone must reconcile canceled checks against requisitions, POs, and receiving documents. The separation of duties and authorities accomplishes nothing without such follow-up. Similarly, in the case of program libraries, someone must reconcile changes to the libraries against requests for changes to the programs. All changes must have such supporting documents.

Data Center Resource Controls

A major difference between personal and workgroup information systems and enterprise information systems concerns the location and environmental control of the processing equipment. Most personal and workgroup systems reside in the

Figure 12-22 Protecting the Data Processing Center
The central processing computer is in an area accessible only by authorized personnel.

users' work spaces. While access to these systems is often controlled by keys and passwords, the equipment is not normally kept in a separate and controlled facility.

The situation is different with enterprise information systems. Because of the value and sensitivity of enterprise data and because of the immense cost of a lengthy disruption in enterprise information systems processing (as when bank teller stations are inoperable for a week or so), most data centers that support enterprise information systems are located in controlled and isolated environments. Twenty years ago organizations proudly displayed their computer centers in ground-floor window locations, but the civil disruptions in the 1960s convinced companies (and their insurance carriers) that it would be better to locate their centers in protected settings.

Today, through **data center resource controls**, most enterprise MIS departments take great care to protect their processing centers. First, the computer is placed in a locked and controlled room accessible only by authorized personnel. Employees allowed in the computer room are identified by special badges or by other means. A log is kept of all visitors and of whether they are employees of the organization or of an outside organization.

Second, the computer centers are located in protected, secure, inside locations. Windows, if any, are located so that they cannot be reached by nonemployees. The room is situated so that no one can inconspicuously observe the activities inside the computer room.

A third data center control consists of operating procedures that are carefully planned and controlled. A schedule of activity is established and followed. Further, the log of activity produced by the OS is examined periodically to ensure that the schedule has been followed and that no important tasks have been omitted or extra tasks added.

In addition, the libraries of computer programs are secure and protected from unauthorized changes. As stated previously, the duties and authorities of changing this library are separated. The libraries themselves are made inaccessible, insofar as they can be and still serve their function. Records are kept of all changes to program libraries and reviewed periodically.

Because enterprise databases are so large and the cost of recreating them is so enormous (if this is even possible), backup and recovery procedures must be carefully planned and executed. Procedures must be documented, and operations personnel, trained. Practice sessions should be held periodically.

Additionally, the data center must be protected from fires, industrial accidents, and natural hazards. Fire extinguishing systems must be operable, and fire drills should be conducted. Further, the enterprise computer center should not be located next to a munitions factory, nor should it be located in a flood plain or on top of an earthquake fault line. Provisions should be made to recover from a total disaster. Critical programs, files, and procedures must be stored in a secure, off-premise storage facility—perhaps in a distant city.

Multinational organizations have additional problems to consider. The data center should be protected from terrorism or danger from disruptive political

Figure 12-23 Data Center Resource Controls

- Control access to data center
- Locate data center in protected environment
- Plan and document operating procedures
- Protect libraries of programs
- Plan and execute backup procedures
- Plan and practice recovery procedures
- Protect data center from natural hazards
- Protect international data centers

situations. Again, copies of critical programs, files, and procedures should be located in out-of-country storage facilities, to the extent allowed by commerce restrictions. Data center resource controls are summarized in Figure 12-23.

I/P/O Controls

The goal of this last category of controls, **I/P/O controls**, is to ensure that all authorized work is performed and that only authorized work is performed. To understand the need for such controls, consider a payroll system designed to operate in the following phases:

1. Departments submit pay rate change requests.

2. Payroll approves pay rate change requests.

3. Payroll clerk makes pay rate changes to payroll database.

4. Payroll supervisor reviews a summary of changes; problems are noted.

5. Mistakes, errors, and omissions are corrected.

6. Payroll produces paychecks.

To ensure that no authorized changes are lost (and that no unauthorized changes are gained), a variety of controls needs to be used at each stage of this process. For example, the departments should submit a batch of pay rate changes with a transmission form that includes the total number of changes being submitted. This sum, called a **batch total**, should be written in ink on a form that is signed by an authorized person.

Figure 12-24 I/P/O Controls

Category	Type of Control
Input	Documentation of authorized input format
	Separation of duties and authorities
	Verification of control totals
	On-line system input controls
Processing	Documented operating procedures
	Reviews of processing logs
	Adequate program testing
Output	Documented output procedures
	Control over disposition of output
	Users trained to examine output

The batch total is then followed through all of these steps. Payroll sums the batch totals from all the departments in step 2, and the system prints a total of the number of changes made in step 3. The clerk compares these two totals. In step 4, the supervisor reconciles the number of changes made on the summary report with the sum of the batch totals from the signed transmission forms. The number of changes due to mistakes is controlled in the same way.

Processing and output must also be controlled. Only a few selected and trained employees can be allowed access to the application used in step 3. Their access to this program must be monitored and controlled, and a summary log of this activity should be printed and reviewed by a supervisor. Output must also be controlled. The report that summarizes pay rate changes should be delivered to only the authorized personnel. Only the employees who need this information should be authorized to receive a copy of the report. Transmission forms may be used when delivering output back to the user as well. I/P/O controls are listed in Figure 12-24.

Summary of Controls

Our brief review of the important controls over enterprise information systems processing leaves much unsaid about this subject. If you become an auditor who specializes in information systems, you will spend weeks learning about computer security and control.

As a business professional, you need to be aware of the possibility of unauthorized activity and crime and to know your responsibilities and those of your department. If you have questions about the appropriate procedures or course of action, contact your MIS department.

Finally, be aware that there is no such thing as a secure information system. All OSs have idiosyncrasies that trained and determined criminals can exploit to compromise security. Furthermore, a leading expert on computer crime, Donn Parker, reports a distressing fact: Most computer criminals are caught by accident. Most crimes are identified in passing while attempting to fix other problems. No one knows the full extent of computer crime.

Because of these facts, it is wise to maintain as little sensitive data as you can to do your job. If you are worried about data being stolen, keep it only on diskettes that you control physically and store in safes. Destroy sensitive data as soon as it is no longer needed.

PEOPLE

People are the final component of an enterprise information system. As with personal and workgroup information systems, people are involved with information systems in four different roles: use, development, operations, and management. With enterprise systems, however, information systems professionals take a larger role than they do with the other two types.

Figure 12-25 contrasts the amount of activity undertaken by users and systems professionals for each of these roles for personal and enterprise systems. As shown, users are far less involved in developing enterprise systems than they are in developing personal systems. Users are still involved, however, primarily in specifying and reviewing requirements. Similarly, users have a small role in operating enterprise systems; it consists of starting and stopping their hardware (and, possibly, programs) and performing limited routine maintenance (e.g., changing printer ribbons). With regard to systems use, users maintain the predominant role for corporate systems. Finally, considering the management of information systems, systems professionals have the primary role, but they are supported by users and users' managers.

Workgroup information systems are not shown in Figure 12-25. If they were, they would lie between personal information systems and enterprise information systems.

Figure 12-26 shows an organization chart of a typical large corporation. User departments are supported by the MIS (or information services or information technology) department. As shown in this figure, the VP of MIS (sometimes called the **chief information officer**, or **CIO**) reports directly to the CEO. This arrangement

Figure 12-25 Responsibilities for Personal and Enterprise Systems

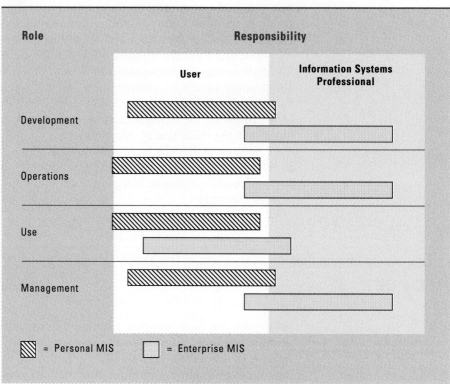

Figure 12-26 Organization of a Large Corporation

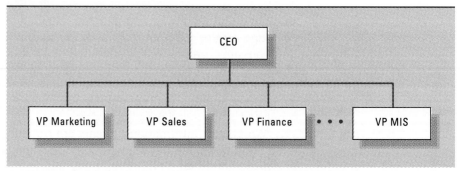

reflects the importance of information and information systems to business organizations today.

In the early days of MIS, many MIS departments reported to the VP of Finance. This structure proved to be suboptimal, primarily because organizations found themselves developing information systems in a wide variety of areas other than Finance. The organization in Figure 12-26 enables the MIS department to best serve the needs of the overall organization as opposed to the needs of any one department.

The roles that enterprise information systems users play are a subset of the roles they have played for the other two types of systems. Consequently, we will only briefly discuss end users' activities before discussing organization and staffing of the MIS department.

User Departments

Although the wording in this text seems to indicate that users are a homogeneous group, this is not the case at all. Users differ in their education, experience, job title, job level, and interest in and desire to learn about information technology. Consequently, users differ in the amount of training, documentation, and other support they need.

Additionally, users' attitudes about information systems vary considerably. Some users couldn't care less about the role of the information systems to the organization whereas others need to understand how each component relates to the others. Some users want to be taught only how to perform a particular function. Others are constantly searching for unknown features, functions, or capabilities in the system.

As a result of these differences, users typically differentiate themselves with regard to the system, quite often informally. One user might become intrigued by computer technology and begin to learn more and more. Eventually, his or her coworkers will come to recognize that person's special skills and knowledge and will bring new, difficult, or anomalous situations to that person's attention. Over time, such people become informal, internal systems consultants.

Some organizations have recognized this situation and created a new job title. Typical names are key user, information systems liaison, even computerist. Here, we employ the term *key user*. A **key user** is a person who holds a job in an end-user department, say accounting, but who, because of an interest in computers and information systems, has gained specialized expertise. This person becomes a local broker of information systems knowledge. End users go to this person when they have problems or need help.

The key user, who often has received special training from the MIS department, answers the other users' questions and calls on the MIS department for help with questions beyond his or her knowledge. In this way, users have someone local whom they trust to go to for answers to their questions; they do not need to exhibit their ignorance in front of strangers in the MIS department, who they fear may not understand their plight. At the same time, the MIS department is not plagued with simple and routine problems or requests.

The MIS Department

The MIS department is the organization's primary source of information technology, and it is responsible for ensuring that the organization uses such technology to best accomplish its goals and objectives. That responsibility breaks into two major functions. One is to develop, operate, maintain, and manage the enterprise information systems. The second is to acquire technology and to facilitate its transfer to appropriate applications.

The nature of this second function was summarized by Cash, McFarlan, and McKenney in a description of three broad objectives of information systems management control:

1. Facilitate appropriate communication between the user and the deliverer of information technology services and provide motivational incentives for them to work together....

2. Encourage the effective utilization of the [MIS department's] resources and ensure that users are educated on the potential of existing and evolving technology....

3. Provide means for efficient management of information technology resources and give necessary information for investment decisions.[7]

Today, the organization of MIS departments recognizes these dual roles. Consider Figure 12-27, which shows the organization chart of a typical MIS department for a large corporation. This organization has two major components. One of them, the data processing department, has responsibility for developing and operating the enterprise information systems. The other component, the information center, facilitates end users in applying computer technology for personal and workgroup systems. Consider each of these departments in turn.

Data Processing The data processing (DP) department is responsible for developing, operating, and maintaining enterprise information systems. As shown

---

7. Cash, James I., Jr., F. Warren McFarlan, and James L. McKenney, *Corporate Information Systems Management,* 2nd ed. Homewood, IL: Irwin, 1988, pp. 135, 136.

Figure 12-27   Organization of a Large Corporate MIS Department

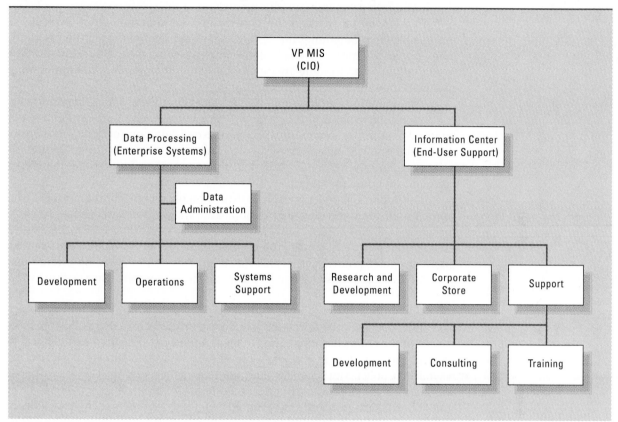

in Figure 12-27, this department normally has development, operations, and systems support groups. Then, too, generally a *data administration* group provides a staff function to the DP director.

The development group consists of systems analysts and programmers who work with users to create enterprise information systems. Typically, an enterprise information system is developed by a team of people that includes systems analysts, users, and programmers. Normally, a senior systems analyst is the leader of the project, although in some cases, a senior end user is the leader.

The systems analysts guide the project through the development process. Either the prototyping process or the SDLC process can be used, described in the next chapter. Systems analysts are responsible to ensure that all five components of an information system be properly developed.

Programming personnel, on the other hand, are concerned only with the program components and, possibly, with data and hardware as they relate to programs. If application programs are custom written, a team of from two to three to several dozen programmers will create them.

In addition to creating the system, the development group typically is responsible for maintaining the system, which involves changing the system to meet new requirements (or making the system do what the users really wanted it to do to begin with). In some organizations, system maintenance consumes more resources than system creation.

The operations group runs the computer hardware. This group normally consists of several shifts of computer operators. It may also include a data-entry group, if the organization requires one, and several data-control clerks who control the receipt and disbursement of data to and from the data center. Operations normally manages the tape or other data library as well, and sometimes it includes a machine maintenance group.

The systems support group consists of highly technical programmers who select, install, tune, and otherwise maintain the systems software. These programs include the OS, the CCP (and other teleprocessing software), the DBMS, the systems utilities, and others. Normally, the programmers in this group are very talented; often they possess advanced degrees in computer science. (Systems analysts and application programmers normally possess degrees in information systems.)

Data Administration   Figure 12-27 shows the **data administration** group as a staff function to the DP director. The **data administrator (DA)** is custodian or trustee of the enterprise data. The DA takes a policy-making role with respect to data for the company as a whole, determining what data should be stored and establishing policies for accessing and maintaining that data. The DA works directly with the CIO and the company's top executives.

The **database administrator (DBA)** plays a more technical role in administering those policies for one or more specific databases. The DBA's functions include establishing data conventions and standards; managing the configuration of enterprise databases; ensuring that adequate backup and recovery procedures exist and are followed and that adequate security controls and procedures exist; and performing other, miscellaneous functions needed to protect the organization's data asset.

Considering the first function, data conventions and standards are required for data consistency. While there may be many views of data and data may occur in many different systems, the organization needs a standard set of data definitions and formats. Consider, for example, a product number. The organization needs to have one standard set of product numbers with one standard set of meanings. If several different product-numbering schemes are allowed to develop, chaos will result; one department or function will be unable to communicate with another. Sometimes, it is impossible to gain consistency. In these cases, the inconsistencies should be defined and documented.

Organizations are dynamic; they change in response to both external stimuli and internal stimuli. As they change, it is often necessary to alter the structure of enterprise databases. Since such databases are shared, however, this change must be accomplished so as to minimize the consequences on other systems and applications.

The data administration function is also involved with the creation and documentation of procedures for backup, recovery, control, and security, as described previously. Data administration is an important function. Much has been written about it. See Lyon in particular.[8]

End-User Support   The purpose of the end-user support department, often called the **information center**, is to help end users employ computer technology to solve their own problems. Whereas the DP department creates, maintains, and operates systems for users, the information center helps end users help themselves create and operate both personal and workgroup applications. It grew out of a support group for end-user DSS in the early days into a wide-ranging set of services to end users of all kinds today.

As we observed earlier in this text, however, while end users develop many of their own personal information systems, it is less likely that they will be able to develop their own workgroup applications. For these applications, end users typically obtain the support of a VAR or of someone from the MIS department. If help is obtained from the former, then the end-user support department will often help in preparing and evaluating the RFP. If help is obtained from the latter, then normally someone from the information center will provide development expertise, and, when necessary, also involve personnel from the development group in the DP department.

Information centers are organized in many ways, one of which is shown in Figure 12-27. Here, there is a group involved with research and development that functions to keep pace with the rapid growth in technology, products, and services available from the micro and end-user support industries. This group typically evaluates new releases and new products and determines whether these releases and products offer potential benefits to the company. The group also has a crucial role in setting enterprise standards.

Many information centers operate their own company microcomputer store. Large companies are often able to negotiate dealer status with many of the vendors, which has the advantage that the MIS department is then able to buy products at the same price as dealers. Large companies take the position that since they may buy as many copies of, say, a spreadsheet program as a small dealer would, they want the same price breaks the dealer obtains.

The third information center shown in Figure 12-27 is the support group, which provides consulting and training services to end users. It may also provide a

---

8. Lyon, John K., *The Database Administrator*. New York: John Wiley & Sons, 1976.

limited amount of development service. For example, an accounts payable department may be able to get along perfectly well with the standard features of a spreadsheet program for all but 5 percent of its work load. For that 5 percent, however, personnel in that department may need specialized programs, or macros. Rather than involving the development group of the DP department, many companies allow personnel in the end-user support group to provide this service, which is generally restricted to a few hours or work days of labor.

Organizations in Smaller Companies

As mentioned at the start of this section, the organization shown in Figure 12-27 is typical for large organizations. For smaller companies, some of these functions are combined. For example, in the DP department, the data administration and systems support functions may be combined into one group. For reasons of control, however, it is never a good idea to combine the operations and development groups.

Considering the information center, smaller companies seldom operate their own computer store. Further, the research and development group is often combined with the support group. In very small organizations, the entire end-user support department is subsumed under the development group in the DP department. In this case, the MIS department and the DP department become one and the same.

SUMMARY

The components of an enterprise information system are the same as those for personal and workgroup information systems: hardware, programs, data, procedures, and people. Since enterprise systems involve more people, departments, and data, however, these components are more complicated and comprehensive than are those for the other system types.

Many types of hardware configurations are used with enterprise systems. This chapter describes four: LANs, teleprocessing systems, internets, and BNs. The structure of LANs is the same for enterprise systems as it is for workgroup systems. The LAN, however, is distributed through several departments, not just one.

The classical approach for supporting enterprise systems is teleprocessing, with which all applications processing occurs on a centralized computer. End users employ either dumb terminals or microcomputers that emulate dumb terminals. In the latter case, terminal emulation cards are inserted into the micros' expansion slots.

The three dimensions of communications media, or communications lines, are speed, mode, and type. When communication lines must cross public roadways or property owned by others, a company usually leases lines from a common carrier. WANs and MANs are services provided by common carriers.

Since most individual users cannot keep a costly communications line busy by themselves, often several or many users are connected to the same line. Polling and multiplexing are used to manage lines. Hardware involved in this process includes front-end processors, multiplexers, and PBXs. Data processing hardware is usually mainframe computers and minicomputers.

Internetworking is the linking of LANs into an internet by devices called bridges, gateways, and routers. Today, organizations sometimes choose to downsize their teleprocessing systems to internets.

A BN is a central data superhighway within an enterprise that provides a general-purpose communications network for the enterprise. It links LANs, mainframe computers, independent microcomputers, and other devices. It may include WAN and MAN links to provide access to geographically remote computers. BNs support at least message passing, such as E-mail, file transfer, and terminal emulation.

Considering programs, enterprise information systems involve systems, horizontal market, vertical market, and custom-developed programs just as personal and workgroup information systems do. The need for controlling communications processing requires special features and functions in systems programs. The communications control program (CCP) manages communications for a teleprocessing system. Network communications control systems follow communications protocols. The OSI model is used as a reference for other models. The Terminal Control Program/Internet Protocol (TCP/IP) is a communications protocol for backbone networks and WANs. Systems Network Architecture (SNA) is an IBM proprietary communications strategy statement that includes protocols for WANs.

Historically, most organizations custom-developed enterprise applications programs. Today, economics favors licensing either vertical market programs or horizontal market programs instead, and most new applications are acquired in this way. Many organizations are converting their custom programs to programs licensed from vendors or VARs.

Enterprise data is stored so that the business can maintain successful relationships among internal departments and employees and external agencies. Enterprise systems store data of use to many departments and, as a result, create dependencies among these departments. Data must therefore be processed with a communitywide perspective. With enterprise systems, the same data can be viewed in multiple ways, depending on the needs of the users.

There are a number of different architectures for enterprise databases, including partitioned or nonpartitioned, replicated or nonreplicated. The advantages and disadvantages of these alternatives are illustrated in Figure 12-16.

When data is shared across international borders, additional factors must be considered. Data communications services in most countries are provided by governmental PTT agencies, whose policies often support national goals. National privacy laws may restrict data transmission across borders. Corporate information systems policy makers must be educated about these factors. The resulting systems often process data locally to reduce transborder data flow and eliminate problems with privacy regulations.

Enterprise systems require the same four types of procedures as do personal and workgroup systems. Because of the importance of enterprise processing, CPAs and others have developed procedural controls over processing. The basic categories are management, organizational, data center resource, and I/P/O controls.

Enterprise information systems involve development, operations, use, and management roles. Because of their complexity and size, such systems require support from professional staff. The professionals play a much larger role in development, operations, and management of enterprise information systems than they do for personal or workgroup information systems.

Most MIS departments have two major divisions. One division is concerned with the development, operations, and maintenance of enterprise information systems. The other division is concerned with transferring technology to individuals and workgroups outside the MIS department. Enterprise databases must be supported by data administration.

KEY TERMS

Teleprocessing
Dumb terminal
Terminal emulation
Port, or line connector
Network server
Voice-grade line
bps
Line conditioning
Wideband line
Analog line mode
Digital line mode
Modem
Full-duplex line
Half-duplex line
Simplex line
Common carrier
WAN
MAN
Communications port
Polling

Front-end processor
Multiplexing
Buffering
Internetworking
Internet
Bridge
Gateway
Router
Downsizing
BN
Teleprocessing
   communications
   control
CCP
Network
   communications
   control
TCP/IP
GOSIP
SNA

Partitioned database
Replicated database
Transborder data flow
Postal, telephone, and
   telegraph (PTT)
EDP controls
Management controls
Organizational controls
Separation of duties
   and authorities
Data center resource
   controls
I/P/O controls
Batch total
CIO
Key user
Data administration
DA
DBA
Information center

REVIEW QUESTIONS

1. List the five components of an enterprise information system.

2. Describe how LANs can be used for enterprise information systems. How does such application differ from the use of LANs with workgroup information systems?

3. Define *teleprocessing* and give an example.

4. Describe two important advantages of teleprocessing systems over LANs.

5. What is the difference between a dumb terminal and a microcomputer? Which will see greatest use in the future? Why?

6. What hardware is required at the user's site in a teleprocessing system?

7. What is a terminal emulation card? Why is it used?

8. List three dimensions for classifying communications lines.

9. Explain the difference between voice-grade communications lines and wideband communications lines.

10. Explain the difference between analog lines and digital lines. What function does a modem serve?

11. Explain the difference between full-duplex lines and half-duplex lines.

12. Differentiate between a LAN, a WAN, and a MAN. For each, who owns the actual communications lines?

13. What role does polling serve? What is its chief disadvantage?

14. What is multiplexing? How does it differ from polling?

15. What role does the PBX play in communications?

16. What types of computers are used for the centralized computer of a teleprocessing system?

17. What is an internet, and how is it used in enterprise information systems?

18. Differentiate between a bridge, a gateway, and a router.

19. What does the term *downsizing* refer to?

20. What is the purpose of a BN?

21. What three basic functions are provided on a BN?

22. What purpose does terminal emulation serve on a BN?

23. List the four categories of programs for enterprise information systems.

24. What is the function of the CCP? Why is it needed?

25. What is TCP/IP? What function does it serve? How is it different from the OSI model?

26. What is GOSIP? How does it differ from the OSI model? What impact will GOSIP have on TCP/IP products?

27. What is SNA?

28. List two enterprise information systems horizontal market applications.

29. List two enterprise information systems vertical market applications.

30. Explain the economic disadvantages of custom-developing programs. When is such development justified?

31. Explain how the views of a vendor might vary between the purchasing department and the accounts payable department.

32. Describe a situation in which two departments have a data dependency.

33. Under what conditions is it acceptable to duplicate data?

34. List four alternative ways to store an enterprise database.

35. Explain the advantages and disadvantages of centralized versus distributed data.

36. How do privacy laws affect transborder data flow?

37. Identify three strategies used by multinational corporations to respond to the challenges of international data communications.

38. List the four types of procedures needed for an enterprise information system.

39. Give an example of the need for controls over the changes that are made to a program library.

40. What are EDP controls? Why are they necessary? List the major categories of such controls.

41. Describe two management control activities.

42. Describe two organizational control activities.

43. Describe two data center resource control activities.

44. Describe two I/P/O control activities.

45. Why does the VP of the MIS department not report to the VP of the finance department?

46. What is the function of a key user?

47. What are the two major branches of the MIS department?

48. Explain the function of each group shown on the organization chart in Figure 12-27.

49. Differentiate between the functions of data administration and database administration. Describe at least three functions of each.

DISCUSSION QUESTIONS

1. Suppose your college or university decides that it should provide computing facilities to every student in every dorm. The stations will be used for word processing, E-mail, and specialized classroom projects. Consider each of the four alternatives shown in Figure 12-3. List criteria for deciding among these alternatives. Using your knowledge of a student's needs and the discussions in this text, score these alternatives and recommend one of them.

2. Suppose that your university uses a teleprocessing system to process all student records including applications, admission scores and other data, class schedules, grades, and withdrawal and graduation data. Further suppose that every department on campus operates its own LAN and that each faculty member has his or her own microcomputer connected to the LAN. Finally, suppose that the department chairperson has account numbers and passwords to access the teleprocessing system. Periodically, the chairperson extracts data about students who major in the department.

   List 10 potential threats, or opportunities, for accidental loss, unauthorized activity, or criminal activity. List controls that should be placed on this system. Include at least two control activities from each of the four major control categories.

PROJECTS

A. Interview (or invite to class for an interview) the VP of the MIS department from a local company. What are the major enterprise information systems in use? What types of communications networks are used? What types of programs? Is any of the data distributed? If so, why? What problems have occurred because of the distribution? What benefits? If not, why not? What types of procedures are in use? What does the organization do to ensure that control procedures are followed? What happens when the control procedures are not followed? What is the organization of the MIS department? How does that department reach out to the rest of the organization? Is there a data administration group? If so, what does it do? If not, why not? What are the two or three major trends or shifts in MIS service that this VP has observed in the past 5 years? How has the function of the MIS department changed? How does the VP view the future for MIS departments? What will be that department's function 10 years from now?

B. Collect further information about computer crime and methods of prevention and report your findings. Consult the references provided in this chapter and other books and periodicals, and, if possible, interview an EDP auditor or a teacher with knowledge of EDP auditing. What are the most common types of computer crime? Illustrate each type with anecdotes. Are statistics on computer crime generally accurate? Why? To what degree do typical, or average, companies protect themselves against computer crime?

C. Interview a data administrator or a database administrator. What is that person's job description? What does the person actually do? Is there a difference between the job description and the job activity? If so, why? What are the two or three most important functions served? Over whom does that person have authority? What does that person have responsibility for? What are the greatest assets that a person in this position can have? How has this field changed in the past 5 years? How does that person expect it to change in the future? Would you like to have the job of data or database administrator? Why or why not?

D. Locate a textbook or professional handbook on data communications published at least 7 years ago. Compare its description of computer networks to the description in this chapter. Skim over the technical details, as much as possible, and concentrate on the overall shape of data communications networking as envisioned at the time the book was written. What major differences do you find? Compare the emphasis on teleprocessing to the emphasis on LANs in the book. Did the author of that book foresee the rapid spread of LANs? Is the concept of internetworking described in any way?

M I N I C A S E

Hackers for Hire

One Sunday afternoon early last year, a team of hackers dressed as phone company workers arrived at the Philadelphia Savings Fund Society, breezed past security guards, and entered the bank's operations center. Once inside, the squad defeated an encryption system on a money machine, withdrew $80,000, and wreaked havoc on the bank's computer systems for three hours.

Sometime later, the same group used wiretaps and other devices to hijack a United Airlines computer. They accessed an airline ticketing center and the Apollo and Sabre computer reservation systems and landed a virtually unlimited supply of airline tickets.

Just two more damning examples of hacker crime? Not quite. In both cases, the hackers were working for their victims, who paid them handsome fees in return for detailed reports on just how their systems were cracked. Not surprisingly, the reports shocked both companies. "Corporations always think they have a fortress around them," says Ian Murphy, leader of the hired guns. "Then we crawl in through the basement window."

Murphy, also known by his nom de guerre, "Captain Zap," is one of a new breed of hackers for hire. It's perfectly legal to hire someone to break into your own computer and communications systems and explore their weaknesses. But some companies understandably shudder at the thought of inviting hackers—some of whom are convicted felons—into their networks.

More sobering is the thought they might be there anyway, hired by some brazen competitors that cross the legal line and hire hackers as spies. "Last week I got a call from some guy who said he could get me anything on anybody for $50," says Winn Schwartau, executive director of Interpact, a security consultancy in Seminole, Fla., and a technical analyst for the National Computer Security Association in Carlisle, Pa. "He had a shopping list of stuff he could get, a whole section on corporations. I hear from these people all the time."

The issue of whether to hire hackers is a source of soul-searching at security conferences and in corporate boardrooms. "It's a real tough call," says Dorothy Denning, a professor of computer science and security at Georgetown University in Washington. "If you really want to find out if your system is protected against hackers, you must have hackers beat away at it. On the other hand, there's a widespread feeling that businesses don't want to promote that kind of activity."

In fact, hiring hackers is an idea many security managers can't stomach. After all, they worry, what's to keep the hackers from coming back later to do damage? Or selling information on the client to other hackers? "It would make me very nervous," says Ernie Arthur, support center manager at American Financial Corp. in Cincinnati. "We don't feel we have enough of a security problem to risk that."

Many of today s hackers-for-hire have in fact been convicted of major crimes in the past. Murphy, for one, was found guilty in 1981 of using Pentagon phone lines for his personal use and breaking into Bell of Pennsylvania systems to reset the phone company's clocks. And all 12 of the hackers he employs at his Gladwyne, Pa.-based security firm, IAM/Secure Data Systems Inc., are convicted felons. ∎

Bob Violino, excerpted from *Information Week*, June 21, 1993, pp. 48–56.

Discussion Questions

1. Why do some companies hire hackers to crack their data security systems?

2. Why do other companies believe that hiring hackers is a bad idea?

3. What controls, as described in this chapter, should have been in place to prevent the security failures described in the first two paragraphs of this minicase?

4. What factors should a manager consider in determining whether to hire hackers as described here?

Copyright© 1993 by **CMP Publications, Inc.,** 600 Community Drive, Manhasset, NY 11030. Reprinted from INFORMATIONWEEK with permission.

13

Developing Enterprise Information Systems

THIS CHAPTER CONSIDERS THE DEVELOPMENT of enterprise information systems. Like Chapters 7 on the development of personal systems and 10 on the development of workgroup systems, it is concerned with the process by which such systems are created. Development activities become increasingly complicated as we move from personal to workgroup to enterprise information systems. One consequence of this movement is that the user role changes; users take less of a leadership role and instead become clients of others' services. For enterprise information systems, users generally become clients of the in-house MIS department.

There are four major sections in this chapter. First, we consider the challenges in developing an enterprise information system. Second, we discuss strategic planning for enterprise MISs, including several ways in which enterprises plan and prioritize development projects. Third, we discuss CASE, or computer-aided systems engineering. The last section discusses two contemporary movements in the development of enterprise information systems: outsourcing and the growth of workgroup MISs.

CHALLENGES IN DEVELOPING ENTERPRISE INFORMATION SYSTEMS

Developing an enterprise information system involves considerably more challenge than does developing personal and workgroup information systems. Some of the reasons for this arise from within the system to be developed; some arise from outside the new system; and some arise from the nature of the enterprise systems themselves. We will address each group of challenges. To understand this discussion, however, first consider the need for a new enterprise system in a manufacturing company.

Scott Orthodontics

Scott Orthodontics manufactures exceptionally high-quality orthodontic appliances for orthodontists, oral surgeons, and dentists. Over 90 percent of the orders that Scott receives are for custom-made items. Depending on the item, it may require from 2 days to several weeks to process the order. On rare occasions, when required raw materials are out of stock, it may take 6 to 8 weeks to manufacture an item.

Scott's customers, the dental professionals, want to provide prompt and efficient service to their patients. When they order from Scott, they need to know how long it will take to process their order so that they can schedule their patients' visits. Further, they need to know whether there are going to be extensive delays in manufacturing an item, so that they can reschedule their patients, order a different product, or order from another source.

When there are delays, the company's sales force bears the brunt of the customers' complaints. The salespeople need to know the status of an order, what problems exist, if any, and how long it will be until the order is shipped. Scott's order-tracking system is informal and inadequate, without a single point of contact for salespeople to call. Consequently, salespeople often are forced to call production supervisors, who, if sufficiently charmed or bludgeoned by the salespeople, will track down an order. The current situation is unacceptable to all, and, as a consequence, Scott has decided to develop an order-tracking information system.

The Flow of Order Processing

The order-processing system is shown in the DFD in Figure 13-1. Customers describe their needs to personnel in Sales, who then create orders. The order is

Figure 13-1 Order Processing at Scott Orthodontics

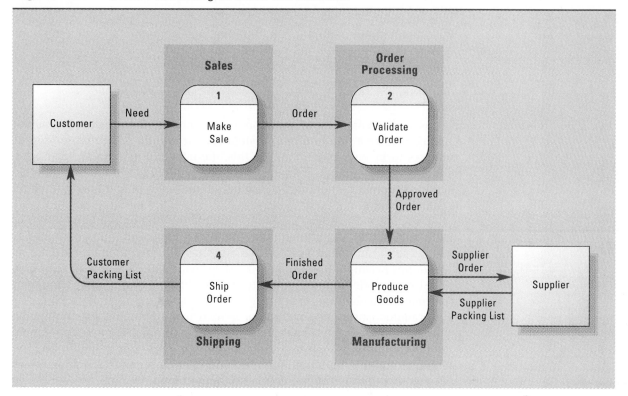

submitted to Order Processing, where it is validated for accuracy (which ensures that Scott can fill the order). The approved order is then sent to manufacturing, where it is produced. Raw materials are received from suppliers to produce an order. Finally, the finished order is transferred to Shipping, where it is sent to the customer.

At a point in time, an order can be in any one of these processes, or it can be in transit between any two of them. When there is a delay with an order, the salespeople need to know not only where an order is in the process but also when the customer will receive the order. Knowing that the order is in Manufacturing is of little value if it will be 6 weeks until a required raw material is received.

Although Scott has no order-tracking information system, it has other information systems. Its revenue-generation system includes Sales, Order Processing, and Accounts Receivable. Information systems in Manufacturing are used to plan production and purchasing activity and to schedule people and machines. There are information systems in Purchasing (not shown in Figure 13-1) and a general ledger system in Accounting. All of these systems are effective in accomplishing their function, but none of them provides information about the status and shipping date of a particular order.

Challenges to Development from Within the System

As stated earlier, enterprise information systems integrate the activities of different departments into a single business system that produces coordinated, consistent responses to its environment. To do this, the information systems must bring together a diverse group of people, policies, procedures, goals, and expectations. This diversity creates a number of challenges to the development activity; they are listed in Figure 13-2.

First, as you have seen, different departments maintain different views of shared data. Further, departments vary in the ways they need to process data. For example, sales can delete a terminated customer's record after the final sale is entered, but Accounts Receivable must keep that record active until the bill is paid. Also, some departments need to enter data that is only used by a different department, in which case, the quality of the data suffers.

In addition, users employ the same terms to mean different things. A shipping date to Manufacturing may be the date the order is completed. To Shipping, such a date is the date it is delivered to the carrier. To Sales, it may be the date the customer receives the shipment. Until the inconsistencies are known and understood, they will confuse the development activity.

Figure 13-2 Challenges to Enterprise MIS Development from Within the System

- Different views of data
- Different ways of processing data
- Different terminology
- Different goals and expectations
- Different types of system desired
- Different levels of competency
- Intrasystem departmental competition
- Fear of organizational change

Additionally, each department has its own goals and expectations. For example, at Scott Orthodontics, personnel in Order Processing are evaluated on the basis of the number of orders they process; personnel in Manufacturing, on the other hand, are evaluated on the quality of their products. As a result, characteristics of the new system that enable orders to be processed more quickly will be applauded by Order Processing; they may, in fact, be resisted by Manufacturing.

Departments also have different goals and expectations regarding the type of system to be developed. Order Processing may want a system that is, basically, a TPS. Manufacturing, on the other hand, may want a system for production supervision. Shipping may want a system that mainly addresses product delivery, while Sales may want a system that improves product quality (where the product includes sales support).

Another complication is that very often major differences exist in the competencies of departments. Because manufacturing quality was of great concern to Scott's founder, Manufacturing is full of well-paid, hard-working, ambitious, capable people. On the other hand, Order Processing was an afterthought. Hiring was done with less care, salaries are lower, promotions have been infrequent, and as a result, the level of competency is lower. When the development team convenes meetings among the Order Processing and Manufacturing personnel, this difference may become a problem. For example, Manufacturing personnel may so overwhelm the discussion that Order Processing's needs never become apparent.

In addition, the departments which are part of the system compete with one another for dollars, management time, promotions, salary increases, and other resources. While it is all very good to state that the new system is to be created for the benefit of all, when the system places (or appears to place) one department in an advantage with respect to another, problems will result. Further, it is possible for one group to gain control over the development activity and to turn the project into an internal competitive weapon. Markus states the following:

> Designers have been known to build systems to change the balance of power among departments or other units in the enterprise. Because this design intention is not viewed as legitimate in most enterprises, systems designed to increase one party's power and control over others are frequently masked in the language and appearances of improved efficiency or decision-making performance.[1]

While such manipulation is undoubtedly rare, elements of it, or the threat of it, do complicate the development activity.

Finally, systems often change the flow of work and the interactions among personnel both within departments and across departments. As this occurs, the enterprise will change. Such change, however, is normally perceived as threatening and is resisted. The enterprise change does not even have to be real; if the system

---

1. Markus, M. Lynne, *Systems in Organizations.* New York: Pitman Publishing, 1984, p. 77.

is perceived as changing the enterprise, it may be resisted. Then, too, such impact of this type of resistance is greater because it is seldom openly stated.

Challenges to Development from Outside the System

Other factors that complicate development arise from sources outside the boundaries of the system. These factors are listed in Figure 13-3. To begin, every information system resides in an environment of other information systems. In the case of Scott Orthodontics, the new order-tracking system will reside amid the existing revenue-generation system, the manufacturing system, the purchasing system, the general ledger system, and others as well.

The development activity of a new system must be cognizant of existing systems. If the new system will obtain data from or send data to an existing system, then this need will form part of the new system's requirements. In many cases, this is no problem. In others, however, the interface will be awkward. Consider an example from Scott. The goal of the new system is to track customer orders. To do this, the new system could utilize data processed by the existing manufacturing scheduling system. That system, however, tracks production work orders, which differ from customer orders. Thus, for the new system to use data from the existing manufacturing system, data conversion must be done.

Another complicating factor is that the new system may require more data from existing systems than they can provide. At Scott, the order-tracking system may be able to obtain 90 percent of the manufacturing data it needs from the current manufacturing systems. Obtaining the other 10 percent, however, may require a substantial change to those systems.

Figure 13-3 Challenges to Enterprise MIS Development from Outside the System

- New system resides in presence of existing systems
- Possible awkward system interfaces
- Data needed from other systems may be unavailable
- Projects compete for development dollars and personnel
- Partial development may be required
- Intersystem departmental competition
- Conflicts with MIS department

When this situation arises, the development team has three undesirable alternatives. It can develop an incomplete system, wait for the manufacturing system to be changed in the necessary way, or duplicate the functionality that properly belongs in a manufacturing system. All of these involve an unwanted compromise.

There are other external sources of complication besides existing systems. One is that the new project competes for both dollars and development personnel with other systems' development projects. Sometimes the development team is forced to compromise and cut back on necessary system capabilities because of a lack of money or time. The users whose requirements are unmet will be dissatisfied, and this dissatisfaction will then pose another problem to be solved. The enterprise prioritization of information systems projects is an important issue and will be discussed later in this chapter.

Another problem is conflict between departments that will be part of the new system and departments that will not. The new system may give departments that use it a competitive advantage over those that do not. With the system, the departments may gain more power, competency, time, or other resource. This change may be viewed jealously by departments that do not benefit from the new system's capabilities.

Sometimes, too, conflict develops between the users' needs and those of the MIS department. The MIS department may believe that it requires control over processing that the users do not want to give. For example, sometimes users want to make changes to enterprise data on their own computers. The MIS department may prohibit this. The reasons may be valid, such as limiting the processing of partitioned, replicated databases, as discussed earlier. Their reasons may also be suspect, such as a concern for loss of budget, personnel, or priority with management.

Challenges from the Nature of Enterprise Systems

In addition to challenges arising from within and from outside the new system, there are challenges that have to do with the nature of enterprise systems. These factors are listed in Figure 13-4.

First, enterprise information systems are often far more complex than are personal and workgroup information systems. Complexity in this sense means more functionality against more types of data. Whereas workgroup systems provide functions needed by the workgroup (a single department), an enterprise system provides functions needed by many departments. Further, the data to be processed is often more complicated. As stated, there may be many views of data as well.

Second, enterprise information systems are larger, with more concurrent users, more data input and stored, and more reports and output produced. Although size does not directly impact the design activity (e.g., given a level of

Figure 13-4 Challenges to Enterprise MIS Development from the Nature of the System

- Complexity—multiple features and functions
- Size—large number of users and amount of data
- Integration of different, possibly inconsistent and incompatible departments
- Considerable work and lengthy periods of time required
- Large development staff
- Possible requirements change during development
- Difficult-to-comprehend system

complexity, it takes as much time to design a small file as to design a large one), size does directly impact the amount of activity necessary for requirements definition and for implementation.

Another complicating factor is that enterprise systems integrate departments whose underlying activities may be inconsistent or incompatible. For the order-tracking system, it might be that Order Processing has been blaming certain delays on Manufacturing for years and that Manufacturing has been blaming other delays on Order Processing for years. To substantiate these claims, the two departments may have set up independent (and incompatible) business reporting systems. The new system may bring these incompatibilities to light.

Enterprise information systems often require considerably more work and longer periods of time to be developed. The increased complexity and size means that more time will need to be spent in all five stages of development.

There are two corollaries to this fact. First, to shorten the development time, enterprises sometimes increase the size of the development staff. Unfortunately, there are diminishing returns on the addition of people to development projects. In short, the more people there are, the more human interfaces must be maintained and the more time must be spent on communication and coordination. Larger projects are harder to manage.

Second, the problem with long projects is not just the delay that occurs before the system's benefits are realized. Another problem of lengthy projects is that, while development is underway, the business will change and the needs for the new system will also change. For a long project, the system is often out of date by the time it has been developed. The enterprise must respond to market needs, new laws, changes in ownership and management; as it responds, the original requirements may be invalidated.

Finally, because of the increased complexity, size, and time required for enterprise information systems development, it is more difficult for the development team and for any one individual to have an overall understanding of the system. In a classic book, Fred Brooks, a pioneer in large hardware systems development, discussed the importance of a single individual having a vision for the conceptual integrity of the entire system.[2] Without such vision, the system is vulnerable to inconsistencies, errors, and omissions. The larger the system becomes, the more difficult it is for anyone to have such vision. Additionally, the longer the project takes, the more likely it is that key personnel will be transferred or will change jobs.

ENTERPRISE MIS PLANNING

As stated, developing an enterprise information system is far more difficult than developing a personal or workgroup information system. Consider an analogy from construction. Building a personal information system is like constructing a single-family house; building a workgroup information system is like constructing a small office building; building an enterprise information system is like constructing a skyscraper. To build a skyscraper, much more planning and organization is required than for building houses or small office buildings.

Further, as described in the previous section, the new system will reside amid existing information systems and compete with other projects for resources. In terms of the construction analogy, the new skyscraper will need to be compatible with existing buildings and will compete with other skyscrapers being constructed or planned.

Business enterprises need a family of enterprise information systems that enables them to accomplish their business goals and objectives. They need a city of skyscrapers. At any one point in time, a number of different groups will propose the construction of a number of different systems. All of these proposed systems may be equally critical; some may be more critical than others; or some may not be critical at all. There may even be other systems not being proposed that are more critical than those that are. To deal with this problem, the enterprise must have some means of planning and prioritizing projects. We will consider a number of planning alternatives in this section. First, however, we will discuss the role of the MIS steering committee.

2. Brooks, Frederick P., Jr., *The Mythical Man-Month*. Reading, MA: Addison-Wesley, 1975.

Figure 13-5   The MIS Steering Committee
This committee of top company executives sets policies and priorities for MIS.

MIS Steering Committee

Every enterprise has some means for setting priorities among information systems development projects. Initially, as enterprises first develop information systems, that means is simply an informal committee. Perhaps the MIS director meets with the CEO and one or two other senior officers before making important or large-dollar decisions. Such an informal committee is not effective in the long run, except for small enterprises. As the enterprise develops more and more information systems, the planning issues become more involved, and it becomes apparent that a formalized forum for such decisions is needed.

To meet this need, most enterprises establish a formal group that sets priorities for information systems development projects. This group, called the **MIS steering committee** or some similar name, consists of senior-level managers or executives from all of an enterprise's major departments. The major functions of the MIS steering committee are listed in Figure 13-6.

First, the steering committee sets priorities among information systems projects. As stated, most often a number of different projects compete for the same dollars and human resources. The steering committee resolves such conflicts.

Figure 13-6 Major Functions of the MIS Steering Committee

- Establishing priorities among information systems projects
- Setting guidelines for MIS architecture and infrastructure
- Approving project plans, schedules, budgets
- Reviewing progress at major milestones; making "go" or "no-go" decisions
- Approving major hardware and program acquisitions
- Helping select and hire key MIS personnel
- Setting high-level policy and standards
- Providing advice and assistance to CEO, board of directors, and other senior executives

It may also take a proactive role in suggesting systems that should be developed or in approving planning projects.

The steering committee determines guidelines for the MIS architecture to be used in the enterprise. For example, if all systems are to be centralized, it is because the steering committee has created that requirement. The steering committee provides guidelines for the enterprise infrastructure needed to support the architecture. For example, if some systems are centralized and some distributed, the steering committee authorizes the creation of a network system to support that architecture. Similarly, if the steering committee determines that all systems are to be distributed, it establishes corporate policies to protect vital enterprise data in the distributed environment.

Another function of the steering committee is to approve project plans, schedules, and budgets. Along with this, the steering committee often has responsibility for reviewing progress at major milestones in large or important projects and in giving "go" or "no-go" decisions for initiating the next project stage.

The steering committee also is responsible for approving the acquisition of hardware and/or major programs. Sometimes, enterprises establish a budgetary limit for the MIS director; if the cost of an acquisition exceeds that limit, then the steering committee's approval is required. Similarly, the steering committee can be involved in selecting and hiring key MIS department personnel.

Additionally, the steering committee often sets high-level policy and standards. For example, it might establish the policy that users can buy only certain types of personal computer hardware or programs. Or, the committee might stipulate that the MIS department is to determine lists of approved hardware and programs from which users must select. Finally, the steering committee advises and assists the CEO, the board of directors, and other senior executives on an as-needed basis. An evaluation of the use of MIS steering committees can be found in an article by Drury.[3]

Top-Down Versus Bottom-Up Planning

There are two general categories of information systems planning: **top-down planning** and **bottom-up planning**. Top-down planning starts with an analysis of the overall business objectives and works down to specific systems. Bottom-up planning starts with the needs of a particular system, develops the needs for that system and other systems on that same level, and works upward toward an integration of systems.

To understand the differences between these two strategies, suppose that Scott Orthodontics sets out, without further planning, to build the order-tracking system. If the company does this, it is following a bottom-up strategy. Now suppose that, while developing requirements for the order-tracking system, it becomes clear that the information systems in manufacturing are totally inadequate, not only for the needs of order tracking but for manufacturing in general. Then suppose the team learns that the order-processing system needs substantial rework as well. As the order-tracking system development progresses, Scott management may decide that an entire revamping of its information systems is in order.

If Scott elects to do this, it will most likely use a top-down strategy. It will review the general business objectives and translate those objectives into the need for specific systems. Then it will prioritize the development of those systems and get to work.

The advantage of top-down strategies is that systems are developed with an overall perspective of the needs of the business. Correct and appropriate systems are developed on a timely basis. The disadvantage is that substantial lead time is required to perform the top-level studies, which results in delays before the first system is developed. Further, because of the lengthy time required, business needs may change before the first system is developed. When this occurs, the top-level analysis may never be finished, a situation sometimes referred to as **analysis paralysis**.

The advantage of bottom-up strategies is that specific systems are developed more quickly. The disadvantages are that the wrong system may be developed, incomplete and ineffective systems may be developed, and the system that is developed may have a short lifetime because it fulfills only a short-term need.

In the next three sections, we consider two top-down planning methodologies and one bottom-up planning methodology.

---

3. Drury, D. H., "An Evaluation of Data Processing Steering Committees," *MIS Quarterly*, Vol. 8, No. 4, December 1984, pp. 257–265.

Critical Success Factor Planning

A **critical success factor** (CSF) is an operational goal that must be attained to achieve success.[4] Individuals, departments, and the overall enterprise all have CSFs. For example, a salesperson may believe it is critical for her to identify at least two new leads per day, or an inventory manager may believe it is critical to turn the inventory at least six times per year. CSFs are used in top-down information systems planning to identify information needs, information systems, and, ultimately, requirements for information systems.[5]

The underlying assumption in CSF-based information systems planning is that the systems must exist that provide the information necessary to help management achieve the CSFs. If the CSFs are unknown, they must be discovered. The first step is to interview managers and to define the CSFs. Then the individual CSFs are combined into departmental and enterprise CSFs. Finally, the CSFs are analyzed to determine which information systems need to be added and which existing systems need to be changed.

Usually all top-level and many midlevel managers are interviewed and asked to specify both personal and departmental CSFs. For example, the manager of Customer Support believes it is critical for him to call three dissatisfied customers per day. That is one of his personal CSFs; typically, a manager will have several or many CSFs. The department will also have CSFs, one of which might be to keep customers on hold less than 30 seconds and in no case longer than 3 minutes.

Senior managers are also asked to specify enterprise CSFs. Examples are that revenue grow at 15 percent per year or that gross profit exceed 20 percent of sales.

Once all the managers have been interviewed, the CSFs are combined. Herein lies one of the problems of this method: There is no clear-cut, well-delineated algorithm for combining CSFs. Four individuals in the customer support department may specify 10 different CSFs, which need to be combined into 2 or 3. Similarly, five different senior managers may specify a large number of enterprise CSFs, which also need to be combined into a few.

One advantage of the CSF method is that, by identifying the most important information needs, it focuses the planning and development of information systems on the highest-priority issues. It also is broad in scope and thus unlikely to leave important information needs unaddressed. Further, it is simple and intuitive to understand.

The disadvantages are that it is time-consuming to perform, the process of combining the CSFs is difficult and sometimes ambiguous, and the result is no better than the ability of people to specify the CSFs. Also, this method focuses

---

4. Rockart, John F., "Chief Executives Define Their Own Data Needs," *Harvard Business Review*, Vol. 57, No. 2, March/April 1979, pp. 77–124.

5. Shank, Michael E., Andrew C. Boynton, and Robert W. Zmud, "Critical Success Factor Analysis as a Methodology for MIS Planning," *MIS Quarterly*, Vol. 9, No. 2, June 1985, pp. 121–129.

primarily on high-level managers. While such managers may be able to specify good CSFs at their level, they may not know and understand how the company functions at lower levels. Thus, the information needs of lower-level personnel may remain unaddressed. This disadvantage is compounded because the CSF method is not concerned with the details that must be specified to develop operational TPS. Because of these disadvantages, the CSF method is most likely to be helpful in developing MIS (narrow definition), DSS, and ESS.

Enterprise Analysis

Enterprise analysis, or **Business Systems Planning,** is a second top-down method for planning information systems. Whereas the CSF method is primarily concerned with generalized objectives, enterprise analysis is concerned with details—with identifying and correlating groups, their processing, and their data use. The CSF method asks each manager to consolidate his or her understanding into a few objectives. Enterprise analysis asks the managers for details about processes and data use; then the myriad details are combined, often with the assistance of computer processing, to identify which information systems are needed and what functions those systems should have. Enterprise analysis was invented by IBM under the name Business Systems Planning.[6]

Enterprise analysis is concerned with processes, organizations, data classes, and logical application groups. A process is an activity performed in the business. Enterprise analysis processes are the same as processes in DFDs. An organization is a group within the overall enterprise; usually organizations are formal groups and have names like *department, office,* and *group.* A **data class** is a group of data items that are created, changed, deleted, or used by one or more processes. A **logical application group** is a group of processes and organizations that utilize the same data.

The first step in enterprise analysis is to select a group of managers who represent all important activities of the enterprise. This group is then interviewed to determine what processes it or its departments perform and what data is involved in those processes. The result of these interviews is recorded in a number of different matrices and other documents.

Figure 13-7 shows a portion of a **process/organization matrix** for an enterprise analysis of activities at Scott Orthodontics. The rows of the matrix list processes and the columns list organizations. An *M* means the organization has a major involvement with the process; an *S* means the organization has some involvement. No letter means there is no involvement in that process.

---

6. Zachman, J. A., "Business Systems Planning and Business Information Control Study: A Comparison," *IBM Systems Journal*, Vol. 21, 1982, pp. 123–154.

Figure 13-7 Portion of Process/Organization Matrix for Scott Orthodontics

Process \ Organization	CEO	Finance	General Ledger	Purchasing	Accounts Receivable	Payroll	Treasury	Sales	Direct	Support	Manufacturing	Scheduling	Production	Inventory	Quality Control	Shipping	•••
Approve Order					M				S	S		S					
Support Customer					S				M	M		S					
Manufacture Order												M	M	S	M	M	
Validate Quality									S	S			S		M	S	
⋮																	

M = Major involvement   S = Some involvement

Figure 13-8 shows a portion of a **process/data class matrix** for Scott Orthodontics. This matrix relates processes (rows) to data groups (columns). A *C* means the data is created by that process, a *U* means the data is updated by the process, and an *R* means the data is read by that process. Processes that utilize the same groups of data are called logical application groups. These are shown by the circled regions in Figure 13-8.

A logical application group identifies processes and data classes. Using the process/organization matrix, processes can be related to organizations. Thus, the result of an enterprise analysis is a set of logical application groups with the data classes, processes, and organization units for each. This set of groups can then be used to plan the development of information systems to support each application group.

Figure 13-8   Portion of Process/Data Class Matrix for Scott Orthodontics

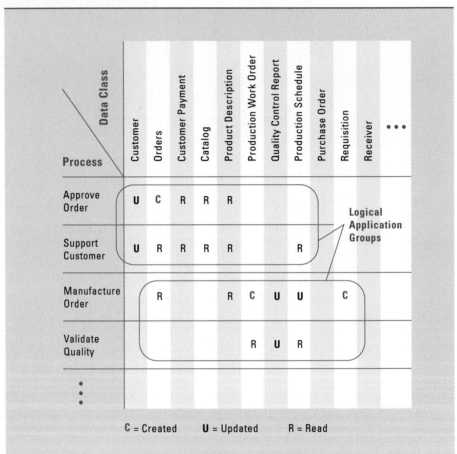

C = Created   U = Updated   R = Read

Logical application groups identify specific systems that need to be developed. Usually, a logical application group involves a mixture of systems types. Often a single logical application group indicates a need for TPS, MIS, and ESS within that group.

The major advantage of enterprise analysis is that it provides a comprehensive review of the information requirements across the organization and documents the use of data for all major processes and organizations. It is particularly useful for large organizations that require a thorough review of their processing and information needs. For example, the Social Security Administration used enterprise analysis in documenting its requirements when revamping its information systems.

There are three major disadvantages of enterprise analysis. First, as with CSF, only managers are interviewed. Critical information needs of workers and first-line managers can be missed. Second, enterprise analysis is a time-consuming and expensive process. The Social Security Administration scheduled 10 years for its systems modernization plan. Over such a long period, major changes may occur in organizational needs. Finally, enterprise analysis documents what is and not necessarily what ought to be. The results of an enterprise analysis are a set of logical application groups required to facilitate the existing processes, data needs, and organizations. Enterprise analysis does not suggest better ways of organizing business activity and data flow.

Evolutionary Planning

Whereas CSF and enterprise analysis are top-down methods, **evolutionary planning** works from the bottom up. With this approach, the need for information systems and their requirements are allowed to evolve as the business evolves. This does not mean that development is unplanned or uncontrolled but rather that projects are proposed as the need for them becomes apparent. The proposals are periodically reviewed by the MIS steering committee and prioritized against projects underway and projects scheduled to be started. Newly proposed projects may preempt existing projects, or they may supplant projects that were about to be started.

The advantage of evolutionary planning is that projects can be started with minimal study time and expense. The intuitive judgment of the steering committee members replaces the lengthy analyses performed using CSF or enterprise analysis. Further, evolutionary planning is adaptive in that priorities for projects change as the business needs change. New system development projects can be started without having to reconsider or repeat portions of an extensive planning process.

The disadvantage of this approach is that it can result in a hodgepodge of systems that have clumsy and ill-fitting interfaces or in a number of separate systems in search of a centralized theme. Further, it places a great burden on the judgment of steering committee members. While these people may be wise and experienced, using this process, they may not have enough data on which to base good decisions. Also, the steering committee typically is a consensus-oriented, group decision-making body. As you have seen, such groups can be dominated by one or two powerful individuals, and if this occurs, the information needs of certain groups may receive undue attention (or inattention).

Finally, evolutionary planning can cause systems development to proceed in fits and starts. It may be that, of three systems—say A, B, and C—C is the most important and A the least important. If, however, at the start of its planning, the steering committee is aware only of A, then it will approve the initiation of this project. If, later, the committee learns about B, it probably will decide to place A on a lower priority and then start B. When, finally, the committee becomes aware of C, it probably will decide to place B on a lower priority and start C. At this point, the management and staff of the MIS department may begin to lose confidence in the directions they are receiving.

Realize that evolutionary planning is not an unplanned or **ad hoc planning** approach. There is a plan, but it is based on the needs that have been discovered, without an active attempt to determine what other needs may exist. A truly ad hoc approach would allow projects to be started as they are proposed to the MIS department, as long as the money holds out, with little intervention or prioritizing.

Choice of Strategic Planning Method

Figure 13-9 summarizes the strengths, weaknesses, and best applications of the three planning methods described in this section. None is superior to the others for all cases; they each have situations in which they excel. Proponents of the top-

Figure 13-9 Strategic Information Systems Planning Methods

	CSF	**Enterprise Analysis**	**Evolutionary Planning**
Type	Top-down	Top-down	Bottom-up
Strengths	Focus on critical information needs Broad in scope Easy to understand	Detailed Comprehensive Useful in complicated situations	Quick Adaptive
Weaknesses	Time-consuming Possibly ambiguous	Very time-consuming Documents only "what is" Only managers' input	Possible hodgepodge of systems Possible domination by a few people Possible erratic development
Best Applications	MIS (narrow definition) DSS ESS	Stable, complicated environment	Dynamic environment

down approaches argue that these approaches are superior because each business needs an overall strategic systems implementation plan to avoid incomplete and duplicative systems and costly rework. Proponents of the evolutionary approach or other bottom-up approaches argue that this approach can build several incorrect systems for the time and cost that must be invested in top-down plans. Even if the systems are ineffective and incomplete, the process of building them will reveal more true requirements than will ever be identified by a strategic study.

Sometimes, businesses elect to follow a hybrid approach. For example, the steering committee might request a quick top-down overview of needs using either CSF or enterprise analysis. Given the results of this review, it would then follow evolutionary planning.

CASE

Computer-aided systems engineering (CASE) is the process of using information systems (having the five components) to build information systems (having the five components). CASE technology developed as information systems professionals sought ways to use computer technology to improve their own productivity. Some professionals found it ironic that so many people in the computer field were attempting to increase others' productivity but ignoring the potential for improving their own.

While many of the ideas that form the foundation of CASE have existed for quite some time, it was not until the advent of the microcomputer that CASE technology began to see widespread use. Today there are dozens of CASE products, and almost every major corporation is experimenting with, if not operationally using, CASE products and methodology.

CASE, however, is more than a set of computer programs. CASE is an information system that includes all five components. Together, CASE hardware and CASE programs are sometimes called **CASE tools**. But, as CASE is used to develop systems, a **CASE repository**—a database of system descriptors and other system parameters—is also developed. Further, procedures for using CASE are sometimes called **CASE methodology**. Finally, CASE requires a staff of systems developers trained in CASE tools and methodology.

It is a mistake to think of CASE as just a set of programs. Technology without methodology is a waste of money. Enterprises that have acquired CASE programs without changing their methodology have found little benefit from the tools.

We now survey the important components of CASE methodology and then discuss the capabilities of CASE tools.

CASE Methodology

While there is no single step-by-step CASE methodology, there is general agreement about the stages and basic activities that need to take place for developing systems using CASE tools. This generally agreed-on process is a variation and extension of the five-stage process you studied in connection with workgroup systems.[7]

Consider Figure 13-10, which summarizes this process. It begins with strategic systems planning, using one of the top-down methods. Enterprise analysis is frequently mentioned in CASE literature, though other methods are feasible. A variety of CASE tools are available to support this planning. The result is a set of specific systems to be developed. These systems are briefly documented, using CASE tools, and submitted to the steering committee for approval.

Figure 13-10   CASE Methodology

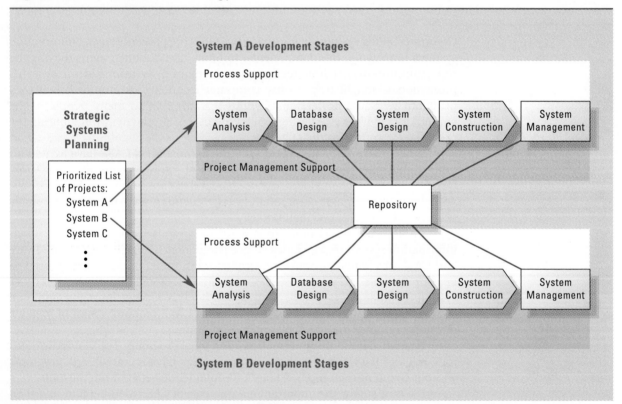

7.   Boone, Greg, *The CASE Experience, CASE Product Profiles.* Publication No. PP-10688. Bellevue, WA: CASE Research Corporation, 1988.

The steering committee creates a prioritized list of projects. The remaining activities are performed for each system to be developed. Figure 13-10 shows the development of two systems, A and B.

First, a system analysis is performed. During this stage, requirements are developed, including DFDs, data dictionaries, and other kinds of documentation. All are created with the aid of CASE tools and stored in the CASE repository. Figure 13-10 shows the repository, which contains data about systems requirements and other data about the various systems being developed. This means that, with some CASE tools, requirements developed for one system can be used as input to others, which is useful when certain operations involving a particular workgroup or department are common to both systems. In this situation, the DFDs and data dictionary that have been developed for one system can be used as a starting point for the analysis of a second.

The next stage is database design. Here, the data dictionary data is used to design the database using a process similar to that described in Module A. Next, system design is undertaken. In CASE literature, the term *system design* refers to the design of programs, user interfaces, forms, and reports. It does not generally include the design of hardware specifications, procedures, or job descriptions.

The next stage is system construction. This term also refers just to the creation of programs, user interfaces, forms, and reports. During the last stage, system management, the system is monitored and changes are made to it. Versions of programs and other system components are managed so that configuration of the system is always known and under control.

Two activities underlie the development of the system. Process support refers to activities to ease the development process and ensure that it complies with the MIS department's development standards. It includes support for group communications; creation, editing, and review of work; security and backup and recovery; and compliance with quality assurance standards. Project management support refers to activities accomplished to plan, schedule, allocate resources, and control the development project.

The process described here is similar to the five-stage process you learned previously, but it emphasizes different aspects of the development effort. With enterprise systems, much more time must be spent coordinating the new system with existing systems. Also, since enterprise systems are more complicated than personal or workgroup systems, this methodology places greater emphasis on design activities. And, since enterprise systems are larger, it places more emphasis on systems management.

This process, however, is compatible with the five stages. The definition stage occurs during strategic systems planning; the requirements and evaluation stages occur during system analysis; the design stage occurs during database and system design; and the implementation stage occurs during system construction and management. Again, this process is an extension and adjustment of the five-stage process.

CASE Tools

The goal of CASE is to use computer technology to facilitate the development of information systems by automating or at least improving human productivity for each activity in Figure 13-10.

Figure 13-11 shows typical components of CASE products, which are collections of CASE tools and a database of systems development data. The database, shared among all the tools, is called the CASE repository. The advantage of sharing the repository is that the results from one stage of development are readily available to tools in a subsequent stage of the process.

Figure 13-11 Typical Components of a CASE Product

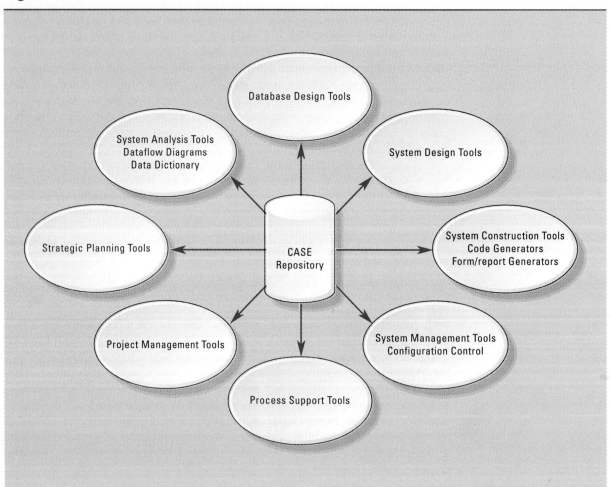

Most CASE products do not have all of these tools, though most CASE vendors are developing a complete set or are cross-licensing tools with other vendors to form a complete set. Not all CASE products have the same strengths. One product may have a particularly good system analysis toolset, while another product has a particularly good database design toolset. Consequently, some enterprises mix and match tools from different products, using tools from one product for one stage and tools from a different product for another stage.

The problem with using multiple CASE products is that there is no standard structure for the repository. The data in a repository for one product may be incompatible with the data in a repository for another product. Different products use different data structures that may not be easily translated. Therefore, enterprises that plan on using several CASE tools must watch out for potential problems.

There are CASE tools for each activity in Figure 13-10. Starting with strategic planning, some tools store, organize, and present the results of enterprise, CSF, or other types of strategic planning analysis. Using these tools helps to organize the strategic plan as well. The matrices in Figure 13-7 and 13-8 are examples of the kinds of output that such strategic planning tools can produce.

There are dozens of CASE tools that facilitate the creation of DFDs. These tools are graphical and mouse driven. They provide a standard set of symbols that can be placed and moved about the screen, and they allow the input of both text and drawn art. When these tools are used, DFDs can be developed with far greater ease and productivity than when drawn by hand. In addition, these tools provide automatic validation checking. For example, they ensure that, as a dataflow process is expanded to another level, no input or output is left out nor is any extraneous one added.

Analysis tools also provide capabilities for creating the data dictionary. Each dataflow, file, and process can be defined as described in Chapter 10. These definitions are then carried forward into the design construction processes.

CASE products generally include a database design tool, although the capabilities vary widely. Some such tools are simply graphical systems that aid humans in documenting a manually developed E-R data model. At the other end of the spectrum, some tools will construct a database design from data descriptions recorded in the repository. Generally, however, automatically generated designs exhibit problems and usually serve only as a starting point for human designers.

CASE products also include system design tools to facilitate the design of programs, menus, forms, and reports. By the time the system design tool is used, the data dictionary data and the database design are stored in the repository. The system design tools can access this data to make it easy for the human designer. For example, the human need only specify the name of a table when designing a report, and the system design tool can obtain the name of all columns of that table and guide the designer through the process of locating the columns on the form.

Some CASE products, called **upper CASE**, focus on systems analysis and design, and other products, called **lower CASE**, focus on system construction and management.

CASE products vary widely in their support for system construction. Some provide little, if any, support. Others provide tools that generate application program code, menus, and form and report descriptions. Many products produce large sections of source code that application programmers then move into the programs they write, which saves considerable time and eliminates the need for much of the programming work that is boring and repetitive.

There are also CASE tools to facilitate systems management. Many of the tools are used for configuration control over programs and database structures. Changes are made to programs or database structures either to correct errors or to adapt the system to changes in system requirements. Either way, it is important to know what changes were made, when they were made, for what reason, and by whom. Such records are also important for control reasons as discussed previously.

Concerning process support, many CASE tools include word processing and other text processing programs, paint and draw programs, and a limited version of E-mail. They also include facilities to control concurrent processing by development personnel and to protect the database against accidental, unauthorized, or criminal losses.

Finally, many CASE products include project management tools, such as programs for developing plans and budgets, for scheduling system development tasks, and for allocating resources. These tools are used to organize and control the project and to report on progress to management and the steering committee.

From this discussion, you can see that CASE is exactly what it sounds like—computer-*aided* systems engineering. CASE is not automated systems development. Instead, it is a methodology and a set of tools for developing systems with higher productivity and quality.

THE CHANGING NATURE OF MIS

For most of the history of information systems, the MIS department has held near-exclusive control over all computing resources. When the microcomputer became available, however, that control began to fade. At first, MIS professionals made fun of the primitive and sometimes erratic personal computers, calling them toys. But over time, as microcomputers and their software matured, end users found that they could accomplish many of their information requirements on their own, without the assistance of the MIS department. Some MIS departments found themselves bypassed by the new technology.

Meanwhile, senior management began to look more closely at the costs and benefits of their investment in information technology. In many cases, it was not clear that the enterprises were obtaining sufficient returns on their investments in information technology.

The emerging independence of end users along with the increasing scrutiny of costs and benefits has placed MIS departments under considerable pressure. As a result, in a number of enterprises, the MIS departments have begun a transformation into much leaner organizations that serve a staff and advisory function. As such, the MIS department is taking a less direct role in developing new information systems. Two new development strategies are emerging as a result: outsourcing and the growth of workgroup MIS. We will consider each.

Outsourcing

The benefits of the rate of change of technology in the information systems industry are well known. Computers have become incredibly more powerful while decreasing in prices; personal computers of incredible power and utility are now available quickly for little money; and so forth.

It is less well known that this rate of change has also been the source of many costs and problems. Hardware has become obsolete so quickly that it is difficult to depreciate it fast enough. MIS personnel need to be constantly retrained on new technologies. Some personnel are unable to adapt to new technologies, methods, and procedures, and they become deadwood in their organizations. Immature products are introduced that cause incredible disruption and stress until their quirks are removed or understood well enough to be overcome or avoided.

These problems are especially troublesome to MIS departments because MIS personnel are constantly just beginning to learn the technology they must work with. Just when the critical problems of one technology are solved, another technology—with a brand new set of problems—pops up to take its place. The knowledge painfully gained to cope with a technology is seldom used more than once.

The situation is different for vendors like Legacy Systems. A Customer Support representative learns to solve a problem and then can use that knowledge to solve many more similar problems for other customers. Vendors are able to reuse their knowledge.

In response to these factors, a number of companies are turning to third-party specialists to run their computing equipment and systems in a process referred to as **outsourcing**. Companies such as Andersen Consulting and Electronic Data Systems are offering to operate enterprise computers and systems for a fixed price, usually less than the cost of developing and operating systems internally. In addition, because the price is fixed, it stabilizes an important business cost and simplifies business planning.

Third-party specialists can perform these services for less money because they are able to gain efficiencies of scale. An outsourcing vendor can negotiate better prices on hardware because it buys the hardware in large volume. Such vendors can train more efficiently because they develop training programs to

Figure 13-12 Outsourcing Vendor
An outsourcing vendor may achieve economies of scale by combining the needs of many clients.

upgrade the knowledge of hundreds of personnel, not just a few. As outsource vendors learn the quirks of new products, they can apply that knowledge to dozens or even hundreds of installations rather than just to one.

An outsource vendor can specialize its human resource function on the particular needs of MIS personnel. In this way, outsource vendors can identify unneeded and ineffective personnel more quickly. Unneeded personnel can be transferred to other sites; ineffective personnel can be retrained, moved to other jobs, or let go. In this way, the MIS personnel function can be made more efficient.

It is not necessary for an enterprise to turn all of its systems over to outsource vendors. Some companies turn over their most stable and standardized systems such as payroll, accounting, purchasing, and so forth. In this way, the MIS department can specialize on the systems that are unique or especially critical to enterprise success.

Outsourcing can also reduce financial risk. A reputable outsource vendor can be depended on to provide services of at least acceptable quality at a fixed price. While the price may be higher than management wants, it at least is a known price. Many enterprises have been seriously harmed by MIS departments and projects that generated very large expenses for little or no return.

Outsourcing is new, and it is not clear how successful it will be in the long term. Some experts would say that by outsourcing, management is abrogating its responsibility to outsiders—that outsourcing is equivalent to admitting, We never figured out how to manage the MIS function, so we'll pour money into another company and hope they can. Others say that, because of economies of scale, outsourcing is an appropriate and wise course of action. In any case, it appears that you can expect to see more and more outsourcing, at least in the early years of your career.

The Growth of Workgroup MIS

The success that end users have had in developing their own personal MIS has given them confidence in their ability to satisfy their own information requirements. This emerging confidence began with simple systems such as a personal word processing application or a single-user spreadsheet analysis. Later, users found that, if they could download enterprise data, they could develop their own personal database applications to format that data as they wish.

In part, this movement arose out of necessity. MIS departments were overwhelmed with requests for service and were unable to satisfy many of the users' needs. Application backlogs of over 2 years were commonly reported. Even though many end users did not want to become involved with information technology, they found that they had to do so in order to accomplish their work.

Thus, many workgroup systems have been those that would have been developed for the enterprise platform by the MIS department previously. Some other workgroup applications were MIS applications that have been downsized to run on workgroup platforms. Yet others are personal systems that have been expanded to allow the sharing of data.

Technology has helped to make users more self-sufficient. Twenty years ago, all applications were developed using custom programming. Several years of training were required to be able to develop even the most rudimentary applications. As application packages that could be altered and adapted became available, the education and training time required to develop applications were dramatically reduced. One consequence has been the rise of **third-party systems integrators**, which are companies that acquire hardware and programs and integrate them on behalf of end users. They also work with their customers to develop the data, procedures, and personnel components of the systems they integrate.

With the growth in the end users' confidence, the simplifications of development due to change in technology, and the emergence of systems integrators, groups of end users have begun to take more responsibility for developing and using their own information systems.

To understand this more fully, examine Figure 13-13, which shows an organization with a traditional MIS function. The shaded portion of this figure represents the control over the MIS systems. While computers (or terminals) reside in the users' departments, the responsibility for developing, operating, and maintaining the information systems lies with the MIS department. When

Figure 13-13 Organization with Traditional MIS Function

Under the traditional organization, the MIS department operates all the multiuser information systems in the organization.

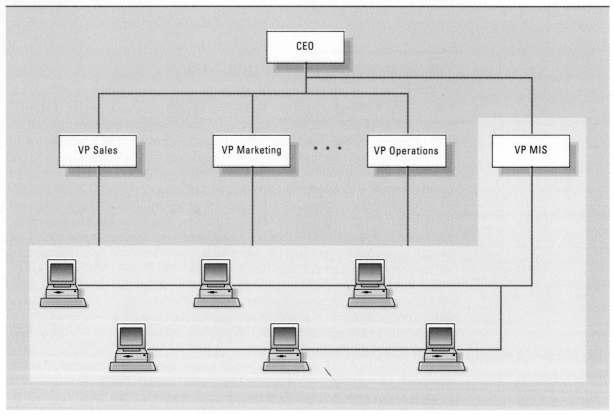

something goes wrong or needs to be changed or a new functionality needs to be developed, the line departments must call and rely on personnel in the MIS department.

Now examine Figure 13-14, which shows an organization with **line MIS** functions. The three shaded portions of the figure represent the control over three separate line MIS functions. Sales, Marketing, and Operations all have taken responsibility for developing, operating, and maintaining their own information systems. The MIS department is responsible for controlling enterprise data, but it does so by developing standards and procedures for using that data.

Figure 13-14 shows three different workgroup information systems in three different departments. Since each department is headed by a single VP, the formal chain of command can be used to manage and administer each system. Standards

Figure 13-14 Organization with Workgroup MIS Functions
Under this organization, each functional area has its own workgroup information systems.

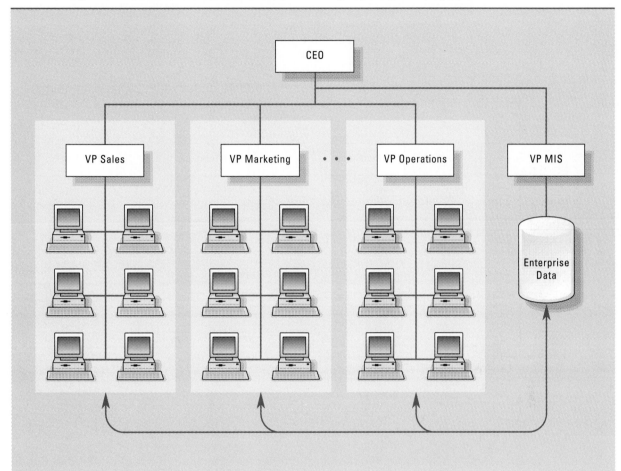

and procedures for using departmental data are established within each department. When a workgroup system uses enterprise data, it is subject to the policies of the MIS department with respect to that data.

Figure 13-15 shows a workgroup information system that spans departments, such as a product introduction team including representatives from various departments. Workgroup data administration may be more difficult in this case, since no single VP or other manager is formally in charge and no obvious chain of command exists for resolving conflicts and differences. Still, there is no reason that such issues cannot be worked out by the departments involved.

Figure 13-15 Organization with Workgroup MIS Shared Among Functions
Under this organization, workgroup information systems cut across functional lines.

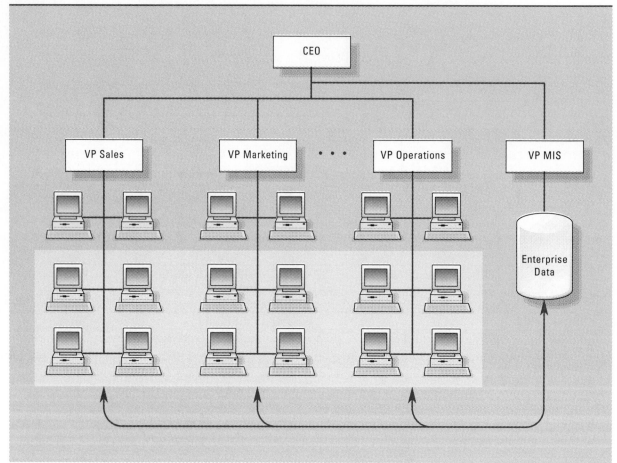

The rise in workgroup MIS will create new and important career opportunities. Over the next few years, many thousands of workgroups will set up information systems, primarily client/server systems based on LANs. Setting up and operating a LAN and operating a client/server information system is a task that an enthusiastic amateur can learn to do, but many of those workgroups will not include such a person. In that case, someone must be hired to take on the workgroup MIS responsibility—a person who has knowledge of a business area, say, manufacturing, and who also knows information technology.

The Future Role of MIS Departments

As outsourcing and workgroup MIS become prevalent in business organizations, then the role of the MIS department will change dramatically. Instead of directly developing and operating virtually all information systems, as it did 10 years ago, the MIS department will begin to serve more of a staff function that oversees, advises, and supports the efforts of others. It will provide the information technology infrastructure for the organization.

In one recent report, John McCarthy of Forrester Research predicted that the MIS department will change to have three primary functions: defining and overseeing procedures, developing high-tech expertise, and operating the enterprise data infrastructure.[8]

Defining and Overseeing Procedures   According to McCarthy, specialists, or **technology practices auditors**, in the MIS department develop standard practices, system processes, data administration guidelines, and other information standards for all shared systems. These standards are developed with cognizance of the needs of the entire enterprise. The technology auditors inspect the work of workgroup system developers, outsourcing vendors, and third-party system integrators to ensure compliance with enterprise standards and contractual terms.

Data security should be monitored in the interest of the enterprise. It is provided routinely in a mainframe-based, centralized system, which is nearly always located in a locked, continuously staffed computer center. Operations personnel are available to perform failure recovery procedures at all times and to do system backups in the middle of the night when loads are light.

By contrast, a workgroup server is typically located in a spare room, such as a departmental mailroom or stockroom, to which many people may have access. The operator typically is a group member who has agreed to take on MIS responsibilities in addition to a regular position. The operator is seldom available outside normal office hours, so if the system fails at 3:00 a.m., it may be out of service until morning. Regular backups and other data security activities are performed only if the part-time operator recognizes their importance. Yet the data in such systems may be critical to the performance of the workgroup, and the workgroup may play a vital role in the success of the enterprise as a whole.

Data security procedures would be one of the areas to be covered by the technology practices auditors. Minimum security standards and backup procedures would be prescribed for every shared information system in the organization, and training would be provided for all shared system operators. Any workgroup that

---

8. McCarthy, John C., "MIS's Mid-life Crisis," *Forrester Professional Systems Report*, October 1990, pp. 2–14.

developed an information system would have to accept the burden of required security procedures as one of the costs of the system.

Developing High-Tech Expertise   An enterprise needs for someone to accept responsibility to maintain a shared pool of expertise on current information technology. The various workgroup system operators address day-to-day business problems, but are unable to stay abreast of emerging high technology. They are supported by personnel in the MIS department who maintain expertise in technical disciplines such as data communications, information modeling, distributed databases, and the like. These experts provide advice on the best ways to utilize emerging technology to accomplish the goals and objectives of the enterprise.

For example, the technology of data communications and networking is changing extremely rapidly, and the many products available on the market have widely varying capabilities. It is beyond the capacity of part-time workgroup LAN managers to maintain current knowledge in this complex field, and that shortcoming may be costly. For example, a workgroup may upgrade its network platform just before the introduction of new products that would have provided far more capability at a lower price. Such changes happen frequently in such a volatile technology and are often predictable to those who can take time to immerse themselves in the literature of the field. That is the role of the MIS department data communications expert, who will then advise those who are making purchase decisions.

Operating Enterprise Data Infrastructure   The **enterprise data infra–structure** includes enterprise-wide databases and associated information systems, along with the backbone networks and WANs that are shared enterprise-wide. It includes the data and the communication systems that everyone shares. It is the data superhighway for the enterprise.

The MIS department ensures that the data is properly administered and protected. In this role, the MIS department maintains data archives, determines data-distribution policies, and serves as the primary point of contact for enterprise data needs.

Today, most MIS departments perform this function, but they also still develop, operate, and maintain enterprise information systems. As a result of the changes described here, however, many applications will access enterprise data (administered by the MIS department), but most of those applications will be operated by workgroups rather than by the MIS department.

The changes described in this section mean a dramatic reduction in the number of personnel in the MIS department and in the power and influence of the MIS director. Hence, there is likely to be considerable resistance to this evolution. Still, there are strong economic and technological pressures on organizations to shift to outsourcing and workgroup MIS, and it is likely that the changes described here will come about eventually.

SUMMARY

Developing enterprise information systems is more challenging than developing personal and workgroup information systems. Some of the challenges arise from the diversity of people and departments who will use the system to be developed. These challenges include the differing views of data among users and the use of inconsistent terminology. Each department involved also has its own goals and expectations, and some of these may conflict across departments. Different departments may want different types of systems to be developed. Also, there may be substantial differences in the competencies of the personnel in the departments. Further, departments also compete with one another and may use, or fear that others are using, the development project to change the balance of power. Finally, new systems often change enterprise structure and dynamics; this fact may cause users to resist the new project.

Other challenges arise from sources outside the new system. The new system will reside in an environment of other systems and may need to obtain data from or send data to those other systems. Even if it does not interface with them, the development effort must be cognizant of them. Further, the new system may require data from existing systems that they cannot provide. The new system will also compete with existing and other development projects for dollars, personnel, and other resources. Lack of budget sometimes forces the development team to constrain its work in a way that is dissatisfying to all. Another problem is enterprise politics. The new system may change the balance of power outside of itself just as it might change it within itself. Finally, sometimes conflict develops between the user departments and the MIS department.

A third group of challenges arises from the nature of enterprise information systems. They are more complex than personal or workgroup information systems; they must provide features, functions, and data views for many different departments. They are larger, with more concurrent users and more data. Enterprise systems also must integrate departments whose underlying activities may be inconsistent or incompatible. They take more work and longer time periods for development. They also often involve larger development staffs, which means more time must be spent in coordination and communication. Also, due to the longer development time, there is a greater chance that the business needs will change before the system is finished. Finally, because of the complexity, size, and time required, it is more difficult for any single person to comprehend all the system. This means that it is more difficult for the system design to be clean and consistent and more likely the system will be incomplete or have errors.

Enterprises need a system of systems. To build it, careful planning is required. At any one point, there will be many requests for new development projects. The enterprise must plan carefully to develop the right systems in the right order.

Most enterprises form an MIS steering committee to guide and direct development projects. The steering committee is composed of senior executives from all the enterprise's major departments. The steering committee sets priorities among projects; approves plans, schedules, and budgets; and monitors development progress. It also approves major hardware and computer program acquisitions, is involved in selecting and hiring key MIS personnel, and establishes high-level policy and standards. Finally, the steering committee provides advice and assistance to the CEO, the board of directors, and other senior personnel.

There are two general categories of information systems planning: top-down and bottom-up. Top-down planning works from the overall enterprise needs down to specific systems. Bottom-up planning starts with the needs for specific systems and works up to the overall needs. The advantage of top-down strategies is that systems that are correct and appropriate for the entire enterprise are more likely to be developed. The disadvantage is that considerable lead time and expense are required to perform the analysis. Further, the business needs can change as the analysis is underway, leading, possibly, to analysis paralysis. The advantage of bottom-up planning is that a specific system can be developed more quickly. The disadvantage is that incomplete, ineffective, or short-term systems may be developed.

One top-down strategy involves the analysis of critical success factors (CSF), which are operational goals. Managers are asked to identify their personal most critical goals and their department's most critical goals that they need to achieve success. Senior managers are also asked to identify such goals for the enterprise. These goals are combined, using an intuitive and fuzzy method, into a few goals for each department and for the enterprise. From this final list, the information needs of the enterprise are determined. The advantage of CSF is that it focuses on the key information needs of the enterprise. The disadvantages are that it is time-consuming, the combination of CSFs is potentially arbitrary, it involves only managers, and specific needs for lower-level systems like TPS are not identified.

Enterprise analysis is a second strategic planning method. Here, representative managers are interviewed, and the enterprise's processes, organization, and data classes are identified. Logical application groups are obtained from processes that involve the same data classes. Using matrices like those in Figures 13-7 and 13-8, logical application groups, data classes, processes, and organization are identified that delineate the need for new systems. The major advantage of enterprise analysis is that it provides a comprehensive review of information requirements. The major disadvantages are that it is very time-consuming and reflects only what is and not what could be.

Evolutionary planning is a bottom-up method in which the MIS steering committee plays a key role in approving and prioritizing projects as they arise. No systematic attempt is made to identify all the enterprise's information needs. Instead, systems projects are considered and prioritized marginally, as new systems are proposed. The advantage of evolutionary planning is that projects can be started with minimal time and expense. The disadvantage is that separate, isolated, and inconsistent systems can result; bad decisions can be made due to a lack of information; and systems development can proceed in fits and starts. Evolutionary planning is not the same as ad hoc planning, however, in which systems are developed as they are proposed, at least as long as the money holds out.

CASE, computer-aided systems engineering, is primarily concerned with analysis of business needs followed by the development of programs and data. Hardware, procedures, and personnel components receive less attention. CASE involves both methodology and tools. The CASE methodology concerns strategic systems planning, system analysis, database design, system design, system construction, system management, process support, and project management support.

There are CASE tools for each activity in the CASE methodology. Such tools are sold as package products by CASE vendors. The products normally involve a centralized database of CASE data referred to as a repository.

The emerging independence of end users together with the increasing scrutiny by management of information systems costs and benefits have placed MIS departments under considerable pressure. As a result, many MIS departments are evolving into smaller organizations that serve a staff and advisory function.

Two movements are key to this transformation: outsourcing and the growth of workgroup MIS. With outsourcing, third-party companies are hired to develop and operate enterprise information systems for a fixed fee. These companies can achieve sufficient economies of scale in that they can provide these systems more cheaply than can the in-house MIS department.

With the growth in workgroup MIS, end-user departments take increased responsibility for developing and operating their own information systems. These departments often hire third-party system integrators to assist them in these endeavors.

The functions of the MIS department are evolving into three primary responsibilities: the definition and administration of procedures; the development of high-technology specialties; and the development and operation of enterprise-wide data utilities.

These changes may mean a reduction in the size and influence of the MIS department. Consequently, they are likely to be met with organizational resistance.

KEY TERMS

MIS steering committee
Top-down planning
Bottom-up planning
Analysis paralysis
CSF
Enterprise analysis, or
   Business Systems
   Planning
Data class
Logical application
   group

Process/organization
   matrix
Process/data class
   matrix
Evolutionary planning
Ad hoc planning
CASE
CASE tools
CASE repository
CASE methodology
Upper CASE

Lower CASE
Outsourcing
Third-party systems
   integrator
Line MIS
Technology practices
   auditor
Enterprise data
   infrastructure

REVIEW QUESTIONS

1. List three sources of challenge in the development of enterprise information systems.

2. Describe the challenges to the development of enterprise information systems that arise from within the system.

3. Explain how the development of a new system can become or can be viewed as an internal competitive weapon.

4. List and briefly explain challenges to the development of enterprise information systems that arise from outside the system.

5. In what ways can conflict arise between user departments and the MIS department? In such a conflict, who is right?

6. Describe the challenges to the development of enterprise information systems that arise from the nature of such systems.

7. What complications arise because enterprise information systems require more work and longer periods of time than other information systems?

8. Why is it important for one person to have a vision of the conceptual integrity of the system?

9. Explain the analogy of system development to building construction.

10. Why do enterprises need a means of planning and prioritizing development projects?

11. Why is an informal steering committee not effective for most enterprises?

12. Who should be members of the MIS steering committee?

13. What are the major functions of the MIS steering committee.

14. Give an example of a policy or a standard that the MIS steering committee might establish.

15. Explain the nature of top-down information systems planning. What are its advantages and disadvantages?

16. Explain the nature of bottom-up information systems planning. What are its advantages and disadvantages?

17. What is analysis paralysis? Give an example.

18. Define *critical success factor*.

19. Summarize the process used to perform CSF information systems planning.

20. Summarize the advantages and disadvantages of CSF information systems planning.

21. Summarize the process used to perform an enterprise analysis.

22. What are the four major entities involved in an enterprise analysis?

23. Explain the meaning and use of the matrices in Figures 13-7 and 13-8.

24. Explain the relationship of a logical application group to information systems.

25. Summarize the advantages and disadvantages of enterprise analysis.

26. Describe the process used to perform evolutionary planning.

27. Summarize the advantages and disadvantages of evolutionary planning.

28. How is evolutionary planning different from ad hoc planning?

29. Explain the statement that CASE refers to the process of using information systems to build information systems.

30. Why is it a mistake to think of CASE only as a set of programs or tools?

31. List the stages and basic steps of CASE methodology. Summarize the activity for each.

32. Explain why the strategic planning step pertains to all systems, but the remaining CASE methodology steps refer to just one system at a time.

33. Explain the meaning of *system analysis* and *system construction* as they are used in CASE methodology.

34. What is the difference between a CASE product and a CASE tool?

35. What is the CASE repository? Why is it important?

36. List the primary CASE tools.

37. What is the disadvantage of using multiple CASE products?

38. Describe two factors that have placed MIS departments under pressure to change.

39. Explain the factors that have led to the rise of outsourcing.

40. Describe the factors that enable a third party to provide information systems for less cost than can an in-house MIS department.

41. Describe the factors that led to the rise of workgroup MIS.

42. Describe the three primary functions of an MIS department in an organization in which there is a substantial amount of outsourcing and line MIS.

43. What factors will cause organizational resistance to the new role for MIS departments?

DISCUSSION QUESTIONS

1. Suppose that every department in the College of Business has its own LAN. One application on the network is a grade-recording system used to track the grades achieved by all students majoring in that department. Each system obtains an extract of the grades recorded by the university's administration computer at the end of every semester. Another application that is available on every network keeps track of the jobs taken by graduates of the department. Although both of these systems are available to every department, not every department uses them, or uses them to the same extent.

The dean of the College of Business needs a new information system that will provide information about the relationship of grades, majors, and graduates' starting salaries. She will use this information to justify the college's budget with the state legislature. Now, consider the College of Business as an enterprise unto itself and the dean's need as one for an enterprise information system that obtains data from the departmental systems.

    a.   List and explain five challenges to the development of this system that will arise from within the system.

    b.   List and explain five challenges to the development of this system that will arise from outside the system.

    c.   List and explain five challenges to the development of this system that will arise from the nature of enterprise systems.

    d.   Suppose the university's MIS department hears about this project and tries to stop it. The MIS department claims that it is quite likely grade data will be incorrect and that faulty information will be given to the legislature, to the embarrassment of the entire university community. The MIS department states that the grade data must be obtained from its computer. How should the dean respond?

2. Suppose you are the manager of the sales department at Scott Orthodontics. The salespeople need an order-tracking system. The MIS department and the MIS steering committee agree to initiate the development of that system, but it will be nearly 12 months before the system will be finished. The MIS department offers to build a simulation prototype and show it at your national sales meeting next month. How do you respond to this offer? How certain are you that the new system will be done in 12 months? What can you do to improve your confidence? What can you do to help the sales force in the meantime? Suppose you start losing a substantial number of sales because of lost or untracked orders. What should you do?

3. Consider the situation in question 2. Suppose that you complain loudly about the delay in the schedule, so loudly that your needs come to the ears of the board of directors. One director manages a company that has drastically reduced its systems development time by using CASE technology. That director tells your CEO about CASE, and the CEO directs the MIS director to employ CASE technology on your project. The MIS director resists, claiming that CASE is inappropriate for your project. You perceive that your project has become a political football between the MIS director and the CEO. What do you do?

4. Consider the situation in question 2. Suppose that you complain loudly about the delay in the schedule, so loudly that your needs come to the ears of the board of directors. One director manages a company that has dramatically reduced its systems development time by outsourcing many of its enterprise information systems. That director tells your CEO about outsourcing, and the CEO directs the MIS director to investigate this possibility. The MIS director resists, claiming that your enterprise will lose too much control. What do you do?

PROJECTS

A. Interview an MIS director or other senior person from an MIS department. How does that person's enterprise plan its information systems? Does he or she use a top-down or bottom-up strategy? How well does it work? Why does he or she choose to use one strategy over another? How frequently does he or she perform strategic systems planning? How is the plan documented and communicated to the rest of the enterprise? What process does the person use for enterprise information systems development? Does the development process vary among enterprise, workgroup, and personal information systems? For enterprise systems, does he or she employ CASE methodology or tools? If so, how does that person use them? How well have the methodology or tools worked? If they have not worked, why not?

B. In your library, find articles about CASE in *Computerworld, Database Programming and Design, Datamation*, or some other computer industry journal. From these articles, select two different CASE products. For each of these products, list the number of different CASE tools that each product offers. Compare the features and functions of each tool to those listed in this chapter for that tool. Are any tools missing from those products? Do either of the products have tools that are not shown in Figure 13-11? If so, what is the function of that tool? Where, in Figure 13-10, would that tool be used? If possible, find out how users have evaluated that particular product. Summarize any case histories for either type of products mentioned in the literature you read.

M I N I C A S E

When Your Back Is Up Against Your Backup

Network *Computing* recently ran a contest in which they asked readers to tell their worst real-life backup disaster stories. This was one of the winners.

• • •

Peter Horwood, vice president of research and development at Auto•Administrator, has learned that what seems obvious to people at his company may not always be obvious to their clients.

One client runs The Software Link's PC-MOS and LanLink. The system is configured as Multiuser DOS plus Satellites on the LAN. The client called one day to report that its 120-Mb server drive was "making screeching noises and then quit." It appeared that something was physically stopping the drive from spinning, and whatever it was also was causing the whole process to take up a lot more wattage than normal.

The folks at Auto•Administrator found that the problems stemmed from a lack of lubricant in the drive. No problem, the support technician thought. He'd just have some hardware people go to the site, swap drives and restore the data via an Everex minicassette drive.

When the switch was completed, they began to restore the data from the client's backup library and found something that made them screech: Every backup tape in the client's library was empty!

Perplexed, they asked the client a few questions about its backup history. The client's procedure appeared to have been correct, and the firm had been running full system backups on a regular basis without any apparent problems.

The full system backups took about an hour, given the amount of data being stored. But the users felt that an hour to back up the entire system was an awfully long time, so when the process suddenly took only 45 seconds to complete, they were thrilled. Indeed, they were so happy that they chose to disregard the "Backup Failed" message that appeared on the screen every time it took 45 seconds—the fact that it had always relayed a "Backup Successful" message after the hour-long backups somehow seemed to have slipped their minds.

Crazy with disbelief at the backup procedure and not at all comforted by the fact that there wasn't even hard copy available, the technicians realized their only hope was the malfunctioning hard drive—all the information for the past five years was on a drive that was dying, slowly but surely. They plugged it directly into a separate power supply to get it running again, which allowed the internal resistance to be overcome long enough for Horwood and the technicians to recover most of the important data from the past five years.

The hard drive and the tape drive were replaced, and the clients were reeducated about the importance of doing complete, successful backups. ■

Debra Ann Townes, excerpted from *Network Computing*, September, 1992, p. 126.

Discussion Questions

1. Summarize the error that created the backup problem described in this article.

2. What lesson should be drawn from this story? Consider the fact that Horwood had no reason to imagine that his client would make this particular error, so a useful lesson will be more general than, say, informing the client how long a backup should take.

3. Since hard disk units fail infrequently, why are backups very important?

4. Explain how the technicians recovered the data from the failing hard disk.

Copyright© 1992 by **CMP Publications, Inc.,** 600 Community Drive, Manhasset, NY 11030. Reprinted from NETWORK COMPUTING with permission.

MODULE C

Development of an Enterprise Information System

MODULE C ILLUSTRATES THE DEVELOPMENT OF AN ENTERPRISE MIS that provides the order-tracking system for Scott Orthodontics (introduced in Chapter 13). In this project, the systems analysis was supported by an outside consultant, and the development was done by an outside vendor. The project illustrates the role of the MIS steering committee in developing such a system. It also illustrates the use of prototyping to clarify and document requirements for a user interface.

THE NEED FOR AN ORDER-TRACKING SYSTEM

Scott Orthodontics manufactures orthodontic appliances and sells them directly to orthodontists, oral surgeons, and dentists. Since Scott's customers are themselves in a service business, it is very important that they receive orders as fast as possible and on a reliable schedule. At the time of an order, Scott's customers need to be given a realistic estimate of when the order will be shipped. If, later, the order is delayed, the customers need to know that the order will be delayed, and they need an accurate projection of when the order will be shipped.

Scott employs its own sales force to call on the dentists. At the time of the call, the salespeople present the product line, explain ordering procedures, answer questions, and handle any objections that may arise. The salespeople also make it clear that the dentists are to call them if problems develop. Thus, when an order is late, the dentists normally call the salespeople first.

As described in Chapter 13, there is no formal system for tracking orders. Often, the salespeople must struggle to obtain any information at all, and, often, the information they do receive is inaccurate, which places the salespeople in an embarrassing and untenable position.

Understanding the Current System

Figure C-1 illustrates Scott Orthodontics' current order-processing and manufacturing systems. Customers submit orders either by mail or over the telephone. Order-entry clerks use computer terminals to key in order data; these terminals are connected to a minicomputer that runs an order-entry application program (labeled O/E). At the time the order is entered, the data is checked for correctness, but no attempt is made to determine how long it will be until the order can be manufactured.

After the order has been entered, order-processing clerks check the customer's credit rating and verify the order for completeness and sensibility. This is necessary because customers fill out their own order forms; due to the complexity of the products, they often make mistakes. If necessary, the order-processing clerks call the customer for clarification.

At no point in this process is the customer given an estimate of a shipping date. If the customers ask for one, Scott employees respond in general terms with a statement such as "Ninety percent of our orders are shipped within 10 days. Yours should be too." Customers who are dissatisfied with this response call their salesperson, who, through an informal network, obtains a more precise estimate.

Figure C-1 Scott Orthodontics' Current Order-Processing and Manufacturing Systems

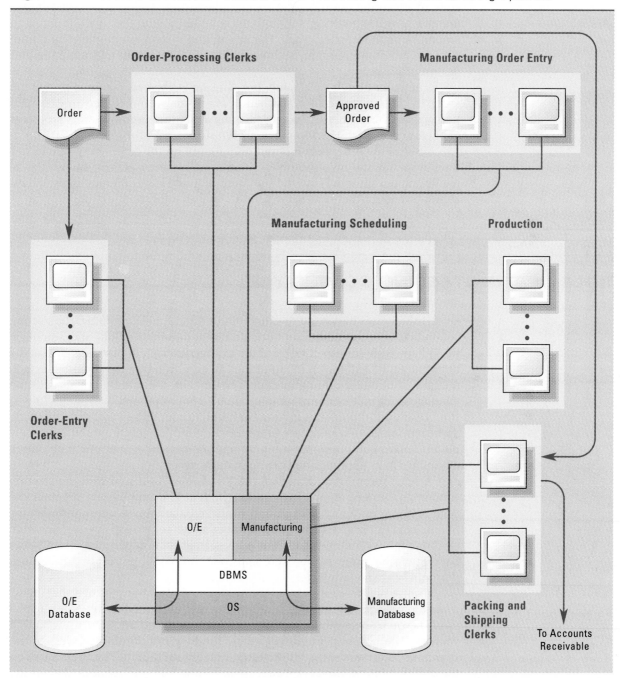

Once the customer's credit has been approved and the order validated, a copy of the order form is sent to Manufacturing. There, it is keyed into a manufacturing scheduling system, which builds production work orders and schedules manufacturing work. The scheduling system is completely separate from the order-entry system, as shown in Figure C-1. It has its own programs and its own database.

The order form is saved, and, once the job is finished, it is used to ship the order to the customer. The finished order form is then routed to Accounts Receivable, which accesses the original order data using the order-entry programs to bill the customer. (This last process is not shown in Figure C-1.)

Most of the order data is keyed twice—once for the order-entry system and then again for the manufacturing system. Scott's management knows this is inefficient, but since the two packages were acquired from different, independent software vendors, there has never been any way to integrate the two.

ROLE OF THE STEERING COMMITTEE

Scott Orthodontics has an MIS steering committee that meets monthly. The steering committee is not particularly sophisticated; it has never done a long-range strategic plan of any type. Initially it followed an ad hoc approach to planning, but, as the company expanded, the problems of such an approach became apparent. In fact, the lack of interface and connection between the order-entry system and the manufacturing system is attributable to that ad hoc approach.

Over time, the steering committee began to adopt an evolutionary planning approach. It made a roster of projects underway and projects proposed. Every new project had to compete against others, and the committee became much more disciplined in its approach and in prioritizing projects.

Over a several-month period, the VP of Sales discussed with the steering committee the need for an order-tracking system. Unfortunately, at the time, the Scott MIS department was extremely overtaxed, with a heavy responsibility for maintaining existing systems. The few resources left to develop new systems were spread so thinly that little progress was being made. The department had a 2-year backlog of new projects that were approved, but could not be begun because personnel were not available.

The VP of Sales was aware of the resource problem but she knew that unless something was done, the problems due to lost revenue from disgruntled customers would become worse. Finally, the VP proposed developing the system using outside vendors. The proposal was accepted by the Steering Committee, despite the strenuous objections of the MIS director, who argued that the resources spent on the outside vendors would be better spent adding MIS staff to tackle the already approved projects.

Selecting the Consultant

A study team was assembled including John Fitzpatrick, a senior sales manager, and Fred Tompkins, one of the more experienced production managers. Its first task was to select and hire a consultant to lead the study. The MIS department suggested two candidates. The team interviewed both. The first, Faye Chou, was an experienced consultant who had developed similar systems for other companies. The second, David Sarkov, was a systems analyst with strong technical skills who was just beginning a career as a consultant after working successfully in the MIS department of a progressive local corporation for 3 years.

The team saw the choice as between an experienced person and one with less experience, but perhaps more energy and enthusiasm for the task—hoping to develop a reputation that would produce more business. After discussion, the team agreed on Faye Chou.

THE ORDER-TRACKING STUDY

Faye and the team met with employees from Sales, Order Processing, Manufacturing, and the MIS department over a 3-day period; then the team members met among themselves for another 2 days. Their goal was not to perform a detailed analysis of requirements, but rather to define the problem and identify a feasible solution. With this in mind, they would then be better able to develop an RFP for potential vendors.

Once it had met with users, the team decided that it would be important to track orders through a number of different stages of processing (see Figure C-2).

Figure C-2 Stages of Customer Order Processing

- Received
- Approved
- Scheduled
- Finished
- Packed
- Shipped

Orders are received (entered into the order-entry database); approved (customer's credit checked and order validated); scheduled for manufacturing; finished; packed; and, finally, shipped. The order-tracking system needs to be able to report which stage a particular order is in and to provide estimates as to the amount of time required to complete the remaining stages.

The study team considered several alternatives for order tracking. Figure C-3 shows the basic architecture of the alternative that the team considered most promising. This alternative not only provided order-tracking capability but also eliminated the need to rekey the order data.

As shown in Figure C-3, a new set of application programs would be developed to provide the order-tracking function (labeled O/T). The new system would operate as follows: Once order data had been keyed into the order-entry program, a copy of the data would be transferred to the order-tracking program. Additionally, after a customer's credit had been checked and the order had been validated, a second message would be sent to the order-tracking program. Both the initial data and the subsequent order acceptance message could be generated by the order-entry system by using a special output option of the order-entry package.

According to the proposed design, the order-tracking system would track each order in a new database, the order tracking (O/T) database. The data in this database would be modified whenever an order made a transition from one stage to the next. To determine order status, this database would be queried by customer service, order tracking, manufacturing scheduling, and packing and shipping personnel.

The team wanted to have the order-tracking program provide order data directly to the manufacturing program. If this could be done, it would eliminate the expensive rekeying of data, with substantial labor savings. To do this, the order-tracking programs would need to structure the order data in a format acceptable to the manufacturing programs. Further, when a production job had been finished, the manufacturing programs would send a message back to the order-tracking programs, indicating the change in status. The last two changes in status—packing and shipping—would be made directly by shipping personnel.

As they developed this proposed design, the study team decided that although it generally understood the data needed for order tracking, it did not know specifically what data would be required nor what format would be most effective. Since the users' need for order-tracking data was the primary determinant of the structure and size of the order-tracking database, the study team believed that such knowledge was crucial.

In light of this uncertainty, the study team decided to prototype the user interface to determine and understand the order-tracking requirements. Faye thought she and John would be able to develop the user-interface prototype in about 2 weeks, assuming they could gain ready access to the key users.

Figure C-3   An Alternative Order-Processing, Order-Tracking, and Manufacturing System

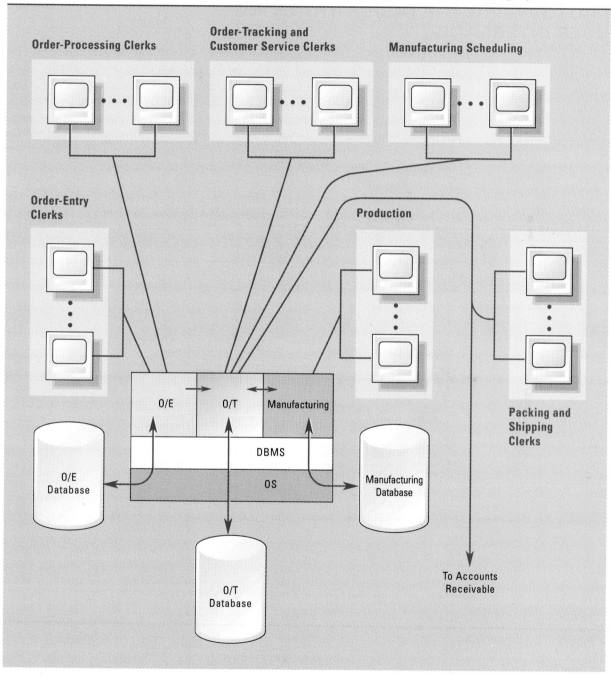

PROTOTYPING THE ORDER-TRACKING
USER INTERFACE

To build the order-tracking user interface prototype, Faye decided to use a commercial slide-show product called DEMO-NOW. With this product, she and John could develop a series of screen images that would simulate the user interface. DEMO-NOW allows the images to be linked together so that, when the users respond to directions via the keyboard, the appropriate simulated screen will be shown next. Thus, in a simulated menu, if one of the choices is "Exit" and if the user picks that choice, then DEMO-NOW could be directed to display the Exit screen image.

Faye spent several hours building demo menu screens. She did this just so the prototype would establish a context in the reviewers' minds. Her primary concern came with the work she did next. She wanted to demonstrate how the system would respond to the users' requests for order-status information. She built a screen like the one shown in Figure C-4 and then showed the prototype to John.

Figure C-4 Order-Tracking Screen, Version 1

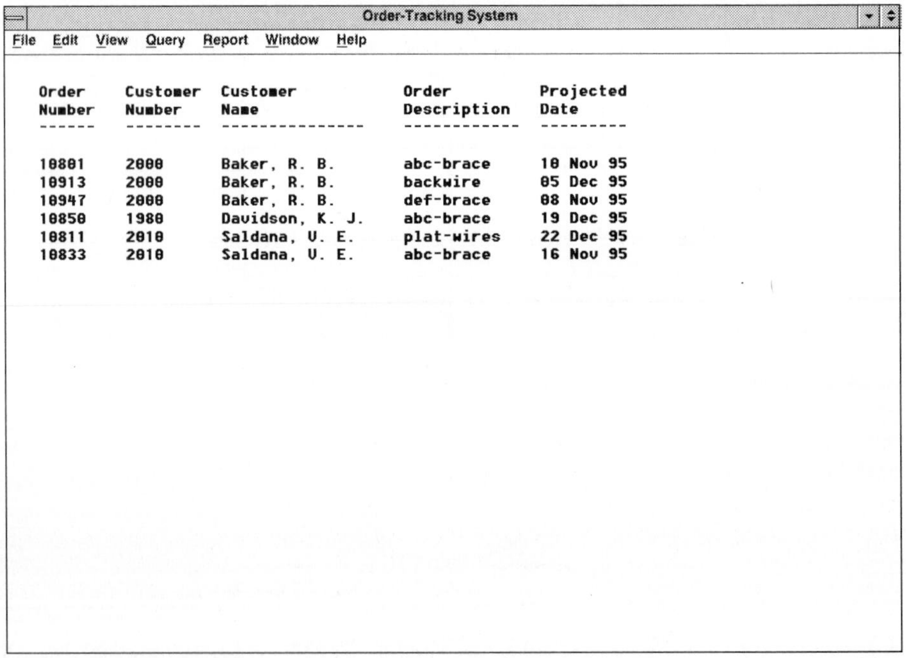

Order-Tracking System				
File Edit View Query Report Window Help				
Order Number	Customer Number	Customer Name	Order Description	Projected Date
------	--------	----------------	------------	---------
10801	2000	Baker, R. B.	abc-brace	10 Nov 95
10913	2000	Baker, R. B.	backwire	05 Dec 95
10947	2000	Baker, R. B.	def-brace	08 Nov 95
10850	1980	Davidson, K. J.	abc-brace	19 Dec 95
10811	2010	Saldana, U. E.	plat-wires	22 Dec 95
10833	2010	Saldana, U. E.	abc-brace	16 Nov 95

He liked the menu interface, but when he saw the screen, he looked so disappointed that Faye had to reassure him they were just getting started, and she told him not to lose confidence. As they talked, it became clear that the orientation of the screen was wrong. The screen (as in Figure C-4) showed all the orders in the system. What a particular salesperson or customer service representative would want, however, are the orders for a particular customer.

Faye went back to her computer and, in an hour, developed the screen in Figure C-5, showing all the orders in process for a given customer. John had told her that, for many queries, the customer number is unknown. Therefore, the system had to be able to access order data by either customer number or customer name. In the case of duplicate names, the system had to show all the records for all the names and let the user pick the correct one.

With John's advice, Faye made several other, less significant changes. They then set up a meeting with several of the system's future users. The users were ecstatic about the system. "Can you really do this?" and "You have no idea how badly we need this information," were some of the comments made. After some probing questions from Faye, however, a number of deficiencies were identified, the most important concerning partial shipments. Sometimes, when some items are finished well before others, the order would be split and the finished items shipped ahead. The screen in Figure C-5 does not allow for this possibility.

Figure C-5   Order-Tracking Screen, Version 2

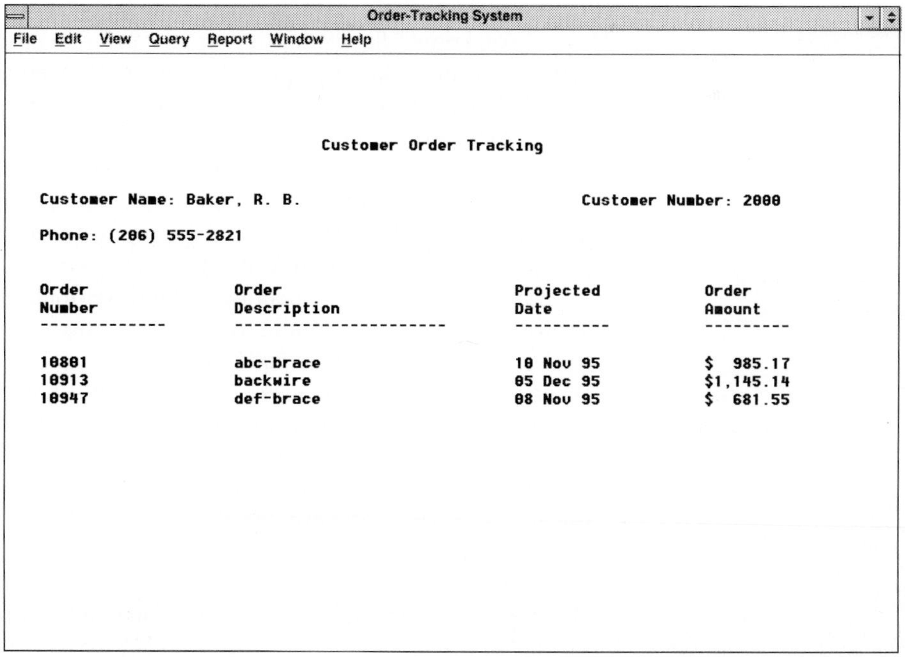

Order-Tracking System			
File Edit View Query Report Window Help			

Customer Order Tracking

Customer Name: Baker, R. B.   Customer Number: 2000

Phone: (206) 555-2821

Order Number	Order Description	Projected Date	Order Amount
10801	abc-brace	10 Nov 95	$ 985.17
10913	backwire	05 Dec 95	$1,145.14
10947	def-brace	08 Nov 95	$ 681.55

Figure C-6 Order-Tracking Screen, Version 3

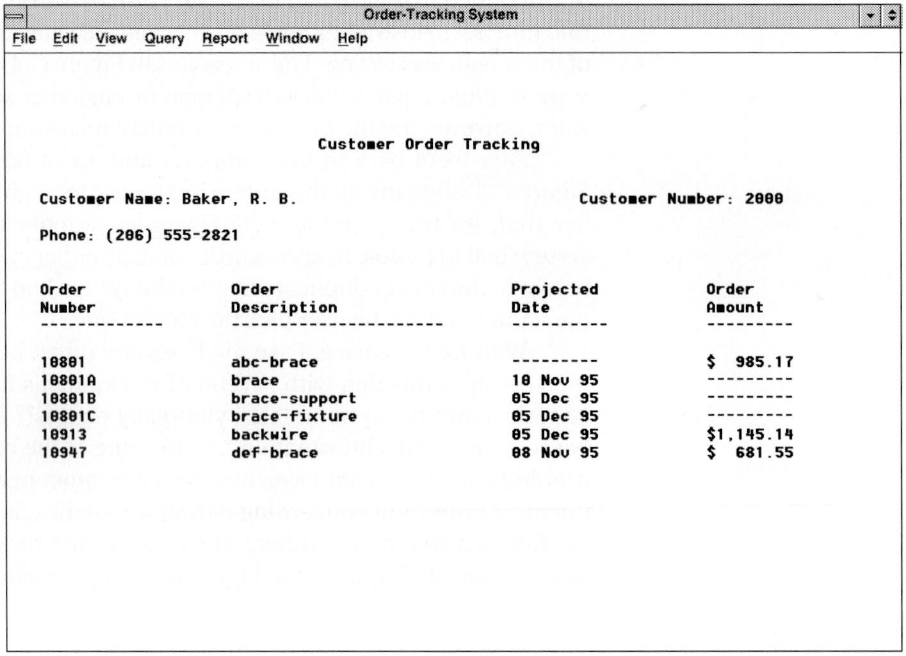

```
┌─────────────────────────────────────────────────────────────────────┬───┬───┐
│                          Order-Tracking System                        │ ▾ │ ▴ │
├─────────────────────────────────────────────────────────────────────┴───┴───┤
│ File  Edit  View  Query  Report  Window  Help                                │
│                                                                              │
│                                                                              │
│                                                                              │
│                          Customer Order Tracking                             │
│                                                                              │
│    Customer Name: Baker, R. B.                    Customer Number: 2000       │
│                                                                              │
│    Phone: (206) 555-2821                                                      │
│                                                                              │
│                                                                              │
│    Order           Order                    Projected        Order           │
│    Number          Description              Date             Amount          │
│    -------------   ----------------------   ----------       ---------        │
│                                                                              │
│    18801           abc-brace                ----------       $   985.17       │
│    18801A          brace                    10 Nov 95        ---------        │
│    18801B          brace-support            05 Dec 95        ---------        │
│    18801C          brace-fixture            05 Dec 95        ---------        │
│    18913           backwire                 05 Dec 95        $1,145.14        │
│    18947           def-brace                08 Nov 95        $   681.55       │
│                                                                              │
│                                                                              │
│                                                                              │
│                                                                              │
└──────────────────────────────────────────────────────────────────────────────┘
```

"You know," Faye said, "it never occurred to us that that might occur. But it's very important to know, especially now. We'll need to change our thinking. Give us a day, and we'll get back to you." Later Faye remarked to John, "That's the reason these prototypes are so useful. Since we know about partial shipments at this point, it will be easy to make the needed changes. Halfway into development, however, and we would have had major changes on our hands. This change means quite a different database structure from the one I was thinking of. It's no problem, just very different from what I had in mind."

In response to this meeting, Faye developed another simulated screen, as shown in Figure C-6. Faye and John had two more meetings with the future users. In these meetings, they learned that the screen in Figure C-6 still needed work. When an order is split, the users need to know what items are on which portion of the order. Also, when orders are late, if possible, the users need to know what the problem is and who is working on it. Sometimes, too, the users are the first people to learn the cause of a delay, and so they need a means of recording that reason in the order-tracking database. In light of this need, Faye developed one more screen, as shown in Figure C-7.

The screen would be used in conjunction with the screen in Figure C-6. Users were to place the cursor on the line of a late order and touch a special key.

Figure C-7 Order-Tracking Screen, Version 4

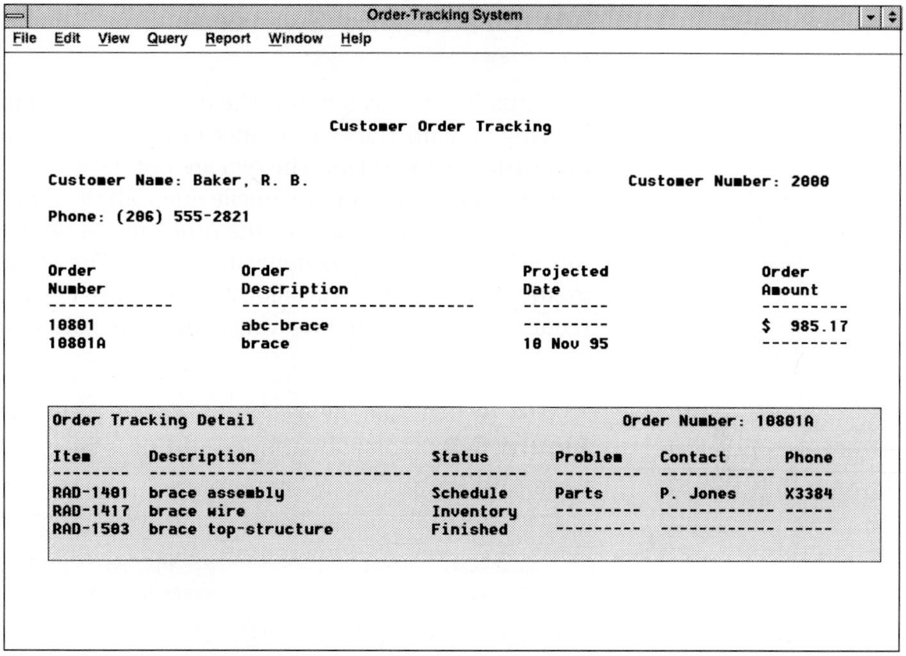

When they did this, the shaded portion of the screen in Figure C-7 would pop up on top of the screen shown in Figure C-6. The users could then read, enter, or modify the data on this pop-up screen.

With these changes, the study team concluded that it had a much better idea of the requirements for the order-tracking user interface. "The biggest lesson," Faye remarked, "was to find out about partial orders. That will save us a tremendous amount of work."

CREATING THE RFP

The remaining area that needed clarification before developing an RFP was the relationship of this new system to the existing manufacturing system. Faye had been working with Fred on an investigation into the issues that needed to be addressed. After several days work, they concluded that the biggest problem concerned the different orientation of the order-entry system and the manufacturing system.

Reconciling the Order-Entry and Manufacturing Systems

The situation was as follows: The order-entry system (along with the new order-tracking system) tracks customer orders, but the manufacturing system tracks production work orders. The two are not the same, and, at the time of the study, there was no easy way to reconcile one with the other.

Figure C-8 summarizes the problem. An order is submitted by a customer; the order potentially has many items on it. The production scheduling personnel examine each order and allocate the items to production work orders. Items requiring similar manufacturing activity are placed on the same production work

Figure C-8   Correspondence of Customer Orders to Production Work Orders

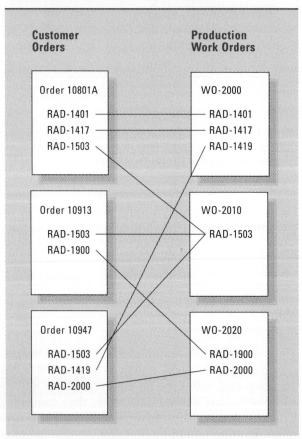

order. Thus, a customer order is broken into pieces and combined with other customer orders. As the production work orders are finished, the customer order is assembled and then packed.

The manufacturing system tracks production work orders, and it is possible to obtain the status of a particular production work order at any time. While an order is in production, however, there is no easy way to relate a customer order to a production work order.

The situation, according to Fred, was as follows: "We need a way to track every production work order involved in every order. If we have that, then we can obtain the dates of completion from the manufacturing system and report them back."

With this knowledge, Faye and Fred developed the design of the order-tracking programs shown in Figure C-9, which is an explosion of the program box

Figure C-9 Design of Order-Tracking Programs

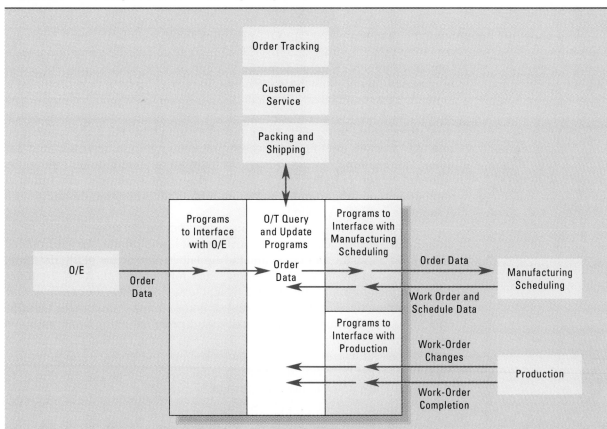

Figure C-10 Tables and Relationships in Order-Tracking Database

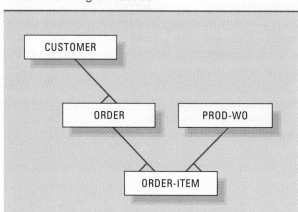

labeled O/T in Figure C-3. The O/T programs would include programs to accept data from the O/E (order-entry) system; programs to provide query and update facilities to order tracking, customer service and packing, and shipping clerks; and programs to interface with the manufacturing system. This latter category includes a program that manufacturing scheduling personnel use when allocating orders to production work orders.

Observe that in Figure C-9, the manufacturing scheduling and production interface program components accept production work order data from the manufacturing system. When an item is assigned to a work order, that fact is recorded. Later, if delays are reported, the order schedules are updated appropriately. Finally, when a production work order is finished, this fact is also recorded in the order-tracking database.

To support these programs, the order-tracking database needed to be designed to track the relationship of customer orders to production work orders. Figure C-10 shows the four tables and the fundamental structure of this database. Since customers can have many orders, each row in the CUSTOMER table is related to many rows in the ORDER table. Further, since each order can have many items, each row in the ORDER table is related to many rows in the ORDER-ITEM table. Finally, since each production work order has many items, each row in the PROD-WO table is related to many rows in the ORDER-ITEM table. A portion of the structure of each of the tables is shown in Figure C-11. Observe that the ORDER-ITEM table contains a column that indicates which production work order a particular item has been assigned to.

Figure C-11 Example Columns in Order-Tracking Database

CUSTOMER			
Customer Number	Customer Name	Customer Address	• • •

ORDER				
Order Number	Order Date	Salesperson Number	Customer Number	• • •

ORDER-ITEM						
Order Amount	Order Number	Line Number	Item Number	Item Cost	Work-Order Number	• • •

PROD-WO		
Work-Order Number	Work-Order Date	• • •

Writing the RFP

At this point, the team was ready to create the RFP for circulation to potential vendors. Members of the study team worked with Faye to write the various sections.

The first section described Scott Orthodontics, its products, and its current processing system. The second provided detailed information, including the material described above, about the new system's requirements. Typical user inquiries were described, along with the anticipated contents of the system's response.

The third section identified constraints on the system. For example, because of its severe resource limitations, the MIS department must be disturbed as little as possible during the development and implementation of the new system. The vendor was to provide system maintenance throughout the lifetime of the system. In addition, the project must add as little as possible to the current MIS workload, operating independently as far as possible. Finally, the current manufacturing programs cannot be modified in any way. They are provided by another vendor, who plans no changes that would support this project. The fourth section of the RFP provided a project schedule.

When the RFP was completed, Faye and the team met with the steering committee. In their presentation, they described the need for the system and overviewed its requirements and schedule. They ended by stressing the benefits of the system in comparison to its cost.

EPILOGUE

Scott Orthodontics did, in fact, develop an order-tracking system. The MIS steering committee was pleased with the work of the study team and authorized the circulation of the RFP to potential vendors. After comparing vendor proposals, the committee selected Ben Saltzer and Associates to develop and maintain the system.

The order-tracking system worked well for about 18 months. As Scott grew, however, the lack of data integration and the duplication of data in the three separate databases started to become a problem. This led to a need for consideration of a new development project.

DISCUSSION QUESTIONS

1. The duplication of keying effort that existed at the time this study was initiated was obviously wasteful. What factors are mentioned in this case that indicate how the situation might have come about? What factors not mentioned in the case do you think might have also contributed to this situation? Describe the essence of an argument to justify the duplication of effort. Describe the essence of an argument to show that such duplication was unnecessary and that it was evidence of inept MIS management.

2. There is considerable duplication of data in the system shown in Figure C-3. List the tables of data that are likely to be duplicated. Describe problems that Scott is likely to have because of this duplicated data. In describing these problems, consider not just the normal operation of the system but also the events such as the definition of a new product, the change in the definition of production items, the elimination of a product, or the decision never to do business with a particular customer again. Define procedures that need to be developed to prevent these problems or to mitigate their consequences.

3. Scott elected to bring in a consultant to perform the system analysis and a vendor to develop the system. Suppose that the steering committee had elected to develop the system using in-house personnel instead. How would the work have been done differently? How could the MIS department resource problems have been overcome so that the project could proceed? Discuss the costs and benefits of the MIS change that you think would be needed. (Why do you suppose such a change has not been made up to now?) Do you think the personnel in manufacturing would have been more or less willing to work with MIS personnel? By developing the system in-house, Scott would have had more direct control over the project. How do you think that fact might have influenced the results?

4. The development team used a prototype in developing the user interface in this case. What organizational and political reasons were there to do this? Without the prototype, how would the project have been started? How does the use of prototypes in this case differ from that described in Chapter 7 on developing personal information systems through prototyping?

5. Suppose that the MIS steering committee had not approved the project for enterprise-level funding. What steps might the VP of Sales have taken? For example, could this system have been developed on the authority of the VP as a workgroup system in sales? What problems might such an approach create? Is this system better treated as an enterprise information system or a workgroup information system? Why?

Decision Support and Expert Systems

PART V ADDRESSES TWO TYPES OF SPECIALIZED INFORMATION SYSTEMS. Chapter 14 discusses decision support systems. Such systems facilitate the solution of problems that arise from semistructured or unstructured domains. Chapter 15 describes knowledge representation and expert systems. These systems store representations of knowledge and provide advice, recommendations, and other assistance, primarily by making logical inferences from the stored knowledge.

The structure of these two chapters is a compressed form of the structure of Parts II, III, and IV. Each considers the why, what, and how dimensions in a single chapter instead of three separate chapters.

14

Improving Decisions with Decision Support Systems

A DECISION SUPPORT SYSTEM (DSS) is a specialized computer-based business information system. DSSs cut across the personal, workgroup, and enterprise MIS categories, and they are used at the operational level, the management control level, and the strategic planning level of organization. Although DSSs were initially developed and used by individuals, today attention is focused on both individual DSS and group DSS applications.

As you read this chapter, keep in mind that DSSs do not solve problems; people do. Consequently, the goal of a DSS is not to solve but rather to support. Managers retain the responsibility for making decisions and implementing them. The DSS is a facility to improve the productivity and quality of human decision making.

The structure of this chapter is similar to the structures of Parts II, III, and IV. First, we survey DSS goals and applications; then we investigate the five components of a DSS; and, finally, we describe the development of DSS applications.

WHAT IS A DSS?

One of the earliest definitions of DSS was developed by Gerrity: A DSS is "an effective blend of human intelligence, information technology, and software, which interact closely to solve complex problems."[1] This definition identifies the basic character of DSSs, but the type of problems that DSSs address can be specified more clearly: A DSS is "an interactive computer-based system which facilitates solution of unstructured problems."[2] The key words in this definition are *facilitate* and *unstructured*.

DSSs facilitate the decision-making process; they do not make decisions. In fact, the term *decision support system* may be misleading. DSSs are not rigid, structured systems with fixed, standardized interfaces like menu-driven TPS applications. Rather, each DSS provides a set of capabilities to assist professionals in decision making. A better term might be **decision support facility**, since the DSS is actually a set of tools, data, models, and other resources that help managers and analysts understand, evaluate, and solve problems.

DSSs address *unstructured* problems that cannot be entirely solved by the application of a known formula to known data.[3] (So, it is not really the problem that is unstructured, but the method of solution.) This characteristic is what most distinguishes DSSs from other types of information systems that you have studied.

Suppose Legacy Systems faces an extended labor strike and needs to determine the impact of reduced operations on the company and its financial position. There is no fixed, predefined set of rules and procedures for producing this information. The problem statement itself is vague, involving terms—like *extended*, *impact*, and *reduced*—that do not have a specific meaning. Further, when the answer is developed, it will be difficult to know how accurate it is, whether a better answer could have been developed, or whether the process used was the best, or even a good, one.

Figure 14-1 shows the fundamental structure of a DSS application.[4] Users interface with the **dialogue management component,** which is a set of programs that manages the user interface and translates the user's requests into commands for the other two components.

1. Gerrity, T. P., "Design of Man-Machine Decision Systems, An Application to Portfolio Management," *Sloan Management Review*, Vol. 59, Winter 1971, pp. 17–25.

2. DeSanctis, G., and R. B. Gallupe, "Group Decision Support Systems, A New Frontier," *Data Base*, Vol. 16, Winter 1985, p. 3.

3. Some authors use the term *semistructured* instead of the term *unstructured*. In truth, the solution process must have some structure to be able to benefit from any computer-based system.

4. Ariav, Gad, and Michael J. Ginzberg, "DSS Design: A Systemic View of Decision Support," *Communications of the ACM*, Vol. 38, No. 10, October 1985, p. 1047.

Figure 14-1   Fundamental DSS Program Structure

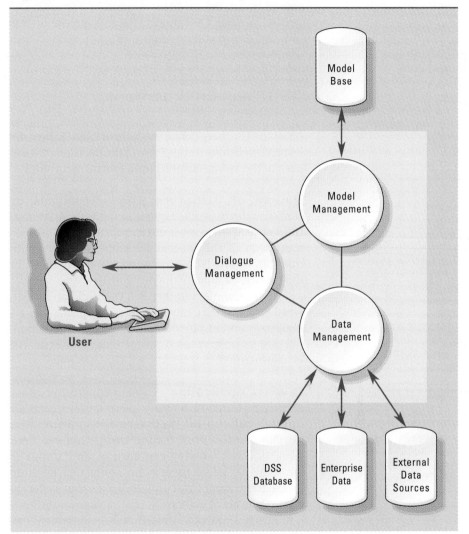

The **model management component** maintains and executes models of business activity, including spreadsheets, operations research models, financial models, and simulation models. The model management component is used to create, store, and modify models and to make them available to the user.

The **data management component** maintains DSS data. Its tasks include managing the DSS database, which contains both intermediate and final results of DSS studies, and managing interfaces to enterprise data and other external sources.

Not all DSSs have all the components in Figure 14-1. The selection of parts should match the problem domain of a specific DSS, so some parts may not be needed. A small DSS created for a single use on a personal computer may have only one or two components.

DSS Task Environment

Ariav and Ginzberg define the tasks of DSSs in three dimensions: degree of structure, level of application, and phase of the decision process addressed.[5] We will consider each of these dimensions plus a fourth, recurrency.

Degree of Structure DSSs are designed to address unstructured (or semistructured) problem environments. As Ariav and Ginzberg point out, however, the degree of structure is not a property of the problem to be solved as much as it is a property of the process for addressing the problem.[6] Thus, the appropriate question is not "How structured is the problem?" but rather "How structured is the process for solving the problem?"

For example, weather is a very fluid and unstructured phenomenon. Most weather prediction, however, is accomplished by a well-known, predefined, and highly structured process. Thus, weather prediction would not be considered to fall into an unstructured problem environment, even though the problem itself is unstructured.

Level of Application Level of application refers to the level of management activity in terms of Simon's three-layered cake and introduced in Chapter 4: operational control, management control, and strategic planning. Early development of DSS theory and technology assumed that DSSs would be used only for strategic planning and upper-level management control applications. While there is no doubt that DSSs do have applications at these levels, more recent research indicates that DSSs can be applied to problems at all three levels of activity.[7]

Thus, DSSs can be used at the operational control level when decisions at that level require a semistructured or unstructured process. The production scheduling activity at Scott Orthodontics in Module C is a good example. Accelerating a critical order is an operational control issue. Yet, to do this within

5. *Ibid.*, p. 1046.

6. Moore, J. H., and M. G. Chang, "Design of Decision Support Systems," *Data Base*, Vol. 11, No. 2, Fall 1980, pp. 10–17.

7. Ariav and Ginzberg, "DSS Design," p. 1046.

the limitations of the Scott manufacturing system, the production schedulers are required to adjust and adapt the week's production activities using a very unstructured process. Thus, do not fall prey to the misconception that DSSs are only applicable at the higher levels.

Phase of the Decision Process The decision process involves three primary phases: intelligence gathering, alternative development, and choice. DSSs can be used for all three phases.

DSSs can be used to investigate, understand, and discuss the problem and its environment. They can be used (1) to produce information that reveals the key elements of problems and the interrelationships of those elements; (2) to identify, create, and communicate alternative courses of action and other decision alternatives; and (3) to facilitate choice by estimating costs and benefits, by projecting other outcomes of decisions, by determining the sensitivity of outcomes to decision variables, and by communicating these projected results to decision makers.

The purpose of DSS applications is not only to generate information but also to facilitate communication about the information among the personnel involved in the problem. Thus, a specific function of a DSS at all levels and in all phases is to generate documents, reports, tables of data, graphs, slides, and other output.

Recurrency Another task dimension is task recurrency. Some DSS applications are developed to address problems that will never occur again. The labor strike at Legacy Systems is an example. At the other end of the recurrency continuum are tasks that regularly recur. Scheduling production at Scott Orthodontics is an example; it must be done every day of every week. Between the extremes are intermittent tasks that recur, but not regularly. The need to assemble a construction crew for an offshore drilling operation is an unstructured problem that recurs, but only irregularly.

Organizations respond to the recurrency dimension in different ways. Permanent DSS applications for regular and recurring needs are developed, supported, and maintained just as other types of information systems are.

To support the development and use of DSSs for intermittent applications, some organizations have established centers of DSS resources that include personnel with DSS expertise, programs, models, and data. Such centers or departments are like internal consulting companies to assist the development of DSS applications. A permanent DSS group facilitates the construction of DSS applications for whatever needs develop.

Where the need for the DSSs is temporary, the MIS department will set up an ad hoc team to build that particular DSS. For the strike at Legacy Systems, for example, the MIS department staffed a temporary team to build and use the DSS to compute estimates of financial impact.

DSS at Amalgamated Mining

Amalgamated Mining, a multinational corporation that operates mines throughout the world, periodically opens and closes mines. In the process, hundreds of decisions must be made concerning the acquisition or disposition of equipment and the relocation of personnel.

The Need for a DSS   In Spring 1993, Amalgamated closed one of its largest copper mines. In planning this closure, Amalgamated needed to decide which equipment to sell, which equipment to move, and which equipment to abandon. Further, it needed to make related personnel decisions. Because of interrelationships among the components inherent in mining operations, this closure was exceedingly difficult to plan.

Consider, for example, the consequences of eliminating 50 bulldozers. Clearly, if the bulldozers are removed, then the drivers of the bulldozers will not be necessary. But if the drivers are unnecessary, then the trainers of the drivers are unnecessary, as are the personnel required to hire both the drivers and the trainers. Further, if the bulldozers are removed, then the bulldozer trailers need to be removed along with the trucks that pull them. But if the trucks are removed, then the truck drivers are not necessary, nor are the truck driver trainers and the personnel who hire the drivers and their trainers. Additionally, the people who maintain the bulldozers, trailers, and trucks will not be needed (and neither will their trainers and support personnel).

Given the reductions in personnel, fewer people need to be supported. Since Amalgamated's mines are located in remote locations, this change has a substantial impact on operations. With the closing of the mine, fewer cooks, food buyers, builders of baths and showers, and people to maintain warehouses of tissue and toilet paper will be needed, and so forth.

This, clearly, is a complicated problem. It is also an important one. Amalgamated wants to make its cutbacks and reductions in a sensible manner. It does not want to harm remaining operations by cutting too far or to leave useless appendages untouched (e.g., truck drivers who have no trucks).

An Example DSS   An example that applies the general structure shown in Figure 14-1 to the DSS at Amalgamated Mining is shown in Figure 14-2. The model files are an important component. Amalgamated keeps a model of mining operations that pertains to the basic operation of all types of mines in all locations. In addition, it has developed more detailed models that pertain to particular types and locations of mines. Depending on the nature and level of detail in the analysis to be performed, Amalgamated may merge the general model with one or more of the detailed mine types or location models for a given study. This structure allows flexibility in the amount of detail considered for different analyses.

Figure 14-2 DSS for Amalgamated Mining

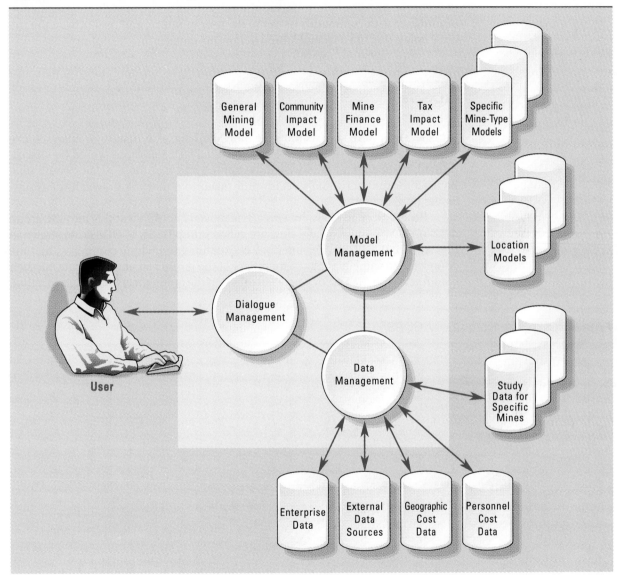

The data management component maintains databases of particular studies of particular mines. Data from all studies is saved so that it can be used for future studies.

To analyze logistics at a particular mine, the user indicates the type of analysis, the type of mine, and the location of the mine. This input enables the model management component to load and invoke the correct models and the data management component to access the correct data. The models are executed in accordance with commands issued to the user interface, and results from the run are displayed to the user and stored in the DSS database.

GDSSs

Initially, DSSs were seen as tools for individual decision makers or analysts. The notion was that the results from an individual's DSS sessions would be viewed, printed, graphed, and otherwise documented and that those results would then be used for the individual's decision or taken to a meeting in which the results would be discussed.

Recent work in DSSs, however, has moved DSS applications into the group decision environment where they are called **group DSSs,** or **GDSSs.** As shown in Figure 14-3, the GDSS user interface is expanded to include computers that are connected in some manner so members of the group can communicate via their computers with the DSS or with each other.[8] If the group meets in a single location,

Figure 14-3   Architecture of GDSS

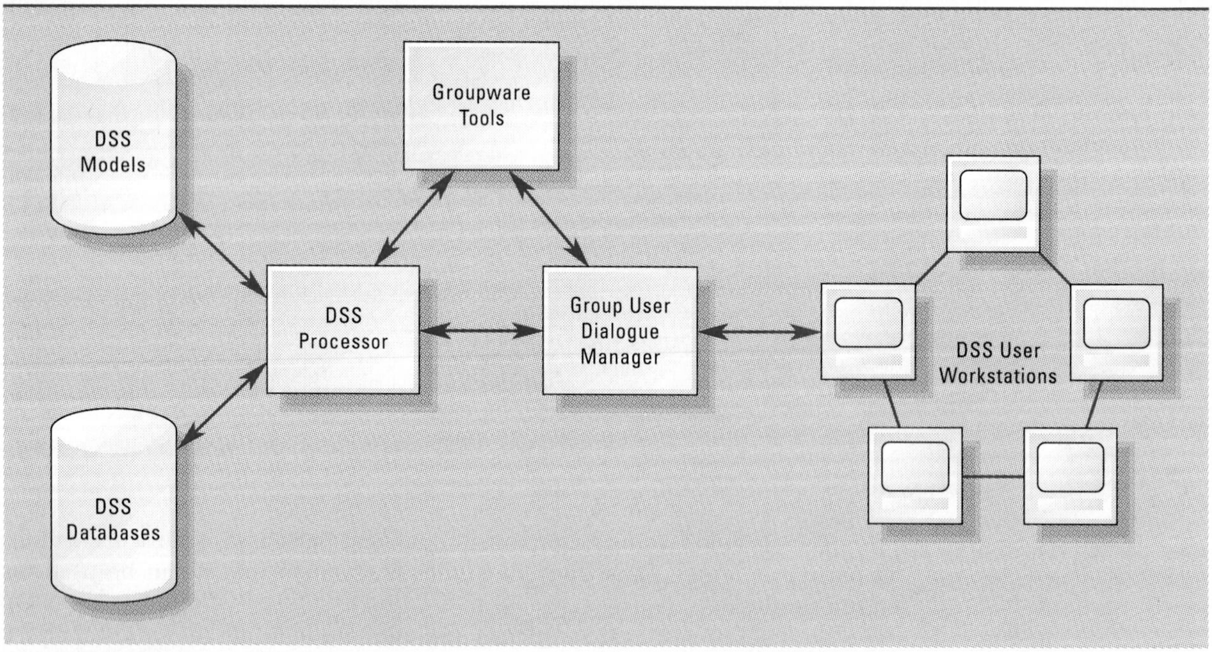

8. DeSanctis and Gallupe, "Group Decision Support Systems," p. 4.

they share a public screen for input and output. If they are geographically dispersed, they each have a window on their computer display that displays the public screen. Also, GDSSs often include special tools for facilitating group work called groupware, described in the following section.

The architecture used to support a GDSS depends on the recurrency of the DSS and the geographic location of the users. Figure 14-4 shows the alternatives

Figure 14-4   Alternative GDSS Architectures

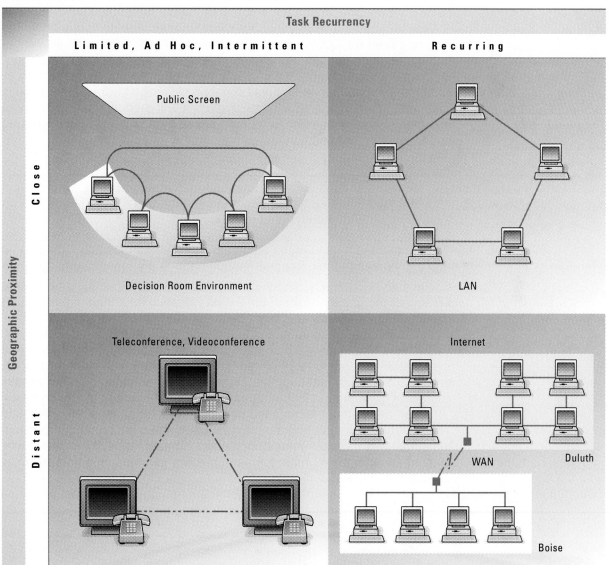

recommended by DeSanctis and Gallupe for combinations of recurrency and geographic proximity.[9] For limited, ad hoc, and intermittent GDSSs, where the members can meet in the same location, they recommend a **decision room environment**. Here, group members each use a computer station to communicate with each other, to obtain stored data, and to alter the display on the public screen.

For limited, ad hoc, and intermittent GDSSs where the members are geographically distributed, DeSanctis and Gallupe recommend **teleconferencing**. Here, desktops or meeting rooms are connected via video displays. For recurring GDSSs where the members are in the same location, DeSanctis and Gallupe recommend microcomputer workstations connected via a LAN. The recurring need for GDSSs justifies the expense of maintaining the permanent LAN connection.

Finally, for recurring GDSSs among geographically dispersed users, these authors recommend "uninterrupted communication between remote 'decision stations.'"[10] Their article, which appeared in 1985, recognized that, at that time, there were few such systems. Today, internets and WANs would be the preferred architecture for this combination.

Groupware

Initially, GDSS products and technology were focused exclusively on group decision making. As the resulting systems were used and more research was conducted on the role of computer systems in group environments, the benefits of using information systems to facilitate group activities beyond just decision making became clearer. The term **groupware** is used today to refer to information systems that facilitate and coordinate group activities, including decision making.

The purpose of groupware is to increase the productivity of workgroups. Valacich et al. stated that the purpose of their work was to "reduce or eliminate the dysfunctions [i.e., process losses] of the group interaction so that a group reaches or exceeds its task potential [i.e., achieves process gains]."[11] The authors summarized a number of factors, listed in Figure 14-5, that lead to **process losses**.

The University of Arizona has developed one of the most successful and popular groupware applications, which it licenses jointly with Ventana Corporation under the name GroupSystems. This product contains specific tools that can be used to facilitate group meetings. For example, the electronic brainstorming

---

9. *Ibid.*, p. 6.

10. *Ibid.*, p. 7.

11. Valacich, Joseph S., Alan R. Dennis, and J. F. Nunamaker, Jr., "Electronic Meeting Support: The Group Systems Concept," *International Journal of Man-Machine Studies*, Vol. 34, No. 2, February 1991, p. 262.

Figure 14-5 Group Process Losses, the Dysfunctions of Group Interaction

Loss Type	Description
Production Blocking	Limit that occurs because only one member can speak at a time
Evaluation Apprehension	Fear of negative response to ideas that are shared with the group
Free-Riding	Tendency of some group members to rely on others to carry the discussion or solve the problem
Cognitive Inertia	Tendency of a conversation to continue along a given course
Socializing	Party time!
Domination	Domination of topic, opinion, or conversational time by one or a few individuals
Failure to Remember	Tendency to forget comments made by others
Incomplete Analysis	Group fails to use data that is available or to challenge assumptions

application provides an interactive computer environment in which participants enter and share ideas about a topic. Participants review ideas and comments entered by other members of the group, usually anonymously.

When participants use such a tool, several of the process losses in Figure 14-5 are eliminated or reduced. Production blocking is reduced because members can enter ideas simultaneously. Anonymity eliminates evaluation apprehension. Records of the number of comments generated at each station can be evaluated to detect free-riding. Since a record is kept of all ideas, the tendency to forget others' contributions is reduced.

Another tool in the GroupSystems application is the idea organizer. With it, participants group the comments that resulted from the electronic brainstorming application into logical categories. Comments on the categories are shared, and eventually, the group combines categories into one shared set.

Other tools prioritize comments and ideas, and still others score alternatives for multiple criteria on a scale of 1 to 10; an important goal of these tools is to reduce incomplete analysis process loss.

Valacich et al. define three modes of groupware use in the facilitation of meetings.[12] In a **chauffeured process**, a meeting facilitator is the only user of the groupware program. As the meeting progresses, the facilitator enters comments

---

12. *Ibid.*, pp. 264–265.

and conclusions on behalf of the group. The primary use of the groupware is to record the progress and findings of the meeting and thus to reduce the failure to remember losses.

In a **supported process**, the group members use both verbal and electronic means to communicate with one another. In an **interactive process**, nearly all the group communication occurs through the groupware application; face-to-face communication is sacrificed, but production blocking, evaluation apprehension, failure to remember, free-riding, socializing, and domination losses are all reduced.

Other types of groupware support activities other than meetings. MIT has developed a groupware application called Object Lens that allows groups to create their own coordination tools, including tailor-made group calendars, Rolodexes, project management tools, and so forth. The format and appearance of these tools can be designed to meet the particular needs of the group.[13]

Still other groupware products focus on facilitating group conversations. For example, a product called the Amsterdam Conversation Environment (ACE) provides a flexible and unstructured common work space in which group members can share and manipulate new constructs and engage in new types of group interaction.

The goal of ACE is to increase the level of meaningful interaction and not necessarily to solve a particular problem. The designers of ACE wanted to create a system that would help increase the competence of the individuals in the workgroup without decreasing the group's collective competence.

> A system which assists the user to mechanically reduce a problem to manageable proportions works in the reductionist paradigm. Our view of a support system moves the user—toward a process of continuous incremental improvement requiring interaction and barring end-state finality.... The effects include a new capability to develop distinctions; a higher degree of interaction; an increased exchange and negotiation of viewpoint; and a richer variety in the conversations among users.[14]

As you can see, groupware lies on the boundary between DSSs and the communications workgroup systems that we discussed in an earlier chapter. No specific line divides these categories; they overlap.

Functions of DSS Applications

Figure 14-6 lists the major functions of DSS applications. First, DSSs can be used to become familiar with the problem domain. For large problems where it is not

---

13. Williams, Daniel, "New Technologies for Coordinating Work," *Datamation*, May 15, 1990, pp. 92–96.

14. Dykstra, Elizabeth A., and Robert P. Carasik, "Structure and Support in Cooperative Environments: The Amsterdam Conversation Environment," *International Journal of Man-Machine Studies*, Vol. 34, No. 3, March 1991.

Figure 14-6 Major Functions of DSS Applications

- Becoming familiar with a problem domain
- Determining sensitivity of results to changes in decision variables
- Identifying patterns and trends
- Predicting decision outcomes
- Developing models of business processes
- Computing optimum mixes
- Facilitating group communication, collaboration, and teamwork

clear which decision factors are dependent on which, a DSS can be used to identify relationships among key elements of the problem.

For example, in Amalgamated Mining's budget reduction problem, a DSS can be used to identify what equipment and personnel are required to support a bulldozer, both directly and indirectly. It is probably easy for analysts to determine direct support; the numbers and skills required for the bulldozer crew are well documented. What is less obvious are questions like "How many trainers are needed to support 100 bulldozer crews?" "What facilities are required to train 100 such crews?" "How much training is required of the trainers?" "How long does it take for a trainer to become qualified?" and so forth. Clearly, the indirect support is not easily determined, and the DSS is useful in determining what is dependent on what.

A second DSS function is determining the sensitivity of outcomes to changes in variables. For example, eliminating 10 bulldozers may save $1 million in logistic support costs. Or perhaps eliminating the 10 bulldozers saves $10 million in support costs; or if support costs are fixed over the relevant period, eliminating 10 bulldozers may save nothing at all because the costs may already have been sunk.

Obviously, the difference is important. Knowing which decision variables have the greatest impact on the outcome enables the decision makers to focus attention on the important matters. Decision makers focus considerable attention on unimportant factors and not enough on critical ones.

A third DSS function is pattern and trend identification. Using both statistical techniques and the visual display of quantitative data, a DSS application can help analysts identify patterns in input data or results. For example, a plot of sales data on a map can reveal differences in market size, market penetration, or sales effectiveness. The same plot repeated over successive time periods can help identify trends.

Another DSS function is the prediction of decision outcomes. For example, a DSS can be used to estimate the impact on sales of doubling the size of the sales force, increasing the advertising budget, or introducing a product in a new market. All such predictions rely on models that relate outcomes to input variables. Next, a DSS can develop models of business processes consisting of one or more equations that relate output to input. For example, an equation may relate sales to the number of sales personnel, sales to advertising, or both. The DSS can include statistical programs that estimate the parameters of such equations.

Computing optimum mixes is yet another DSS function, such as the problem of allocating people to jobs. Suppose Amalgamated eliminates 50 bulldozers, and, as a result, 500 employees become available for reassignment. Some of them will have other skills and training; some will not. Some of their skills will be in demand; some will not. Unless there is a match between alternative skills and available jobs, some people must be retrained or laid off. Amalgamated's problem may be allocating people to jobs to minimize retraining and moving costs. OR techniques like linear programming can be used to compute the optimum solution.

The last major function of a DSS is to facilitate group communication. Problems that require DSS applications nearly always involve group decision making, and decisions are often made by consensus. Even when the decision is made by a single authority, that person relies on the input of other team members. This means that a group must have a common understanding of the problem, the available solutions, and the criteria for choosing among alternatives.

Single-user DSSs facilitate communication not only by producing output that can be easily copied but also by producing overhead transparencies, 35-millimeter slides, and even video images and animation. GDSSs facilitate communication by making the facilities of the GDSS available to all group members.

COMPONENTS OF A DSS

A DSS is a computer-based information system. As such, it has the five components that all such systems have. This section briefly discusses these components. Most of what you need to know about these components you learned in Chapters 6, 9, and 12. Therefore, we now are concerned only with the special aspects of these components that relate to DSSs.

Hardware

Hardware for DSS applications falls into three groups: processing, communications, and special output. DSSs are supported by two different types of processing hardware. The first and oldest consists of a minicomputer or mainframe computer that stores key company databases to be accessed. The DSS facility on such a computer allows easy access to the system's data and programs. In contrast to a TPS or other structured system, control and standardization are less important in a DSS, and flexibility, adaptability, and ease of use are more important. Managers use DSSs to respond to complex problems that dynamically change.

The second type of DSS hardware consists of networked microcomputers. Microcomputers today not only provide a cheap alternative but also can deliver more power to a user. Since a microcomputer is normally dedicated to a single person, much more power can be dedicated to managing the user interface, and windows, graphics, and mice can be supported, making microcomputers easier to use. Most DSS applications you encounter probably will use microcomputers.

Communications hardware is the second category of DSS hardware. The most commonly used communications facilities are LANs, internets, and WANs. In addition, video-conferencing facilities are sometimes used. These alternatives are illustrated in Figure 14-4.

Special output equipment is the last category of DSS hardware, which includes high-resolution display screens and graphics printers as well as multicolored printers and plotters. In addition, some DSSs can produce 35-millimeter slides and images in other photographic media, such as digitized video, which can be input to DTP systems for the preparation of high-quality documents. Finally, GDSSs include large group display screens and visual output projection equipment.

Programs

The DSS architecture shown in Figure 14-1 illustrates the major categories of DSS programs. They include dialogue managers, model managers, and data managers. Details of each type are shown in Figure 14-7. This figure is a continuation of the structure developed by Ariav and Ginzberg.[15]

Dialogue Management   As Figure 14-7a shows, the dialogue management component has three subsystems. The user interface subsystem manages the physical user interface. It controls the appearance of the screen, accepts input from the user, displays the results, and checks user commands for correct syntax.

The dialogue control subsystem maintains a processing context with the user, ranging from a very structured menu-driven system in which the DSS application maintains control (rare with DSSs) to a loosely structured command-driven system in which the user maintains control. Since flexibility and ease of use are of paramount importance in DSSs, GUIs are becoming the standard for DSS applications. Database access in DSSs is normally performed with SQL. Natural

---

15. Ariav and Ginzberg, "DSS Design," pp. 1048, 1049.

Figure 14-7   Categories of DSS Programs
(a) Dialogue management. **(b)** Model management. **(c)** Data management.

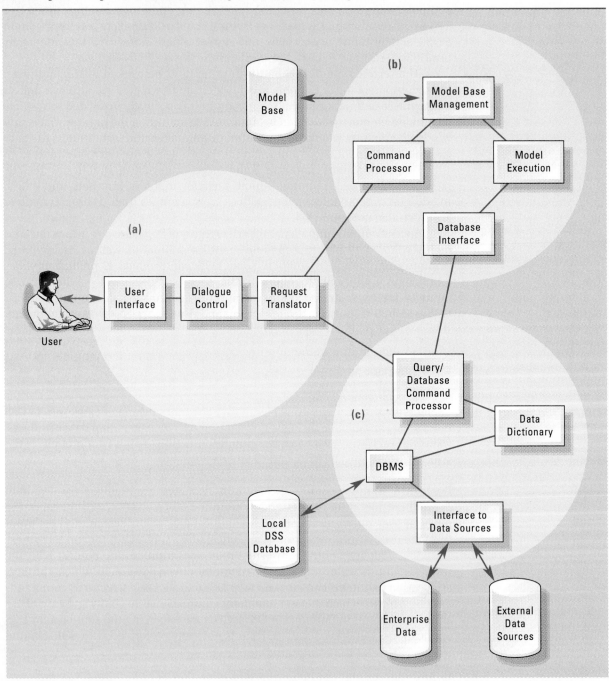

language interfaces, in which users interact with the system using free-form English or another language, are also becoming important for DSSs.

The request translator, the third subsystem, translates user commands into actions for the model management or data management components and translates responses from those components into a format and vocabulary understandable by the user.

Model Management The structure of the second component, the model manager, is shown in Figure 14-7b. The command processor receives commands from the dialogue management components and delivers them to either the model base management system or the model execution system.

A model is a generalized representation of some aspect of the organization's activity and its internal or external environment. The model manager must process spreadsheets, OR models, financial and accounting models, business simulations, and other similar models. The model manager stores the model and is used to make changes to it. The model execution system invokes the model, causing data to be retrieved from the data management component and processed in accordance with the model. Results from model execution can be stored in the DSS database via the data management component, communicated to the user via the dialogue management component, or both.

Data Management The data management component has two functions. First, it stores and manipulates the DSS database as directed by either the model management component or the dialogue management component. Second, it maintains an interface with data sources that are external to the DSS, such as enterprise TPS databases, interenterprise systems, external data utilities, and other DSS applications.

The structure of the data management component is illustrated in Figure 14-7c. Either the model management component or the dialogue management component can issue requests for data service. These requests are interpreted by the query processor, which may consult its own data directory (most likely part of the DSS database). They are then executed by a DBMS or equivalent.

The DSS program models illustrated in Figures 14-1 and 14-7 are generalized to all DSS applications. A particular application may be strong in one or a few of these components and weak in others. The model provides a way of understanding and evaluating DSS products. When reviewing a product or an application, consider each subsystem in Figure 14-7.

Figure 14-8 is a checklist of subsystems and their features and functions. All products may not have subsystems with the same names and features as these. However, all of these features and functions should be present in some part of the product.

The four categories of programs defined for personal, workgroup, and enterprise MIS also apply to DSS applications. They are systems programs,

Figure 14-8   Checklist for DSS Program Component Characteristics

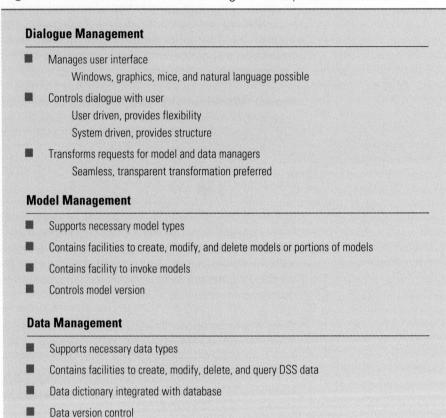

horizontal market programs, vertical market programs, and custom-developed programs. For historical reasons, however, horizontal and vertical market programs go by other names when applied to DSSs.

Systems Programs   DSS applications almost always require a DBMS, which serves the major role in the data management component shown in Figure 14-7c. The DBMS used, however, may be different from one used for TPS applications, since flexibility and ease of use are more important than control and performance. Nearly all the DBMS products used in DSS applications are based on the relational model that represents data in tables.

Figure 14-7a shows a subsystem that transforms requests into data management system operations, and Figure 14-7c shows another subsystem that

Figure 14-9   Role of Extraction Program on Enterprise Computer

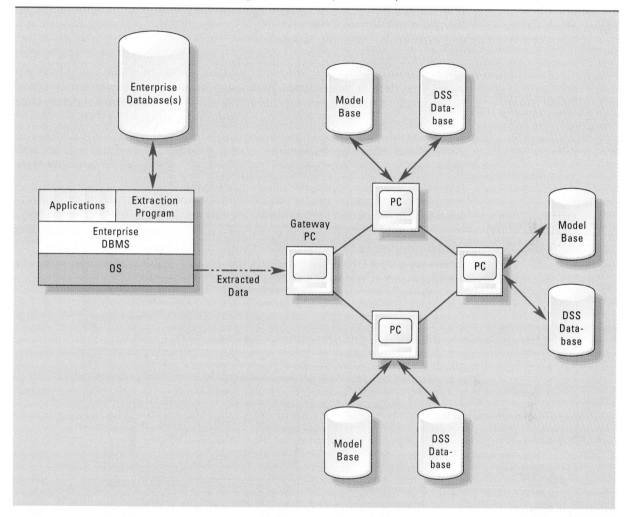

provides a data interface to external data sources. These components provide critical services to the DSS. Figure 14-9 shows why.

In Figure 14-9, three microcomputers are running different DSS applications. The DSS on each microcomputer has the structure shown in Figure 14-7, and each has its own data-interface program that obtains external data through the gateway micro. These programs communicate with a program on the mainframe called an **extraction program**. It translates the DSS data-interface program's requests into commands for the DBMS that processes the enterprise database or other data source; thus, it allows the user's data-interface program to perform as a client to the mainframe, which acts as a database server. Normally, too, the extraction program is responsible for providing security and control over the incoming requests.

In a well-designed DSS, the interface between all these computers is hidden from the user. In fact, some DSS applications are designed so the user is not even aware that data is downloaded from other computers. The user may know, conceptually, that the data comes from the enterprise's operational database or some other source, but data access is transparent to the user.

Horizontal Market Programs (DSS Shells)   Horizontal market DSS **programs** provide features and functions for dialogue, model, and data management for a wide class of DSS applications. Like word processors or spreadsheets, these programs can be used for widely varying applications and across many industries. Such products are called **DSS shells** or **DSS generators**.

Just as a DBMS is used to construct a database application, a DSS shell is used to construct a DSS application. A shell can be a spreadsheet like Lotus 1-2-3 or an easy-to-use DBMS like Paradox. Other possible shells are financial-modeling packages such as IFPS and other simulation languages.

Figure 14-10   DSS Shell Composed of Horizontal Market Applications

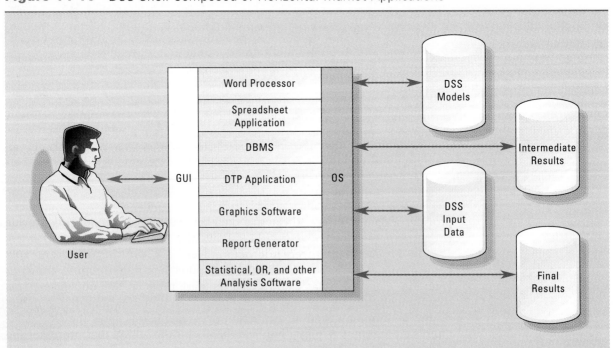

DSS shells do not require procedural language programming, as is required when using languages like COBOL and BASIC. Consequently, they are fast to use, and the DSSs they create can be readily changed. Recall that procedural language programming arose in third-generation languages. DSS shells are an example of the fourth-generation languages defined in that chapter. As such, DSS shells can be used to create DSS applications with far greater ease and rapidity than can general-purpose programming languages.

In some cases, no single horizontal market program can fulfill all the requirements for a DSS application. When this occurs, a DSS shell is created by integrating a number of different horizontal products, as Amalgamated Mining did. Figure 14-10 shows an example in which several off-the-shelf microcomputer programs are brought together to form a DSS shell. The roles taken by DSS subsystems shown in Figure 14-7 are fulfilled by commercial packages.

A DSS shell constructed from off-the-shelf components is an example of an integrated application. These applications share files; for example, the results from a spreadsheet analysis are input to a presentation program which creates 35-millimeter slides. Similarly, data from a DBMS is input to a statistical analysis program, which sends its results to a report generator, which sends its output to the DTP program that produces a newsletter. These programs can share files either statically or dynamically.

The integration of disparate horizontal market programs is easier in a GUI environment because the applications in a GUI environment have a more consistent user interface. Also, most GUI environments provide for dynamic data sharing (e.g., Dynamic Data Exchange in Microsoft Windows).

In some situations, custom-written applications are needed to integrate these applications. Such programs are sometimes needed to smooth the interfaces between component programs when the output format of data from one program is incompatible with the input data format of another. The services of a professional programmer are usually required to create such custom programs.

Vertical Market DSS Programs **Vertical market DSS programs** provide support for a specific class of problems and for problems in a particular industry. In the same source cited above, Ariav and Ginzberg refer to these programs as **generalized DSSs.**

For example, one vertical market DSS program has features and functions that enable manufacturing scheduling DSSs to be rapidly developed. Although the program cannot be used for other applications, the high productivity it provides for its particular vertical market segment may justify its acquisition.

Figure 14-11 lists popular vertical market DSS program products. Some are used to process geographic data; others, for financial modeling; and still others, to model decision-making processes.

Custom-Developed DSS Applications The custom development of DSS applications through the use of a general-purpose programming language such as

Figure 14-11   Vertical Market DSS Program Packages

DSS Name	Purpose	Vendor
BRANDAID	Facilitates the development of marketing plans for packaged goods	J. D. C. Little
GADS	Performs geographic problem analysis such as redefining political boundaries, planning territory assignments, and the like	IBM
MAPP	Facilitates financial planning and budgeting for a portfolio of products	Citibank
EIS	Performs financial planning and modeling for major corporations and projects	Boeing Computer

COBOL or C is seldom done. While this approach is technically feasible, it is seldom cost- or schedule-feasible. **Custom-developed DSS applications** are expensive and difficult to justify when so many horizontal market programs are available. Also, time-consuming custom development does not meet the schedule requirements of most DSS problems. The Amalgamated Mining DSS described earlier in this chapter would have been both cost-infeasible and schedule-infeasible if entirely custom-developed.

As with other types of custom programming, if the requirements are rare or unique and if the value of the information produced is exceptionally high, building from scratch can make sense. This is rare, however, and should only be a last resort.

Data

Examine Figure 14-1 again; there are two kinds of data: model data and DSS database data. Facilities must exist to create, modify, delete, and retrieve both types. Often, as suggested by Figure 14-1, the model manager and the data manager are different programs, sometimes from different vendors. This means that the coordination of model data and DSS data can become a problem. Care must be taken to match the correct data with the correct model.

Two other problems concern data in DSS applications: the risk of data incompatibilities and the need for multiple versions of the same data.

DSS Data Compatibility   DSS databases are usually composed of data from a variety of sources and time periods. Sometimes the data is taken from various databases in the same department, but more often it is taken from databases in different departments, divisions, or even companies. Additionally, data from different time periods must sometimes be combined, as when last year's sales data must be compared to this year's market data. Because of the different sources and different time periods, incompatibilities in the data are almost inevitable.

For example, suppose you have the task of assessing sales region effectiveness over the past 24 months. You gather quarterly data about sales that includes the following table:

ORDER [Cust#, SP#, Region#, Date, Amount]

You want to relate this data to sales regions. You access a database that supports a workgroup MIS in the sales department, and obtain this table:

REGION [Region#, Manager, Location, Phone, TerCode]

Using SQL, you combine the rows in these two tables where Region# is identical and generate this table:

REGSALES [Cust#, SP#, Region#, Date, Amount, Manager, Location, Phone, TerCode]

From this table, you extract just the columns you want to form a final table:

REGIONSALES [Region#, Date, Amount, Manager, Location]

You sort this table by region, as shown in Figure 14-12. From the sorted table you can compute region totals by quarter, and so forth.

There is only one problem: Much of the ORDER data has disappeared! When you add the regional sales totals to obtain a grand total, it does not come close to the accepted value of total sales for the company's past 2 years. What's wrong?

The problem is that Region# in the ORDER table and Region# in the REGION table are not the same! Region# in ORDER is the number of the region as of each order's date. Region# in the REGION table is the current number of the region. Unknown to you until now, in the past few months, regions have been created, eliminated, and changed. To solve this problem, you will need to obtain region data that corresponds to the dates on which orders occurred. Unless you are lucky, this data most likely will not exist in any convenient place or format, and you will have to dig through paper files to obtain it.

This example is a typical situation that occurs in DSS applications. Since such applications often combine data from different sources and different time periods, incompatibilities like this are common.

Consider this problem in light of Amalgamated's mine closures. Can you imagine the number of data items that seem to have the same meaning but actually do not? In fact, a data item as simple as a department number is a source

Figure 14-12 Data-Inconsistency Problem

ORDER				
Cust#	**SP#**	**Region#**	**Date**	**Amount**
1200	798	84	30 Apr 94	$589.77
2000	900	12	12 Mar 95	$300.17
1000	800	10	14 Feb 95	$700.89
1000	810	10	27 Feb 95	$312.56
3000	950	15	18 Mar 95	$415.88
4000	975	20	15 Apr 95	$987.65

REGION				
Region#	**Manager**	**Location**	**Phone**	**TerCode**
10	Jones	Dallas	555-1000	17
15	Code	San Fran	555-2345	08
20	Eastman	NYC	555-4567	99

REGIONSALES				
Region#	**Date**	**Amount**	**Manager**	**Location**
10	14 Feb 95	$700.89	Jones	Dallas
10	27 Feb 95	$312.56	Jones	Dallas
15	18 Mar 95	$415.88	Code	San Fran
20	15 Apr 95	$987.65	Eastman	NYC

of major problems. Department numbers change format and meaning over time and between nations, divisions, and mines. The management of data with different meanings is, in fact, one of the greatest problems for Amalgamated's DSS.

Recall that, in the case of the sales example, you did not notice a problem until you examined the answer. You should take two lessons from this. First, data-item incompatibilities are often not visible until the analysis is nearly complete. If you can anticipate such problems, you can save considerable work.

Second, with DSS applications of all types, examine your results for reasonableness! Do not assume that the answers you obtain are necessarily correct.

Incompatibilities and other types of problems can bring all sorts of errors into your results. Check your results before you embarrass yourself in front of critical audiences. Be certain you can explain what you present!

Multiple Versions of Data   Unlike transaction-oriented systems, DSSs often involve many different versions of the same data. For a revenue-generation TPS, there is one and only one record for customer 1000, but in a DSS there may be multiple versions of the record for that customer, depending on the studies undertaken.

Consider the problem of evaluating three marketing strategies. Suppose that each strategy is applied to four different portfolios of products. Further suppose that these strategies and portfolios are used to project 5 years of quarterly sales performance for each sales region.

There are 12 different sales estimates—one for each strategy and portfolio. Each of these iterations produces 5 years of sales data. In making these projections, suppose that the marketing analysts make a year's projection, evaluate the results, change allocations of marketing dollars according to the strategy being studied, and make the next year's projections. Operating in this way, the team will have a total of 60 different files of annual sales data. See Figure 14-13.

In addressing this problem, the analysts are creating a large data administration problem. Whereas in a TPS there is 1 table for each year's sales, in this DSS there will be 12 tables for each year's sales. Unless the versions are carefully administered, confusion and errors will result. We will consider such administration in the procedure section later in this chapter.

The need for careful administration of data versions sometimes continues past the life of the project. It may be that, unknown to anyone at the time of the analysis, all 60 files of sales projections will be helpful in resolving a sales territory allocation problem at some later date. If so, records showing what is contained in each file, how the file was generated, what assumptions were made, and so forth, will be very useful.

Also, as with the problem of inconsistent data items, errors generated by using the wrong data for an analysis will not be immediately evident. Such errors may not be visible until the end of the project, if then. In the worst case, incorrect decisions are made and the business suffers. No one may ever know that the analysis was based on inconsistent versions of data.

People

Personnel involved in the use, development, and operation of a DSS are summarized in Figure 14-14. First, the *clientele* of a DSS are the business managers for whom the system is created. These are the people who make the business decisions on the basis, in part, of the results produced by the DSS. Typically, they

Figure 14-13 Origin of 60 Versions of Sales Projections

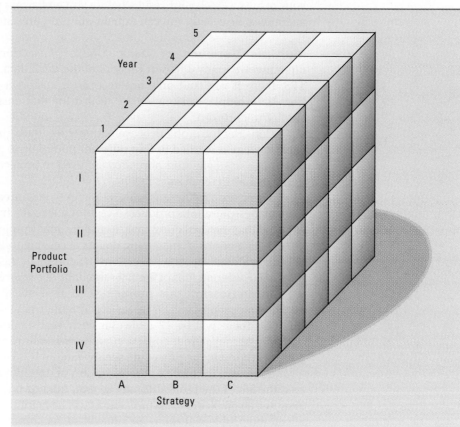

include such people as vice presidents, division managers, shop floor managers, warehouse managers, and fleet dispatchers. In some situations, these people make decisions as a single authority; in other situations, they make decisions in concert with other people, as part of a team.

Business analysts are assistants to the decision makers who serve as staff analysts and administrative assistants. They normally have experience and expertise in a functional area of business and also in the use of information technology—especially technology that can facilitate decision making. They plan and execute the studies, and they interpret and prepare the results for presentation. They usually are responsible for keeping the study on track and on schedule. They are the primary users of the DSS.

DSS Support Personnel End-user support personnel may be organized in several ways. If the company has a permanent DSS group, it may be a part of the

Figure 14-14   Personnel Involved with DSS Applications

End-User Personnel

Clientele	Managers for whom project exists
Business Analysts	Assistants who have expertise in the problem domain

DSS Support Personnel

Operations Personnel	Run computer equipment
Program Development and Support Personnel	Develop DSS applications software; support and service purchased programs
Data Administration Personnel	Administer DSS data
Consultants	Provide liaison with user personnel; provide advice and assistance, may join DSS project team
Facilitators	Plan, conduct, and follow up on group meetings

MIS end-user support department, or it may report directly to the president or CEO. Alternatively, DSS support personnel may be located directly in the various end-user departments.

Whether it is located in an MIS end-user support department, sometimes called the information center, or reports directly to the president or CEO, DSS group provides facilities to support the development, operation, and maintenance of DSS applications. Such a group may operate its own minicomputer or mainframe computer, and it may support users in acquiring their own hardware resources. Additionally, DSS groups provide DSS programs and libraries of both model data and other DSS data, along with a professional staff.

The staff in a DSS group is analogous to the staff in an enterprise MIS department. Personnel may be involved in supporting DSS operations, developing and supporting programs, and administering data. In addition, consultants may assist users in utilizing the department's resources.

Operations personnel include people who run and maintain DSS hardware, if separate from other systems, and people who decide what hardware is needed and spearhead its acquisition. *Program development and support personnel* are primarily involved with procuring and supporting DSS software. Also, when there is a need for tailored programs, these people develop them. *Data administration personnel* are specialists in DSS data. They have the same responsibilities for data administration as described earlier for enterprise MIS data administration.

However, the DSS data administration job is more complicated because data is obtained from widely varying sources, may be inconsistent, and exists in many versions.

Consultants advise, support, and guide business analysts in planning and executing DSS studies. They serve as the liaison between the DSS group and the analysts. Consultants can be assigned to study teams, sometimes for extended periods of time. Over time, they become experts within the DSS group about particular end-user departments' problems. One individual, for example, may come to be known as the DSS person who understands marketing problems. That person will speak on behalf of the marketing department within the DSS group.

Facilitators are involved with the application of GDSS software. They are trained in the dynamics of group processes and also in the technology of groupware. They help the group users plan, conduct, and follow up on group meetings.

Organizational Placement of the DSS Group   Where a permanent DSS group exists, its relationship to the enterprise MIS department is an interesting one.

In some companies, the DSS group resides within the MIS department. However, there are two problems with this arrangement. First, DSS applications and the TPS applications that are the main focus of the MIS department are antithetical; TPSs focus on control and DSSs focus on flexibility. This difference creates difficult management problems. Second, when the DSS group is located within the MIS department, it tends to lose its value to its customers, becoming more responsive to the needs of the MIS department than to the needs of DSS users.

Because of these problems, many companies pull the DSS group out of the MIS department and establish it as a staff function to the president or the CEO. Figure 14-15 diagrams the MIS department and the DSS group for Amalgamated Mining.

The problem with separating MIS from DSS is that they tend to step on one another's toes. There may be a continuing turf battle over which department has the authority to perform particular services. The MIS department tends to wage a continuing battle to pull the DSS group inside itself. There may also be duplication of hardware, programs, data, and personnel between the two units.

It is impossible to say, unequivocally, which is the better arrangement, since the answer depends on the company, the roles of the departments, and the personalities of key personnel. It is true, however, that the DSS group and the MIS department are often at odds, and if the DSS manager reports to the MIS manager, the losers in the battle tend to be the DSS customers. Therefore, in many companies, a separation of the two departments is desirable.

Personnel in the Absence of a DSS Group   If the company does not support a formalized DSS group, then selected personnel within user departments (or, less often, the MIS department) are identified as DSS experts or proponents.

Figure 14-15 Organization of Amalgamated Mining's DSS Group and MIS Department

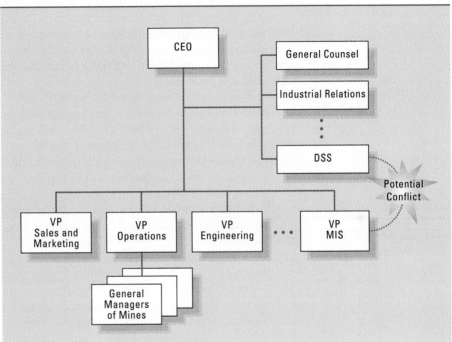

They form the teams created to develop or operate DSS applications and to perform particular studies. The same job descriptions exist as described previously. Sometimes end-user departments allocate personnel permanently to these jobs. The job of meeting facilitator, for example, is likely to be a full-time, permanent job.

Procedures

Two types of procedures are required for DSS applications. First are procedures to maintain the DSS resources. The DSS group must have procedures for operating the hardware, for maintaining and changing the programs, for administering the data, and so forth. These procedures are the same four types we have discussed before: normal and failure recovery procedures for both users and operators. The only addition to these procedures is extended data administration procedures to account for the possibility of incompatible domains and multiple versions.

If there is no permanent DSS group, then these standard types of procedures need to be created at the start of each DSS project. While some teams do not want to take the time to do this, not doing so is usually a mistake.

The second type of procedure concerns the use of a DSS facility to solve a business problem. Unfortunately, since each study is different, it is not possible to formulate generalized procedures. The work to be done is too varied; the process involved is too convoluted; and there is insufficient repetitiveness for standard procedures to be useful.

Instead, most DSS groups (or teams) agree on a set of policies that are interpreted and implemented in accordance with situations as they develop. For example, one policy might be that records will be kept of the origin of every data file so that, in the case of inconsistent or unexplainable results, the ancestry of the data can always be traced. This is an important policy because months may go by before users realize it is important to know a file's heritage.

Other policies concern the management of the DSS group, and they are akin to the policies established by consulting companies. For example, a single spokesperson may be identified for each DSS project. Only that person is allowed to disseminate or to approve the dissemination of results. This is especially important in DSS work because such work is iterative; what appears to be a sound conclusion one week may be invalidated by work undertaken in the next week. The DSS project can lose credibility if a different opinion is issued each week. The identification of a single spokesperson reduces such risks.

Additional policies concern quality of work. If the use of particular tools or the processing of particular data is complicated and, hence, error-prone, the DSS team may establish a policy that all work is to be checked by a second person. Similarly, there may be a policy that all reports are reviewed by a copy editor for clarity, consistent terminology, and so on. The DSS team may require that critical input data, formulas, and models be corroborated by at least two authorities before they can be used.

The particular policies that a given DSS group or team establishes depend very much on the organization and the nature of the work. The point is that, since DSS work is not standardized and must be flexible and creative, rigid procedures are often not realistic. However, there can and should be policies that govern the process by which the DSS team accomplishes its work.

DEVELOPING DSS APPLICATIONS

The process used to develop a DSS application depends on the recurrency of the tasks. Sometimes DSS applications must be developed on a "crash" basis to respond to one-of-a-kind emergencies. In this case, they are developed using an adaptive process like the one described in Chapter 7. At other times, they are developed to support recurring needs, and they can be developed using the structured development processes described in Chapters 10 and 13.

Since you have learned the basic processes used for developing information systems in those chapters, we will not repeat the discussion here. Instead, we will focus on the development of DSS applications for a one-of-a-kind crash project.

Developing Unexpected, Nonrecurring, High-Priority DSS Applications

In many cases, the need for a DSS application arises suddenly and unexpectedly, as in the event of a labor strike, a sudden threat such as product poisoning, an explosion or major industrial accident, an opportunity to effect a hostile takeover, the need to blunt a hostile takeover attempt, a lawsuit, a stock market crisis, an earthquake, a war, a Federal Trade Commission (FTC) investigation, a change in government policy, and so forth. These events cannot be anticipated, and the need for information that will arise cannot be known in advance.

The flow of events often dictates that the response time for developing a DSS application is short, often unrealistically short. Still, however, some response must be made to the labor strike, the accident, the takeover attempt, or the FTC investigation, and the response must be made within the time frame of events, not within the time frame that is appropriate for effective systems development.

The subject of a DSS application is often one of great concern to very senior managers, which means that considerable expense and inconvenience is tolerated, and, at times, even expected. In the words of one senior manager, "I know it's impossible, but do it anyway." That kind of statement from an executive vice president of operations authorizes activity and sets expectations that seldom occur in developing other types of information systems.

For these reasons, people may reasonably begin solving the problem before defining it—or at least before they have defined all of it. Such projects are like learning to play the violin while playing a concerto in public. First you start; then you learn that there's an orchestra behind you, and a conductor, and that the marks on the pieces of paper in front of you have something to do with the sound you are expected to make with the violin.

Getting started before you have fully defined the problem flies in the face of the systems development discussions in previous sections of this text. You know from those chapters that starting before you understand the problem is an invitation to disaster. The difference here is that, with this type of need, disaster is certain if you do *not* start immediately. So you start, and you hope that you can learn enough as you continue to be able to contribute information of value to the problem.

Figure 14-16 DSS Applications Are Often Created Under Emergency Conditions
When the fire trucks leave, what resources are needed to get the plant back into full operation?

Further, since you may be forced to start the project before understanding the problem, you are likely to waste considerable time and resources. Development in such a situation must be iterative, even more iterative than developing with prototypes. You start, define a problem, and create a platform; then you realize that you are working on the wrong problem; you back up and regroup, redefine the problem, and build another platform; and so forth. The process often involves two steps forward and one step backward. This is an exceptionally expensive way of solving a problem, but at times it cannot be avoided.

Contributing to the lack of time and understanding is the fact that some DSS applications require unstructured solution processes that *nobody* truly understands. Sometimes the only way to understand what needs to be done is to do it; other times, the process of addressing the problem is only understood well enough to circumvent the issue, and the organization moves on to other things without ever understanding the problem.

In this setting, the efficient use of hardware that is essential in TPSs may not be as important as development speed and flexibility. Therefore, DSS tools may emphasize fast development more than operational efficiency. For example, fourth-generation programming languages, which are notorious for their inefficient use of hardware, may be the most appropriate development tools for any custom-developed part of a DSS. Once developed, the DSS may be used infrequently and in situations that impact the company's bottom line quite directly. Therefore, operational inefficiency may be readily tolerated.

An Adaptive Development Process

All of this is not to say that the process you learned in Chapter 7 has no utility for this type of DSS application development. In fact, it does. But the process must be modified to be much more adaptive, and its application will be piecemeal and iterative. We call this method the **adaptive development process**.

Using such a process, you may repeat the same stages many, many times for one DSS application. You may address part of the problem and solve it, then find out that the solution was incomplete or erroneous or turned out to be unhelpful. Or the problem may change part way through a solution in a way that invalidates much of the work done to that point.

Figure 14-17 summarizes this process. You pick part of the problem, and you begin work. You define the problem, classify the solution, build a platform, and then, instead of developing a prototype (as in Chapter 7), you generate your first study results. In a sense, these are prototypes, but they are prototypical study results. The results are evaluated, and at this point, in the presence of new information, you may redefine the problem, rebuild the platform, spawn another subproject, generate more results, integrate subproject results, or report your results. In fact, you may take all of these actions.

Developing a DSS for the Amalgamated Mine Closure

In the Amalgamated mine closure, suppose that the decision to close the mine was made suddenly and that no one knew it was coming. You arrive at work one day and are told to get on an airplane, go to the mine, and help the general manager

Figure 14-17   Example of the Adaptive Development Process

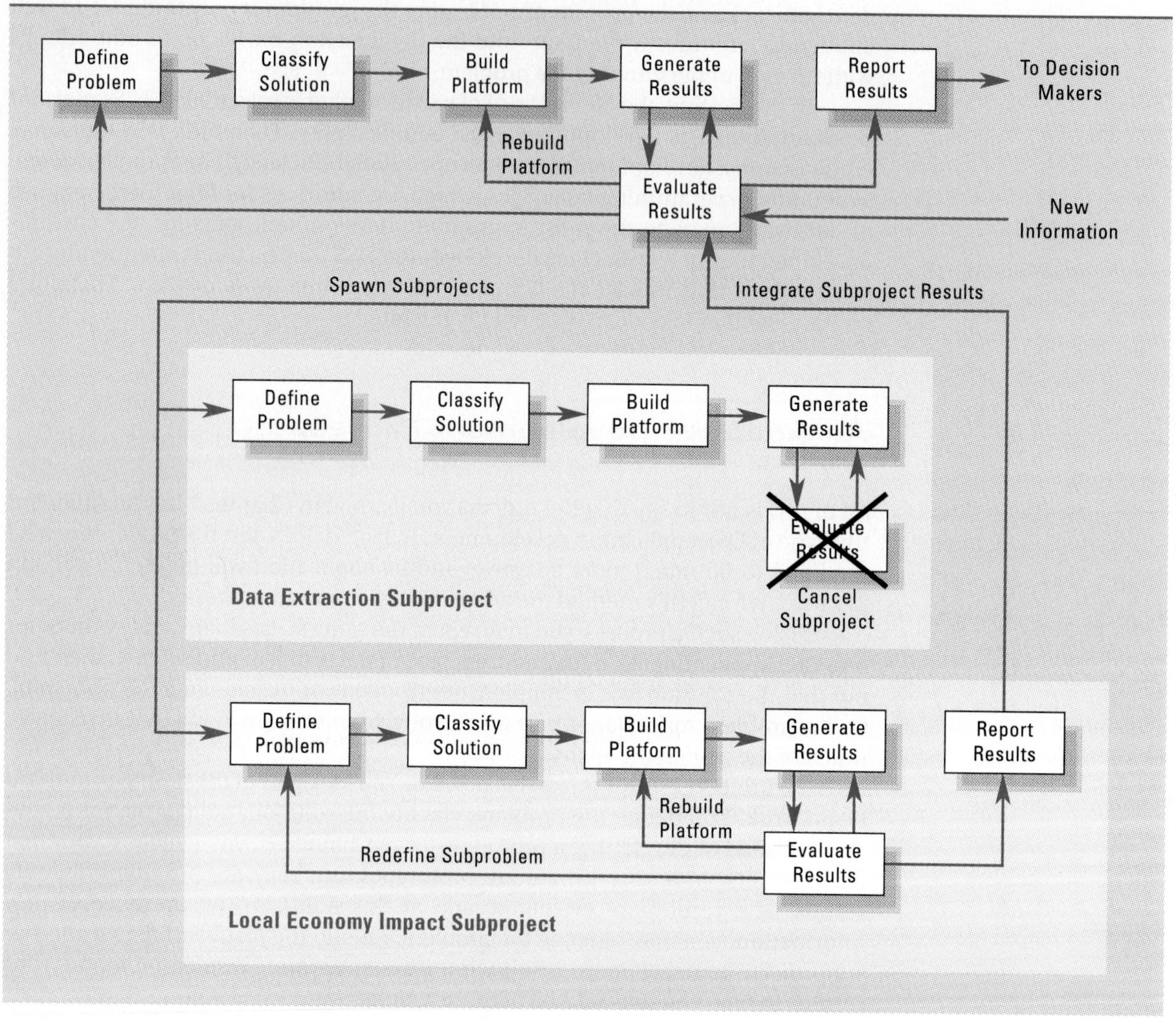

determine the impact of eliminating 50 bulldozers, crews, and related equipment and personnel.

Given this assignment, you begin by clarifying the problem definition. What does *impact* mean? Impact on cost? Impact on Amalgamated's ability to open future mines? Impact on the local country's economy? Suppose you find out that *impact* isn't the problem at all and what the company really wants is a way to eliminate equipment and personnel with minimum cost.

A concern is the scope of the project. At the extreme, you know that the removal of the bulldozers will impact the corporation's need to purchase steel wool and screwdrivers. But do you need to go into that depth of detail? Thus, you consider alternative scopes and choose one of them.

Next you classify the solution and build a platform. You focus on the essence of a problem statement. What do you need to determine costs? Since this is a one-of-a-kind application, you will not spend time developing prototypes to evaluate niceties like report formats and arrangements of menu choices. Since the compnay needs an answer as soon as possible, you will need to focus your activity on solving the problem.

Suppose the following situation: While building the platform, you find out that, for at least 2 weeks, you cannot obtain data on the personnel who support bulldozers. Since you cannot wait for 2 weeks, you set those requirements aside and begin working on the data needed for equipment decisions. Now, you know that separating the analysis of personnel and equipment may be a serious mistake. If you had more time, you would check out that possibility. Time is your most critical resource, however, so you press on and hope you will recover as best you can, if you later have to.

Suppose you learn that the data you need is in a corporate data center in St. Louis; you spawn a subproject to obtain that data. The subproject team classifies the solution and builds a platform to extract the data. At that point, you learn that part of the data is restricted and that the MIS department must have three levels of approval authority before it will release the data to your team. From past experience, you know that it will take 3 weeks to obtain the approvals. That is too long to wait, and you cancel the subproject.

As soon as you can, you assemble the components for one platform and begin generating the initial results. You are concerned because there are probably errors in the data, and you are not certain you have combined compatible data; so you show these initial results to people who are knowledgeable about mine operations and ask them to make reasonableness checks for you.

Just about now, the word reaches you: "Yes, impact does mean cost impact, but it is also of great concern to know how this cut will impact the local economy. Local politicians are up in arms about the mine closure, and the PR department needs to know exactly how many people will be laid off and how many will be offered employment in other mines or divisions. Get the data as soon as possible." Given this knowledge, you spawn another subproject to address these concerns. This subproject will also follow the adaptive process, independently.

Now, as the feedback on the initial results arrives, you discover that the data you received is not what you expected and that there are serious problems with inconsistencies between seemingly identical data items. You realize that you used the wrong terms when asking for the data. You could have found this out if you had talked with Ms. Blum in the Miami data center. It was only by having the problem, however, that you learned of the existence of Ms. Blum.

Given this new knowledge, you back up, redefine the problem, and reclassify the solution. Then you recreate the platform, create another round of study results, and continue iterating on them. Meanwhile, the local results project continues.

All of this work proceeds until, most likely, some event occurs external to the system. And, most likely, the senior manager you are supporting reaches a deadline and is forced to ask for the best results you have at some point. You do the best you can to meet the decision maker's needs. After the crisis is over, you are sent back to your regular duties, and you never know how well you did, how accurate your results were, or whether or not you even studied the correct problem.

Justifying the Costs of Adaptive Systems Development

This, in a rough sense, is the nature of crash application development. You plan where you can; you follow the adaptive process as best you can; and often, as you learn and see the results of your mistakes, you back up and repeat much work. This is an expensive way to solve a problem. You probably could cut the development costs by a factor of five or more if you had the time to follow either the prototyping process or the five-stage process on a reasonable schedule.

You may be wondering why anyone would want to pay five times more than they need to for an information system. Suppose you are given the task of analyzing the costs in a $3.5 billion procurement. The interest cost on $3.5 billion is roughly $1 million per day. If the DSS application development is holding up a decision on the contract, every day of DSS development costs $1 million. Thus, the premium is on speed, flexibility, and results—costs are simply not significant.

This is an exaggeration to make a point. Chances are slim that you will be involved with very many $3.5 billion procurements. It is always important to consider development cost and effectiveness. Further, in a time-constrained process, good planning may be more important than in a less time-pressured process. The difference is that sometimes, in DSS application development, there is no time to measure twice before cutting. Instead, you measure once, cut, and hope. Now and then you have to cut two or three times to get the right result. The cost of the wasted labor can often be less than the cost of a delay in a DSS project, however.

SUMMARY

Decision support systems (DSSs) are a specialized type of business information system that cuts across personal, workgroup, and enterprise levels. A DSS is an interactive computer-based system that facilitates the solution of unstructured (and semistructured) problems.

There are four dimensions to the DSS task environment: degree of structure, level of application, phase of application, and recurrency. DSSs are used in situations in which the solution process addresses semistructured or unstructured problems. Second, DSSs can be used for operational, management control, and strategic planning levels. They can also be used for all three phases of decision making: intelligence gathering, alternative development, and choice. Finally, DSS tasks may or may not recur. Some DSSs are used regularly as part of operations; some are intermittent; and others are developed for unique problems.

There are three primary program components in a DSS application: dialogue management, model management, and data management. The dialogue management component maintains the interface with the user; model management stores and executes business models; and data management maintains the DSS data and provides an interface to external sources of data.

Group decision support systems (GDSSs) move the DSS into the group environment. Members of a group communicate with each other and with the DSS facilities via computer workstations. Members can meet in the same location, or they can be geographically separated. Possible GDSS architectures include decision room environments, teleconferences, LANs, internets, and WANs as summarized in Figure 14-4.

The purpose of groupware is to reduce or eliminate the dysfunctions of group interaction so that the group reaches or exceeds its task potential. Possible group process losses are listed in Figure 14-5. Some groupware products address the needs of meetings; typical tools involve electronic brainstorming, idea organization, alternative prioritization, and alternative scoring. Processes using groupware can be chauffeured, supported, or interactive. Other types of groupware address workgroup coordination of activities and workgroup conversations.

DSSs provide a number of important functions: They can be used to become familiar with a problem environment, to determine the sensitivity of results to changes in decision variables, to identify patterns, and to predict decision outcomes. DSSs can also be used to develop models of business processes, compute optimum mixes, and, finally, facilitate group communication.

DSSs have the same five components as other business systems. Considering hardware, DSSs are supported either by shared mainframe computers or by personal computers. They often require communications hardware including LANs and WANs. They also use special-output equipment, including large display screens, high-quality printers, cameras, and video displays.

DSS programs provide support for dialogue management, model management, and data management. The basic functions for each of these are listed in Figure 14-8. They almost always involve a DBMS. An extraction program on the organization's operational computers may be required to interface with the data management component of the DSS on other computers. In a well-designed DSS, the particulars of the interfaces among computers are hidden from the DSS user.

Horizontal market DSSs, or DSS shells, generalize facilities to construct DSSs across many industries. Sometimes DSS shells are constructed from off-the-shelf horizontal market applications called DSS shells or DSS generators. Vertical market DSSs, or generalized DSSs, support a particular class of programs. DSSs can be custom-developed using conventional programming languages, but this activity can seldom be cost- or schedule-justified.

Two types of data are managed for DSS applications: model data and DSS database data. Because of the wide variety of sources of DSS data, data incompatibilities can arise and can be particularly problematical because they are very difficult to predict or even to detect. Further, DSSs, unlike operational systems, maintain a number of different versions of the same data. Keeping track of these versions can be as difficult as it is important.

Clientele are the people the system exists to serve. Business analysts are assistants to senior decision makers who have knowledge about their business area, but who may have limited knowledge of computer technology. They typically are the users of the DSS. Personnel in a DSS group include operators, program development and support personnel, data administration personnel, consultants, and facilitators.

The DSS group can reside on a staff function to the CEO or some other, very senior executive, or it can be part of the MIS department. Both arrangements can work, and both can be problematical. Alternatively, the DSS function may be performed entirely by personnel in the various user departments.

DSS procedures include the four types that exist for all information systems: normal and failure recovery procedures for both users and operators. These may need to be extended to include more comprehensive data administration procedures. Procedures also must be devised for group activity during the solution of a problem. Most study teams agree on a set of policies that guide their activities.

The development process used for DSS applications depends, in large measure, on the recurrency of the problem to be solved. If the problem recurs or is intermittent with high frequency, then either the prototyping or the structured processes described in Chapters 7 and 10 should be used. If, however, the problem is a high-priority, short-schedule, unique situation, then a less orderly, less well-planned process is often used. Such a process, called adaptive systems development, can waste time and resources and, consequently, is expensive. It can be justified only in situations where time pressure and importance dictate that no other choice can be made.

KEY TERMS

DSS	Teleconferencing	Vertical market DSS program
Decision support facility	Groupware	Generalized DSS
Dialogue management component	Process loss	Custom-developed DSS application
Model management component	Chauffeured process	Facilitator
Data management component	Supported process	Adaptive development process
GDSS	Interactive process	
Decision room environment	Extraction program	
	Horizontal market DSS program	
	DSS shell	
	DSS generator	

REVIEW QUESTIONS

1. State two definitions for *DSS*. Explain the differences between the two definitions.

2. Explain the importance of *facilitate* and *unstructured* in the definition of DSS.

3. Explain why some authors prefer *semistructured* to *unstructured*.

4. Describe the three major components of a DSS program.

5. Explain the difference between a DSS model and a DSS database.

6. What are the four dimensions of the DSS task environment described in this chapter?

7. Explain why degree of structure is not a property of the problem to be solved.

8. What levels of application do DSSs serve?

9. Which phases of the decision process do DSSs serve? What does a DSS do for each?

10. Describe the recurrency dimension. Why is it important to DSSs?

11. How does a GDSS differ from an individual DSS?

12. Explain the appropriate role for decision room environments, teleconferences, LANs, and internets in GDSSs.

13. What is the function of groupware?

14. List and briefly describe five common sources of group process loss.

15. Describe three groupware tools that can be used to facilitate a meeting.

16. Explain the differences among a chauffeured process, supported process, and interactive process.

17. Describe a role for groupware besides the facilitation of meetings.

18. Explain how DSSs can be used to become familiar with the problem domain.

19. Explain how DSSs can be used to determine the sensitivity of results to changes in decision variables.

20. Explain the role of a DSS in pattern recognition.

21. How can DSSs be used to predict decision outcomes?

22. How can DSSs be used to develop models of business processes?

23. Explain how a DSS can be used to compute optimum mixes.

24. How do both individual DSSs and GDSSs facilitate communication?

25. What special requirements do DSSs pose for hardware?

26. Explain the basic structure and process of the dialogue management portion of a DSS program.

27. Explain the basic structure and process of the model management portion of a DSS program.

28. Explain the basic structure and process of the data management portion of a DSS program.

29. Explain the relationship of the data-interface program in the DSS and of extraction programs on an enterprise computer.

30. Describe the character of a DSS shell.

31. Explain how a DSS shell can be constructed from off-the-shelf programs.

32. Describe the character of a vertical market, or generalized, DSS program.

33. Under what conditions does it make sense to custom-develop a DSS using a conventional programming language?

34. Give an example, other than the one in this text, of a data-incompatibility problem. Show sample data for your example, and indicate one specific problem that could occur.

35. Summarize the problems posed by the need to maintain multiple versions of data for a DSS.

36. Describe the role of DSS clientele and business analysts.

37. Explain the role of each category of personnel in a DSS group.

38. Describe two organizational arrangements for the location of the DSS group. Which is better?

39. Under what circumstances can the enterprise systems development processes you learned in Chapter 13 be applied to the development of a DSS?

40. Describe the adaptive development process. When should it be used?

DISCUSSION QUESTIONS

1. Consider two dimensions of level of business activity—strategic planning and operational control—and two dimensions of structure—structured decision making and semistructured decision making. Now, identify four business problems, decision opportunities, or situations—one for structured strategic planning, one for semistructured strategic planning, one for structured operational control, and one for semistructured operational control. Describe each of these four situations. For each, identify two or three key decisions that must be made. Characterize what you think would be the most important aspects of an information system to facilitate these key decisions. Briefly describe the five components of an information system for each situation. What type of development process would you follow for each?

2. Pick one of the interdepartmental information system applications described in Chapter 11 (revenue generation, purchasing, payroll, and manufacturing). For your application, list five important problems that

require a semistructured decision process. Describe the characteristics of one or more DSS applications to facilitate solutions to these problems. Describe the level, phase of decision process, and recurrency of these DSS applications. Briefly describe the five components of each. What style of systems development do you think would be appropriate for developing these applications?

3. Take the position that the adaptive decision process is just a name that attempts to legitimize an inexcusably chaotic and unplanned management style. Argue that every project should be able to fit either the workgroup development process described in Chapter 7 or the enterprise development process described in Chapter 10. Describe problems that are certain to occur using the so-called adaptive process. Indicate better ways of proceeding for high-priority, crash projects.

PROJECTS

A. Interview whoever plans class schedules for your major department. Determine what process is used to establish a course schedule. Is this a structured or a semistructured process? What level is this process? Does the decision maker employ an information system or any product of an information system in this process? If so, describe what is used. What are the biggest frustrations in planning the schedule? What are the most important outcomes by which the person judges the success or failure of the schedule? Describe any forms of DSS not currently used that you think would be helpful to the schedule planner.

B. Play the role of information center manager for a company that typically spends about $200,000 per year on personal computer hardware and programs. The company has recently adopted a policy of buying only GUI-based personal computers rather than the current standard character-based computers. As a result, the typical new system now requires 8MB of memory costing $230 rather than 2MB costing $61, a 230MB hard disk costing $435 rather than a 65MB hard disk costing $230, and a super VGA display system with high-resolution monitor costing $685 rather than a VGA system with lower-resolution monitor costing $290. (A complete PC consists of a system unit, memory, a hard disk, and a display system with monitor; printing services are provided on LANs.)

Because of recent price reductions, the cost of 20 Mh 386-based system units capable of only modest GUI performance have dropped from $940 to $710; 50 Mh 386 units capable of adequate GUI performance have dropped from $1,095 to $930; and 66 Mh 486 units capable of impressively fast GUI performance have dropped from $1,295 to $970. Users would much prefer the higher performance units.

Your reading of computer trade journals suggests two major trends. First, new versions of horizontal application programs currently being developed are likely to be slower than today's typical programs, requiring faster computers for adequate performance. Second, recent changes in federal trade policies make it likely that memory prices may increase beginning in about 6 months. It is not clear whether the increase will double the price of memory chips or increase prices by only about 10 percent.

Create a DSS to support your analysis of these factors. Use your DSS to help propose a revised company personal computer budget for the year. Should the company spend more or less than typical? Which system unit should typically be purchased? Provide specific figures to support your conclusions. In addition, describe the DSS that you created. In your analysis, you will surely need to make reasonable assumptions beyond the facts provided here; document those assumptions.

C. Locate a manager on your campus (or other organization) who has budgetary authority over some aspect of the university. Consider a department chairperson, a library director, an athletics director, or a residential director. If that person were to learn tomorrow that his or her budget had been reduced by 25 percent, across the board, what would he or she do? What would be the major problems to be addressed? How would those problems be addressed? What actions would be taken for the intelligence phase? The alternative development phase? The choice phase? Would the person use an information system or any product of an information system? Which would be more important to the manager, capability to perform analysis or capability to communicate? Describe any form of DSS not currently used that you think would be helpful.

D. Research the topic of DSS in the literature at your library. In particular, find articles about the use of DSSs in actual business settings. For these applications, describe the problems to be solved. Indicate the degree of structure, level, phase, and recurrency of the tasks that were processed. What hardware and programs were used? What models? Procedures? Personnel? Was the application judged a success? Why? Do you think the application was a success? What, if any, lessons were learned from the experience?

Businesses Are Making the Internet Connection

Once the exclusive backwater of the federal government and academic researchers, the Internet, the world's largest computer network, has emerged as a giant "infomart" for Fortune 500 companies. Propelled by advances in computer power and packet-switched networks, the Internet is poised to become a staple of modern business communications.

Since June 1991, the Internet has jumped from 2,982 interconnected networks supporting about 130,000 computers to more than 10,500 networks with more than 8 million users, according to a database maintained by Merit Inc., an Ann Arbor, Mich., firm that manages the National Science Foundation component of the Internet. The total number of users is expected to top 100 million by 1998, Merit officials say.

"In business terms, it's [certainly] a success," agrees John Shore, president of Entropic Research Laboratory Inc., a Washington start-up that designs software tools used to study human speech and develop voice-controlled computers

By using the Internet as a delivery vehicle, Shore met a March 31 deadline for shipping the first commercial release of a new software product to reviewers at Cambridge University in Great Britain.

"The Internet speeds up development of products created entirely in-house," Shore says. "We can work quickly with experts around the world, and we can get feedback on our early revisions. It [also] improves our customer support, which increases our income."

Rapid communication over the Internet is helping to shorten the development cycle for new medicines and chemicals. Dr. Gregory S. Shotzberger, manager of Technical Assessment for Du Pont Merck Pharmaceuticals Co., in Rahway, N.J., uses public medical databases to explore new areas of research in the treatment of central nervous system disorders. The Internet helps Shotzberger quickly find experts for collaborative research and scan hundreds of reports to help Du Pont Merck bring new drugs to market faster, he explains.

Other drug and chemical companies are getting in on the Internet act, too. Rohm and Haas, the Philadelphia-based company best known for inventing Plexiglas, has used the Internet for research activities since 1988.

Using the Internet to gain access to Minnesota Supercomputer Center Inc.'s high-powered systems, Thomas Cozzolino, a scientific programmer and analyst for Rohm and Hass, is able to analyze molecular structures of new chemicals. For example, to make a new plastic with certain strengths or insecticide with certain reactive properties, Cozzolino uses a computer simulation to "build" a molecule and then watches the behavior of the molecule under different temperatures.

The Internet is "a great time and money saver," Cozzolino said in an exchange of E-mail messages. "We get software fixes from vendors over Internet, write collaborative papers with academic and industry leaders. and search numerous on-line databases from

our desktops. The days of slow, complex modem connections are over."

By far, the largest use of the Internet is E-mail. Internet E-mail services span the globe, making just about anyone at or near a computer available. At CapDisc, a unit of Capitol Multimedia Inc., producer Tim Phillips says he sends about 25 E-mail messages a week to clients in Europe to discuss a project to translate interactive compact discs from English to French, Spanish, Italian, German, and Dutch.

"With electronic mail. I can say, 'Here's a script,' or 'Here's a moving image,' and I can send it to somebody who can see exactly what I'm doing," Phillips said. Using Unix-to-Unix Copy Program E-mail over UUNET Technologies Inc. links, he can participate in news groups to develop new products. ■

Jayne Levin, excerpted from *Infoworld*, May 24, 1993, p. 71.

Discussion Questions

1. Describe the Internet. Indicate its size and growth rate.

2. List some of the Internet's resources, as described in this article.

3. Compare and contrast the Internet, described in this article, and an internet, as described in Chapter 12. Consider both differences and similarities.

4. How can the Internet add value to an enterprise?

15

Improving the Use of Knowledge: Knowledge Systems

THIS CHAPTER CONSIDERS KNOWLEDGE SYSTEMS, which go beyond the storage of data and the functions of communications, analysis, and tracking that we discussed previously. Instead, these systems store knowledge and make that knowledge available to businesspeople, sometimes in novel ways.

The structure of this chapter is similar to that of Chapter 14. First we survey goals and applications of knowledge-based systems in general. Then we discuss one particular type of system, expert systems, in detail. After this overview of expert systems, we discuss their five components, and, finally, we consider expert systems development.

ADVANTAGES OF KNOWLEDGE SYSTEMS

A **knowledge system** is a computer-based information system that represents knowledge and makes it available to users for the solution of semistructured, knowledge-related problems. The representation format depends on the nature of the problem to be solved. To understand this definition and how such systems differ from other types of information systems, consider some of the goals of such systems.

Reducing Training Time

The following conversation took place prior to a major product introduction at Legacy Systems:

> "Look, we've hired 15 new people in the past two months. There's no way we can train all of them in time for the new product launch."

> "John, we've got to do something. I've been wondering, though, don't most of the calls after a new launch have to do with installation problems?"

> "Sure, but so what? We've still got to train the people."

> "Have you ever heard of an expert system?"

> "Well, yeah, isn't that a program that gives advice? No, now wait a minute. No way! It's one thing for a million doctors to build a system to diagnose diseases and another for a company like ours to create one in time for the new launch."

> "You're right, John, we can't build a complicated system in that time. But, to handle, say, the top 20 questions for installing the new product, I wonder..."

Suppose, as in this scenario, you manage Customer Support and your department will soon be inundated by calls from customers wanting to know how to install a new product. If you had the time, you would conduct training classes for all of your representatives and teach them about the new product. Your staff, however, is very busy; you cannot devote more than two half-days of training to the new product.

You wish there were some way you could package the knowledge required to support the installation of the new product. You would like to have a computer-based system that could lead your representatives through a diagnostic procedure

Figure 15-1 Expert System Dialogue for a Help Desk Application

Expert System Query/Commentary	User Response
IS THE COMPUTER AN IBM PS/2?	Yes
ENTER THE MODEL TYPE. CHOOSE ONE OF: 30, 40, 50, 60, 70, 80	80
HAS THE USER INSTALLED WINDOWS, VERSION 3.1?	Yes
WHAT IS THE NAME OF THE DIRECTORY CONTAINING THE FILE PROGRAM.EXE?	Windows
HAS THE USER INSTALLED THE LEGACY 400 PROGRAM?	Yes
WHAT IS THE NAME OF THE DIRECTORY CONTAINING LEGCY.EXE?	leg400
IS THERE A PATH STATEMENT TO LEG400 IN THE LEGACY STARTUP FILE?	No
SUSPECTED PROBLEM:	
MISSING PATH STATEMENT	Why?

EXPLANATION:
    IF WIN.EXE AND LEGCY.EXE ARE IN
        DIFFERENT DIRECTORIES	

THEN THERE MUST BE A PATH STATEMENT IN THE LEGACY STARTUP FILE.	
SEE INSTALLATION PROCEDURE 4.3.6	

to identify the source of a customer's installation problem. Figure 15-1 shows the dialogue that you wish your representatives would be guided through.

Reducing Training Cost

Consider another situation. Suppose you manage the national sales force of a large life insurance company. Congress has enacted a new tax law that has impacted the way many of your customers should plan insurance for paying estate taxes. Unfortunately, the law is complicated; it is difficult to determine whether a customer is affected and how much. The home office staff has developed a procedure for evaluating a customer's situation, but the procedure is 37 pages long. You cannot just mail such a complicated procedure to the salespeople and rely on them to follow it.

An alternative is to bring the sales force into the home office for training. However, you do not want to pay to fly everyone in just to learn this new procedure. If a computer-based system could guide the salespeople through the procedure, they would not need to read and understand all 37 pages. Further, you could mail such a system to them and save the expense of flying them to the home office. Also, no matter how well they are trained, salespeople hate this type of work, so having an information system directing the process undoubtedly would result in higher-quality service to your customers, as well.

Replicating Valuable Expertise

Consider a third situation. You manage engineering operations for Amalgamated Mining (from Chapter 14). Your company has pioneered the use of a specialized, high-technology technique for extracting minerals from ore. Unfortunately, the technique is tricky. A highly skilled operator is required, and if the operator makes an error , serious problems can result. Equipment may break, the product quality may fall, or a serious accident could occur. The accident risk has your management, your attorneys, and your insurance company concerned.

Because of the complexity of this work, you have only four fully trained operators, all of whom are working long hours at a single site. If you had more fully qualified operators, you could open more mines. In fact, you have identified 27 such mining opportunities throughout the world.

Even though you are training new operators as fast as you can, you will be able to address only 10 of the opportunities in the next 4 years. Your manager has told you that you must do more.

If you could capture the knowledge required to monitor the equipment, you would develop an information system that you could install at the new mines. Such a system would be connected to sensors that monitor the machinery's operation. When adjustments need to be made, the computer system either makes a recommendation to an operator, or, if the system's reliability is great enough, issues instructions directly to the equipment. In this way, you could reduce both the number of operators and the training they require.

Reducing Operational Response Time

Suppose you manage a motor vehicle repair shop for a utility company. Trucks, vans, and cars are brought to the shop in the evening for repair. You are supposed to return every vehicle to service within 24 hours unless you cannot obtain parts. Further, some vehicles are so critical to operations that they must be repaired overnight. Because of these constraints, your shop places a premium on speedy work.

Unfortunately, for a variety of historical reasons, your company has a hodgepodge of vehicles. In fact, your staff once calculated that it must repair 117 types of vehicles from 18 manufacturers, each with different maintenance programs, different parts descriptions and numbers, and different problems and repair techniques.

You have acquired repair manuals for all these vehicles. Mechanics constantly refer to manuals to determine maintenance schedules and procedures for repair work. Replacing a clutch on a telephone pole installer, for example, differs substantially from replacing one on a five-passenger sedan.

If you could place all these manuals in a more readily usable format, such as a text processing information system, then a mechanic would enter the brand, type, model, and year of the vehicle, along with the work to be done, and the system would locate procedures, pictures, diagrams, and part numbers relevant to the job. Such a system would increase the throughput of the repair shop by 40 percent or more.

Figure 15-2 Preserving the Knowledge of a Human Expert

An original goal of knowledge systems was to capture and preserve the full, complex knowledge of a human expert, but this goal has proven much more difficult to achieve than expected. Today's knowledge systems have more limited domains.

Preserving Valuable Knowledge

Suppose you manage research and development at Specialty Chemicals Corporation. One of your employees, Dr. Elizabeth Smith, has devoted the past 45 years of her life to analyzing the chemical composition of compounds. Whenever lab personnel cannot determine the composition of some compound, they turn to Dr. Smith. She is held in awe by your employees.

Dr. Smith has indicated her intention to retire in 6 months. The loss of her expertise will cause a serious reduction in the amount of work your department can do.

You wish there was some way of saving Dr. Smith's expertise. She has written many papers about her methods, but much of her experience cannot be readily documented. Her general notions and hunches about things cannot be written in a way that a novice can understand. However, some of what she knows can be put in the form of rules such as, If the compound can be ignited at less than 120 degrees centigrade, then it must contain oxygen.

Other aspects of Dr. Smith's knowledge are not so specific. Some of her knowledge takes the form of **heuristics**, or rules of thumb. An example: If the substance is yellow and it originated in the Paint and Adhesives division, then it probably contains sulfur. This rule is not ironclad. She has learned over the years, however, that most of the compounds from Paint and Adhesives do contain sulfur if they are yellow. She starts with that assumption and rules it out later if she has to.

If Dr. Smith's knowledge could be stored in a computer-based knowledge bank, it would remain available for your department (and for posterity). You could add other people's knowledge to this bank as well.

The State of the Art

Figure 15-3 summarizes typical goals of knowledge-based systems. Not all of these goals can currently be realized. As you will learn, well-defined procedures are not too difficult to represent and process, especially if the procedures are not too complicated, but representing the knowledge of an expert like Dr. Smith is difficult. While some systems have been created to do that, they are the experimental products of university research groups. Such systems are large and expensive, and they have consumed dozens or hundreds of years of the labor of talented and well-educated people. The true feasibility of such systems, on a cost-benefit basis, is not really known.

One of your goals in reading this chapter should be to learn about the potential of knowledge systems, and another should be to understand that many systems that have been envisioned are not commercially feasible today. At the

Figure 15-3 Some Goals of Knowledge-Based Systems

- Reduction of training time
- Reduction of training cost
- Replication of valuable expertise
- Reduction of response time
- Saving of valuable knowledge

same time, organizations have found value and utility in small expert systems. More comprehensive and accurate knowledge systems will be developed during your career.

Types of Knowledge Systems

Knowledge systems technology is evolving. This chapter considers the three types of knowledge systems shown in Figure 15-4: hypermedia, interactive video, and expert systems. Expert systems are generally considered the predominant form of knowledge system. There is disagreement today about the other two types. Not everyone would agree that these are knowledge systems. Further, some experts would include knowledge systems not shown in this figure.

For example, Microsoft provides in some programs step-by-step support, called **Wizards**, to help a user perform complex tasks such as setting up a mail merge document in a word processor or creating a crosstab report in a spreadsheet program. For example, to create a crosstab report, the user selects the Crosstab ReportWizard and then follows a series of step-by-step instructions to complete the task.

Although Wizards have some characteristics of knowledge systems, many experts would not include them as knowledge systems. There is no definite boundary around knowledge systems; in fact, as expert systems technology matures, it is being combined with other types of systems into mainstream information processing applications.

Figure 15-4 categorizes knowledge systems along two dimensions: degree of formalized structure and degree of computer control. In this figure, the vertical dimension shows form of knowledge—from free-form, natural-language text, to structured and highly formalized rules and formulas. The horizontal dimension shows the degree to which a computer system controls the use of the knowledge.

Figure 15-4   Knowledge Processing Alternatives

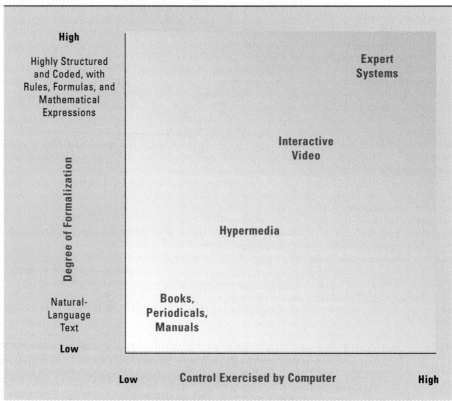

Books and publications, shown near the origin in Figure 15-4, need not involve computers and are not considered knowledge systems. They are shown here to establish an end point of a continuum. The processing of the knowledge in a book or a publication is entirely directed by a person. An example of this situation is the manuals read by the vehicle mechanics at the utility company.

Hypermedia Systems   A **hypermedia system** provides computer-based storage of documents composed of text, graphs, diagrams, sound, schematics, pictures, motion video, and the like. Hypermedia documents include not only the document but also indexes for cross-referencing its material.

Imagine an encyclopedia stored as a hypermedia document. All of the text, pictures, and graphs are stored on computer files and displayed on the computer's screen. Further, links are maintained so that, when you encounter a reference to another topic (e.g., *see also* references), you simply click with the mouse and that material is presented. Thus, you can dynamically organize the presentation as you use the encyclopedia. Figure 15-5 shows an example hypermedia document.

Figure 15-5 Hypermedia Document

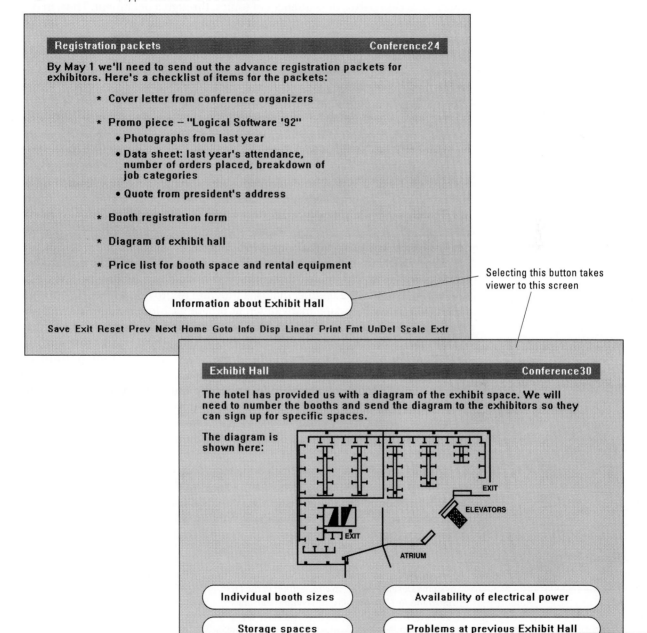

Hypermedia documents are knowledge systems because developers can predefine **access paths**, or sequences of topics, through a document. Thus, in the vehicle repair shop, paths through repair documents could be constructed for the most common types of repairs or problems. These paths are sometimes constructed by the publisher and are part of the original document, or they can be constructed by a user. In the repair shop, a senior mechanic might construct paths for common problems or repairs. The paths represent the senior mechanic's expertise, so the hypermedia document represents knowledge.

Hypermedia applications are especially useful for technical documents that contain a mixture of text and engineering drawings. These systems not only present the material in an efficient and easy-to-use format, they also facilitate changes. Given the multiple indexes to topics, drawings, parts, and so on, when a part or a drawing changes, it is easy to determine where the hypermedia will need to be altered. In fact, with most systems, the drawing or description is stored only once. All references to it are simply pointers to the location where the drawing is stored. Thus, making a change simply means substituting the new drawing, and all references to it are automatically adjusted.

One widely used hypermedia application is the Windows Help system that provides access to on-line documentation for Windows programs. The Help system is a **hypermedia engine**, that is, a program to provide user access to help documents that accompany many different programs. Most vendors of Windows programs provide on-line documentation that uses that Help system. In addition to the Help engine, Microsoft suggests a standard form for on-line documentation, which helps vendors maintain a consistent pattern of documentation from program to program.

For large documents, hypermedia typically uses optical disk storage. But since most optical storage devices are read-only devices, users of larger documents cannot modify text or access paths themselves. When optical disks that allow writing become less expensive, this limitation will disappear. This should occur soon.

A number of studies have been done regarding the use of hypermedia. See, for example, Akscyn, Bieber, and van Dam.[1] Proponents of this technology believe that full-functioned, flexible hypermedia systems allow people to think in multiple directions at once and to develop ideas in parallel. The hypermedia system helps the user to track the multiple paths. If this claim is true, such systems will facilitate

---

1. Akscyn, Robert M., and Donald L. McCracken, "ZOG and the USS Carl Vinson: Lessons in Systems Development," in *Proceedings of the First IFIP Conference on Human-Computer Aided Interaction.* Amsterdam, Netherlands: Elsevier Science Publishers, 1984. van Dam, Andries, "Hypertext '87: Keynote Address," *Communications of the ACM*, Vol. 31, No. 7, July 1988. Bieber, Michael P., and Steven O. Kimbrough, "On the Concept of Hypertext," *MIS Quarterly*, March 1992, pp. 77–93.

both the creativity and the productivity of knowledge workers in professions such as law, public accounting, medicine, engineering, and all types of consulting.

Interactive Video   In **interactive video**, another type of knowledge system, video segments are integrated via a menu-processing application. Interactive video applications overcome one of the biggest disadvantages of video media: the requirement of sequential access. Instead, users are presented with video segments that they can control through selection from menus.

In Figure 15-6, the user selects from a menu and is presented with a video segment on a topic. From time to time, the user is presented additional menus, usually including options to repeat the last segment, continue with the next segment, or jump to some other segment.

With interactive video applications, the application takes more responsibility (and control) for the presentation of the material. The menus provide more structure to the process than is provided by a hypermedia application, which may include video segments. On the other hand, the hypermedia system allows for greater flexibility in use.

Interactive video is used primarily in training and advisory capacities. Airlines, for example, use interactive video to train personnel on procedures

Figure 15-6   Interactive Video System Menu

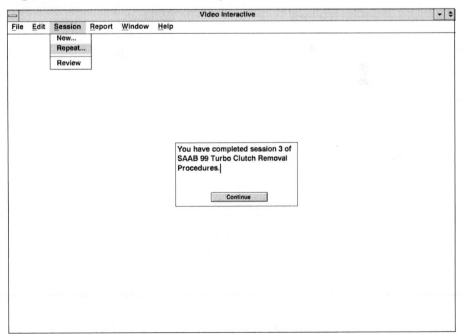

for new equipment. Interactive video is also used to guide the repair of expensive equipment.

The advantages of interactive video are that it provides multimedia—music, voice, video, sketches, animation, text, pictures, and so forth—all under the user's control. The disadvantage is that it is expensive to develop and to change. It has, therefore, found the greatest use in training and advisory capacities in stable situations. It is also used when the cost of a mistake is so high that the expense of interactive video is justified, for example, the repair of a critical airplane component.

Because of the amount of data required to store video images, interactive video applications require large-capacity storage devices. These can be either optical disk or very large magnetic media. Research is underway to develop techniques for compressing data, however, and the storage required per image is rapidly decreasing.

Consider the horizontal dimension of Figure 15-4 again. Moving from left to right the computer is assuming more and more control over the use of the knowledge. On the far left, when using free-form text materials such as manuals, the user has complete control. You, the reader of this text, can turn to any page at any time, and you decide when to change topics, use the index, and skip to a figure. The cost of such complete control is that you receive no automated assistance in learning. You must provide all of the learning expertise yourself.

With hypermedia, the system removes some control from the user, but it also helps the user learn and the knowledge. By following a predefined path through a hypermedia document, you are using someone's expertise concerning the appropriate progression of material. With interactive video, the menu system defines fixed ways in which the video knowledge can be accessed. Finally, with expert systems, the information system takes even greater control over the processing and use of the knowledge.

EXPERT SYSTEMS

An **expert system** is a computer-based information system in which knowledge is represented in data and in which the processing of that knowledge is directed, primarily, by programs. The term *expert system* originated because these systems were aimed, initially, at replicating the abilities of true human experts. The goal was to create a system that could, for example, diagnose human diseases as well as or better than a human expert.

The development of true expert systems has been difficult and expensive, but the technology developed in the process has solved many, smaller problems that occur in the business world. Thus, many of the expert systems encountered in business do not have the abilities of a true human expert. Instead, they have expertise in some limited problem domain, such as the problems that occur during the installation of a personal computer software product.

What Is Artificial Intelligence?

Expert systems technology is an outgrowth of a field of study called **artificial intelligence (AI)**. Unfortunately, this term has been abused and misused by the press and by the marketing departments of computer and software companies. Before continuing, we need to debunk this term.

The truth is, nobody knows what AI means. It is used for its emotional impact, mostly in advertising or in news articles as an adjective rather than as a noun. In those sources, it seems to mean interesting, "hot" (in the marketing sense), valuable, or ethically frightening.

Consider the words *artificial intelligence*. What does artificial mean? It could refer to anything that is manufactured—anything that is not biological in origin. Or, given recent work in genetic engineering, it could refer to anything that is not the product of natural biological development.

What is intelligence? Is it performance on an IQ test? Is it the ability to engage in goal-directed activity? Is it the ability to sacrifice gains in the short term for greater gains in the long term? And, even if we can define these two terms, how can we decide if an artificial device has intelligence?

In 1950 a British mathematician, Alan Turing, proposed a test for determining whether or not a machine has human intelligence. In brief, the test is to connect a human, via a teletype (the terminals of 1950), with either another human or a computer. The two entities engage in a conversation. If a computer is able to respond so that the human cannot tell on the basis of the conversation whether the other entity is a computer or a human, then, according to this test, the computer evidences human intelligence.

This test, called the **Turing test**, avoids many of the problems due to word meanings. It also avoids the issue of whether or not the machine understands the conversation. It is a test based entirely on behavior. Does the machine create sentences that are understandable by humans and appropriate in context? Today, no computer system can pass this test.

Among computer scientists, AI refers to a group of related disciplines, summarized in Figure 15-7.

Natural language concerns the development of human language computer interfaces and with the translation of human languages. **Pattern recognition** systems identify patterns in visual, auditory, or other signals, and in data. **Vision systems** provide the technology to enable computer systems to "see." **Robotics** concerns the development of, primarily, industrial robots. Finally, expert systems attempt to capture the essence of the human knowledge in a specific domain and

Figure 15-7   The AI Disciplines

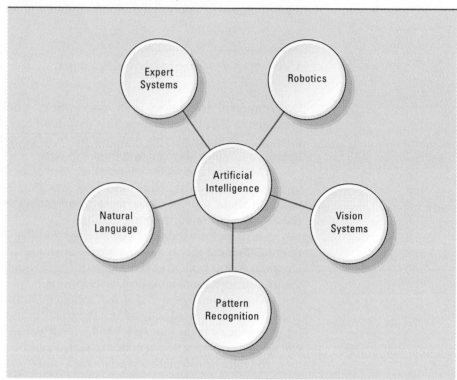

to apply that knowledge to solve real-world problems. This chapter considers only expert systems because they are the primary business application of AI technology.

As progress in one of these fields leads to commercial products, that domain tends to assume an identity of its own and cease being identified as artificial intelligence. This has happened to expert systems, which are now recognized separately from their artificial intelligence roots. It is happening today with **neural networks**, a sophisticated pattern-recognition technique originally developed by artificial intelligence researchers. Neural networks model the pattern-recognition activities of biological neurons.

Neural network programs are used in recognizing all kinds of patterns: patterns of marks making up handwritten characters (handwriting recognition), patterns of sounds (voice input), patterns of stock prices (financial analysis), even patterns of clinical disease symptoms (medical diagnoses). A few years ago, neural networks existed primarily in artificial intelligence laboratories; today, they are developed by commercial neural network vendors and applied in all sorts of enterprises. Thus, they are no longer generally considered as a part of artificial intelligence.

Architecture of an Expert System

The structure of a generic expert system is summarized in Figure 15-8. The **knowledge base** contains rules, facts, and descriptions of objects. The first expert systems encoded knowledge in programming language statements, an undesirable approach because the knowledge was difficult to find, understand, and change. With today's products, the knowledge base is almost always stored in data.

Figure 15-8 shows the structure of an **expert system shell**, which is a collection of programs for defining, administering, and processing an expert system. Just as a DBMS is used to define, administer, and process a particular database application, an expert system shell is used to define, administer, and process a particular expert system.

An expert system has four major components, as shown in Figure 15-8. The **inference engine** processes the knowledge base to achieve the goal stipulated by the user, who is communicating via the **user interface**. The **explanation system** helps the user by describing the need for certain information or by explaining the basis for recommendations that are produced. Finally, the **knowledge acquisition**

Figure 15-8 Structure of an Expert System Shell

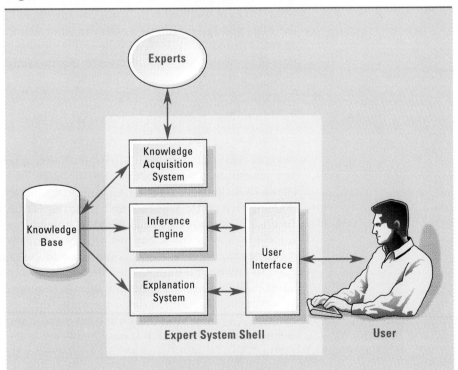

system is used by someone who has expertise in the problem to create, add to, or change the knowledge base.

To understand the processing of an expert system, you must understand the concept of **inferencing**. Suppose you have the following set of rules and facts:

1. Employees with skill 100A can operate lathes or drill presses.

2. The pay range for those employed at skill 100A is $27,000 to $38,000.

3. Employee Jones operates a drill press.

4. Employee Smith operates an articulated front-end loader.

Given these facts, you could make inferences to answer the question "What is the most that employee Jones can be paid?" by connecting the third item with the first and the first item with the second. From this you conclude that Jones's maximum salary is $38,000. Suppose you are asked "What is the most that employee Smith can be paid?" You examine these rules and facts and determine that you do not have enough data to answer the question. You need to know the skill code for operators of articulated front-end loaders and the pay range for that skill code. You would respond by asking for these rules.

Suppose that, instead of 4 facts, you had 400. Some of the paths through the 400 items (like the path from item 3 to item 1 to item 2) could be 10, 12, or 15 steps deep. Keeping track of where you are, what to do next, what you have tried, and what you have not tried is difficult. You might get lucky and find a path through the rules and facts right away. On the other hand, you might not. And, if your question cannot be answered by the knowledge base, it might take you a very long time to figure that out. The inferencing engine establishes such paths.

How Inference Engines Operate

The goal of the inference engine in Figure 15-8 is to process the rules systematically and efficiently. To understand how it might proceed, consider the rules in Figure 15-9. Consider question A. Suppose the inference engine is programmed to examine each rule in sequence and, if the rule is true, to take the indicated action. To do this, the engine needs working storage in which to store values of the variables and other data. For this problem, it needs to store values for variables *name, operate, jobcode, minpay, maxpay,* and *lifeinsurance.*

To answer question A, the inference engine sets the value of the variable *name* to "Jones" and examines the rules in sequence. Only rule 7 is true, and the inference engine sets the variable *operate* to "drill press." It then proceeds through the rules again and finds that both rules 3 and 7 are true. (The engine will have a means for determining that it has already taken the action for rule 7 and that it

Figure 15-9　Sample Rules and Questions for an Inference Engine

Rule Number	IF	THEN
1	jobcode = 100A	minpay = 27,000 and maxpay = 38,000
2	jobcode = 200A	minpay = 23,000 and maxpay = 25,000
3	operate = lathe or drill press	jobcode = 100A
4	operate = articulated front-end loader	jobcode = 200A
5	minpay > 25,000	lifeinsurance = 250,000
6	minpay <= 25,000	lifeinsurance = 200,000
7	name = Jones	operate = drill press
8	name = Smith	operate = articulated front-end loader
9	name = Parks	operate = drill press

Possible Questions

A. What is Jones's maximum pay?

B. What is Jones's life insurance?

C. Person X has a life insurance policy of $250,000. Who could person X be?

must stop considering that rule.) Since rule 3 is true, the engine sets the value of the variable *jobcode* equal to "100A."

Working in this way, the engine will keep examining rules until it obtains a value for the variable *maxpay* or until no new rules become true. In that case, it will set the value of the variable *maxpay* to 38,000 and thus answer the question.

Consider question C. Here the engine is given a conclusion and asked to determine how that conclusion could have come about. To answer this question from the rules, the engine cannot make a definitive answer. Instead, it can identify possible answers. To see why, consider rule 5: If the variable *lifeinsurance* equals "250,000," then one possibility is that the person has pay greater than 25,000. However, this rule does not eliminate other possibilities. For example, the employee could have purchased his or her own insurance. Thus, when working backward from these rules, the engine can identify only possibilities.

These two questions illustrate the two most popular strategies for processing rules. The first, called **forward chaining**, starts with the given data and works forward, determining what results can be concluded from that data. The second, called **backward chaining**, starts with a possible conclusion or hypothesis and works backward to determine what might have held. Both humans and expert systems use backward chaining when the number of possible outcomes is small (hire/don't hire) and forward chaining when there are many possible outcomes (species identification). Many inferencing engines use a combination of the two strategies.

An important capability of an inference engine is its ability to explain itself. At any point in the dialogue, in some expert systems, the user can command the system to explain its reasoning or why it is asking for specific information. The system explains by indicating the rules that have led to its current status. For example, in the sample expert system dialogue in Figure 15-1, the user ends by entering the command "Why?" The system responds by explaining how it reached its conclusion.

What Problems Can Expert Systems Solve?

Expert systems cannot solve every problem, nor are they as effective at solving some problems as others. Figure 15-10 shows a continuum of problems, in conceptually increasing order of difficulty, that have been solved by expert systems. The word *conceptually* here means that a problem from a domain on the left is easier than an equivalent problem from a domain on the right. Thus, in general, diagnosis problems are easier than configuration and design problems, but a difficult diagnosis problem may be harder than an easy design problem.

Procedural problems concern the representation and processing of well-defined, ordered procedures. They provide instructions and advice, and they can perform classifications. Examples include instructions to assemble components into a whole, advice for using a new form, and classifications of things based on data about their observed characteristics. The life insurance client-evaluation problem is an example of a procedural problem.

Figure 15-10 Continuum of Expert System Problem Domains

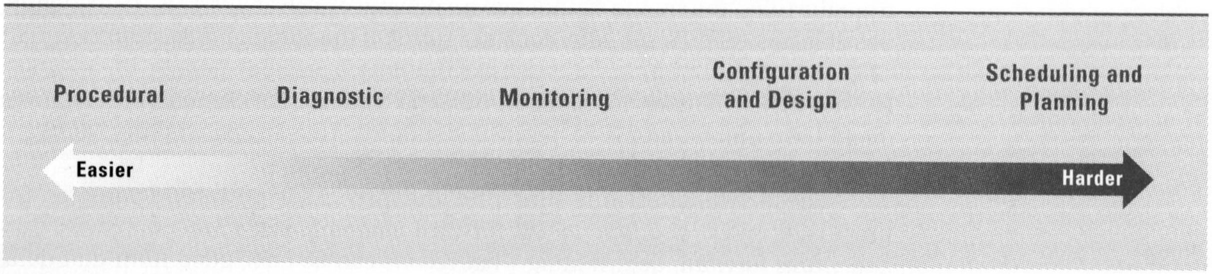

Diagnostic problems involve the identification of the possible causes of a situation. Examples include the causes of an automobile malfunction, the source of failure in an electronic system (say a TV), and the cause of disease. The customer support problem with which this chapter began is an example diagnostic problem.

Many of the expert systems that address diagnostic problems also provide suggestions for the solution. Thus, MYCIN, which is one of the first large diagnostic expert systems (and the grandfather of many others), not only identifies potential causes of infectious human disease but also produces a suggested treatment plan.

Expert systems that address **monitoring problems** gather data from a process, evaluate that data, and, if appropriate, issue instructions to people or equipment to make changes to the process. Examples include monitoring an assembly line or monitoring the life signs of a critically ill patient. Monitoring systems are diagnostic systems that run iteratively. They examine data, look for out-of-ordinary conditions, and issue treatment recommendations or instructions. Then they repeat the cycle. The mining company referred to at the beginning of this chapter needs a monitoring expert system to run (or help to run) its sophisticated mining equipment.

Configuration and design problems involve expert systems that accept requirements statements and constraints and build a list of components or other designs that will fit those requirements. Examples are expert systems that determine all the required components and subcomponents of a complicated machine that must be tailored to a given environment, such as a spaceship, or systems that recommend the best way to integrate a large number of components into a constrained space, such as the best way to route wires through the walls of an airplane.

XCON, one of the earliest design expert systems, builds a list of components required to configure VAX computers. Given the requirements of the basic components (CPU type, amount of memory, number and size of peripheral storage units), XCON determines the entire equipment configuration, including power supplies, cabinets, cables, and the like.

Scheduling and planning problems, conceptually the most difficult type, involve determining the best allocation of people, equipment, money, and time to accomplish specified tasks. This is a broad management goal, and you can think of expert systems that do planning and scheduling as management expert systems.

Scheduling and planning systems often require more knowledge than just rules and facts. Information about the characteristics of the entities involved is often necessary. For example, consider the problem of assigning people and machines in a machine shop. Suppose each week the shop is given a list of products to construct. To make a schedule for this shop, an expert system must consider not just the rules of production but also the characteristics of the machines, the machine setups, the skills of the employees, and the use of space in the workshop. This difficult assignment is probably beyond the current state of expert systems technology and practice.

Problems with Expert Systems

Although expert systems present a novel way of applying knowledge to problems, they are not without problems or critics. Some MIS professionals believe that such systems cannot add value to the practical day-to-day world of business. They contend that the only problems solvable by expert systems are so simple that the value of the solution is low and that important problems with a high solution value are too complex to be solved by today's expert systems. Consider some of the disadvantages claimed against expert systems.

High Development and Maintenance Costs   Perhaps the most common claim against expert systems is that they are difficult and expensive to develop and maintain. This claim arose partly because early expert system programs were written in symbolic processing languages like LISP and Prolog (discussed briefly below). While these languages offer great productivity under certain circumstances, they require specific programming knowledge not commonly found in a business MIS department. As a result, specialized programmers are needed to write and maintain programs in these languages. Today, however, with expert systems shells, such programming is not required.

Even with the availability of shells, however, critics of expert systems argue that they are hard to use for anything other than the simplest applications. They argue that realistic problems require a sophisticated specialist trained in the use of the shells and in the modeling of knowledge. Such people are both hard to find and expensive. Thus, these critics argue, the cost of developing expert systems is too high.

The introduction of new rules in a rule base can have unexpected and largely unpredictable side effects. Unlike conventional programming, there is no fixed logic path through a rule base. Rules are evaluated as they are encountered, and the appropriate action is taken. A new rule can change the order of rule execution in unexpected ways. Thus, when a problem is encountered and a rule is inserted to correct the problem, new difficulties may be introduced because the processing order of inferences has changed.

Traditional program-testing methodologies rely on the segregation and partitioning of potential sources of error. These methodologies are less effective for expert systems, and new techniques for verifying and validating expert systems logic need to be developed. Meanwhile, many people feel that the reliability of expert systems is lower than that for conventionally programmed systems.

Preference for Conventional Programming   Because of the potentially high development and maintenance costs, some critics argue that expert systems should be used only as prototyping tools to learn and demonstrate user requirements. An expert system can be used as an easy, fast way to apply and illustrate the rules, constraints, and logic of an application. Once the requirements are understood, however, then the system should be developed using conventional programming methodologies.

Those who disagree with this argument feel that expert systems provide an alternative way of viewing and, possibly, implementing solutions to knowledge processing. Expert systems methodology differs substantially from that of procedural programming. This means that expert systems can provide solutions to problems that cannot easily be solved by conventional programming. Some argue that any attempt to solve expert systems problems with conventional languages would reveal the necessity for developing the expert systems shells that already exist.

Further, many expert systems shells can be used by nonprogramming businesspeople. The inductive shells, for example, can be used by business managers to build small, but useful, expert systems. The systems developed may not be as effective as a program written in a conventional language, but they do work, and, in the absence of a programmer, they can be better than nothing. Thus, expert systems open a new avenue for the non-information systems professional to obtain value from information technology.

Expert Systems as Philosophically Unsound

Some authors have challenged expert systems on philosophical grounds. Winograd and Flores, for example, argue that it is impossible to build any useful system using rules that have been removed from the context in which they are stated.[2] All rules contain implicit assumptions that cannot be represented in sufficient detail in expert systems.

Consider, for example, the statement "Thou shalt not steal." At first glance, this statement appears to be clear and its meaning obvious. However, we can understand this statement only in a complex mental context with hundreds of assumptions and linkages. Implicit in this statement, for example, is the assumption of a social structure that allows ownership among identifiable entities. That set of assumptions, which is obvious to humans, is essential for the proper application of this rule. Winograd and Flores argue that taking sentences out of context and placing them in rule bases or other decontextualized forms implies a degree of independence that can never exist.

Consider the mundane example of selecting a wine that is appropriate for a given meal. Consider the rule "If maincourse = meat then wine-color = red." Now, during an execution of the expert system, suppose the system asks you, "Is the maincourse meat?" If you are having beef or chicken, the answer to this question is obvious. But suppose you are dining on ostrich. How do you respond? Ostrich is red like meat, but it has the nutritional properties of chicken.

Supporters of expert systems would say this is a silly example, since people seldom dine on ostrich. Critics might agree that ostrich is rare, but they might also

---

2. Winograd, Terry, and Fernando Flores, *Understanding Computers and Cognition.* Norwood, NJ: Ablex Publishing, 1986.

counter that only such seldom-seen cases require the expert system's assistance: "When I'm dining on beef, I already know to pick a red wine. It's the rare cases in which I need the help, and those are the very cases in which decontextualization makes expert systems useless."

This example illustrates a general property of expert systems: They are *brittle*. That is, their performance degrades dramatically—they suddenly break—as a problem leaves the area in which their rules apply. In addition, the expert system cannot usually detect that this has occurred, so the system cannot readily monitor its own ability to solve a given problem.

This brittleness underlines the need for the explanatory capability of an expert system inference engine. Although an expert system may appear to provide sensible advice when it is used in cases not within its domain, the explanation it provides of its reasoning often reveals that the reasoning is spurious. Therefore, as a user of expert systems, you should frequently invoke the explanatory capability and test the reasonableness of the answers you receive against your own judgment. You should do this especially when the system is giving unexpected responses. Doing so may reveal weaknesses or errors in the expert system.

Many of the difficulties with expert systems may arise from unfulfilled expectations created by their name. The term *expert system* is too ambitious and presumptuous for the level of technology that exists today. Winograd and Flores suggest that *idiot savant* would be a better term. (Recall Raymond, played by Dustin Hoffman in the movie *Rain Man*.)

Where to Use Expert Systems Successfully

As you can see, there is considerable controversy about the value of expert systems. Large, sophisticated expert systems are incredibly expensive and hard to maintain, and most such systems have only been of academic interest. On the other extreme, many simple systems have been implemented, but they are of questionable value. Somewhere between these two extremes lies a gray area in which expert systems will most likely find their niche.

In a recent study, Schutzer investigated several expert systems failures in the financial industry.[3] Among them were several projects that were developed and abandoned, including Paine Webber's Financial Hedging Advisor, Shearson's Interest Rate Swap, and Information Analytic's Market Minder. Schutzer found several common threads that he believed led to the failure of these projects. These failures can help us define the proper role for expert systems.

For one, these expert systems were too simple. The domains in which they were supposed to operate were far more complicated than the models used in the

---

3. Schutzer, Daniel, "Business Expert Systems: The Competitive Edge," *Expert Systems with Applications*, Vol. 1, No. 1, 1990, pp. 17–21.

expert systems. The advice was too simplistic and did not consider enough factors. Also, the expert systems Schutzer studied tended to consider complicated issues from only a single viewpoint. The users of these systems were accustomed to addressing their problems from several vantage points.

Another problem was that the input of financial analysts, the system users, was not sufficiently considered during the requirements phase. Finally, the users judged the expert systems to be too inflexible. The problems that the analysts needed to address were dynamic; as important factors changed, the analytical approach needed to be adjusted, but the expert systems could not be changed quickly enough.

From these and other experiences in the past few years, we can conclude that it is vitally important to match expert systems technology with problems of appropriate scope and complexity. Both ends of the spectrum should be avoided. Expert systems that solve trivial problems are a waste of time and money; expert systems that provide simplistic answers to complicated problems are also wasteful and possibly even dangerous. One heuristic in the industry is that any problem solvable in less than 15 minutes by two strangers talking over the telephone is at the right level of complexity for an expert system.

A Successful Expert System   Simple expert systems that provide great savings are the most likely to be successful. For example, many employees in all parts of a large company occasionally ship documents and parcels, either among company locations or to recipients outside the company. If George Chen in the home office must send an important contract to salesperson Viviana Ochoa in Spokane, he must select fax transmission or a method of shipment that is economical, yet reasonably ensures its arrival in time to serve its purpose. Because George ships only half a dozen parcels a year, he has little basis for comparing shipment methods. One method may usually provide on-time delivery for less than half the cost of another that guarantees it, but George lacks the knowledge to make this judgment.

George typically has a great incentive to get the parcel delivered on time, but he feels less incentive to save what seem like small amounts of money by seeking the most economical shipping method. If the parcel arrives late, he will be blamed. But if he spends a few extra dollars to use a more expensive shipper that advertises widely on TV, for example, no one is likely to notice. After all, the total cost of the half-dozen parcels he ships per year is very small, even if he selects unnecessarily expensive shippers. Thus, he has little sense of the enormous cost incurred when individuals all over his company each follow this pattern of shipping choices.

In this situation, a simple expert system available to all employees through the company computer network can provide substantial overall savings. If George's company had such a system, he could access it through his PC. It would ask several questions about the size and weight of his parcel, contents, its destination, and its required arrival time, as Figure 15-11 shows. Then it would recommend the most economical shipping method that reasonably ensures the required delivery. If the parcel does not arrive on time, the expert system, not

Figure 15-11 An Expert System Shipping Advisor

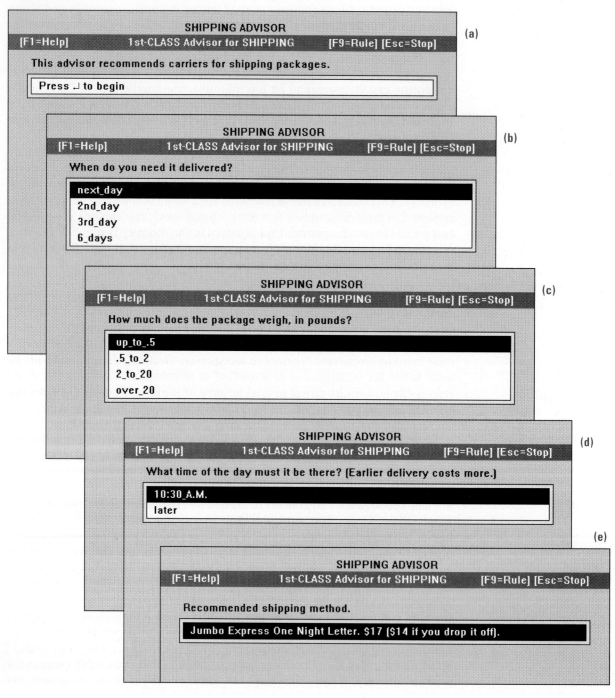

George, is blamed. Therefore, George has no reason to spend more than the expert system recommends.

The substantial savings of such a system throughout a large company repays its development cost very quickly. The savings also pays for continuing maintenance and modification of the system as shippers change rates and the company gains experience with various shipping methods. For example, if an economical shipper shows a pattern of late deliveries, the expert system rules can be modified to take this performance into account. Thus, each employee has access to the best expertise available in the company about shipping methods.

In the long run, this simple high-return system may be the most common expert systems application. Its simplicity makes it manageable, and its savings makes it attractive. The fact that today's PCs are usually networked makes it available wherever it is needed.

Another niche for expert systems technology may be as part of other information systems. For example, the spreadsheet application of the future may question you about the nature and characteristics of data you want to display and it may use an internal expert system to select the best type of graphic for that data. (Further in the future, it may analyze the data itself and make the determination.) Similarly, a statistical analysis package may assist you in selecting an appropriate statistical test for your data. It may also help interpret the results, explaining what they mean and cautioning against common misinterpretations.

COMPONENTS OF AN EXPERT SYSTEM

An expert system has the same five components as other computer-based information systems: hardware, programs, data, people, and procedures.

Hardware

Expert systems shells operate on all types of hardware—microcomputers, minicomputers, and mainframe computers. Some shells, in fact, run on all three. As microcomputers become more and more powerful, however, it is likely that they will come to be the standard expert system hardware platform.

Some special-purpose hardware was developed just for expert systems. Special-purpose computers were designed to be especially fast at symbolic (as opposed to numeric) processing. Since symbolic processors were low-volume machines, manufacturers had to charge premium prices to recover the substantial development costs. As a result, the machines have not been commercially successful. The microcomputer price/performance ratio has improved so much that today's powerful microcomputers are feasible for most expert systems applications.

Programs

There are two major program categories in expert systems. First are symbolic programs that are custom-developed for specific applications. The second is expert system shells.

Symbolic Programming   The earliest expert systems were developed in **symbolic programming languages**, which are designed to facilitate the processing of symbols rather than the processing of numbers. For example, a symbolic program can be written to prove trigonometric identities (such as $\sin^2 x + \cos^2 x = 1$) or solve fundamental integration problems in calculus. These languages also can be used to write expert systems.

Of many symbolic languages, two have gained the most prominence. **LISP** (for list processor) was developed in the early 1960s by John McCarthy, one of the pioneers of AI. A major strength of LISP is that programs and data are structured in the same way. This means that one LISP program can be written to accept another LISP program as data. Thus, one program can be written to change another. In fact, a LISP program can accept itself as data and modify itself while it is in execution. The chief disadvantage of LISP programs is that they require specialized programmers, since most business programmers view LISP as difficult to use.

Prolog, a second language that has received widespread use for symbolic programming, was developed about 1970 by Alain Colmerauer at the University of Marseilles. It enjoyed a spurt of great popularity worldwide in the 1980s, although today its popularity has waned. Figure 15-12 shows a simple Prolog program.

Developing expert systems in symbolic programming languages requires the expertise of sophisticated (and expensive) computer professionals. It is also slow. Therefore, these languages are not normally used for developing expert systems in the commercial world. Instead, expert system shells are more often used.

Expert System Shells   An expert system shell is a set of programs that is used to create, administer, and process an expert system. The general structure of an expert system shell was shown in Figure 15-8. Such shells provide a development environment in which a nonprogrammer (at least for the simpler shells) can declare rules and other knowledge and develop the expert systems user interface.

Expert system shells can be classified into the five groups listed in Figure 15-13.[4] **Inductive shells** and **simple rule-based shells** represent knowledge

---

4. Harmon, Paul, and David King, *Expert Systems: Artificial Intelligence in Business.* New York: John Wiley & Sons, 1985, p. 45.

Figure 15-12   Simple Prolog Program

(a) Sample Prolog program. (b) Execution of program.

(a)

```
person (X, gotbucks) :-
    club (X, Y),
    cost (Y, Z),
    Z > 200

person (X, fewbucks) :-
    club (X, Y),
    cost (Y, Z),
    Z < 101

club (john, ski).
club (mary, scuba).
club (fred, jogging).
club (rosemary, racketball).
club (roger, mountaineering).

cost (ski, 500).
cost (scuba, 650).
cost (jogging, 5).
cost (racketball, 100).
cost (mountaineering, 125).
```

(b)

```
>club (Who, ski)?
Who = john
>
>
>club (rosemary, Which)?
Which = racketball
>
>
>person (Who, gotbucks)?
Who = john
Who = mary
>
>
>
>
>person (Who, fewbucks)?
Who = fred
Who = rosemary
>
>
>
>
>person (Who, nobucks)?
NONE
>
```

in terms of IF-THEN rules. The difference between the two types is that inductive shells derive the rules from a set of examples provided by the user. For simple rule-based shells, the user must enter in the rules directly.

Figure 15-11 shows an example use of an inductive rule tool called 1st-Class. The developer has input a number of case examples. 1st-Class uses these cases to derive a set of IF-THEN rules that will be stored in the knowledge base. These rules are used to create a shipping recommendation, as shown in Figure 15-11.

Structured rule-based shells are recommended for problems that have several hundred or more rules. These systems allow rules to be grouped (or structured) so that the inference engine need not process every rule every time. Instead, the inference engine processes one group of rules until a rule triggers

Figure 15-13 Five Types of Expert System Shells

- Inductive rule-based
- Simple rule-based
- Structured rule-based
- Hybrid
- Domain-specific

another group or until all the rules in a group have been processed. The structuring of rules not only simplifies the task for the inference engine but also makes it easier for humans to maintain and modify the rule base.

Hybrid shells represent knowledge by a combination of rules and other more comprehensive data structures called frames and objects defined in the next section. Because of their richer set of data structures, hybrid shells can be used to model more complicated situations than those modeled with rule-based systems.

Finally, **domain-specific shells** can be used to generate expert systems in particular problem domains. Since they are restricted in scope, they can be used to develop expert systems applications in their domain more quickly and with greater ease than the systems developed with general-purpose shells. A domain-specific tool can be any of the other four types.

Figure 15-14 combines Figures 15-10 and 15-13 to show what Harmon and King consider to be the appropriate use of expert system shells.[5] They recommend that the inductive and simple rule-based systems be applied to easier problem domains, that simple and rule-based shells be used for the more difficult domains, and that hybrid shells be used for the most complicated problem domains. These recommendations are heuristics, however, rather than absolute rules.

Expert Systems Integrated with Database and DSS Data   A number of enterprises have found that they can gain more value from expert systems that can access other sources of data. Figure 15-15 shows the structure of such a system. Data is extracted from workgroup and enterprise databases and made available to the expert system. Similarly, data can be extracted from DSS applications.

The extracted data can be used in two ways. First, it can be used to update the knowledge base. In an inductive knowledge base, the extracted data can be used as a source of examples to update the rules. In other types of shells, it can be used as a source of information for obtaining other knowledge-based structures, as described in the next section.

---

5. *Ibid.*, pp. 51–53.

Figure 15-14   Appropriate Use of Expert System Shells

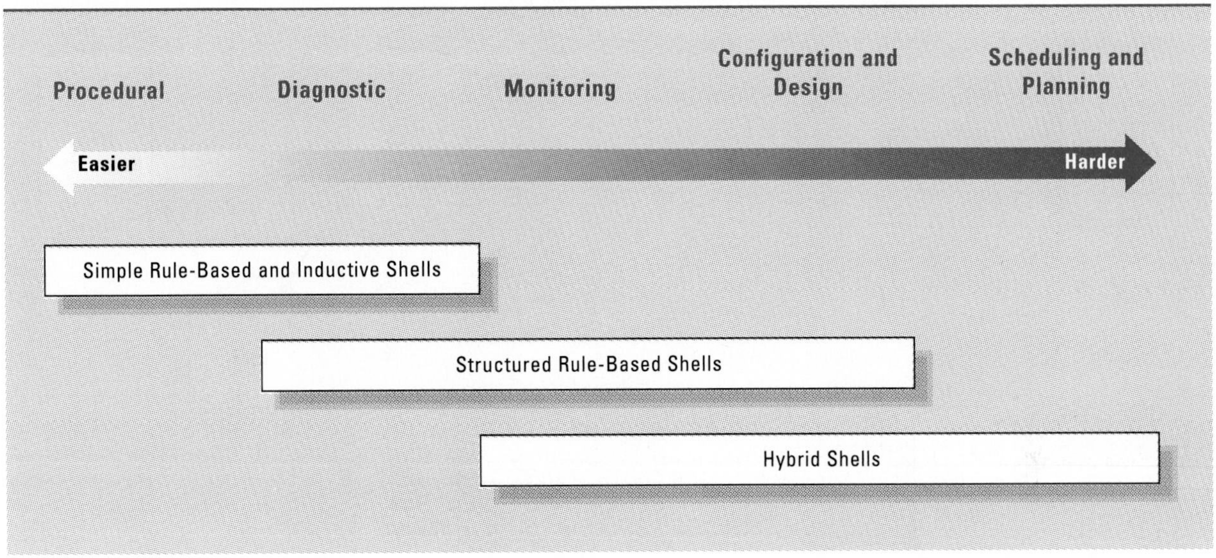

Procedural	Diagnostic	Monitoring	Configuration and Design	Scheduling and Planning

Easier ←──────────────────────────────────→ Harder

Simple Rule-Based and Inductive Shells

Structured Rule-Based Shells

Hybrid Shells

Second, the extracted data can serve as input during execution of the expert system. For example, an expert system might be used in accounts receivable to classify the credit-worthiness of customers. To evaluate a customer's most recent payment history, the expert system may obtain the data directly from a database extract.

The integration of expert systems, databases, and DSS is sometimes called **intelligent DSS**. King describes several strategies for creating such systems.[6]

Data

Expert systems store knowledge in three different ways. Some expert system shells use just one of these ways, some use two, and some use a combination of all three.

First, some expert systems store knowledge in the form of IF-THEN rules. (Inductive shells store both the input examples and the derived rules.) The rules may be a simple list like the one in Figure 15-9, or, for expert systems with hundreds of rules, the rules may be clustered into structural sets.

A second way expert systems represent knowledge is in the form of **frames** representing the entities or objects to which procedures or rules refer. Frames are

---

6. King, David, "Intelligent Decision Support Systems for Integrating Decision Support, Database Management, and Expert Systems," *Expert Systems with Applications*, Vol. 1, No. 1, 1990, pp. 22–31.

Figure 15-15   Expert System Using Database and DSS Data

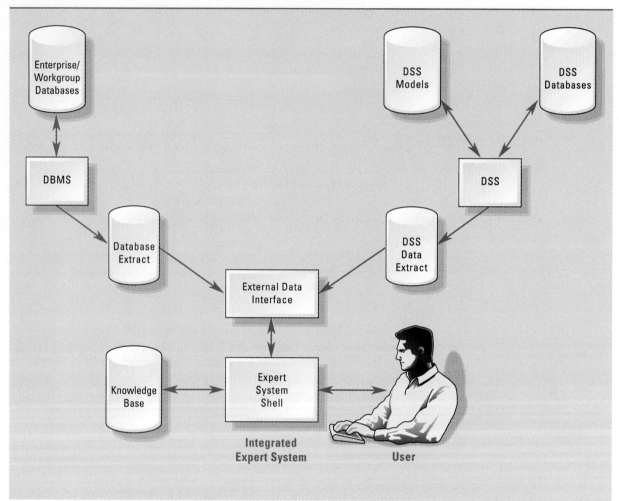

used in conjunction with rule processing. With frames, the parameters of a rule can be more than just simple data items.

Figure 15-16 shows several frames. Each frame has **slots,** which are locations where data items, procedures, or references to other frames can be stored. In the first frame of Figure 15-16, STUDENT, slots contain data about a person. A slot also contains a pointer to other frames describing courses taken: Biology and Chemistry. COURSE frames also contain slots with data items and possibly with pointers to other frames.

Figure 15-16 Frames to Represent Data

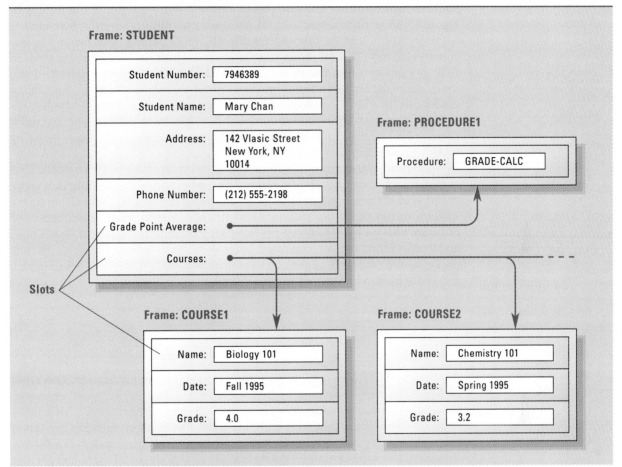

One of the slots in STUDENT contains a pointer to a procedure contained in another frame, GRADE-CALC. This procedure is a program that computes a student's current grade point average. When the user asks for a grade point average, the expert system invokes GRADE-CALC, which then computes it using the most up-to-date data. Thus, no static value (that may later fail to reflect subsequent changes) need be stored in that slot.

A third way expert systems represent knowledge is with **objects**. Expert systems objects are extensions of frames. They marry extended data structures with program procedures, or **methods**, as they are called. Objects are processed by special languages called **object-oriented languages**. Examples of such languages are Smalltalk and C++.

Object-based systems provide **method inheritance**. An object inherits methods (procedures) from its parent objects. For example, if the frames in Figure 15-16 were represented and processed as objects, then the procedure GRADE-CALC could be invoked for the object STUDENT and for any object subordinate to STUDENT. Thus, if someone asked for a student's average grade in Biology courses only, the procedure GRADE-CALC could be invoked. If the developer of the expert system wanted a COURSE to have its own grade-calculating procedure, then he or she would write it and store the new procedure, say GRADE-CALC-2, as a method associated with that COURSE. In this case, the grade point average for COURSE and all of its subordinate objects would be computed by invoking procedure GRADE-CALC-2.

Method inheritance shortens the development time of sophisticated applications because developers can build on one another's objects. In fact, some expert system shells contain libraries of objects for just that purpose. Using such a library, one developer can add to the knowledge base of another; developers need not start with an empty knowledge base. Object-oriented programming is new, and its true utility not yet confirmed. Some developers believe, however, that it is the key to the next stage of development in expert systems. Because it is so useful, inheritance is now supported in many frame-based systems.

People

Expert systems involve some of the same personnel as are involved in other types of MIS, and they also require personnel with new and different expertise. Figure 15-17 (which is adapted from a graphic by Merrill Warkentin & Associates) shows the important personnel and their roles. **Knowledge engineers** use expert system shells or programming languages to create the expert system. To do this, they interview **subject matter experts (SMEs)**, who understand the subject matter of the expert system. For example, a domain expert for the development of an insurance-claims-processing expert system would have years of experience in processing claims and a knowledge of enterprise goals, objectives, policies, and procedures that pertain to claims processing.

The domain expert often maintains the expert system, testing it for appropriate responses and modifying it, possibly with the assistance of the knowledge engineer. The expert system is then employed by the end user, who provides services to the clientele.

Knowledge engineers must be able to perform three fundamental tasks: acquiring knowledge, modeling knowledge, and encoding knowledge.[7] The

7. Harman and King, p. 163.

Figure 15-17 Expert Systems Personnel and Their Roles

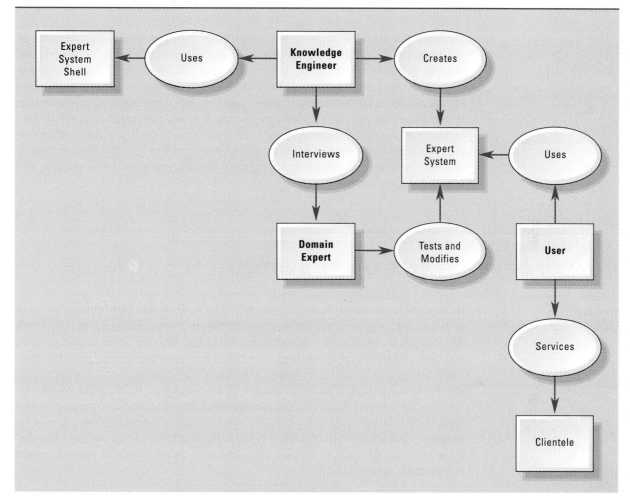

process by which this is done is summarized later in the section on developing expert systems.

If the expert system does not use a shell, then it may be custom-developed. In this case, an **expert system tool** may be used or the services of a **symbolic language programmer** may be required. Since symbolic programming is difficult for most business programmers, good symbolic programmers are in demand. Consequently, they are hard to locate and expensive to employ.

Procedures

For both users and operators, the procedures required when working with an expert system are similar to those required for other types of MIS. Procedures must be defined for both normal operations and failure and recovery operations.

Since expert systems are difficult to test, errors or ineffective and misleading results are more likely than with other types of MIS. Consequently, most expert systems include special procedures by which users can report expert system behavior that they consider suspicious. A procedure must be established so that these error reports are delivered to the developers on a timely basis. The developers, in turn, need procedures for ensuring that all such reports receive prompt and appropriate attention.

HOW TO DEVELOP AN EXPERT SYSTEM

In most cases, expert systems are developed using the prototyping process discussed in Chapter 7. As summarized in Figure 15-18, the problem is defined, the solution is classified by determining the scope and size of the expert system, and then a platform is constructed. The expert system is then developed iteratively using prototypes. When the system is judged to be complete and accurate, it is implemented, which, for historical reasons, is often called **fielding the system**.

In this process, the definition, classification, and platform construction stages are normally done once. On occasion, if the solution is misclassified, it may be necessary to back up and reconstruct the platform. This would occur, for example, if the number of rules is underestimated and a more powerful type of expert system shell needs to be used.

Defining the Problem

The problem definition stage has the same three tasks we have discussed before: defining the problem, assessing the feasibility of solving it, and building a project plan. A problem is a perceived difference between what is and what should be. Problems that are amenable to expert systems solutions usually involve a shortage of personnel with knowledge to perform some task. This lack becomes evident because there are too few people to perform a critical task, because people must stop what they are doing and find someone who does have the expertise to perform the task, or because people who lack expertise are performing the task inadequately.

Figure 15-18 Prototyping Process Applied to Expert Systems

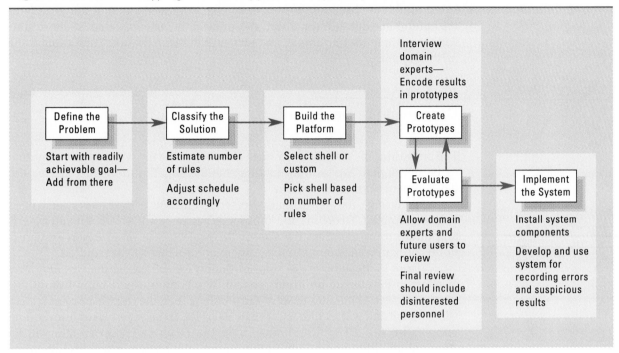

Considering feasibility, Harmon warns: "Expert systems do not create knowledge, and they do not learn on the job. They simply store and play back knowledge that some human expert has already developed. If no one knows how to analyze and solve the problem now, an expert system will not improve the situation."[8] There is no magic, and an expert system is no panacea for finding out how to solve a problem.

When building the project plan, experience shows that considerable caution and conservatism is appropriate. Expert systems projects are almost always more difficult than imagined. Even the simplest task has, embedded within it, assumptions and prior knowledge that will need to be formalized.

In most situations, it is best to start with a small system, develop and implement it, and then add functionality to future versions of the system. In this way, the enterprise can gain a return (and confidence) from its use. Once an expert system has been successfully implemented, there will be support among the users and their management to devote resources for expanding the system to a larger domain.

---

8. *Ibid.*, p. 176.

Further, if too much is attempted too soon, the project may lose credibility in the users' eyes because the benefit will be postponed too long. Large projects are hard to manage and run a high risk of never being completed. In short, start with something useful, simple, and achievable. Make it work. Then expand the existing system.

Classifying the Solution

The purpose of the classification stage is to determine the type and size of system to be developed. We assume in this chapter that the problem requires the development of an expert system.

At this stage, the approximate size, scope, and type of the expert system need to be determined. To do this, the knowledge engineer works with domain experts and future users to assess the size of the project. Size of an expert system is normally expressed in terms of the number of rules that will be required.

Figure 15-19 summarizes rules of thumb for estimating the size and level of effort in developing an expert system. If a human expert takes from a few seconds to several minutes to solve the problem, then the resulting expert system will be small and will require fewer than 500 rules. If the expert takes from several minutes to, say, 20 or so minutes, then the resulting expert system will be midsized and will require 500 to 1,500 rules. If the human expert requires more than 20 minutes, up to several hours, then the resulting system will be large and will require more than 1,500 rules and probably the definition of frames, objects, and other types of knowledge.

In general, small expert systems can be developed in a few months; midsized expert systems typically require from 6 to 18 months; and large systems require 2 to 4 years or more. With an estimate of the number of rules, it may be appropriate to revise the dates set out in the project plan during the problem definition stage.

Figure 15-19 Classification of Expert System Problems and Recommended Shells

Time Required for Human to Solve	Size	Approximate Number of Rules	Recommended Shell
< a few minutes	Small	< 500	Inductive or Simple Rule-Based
> a few minutes but < 20 minutes	Medium	> 500 and < 1,500	Structured Rule-Based or Hybrid
> 20 minutes	Large	> 1,500	Hybrid

Building the Platform

Once the expert system has been classified, the next task is development of the platform. A major decision is whether to use an expert system shell or to custom-develop the expert system using a symbolic programming language. In almost all cases, shells are used. Symbolic programming is too labor-intensive, slow, and expensive to be used for all but the most specialized and expensive situations. Further, as stated, good symbolic programmers are difficult to locate and expensive.

Here we assume that the decision has been made to use an expert system shell. The next decision is the type of shell to use. As shown in the last column of Figure 15-19, an inductive shell or a simple rule-based shell is recommended for small problems, and a structured rule-based shell or hybrid shell for medium problems. Hybrid shells must be used for large problems.

At this point, the developers evaluate available shells in the appropriate category. Of the dozens of products in each category, the team must decide which particular product to use. The product evaluation should follow the process described in Chapter 10.

Creating the First Prototype

Following the general strategy of developing with prototypes, the next stage is to develop an initial prototype. No attempt is made to build a complete and comprehensive system; instead, the goal is a prototype that will increase the developer's understanding of the problem.

Development via prototypes is especially appropriate for expert systems. Human experts seldom know how they do what they do. When asked to formalize their knowledge, they struggle because so much seems obvious to them.

During this stage, the knowledge engineer interviews the domain experts and attempts to understand their knowledge and decision processes and to encode that understanding (or portions of it) in the first prototype. The knowledge engineer also needs to investigate and resolve differences of opinion (usually plentiful).

The work at this stage is not straightforward. All the problems of systems development occur here: Users employ inconsistent terminology; they use different views of data; they are motivated, in part, by political concerns.

Further, there is often considerable disdain among domain experts for the very notion of an expert system: "No machine can do what I do!" There is also considerable fear: "What if a machine can do what I do?" These concerns are similar to those of users who may fear job displacement in the development of other kinds of systems. One difference, which can be important, is that domain experts are typically well educated and connected to sources of enterprise power. Displacing a seasoned and experienced production manager invokes more dramatic forms of organizational resistance than does displacing a part-time data-entry person.

Another problem is that experts, because they possess valuable and needed expertise, have limited time for interviews and reviews. Sometimes it is difficult to obtain the time and attention of needed experts. As a result, the knowledge engineer may be assigned to a junior expert and build the system on the basis of that person's expertise. Later, when the application is shown to the senior expert, deficiencies in the junior person's knowledge and approach emerge. For this reason, it is advantageous for the knowledge engineer to work with the most senior experts available for as much time as possible.

The prototype need not have all the essential features of the completed system, but it should have sufficient capability to be taken seriously by domain experts and others who review it. At least several key elements of the problem should be visible in the prototype. If not, skepticism for the project may develop among the domain experts and future users.

Modeling knowledge is not a linear or straightforward process. For any but the simplest expert systems, there are myriad ways of modeling the knowledge. Design choices made during the construction of the model will have a great impact on the performance and usefulness of the resulting expert system. Since this activity is both difficult and important, knowledge engineers often try a number of different alternatives in several development iterations.

Iterating on the Prototypes

Once the first prototype has been constructed, domain experts, users, and other appropriate personnel review it. Prior to the review, these people should be informed of the incomplete nature of the prototype. They should be told what the goals in developing the prototype were and reminded of these goals from time to time in the review process.

Knowledge modeling is an artistic process and one that is not well understood. Often, the answer to the question "What happens if we do this?" is "Well, we don't know. Try it and see." Consequently, many prototypes are likely to be developed. More than any other information system type, developing an expert system is an experimental process.

Do not be surprised if five or more iterations of prototypes are required before the domain experts find the system satisfactory. At the end of each iteration, the developers refine the design and develop and implement the refined design.

Once the domain experts judge a prototype ready for implementation, it should be reviewed by a pilot group of users and one or more domain experts who have not been involved in the project. After it is approved by this group, it can be installed in the user environment—a task generally called fielding the expert system.

Implementing the System

When the system is implemented, all the procedures described in Chapters 7 and 10 are followed. If new hardware is necessary, it is installed in the user area and tested. Expert system shell programs are installed, and data is stored on the user computers. Documentation is written, and users are trained. Finally, the system is installed. Most often the system is tested by running it in parallel with human experts until the developers and users are confident it works correctly.

Since an expert system is very difficult to test, users should be trained to use the explanatory capability frequently and compare the system's reasoning with their own common sense. In addition, procedures must be established to let users report problems to the developers. Developers need to be aware of the need for continued testing and refinement of the expert system.

SUMMARY

A knowledge system is a computer-based system that represents knowledge and makes it available to users in a form tailored to solving specific problems. Knowledge systems are used for many purposes. Some such systems reduce training time or training cost. Others replicate valuable expertise, and still others reduce operational response time. Another type of knowledge system stores and saves valuable expertise.

Knowledge-based system technology is evolving. More knowledge-application problems have been envisioned than have been solved. There is even disagreement over what constitutes a knowledge-based system. This chapter considers three types: hypermedia systems, interactive video systems, and expert systems.

Hypermedia documents store text, graphs, diagrams, schematics, and other graphics in computer media. What makes such documents knowledge systems is not the computer storage, however, but rather the capacity to store access paths in the document. Thus, experts can establish access paths for nonexperts to follow.

Interactive video links video segments via menu-processing applications. This process allows knowledge stored in video media to be accessed nonsequentially. Such applications involve a greater degree of computer control than do hypermedia applications. Interactive video is used primarily in training and advisory capacities.

An expert system is a computer-based information system in which knowledge is represented in data and in which the processing of that knowledge is directed primarily by computer programs. Expert systems have the greatest degree of computer control of the three systems studied in this chapter.

The development of systems that process the knowledge of a true human expert has been difficult and expensive. The technology is useful in solving many smaller problems, however.

The term *artificial intelligence* (AI) is often used in marketing for its emotional impact. Many experts believe that an information system that could pass the Turing test would have AI. To date, however, no such system exists. In a practical sense, AI refers to the group of disciplines shown in Figure 15-7.

An expert system shell is a set of programs used to develop, administer, and process an expert system. A shell contains a knowledge acquisition system, an inference engine, an explanation system, and a user interface.

The inference engine applies rules and other forms of knowledge in an attempt to make sequences of logical conclusions that will solve a user's problem. Forward and backward chaining are the two major inferencing strategies.

Expert systems can be used to address problems in a number of problem domains. In increasing order of difficulty, these domains are procedural, diagnostic, monitoring, configuration and design, and scheduling and planning.

There are a number of problems with the use of expert systems. These systems have had only limited exposure in the commercial world and only limited success. The demand has not met early expectations. Some say expert systems are exceptionally difficult to develop and hard to use for any but the simplest applications. They are hard to maintain; the introduction of new knowledge can have spurious side effects.

Some critics maintain that expert systems technology results in high development and maintenance costs. Others believe that expert systems should be used only to develop prototypes of systems; they believe that operational knowledge systems should be written in conventional programming languages. Still others argue that expert systems are philosophically unsound. They believe that the decontextualization of rules renders them useless, and that, consequently, expert systems can help only in the simplest interpretations.

The proper niche for expert systems lies between simplistic applications and true human experts. Analysis of failures of expert systems indicates that they should be carefully matched with problems of appropriate scope and complexity. One suggestion is that expert systems can help with problems that can be solved in less than 15 minutes by two strangers talking on the telephone.

Considering the five components, most expert systems run on conventional computers, especially microcomputers. Expert systems programs can be written in special-purpose, symbolic programming languages such as Prolog and LISP. These languages require specialized programmers, however, and most expert systems programs are developed using specialized shells. The five categories of such shells are: inductive rule-based, simple rule-based, structured rule-based, hybrid, and domain-specific shells. Intelligent DSSs integrate expert systems with enterprise and workgroup databases and with DSSs.

Expert systems store knowledge in three ways: with rules, frames, and objects. Rules state IF-THEN logic. Frames represent properties of entities to which rules may refer. Objects are extensions of frames that combine data structures with program procedures so as to provide method inheritance. Some developers consider objects to be the key to the next stage of development in expert systems.

Expert systems are created by knowledge engineers who interview subject matter experts (SMEs). The SMEs test and modify the expert systems. Users employ the expert systems to provide services to clients.

The same four types of procedures are required for expert systems as for other information systems. These procedures need to take special cognizance of the fact that expert systems are difficult to test and validate.

Most expert systems are developed using the prototyping process described in Chapter 7. The stages of activity are: defining the problem, classifying the solution, creating the platform, iteratively building the prototypes, and implementing (fielding) the system.

KEY TERMS

Knowledge system
Heuristic
Wizard
Hypermedia system
Access path
Hypermedia engine
Interactive video
Expert system
AI
Turing test
Natural language
Pattern recognition
Vision system
Robotics
Neural network
Knowledge base
Expert system shell
Inference engine
User interface

Explanation system
Knowledge acquisition
    system
Inferencing
Forward chaining
Backward chaining
Procedural problem
Diagnostic problem
Monitoring problem
Configuration and
    design problem
Scheduling and
    planning problem
Symbolic programming
    language
LISP
Prolog
Inductive shell
Simple rule-based shell

Structured rule-based
    shell
Hybrid shell
Domain-specific shell
Intelligent DSS
Frame
Slot
Object
Method
Object-oriented
    language
Method inheritance
Knowledge engineer
SME
Domain expert
Symbolic language
    programmer
Expert system tool
Fielding the system

REVIEW QUESTIONS

1. What is a knowledge system?

2. Explain how a knowledge system can reduce training time.

3. Explain how a knowledge system can reduce training cost.

4. Explain how a knowledge system can replicate valuable expertise.

5. Explain how a knowledge system can reduce operational response time.

6. Explain how a knowledge system can save valuable knowledge.

7. Summarize what seem to be the best applications for knowledge systems.

8. Explain the knowledge processing alternatives presented in Figure 15-4.

9. What characteristic of hypermedia systems allows them to represent knowledge?

10. Explain an appropriate application for a hypermedia knowledge system, other than one in this chapter.

11. How does an interactive video system represent knowledge?

12. Explain an appropriate application for an interactive video knowledge system, other than one in this chapter.

13. What is an expert system?

14. Do most expert systems in use today replicate the abilities of a human expert? What do they do?

15. Explain the problems with the term *artificial intelligence*.

16. Describe the Turing test. What systems today can pass this test?

17. List and briefly describe the disciplines that constitute the subject of AI.

18. What are the functions of an expert system shell?

19. Describe the purpose of the knowledge acquisition system, the inference engine, the explanation system, the user interface, and the knowledge base in the operation of an expert system.

20. What is the difference between an expert system and an expert system shell?

21. Give an example of inferencing that involves four or more rules, other than the one in this text.

22. For problem 21, show how an inference engine might process the rules to form a conclusion.

23. List the domains of expert systems applications from easiest to hardest. Briefly describe each.

24. Summarize the arguments claiming that expert systems involve high development and maintenance costs.

25. Summarize the reasons why some people believe expert systems should not be used for operational systems.

26. Summarize the philosophical arguments against expert systems.

27. Describe the characteristics of expert systems that are likely to be successful.

28. What is a symbolic programming language? Name two.

29. List and briefly describe five different types of expert system shell.

30. What are the components of an intelligent DSS? Describe one application for such a system.

31. List the three ways in which knowledge is represented in expert systems.

32. What is a frame? Give an example. How are frames used in expert systems?

33. What is an object? How does an object differ from a frame?

34. What is method inheritance? Why is it useful?

35. Describe the categories of personnel involved in the development or use of expert systems.

36. What are the three primary tasks of a knowledge engineer?

37. What role does an SME serve?

38. What characteristics of expert systems pose special requirements on procedures?

39. List the stages of activity in the development of an expert system. List features of the process that are unique to the development of expert systems.

40. Summarize the rules of thumb for estimating the size and level of effort in developing an expert system.

41. Why are special procedures needed for reporting errors and suspicious responses in an expert system?

DISCUSSION QUESTIONS

1. Do you believe that hypermedia and interactive video applications should be considered knowledge systems? To answer this question, first define the terms *data, information*, and *knowledge*. Compare and contrast these terms. Given your definitions, what is the essential difference between an information system and a knowledge system? Now, should hypertext and interactive video be classified as knowledge systems? Can you think of other systems not discussed in this chapter that should be considered knowledge systems?

2. Suppose you are going to build an expert system to advise incoming students on the best teacher to take for American History. First list the various goals that a freshman might have in selecting a teacher. From these goals, develop a list of criteria for selecting a professor. Express these criteria in a list of rules and facts. Demonstrate that your rules work for a student who wants a professor to be interesting and humorous, who is willing to do considerable amounts of reading, and who does not care how old the professor is. Do not restrict your expert system to the criteria listed in the last sentence, however.

3. In 1986 the venture capital and investment banking communities were looking for exciting opportunities in high technology. They invested heavily in expert systems and symbolic logic companies. When demand for products was substantially less than anticipated, interest faded quickly. Today, it is very difficult for companies that work in the field of AI to obtain financing. What role do you think the government should play in encouraging the development of this technology? What role should universities play? Suppose you are in charge of allocating research funds for computer technology at your campus. How would you prioritize your funds for this technology as opposed to hypermedia or interactive video? As opposed to DSS, GDSS, and other information systems? How would your answer change if you worked for the government? How would it change if you worked for a profit-making company?

PROJECTS

A. Obtain a copy of *Developing Expert Systems Using 1st-Class* by Christopher Ruth and Stephen R. Ruth (Santa Cruz, CA: Mitchell Publishing, 1991). A tutorial version of 1st-Class is shipped with this book. Use the tutorial to learn about the product. Answer discussion question 2, and then use the tutorial product to implement your expert system in 1st-Class.

B. Obtain a copy of *Developing Expert Systems Using EXSYS* by Kristopher G. Sprague and Stephen R. Ruth (Santa Cruz, CA: Mitchell Publishing, 1991). A tutorial version of EXSYS is shipped with this book. Use the tutorial to learn about the product. Answer discussion question 2, and then use the tutorial product to implement your expert system in EXSYS.

C. Repeat project A using any other expert system shell at your disposal.

D. Interview someone who has developed an expert system in business. What were the goals of the project? Was the project successful? What process was used to develop the expert system? Were prototypes used? If so, how? Was the expert system implemented using a symbolic programming language or an expert system shell? How was the choice between the two justified? What advice would the developer give anyone contemplating developing an expert system?

M I N I C A S E

How Many Lawyers Can You Fit on a Floppy Disk?

When Metropolitan Life Insurance Co. gets ready to close big commercial real estate financing, it doesn't automatically call in its top legal guns. Often, the financial-services company has its paralegals call up a software program called CLINT, which asks questions about the property, type of borrower, and so on. In 15 minutes—*voilá*—the computer spits out a checklist of the documents and research needed to complete the loan.

It's almost every company's dream: getting rid of the lawyers. Although replacing lawyers with robots is still a fantasy, leading-edge companies increasingly are turning to software for legal expertise. The programs help assemble contracts and close deals. In some cases, "expert systems" let lay people do the work of senior partners.

In recent years, "smart" programs that incorporate human expertise or knowledge have been catching on in diverse areas—finance, energy, and marketing, to name a few. Law has been lagging. But in a scramble to control spiraling legal bills, more general counsels are embracing the software and other technology, such as electronic mail, to boost productivity and cut costs. Yet for those very reasons, outside law firms that bill by the hour "view this technology as a threat," says lawyer Henry Koltys, chairman of the American Bar Association's expert-systems group.

But Motorola Inc., for one, views legal-services software as a competitive edge. As part of a companywide quality program, Motorola last year created a data base for drafting speedier contracts. Before, in-house lawyers would rifle through files searching for contracts from similar prior transactions.

Then, they would cut and paste the old forms to create a new document.

Now, with the push of a computer button, the lawyers can retrieve clauses from Motorola's 100 "best" contracts that are on-line, says Edward W. Jacobs, senior division counsel, who helped devise the system. That's just the first step, he says, toward a more ambitious program of "pushing down" legal knowledge to sales and administrative workers, who'll be able to design contracts on their own.

At Sears, Roebuck & Co., the search for efficiencies has progressed even further. A legal program, known as Matter Manager, can track lawsuits and then use the data to draft summonses and form letters. It can even provide information for answering pretrial "discovery" requests. Besides saving time on drafting, the program lets administrative assistants do paperwork once handled by attorneys, says Matthew Petrich, legal-systems analyst at Sears.

Cost-conscious general counsels such as Chrysler Corp.'s Leroy C. Richie also are pushing law firms to exploit technology. As a result, small and medium-size law firms that use software can win market share. In the mid-1980s, attorney Charles E. Pear Jr. developed a program that could draft documents for conveying real estate. In a year, his small Hawaii law firm saw such business jump from about $10,000 annually to about $250,000, and it continued to rise. While the firm didn't undercut rivals on price, it did work faster and with fewer errors, says Pear, now a visiting professor at the University of British Columbia's law school. By the time a competitor recruited Pear to design a similar system, its real estate work for a common corporate client had evaporated, he says.

Forward-thinking large firms are turning to advanced software to provide better service to demanding clients. Washington's Wilmer, Cutler & Pickering is using software technology known as hypertext. Similar to an electronic book, it lets users browse instantaneously through relevant information about a law or legal issue—and answer client inquiries more rapidly and thoroughly.

Despite exceptions, most law firms remain convinced that what they do is unique and cannot be programmed into a computer. Often, that's true—no software in the world could defend against a hostile takeover. Still, it's amazing what some programs can do. And in the face of increasing competition, law firms may have little choice but to turn to computer technology for help. "If they have the capacity, I want to use them," says Richie. "If not, I wish them luck." ∎

Michele Galen, from *Business Week*,
December 21, 1992, p. 63.

Discussion Questions

1. Summarize the capabilities of the expert systems described in this article.

2. The article jokes about "every company's dream: getting rid of lawyers." Describe more realistically the results reported in this article.

3. Despite reports like this, many lawyers remain convinced that what they do is unique and cannot be programmed into a computer. How would you respond to such an assertion?

4. How can expert systems of the type described here add value to an enterprise?

Glossary

Application program (1) A computer program that provides features and functions particular to the user's information needs; (2) a component of a database application that provides such features and functions.

Artificial intelligence (AI) An ambiguous term with little definitive meaning. Among computer scientists, AI refers to a group of related disciplines that provide capabilities in the past attributed only to humans. Vision, robotics, and expert systems are branches of artificial intelligence. Otherwise, in information systems, a vague term, often laden with emotion, used in marketing literature to mean new and exciting. *See also* Turing test.

Assembly language A second-generation computer language in which commands are close to machine language. Programming in assembly is slow and tedious and, therefore, expensive, but such programs can be made very efficient in using both memory and CPU time. Because of the speed and size of today's computers, such efficiency is less important than it used to be.

Asynchronous meeting A meeting that takes place electronically, potentially over a several-day or even several-week period. The leader establishes an agenda and a time frame, and participants use electronic mail or a similar facility to make comments and to respond to one another's comments. Participants need not meet at the same time.

Backbone network A network that interconnects the various computer networks and mainframe computers in an enterprise. The backbone provides the infrastructure through which application-processing computers communicate.

Baseband transmission A type of transmission in which a single signal at a time is transmitted on the medium. Cheaper than broadband transmission.

BASIC A third-generation computer language that can be used to develop application programs. The term is an acronym for beginner's all-purpose symbolic instruction code. There are many variations of this language; some are rudimentary and some are quite powerful.

Batch TPS A style of transaction processing in which transactions are grouped and processed as a unit; usually associated with sequential file processing. Applications that require periodic processing of a large portion of a file are often designed to use batch processing; payroll is a typical example.

Bit A binary digit—a 1 or a 0; used to represent data in a computer because binary digits are easy to represent electronically. A switch can be on or off, for example.

BPS Bits per second. A measure of communications line speed.

Bridge A computer, most often a microcomputer, that connects one local area network (LAN) to another LAN of the same type. Contrast with Gateway.

Broadband transmission A type of transmission in which multiple signals are carried at different frequencies at the same time. Similar to the system used for cable TV. More expensive than baseband, but broadband products often have higher capacity.

Business network redesign The use of technology to change the way an enterprise interacts with its suppliers, customers, and other entities in its business environment.

Business process redesign   An emerging trend in enterprise systems development. Instead of automating processes as they exist, the systems developers first redesign the business system to better accomplish the enterprise's goals and objectives. Then, after this redesign, the potential application of technology is considered.

Business scope redefinition   The use of technology to change an enterprise's products or markets, particularly where that application results in a revision in the enterprise's strategic plan and direction.

Business systems planning   *See* Enterprise analysis.

Byte   A group of bits that represents a character. Typically today a byte is comprised of eight bits using either the ASCII or EBCDIC character codes. Most often in business applications, byte and character are synonymous.

C   A third-generation computer language used primarily for programming on microcomputers. Most microcomputer program products such as spreadsheets and DBMS programs are written in C. Has some characteristics of assembly language.

CASE   Computer-aided systems engineering is the use of computer technology to improve the productivity of systems development.

CASE repository   A database about systems processes, dataflows, data structures, processing constraints, and other system structure information. Created, modified, and used by CASE tools. Same as CASE repository.

Character code   A coding system that relates patterns of bits to particular letters or other characters. This enables numbers to be used to represent character data. One byte is used to represent each character. Two codes are commonly used: ASCII and EBCDIC. See Figure 3-18 for portions of each.

CD-ROM   A compact disk, similar to an audio compact disk, used to store computer programs and data.

CISC   Acronym for complex instruction set computer. A CPU that processes a large number of different types of instructions. Consequently, its circuitry is complicated; as a result, CISCs can be slower than RISCs. *See also* RISC.

Clientele   The people for whom a system is developed; the beneficiaries of the system. The clientele of an airline reservations system is comprised of people who take flights. The clientele of a payroll system is comprised of employees.

Client/server architecture   A local area network in which specially designated microcomputers called servers provide specialized service on behalf of the users' computers, which are called clients. Often used for database applications in which the database is processed by a DBMS located on the database server computer; application programs on client computers call on the DBMS on the database server for database processing.

Coaxial cable   A medium used for telecommunications. It is similar to the coaxial cable used for television signals. With it, transmission speeds can be faster than twisted pair wires, but not as fast as with optical fiber.

COBOL   A third-generation computer language. The acronym stands for common business oriented language. COBOL has been the language most used for enterprise information systems for many years.

Collaborative writing system   A system to let members of a group work together through a LAN to create documents.

Common carrier   An organization that provides data communications services (or other communications or transportation services) for a fee. In the United States, common carriers are typically governmentally regulated private enterprises.

Communications control program (CCP)   A systems program to coordinate the transmissions of many users in a teleprocessing system. On a mainframe, the CCP is licensed separately from the operating system. On a minicomputer, the functions of the CCP are built in to the operating system.

Communications line   The medium used for telecommunications between computers or between a terminal and a computer. Twisted pair, coaxial, and optical fiber media are used.

Compiler   A computer program that translates computer programs from source language, understandable by humans, into machine language, understandable by the hardware.

Computer-based information system   A system comprised of hardware, programs, data, procedures, and people with the goal of producing information. In this text, the term *information system* is used synonymously with computer-based information system, although an information system can sometimes consist of only people, procedures, and data.

Concentrator A computer that consolidates the signals from many slower-speed transmission lines into a single faster line (or the reverse); also often provides other services such as error detection and correction.

Concurrent server On a local area network, a computer that is processing the network operating system and is also performing applications processing. Contrast with dedicated server.

Consensus Understanding, acceptance, and support for a definition, course of action, or other group decision. Differs from agreement. Group members may disagree, but still reach consensus. Important for problem definition in multiuser systems development.

Context-sensitive help On-line system documentation in which the information presented is selected to be specifically applicable to the user's current activity.

Controlled sharing In multiuser (workgroup and enterprise) systems, the sharing of hardware, data, or other resources such that the activities of one user do not conflict with the activities of another.

CPU Central processing unit, which contains the arithmetic-logic unit (ALU) and other components. In some uses of the term, CPU includes main memory; in others, it does not. Speed of the CPU is measured in millions of instructions per second (MIPS) or in millions of cycles per second (megahertz).

Critical success factor (CSF) planning A top-down method for strategic planning of enterprise information systems. With it, managers are asked to identify factors most important to their individual success and their group's success. The factors are then combined into enterprise factors. The results are used to plan and prioritize the development of enterprise infor–mation systems.

CSMA/CD Acronym for carrier sense multiple access with collision detection. A protocol used for local area networks in which the network-access cards manage the line like a polite human conversation. Contrast with token passing. To the level of detail described in this text, Ethernet and IEEE 802.3 are synonyms for CSMA/CD.

Custom-developed programs Application programs created for a particular user, workgroup, or enterprise. The most expensive style of application program development, because the cost of development must be carried by one organization. *See also* In-house-developed programs.

Data Recorded facts and figures; one of the five components of a computer-based information system.

Data administration The process and function of managing and protecting data. Data administration must be done for personal, workgroup, and enterprise systems. Most companies staff an office of data administration for enterprise data. In a workgroup, one or more workgroup members provide data administration services on a part-time basis. Individuals usually provide their own administration for personal systems.

Database A self-describing collection of integrated records; used to hold multiple tables of data. The primary purpose of a database is to track facts about entities important to the users.

Database application Menus, data-entry forms, reports, queries, and application programs that users employ to process the database. Database applications are commonly created by users of systems developers.

Database management system (DBMS) A set of computer programs used to define, process, and administer a database and its applications. DBMSs are commonly created by commercial software vendors and licensed as horizontal market applications.

Database processing One of two fundamental styles of data processing. With it, multiple files of data are integrated in a single repository. Data duplication is reduced or eliminated, thus improving data integrity.

Data dictionary A database that describes the structure, content, meaning, processing restrictions, and other characteristics of data; used most often in conjunction with data administration.

Dataflow diagram A graphical chart that depicts the flow of data among internal processes, external entities, and data stores.

DBMS *See* Database management system.

Deadlock A condition that occurs when two users invoke conflicting locks. User A is waiting for a record that user B has locked, while user B is waiting for a record that user A has locked.

Decision making The first three stages of the problem-solving process, consisting of intelligence gathering, alternative selection, and choice.

Decision support system (DSS) An interactive computer-based system that facilitates the solution of unstructured (or semistructured) problems.

Dedicated server A microcomputer used exclusively to process the network operating system.

Definition stage The first stage of all three of the systems development processes described in this text; in this stage, the problem is defined, feasibility is assessed, and a project plan is created.

Design stage A stage in the systems development process in which the specifications and characteristics of each of the five components are determined. Most often used in conjunction with the classical systems development life cycle.

Desktop publishing The use of microcomputer-based programs to integrate text, art, graphics, and other design elements into typeset-quality documents.

Direct-access file processing One of two types of file processing. With direct access, records can be read or written in any order, and a record can be updated in the middle of a file. Transactions need not be sorted before processing. Requires disk or other direct-access storage device. Contrast with sequential file processing.

Disk A hardware storage device that allows records to be accessed in any order and allows records to be updated in the middle of the file. Disks can be fixed or flexible, removable or permanent.

Distributed processing system A type of computer-based information system in which applications processing is distributed on two or more different computers.

DOS Acronym for disk operating system. (1) The operating system used on the IBM personal computer and compatibles; (2) any modern operating system.

Downsizing The process of converting applications from a minicomputer or a mainframe computer to a local area network.

DSS shell A set of programs for constructing a decision support system.

Dynamic Data Exchange (DDE) A feature of Microsoft Windows that allows output (such as a graph) to be dependent on and linked to specific data. When the data is later changed, the graph is automatically updated to reflect the change.

EDP controls Procedures developed to control the processing of an information system and to protect the system's assets; usually used with regard to enterprise transaction processing systems. EDP stands for electronic data processing.

Electronic bulletin board A program that lets users contribute messages via E-mail or similar means to a common pool of text that all may share.

Electronic data interchange (EDI) The situation that results when a number of enterprises agree on a common standard format for specified data. Banks, for example, have defined a common EDI standard for the processing of automated teller machine transactions.

Electronic mail (E-mail) A communications system that supports the creation and distribution of messages via electronic media. Can be supported by microcomputers connected via a LAN or a teleprocessing system.

Enterprise analysis A detail-oriented, top-down method for information systems strategic planning. Specific business functions, organizational groups, and data needs are studied systematically and comprehensively. Also called business systems planning.

Ergonomics The study of human physical characteristics in relation to working environments. The result is designs for workstations that maximize comfort, efficiency, and safety.

Ethernet Synonym for the CSMA/CD protocol.

Evaluation stage A stage in the classical systems development life cycle in which alternative strategies for meeting the system requirements are identified and evaluated. May involve the evaluation of responses to a request for proposal.

Exception reports   Reports produced by a management information system application only when a specified condition occurs in the data.

Executive support system (ESS)   A type of computer-based information system that supports very senior executives. ESSs summarize and present information at the highest level of aggregation; they employ easy-to-use interfaces with high-quality graphics and often include the ability to drill down or to expand high levels of abstraction to more detailed levels.

Expert system   A type of knowledge-based system that provides advice and recommendations based on inferences from coded sources of knowledge. Originally used to describe systems that were intended to provide expertise equivalent to a human expert; in practice, they provide far lesser levels of expertise.

Expert system shell   A set of programs used to develop an expert system application. Normally refers to programs that can be used to create a knowledge base and construct a user interface, without having to program in a symbolic language such as LISP or PROLOG.

Facilitator   A professional who designs and conducts computer-mediated meetings.

Facsimile (fax)   A system for reproducing images on paper at a remote location, often by data transmission through telephone lines.

Feasibility   In developing an information system, an assessment as to whether the proposed system makes sense in terms of cost, schedule, available technology, and political environment. Normally assessed during the definition stage but may be assessed during other stages as well.

Feedback   An essential component of quality improvement. Feedback is a method of measuring output, comparing it to a standard, and adjusting the process or input, if necessary, to meet the standard.

File processing   One of two fundamental styles of data processing. With it, files are stored as separate physical entities. Data must often be duplicated, thus creating the possibility of data integrity problems. Data integration is also more difficult. For business applications, file processing is gradually being replaced by database processing.

File server   In a local area network, a microcomputer that processes a shared disk on behalf of other microcomputers.

Floppy disk   A flexible removable disk used for magnetic data storage. Contrast with hard disk.

Gateway   A computer, most often a microcomputer, that connects a local area network to a minicomputer or a mainframe computer or to a second LAN of a different type. Contrast with bridge.

Gigabyte   1,000 megabytes, or approximately 1 billion bytes.

Government OSI Protocol (GOSIP)   A protocol based on the ISO OSI reference model promulgated by the U.S. government.

Granularity of sharing   In a data-sharing system, the size of the data units allocated to particular users. A system with large granularity allocates entire files; a system with small granularity allocates columns of a particular row in a table of a database.

Graphical user interface (GUI)   An interface such as in Macintosh, Microsoft Windows, or Motif, in which the user can manipulate icons, windows, pop-down menus, and related constructs.

Group decision support system (GDSS)   A decision support system used to facilitate group decision making. Generally includes group displays, networked micro-computers, shared databases, and so forth.

Group scheduling system   A system that accesses group members' schedules to seek times when members are available for group meetings.

Groupware   Horizontal market applications marketed to support group operations.

Handwriting input   Data input by handwriting (or, more likely, printing) on a sensitized surface.

Hard disk   A fixed, permanent disk storage system permitting rapid direct access to data. Contrast with floppy disk.

Hardware Physical equipment. One of the five components of a computer-based information system. Can be classified as input, processing, output, or storage.

Hardware-sharing system A system in which users share hardware devices, usually via a local area network. Typical hardware shared in this way includes laser printers, high-speed, large-capacity disks, and plotters.

Higher-level language Synonym for third-generation language.

Horizontal market application program A type of computer program that provides features and functions useful to organizations in a wide range of industries. Word processing, spreadsheet, and DBMS products are horizontal market application programs.

Hypermedia An extension to hypertext in which frames contain text, graphics, images, illustrations, audio, animation, and other forms of knowledge.

Hypertext system Computer-based processing of text documents. Text is held in frames, and authors define links between frames.

Icon A pictorial symbol used to represent data or a program on a GUI screen.

IEEE 802.3 A standard established by the Institute for Electrical and Electronic Engineers. Concerns CSMA/CD protocol on a bus architecture.

IEEE 802.4 A standard established by the Institute for Electrical and Electronic Engineers. Concerns token passing protocol on a bus architecture.

IEEE 802.5 A standard established by the Institute for Electrical and Electronic Engineers. Concerns token passing protocol on a ring architecture.

Implementation stage A stage in the systems development life cycle in which the system is constructed, tested, and installed.

Inconsistent read problem A problem that can occur when one user is reading data while a second user is concurrently updating the same data. Can be prevented with record locking.

Inference engine The portion of an expert system that processes rules or other computer-encoded forms of knowledge and draws logically consistent conclusions. In a rule-based system, the program that processes the rule base.

Informating A term that refers to the use of data generated by transaction processing systems to create reports and other information useful for managing the activity.

Information (1) Knowledge derived from data; (2) reduction of uncertainty that occurs when a message is received; (3) a "difference that makes a difference".

Information center An organizational unit with the goal of supporting end users in their information systems activities.

Information system An open, purposive system that produces information using the input/process/output cycle. The minimal information system consists of people, procedures, and data. People follow procedures to manipulate data to produce information. Computer-based information systems include these three components plus hardware and programs.

In-house-developed programs Custom-developed programs that are created by personnel who work for the enterprise that will own the new system.

Intel 8088, 80286, 80386, 80486 and Pentium microprocessor The family of microprocessors used in the IBM personal computer and compatible computers.

Interactive video A system in which video segments are integrated via a menu-processing application. Users can control the segments they see through menu selections.

Internet (1) A collection of LANs interconnected into a single data communications system; (2) an international data communications network linking thousands of regional networks using TCP/IP protocol.

Kilobyte 1,024 bytes; generally understood to be 1,000 bytes.

Knowledge engineer A specialist who uses expert system shells or other tools to develop an expert system. The knowledge engineer works with domain experts to acquire knowledge; this knowledge is then modeled and encoded using the expert system tool or shell.

LAN topology The configuration of computers in a local area network. The most common topologies are bus and ring.

Laser printer A printer that employs xerographic technology. Typical personal computer systems use laser printers, as do high-speed mainframe output systems.

License A contract to use a program product for a specified purpose, as distinguished from purchasing the program itself. Almost all programs are licensed, not sold.

Line MIS An emerging trend in which end-user departments develop, operate, administer, and use their own information systems, with limited assistance from the enterprise MIS department.

Linked local area networks A system of two or more local area networks connected via bridges and gateways.

LISP A third-generation language used for the development of expert systems and other artificial intelligence applications. LISP stands for list processor. It is a specialized language, and LISP programmers are therefore expensive to hire.

Local area network (LAN) A group of computers connected via a transmission medium. The computers usually reside within a few thousand feet of each other; they can share hardware and data and can communicate via electronic mail and other forms of electronic communications.

Lost update problem A situation that can occur when data is concurrently shared. Two users read the same data with intent to update it. One user stores his or her changes, and those changes are lost when the second user stores his or her changes on top of them. Can be prevented with record locking.

Machine language (1) The first-generation programming language in which programs were written in the binary code of the computer; (2) the program code that results from the translation of source language by a compiler.

Macro A series of stored instructions that perform a task. Often used in spreadsheet and word processing applications.

Magnetic tape A form of computer storage in which data is recorded sequentially. Records must be read in order for processing; records cannot be updated in the middle of the file. Used for backup and sometimes for batch transaction processing with enterprise systems.

Mainframe computer The largest type of computer normally used to support enterprise information systems. Mainframe computers reside in locked, controlled environments.

Main memory The component of the computer in which instructions and data are stored during processing. May include ROM (read-only memory) and RAM (random-access memory). ROM contents are set by the chip's manufacturer and are nonvolatile. RAM, which stores systems and user programs and data, is normally volatile in today's technology.

Management control The process by which managers ensure that resources are obtained and used effectively and efficiently; one of three primary processes to which information systems can add value. Contrast with operational control and strategic planning.

Management information system (MIS) (1) The design and use of effective information systems in business (broad definition); (2) an information system that facilitates management control by producing structured, summarized reports on a regular and recurring basis (narrow definition).

Megabyte 1,000 kilobytes, roughly 1 million bytes.

Microcomputer A computer based on a microprocessor; it is generally used to support personal computer systems. Can be connected into local area networks for workgroup applications and also can emulate dumb terminals for enterprise systems. Microcomputer capabilities have increased so dramatically that their specifications have overrun minicomputers and even many mainframe computers.

Microprocessor The portion of a microcomputer that contains the arithmetic-logic unit, a clock, a decoder, and other components on a single chip. A microcomputer is a microprocessor plus main memory, a data bus, and a power supply.

Minicomputer Midsized computers that are sometimes used to support workgroups and small enterprises. This category of computer has been overrun by microcomputers; gradually it will disappear.

MIS steering committee A formal group consisting of senior-level managers or executives from all the enterprise's major departments. This group sets priorities for information systems development projects.

Modem Acronym for modulator/demodulator, a device that converts digital (computer) signals into analog (voice-like) signals. Used to transmit computer signals over analog telephone lines.

Motorola 68000 microprocessor family The microprocessors used in the Macintosh family of microcomputers.

MPC mark A multimedia standard developed by Microsoft and other vendors. It specifies the minimum hardware requirements for running a multimedia application.

Multimedia system A system capable of storing and processing still image data, sound data, motion video data, and other data representations in addition to traditional types of computerized data.

Multiplexing The process by which the signals from several slower-speed lines are combined into one faster line. The signals are combined on a round-robin basis.

Musical Instrument Digital Interface (MIDI) A standard system for representing data in the composition and production of music.

Natural language interface The processing of human language by computer systems; with such an interface, humans can enter normal English (or some other human language) to communicate with the application.

Network operating system A systems program for coordinating activity among microcomputers on a local area network. Fulfills the functions at layers 3 through 6 of the ISO OSI model.

Neural network A type of system developed by artificial intelligence researchers used for pattern recognition.

Nonprocedural language A fourth-generation com–puter language in which the user or the programmer issues commands that indicate what results are wanted and not what procedure is to be followed in processing data. SQL is the most popular nonprocedural language.

Normalization A process for constructing a set of database tables so as to minimize modification problems. Roughly, every table should have a single theme.

Notebook computer A portable, battery-powered computer with display screen designed to be carried in a briefcase and used away from a user's desk.

Object code The form of a computer program after it has been processed by a compiler.

Object linking and embedding (OLE) A feature of Microsoft Windows that allows data (such as a graph) created by one program to be contained within a document (such as a word processing report) created by another. When the user clicks on the graph, the program that created it is automatically invoked to process it.

Office automation system (OAS) An information system used to create, store, modify, display, and communicate business correspondence, whether in written, verbal, or video form.

Open systems interconnection (OSI) A data communications model developed by the International Standards Organization (ISO). It has seven layers. This model can be used to compare and contrast communications strategies, protocols, and products.

Operating system (OS) A set of computer programs that controls and manages hardware and provides an interface among programs and between programs and hardware. It allocates resources, manages access to the CPU, and provides data management services.

Operational control The process of controlling day-to-day activities; one of three primary processes to which information systems can add value. Contrast with management control and strategic planning.

Operations personnel People who run the computer hardware, start and stop programs, manage removable data storage, and provide certain types of routine maintenance. Enterprise systems are supported by professional operations personnel; the operations functions for workgroup and personal systems are normally done by users themselves.

Optical disk storage Storage devices that use light to sense data encoded on an optical disk. CD-ROM devices are read-only devices; WORM devices can be written once;

erasable optical disk, which is under development, allows data to be both read and written. Generally have much higher capacity than magnetic storage devices.

Optical fiber A form of transmission medium that uses light to encode signals. It has the highest transmission rate of any medium and is also normally the most expensive, though the comparison with some alternatives may soon shift in its favor.

OS/2 A GUI operating system marketed by IBM. It was intended as an alternative to DOS with Windows. It is the third most widely used GUI.

Outsourcing The process of contracting with outside vendors to develop and operate enterprise information systems. The internal MIS department is replaced by the outside contractor.

Pen-based system Microcomputer systems that obtain input through the manipulation of a stylus touching the display screen. Users input data by printing and drawing on the screen.

Personal computer (PC) A microcomputer supporting a single user at a time. Typically, a PC is permanently allocated to a single user to support that person's business activities, though a PC may be shared by several users who use it one at a time.

Postscript A language used to describe the printing of text and images. Used with laser printers. The application, such as a word processor or a desktop publishing program, generates Postscript code, which is then processed by a microprocessor on the laser printer.

Private branch exchange (PBX) A telephone exchange local to an enterprise. PBX can process both voice and data signals. Can provide low-capacity communication among microcomputers and also can be used to concentrate terminal transmissions to a centralized minicomputer or mainframe.

Problem A perceived difference between what is and what ought to be. The word *perceived* is crucial; if many people view a situation, there will be many perceptions, hence many different definitions of the problem.

Problem solving A five-stage process that includes intelligence gathering, alternative specification, alternative selection (choice), implementation, and moni–toring. Systems development processes are a special case of problem solving.

Procedure One of the five components of a computer-based information system; procedures are instructions for people. There are four main types: user procedures for normal processing, user procedures for failure recovery, operations procedures for normal processing, and operations procedures for failure recovery.

Procedure specification A statement of the logic within a process in a dataflow diagram. A procedure specification explains how an input to a process is transformed into an output.

Program One of the five components of a computer-based information system; programs are instructions for hardware. There are four types of programs: systems programs, horizontal market programs, vertical market programs, and custom-developed programs.

Programmer An information system professional who specializes in the design, coding, and testing of computer programs. Primarily works with the hardware, program, and data components of a computer-based information system.

PROLOG A special-purpose language used for developing expert systems and other artificial intelligence applications. PROLOG is a specialized language, so PROLOG programmers are expensive to hire.

PROM Acronym for programmable read-only memory. The contents of PROM are programmed by special-purpose hardware and cannot be changed by the user. To the user, then, PROM is a form of read-only memory.

Protocol An agreed-on method for packaging and processing data communications messages.

Prototype (1) A version of an information system or an information system component. For systems development via prototyping, prototypes are developed, evaluated, redeveloped, reevaluated, and so forth, until a usable system is created; (2) a simulation, a demonstration, a piece of a system, or the first instance of a system. Used to document and verify requirements. In this sense, a rapid prototype is a mockup of a piece of a system. Rapid prototypes are thrown away. Other types of prototypes may be extended and evolve into the actual system.

Quality   A measure of the output of a process as compared to a defined goal. Quality can be increased by improving either product or process or by innovating either product or process.

Query processor   A subsystem of a DBMS that allows generalized, ad hoc query against the database. Query processing language can be learned by nontechnical personnel without much difficulty. The most common query processing language is SQL.

RAM   Acronym for random-access memory. The portion of the computer that holds programs and data as they are processed. Today's standard RAM is volatile, meaning its contents are lost when power is turned off. If the contents of RAM will be needed, they must be stored on external media such as disks when the computer is unpowered.

Record locking   The allocation of a record to a particular user. Used to prevent the inconsistent read and concurrent update problems. Can result, however, in deadlock.

Request for proposal (RFP)   A document that describes the requirements for an information system and is sent to vendors. Vendors are requested to respond with a proposal for a specific system to meet those requirements. Can also serve as system requirements documentation.

Requirements stage   A stage in the classical systems development life cycle in which the input/processing/output scale and the constraints are determined and documented. Requirements can be documented with prototypes, dataflow diagrams, a data dictionary, and procedure specifications.

RISC   An acronym for reduced instruction set computer. A CPU that processes a smaller set of instructions than a CISC computer. Complicated, seldom-used instructions are processed by programs rather than by electronic circuitry in the CPU. RISC CPUs are therefore less complex and can execute more commonly needed instructions faster than can CISC CPUs.

ROM   Acronym for read-only memory. The contents of ROM are preset at the factory; ROM is not volatile. ROM generally is used to hold initialization and other special-purpose programs.

Router   A device to link networks and determine the most efficient route for transmitting messages to particular destinations.

Rule   In an expert system, a statement about conclusions to be made when a specified condition is met. Collections of rules are referred to as a *rule base*.

Sequential file processing   One of two types of file processing. With sequential file processing, records can be processed in a predefined order. Records cannot be updated in the middle of a file. Used primarily for batch-oriented transaction processing systems. Less commonly used now than in the past.

Source code   The form of a computer program before it has been processed by a compiler. Programs in source code form can be read by humans.

Spreadsheet program   A program used to perform repetitive calculations on potentially complicated data interrelationships. The interrelationships are expressed in formulas.

SQL   An acronym for structured query language, a database processing language endorsed by the American National Standards Institute. Important to businesspeople as a query language that can be learned without too much difficulty. Can also be used by application programs to access the database.

Strategic planning   The process by which goals are defined and changed; one of three primary processes to which information systems can add value. Contrast with operational control and management control.

Strategic systems planning   The process of deciding on the objectives and needs for enterprise information systems. Both top-down and bottom-up methods are used. *See also* critical success factor planning and enterprise analysis.

Subject matter expert (SME)   Used in conjunction with expert systems. The SME (pronounced "smee") has knowledge about a particular type of problem and problem environment. A seasoned and experienced accounts payable clerk, for example, could be a SME in developing an accounts payable expert system.

System Network Architecture (SNA) A set of processing concepts developed by IBM to document its data communications strategy. SNA is more than a protocol; it also includes rules, procedures, structures, and statements of strategic direction. Primarily used for wide area networks.

Systems analyst An information systems professional specializing in the development of computer-based information systems. A systems analyst is concerned with all stages of the systems development process and with all five components of an information system.

Systems development life cycle (SDLC) The process used for developing information systems. Two different styles of SDLC are described in this text: classical and prototyping.

Systems programs Computer programs that provide an interface between the hardware and the horizontal market, vertical market, and custom-developed application programs. This category includes the operating system, the database management system, and the communications control program.

Teleprocessing system Data processing from a distance; usually means the processing of application programs and data on a centralized computer from remote, dumb terminals or from microcomputers emulating dumb terminals.

Terminal A user workstation. Normally this term refers to video display and keyboard equipment that does not include a CPU. Sometimes called a dumb terminal. Terminals can be emulated by microcomputers.

Terminal Control Program/Internet Protocol (TCP/IP) A vendor-independent protocol used in the Internet initially sponsored by the U.S. military. It concerns levels 3 through 7 of the OSI model. TCP/IP is often used to connect terminals or microcomputers to minicomputers or mainframe computers.

Textbase A collection of text documents that can be searched for particular information.

Text processing An information system whose primary purpose is to facilitate the creation, storage, and printing of text documents.

Third-generation language A computer programming language in which the procedure a computer should follow in processing data is expressed in human-understandable instructions and algebraic-like formulas.

Token passing A protocol primarily used for local area networks. With it, a communications node must first possess the token before it can use the network. Can be implemented on a bus (IEEE 802.4), but more commonly is implemented on a ring (IEEE 802.5).

Transaction processing system (TPS) An information system that supports day-to-day operations. Examples are ticket reservation systems, order-entry systems, and check-processing systems. TPSs are the oldest type of information system and were developed in the 1950s to support enterprise accounting functions.

Turing test An ingenious test devised by British mathematician Alan Turing to connect a human, via a teletype (the terminals of the 1950s), with either another human or a computer. The two entities converse. If a computer system is able to respond so that the human cannot tell whether it is a computer or a human, then the computer system passes the Turing test and is said to evidence artificial intelligence.

Twisted pair A form of transmission media consisting of pairs of wires, as is used with telephones. This is the cheapest and slowest data transmission medium.

UNIX An operating system initially developed by Bell Labs and used on engineering workstations. UNIX is difficult for nontechnical personnel to use. May increase in popularity in business as GUI environments are added to it. Also, may be used as a multiuser operating system for microcomputers that operate servers on a local area network.

User A person who employs a computer-based information system to accomplish his or her job.

User interface That portion of an information system directly employed by the user. Normally refers to menus, forms, reports, commands, GUI environments, and other structures available to the user.

Value-added reseller (VAR) A company that develops and licenses computer programs, normally for a vertical market niche. The term arises because VARs often acquire hardware and systems programs, add application programs, and resell the entire package. The application programs add value to the hardware and systems programs.

Vertical market application program   An application program developed to meet the needs of a particular market. Examples are programs to manage inventory for an auto parts distributor and programs to support project management for a highway construction company.

Voice-grade line   A form of transmission medium capable of carrying voice transmissions, typically a normal telephone line. Voice-grade lines support data transmission up to about 15,000 bits per second, although 2,400 and 9,600 bits per second are more common today.

Volatile memory   Memory whose contents are lost when the computer system is unpowered. RAM memory is volatile; magnetic and optical storage media are nonvolatile.

von Neumann architecture   The architecture of all commercially successful computers today. Developed by the mathematician John von Neumann, this architecture provides for just one processing CPU. May be supplanted in the next decade by computers that allow for multiple, parallel-processing CPUs.

Wide area network (WAN)   A network that interconnects geographically separated LANs, minicomputers, and mainframe computers.

Word processing   A form of text processing concerned with the preparation, storage, display, and printing of text documents. Most word processing programs include a spelling checker, thesaurus, and facilities for mail merge and boilerplate documents. May also include a macro or a programming language.

Workflow automation   A system to automate the paperwork flow in an office. The system passes forms, using E-mail or a similar system, from one person to another who must take action relative to a form.

Workgroup   A group of, usually, 2 to 25 people who work together to achieve a common goal or set of goals. Can be temporary or permanent; can be located at a single site or distributed at many.

Workstation   A high-performance microcomputer used in engineering applications such as computer-aided design. More expensive than personal computers; may see increased use in business as they become less expensive and as the operating system Unix, with a GUI interface, gains in popularity in the business community.

References

CHAPTER 1

Acoff, Russell L. "Management Misinformation Systems," *Management Science*, Vol. 14, No. 4, December 1967.

Anthony, Robert N. *Planning and Control Systems: A Framework for Analysis.* Cambridge, MA: Harvard University Press, 1965.

Bateson, Gregory. *Steps to an Ecology of the Mind.* New York: Ballantine, 1978.

Clemmons, Eric K. "Evaluation of Strategic Investments in Information Technology," *Communications of the ACM*, Vol. 34, No. 1, January 1991.

Culnan, Mary J. "Mapping the Intellectual Structure of MIS, 1980–1985: A Cocitation Analysis," *MIS Quarterly*, Vol. 11, No. 3, September 1987.

Daft, Richard L., and Richard M. Steers. *Organizations, A Micro/Macro Approach.* Glenview, IL: Scott, Foresman, 1986.

Fayol, Henri. *General and Industrial Management.* London: Pitman, 1949.

Kallman, Ernest A., and John P. Grillo. *Ethical Decision Making and Information Technology: An Introduction with Cases.* Watsonville, CA: Mitchell McGraw-Hill, 1993.

Keen, Peter G. W. "MIS Research: Reference Disciplines and a Cumulative Tradition," *Proceedings of the First International Conference on Information Systems*, Ephraim R. McLean, ed. Philadelphia, PA, 1980.

Leitheiser, Robert L. "MIS Skills for the 1990s: A Survey of MIS Manager's Perceptions," *Journal of Management Information Systems*, Summer 1992, pp. 69–91.

Schermerhorn, John R., Jr. *Management for Productivity.* New York: John Wiley & Sons, 1984.

Simon, Herbert A. *The New Science of Management Decision.* New York: Harper & Row, 1960.

CHAPTER 2

Culnan, Mary J., and M. Lynne Markus. "Information Technologies," in *Handbook of Organizational Communication*, Jablin et al., eds. Newbury Park, CA: Sage Publications, 1987.

Felician, Leonardo. "Image Base Management System: A Promising Tool in the Large Office Environment," *ACM Data Base*, Vol. 19, No. 1, Fall/Winter 1987/1988.

Gait, Jason. "The Optical Filing Cabinet: A Random-Access File System for Write-Once Optical Disks," *IEEE Computer*, Vol. 21, No. 6, June 1988.

Grief, Irene (ed.). *Computer-Supported Cooperative Work: A Book of Readings.* San Mateo, CA: Morgan Kaufmann, 1988.

Hackathorn, Richard D. "End-User Computing by Top Executives," *ACM Data Base*, Vol. 19, No. 1, Fall/Winter 1987/1988.

Keen, Peter G. W. "A Walk through Decision Support," *Computerworld*, 14 January 1985.

Markus, M. Lynne. *Systems in Organizations: Bugs and Features.* Boston: Pitman Publishing, 1984.

Mills, Carol Bergfeld, and Linda J. Weldon. "Reading Text from Computer Screens," *ACM Computing Surveys*, Vol. 19, No. 4, December 1987.

Mohan, Lakshmi, William K. Holstein, and Robert B. Adams. "EIS: It Can Work in the Public Sector," *MIS Quarterly*, December 1990, pp. 435–448.

Rockart, John F., and Michael E. Treacy. "The CEO Goes On-line," *Harvard Business Review*, Vol. 60, No. 1, January/February 1982.

Sprague, Ralph H., Jr., and Eric D. Carlson. *Building Effective Decision Support Systems*. Englewood Cliffs, NJ: Prentice-Hall, 1982.

Turban, Efraim. *Decision Support and Expert Systems*, 2nd ed. New York: Macmillan, 1990.

Turner, Jon T. "Computer Mediated Work: The Interplay between Technology and Structured Jobs," *Communications of the ACM*, Vol. 27, No. 12, December 1984.

Watson, Hugh J., and Mark Frolick. "Executive Information Systems: Determining Information Requirements," *Information Systems Management*, Spring 1992, pp. 37–43.

CHAPTER 3

Hale, David P., William D. Huseman, and Frank Groom. "Integrating Islands of Automation," *MIS Quarterly*, December 1989, pp. 433–445.

Morris, Charles R., and Charles H. Ferguson. "How Architecture Wins Technology Wars," *Harvard Business Review*, March/April 1993, pp. 86–96.

CHAPTER 4

Anthony, Robert N. *Planning and Control Systems: A Framework for Analysis*. Cambridge, MA: Harvard University Press, 1965.

Burns, O. Maxie, David Turnipseed, and Walter E. Riggs. "Critical Success Factors in Manufacturing Resources Planning," *International Journal of Operations & Production Management*, Vol. 11, No. 4, 1991, pp. 5–19.

Carlson, Sune. *Executive Behavior: A Study of the Work Load and the Working Methods of Managing Directors*. Stockholm: Strombergs, 1951.

Clemons, Eric K. "Evaluation of Strategic Investments in Information Technology," *Communications of the ACM*, January 1991, pp. 22–36.

Clemons, Eric K., and Michael Row. "Sustaining IT Advantage: The Role of Structural Differences," *MIS Quarterly*, September 1991.

Clemons, Eric K., and Michael Row. "Information Technology and Industrial Cooperation: The Changing Economics of Coordination and Ownership," *Journal of Management Information Systems*, Summer 1992, pp. 133–163.

Daft, Richard L., and Richard M. Steers. *Organizations, A Micro/Macro Approach*. Glenview, IL.: Scott, Foresman, 1986.

Davenport, Thomas H., Michael Hammer, and Tauno J. Metsisto. "How Executives Can Shape Their Company's Information Systems," *Harvard Business Review*, March/April 1989, pp. 130–134.

Deming, Edward. *Out of the Crisis*. Boston, MA: MIT Press, 1986.

Drucker, Peter F. *The Practice of Management*. New York: Harper & Row, 1954.

Fried, Louis, and Richard Johnson. "Gaining the Technological Advantage: Planning for the Competitive Use of IT," *Journal of Information Systems Management*, Fall 1991, pp. 7–15.

Fuller, Joseph B., James O'Conor, and Richard Rawlinson. "Tailored Logistics: The Next Advantage," *Harvard Business Review*, May/June 1993, pp. 87–98.

Goodhue, Dale L., Laurie J. Kirsch, Judith A. Quillard, and Michael Wybo. "Strategic Data Planning: Lessons from the Field," *MIS Quarterly*, March 1992, pp. 11–34.

Gorry, G. Anthony, and Michael S. Scott Morton. "A Framework for Management Information Systems," *Sloan Management Review*, Fall 1971.

Gurbaxani, Vijay, and Seungjin Whang. "The Impact of Information Systems on Organizations and Markets," *Communications of the ACM*, Vol. 34, No. 1, January 1991.

Higby, Mary A., and Badie N. Farah. "The Status of Marketing Information Systems, Decision Support Systems, and Expert Systems in the Marketing Function of U.S. Firms," *Information and Management*, January 1991, pp. 29–35.

Hopper, Max D. "Rattling SABRE—New Ways to Compete on Information," *Harvard Business Review*, May/June 1990, pp. 118–120.

Ives, Blake, and Gerard P. Learmonth. "The Information System as a Competitive Weapon," *Communications of the ACM*, Vol. 27, No. 12, December 1983.

Mintzberg, Henry. *The Nature of Managerial Work.* New York: Harper & Row, 1973.

Neiderman, Fred, James C. Brancheau, and James C. Wetherbe. "Information Systems Management Issues for the 1990s," *MIS Quarterly*, December 1991, pp. 475–499.

Notowidigdo, M. H. "Information Systems: Weapons to Gain the Competitive Edge," *Financial Executive*, Vol. LII, No. 2, February 1984.

O'Reilly, Charles A., III. "The Use of Information in Organization Decision Making," *Research in Organizational Behavior*, Vol. 5, 1983.

Orilkowski, Wanda J., and Daniel Robey. "Information Technology and the Structuring of Organizations," *Information Systems Research*, June 1991, pp. 143–169.

Porter, Michael E., and Victor E. Millar. "How Information Gives You Competitive Advantage," *Harvard Business Review*, Vol. 63, No. 4, July/August 1985.

Sayles, Leonard. *Managerial Behavior: Administration in Complex Organizations.* New York: McGraw Hill, 1964.

Scott, Michael S. (ed.). *The Corporation of the 1990s: Information Technology and Organizational Transformation.* New York: Oxford University Press, 1991.

Simon, Herbert A. *The New Science of Management Decision.* New York: Harper & Row, 1960.

Simon, Herbert A. *Administrative Behavior,* 3rd ed. New York: Free Press, 1976.

Simon, Herbert A. "Rationality as a Process and as Product of Thought," *American Economic Review*, Vol. 68, 1978, pp. 1–16.

Szewcak, Edward, Coral Snodgrass, and Mehdi Khosrowpour (eds.). *Management Impacts of Information Technology: Perspectives on Organizational Change and Growth.* Harrisburg, PA: Idea Group, 1991.

Tufte, Edward R. *The Visual Display of Quantitative Information.* Cheshire, CT: Graphics Press, 1983.

CHAPTER 5

Ageloff, Roy. *A Primer on SQL.* St. Louis, MO: Times Mirror, 1988.

Armoso, Donald L., and Paul H. Cheney. "Testing a Causal Model of End-User Application Effectiveness," *Journal of Management Information Systems*, Summer 1991, pp. 63–89.

Brancheau, James C., and James C. Wetherbe. "The Adoption of Spreadsheet Software: Testing Innovation Diffusion Theory in the Context of End-User Computing," *Information Systems Research*, June 1990, pp. 115–143.

Cotterman, William W., and Kuldeep Kumar. "User Cube: A Taxonomy of End Users," *Communications of the ACM*, November 1989, pp. 25–34.

Cronan, Timothy P., and David P. Douglas. "End-User Training and Computing Effectiveness in Public Agencies: An Empirical Study," *Journal of Management Information Systems*, Spring 1990, pp. 21–39.

Hackman, J. R., and G. R. Oldham. "Motivation through the Design of Work: A Test of Theory," *Organizational Behavior and Human Performance*, Vol. 16, 1976.

Kroenke, David, and Donald Nilson. *Database Processing for Microcomputers.* Chicago: Science Research Associates, 1986.

Microsoft Corporation. *Microsoft Word Technical Reference.* Redmond, WA: Microsoft Press, 1990.

Pitter, Keiko M., and Richard L. Pitter. *Using IBM Microcomputers with WordStar, Lotus 1-2-3, and dBASE II/III.* Santa Cruz, CA: Mitchell Publishing, 1986.

Trauth, Eileen M. "The Organizational Interface: A Method for Supporting End Users of Packaged Software," *MIS Quarterly*, March 1992, pp. 35–53.

Turner, Jon. "Computer Mediated Work: The Interplay between Technology and Structured Jobs," *Communications of the ACM*, Vol. 27, No. 12, December 1984.

C H A P T E R   6

Bock, Douglas B., and John F. Schrage. "Computer Viruses: Over 300 Threats to Microcomputing... And Still Growing," *Journal of Systems Management*, February 1993, pp. 8–13.

Briggs, Robert O., Alan R. Dennis, Brenda S. Beck, and Jay F. Nunamaker, Jr. "Whither the Pen-Based Interface?" *Journal of Management Information Systems*, Winter 1992–93, pp. 71–90.

Davis, Sid A., and Robert P. Bostrom. "Training End Users: An Experimental Investigation of the Roles of the Computer Interface and Training Methods." *MIS Quarterly*, March 1993, pp. 61–85.

Todd, Peter, and Izak Benbasat. "The Use of Information in Decision Making: An Experimental Investigation of the Impact of Computer-Based Decision Aids," *MIS Quarterly*, September 1992, pp. 373–393.

Webster, Jane, and Joseph Martocchio. "Microcomputer Playfulness: Development of a Measure with Workplace Implications," *MIS Quarterly*, June 1992, pp. 201–226.

C H A P T E R   7

Black, Roger. *Roger Black's Desktop Design Power*. New York: Bantam, 1991.

Brooks, Frederick P. *The Mythical Man-Month*. Reading, MA: Addison-Wesley, 1975.

Cerveny, Robert P., Edward J. Garrity, and G. Lawrence Sanders. "A Problem-Solving Perspective on Systems Development," *Journal of Management Information Systems*, Spring 1990, pp. 103–122.

Date, C. J. *An Introduction to Database Systems*, 5th ed. Reading, MA: Addison-Wesley, 1990.

Harrison, David, and John W. Yu. *The Spreadsheet Style Manual*. Homewood, IL: Dow Jones–Irwin, 1990.

Hoover, Rodger. "Don't Trust Your Spreadsheet," *Government Data Systems*, May 1987.

Naumann, J. D., and A. M. Jenkins. "Prototyping: The New Paradigm for Systems Development," *MIS Quarterly*, September 1982, pp. 29–44.

Nelson, R. Ryan. "Educational Needs as Perceived by IS and End-User Personnel: A Survey of Knowledge and Skill Requirements," *MIS Quarterly*, December 1991, pp. 503–525.

Shusshan, Ronnie, and Don Wright. *Desktop Publishing by Design*. Redmond, WA: Microsoft Press, 1989.

Vick, Nichoel J., Audrey Thompson, and Anne Milkovich. *Designs for Business Communications*. Seattle, WA: Aldus Corporation, 1988.

C H A P T E R   8

Akscyn, Robert M., Donald L. McCracken, and Elise A. Yoder. "KMS: A Distributed Hypermedia System for Managing Knowledge in Organizations," *Communications of the ACM*, Vol. 31, No. 7, July 1988.

Alavi, Maryam. "Group Decision Support Systems: A Key to Business Team Productivity," *Journal of Information Systems Management*, Summer 1991, pp. 36–41.

Bieber, Michael P., and Steven O. Kimbrough. "On the Concept of Hypertext," *MIS Quarterly*, March 1992, pp. 77–93.

Bush, Vannevar. "As We May Think," *Atlantic Monthly*, Vol. 176, No. 1, July 1945.

Casey, Richard G., and David R. Ferguson. "Intelligent Forms Processing," *IBM Systems Journal*, Vol. 29, No. 3 (1990), pp. 435–450.

Daft, Richard L., and Richard M. Steers. *Organizations, A Micro/Macro Approach*. Glenview, IL: Scott, Foresman, 1986.

DeSanctis, G., and R. B. Gallupe. "Group Decision Support Systems, A New Frontier," *Data Base*, Vol. 16, Winter 1985.

Dennis, Alan R., Jay F. Nunamaker, and David Paranka. "Supporting the Search for Competitive Advantage," *Journal of Management Information Systems*, Summer 1991, pp. 5–36.

Felician, Leonardo. "Image Base Management System: A Promising Tool in the Large Office Environment," *ACM Data Base*, Vol. 19, No. 1, Fall/Winter 1987-88.

Huber, George P. "Issues in the Design of Group Decision Support Systems," *MIS Quarterly*, Vol. 8, No. 3, September 1984.

Huber, George P. "The Nature of Organizational Decision Making and the Design of Decision Support Systems," *MIS Quarterly*, Vol. 5, No. 2, June 1981.

Kimbrough, Steven O., and Scott A. Moore. "Message Management Systems: Concepts, Motivations, and Strategic Effects," *Journal of Management Information Systems*, Fall 1992, pp. 29–52.

Kling, Rob. "Cooperation, Coordination, and Control in Computer Supported Work," *Communications of the ACM*, December 1991, pp. 83–87.

Kraemer, Kenneth L., and John Leslie King. "Computer-Based Systems for Cooperative Work and Group Decision Making," *Computing Surveys*, Vol. 20, No. 2, June 1988.

Lee, Soonchul. "Impact of Office Information Systems on Potential Power and Influence," *Journal of Management Information Systems*, Fall 1991, pp. 135–152.

McDavid, J., and M. Harari. *Social Psychology: Individuals, Groups, Societies*. New York: Harper & Row, 1968.

McLeod, Poppy Lauretta, and Jeffrey K. Liker. "Electronic Meeting Systems: Evidence from a Low Structure Environment," *Information Systems Research*, September 1992, pp. 195–223.

Nadler, David A., J. Richard Hackman, and Edward E. Lawler, III. *Managing Organizational Behavior*, Boston: Little, Brown, 1979.

Nunamaker, J. F., Alan R. Dennis, Joseph S. Valacich, Douglas Vogel, and Joey F. George. "Electronic Meeting Systems to Support Group Work," *Communications of the ACM*, July 1991, pp. 40–61.

Scott Morton, Michael S. (ed.). *The Corporation of the 1990s*. New York: Oxford University Press, 1991.

Smith, John B., and Stephen F. Weiss. "Hypertext," *Communications of the ACM*, Vol. 31, No. 7, July 1988.

Tyran, Craig K., Alan R. Dennis, Douglas Vogel, and Jay F. Nunamaker. "The Application of Electronic Meeting Technology to Support Strategic Management," *MIS Quarterly*, September 1992, pp. 313–334.

Yankelovich, N., N. Meyrowitz, and A. van Dam. "Reading and Writing the Electronic Book," *IEEE Computer*, Vol. 18, No. 10, October 1985.

Zuboff, Shoshana. *In the Age of the Smart Machine*. New York: Basic Books, 1988.

C H A P T E R   9

Bieber, Michael P., and Steven O. Kimbrough. "On Generalizing the Concept of Hypertext," *MIS Quarterly*, March 1992, pp. 77–93.

Bly, Sara A., Steve R. Harrison, and Susan Irwin. "Media Spaces: Bring People Together in a Video, Audio, and Computing Environment," *Communications of the ACM*, January 1993, pp. 28–47.

Ellis, C. A., S. J. Gibbs, and G. L. Rein. "Groupware: Some Issues and Experiences," *Communications of the ACM*, January 1991, pp. 38–58.

Loomis, Mary. *Data Communications*. Englewood Cliffs, NJ: Prentice-Hall, 1983.

Madron, Thomas W. *Local Area Networks*, 2nd ed. New York: John Wiley & Sons, 1990.

Martin, James. *Computer Networks and Distributed Processing*. Englewood Cliffs, NJ: Prentice-Hall, 1981.

McLean, Ephraim R., and Leon A. Kappelman. "The Convergence of Organizational and End-User Computing," *Journal of Management Information Systems*, Winter 1992–93, pp. 145–155.

Misra, Jay, and Byron Belitsos. *Business Telecommunications*. Homewood, IL: Irwin, 1987.

Tanenbaum, Andrew S. *Computer Networks*. Englewood Cliffs, NJ: Prentice-Hall, 1981.

C H A P T E R   1 0

Avison, David, and David Wilson. "Controls for Effective Prototyping," *Journal of Management Information Systems*, Vol. 3, No. 1 (1991), pp. 41–53.

Bikson, Tora K. "Understanding the Implementation of Office Technology," *Technology and the Transformation of White-Collar Work*, Rand Corp., N-2619-NSF, June 1987.

Bikson, Tora K., Barbara A. Gutek, and Don A. Mankin. *Implementing Computerized Procedures in Office Settings*. Rand Corp., R-3077-NSF/IRIS, 1987.

Brooks, Frederick P. *The Mythical Man-Month*. Reading, MA: Addison-Wesley, 1975.

Christensen, Dawn M. "The Gap Between Systems Developers and Users," *Journal of Information Systems Management*, Fall 1991, pp. 73–75.

Cooprider, Jay G., and John C. Henderson. "Technology-Process Fit: Perspectives on Achieving Prototyping Effectiveness," *Journal of Management Information Systems*, Winter 1990–91, pp. 67–87.

Dolan, Kathy. *Business Computer Systems Design.* Santa Cruz, CA: Mitchell Publishing, 1983.

Fossum, E. *The Computerization of Working Life.* New York: John Wiley & Sons, 1983.

Gane, Chris, and Trish Sarson. *Systems Analysis, Tools and Techniques.* Englewood Cliffs, NJ: Prentice-Hall, 1979.

Jackson, Michael A. *Principles of Program Design.* New York: Academic Press, 1975.

Orr, Ken. *Structured Requirements Definition.* Topeka, KS: Orr & Assoc., 1981.

Senn, James A. "User Involvement as a Factor in Information Systems Success: Key Questions for Research," *Journal of Management Information Systems*, Vol. 3, No. 1 (1991), pp. 31–40.

Warnier, Jean Dominique. *Logical Construction of Systems.* New York: Van Nostrand Reinhold, 1979.

Weinberg, Victor. *Structured Analysis.* New York: Yourdon Press, 1978.

CHAPTER 11

Ahituv, Niv, and Seev Neumann. *Principles of Information Systems for Management,* 2nd ed. Dubuque, IA: W. Brown, 1986.

Bakos, J. Yannis. "A Strategic Analysis of Electronic Marketplaces," *MIS Quarterly*, September 1991, pp. 295–310.

Benjamin, Robert I., Charles Dickinson, Jr., and John F. Rockart, "Changing Role of the Corporate Information Systems Officer," *MIS Quarterly*, Vol. 9, No. 3, September 1985.

Cash, James I., Jr., F. Warren McFarlan, and James L. McKenney. *Corporate Information Systems Management,* 2nd ed. Homewood, IL: Irwin, 1988.

Delligatta, Ann. "System Reengineering and the User," *Information Systems Management*, Winter 1992, pp. 76–77.

Drucker, Peter F. "The Coming of the New Organization," *Harvard Business Review,* Vol. 66, No. 1, January/February 1988.

Gilder, George. "Into the Telecosm," *Harvard Business Review*, March/April 1991, pp. 150–161.

Karmarkar, Uday. "Getting Control of Just-In-Time," *Harvard Business Review,* Vol. 67, No. 5, September/October 1989.

Miles, Kimberly, and Associates. *The Enterprise Life Cycle.* San Francisco: Jossey-Bass, 1981.

Porter, Michael E., and Victor E. Millar. "How Information Gives You a Competitive Advantage," *Harvard Business Review*, Vol. 63, No. 4, July/August 1985.

Schnitt, David L. "Reengineering the Organization Using Information Technology," *Journal of Systems Management*, January 1993, pp. 14–20, 41–42.

Scott Morton, Michael S. (ed.). *The Corporation of the 1990s.* New York: Oxford University Press, 1991.

Senn, James A. "Electronic Data Interchange: The Elements of Implementation." *Information Systems Management*, Winter 1992, pp. 45–53.

Steinbart, Paul John, and Revinder Nath. "Problems and Issues in the Management of International Data Networks: The Experience of American Companies," *MIS Quarterly*, March 1992, pp. 55–76.

Zuboff, Shoshana. *In the Age of the Smart Machine.* New York: Basic Books, 1988.

CHAPTER 12

Anderson, Ronald E., Deborah G. Johnson, Donald Gotterbarn, and Judith Perrolle. "Using the New ACM Code of Ethics in Decision Making," *Communications of the ACM*, February 1993, pp. 98–107.

Bergeron, Francois, Suzanne Rivard, and Lyne De Serre. "Investigating the Support Role of the Information Center," *MIS Quarterly*, September 1990, pp. 247–262.

Blanton, J. Ellis, Hugh J. Watson, and Janette Moody. "Toward a Better Understanding of Information Technology Organization: A Comparative Case Study," *MIS Quarterly*, December 1992, pp. 531–555.

Bureau of Justice Statistics. *Criminal Justice Resource Manual*. Washington, DC: U.S. Department of Justice, 1979.

Cash, James I., Jr., F. Warren McFarlan, and James L. McKenney. *Corporate Information Systems Management*, 2nd ed. Homewood, IL: Irwin, 1988.

Chen, C. William. "The DBA's Changing Role," *Database Programming and Design*, Vol. 1, No. 10, October 1988.

Drucker, Peter F., "The Coming of the New Organization," *Harvard Business Review*, Vol. 66, No. 1, January/February, 1988.

Flynn, Laurie. "IBM Changes Its Strategy on Protocols," *Infoworld*, Vol. 9, No. 7, February 16, 1987.

Gillett, Craig A., and Cheryl C. Currid. "Backbones and Bridges: Connecting It All Together," *Netware*, Vol. 1, No. 1, October 1988.

Goodhue, Dale L., Laurie J. Kirsch, Judith A. Quillard, and Michael D. Wybo, "Strategic Data Planning: Lessons from the Field," *MIS Quarterly*, March 1992, pp. 11–34.

Lew, H. Kim, and Cyndi Jung. "Getting There from Here: Mapping from TCP/IP to OSI," *Data Communications*, Vol. 17, No. 8, August 1988.

Loch, Karen D., Houston H. Carr, and Merrill E. Warkentin. "Threats to Information Systems: Today's Reality, Yesterday's Understanding," *MIS Quarterly*, June 1992, pp. 173–186.

Lyon, John K. *The Database Administrator*. New York: John Wiley & Sons, 1976.

Madron, Thomas W. *Local Area Networks*, 2nd ed. New York: John Wiley & Sons, 1990.

Madron, Thomas W. *Micro Mainframe Connection*. Indianapolis, IN: Howard W. Sams, 1987.

Martin, E. W. "Critical Success Factors of Chief MIS/DP Executives," *MIS Quarterly*, Vol. 6, No. 2, June 1982.

Oz, Effy. "Ethical Standards for Information Systems Professionals: A Case for a Unified Code," *MIS Quarterly*, December 1992, pp. 423–433.

Parker, Donn B. *Computer Security Management*. Reston, VA: Reston Publishing, 1981.

Smits, Stanley J., Ephraim R. McLean, and John R. Tanner. "Managing High-Achieving Information Systems Professionals," *Journal of Management Information Systems*, Spring 1993, pp. 103–120.

Stephens, Charlotte S., William N. Ledbetter, Mitra Amitava, and F. Nelson Ford. "Executive or Functional Manager: The Nature of the CIO's Job," *MIS Quarterly*, December 1992, pp. 449–467.

CHAPTER 13

Banker, Rajiv D., and Robert J. Kauffman. "Reuse and Productivity in Computer-Aided Software Design: An Empirical Study," *MIS Quarterly*, September 1991, pp. 375–401.

Beath, Cynthia Mathis. "Supporting the Information Technology Champion," *MIS Quarterly*, September 1991, pp. 355–372.

Boone, Greg. *The CASE Experience, CASE Product Profiles*. Publication No. PP10688. Bellevue, WA: CASE Research Corporation, 1988.

Brooks, Frederick P., Jr. *The Mythical Man-Month*. Reading, MA: Addison-Wesley, 1975.

Chikofsky, Elliot. *Computer-Aided Software Engineering (CASE)*, 2nd ed. Los Alamitos, CA: IEEE Computer Society Press, 1993.

Couger, J. Daniel, Scott C. McIntyre, Lexis F. Higgins, and Terry A. Snow. "Using a Bottom-Up Approach to Creativity Improvement in IS Development," *Journal of Systems Management*, September 1991, pp. 23–27, 36.

Drury, D. H. "An Evaluation of Data Processing Steering Committees," *MIS Quarterly*, Vol. 8, No. 4, December 1984.

Ford, Robert C. "Is Your Organization Ready for Telecommuting?" *SAM Advanced Management Journal*, Autumn 1991, pp. 19–23, 33.

Higgins, Lexis F., Scott C. McIntyre, and Cynthia G. Raine. "Design of Global Marketing Information Systems," *Journal of Business & Industrial Marketing*, Summer-Fall 1991, pp. 49–58.

Huber, Richard L. "How Continental Bank Outsourced Its 'Crown Jewels'," *Harvard Business Review*, January/February 1993, pp. 121–129.

IBM Corporation. *Business Systems Planning: Information Systems Planning Guide.* Publication GE20-052701. White Plains, NY: IBM, 1975.

Kador, John. "Outsourcing Application Development: Does It Pay?" *System Builder*, April/May 1991.

Kendall, Kenneth E. "Behavioral Implications for Systems Analysis and Design: Prospects for the Nineties," *Journal of Management Information Systems*, Vol. 3, No. 1 (1991), pp. 1–4.

Lederer, Albert L., Rajesh Mirani, Boon Siong Neo, Carol Pollard, Jayesh Prasad, and K. Ramamurthy. "Information System Cost Estimating: A Management Perspective," *MIS Quarterly*, June 1990, pp. 159–176.

Lederer, Albert L., and Raghu Nath. "Managing Organizational Issues in Information Systems Development," *Journal of Systems Management*, November 1991, pp. 23–27, 39.

Loh, Lawrence, and N. Venkatraman. "Determinants of Information Technology Outsourcing: A Cross-Sectional Analysis." *Journal of Management Information Systems*, Summer 1992, pp. 7–24.

Markus, M. Lynne. *Systems in Organizations.* New York: Pitman Publishing, 1984.

McCarthy, John C. "MIS's Mid-life Crisis," *Forrester Professional Systems Report*, October 1990.

McClure, Carma. *CASE Is Software Automation.* Englewood Cliffs, NJ: Prentice-Hall, 1989.

Merlyn, Vaughn. "Orderly Paths to Automation," *Computerworld*, November 9, 1987.

Neidermann, Fred, James C. Brancheau, and James C. Wetherbe. "Information Systems Management Issues for the 1990s," *MIS Quarterly*, December 1991, pp. 475–499.

Norman, Ronald J., and Gene Forte. "A Self-Assessment by the Software Engineering Community," *Communications of the ACM*, Vol. 35, No. 4, April 1992.

Ryan, Hugh W. "Systems Development: The Human Metaphor," *Information Systems Management*, Winter 1992, pp. 72–75.

Shank, Michael E., Andrew C. Boynton, and Robert W. Zmud. "Critical Success Factor Analysis as a Methodology for MIS Planning," *MIS Quarterly*, Vol. 9, No. 2, June 1985.

Wilder, Clinton. "IBM Users Get Outsource Itch," *Computerworld*, Vol. 25, No. 9, March 4, 1991.

Winsberg, Paul. "CASE: Getting the Big Picture," *Database Programming and Design*, Vol. 1, No. 3, March 1988.

Yourdon, Edward. *Decline and Fall of the American Programmer.* Englewood Cliffs, NJ: Prentice-Hall, 1992.

Zachman, J. A. "Business Systems Planning and Business Information Control Study: A Comparison," *IBM Systems Journal*, Vol. 21, 1982.

CHAPTER 14

Ariav, Gad, and Michael J. Ginzberg. "DSS Design: A Systemic View of Decision Support," *Communications of the ACM*, Vol. 38, No. 10, October 1985.

Azine, Bay. "A Contingency Model of DSS Development Methodology," *Journal of Management Information Systems*, Summer 1991, pp. 149–156.

Chen, Minder, and Jay F. Nunamaker, Jr. "The Architecture and Design of a Collaborative Environment for Systems Definition," *Data Base*, Vol. 22, No. 1/2, Winter/Spring 1991.

DeSanctis, G., and R. B. Gallupe. "Group Decision Support Systems, A New Frontier," *Data Base*, Vol. 16, No. 2, Winter 1985.

Dykstra, Elizabeth A., and Robert P. Carasik. "Structure and Support in Cooperative Environments: The Amsterdam Conversation Environment," *International Journal of Man-Machine Studies*, Vol. 34, No. 3, March 1991.

Forgionne, Guisseppi A. "Decision Technology Systems: A Step Toward Complete Decision Support," *Journal of Information Systems Management*, Fall 1991, pp. 34–43.

Guimaraes, Tor, and Jayant V. Saraph. "The Role of Prototyping in Executive Decision Systems," *Information & Management*, December 1991, pp. 257–267.

Huber, George P. "Issues in the Design of Group Decision Support Systems," *MIS Quarterly*, Vol. 8, No. 3, September 1984.

Jacob, Varchese S., and Hasan Pirkul. "A Framework for Supporting Distributed Group Decision-Making," *Decision Support Systems*, January 1992, pp. 17–28.

Keen, Peter G. W., and M. S. Scott Morton. *Decision Support Systems: An Organizational Perspective*. Reading, MA: Addison-Wesley, 1982.

Kraemer, Kenneth L., and John Leslie King. "Computer-Based Systems for Cooperative Work and Group Decision Making," *Computing Surveys*, Vol. 20, No. 2, June 1988.

Le Blanc, Louis A., and Kenneth A. Kozar. "An Empirical Investigation of the Relationship Between DSS Usage and System Performance: A Case Study of a Navigational Support System," *MIS Quarterly*, September 1990, pp. 263–277.

Liou, Yihwa Irene, and Jay F. Nunamaker. "An Investigation into Knowledge Acquisition Using a Group Decision Support System," *Information and Management*, Vol. 24 No. 3 (1993), pp. 121–133.

Silver, Mark S. "Decision Support Systems: Directed and Nondirected Change," *Information Systems Research*, March 1990, pp. 47–70.

Sisodia, Rajendra S. "Marketing Information and Decision Support Systems for Services," *Journal of Services Marketing*, Winter 1992, pp. 71–80.

Sprague, Ralph H., Jr., and Eric D. Carlson. *Building Effective Decision Support Systems*. Englewood Cliffs, NJ: Prentice-Hall, 1982.

Valacich, Joseph S., Alan R. Dennis, and J. F. Nunamaker, Jr. "Electronic Meeting Support: The GroupSystems Concept," *International Journal of Man-Machine Studies*, Vol. 34, No. 2, February 1991.

Williams, Daniel. "New Technologies for Coordinating Work," *Datamation*, May 15, 1990.

C H A P T E R 1 5

Amaravadi, Chandra S., Olivia R. Liu Sheng, Joey F. George, and Jay F. Nunamaker, Jr. "AEI: A Knowledge-Based Approach to Integrated Office Systems." *Journal of Management Information Systems*, Summer 1992, pp. 133–163.

Barr, Avron, and Edward A. Feigenbaum (eds.). *The Handbook of Artificial Intelligence*. Stanford, CA: HeurisTech Press, 1981.

Buchanan, Bruce G., and E. H. Shortliffe. *Rule-Based Expert Systems: The MYCIN Experiments of the Stanford Heuristic Programming Project*. Reading, MA: Addison-Wesley, 1984.

Chase, Michael D., and Jae K. Shim. "Artificial Intelligence and Big Six Accounting—A Survey of the Current Uses of Expert Systems in the Modern Accounting Environment," *Computers and Industrial Engineering*, Vol. 21, 1991, pp. 205–209.

Clocksin, W. F., and C. S. Mellish. *Programming in Prolog*. Berlin, West Germany: Springer-Verlag, 1981.

Cox, Brad J. *Object Oriented Programming: An Evolutionary Approach*. Reading, MA: Addison-Wesley, 1986.

Deschamps, Paul B. "Standards for Expert System Tools: Reporting the Technology's Integration," *Information System Management*, Winter 1992, pp. 8–14.

Freedman, Roy S. "AI on Wall Street." *IEEE Expert*, April 1991, pp. 3–9.

Harmon, Paul, and David King. *Expert Systems: Artificial Intelligence in Business*. New York: John Wiley & Sons, 1985.

Harmon, Paul, Rex Maus, and William Morrissey. *Expert Systems Tools and Applications*. New York: John Wiley & Sons, 1988.

Haugeland, John. *Artificial Intelligence: The Very Idea*. Cambridge, MA: MIT Press, 1985.

Jain, Sanjay, and David H. Osterfield. "Applying Expert Systems in Automated and Traditional Environments," *Manufacturing Systems*, August 1991, pp. 24–31.

Kattan, Michael W., Dennis A. Adams, and Michael S. Parks. "A Comparison of Machine Learning with Human Judgment," *Journal of Management Information Systems*, Spring 1993, pp. 37–57.

Kraft, A. "XCON: An Expert Configuration System at Digital Equipment Corporation," in P. H. Winston and K. A. Prendergast, eds., *The AI Business: The Commercial Uses of Artificial Intelligence*. Cambridge, MA: MIT Press, 1985.

Liou, Yihwa Irene, and Jay F. Nunamaker. "An Investigation into Knowledge Acquisition Using a Group Decision Support System," *Information and Management*, Vol. 24, No. 3 (1993), pp. 121–133.

McCorduck, Pamela. *Machines Who Think*. San Francisco: Freeman, 1979.

Minsky, Marvin L. *Semantic Information Processing*. Cambridge, MA: MIT Press, 1968.

Nilsson, Nils J. *Problem-Solving Methods in Artificial Intelligence*. New York: McGraw-Hill, 1971.

Ruth, Christopher, and Stephen R. Ruth. *Developing Expert Systems Using 1st-Class*. Santa Cruz, CA: Mitchell Publishing, 1991.

Schutzer, Daniel. "Business Expert Systems: The Competitive Edge," *Expert Systems with Applications*, Vol. 1, No. 1, 1990, pp. 17–21.

Sprague, Kristopher G., and Stephen R. Ruth. *Developing Expert Systems Using EXSYS*. Santa Cruz, CA: Mitchell Publishing, 1991.

Sviokla, J. J. "An Examination of the Impact of Expert Systems on the Firm: The Case of XCON," *MIS Quarterly*, June 1990, pp. 127–140.

Watkins, P., and L. Eliot (eds.). *Expert Systems for Business and Management*. Englewood Cliffs, NJ: Prentice-Hall, 1991.

Winograd, Terry, and Fernando Flores. *Understanding Computers and Cognition*. Norwood, NJ: Ablex Publishing, 1986.

Yoon, Youngohc, and Tor Guimaraes. "Selecting Expert System Development Techniques," *Information and Management*, Vol. 24, No. 3 (1993), pp. 209–223.

Young, Lawrence F. "Knowledge-Based Systems for Idea Processing," *Data Base*, Vol. 22, No. 1/2, Winter/Spring 1991.

Index

Photo Credits

Figures 1-3, 3-7, 3-9,
5-24, 6-1, 6-6, 7-5, 10-2,
10-9, 11-2, 12-15, 12-22,
13-5, 13-12, 15-2:   Courtesy of International Business Machines.

Figures 2-4, 2-16,
6-4, 6-8, 9-6, 9-18:   Courtesy of Hewlett-Packard Company.

Figure 1-4:   Courtesy of GRID System.

Figure 2-22:   Courtesy of COMSHARE.

Figure 3-4:   Bachmann/Profiles West.

Figure 3-5:   Courtesy of Intel Corporation.

Figure 4-4:   Courtesy of Microsoft Corp.

Figure 5-2:   Courtesy of The Interface Group.

Figure 5-9:   Software Publishing Company has granted permission to use this illustration of the software screen capture from Harvard Graphics 3.0.

Figure 6-2:   Courtesy of Texas Instruments.

Figure 6-3:   Courtesy of Toshiba America Information Systems, Inc.

Figures 8-7, 8-8:   Courtesy of Lotus Development Corp.

Figure 8-10:   Steven Mechler.

Figure 11-17:   Hank Morgan/Rainbow.

Figure 14-16:   UPI/Bettmann.

DCCC
BOOKSTORE

$42 75

USED PRICE